Byrdcliffe

An American Arts and Crafts Colony

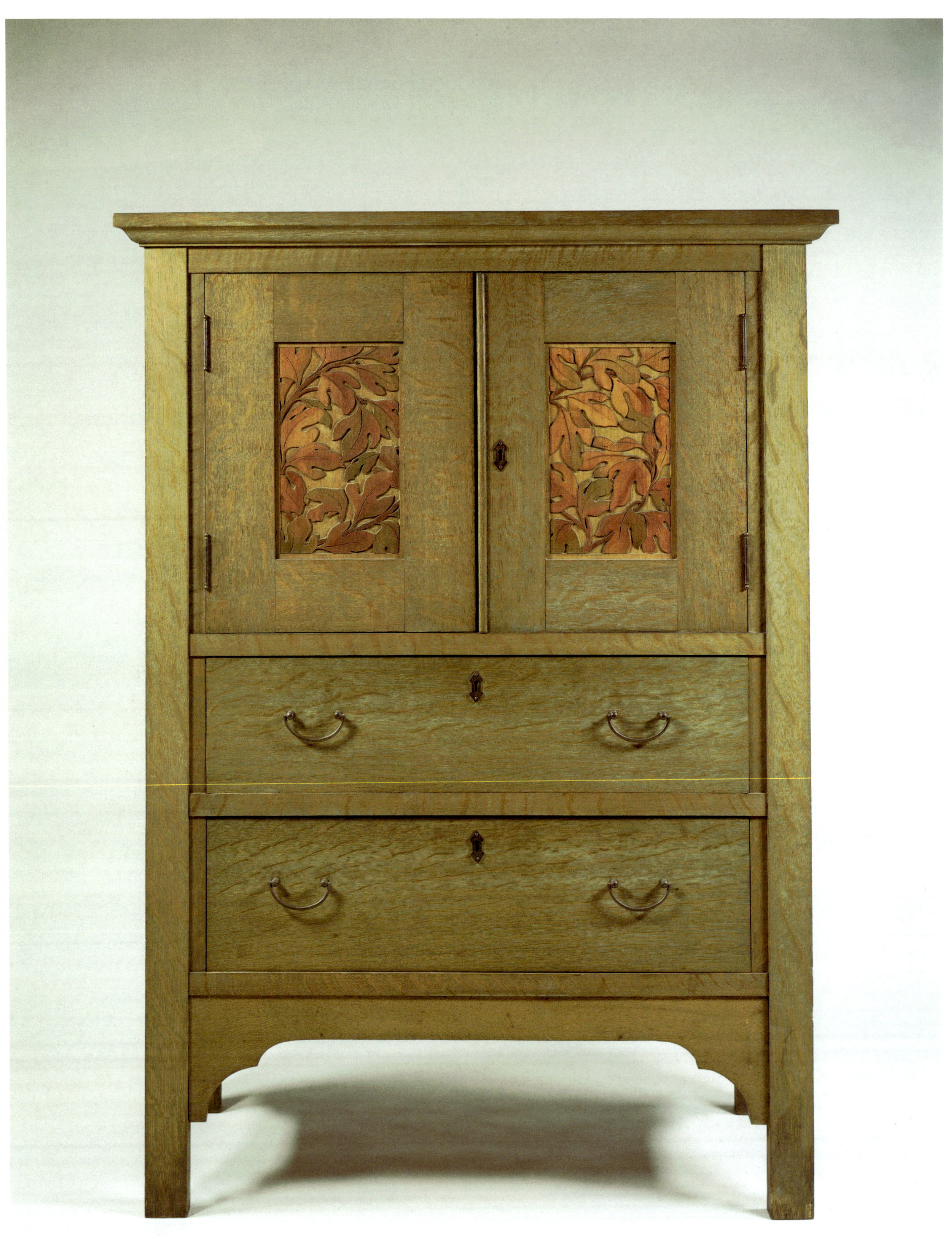

Byrdcliffe

An American Arts and Crafts Colony

Ellen Paul Denker

Robert Edwards

Heidi Nasstrom Evans

Nancy E. Green

Cheryl Robertson

Tom Wolf

Edited by Nancy E. Green

Herbert F. Johnson Museum of Art

Cornell University
Ithaca, New York

2004

This book was designed and set in type by
Abigail Sturges Graphic Design, New York, New York.

It was printed by Brodock Press, Inc.
on Lustro Dull Text and Cover paper
and bound at The Riverside Group.

The typeface is Trump Medieval and Franklin Gothic No. 2.

3200 copies on the occasion of the exhibition
June 2004

Cover: Jessie Tarbox Beals, *View from White Pines Front Porch* (see page 13)

Inside Front and Back Covers: Zulma Steele, *Dragonfly Wallpaper* (cat. 178)

Frontispiece: Edna Walker, designer, *Linen Press with Sassafras Panels* (cat. 38). The Metropolitan Museum of Art, Purchase, Friends of the American Wing Fund, and Mr. and Mrs. Mark Willcox Jr. Gift, 1991. (1991.311.1) Photograph ©1992 The Metropolitan Museum of Art

This exhibition has been made possible in part by the **National Endowment for the Humanities**, promoting excellence in the humanities.

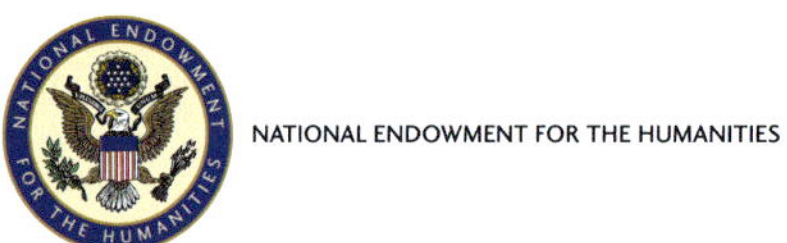

Any views, findings, conclusions, or recommendations expressed in this publication do not necessarily represent those of the National Endowment for the Humanities.

This exhibition is also supported in part by
The Henry Luce Foundation
The National Endowment for the Arts
Public funds from the **New York State Council on the Arts**, a state agency
The New York Council for the Humanities, a state program of the National Endowment for the Humanities

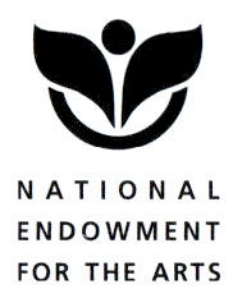

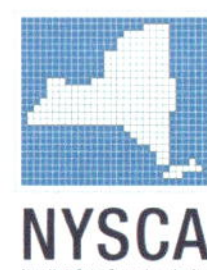

Additional support was provided by
The Getty Curatorial Research Program
Winterthur Fellowships
Furthermore: a program of The J. M. Kaplan Fund

The Institute of Museum and Library Services, a federal agency that fosters innovation, leadership, and a lifetime of learning, supports the operating expenses of the Johnson Museum.

Library of Congress Control Number: 2003115028
ISBN: 0964604205

Published by
Herbert F. Johnson Museum of Art
Cornell University
Ithaca, NY 14853
www.museum.cornell.edu

Museum Editor: Andrea Potochniak

Contents

Exhibition Itinerary

This catalogue accompanies an exhibition organized by the Herbert F. Johnson Museum of Art at Cornell University.
This project was organized by the curator, Nancy E. Green, senior curator of prints, drawings, and photographs; the exhibition has been co-curated by Tom Wolf.

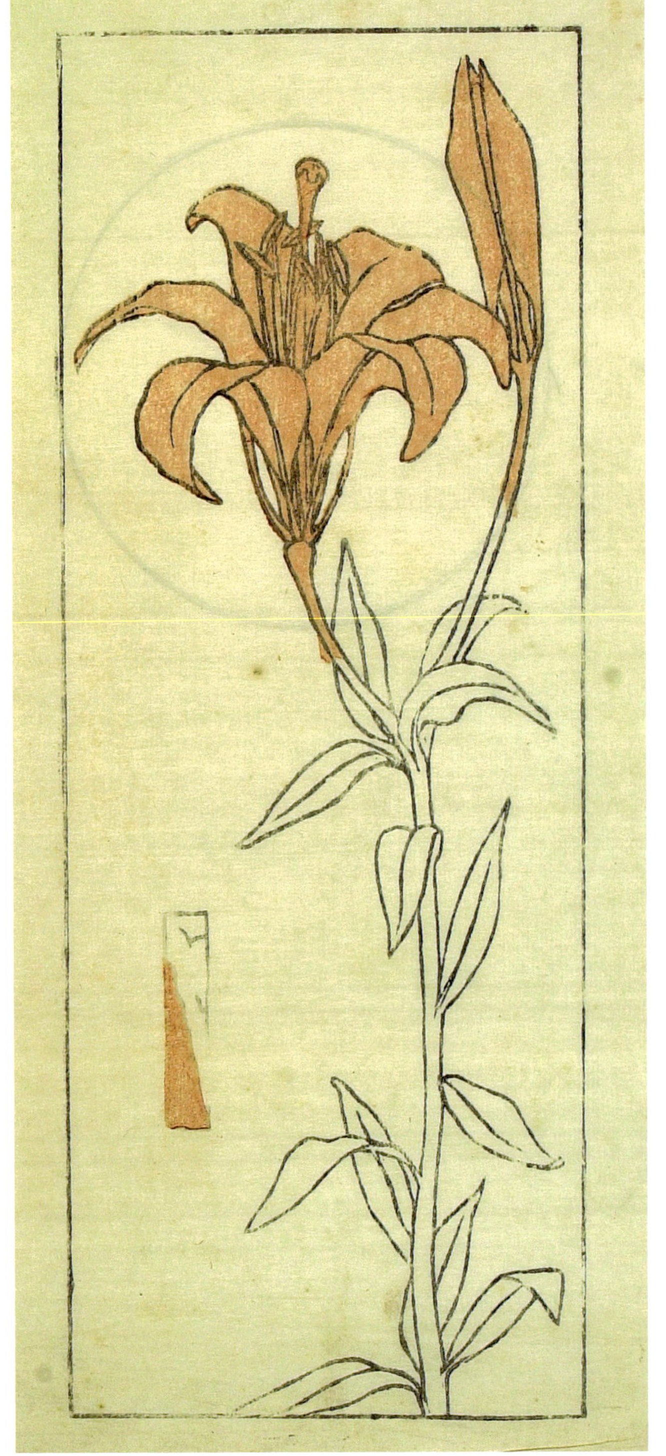

cat. 172

Exhibition Itinerary

Milwaukee Art Museum
Milwaukee, Wisconsin
June 25 to September 19, 2004

Herbert F. Johnson Museum of Art
Cornell University
Ithaca, New York
October 16 to December 5, 2004

Albany Institute of History and Art
Albany, New York
December 28, 2004, to February 28, 2005

The New-York Historical Society
New York, New York
March 15 to May 15, 2005

Winterthur Museum, Garden & Library
Winterthur, Delaware
June 11 to September 5, 2005

Lenders to the Exhibition

The Arts and Clay Company
Berry-Hill Galleries, New York
The Bigelow Homestead
The Brooklyn Museum of Art
The Byrdcliffe Art Colony of the Woodstock Guild
The Center for Photography at Woodstock
David Cook Fine Art, Denver
Drs. Joseph Cunningham and Bruce Barnes
Amy and David Dufour
The George Eastman House
Robert Ellison
Debra Force Fine Art, Inc., New York
Johanna and Leslie Garfield
Howard Greenberg Gallery, New York
Linda and Donald Gregorius
Maribeth Harmes
Hirschl & Adler Galleries
The Historical Society of Woodstock
Robert Inglish and Craig Wood
Douglas C. James
Greg and Kathleen Eagen Johnson
Janet Keep
Abby and Mark Lerner
Gregory E. and Eleanor Lindin
The Metropolitan Museum of Art
Henry T. Michie
Thomas Michie
The Milwaukee Art Museum
Morgan Anderson Consulting
The Museum of Fine Arts, Boston
The National Academy of Design
The National Arts Club
The Nelson-Atkins Museum of Art
The Newark Museum
Dr. Frederica P. D. Perera
Guido Perera
Previti Gallery, New York
Private collections
Suzanne Schutz
The Schlesinger Library, Radcliffe Institute, Harvard University
Edward Shlasko
Hollis Taggart Gallery, New York
The Toledo Museum of Art
The University of Chicago Library, Special Collections
Lawrence Webster
The Henry Francis Du Pont Winterthur Museum Inc.
Tom Wolf
The Woodstock Artists Association
Jean and Jim Young

Preface

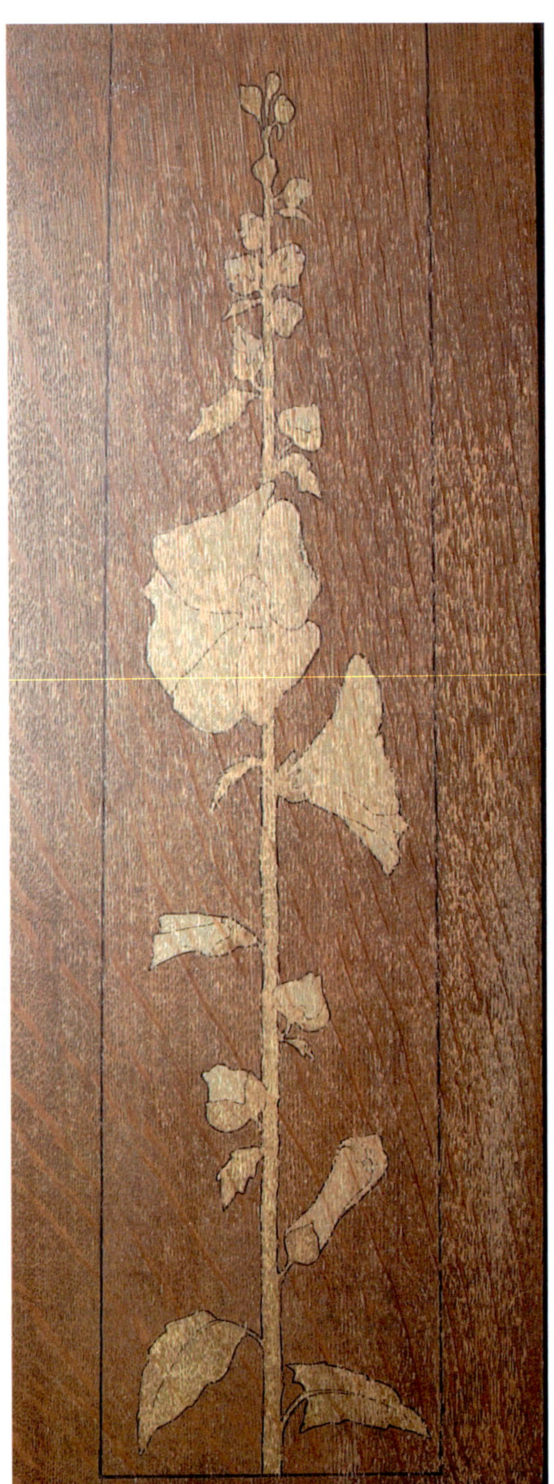
cat. 37 (detail)

Just over a hundred years ago, Ralph Whitehead, his wife Jane, Hervey White, and Bolton Brown shared a dream of forming an idyllic arts colony that would educate young students, provide a haven for writers, musicians and craftspeople, and establish a healthful life for their families in the beautiful natural surroundings of the Catskill Mountains. Over the next hundred years that vision would grow and change and numerous artists would visit or move to the community, while others left, creating a panoply of intellectual interchange. The germ of the original ideal remains and today Byrdcliffe is still an active arts colony, fulfilling some of the dreams of the those four founders.

This type of project takes a battalion of helpful colleagues to make it work, and I can only begin to thank all those who have contributed to this exhibition and catalogue. At Winterthur, the home of the Byrdcliffe archives in the Joseph Downs Collection of Manuscripts and Printed Ephemera, I would like to thank Jeanne Solensky, Laura Parrish, and Rich McKinstry for both their patience and good humor. They have helped in so many ways to see this project come to fruition, and it would not have happened without their cheerful assistance. I am also grateful to Gary Kulik and Neville Thompson for their support. Jill and Mark Willcox Jr. shared their enthusiasm and Byrdcliffe recollections and were extremely generous with their time as well. The team in Woodstock has been unwavering in their help, and I would like to thank Linda Freaney at the Woodstock Artists Association and Ariel Shanberg at the Center for Photography for their aid. I am particularly grateful to Carla Smith at the Woodstock Guild and Doug James, who made my visits so enjoyable and the work a pure pleasure. Historian Alf Evers, whom I consider the "voice of Woodstock," has been unstintingly helpful with information and suggestions. Also at the Woodstock Guild, Franne Entelis and Peter D. Hallsworth were of great help, and Joanne Anthony and Kathy A. Longyear at the Historical Society of Woodstock lent their enthusiam and expertise.

Special kudos to my fellow Byrdcliffe contributors: Ellen Denker, Robert Edwards, Heidi Nasstrom Evans, Cheryl Robertson, and, particularly, Tom Wolf, who has shared his dream of this show with all of us. He would like to add his thanks to D. J. Stern, librarian of the Woodstock Library, and Edwina Hoffman, former president of the Woodstock Guild.

Funds came from many sources and we are very grateful for all those who contributed to this project—particularly to the National Endowment for the Humanities, whose generous support has shaped this project at every stage. The Henry Luce Foundation, the New York State Council on the Arts, the New York Council for the Humanities, and the National Endowment for the Arts have also aided in making this exhibition and catalogue a reality. Furthermore: a program of The J. M. Kaplan Fund, was responsible for showing faith in this project in its earliest stages, and their initiative helped get it off the ground. Winterthur Fellowships have been crucial to many of us in our research support.

I would like to thank the Getty Curatorial Research program for supporting my own research on this project. With their sponsorship I was able to track down important information on Ralph Whitehead's early years in England. I was helped along the way by many colleagues and friends, and to them I would like to offer my sincere gratitude. At the Saddleworth Historical Society, Mike Buckley, Jean Saunders, and the late Maurice Dennett were welcoming and generous with their time and their knowledge. Mrs. Joyce Pearson kindly offered me a glimpse of Ralph's childhood by showing me around his familial home, Beech Hill. Stephen Wildman at the University of Lancaster's Ruskin Library graciously answered all my questions concerning Ruskin, and Hannah Neale at the Abbot Hall Art Gallery in Kendal and Julian Brooks at the Ashmolean Museum, Oxford University, shared their Ruskin watercolor collections with me. Others who have kindly shared information, filling in many answers to my barrage of questions, are Robin Fanshawe, Mark Bertram, Claire Longworth, Philip Gorton, and Nick Marmont, and to all of them I am very grateful. A very special thank you to Professor Glenn Altshuler and Pat and David Atkinson for their enthusiasm and generosity in sponsoring the Byrdcliffe symposium and other public programming at Cornell under the aegis of the Atkinson Forum in American Studies.

The staffs of the other venues have also been extremely helpful. Glenn Adamson, Nonie Gadsden, and David Gorton at the Milwaukee Art Museum; Tammis Groft and Christine Miles at the Albany Institute of History and Art; Jan Seidler Ramirez, Rob Del Bagno, and Kenneth T. Jackson at the New-York Historical Society; and Felice Lamden, Grace Eleazer, and Leslie Greene Bowman at Winterthur have all been a pleasure to work with, promptly answering my e-mails and phone calls.

The staff at the Johnson Museum has done their usual thorough and superb job helping out with every major and minor detail. Curatorial assistants Kasia Maroney, Jane Terrell, and Michael Sampson provided seemingly endless support. Registrar Matt Conway has lent his expertise on many questions and has helped make this complicated exhibition much less confusing. Andrea Potochniak offered her expert help and assistance (as well as her much-needed good humor) to all aspects of publicity and the publication, and Meg Elliott, Elizabeth Byrne, Jessica Evett-Miller, Leah Walczak, and Cathy Klimaszewski have brought focus to the planning of the educational programs. Rita Townsend-Boratav has patiently seen me through the grants process time and again, and Matthew Ferrari and Michael Holobosky provided most of the beautiful photography for this project. George Cannon has been an immense help in conceptualizing the exhibition design. Wil Millard; Nancy Haffner and Steve Brosnahan at RBH Media; Gregory McCartney and the staff at Artistry in Wood; and the late John Matherly have all been invaluable in their contributions to the final configuration of the show. To Frank Robinson, I would like to offer my sincere and heartfelt thanks for this opportunity to work on the Byrdcliffe project and for his support throughout the years it has been in progress.

Such an exhibition could not happen without the generosity and enthusiasm of all the lenders, and we are very grateful to all of them for their support throughout. I would also like to thank friends, family, and colleagues who have helped me at various steps of the way: Betty Krulik Alvarez, David Beevers, Mary Jayc Bruce, Beth Cathers, Janice Coco, Susan Dixon, Kathy Green, Phil Green, Robert Green, Nancy Jarzombek, Barbara Krulik, Ellen Leerberger, Carrie McDade, Marilee Boyd Meyer, Susette Newberry, Christine O'Malley, Kathryn Slocum, Henrietta Usherwood, and Marcia Vose. Lastly, I would like to thank my husband, Douglas Fowler, who has lived and breathed this project almost as intensely as I have and without whose support this would not have been possible.

NANCY E. GREEN
Senior Curator
Prints, Drawings, and Photographs
Hebert F. Johnson Museum of Art

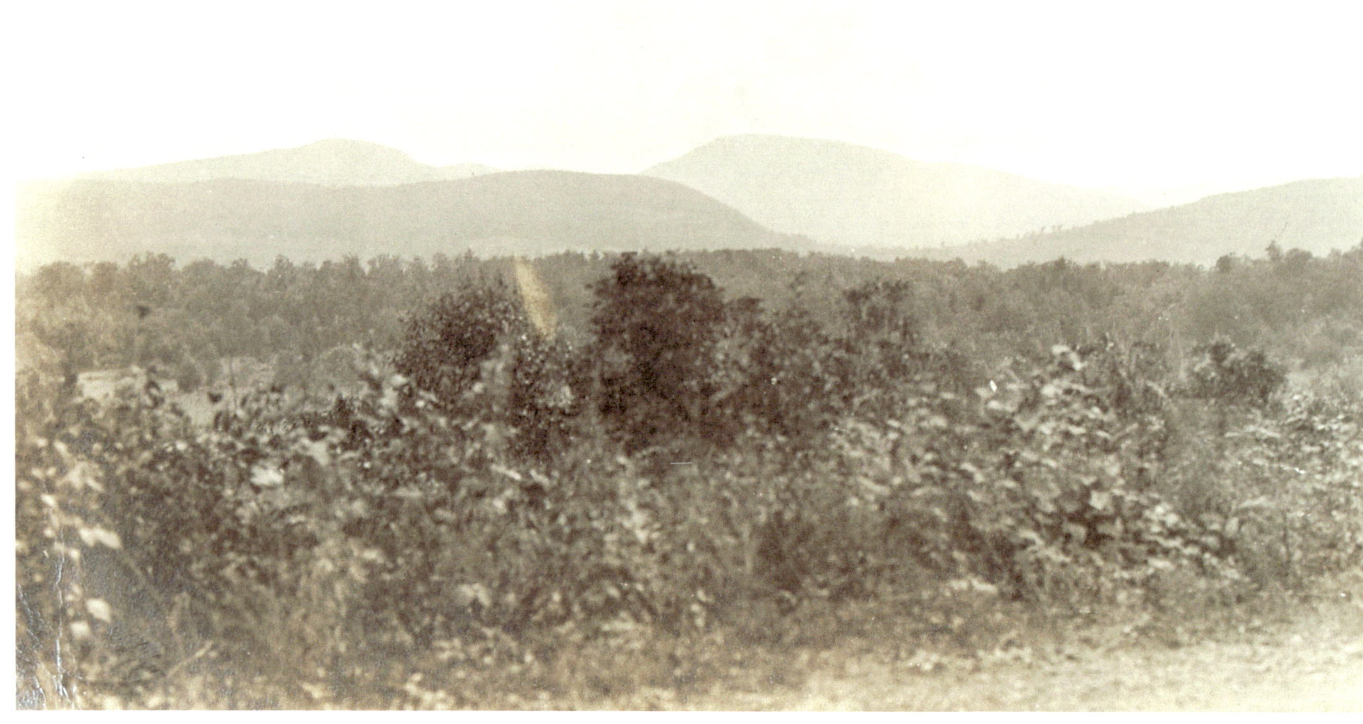

fig. 1 Unidentified photographer, *Catskill View, Woodstock, New York*, ca. 1905. Silver print. Winterthur Library, Downs Collection, 92x39.1140.272.

Introduction

NANCY E. GREEN

It was early in June 1902 when three men gathered on top of Overlook Mountain and gazed down the valley at the hamlet of Woodstock below (fig. 1). For all three it was a triumphant moment. After several months of searching, they had finally found an idyllic spot for their future arts colony. Ralph Radcliffe Whitehead (fig. 2), the man who would finance the project, wrote exultantly to his wife Jane (fig. 3) a couple of days later,

> We have found a country with a sky—such beauty of sky I have not seen except in France, I mean of Northern skies. Such a sky for any painter, a transparent blue with wonderful gradation towards the horizon and such beauty of cloud forms & of distant blue landscape as I never expected to see in N. Y. State. ... Here is an atmosphere for you, dear, which I did not hope for and the beauty of the landscape is very great.[1]

Byrdcliffe,[2] Whitehead's dream of an artists' community, had found its home.

Writer Hervey White (fig. 4), associated with Jane Addams's Hull House in Chicago, and painter Bolton Brown (fig. 5) shared that mountaintop vision with Whitehead, and both men put all their energies into establishing the community and attracting like-minded creative people. Unlike other similar Arts and Crafts colonies in America and in Europe, Byrdcliffe had a threefold mission: to produce beautiful handmade objects that, when sold, would finance the colony; to offer classes in all the crafts so that the colony's success would go forward for future generations; and to lead a healthful life on a working farm that would help to support the inhabitants and provide the best of a rural environment in terms of beauty and simplicity of lifestyle.

For nearly three decades the Whiteheads would summer, and occasionally winter, at Byrdcliffe. The campus became host to numerous writers, artists, and musicians who came and stayed, sometimes for a summer or two or even more. Some bought land from Whitehead and built permanent summer residences; some visited annually but stayed at the inn, the Villetta (fig. 6). It was a complex group that came and, inevitably, personalities clashed. But the variety of participants was impressive. Among the artists, Hermann Dudley Murphy, Dawson Dawson-Watson, John Carlson, Carl Lindin, Birge Harrison, William Schumacher, Blanche Lazzell, Ellen Gates Starr, and Laurin Martin all brought skill and professionalism to the colony. The diverse group of writers included Charlotte Perkins Gilman, Elizabeth von Arnim,

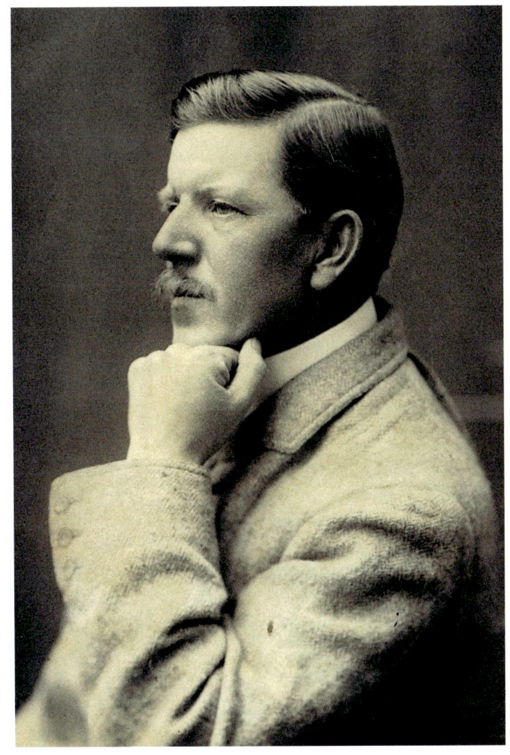

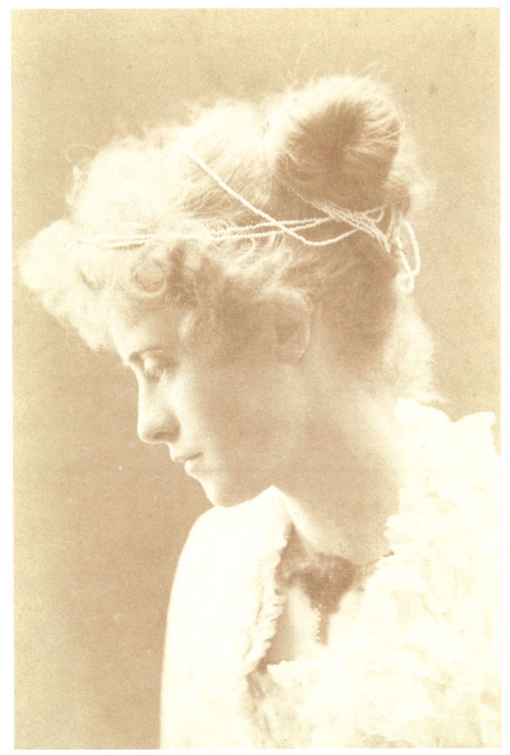

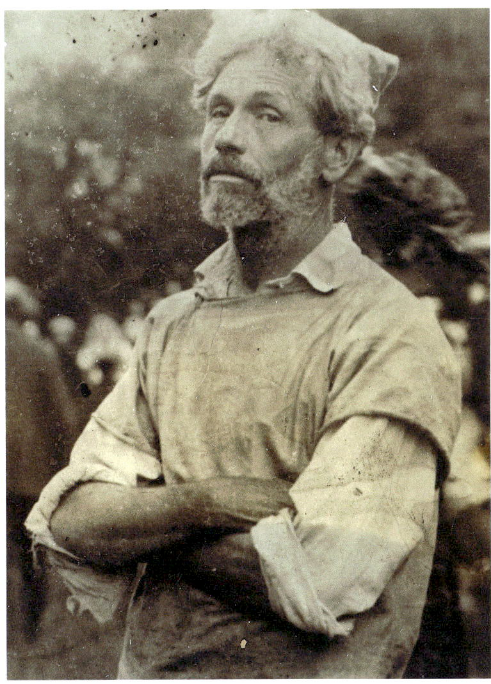

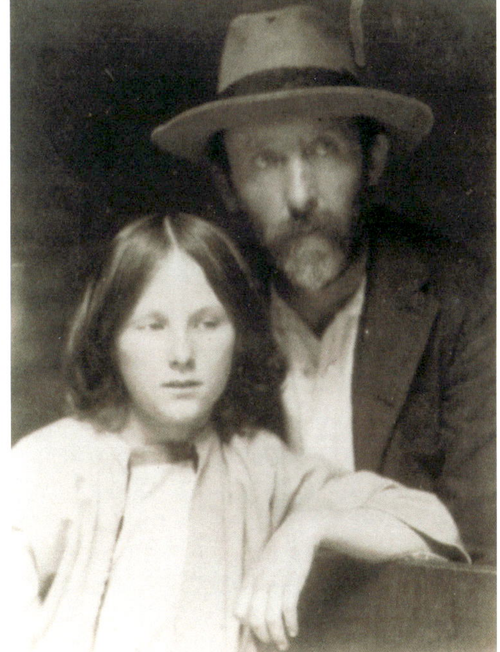

Above
fig. 2 J. Caswall Smith, British, active ca. 1890s, *Ralph Radcliffe Whitehead*, ca. 1895. Platinum print. Collection of the Byrdcliffe Art Colony of the Woodstock Guild.

Below
fig. 4 Unidentified photographer, *Hervey White*, ca. 1915. Silver print. Collection of the Byrdcliffe Art Colony of the Woodstock Guild.

Above
fig. 3 H. S. Mendelssohn, British, active ca. 1880s–1910s, *Portrait of Jane Byrd McCall in Court Dress*, 1886. Albumen print. Collection of the Byrdcliffe Art Colony of the Woodstock Guild. Gift of Jill and Mark Willcox Jr.

Below
fig. 5 Eva Watson-Schütze, American, 1867–1935, *Bolton Brown with His Daughter Eleanor*, ca. 1905. Reprint of original platinum print. Collection of the Byrdcliffe Art Colony of the Woodstock Guild, Alf Evers Collection. Gift of the Douglas C. James Charitable Trust.

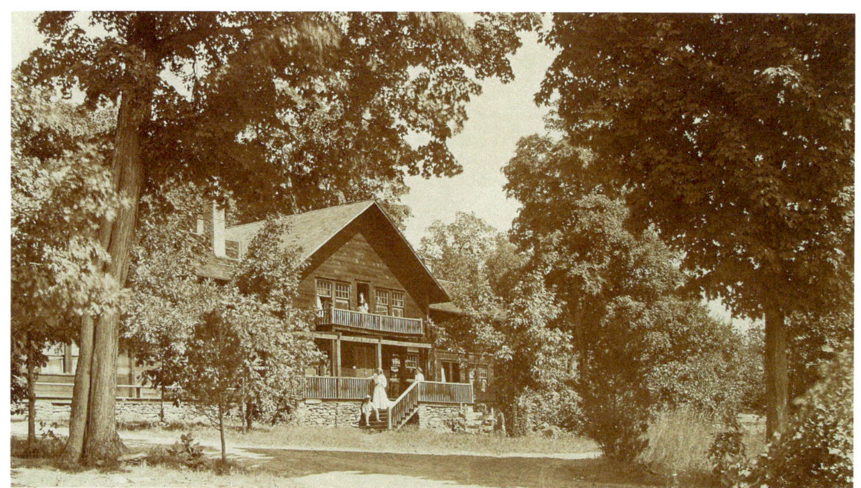

fig. 6 Unidentified photographer, *The Villetta Inn at Byrdcliffe*, ca. 1910. Silver print. Winterthur Library, Downs Collection, 92x39.1140.239.

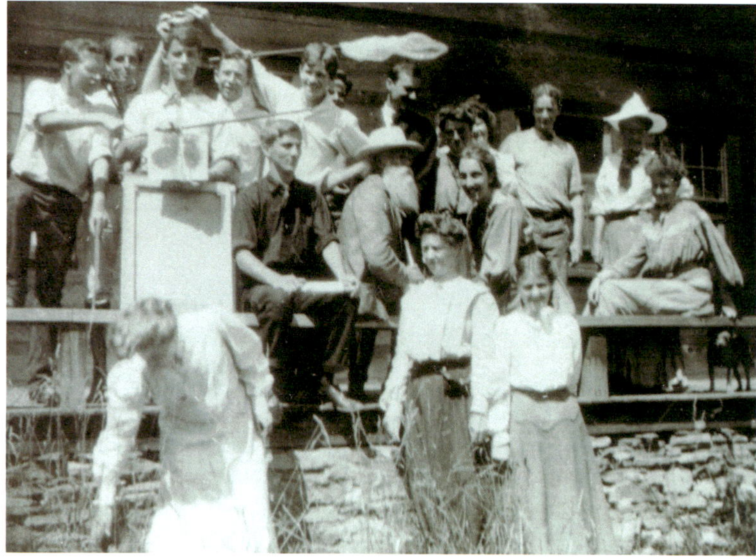

fig. 7 Unidentified photographer, *Group Photograph at Byrdcliffe*, 1905. Artist A. Harold Knott in center with dark shirt and pants; naturalist John Burroughs next to him and writer Isabel Moore in hat at far right. Silver print. Collection of Harleigh Knott.

Oscar Lovell Triggs, Owen Wister, James Shotwell, John Dewey, and John Burroughs (fig. 7).

Despite Byrdcliffe's failure as a commercial venture, Whitehead succeeded in some ways where previous such ventures had failed. Whitehead, raised in Victorian England, was enamored of the teachings of William Morris and John Ruskin and, while he did not follow the socialist views of Morris[3] nor the humanitarian, moralizing approach of Ruskin, he did believe that a community with shared artistic goals could thrive. He successfully encouraged women working within the sphere of decorative arts. Though it was commonplace for women to be thus employed at the turn of the century, Whitehead did not pigeonhole them into gender-oriented crafts or assign credit for their work to their male collaborators. Women at Byrdcliffe were involved in metalwork, weaving, pottery making, painting, furniture design, and even architectural design. Men, too, like many of their counterparts involved with the Arts and Crafts aesthetic, worked in the fields of weaving and pottery decoration. In most cases, each person was given due credit for his or her work, though some of the collaborative pieces remain anonymous.

At the time that Byrdcliffe was founded, one of the most crucial debates among Arts and Crafts practitioners revolved around the use of machines for mundane chores, leaving the creative work to be done individually by the artist. Many thought that the machine had a purpose and that a complete rejection of it in favor of the purely handwrought displayed a foolish romanticism. Others, adhering to a complete medieval guild approach, felt that use of a machine dehumanized the worker. At Byrdcliffe, machines were in use and, like Frank Lloyd Wright,[4] Whitehead felt that the machine did not cause an artist to lose interest in his work but rather enabled him to get on with the business of creating in a timely way. While a seemingly simple point, this made a huge difference in the production schedule of any such enterprise and also dramatically cut the time that was spent on menial work.

The very atmosphere of the community itself was important to Whitehead. He envisioned a colony where the children of the inhabitants would live healthy lives, learning their lessons outdoors when weather permitted, being trained in the crafts at a young age while also learning to distinguish beauty in their surroundings. He

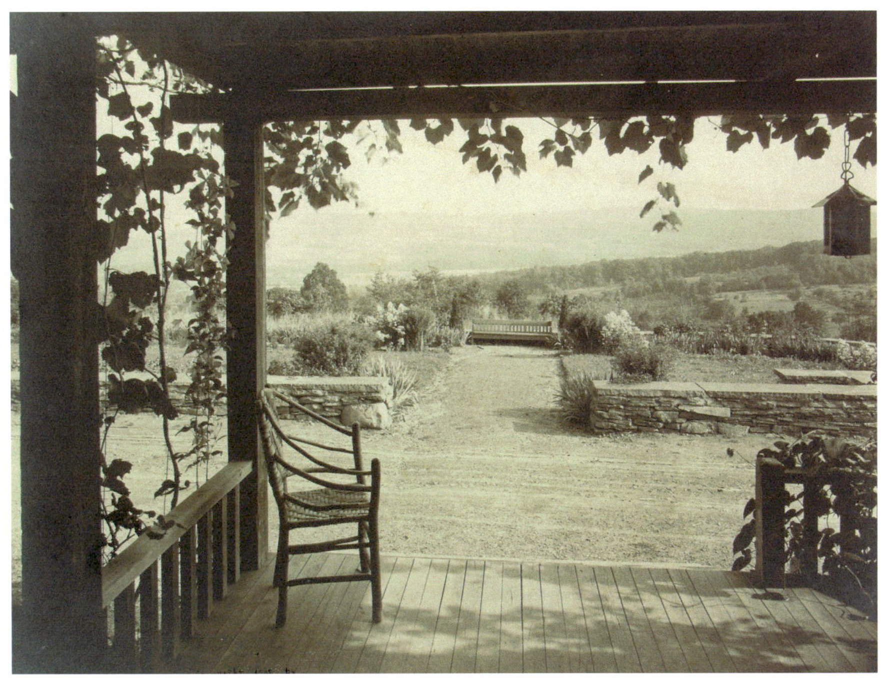

fig. 8 Jessie Tarbox Beals, *View from White Pines Front Porch*, 1908. Silver print. Winterthur Library, Downs Collection, 92x39.1140.604.

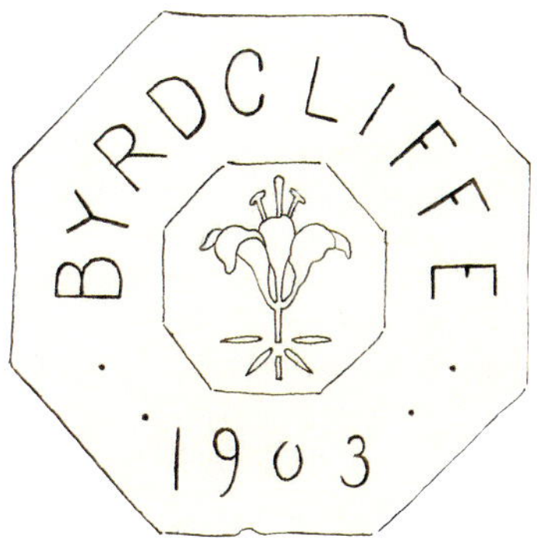

thought the art school would attract a new, active group of like-minded practitioners who would carry on the dream into future generations. To this end he sought out gifted teachers active in the Arts and Crafts movement.[5] He traveled from New York to Philadelphia to Boston in search of artists he thought would inspire and develop the skills of these students. He wanted these artists themselves to achieve a complete satisfaction in their work, and so he provided the most up-to-date equipment, offered them access to his superb personal library, hosted cultural evenings, and hoped the furniture they produced would find serious buyers. When this market failed to materialize, Whitehead cut his losses and closed the furniture shop in 1905.

The colony would continue in many configurations until the death of Whitehead in 1929. His dream of a community of like-minded artists working together in harmonious collaboration was an unrealistic one, yet, unlike other such enterprises, the Byrdcliffe campus still exists as an artist's colony today. Though the concept has changed from Whitehead's original intention, a nugget of his ideal remains—nurturing artists in a place of unparalleled beauty and inspiration (fig. 8).

Notes

1. RRW to Jane, June 5, 1902, Kingston, New York. Winterthur Library, Downs Collection.

2. At the beginning there was some debate as to the name of the colony: "As to names, I think really you must simplify—the address must have as few names as possible... let the estate & the company be the same name, 'Yggdrasil' our house might be, 'Ye House of Yggdrasil' & the company 'The Looms of Yggdrasil' I like very much, & am quite willing to give up 'Byrdcliffe'" (Jane to RRW, undated letter, Wednesday, 6:00 p.m., Winterthur Library, Downs Collection). "Yggdrasil," the tree of life in Norse legend, was a favorite of William Morris. "Igdrasil" was also the name of a literary journal published in England in the late nineteenth century to which Ruskin periodically contributed. The Whiteheads ultimately decided to stay with "Byrdcliffe," a combination of Jane's middle name, Byrd, and the second half of Ralph's middle name, Radcliffe.

3. Though Whitehead would have agreed with the motivation that led Morris to his socialist ideas: "We were borne into a dull time oppressed by bourgeoisdom and philistinism so sorely that we were forced to turn our back on ourselves, and only in ourselves and the world of art and literature was there any hope." Morris to Fred Henderson quoted in E. P. Thompson, *William Morris: Romantic to Revolutionary* (Stanford, 1955, [reprint 1988]), 14.

4. As early as 1901 Wright was writing, "In time, I hope to prove that the machine is capable of carrying to fruition high ideals of art—higher than the world has yet seen!" Frank Lloyd Wright, "The Art and Craft of the Machine," *Brush and Pencil* (May 1901): 84.

5. It was T. J. Cobden-Sanderson who first coined the phrase "Arts and Crafts" on May 25, 1887, at an early meeting of what became the Arts and Crafts Exhibition Society, established in 1888. Alan Crawford, *C. R. Ashbee: Architect, Designer & Romantic Socialist* (New Haven & London, 1983), 31.

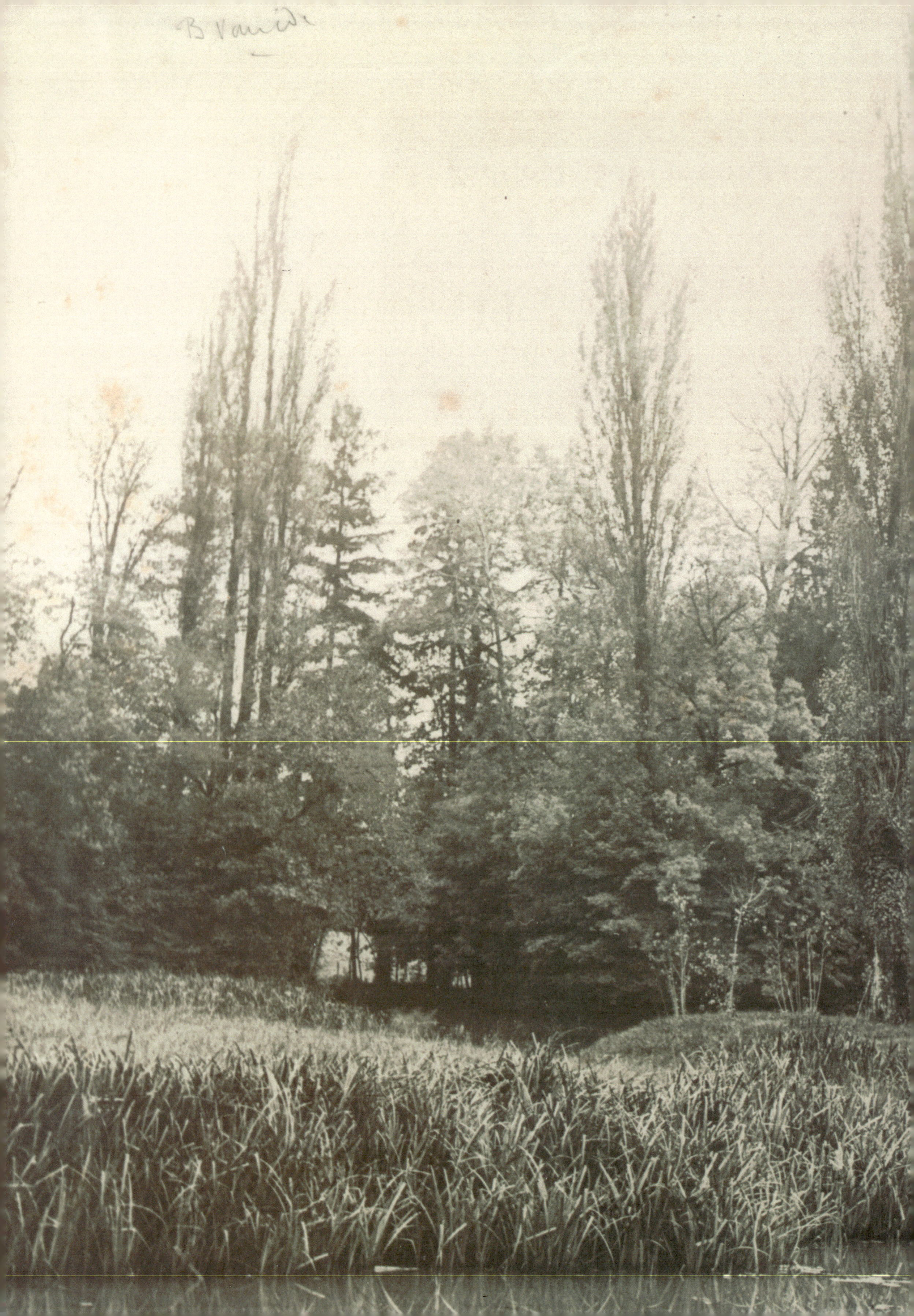

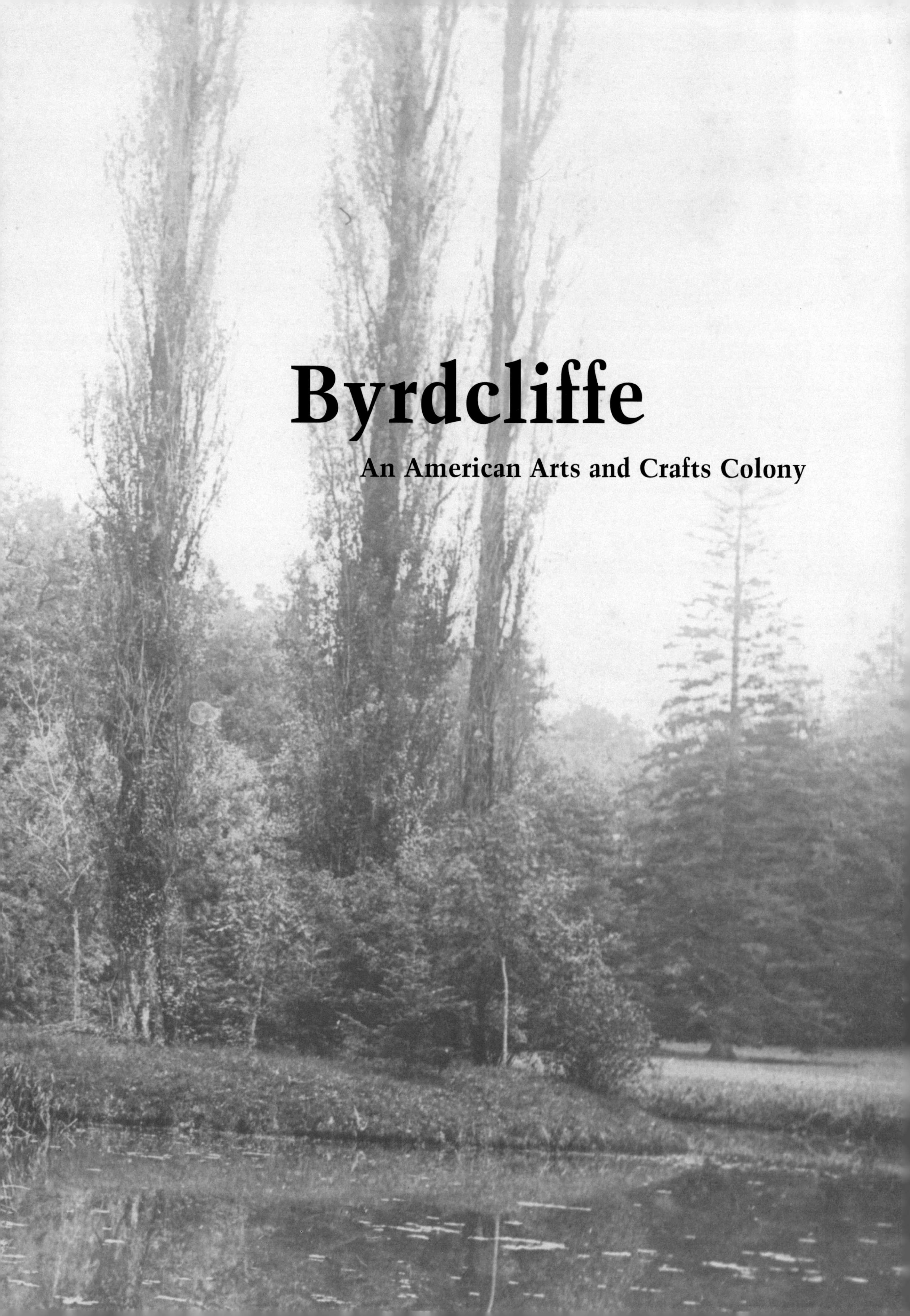

Byrdcliffe

An American Arts and Crafts Colony

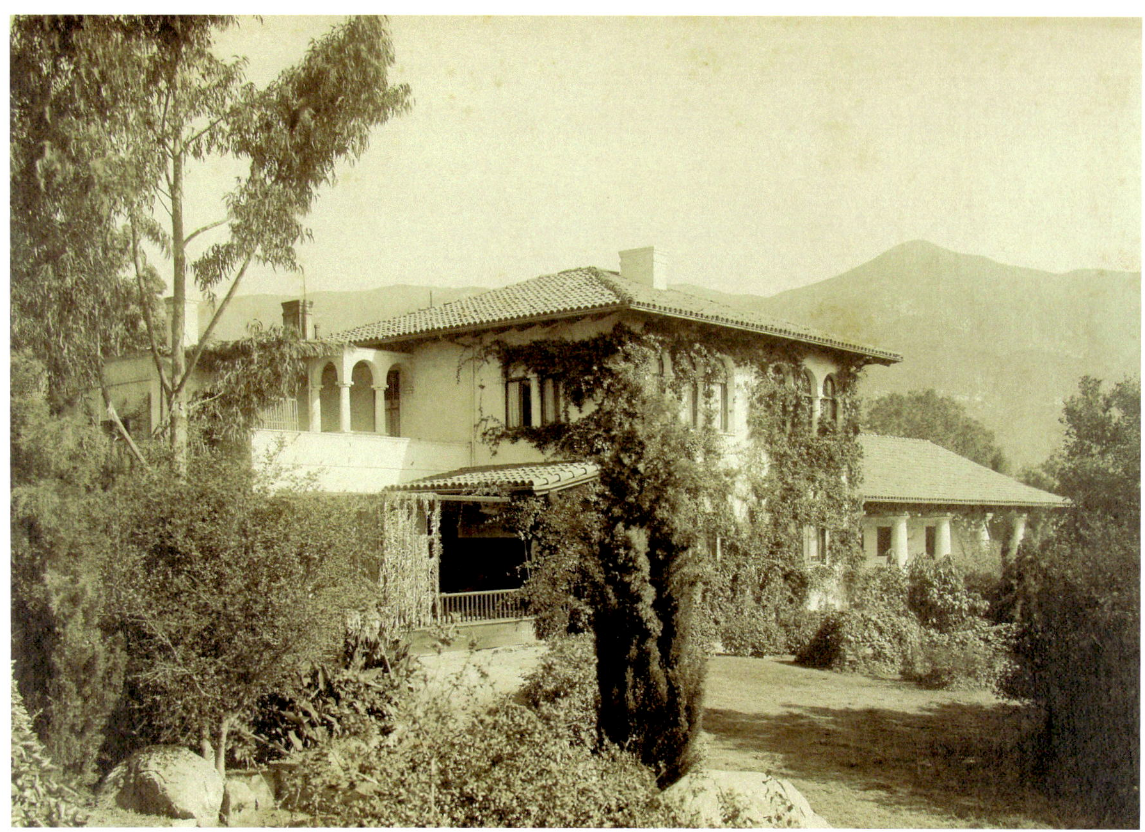

fig. 1 Attributed to Ralph Whitehead, *Arcady*, ca. 1895. Winterthur Library, Downs Collection, 92x39.1140.296.

Byrdcliffe's History

Industrial Revolution

TOM WOLF

When Ralph Radcliffe Whitehead and Jane Byrd McCall became romantically involved in 1890, both were disciples and acquaintances of John Ruskin. They shared his belief in the spiritual value of the arts and his hatred of the dehumanizing effects of the Industrial Revolution. Whitehead's family, felt manufacturers from Saddleworth in Yorkshire, England, were immensely wealthy thanks to industrialization, and he sought a purpose for his life and his inheritance. When he met Jane McCall, an aspiring artist from Philadelphia on an extended tour of Europe with her mother and sister, he found a kindred spirit. Together they developed an idea of a community of men and women making arts and crafts in a healthy, beautiful natural setting. It took more than a decade for them to actualize their fantasy, but they did make it real as Byrdcliffe, the art colony that they founded in Woodstock, New York, in 1902. Byrdcliffe became a link in a chain of Arts and Crafts enterprises throughout the United States, and transformed the little town of Woodstock into a center for the arts and for alternative lifestyles that would have a powerful impact on the culture of the United States.[1]

Whitehead and McCall fell in love during an art-filled tour of Italy. She was thirty years old; he, thirty-five and already married. His wife, Marie, was reluctant to divorce, and in the 1890s divorce was controversial and legally difficult. In the early stages of their courtship Ralph and Jane kept their relationship a secret. Once they had decided to make it permanent, Jane McCall returned to the United States with her skeptical mother, and he established residence in Germany to get a speedy divorce from his Austrian wife. After six months in Berlin, where he apprenticed with a master carpenter and lived in an apartment decorated with Arts and Crafts fabrics by William Morris, the divorce was final. Then Marie Whitehead wrote her former husband a painful letter to be opened at her death that included a prophetic analysis of his personality: "You request too much, you long for something impossible, and therefore, you must be discontented with reality."[2] She came from a humble background, and little is known about her—but the opposite is the case with Ralph and Jane Whitehead. Their relationship is extremely well documented, and over 1500 letters between the two of them are available in the library of the Joseph Downs

Collection in the Winterthur Museum in Delaware. We know that from the outset of their romance they planned to create an ideal Arts and Crafts community, and that Whitehead's hopes of being trained by the great craftsman William Morris were disappointed: "Morris will not take me as a pupil. . . he thinks tapestry is too difficult for me who by own confession have no artistic facility."[3]

Whitehead's self-deprecation is typical; he measured himself by the highest standards, and usually saw himself falling short. "The greatest difficulty is to be content with one's own small capacity," he wrote to Jane McCall early in their relationship.[4] He believed the Arts and Crafts dogma that a fulfilled life is realized through manual labor, but because of his inherited wealth he did not have the usual necessity: "Oh, that I had daily work!" he exclaimed somewhat improbably to his future wife.[5] His desire for work comes up often in his correspondence, usually accompanied by declarations of failure and moods of depression, and it helps explain his admiration for artists, who felt compelled to work.

Following their marriage in 1892 the Whiteheads spent much of 1893 in Paris, where Jane studied painting at the Académie Julian. They then returned to the United States to build a new home, and to realize their dreams of a colony. Whitehead had already articulated the concept of that colony in *Grass of the Desert*, a book of meditations he published in 1892. Its title was derived from one of his literary idols, Walt Whitman, and its content reflected the philosophies of his mentors, Ruskin and Morris.[6] It included chapters devoted to "Dante" and to "Modern Painters," and featured a discussion of Plato's *Phaedrus* that Whitehead concluded by quoting directly from Plato for fourteen pages. In the chapter entitled "Work," he set out his ideas for a "convent" whose members would live rational lives, each doing several jobs, including making crafts and farming.

Why did the Whiteheads choose to relocate to the United States? It was Mrs. Whitehead's native land and she had family there, while he had virtually no family left, and they were nervous about the scandal his divorce and immediate remarriage might produce in Europe. He had not defined himself professionally in Europe and could start over in America. Also, he was a social progressive who felt guilty about living lavishly from the labor of others, and he admired democracy and the ideal of social equality.[7] At the same time his idealism was complemented by a pervasive snobbism that led him to judge people and find them lacking in refinement, a snobbism that was probably inherited but also his way to elevate himself above his continual sense of failure.[8]

The Whiteheads settled in Montecito, a suburb of Santa Barbara, California, beautifully sited near the Pacific Ocean. In 1894, when they bought seventy mountaintop acres for their new home, Montecito retained traces of its Native American and Spanish history, but it was becoming a community of mansions owned by wealthy residents, many based in the Midwest or on the East Coast. In collaboration with the architect Samuel Ilsley and the builder and Arts and Crafts metalworker Christoph Tornoe, the Whiteheads created Arcady, an Italianate white stucco mansion that consisted of a square, two-story tower with bedrooms above, joined to a long, spacious room flanked by a colonnaded porch that the Whiteheads called the "stoa" (fig. 1). The room was used as Mrs. Whitehead's studio and a music room; the porch faced the ocean and had plaster cast reliefs of horsemen from the Parthenon frieze set into its wall. Although grand, the building's simple plan recalls photographs of rustic Italian architecture that Whitehead

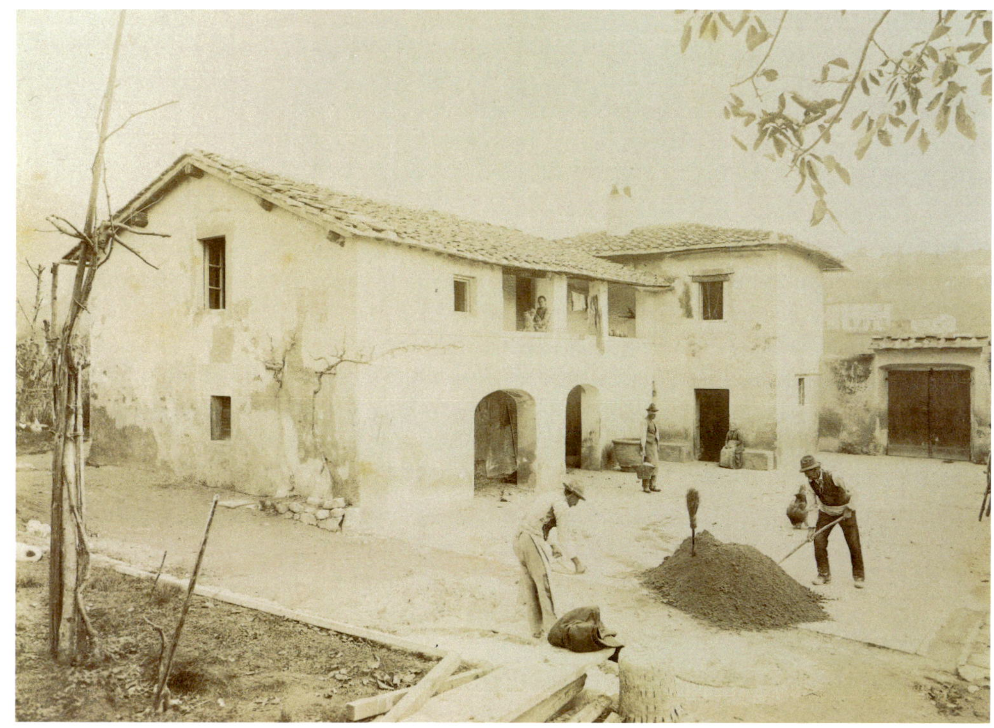

fig. 2 Flli. Alinari, Italian, 19th century, *Villa Salviati*. Albumen print. Winterthur Library, Downs Collection, 92x39.1140.842.

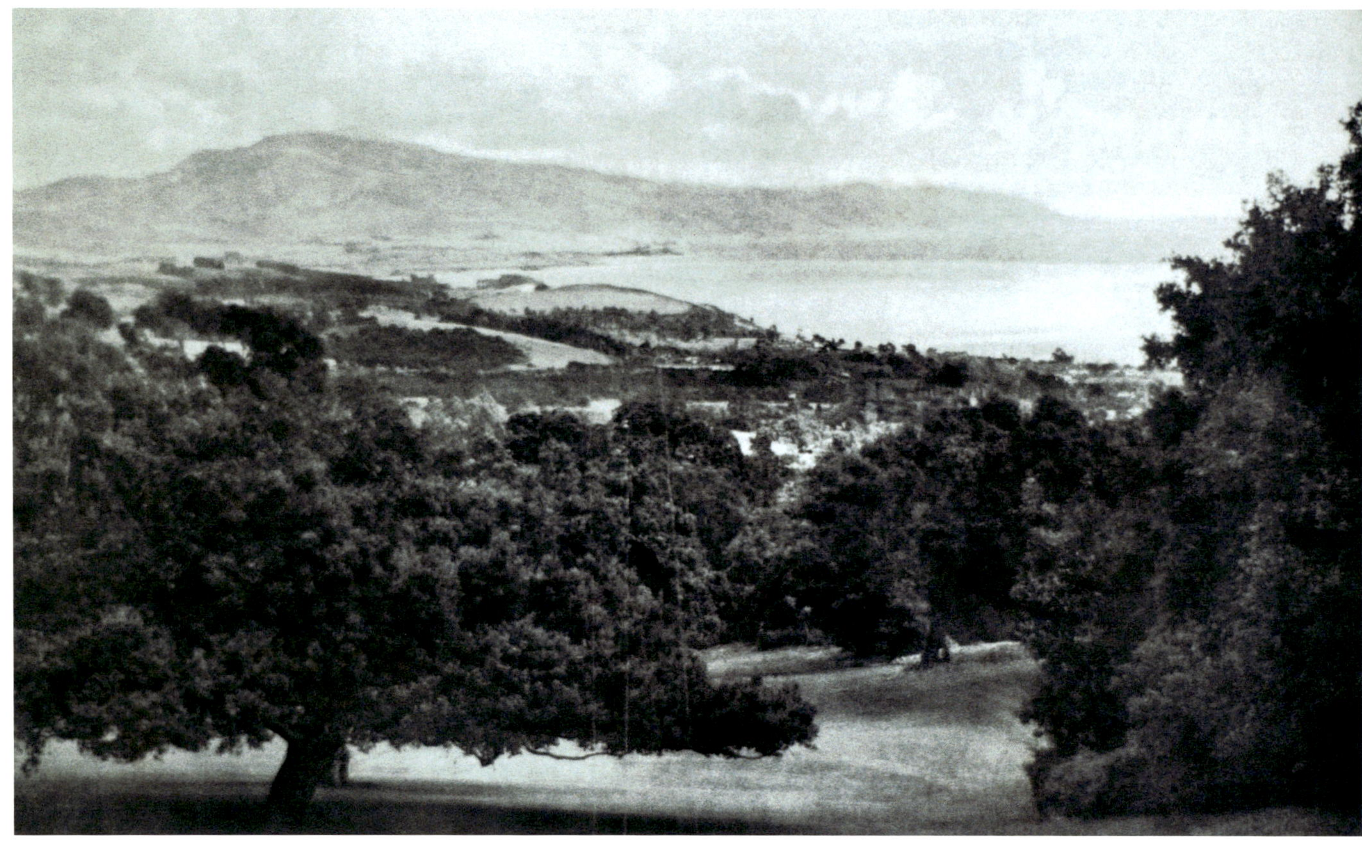

fig. 3 J. Walter Collings, Amercan, active 1920s–30s, *View of the Pacific Ocean from Arcady*, ca. 1920. Published in *"Arcady" Montecito*, The Garden Club of America, 1926. Collection of the Santa Barbara Historical Society. Courtesy of the author.

brought with him from Europe (fig. 2). Located on the top of a mountain, Arcady commanded spectacular views of both mountains and the ocean, most strikingly from the second floor bedroom (fig. 3).

Ralph and Jane were making a family at Arcady; their first son, Ralph Jr., was born in 1899, and Peter followed in 1901. But Jane suffered from ill health, including miscarriages and stomach tumors.[9] Much of her time was spent resting and convalescing, struggling to find energy to work on her paintings. A family friend remembered she "appeared to be an invalid."[10] Still, the Whiteheads had the energy to host elegant dinner parties, and they improved their property, working with other landowners to build roads and plumbing. Although altered over the years, Arcady is still extant and retains its magnificent view and some sense of the lush gardens that the Whiteheads cultivated with the help of an old English gardener they met in California.[11] Whitehead hired a team of Mexican workers, who took the soil from excavating a road and constructed a terraced garden below the house. Some large rocks were deliberately retained to serve as visual foils to the hollyhocks and Easter lilies that flanked "their lawn of native grasses, unmown and sprinkled in with flowers introduced with such modest art of the gardener as to yield the effect of a natural bloom-strewn meadow."[12] Terraces of olive trees and grape vines gave way to orchards of tangerines and grapefruits that underlined the ocean view.

Despite many modifications at Arcady, the former studio still retains two plaster casts of singing angels by the Renaissance sculptor Luca della Robbia, a detail typical of Whitehead's ambition to bring the art of the European old masters to the United States. Along with plaster casts, he bought hundreds of photographs of Italian Renaissance and English Pre-Raphaelite paintings and sculptures which he made available to the Santa Barbara school system in frames stained by Mrs. Whitehead. He wrote a small pamphlet, modeled after William Morris's socialist tracts, titled *Pictures for Schools*, where he defined the moral and intellectual value of being exposed to artistic masterpieces in facsimile.[13] In this period reproductions of works by Renaissance masters frequently adorned the walls of liberal, socially concerned institutions, such as Hull House in Chicago, particularly in their classrooms. This was not just a condescending attempt to educate the lower classes, for the Whiteheads themselves lived with framed reproductions as part of their carefully planned decors in both Montecito and Woodstock. Mrs. Whitehead may have insisted that their architect not use "one commonplace stock machinery door . . . they are to be squat or round or nailed or paneled across," but a framed reproduction of a Raphael Madonna was acceptable because it carried with it the forms of the great European artistic tradition.[14]

Whitehead's interest in education, with his two sons and the philanthropic uses of his fortune in mind, led him to build and staff a small school on his Montecito property—a school that practiced the Sloyd method of teaching. This Swedish technique emphasized manual training, and, being consonant with the ideals of the Arts and Crafts movement, it spread through Europe and the United States in the second half of the nineteenth century. When Whitehead started his school there already was another Sloyd school in Santa Barbara, one that would eventually evolve into the Santa Barbara branch of the University of California. Sloyd was intended to supplement, not replace, normal public school, and it involved about six hours of manual work per week. It focused on woodworking as the ideal craft for its ends, which were "not to turn out Carpenters, but to develop the mental, moral, and physical powers of children."[15] In 1900 Miss Annette Butler taught at the Arcady school and the next year the Whiteheads hired the daughter of Philadelphia educator J. Liberty Tadd to teach there. Although Tadd was critical of the Sloyd method, his step-by-step system of manual training had much in common with it. He is known for his emphasis on ambidextrous drawing, and his Philadelphia school was notable for reaching out to minorities.[16] Similarly, a roster of students from Whitehead's Sloyd school includes not only the names of children of his prosperous friends, but also those of Hispanic children from the local working class[17] (fig. 4).

While Mrs. Whitehead convalesced in Montecito, her husband traveled frequently. He visited Chicago to interview mediums for the American Society of Psychical Research.[18] While there he got to know many of the progressive thinkers of the period, including philosopher John Dewey and Jane Addams, founder of Hull House, the settlement house dedicated to helping impoverished immigrants. His main contact was writer Hervey White, who would be a key participant in the founding of Byrdcliffe. White's gregarious personality kept him always surrounded by friends, and he introduced his bohemian acquaintances to the reserved Englishman, who would

fig. 4 Unidentified photographer, *Sloyd School at Arcady*, ca. 1899. Silver print. Collection of the Byrdcliffe Art Colony of the Woodstock Guild, Alf Evers Collection. Gift of the Douglas C. James Charitable Trust.

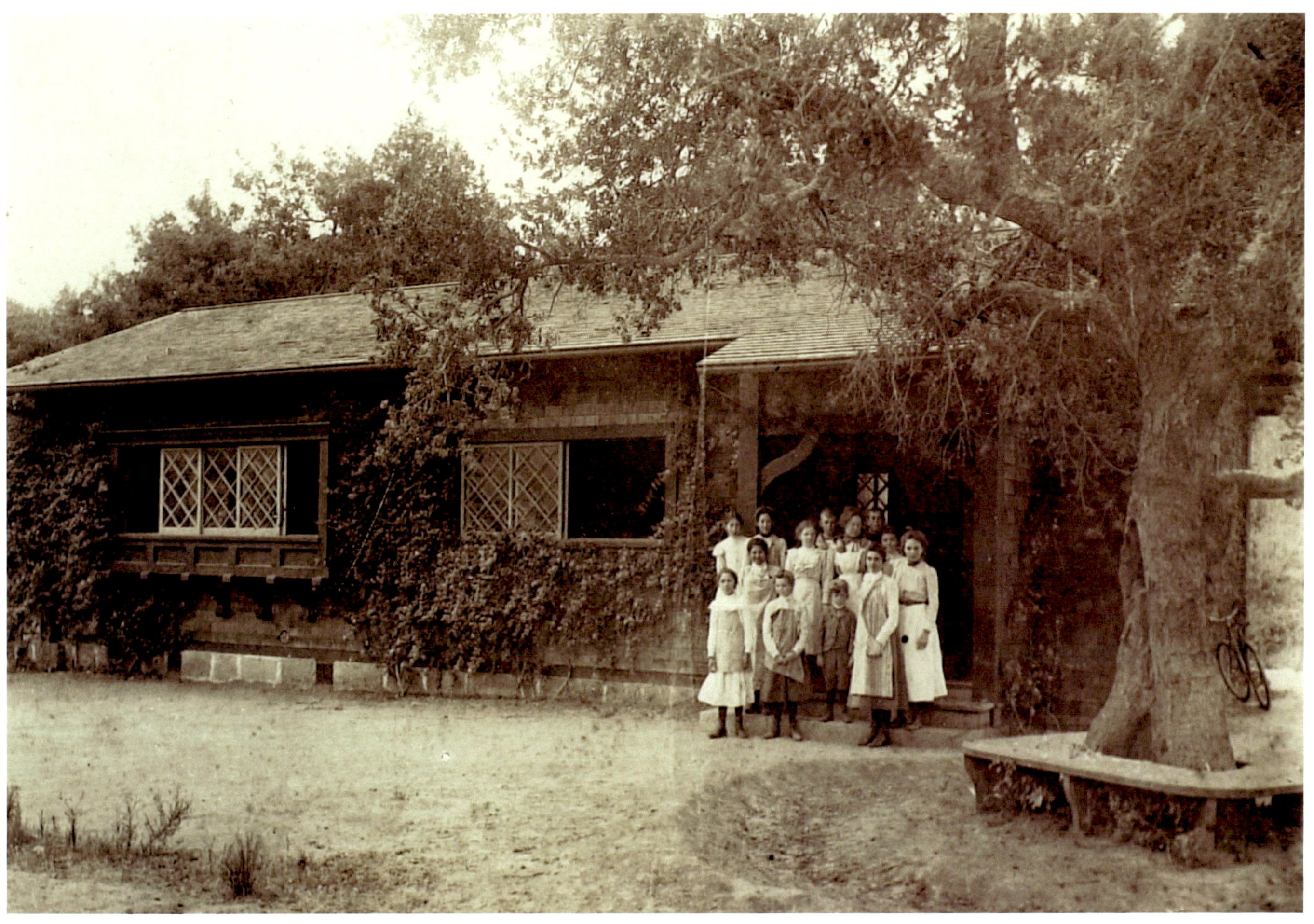

take them out and pay for everything, "a privilege he insisted on with artists."[19] Whitehead also frequently visited Los Angeles, where he kept the company of artists and musicians. These included painters William Wendt, Leonard Lester, and Charles Walter Stetson, whose wife Charlotte Perkins had spent time at Hull House and was one of Hervey White's many friends. Mrs. Perkins became one of the most influential feminist thinkers of her time with her book, *Women and Economics*, published in 1898. In 1894 she and Stetson divorced, with much attendant publicity, and in 1900 she married her cousin, George Houghton Gilman, who subsequently served as Whitehead's lawyer in the creation of Byrdcliffe. Stetson, soon after divorcing his wife, married her good friend Grace Ellery Channing, and the three jointly parented Katharine, the child of the original marriage. For much of the 1890s Stetson and Channing, and sometimes Perkins, lived in Pasadena where Whitehead visited them. He also cultivated a group of musicians; he invited them to perform chamber music at Arcady, and provided living and studio space at the bottom of his hill to White, Wendt, and Lester. Landscape painter Birge Harrison worked in a building supplied by Whitehead, while Mrs. Whitehead benefited from having professional artists to paint with, and in Harrison's case, a veteran art teacher to critique her efforts. The other side of the Whiteheads' California life involved wealthy friends who were part of their social circle, including Charles Frederick Eaton, who bridged the two groups since he was both affluent and an important Arts and Crafts designer, who used local sea shells in his designs for book bindings and frames. Mrs. Whitehead was thrilled to work with him on an elaborate, horse-drawn float for one of Santa Barbara's famous floral parades in 1895. Shaped like a Venetian boat, it was called "Flowers of the Sea and Seashore" because it featured abalone shells and seaweed along with local flowers. It was topped by a lateen sail from Mrs. Whitehead, while below hung fabric painted with waves by Eaton and Birge Harrison. After the parade Mrs. Whitehead planned to use the sail and shells to decorate her studio.[20]

fig. 5 Attributed to Charles Frederick Eaton, *Leather Photograph Album*, ca. 1900. Winterthur Library, Downs Collection, 92x39.661.

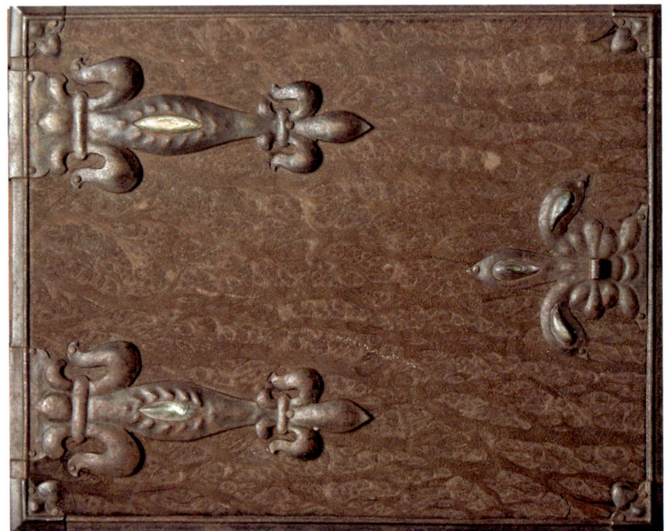

A striking photo album that the Whiteheads used for pictures of Arcady and Byrdcliffe was probably made by Eaton (fig. 5). It is bound with leather, secured by metal straps that have pieces of blue shell set into them, an unusual combination of materials characteristic of Eaton's workshop. Here the metal straps were cut into fleurs-de-lys shapes, incorporating a favorite symbol of the Whiteheads, who would adopt the *giglio*, the Italian version of the fleur-de-lys, the emblem of the city of Florence, as one of their images of Byrdcliffe.[21]

In 1896 the Whiteheads took part in a flower festival by constructing an ornate float on the theme of *Primavera*. It was covered with sod planted with pink daisies; a woman dressed as Spring stood under a baldacchino accompanied by children holding garlands of daisies (fig. 6). A team of four chestnut horses was rented to pull the float, wearing harnesses that three women had spent five days covering with green silk. When the horses balked and a pair of "ugly old cart horses" had to be substituted, Mrs. Whitehead was distressed that this would cost the Whiteheads the first prize—in fact, they won second.[22]

The Whiteheads named Arcady after antiquity's imaginary land of peace and serenity, but it proved less than idyllic once Ralph became involved in a scandalous relationship with Louise Hart, the artistic daughter of a friend. The liaison caused the Whiteheads to be ostracized by Montecito acquaintances, and some have thought that their decision to pursue their plan to create an ideal colony in an environment far from Santa Barbara was catalyzed by the Hart affair, but this was probably not the case.[23] Several documents attest to the compromising relationship, but only one is dated: Mrs. Whitehead's, where she demands that her husband see less of Miss Hart. Its date is 1896—and it is unlikely that she allowed the affair to continue for five years before insisting on a move.[24] Rather, the motive that impelled them to finally act on the colony idea can be found in a heartfelt letter from Whitehead to his wife written on a gloomy night in Chicago in 1901:

> I feel so terribly that it haunts me day and night that I have made myself no definite place of usefulness anywhere in this wide world. And I feel that for the boys' sake I must make some place that as they grow up they may be able to respect me as one who bears his part in the march of humanity, as one who is doing his share of the work of the world. . . . To be a country gentleman is no longer sufficing.[25]

This letter was written on Whitehead's way to England, where he researched aspects of the Arts and Crafts movement in preparation for his own colony. He spent time with designer C. R. Ashbee, who was running a crafts factory with forty employees, and with architect Halsey

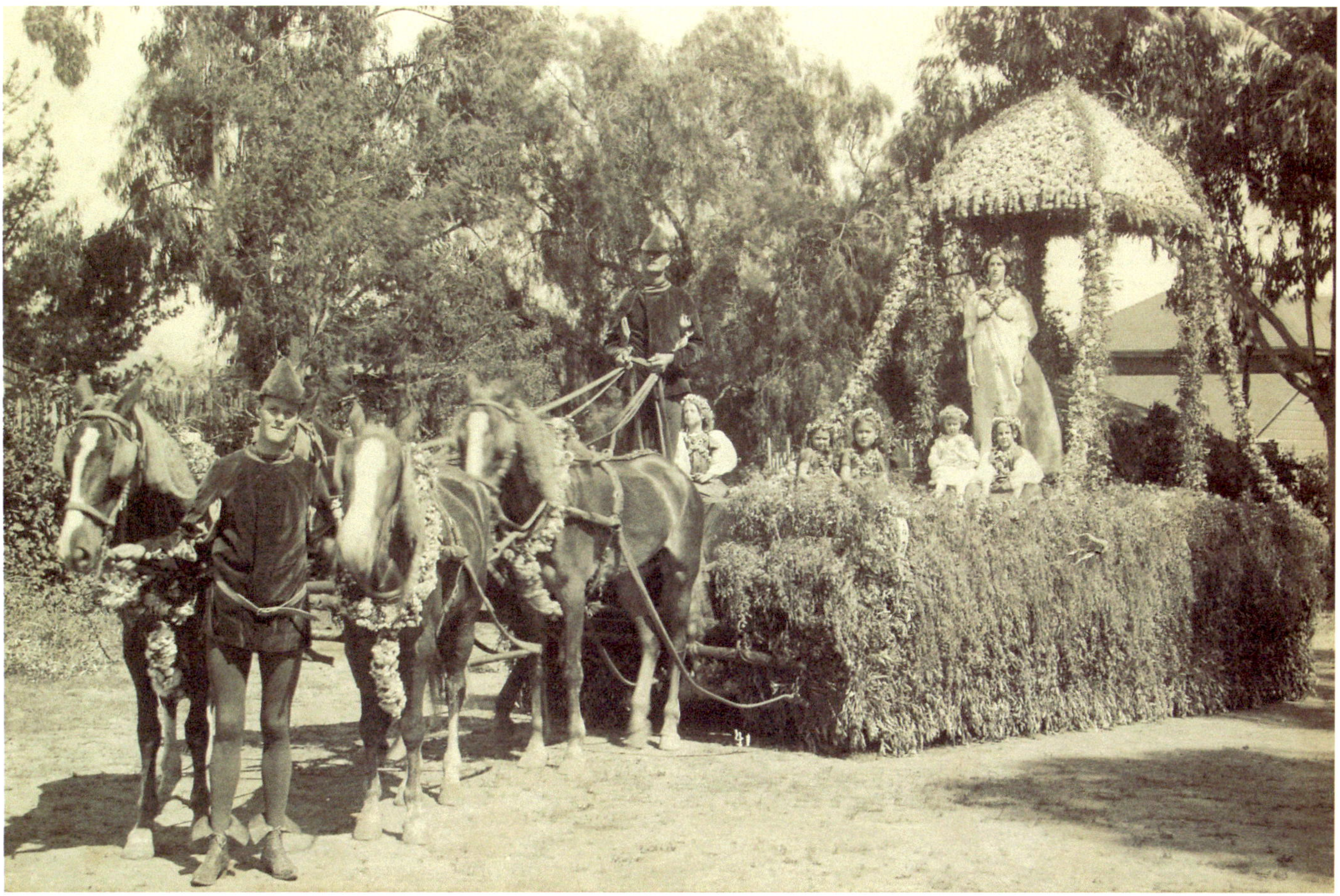

fig. 6 Unidentified photographer, *Primavera Float*, 1896. Albumen print. Winterthur Library, Downs Collection, 92x39.1140.283.

Ricardo. Then he met his American friend Hervey White in Paris; White would be one of the two men he enlisted to realize his vision back in the United States; the other was Bolton Brown.

Brown was an energetic, self-confident, and opinionated man. His strong personality was forged in conflict with his equally strong-willed father, a strict Presbyterian minister who refused to accept the fact that his son was a freethinker.[26] Brown grew up in northern New York and studied art at Syracuse University. By the age of nineteen he was teaching drawing at Cornell, and over the next decade he taught at various colleges, made two trips to Europe, and pursued his passion for mountain climbing (a California mountain bears his name, in honor of his exploring and mapmaking activities).[27] Today Brown is best known as a popularizer of the art of lithography, which he practiced and wrote about in the later 1910s. But in 1902, when he joined Whitehead's project, he was a painter. He had just finished a decade-long stint as the first head of the art department at the newly established Stanford University, where he had encountered resistance to his practice of posing models nude for his coeducational drawing classes. While at Stanford he built a small house, an experience that gave him the confidence to convince Whitehead that he was qualified to direct the building of the new art colony. His Palo Alto house, with its irregular silhouette, walls of exposed wood, and built-in window seats, looked forward to the houses at Byrdcliffe.[28] It also presented an extreme instance of the Arts and Crafts ideal of integrating architecture with the surrounding landscape as the floor of the porch and the roof overhanging it were built around a large oak tree already on the site (fig. 7).

In California, Brown had made himself an expert on Japanese prints; he would buy them from the boats in San Francisco Harbor and sell them to collectors. When he lost his job at Stanford he entertained the idea of moving to Japan, not a practical plan for a man with a wife, three small children, and no income. When Whitehead offered Brown a good salary to help start his art colony, the artist agreed and embarked on a search for the ideal spot.

Whitehead admired Brown for his self-confidence and his talents, but he had a closer personal relationship with Hervey White. They shared many of the same ideals while White's open, freewheeling personality complemented the Englishman's formality—White described Whitehead as

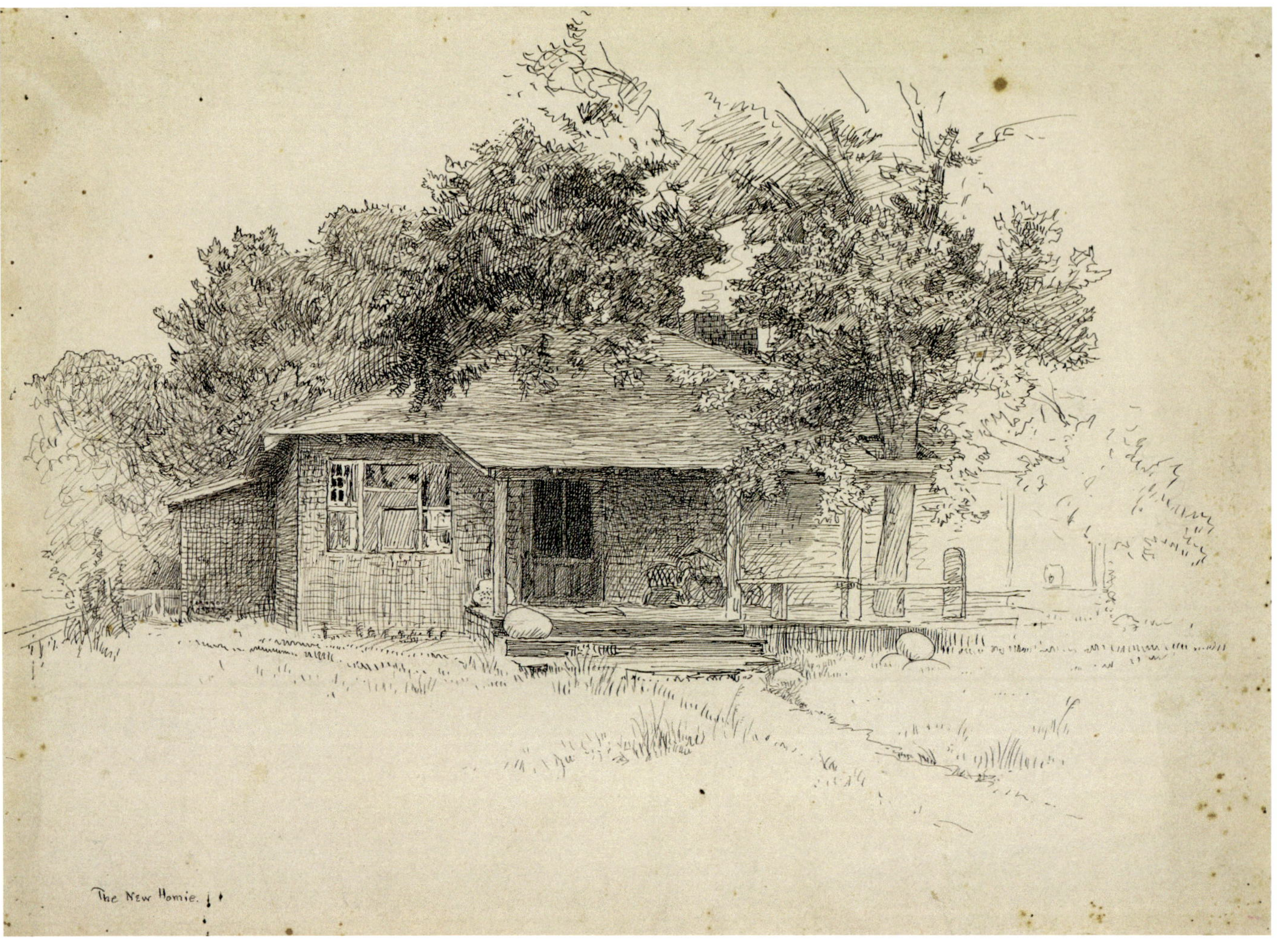

fig. 7 Bolton Brown, *My Homie*, ca. 1895. Ink on paper. Collection of Millicent Coleman.

"the most reserved person I had ever met."[29] In contrast to Whitehead, White grew up in quite impoverished circumstances in Iowa and on his brother's struggling farm in Kansas. But he was well-versed in literature thanks to his maternal grandfather, who was a schoolteacher. White realized that he wanted to be a writer at an early age, and was teaching in a rural school in Kansas by the time he was sixteen. He went to Kansas State University and transferred to Harvard for his senior year, walking and riding freight trains to get from Kansas to Cambridge. At Harvard, where Charles Eliot Norton, Ruskin's close friend, was a big influence, White read Ruskin and admired his social and artistic theories. After graduation he spent a year traveling through Italy, and when he met Whitehead the two men shared a love of that country, as well as the ideals of the Arts and Crafts movement.

The two met in Chicago, where White settled after his return from Europe. He worked at Hull House, an institution that reflected the social criticism of Ruskin and Morris, and in fact was British-inspired—Jane Addams got the idea of founding a charitable settlement house after visiting Toynbee House in London.[30] In Chicago, White worked as a librarian (at the Creor Library) and organized theatrical events for Hull House. For a time he was one of four men who actually lived at Hull House, an organization dominated by well-educated, well-to-do women, and while there he and two friends tried to start an Arts and Crafts furniture company. The Krayle Co. was short-lived, but it planted the idea of a cooperative Arts and Crafts organization. In 1899 White published his first novel, *Differences*, the story of a young society woman working at a settlement house who falls in love with a client, an impoverished, widowed father. Despite its sentimental premise, *Differences* is full of compelling descriptions of lower-class life in Chicago, and it received good reviews. White followed with *Quicksand*, published in 1900, a grim, depressing story of a midwestern farming family whose children's lives are thwarted by the religious orthodoxy of their domineering mother. It was highly praised by Theodore Dreiser, but White's publisher went out of business, stranding his novel in warehouses and slowing the rise of his literary career, although he continued to write and publish for the rest of his life.

According to White, he was introduced to Whitehead by Charlotte Perkins Stetson, who wrote to him, "I am sending you a Yankeeized Englishman, a socialist who intends to spend a few days in Chicago. He is worthwhile."[31] Their meeting set off a sequence of events that included White's extended visit to Arcady in 1900, the introduction of Whitehead to many of White's friends who would become important in the history of Woodstock, and the forming of the group of four—Mr. and Mrs. Whitehead, White, and Brown—who in 1902 began looking for the ideal setting to create an Arts and Crafts colony.[32]

The Whiteheads and White explored Virginia and North Carolina while Brown returned to his native New York to search—but Brown and White preferred New York for practical reasons. The colony was intended to manufacture and sell art and crafts to support itself, so it should be near a commercial center, and New York City was the natural choice. Brown made use of his mountaineering experience to hike through the Catskills, until he trekked to the top of Overlook Mountain and saw the village of Woodstock on the other side. In later years he likened himself to the explorer Balboa when he first saw the Pacific Ocean, overcome by "that extraordinarily beautiful view, amazing in extent, the silver Hudson losing itself in remote haze, those farthest and faintest humps along the horizon being the Shawangunk Mountains."[33] The site satisfied Whitehead's Ruskin-inspired desires for an altitude over fifteen hundred feet, with a view of water, and Brown immediately telegraphed the others to join him in New York. He was hoping to overcome Whitehead's bias against the Catskill region, which the anti-Semitic Englishman had heard was full of Jews. When he arrived Whitehead was pleasantly surprised, as revealed in his first letter from Woodstock, which was addressed to his three-year old son, Bim (Ralph Jr.). He began, "here's a little spray of spruce and some fern and some of your own blue grass flowers from this lovely country," and went on to praise the local landscape and its trees, "chestnuts and maples, and oaks and glorious old apple trees in the orchards and white acacias...":

> Tell mother that Mr. Brown's country is much better than I expected... there's good water and fine air and painters country within five hours of New York... the little hotels are clean and much nicer than either in the west or in the south and that there are no Jews at this season and that even in the summer they are confined to the railroad and to the district where the big hotels are.[34]

Two days later he wrote his wife in a similar vein: "I have had a pleasant surprise in this district both as regards the beauty of the landscape and the character of the people.... And so far we have met only three Jews in four days of journeying."[35]

Most people in Whitehead's milieu shared his anti-Semitism, despite their liberal politics. In a memorial essay about Whitehead, Hervey White described him as "a Socialist, a radical, an idealist... to the day of his death," but also wrote, "he hated Germans and Jews from tradition, but always seemed to have them for companions."[36] Whitehead was not an obsessive anti-Semite; in his various writings he praised the Jewish civilization of the past. For example, discussing how great ideas build on earlier ones, he wrote, "the Christian teaching did not make the law of Moses of no effect," and a few months after his first letter from Woodstock he wrote his wife about his desire to inculcate in their sons "an intimacy with some of the great ones of all time: the Greeks and the Hebrews, and Virgil and Dante, and Shakespeare and Keats and Browning."[37] He praised Zola for his pro-Dreyfus position during the Dreyfus affair, the scandal which divided the French public between those for and those against the Jewish military officer.[38] He admired the eminent Jewish political economist Walter Weyl, and offered him property at Byrdcliffe that Weyl politely declined, electing to buy his own land in a different part of Woodstock.[39] But less distinguished Jews were to be avoided in everyday life, and this sort of genteel anti-Semitism, repellent though it seems today, was shared by his friends, who nevertheless saw themselves as among the most liberal and forward-looking people of the early twentieth century. If they were alive now, progressives like Charlotte Perkins Gilman probably would be horrified by their own casual prejudices.[40] Even Hervey White, the great humanitarian protohippie, wrote a tract about Jews where he argued that they are "arrogant" and "parasitic." He concluded his essay with the suggestion that Jews learn to work more as farmers and laborers: "then we will cease to have the universally hated Jew, the pariah of all peoples of the earth."[41] It is hard to reconcile such negative sentiments with the almost saintly image of Hervey White that has come down in Woodstock, and his anti-Semitic attitudes must have been tempered in his daily life. He started his Maverick art colony in Woodstock with three artist couples, including Eugenie Gershoy and Harry Gottlieb, both Jewish, who in later years had nothing but good to say about him.

Whitehead's anti-Semitism was social and elitist. His remarks about a painter who taught at the Pratt Institute named Paddock illustrate the flexibility of these prejudices: "I like him although he is a Jew! He is a great friend of Lindin and [Hervey White] and they will spend the summer together.... "[42] Anti-Semitism was widespread in the United States in these years, fueled by massive immigration during the late nineteenth century and by the fact that Jews were not only different in style and custom from the establishment, but were also the most upwardly mobile group among the immigrants. Alf Evers has documented that anti-Semitism continued to be a factor at Byrdcliffe in the years after World War I, including a physical assault on a Jewish hotel owner in 1922 by three men, including Ralph Whitehead Jr.[43] By that time anti-Semitic remarks had disappeared from Whitehead's letters, and he wrote his son cautioning him about intolerance: "Watch out for prejudices, which are apt to harden into 'complexes.' They are a great nuisance to oneself."[44] It took Hitler and Nazism to prove the horrifying ends to which bigotry could lead, and anti-Semitism before World War II was a different strain than after the war years, during which time it completely subsided in Woodstock.[45]

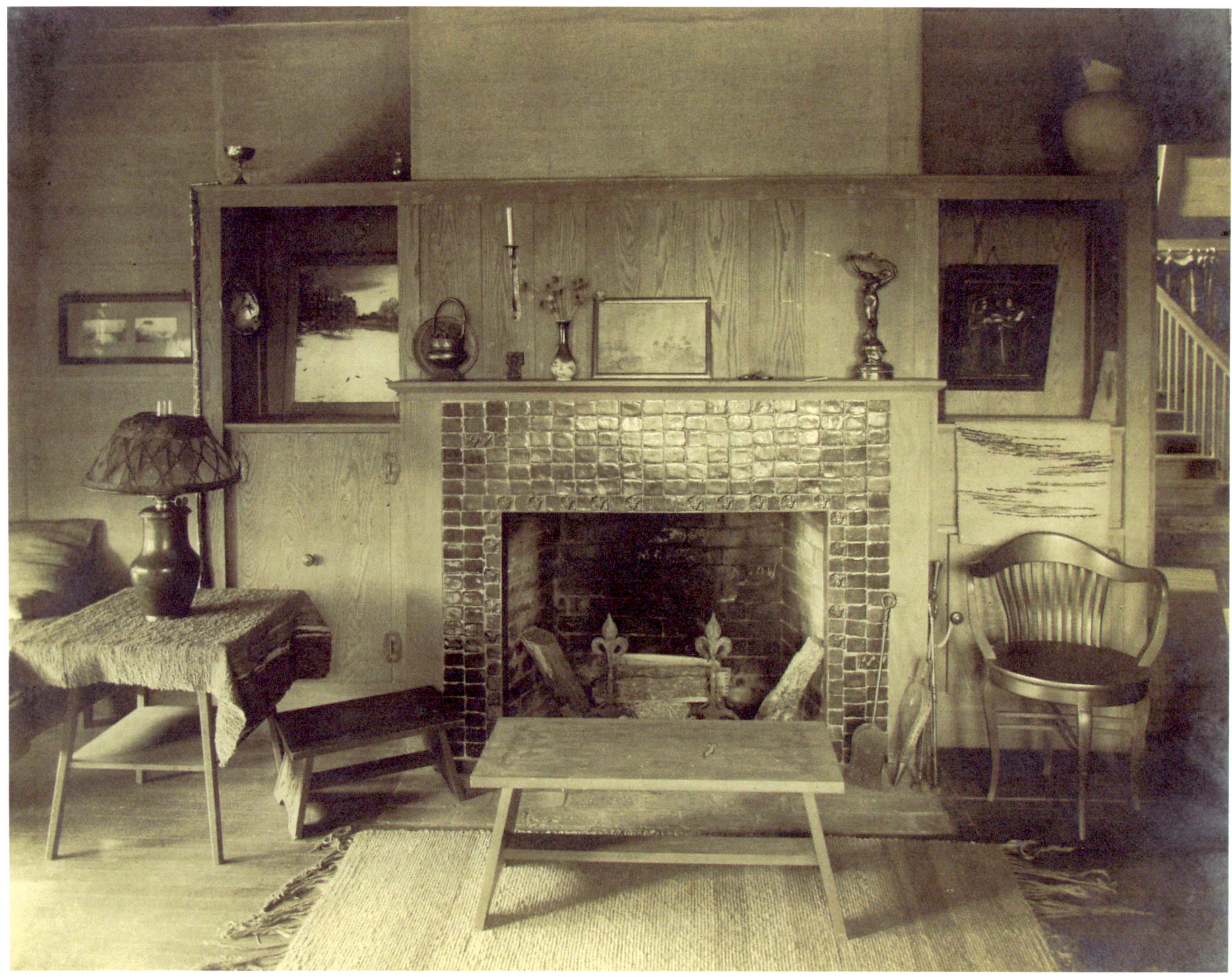

fig. 8 Jessie Tarbox Beals, *Henry Mercer Fireplace, White Pines,* 1909. Silver print. Winterthur Library, Downs Collection, 92x39.1140.546.

Eight days after his initial letter from Woodstock, Whitehead's enthusiasm about the new site had steadily grown, and he solicited his wife's approval. "You have only to wire 'Proceed,'" he wrote her, and then he left Brown to negotiate with the local farmers to buy their land. In the end seven large farms were purchased, totaling around 1200 acres. Whitehead had hired White and Brown as supervisors of the building project, and they worked intensely getting five buildings with roofs on them before winter became too severe. They were joined by friends of White's: a Dutch military man named Fritz Van der Loo, and Carl Eric Lindin, a painter from Sweden who had moved to the United States and became a close friend of White's at Hull House.

Whitehead gradually grew skeptical about Brown, who had great intelligence and energy, but who was slow to produce the architectural drawings Whitehead required. Brown had some experience building his own house in Palo Alto, but Whitehead had twice served apprenticeships with carpenters, once in Paris and once in Germany, and he soon found Brown overconfident about his abilities.[46] Meanwhile, they were working from early morning into the night, employing over fifty men and eight teams of horses to get their job done. For once Whitehead found the labor that he so desired: "I have not worked so hard since I was at college and it suits me."[47] They planned and built roads, felled huge oak and chestnut trees and milled them into beams for their houses. By the time winter hit the main buildings were up, and by spring the colony had enough buildings to begin functioning. Five main structures formed its nucleus, including Whitehead's fifteen-room house, White Pines, which featured a fireplace with green glazed tiles made by Henry Chapman Mercer, Mrs. Whitehead's cousin, who ran a successful Arts and Crafts tile business in Doylestown, Pennsylvania (fig. 8). Also completed were Brown's thirteen-room house, Carniola; the farmhouse where Hervey White would live; an art studio with a library annexed to it; and the Villetta Inn, a boarding house for students.[48] Carniola was destroyed by fire, but the other original buildings plus more than twenty others from the colony still stand today. On the whole they conform to many of the ideals of Arts and Crafts architecture: they are built from local wood, which is left exposed. On the exterior they are characterized by irregular silhouettes, punctuated by big overhanging eaves, balconies, porches, and sleeping porches, all of which were intended to integrate the structures with the surrounding nature. Inside they again feature exposed wood, often stained; built-in furniture; and simple, clear rectilinear forms, as can be seen in the staircase of Eastover (fig. 9). Today these houses are surrounded by forest, making a peaceful living environment both close to and removed from the busy town of Woodstock in the valley below. But originally they were in the middle of cultivated fields with a few patches of forest for shade. Instead of the present feeling of being in a forest interior, there were spectacular views down the mountain through miles of space.

When the Whiteheads arrived Woodstock was a small community of rural industry and farming, and in fact Whitehead planned to continue farming as one of the ways his colony would support itself. A large, handsome barn was built to assist with this project, and Hervey White was put in charge. In the previous century glass had been Woodstock's major business, but this declined in the 1850s. The town provided bluestone for New York City sidewalks, but that was threatened by the growing use of concrete. The sudden influx of artists was greeted with some reserve on the part of the townspeople, but it also stimulated the local economy.

By the spring of 1903 the five main buildings were up, and there were other smaller houses, intended as workshops, or studios and living spaces for artists. There was a wood shop for furniture making and a metal shop, and the original settlers got busy inviting people to join the enterprise. Whitehead had been searching for artists and craftsmen for much of the year. In Boston he was impressed by painter Hermann Dudley Murphy and hired him to head

fig. 9 Les Walker, *Staircase in Eastover*, 2002. Courtesy of the photographer and the Woodstock Guild.

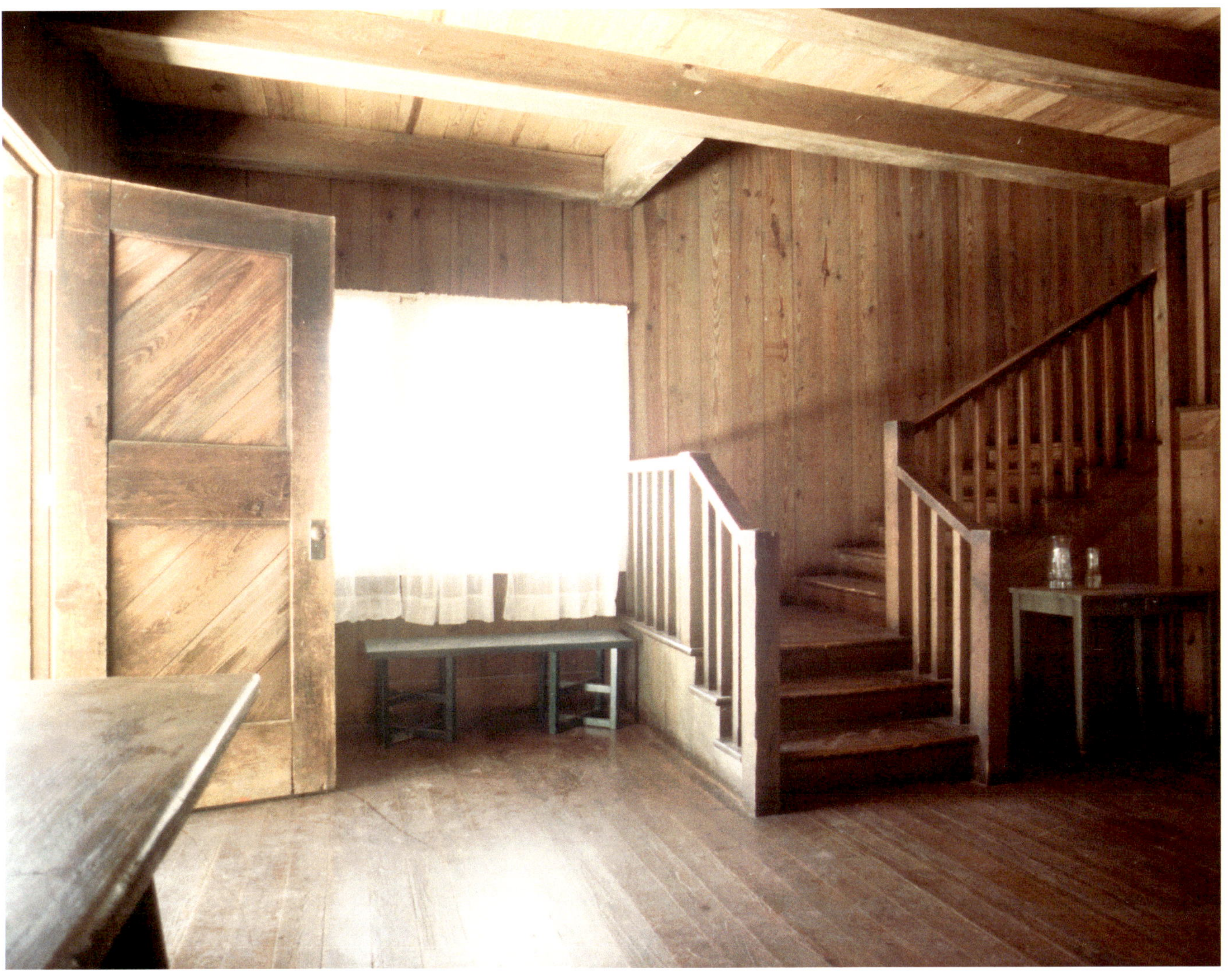

Byrdcliffe's art school, to Brown's chagrin, as he thought that post was his. John Duncan, a Scottish artist working in a tight, Pre-Raphaelite style, was another recruit from Hull House; Brown described him as "the only one in the crowd who could draw."[49] Birge Harrison, who came in 1904, would be an influential presence in Woodstock's art world for years. Lindin and White, in their house, Yggdrasil, invited friends and kindred spirits from the orbit of Hull House in Chicago, including German historian Martin Schütze and his photographer wife Eva Watson-Schütze, who became the main photographic documentarian of the people of Byrdcliffe. Ellen Gates Starr, founder of Hull House with Jane Addams, was also an early resident at Byrdcliffe. She had studied with the leading British Arts and Crafts bookbinder, T. J. Cobden-Sanderson; Starr's binding of Martin Schütze's *Poems* is a beautiful example of her style of embossing fine, gold lines in a complex symmetrical design on dark brown leather (cat. 7). Also from the Hull House circle were writers Charlotte Perkins Gilman, Edith Wherry, Marie Manning, and Harriet Howe.

Pratt Institute, the progressive art school in Brooklyn, was another major source of talent for Byrdcliffe, which attracted several students of the renowned art teacher Arthur Wesley Dow. Zulma Steele and Edna Walker, who became the chief designers of ornament for Byrdcliffe furniture, came from Pratt, as did George Eggers, who went on to a career as a museum director; Edward Thatcher, who made metal fixtures for the furniture; and Marie Little, a weaver who would spend most of her life in Woodstock. Byrdcliffe pottery was made by the team of Elizabeth Hardenbergh and Edith Penman.

Today Byrdcliffe is best known in Arts and Crafts circles for the splendid furniture produced there, between 1903 and 1905. Whitehead put considerable energy in finding a cabinetmaker, and the Norwegian Riulf Erlenson was hired, along with Olaf Westerling, a Swedish woodcarver. Fordyce Herrick, a carpenter who worked on the Byrdcliffe houses, became shop foreman.[50] The furniture seems to have been created through a collaborative process. Zulma Steele and Edna Walker designed the distinctive ornamentation, based on their drawings from local plant life, and they made working drawings for the cabinetmakers. As noted by Robert Edwards, the forms of the pieces apparently were derived by Whitehead from prototypes published in British art magazines *The Studio* and *International Studio*, specifically from works by the architect and designer Mackay H. Baillie Scott[51] (fig. 10). The furniture exemplified the Arts and Crafts ideal of simplicity—most examples are boxy and rectilinear in silhouette, with unfinished or stained wood surfaces. This simple, unadorned perpendicularity enables their doors to function as frames for inset floral designs, or even landscape paintings. There was a tradition among William Morris and his followers to incorporate paintings into rectangular panels in their furniture, but those paintings are generally of medieval figures in shallow spaces flush with the flat surfaces of the objects.

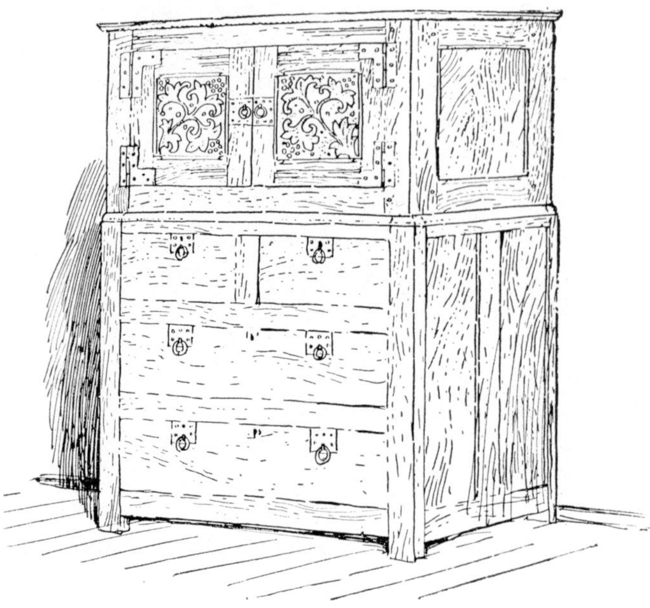

fig. 10 M. H. Baillie Scott, *Clothes Press Design*, from *International Studio*, vol. 10, no. 49 (April 1897). Courtesy of the Division of Rare and Manuscript Collections, Cornell University Library.

In contrast, the door panels of some Byrdcliffe cabinets feature landscapes with deep space that is dramatically interrupted by the framing elements. This boldly disobeys one of the cardinal rules of decoration, that it should be flat and affirm the flatness of the object's surface. One of the best preserved of these cabinets includes two panels of a continuous landscape by Hermann Dudley Murphy set into its doors (cat. 20). This unusual format joins the tradition of landscape painting, here produced by painters who were veterans of French art colonies, with the British Arts and Crafts movement, which urged the integration of fine art with crafts. Select Byrdcliffe objects represent some of the most thorough fusions of "high" and "decorative" art produced in the period—for example, the landscape painting by Dawson Dawson-Watson which depicts a river scene in the Catskills and which is held in a custom-made frame with the names of the plants in the painting engraved into the frame (cat. 60). Here the craft of frame making and the art of painting are joined in a total unity.

In the end the colony produced only about fifty pieces of furniture. They were expensive to make and to ship, and although they were sold at McCreery's department store in New York, they could not compete with other brands of simply contoured Arts and Crafts furniture made in New York with more efficient means of production by Gustav Stickley and his brothers, and by Elbert Hubbard's Roycrofters. Whitehead's plan was to have Byrdcliffe's crafts pay for themselves. After he provided the land, the facilities, and the initial investment, the salaries of the craftsmen and their materials should come out of money earned by the business.[52] When the crafts enterprises were about to begin, in spring 1903, he wrote to his wife:

> I want to reassure you about our scheme here. Of course I am putting capital into it, but I am not putting more than we can at our age afford to risk, without crippling ourselves or our children, even if we fail to make a business success.[53]

He had spent a tremendous amount of money to purchase the land and erect the buildings, far beyond the ten thousand dollars he had originally given Brown to buy property, and by early 1905, when the furniture proved slow to sell, he ended that part of the project. But Byrdcliffe went on; he continued to invite artists and craftsmen and help them with facilities, and many of those who had initially settled there stayed. Whitehead was a complex person, with many sides to his personality. Another man with his inherited fortune might have built a lavish estate in England and lived to please only his refined tastes, but Whitehead put his money at the service of his idealistic vision, and the many people who recorded their impressions of him all agreed that he was a generous man.

Although furniture making was abandoned fairly quickly, other art making enterprises at Byrdcliffe continued—the art school, for example, went on with a succession of instructors, most of whom specialized in landscapes painted in a broad, painterly style influenced by Impressionism. Most of them had spent time in art colonies in France, and were drawn to Woodstock in part because of its unspoiled and varied landscape. The Byrdcliffe school started with a faculty of three. Hermann Dudley Murphy, introduced to Whitehead by Boston educator and collector Denman Ross, was recruited for the first season at the colony, bringing with him his experience as a frame maker along with his prestige as a painter. John Duncan, from Scotland, who was drafted from Chicago, apparently quit when Whitehead refused to buy a lithograph press for him to teach lithography. And Brown, displeased with his demotion from head of the art school to drawing instructor, later wrote, "The first man in, I now became the first man out."[54] With Whitehead's blessing, he bought land near Byrdcliffe, and remained part of the artistic culture of Woodstock, as a painter, a lithographer, and finally a ceramist. This trio was followed by the worldly landscape painter Birge Harrison, who would leave Byrdcliffe in 1906 to head the summer school of the Art Students League in Woodstock, which brought hundreds of art students to the town. Carl Eric Lindin never taught at Byrdcliffe, but he was another painter attracted to the area by the fledgling colony, who settled there and became an important part of the local art culture, serving for twenty years as the President of the Woodstock Artists Association, founded in 1919. After Harrison left the Byrdcliffe school, another landscape painter, Leonard Ochtman, from the Cos Cob art colony in Connecticut, briefly replaced him. As the school declined, William Emile Schumacher, trained in Paris, established art classes in Byrdcliffe every summer and ensured that painting continued to be taught there through the teens. Schumacher developed a more modern style than his Byrdcliffe predecessors, painting with large areas of flat color (cats. 74 and 75). Among his students in Woodstock in 1915 were the photographer Eva Watson-Schütze; the printmaker Blanche Lazzell; and Elsie Moll Stevens, the wife of poet Wallace Stevens. Elsie's presence in the colony brought Stevens there on occasional visits when he made use of Whitehead's extensive library. In later years he wrote of Byrdcliffe, "There, the driving force was Whitehead, an Englishman."[55]

Brown was the first to leave, and Hervey White departed after the summer of 1904. He bought some land a few miles from Byrdcliffe and established his Maverick art colony, which would contribute bohemian energy and talent to the growing art scene in Woodstock. He left Byrdcliffe ostensibly because of an argument about milk with Whitehead, but it would seem that this small matter was the catalyst for tensions already underlying their relationship. In 1907 and 1909 two articles appeared in the national press about the colony, and both writers, Alvin F. Sanborn and Poultney Bigelow, made the point that at this colony of artists and craftsmen the man furnishing the funds made the decisions.[56] Whitehead's inspiration was his teacher, Ruskin, who formulated his own plans for an ideal colony, the Guild of St. George, in the 1870s at Oxford while Whitehead studied there. Ruskin's project featured a paradoxical blend of socialism and dictatorship comparable to, if more severe, than what Whitehead would try to practice. In Ruskin's words:

> The first essential point in the education given to the children will be the habit of instant, finely accurate, and totally unreasoning, obedience to their fathers, mothers, and tutors; the same precise and unquestioning submission being required from heads of families to the officers set over them.[57]

Such a climate was intolerable for many of the artists who were enticed to come to the colony to practice their art, and it explains their steady exodus. Hervey White in particular was not the type to live under somebody's rules when he could establish his own low-budget, do-it-yourself art colony.

While some artists were quick to depart, others came, some to stay. A dazzling variety of people took part in the Byrdcliffe project in various ways, including the naturalist John Burroughs, who would emerge from the woods to have meals at the colony. Philosopher John Dewey—whose ideas about education greatly interested Whitehead, and who knew a number of Byrdcliffe colonists from his days teaching at the University of Chicago and working with Hull House—came for one summer. Dewey believed in the educational value of hands-on experience and he

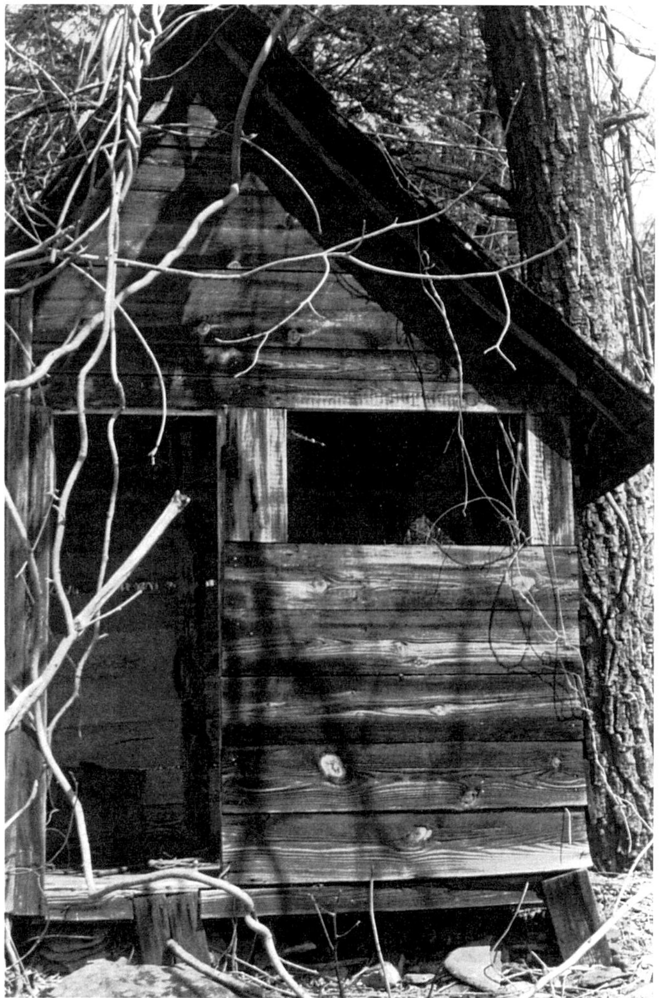

fig. 11 Unidentified photographer, *Playhouse made by John Dewey's Children*, 1906. Silver print. Courtesy of the Woodstock Guild.

helped his children build a little playhouse up on the hill, between White Pines and the Villetta[58] (fig. 11).

Bolton Brown recounted an episode where Ellen Gates Starr, one of the founders of Hull House, complained to Whitehead about a young art student kissing a serving girl, and Whitehead replied, "This isn't Hull House."[59] The anecdote reveals Whitehead's tolerance when it came to sexual mores, and it also reflects the fact that these artists came to live and practice their art in unspoiled natural surroundings—with servants. Beyond the staff they hired for the colony, the Whiteheads themselves always had the help of at least a nanny, a cook, and a driver/handyman, and the fluctuating cast of characters who made up their staff is a recurrent subject in their letters.

Saturday night dances held in the art studio, where the community dressed up and went to party, were a social highlight of the colony. Metalworker Bertha Thompson wrote about the summer of 1904, "The days were sacred to work—we did not intrude upon each other, but when late afternoon and evening came our exuberant spirits broke loose!!"[60] Each summer ended with a big, fancy dress costume ball, and after Harrison started his Art Students League summer school many of those students came to dance along with the Byrdcliffe residents. As he had in California, Whitehead sponsored musicians to provide concerts, including the famed British pianist and instrument maker Arnold Dolmetsch. When he saw the keyboardist perform in New York City in 1903, Whitehead described him as "very picturesque, dressed in a seventeenth-century black velvet coat and breeches with lace ruffles."[61] Dolmetsch and his instrumentalist wife began visiting Byrdcliffe in 1908, and Whitehead bought a clavichord made under his supervision. A program exists of three concerts the Dolmetsches performed in 1908, including pieces by Handel, Bach, and Purcell, as well as anonymous traditional songs.[62] Dolmetsch had serenaded William Morris on his deathbed with traditional English songs, an example of the 1890s interest in folk music among British Arts and Crafts practitioners such as C. R. Ashbee.[63] Paralleling Ashbee, who published *The Essex House Song Book* in 1903, the Whiteheads published *The Morning Stars Sang Together: Folk-Songs and Other Songs for Children* the same year with a handsome cover designed by Mrs. Whitehead, a landscape in flat blues and yellows (cat. 11).[64] In 1912 they published a second volume, *Folk-Songs of Eastern Europe*. Whitehead felt that the lyrics, which were added to the traditional melodies in the nineteenth century, were often unsuitable: "in most cases they are commonplace; sometimes they are vulgar."[65] So he and his friends, such as Martin Schütze, wrote new words for the old tunes.

Looking at Byrdcliffe one hundred years later, it is surprising to see how many young artists who came to the colony full of energy and ambition have been forgotten. This has happened especially with the craftspeople, in part because they made functional objects, which are often used for a time and then discarded. Many of the craftspeople were women, a gender division typical of the Arts and Crafts movement, although there were exceptions on both sides. Zulma Steele, for instance, worked as a painter at Byrdcliffe as well as a designer, while Edmund Rolfe came as a jeweler but also made paintings.

Marie Little was known in the colony for her subtle weavings and her hooked rugs made from rag remnants. Today, many more of her color studies on paper—bands of color organized in parallel rectangles—exist than the actual textiles made after them. Whitehead, too, was involved with hand weaving, a significant choice for a man who owed his fortune to his family's business in machine-made textiles. In the 1890s he wove on a hand loom that he carried on trains in England, and at Byrdcliffe in 1906 he built a large Loom Room as an annex to White Pines. There, he made his weavings, including silk scarves sold at the Handicraft Society in Boston, assisted by Edna Walker, who later worked for Herter Looms in New York City.[66]

Louise Hastings Lindin is a good example of a craftswoman whose works are almost totally unknown today. From Chicago, she studied bookbinding with

Ellen Gates Starr at Hull House, where she met her future husband, painter Carl Lindin. Although she worked seriously in her studio in Woodstock for years, only a handful of books bound by her are locatable, sketchbooks handmade for her husband. An early one is beautifully crafted in the style of Starr; with deep green tooled leather ornamented by precise gold lines set in (cat. 4). Ornate organic units are held in check by a rigid geometrical superstructure, a juxtaposition typical of much decorative art, including some of the Byrdcliffe furniture that features floral ornament set within rectilinear frames. In other works she developed a less formal style of binding, with areas of raw canvas serving as a ground on which are pasted swatches of paper washed with fluid colors (cat. 3). With money she had inherited from her father, a successful civil engineer and banker, the Lindins could afford to buy the abandoned Lutheran church he had originally shared with Hervey White in 1902 and customize it into an Arts and Crafts home, with the help of Fordyce Herrick, who had worked as carpenter on many of the Byrdcliffe houses. The Lindins used their talents to decorate their house, about a mile east of Byrdcliffe, with glazed tiles, carved stair posts, and with Carl's paintings set into the walls, made of local chestnut wood (fig.12).

Objects by Byrdcliffe's metalworkers are also hard to find.[67] In his 1907 article, Alvan Sanborn described the metal shop Whitehead set up (cat. 1):

> The metal workshop is admirably equipped. It contains four rooms: the first room has a forge, a lathe and stakes for metal raising; the second is for jewelry and chasing; the third, for the coloring, polishing and cleaning of metals; and the fourth contains furnaces, etc., for enameling.[68]

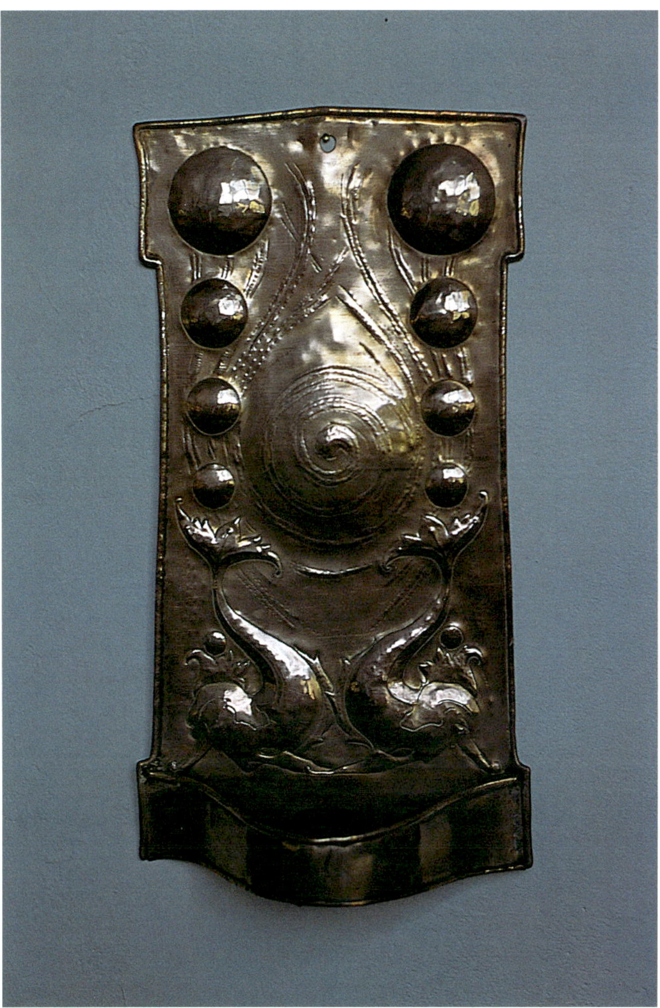

fig. 13 Attributed to Ned Thatcher, *Brass Sconce*. Leaycraft Collection. Photograph from the author's collection.

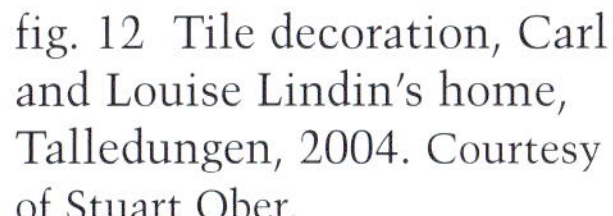

fig. 12 Tile decoration, Carl and Louise Lindin's home, Talledungen, 2004. Courtesy of Stuart Ober.

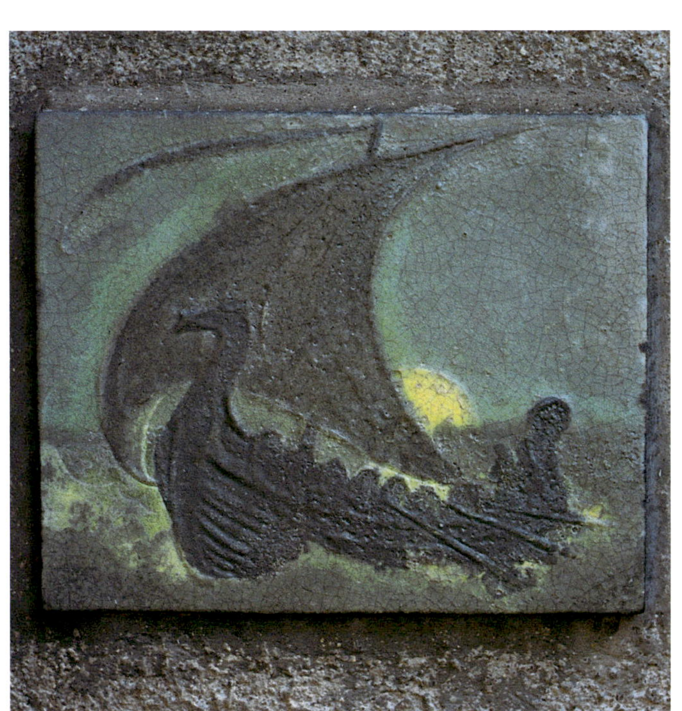

Who used these facilities? Laurin Martin, who had worked with Arts and Crafts organizations in Boston, did, but little is known about his work at Byrdcliffe. In 1909, Franz Hazenplug, the noted Chicago illustrator associated with Hull House, joined the staff at Byrdcliffe in charge of the metal shop. Edward Thatcher was one of the craftspeople who trained with Arthur Wesley Dow at Pratt Institute and then came to Byrdcliffe. He remained in Woodstock as a metalworker and local character for many years, but few works are clearly attributable to him. He made some forged fixtures for Byrdcliffe furniture, and there are several drawings for jewelry, handles, and doorknobs on scraps of paper signed by him.[69] Andirons found on the Byrdcliffe property may have been made by Thatcher, and a few other works in metal have been associated with his name, including an elaborate brass sconce[70] (fig. 13) and an iron chandelier.

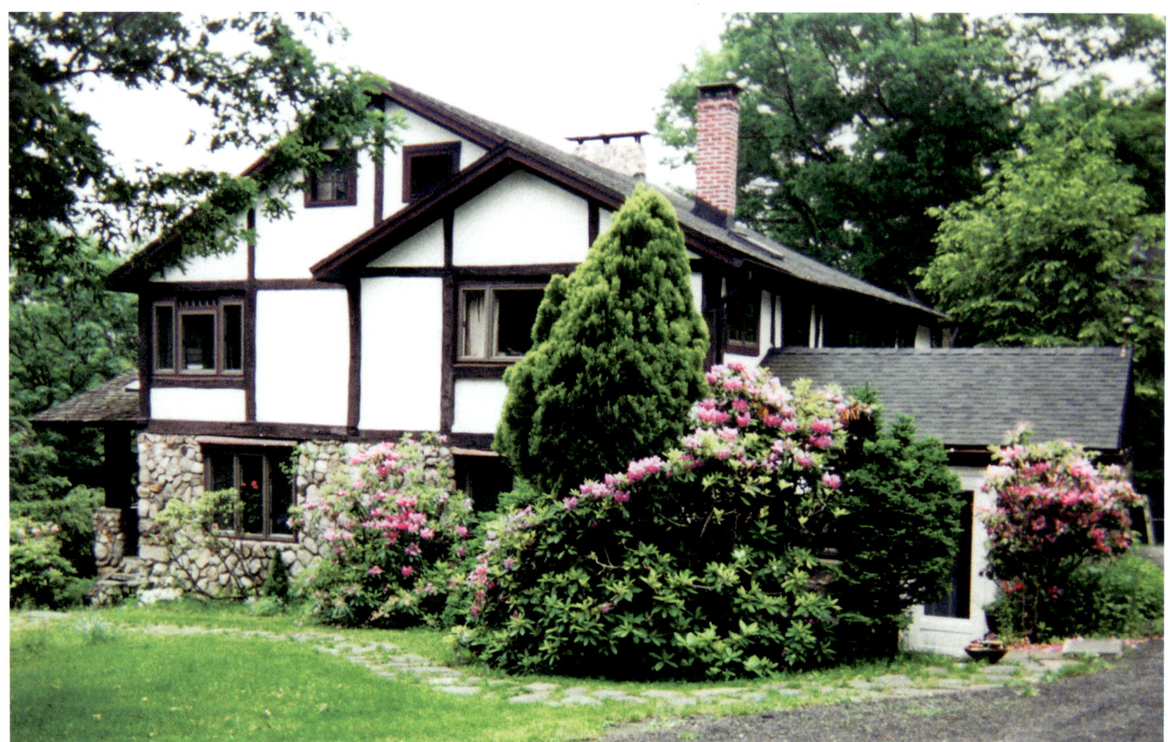

fig. 14
Maribeth Harmes,
The Boulders, Edmund Rolfe's home, 2002.
Courtesy of the photographer.

In 1905 Edmund Rolfe followed Laurin Martin from Boston, where he was affiliated with the Society of Arts and Crafts, to Byrdcliffe to teach metalworking in the art school. One of his necklaces features an elaborate pendant with fine curving bands of gold holding small pearls and assorted stones that frame a large freshwater pearl (cat. 43). It is a good example of Arts and Crafts jewelry, with Rolfe's artistry put at the service of the irregular pearl, created by nature. Rolfe and his painter wife, Florence, were among the first Christian Scientists in Woodstock. They bought land near Byrdcliffe and built their rugged and picturesque house, The Boulders, out of local stone (fig. 14). Hervey White wrote of Rolfe:

> He must experiment on some new problem till he had the solution, and having succeeded, he was no longer interested. There were always new worlds to conquer and he moved on to financial ruin and destitution with a placid optimism that was the despair of his friends.[71]

Rolfe's career was cut short by a fatal car accident in 1917, when he was thirty-nine years old. Before his early death, Rolfe had added painting to his repertoire of activities. His *Girl in Interior* exemplifies the broadly painted realism popular among the first generation of Byrdcliffe painters (cat. 73). Its subject is most likely his young daughter sitting in a Byrdcliffe house, wearing a simple Arts and Crafts smock. The rustic, handmade frame adds a craft element to the work.

Bertha Thompson was another metalworker who lived much of her life at Byrdcliffe; she heard about the colony from some of her artist friends in Chicago and spent the summer of 1904 studying with Laurin Martin in the metal shop. For the next few years she studied in various Arts and Crafts centers, including Boston, where she continued working with Martin, and then with George Gebelein. She also studied with Dow at his Ipswich summer school, but in 1908 she returned to Byrdcliffe where she settled for most of the rest of her life, building a house in 1913. She is one of the serious, career craftspeople from whom we have little identified work. Exceptional are a lovely silver sugar bowl and creamer which are characterized by their simplicity of form, which emphasizes the glistening reflectiveness of the metal, and by their unusual little legs, both functional and idiosyncratic (cat. 50).

Thompson's sister, Annie, who learned weaving at Byrdcliffe, lived with her sometimes, and the two were typical of the women art workers who made up an important part of Byrdcliffe's population. When the renowned British Arts and Crafts designer C. R. Ashbee visited in 1915, seven years after the demise of his Chipping Camden crafts colony, he wrote:

> The landscape is lovely, the conception superb, the craftsmen's houses with delightful workshops—finely placed. . . . The shell of a great life is all here and all empty except for two or three lonely spinsters.[72]

These spinsters might have included Thompson and her sister, Steele and Walker, the potters Penman and Hardenbergh, and the weaver Marie Little. Earlier there had also been several other single-women artisans, including Ellen Gates Starr, who came with a companion from Hull House, which was itself staffed primarily by single women who had close personal relationships with each other. This period marked a time when considerable numbers of American women were permitted to go to college, and some of these educated women chose same-sex living partners and experimented with gender identities that departed from the traditional, subservient role of wife. Perhaps Whitehead's benevolent rule appealed to some of them, like metalworker Bertha Thompson, who was handicapped from a childhood bout with polio which left her permanently hobbled, needing a cane to walk. She recounted that in 1912 she decided to build a house at Byrdcliffe but picked a site that another family also wanted. To induce her to change her mind, Whitehead sold her property close to Steele and Walker's house at a low price, built a road to her property, and installed plumbing so she had water from a nearby spring. Although she did not get what she originally wanted, in the end she was happy with her new location and spent many productive years there, grateful to Whitehead for his generosity.[73]

Zulma Steele's painting *Woodstock*, dated 1903, is typical of Byrdcliffe's paintings—a broadly painted, delicately hued landscape in the Tonalist tradition (cat. 76). The figures in the sylvan scene, three women and only one man, reflect the Byrdcliffe's population. Bertha Thompson's sister, Annie, recalled "an unusual party at the Angelus: There were few of the younger men around, so we decided to have half of our special group come in male costumes to remove that social deficiency." One came as a Chinaman with a pigtail, one as an organ grinder, and Steele and Walker as art students. In those times, more innocent and less sexually self-conscious than today, they had a "merry evening," with punch on the porch and a victrola for music.[74] What started at Byrdcliffe seems to have made Woodstock a magnet for women who were in pursuit of independent artistic careers. Dewing Woodward, a painter forgotten today, had lived in French art colonies as did the male painters at Byrdcliffe. Then she moved to Woodstock with her companion, Louise Johnson, and drew portraits of Byrdcliffe figures like Hervey White and Birge Harrison.[75] Abastenia St. Leger Eberle, a sculptor active in the suffragist movement, who lived for years with a woman companion and willed her estate to another woman friend, is admired today for the sculptures she made of members of the immigrant population on New York's Lower East Side. Despite her urban subject, she spent several summers in Woodstock in the second decade of the twentieth century, and one can guess that she was drawn there by the community of women artists living outside of the roles traditionally defined for their gender. There was also the presence of Charlotte Perkins Gilman, whose *Women and Economics* (1898) is one of the foundational texts of modern feminism. What today can be seen as an early feminist enclave at the time was perhaps unconsciously so, as the shortage of men was a "social deficiency" in Annie Thompson's words, and others shared her attitude. Mrs. Whitehead wrote in 1910: "This place has improved, but there is a lack of men, as usual. Stevens and the two engineers are good, but the thirty women want some more and some older men."[76]

Most of Byrdcliffe's residents were there only during the summers. As Sanborn pointed out in his 1907 article, this was a pattern encouraged by the example of the Whiteheads, who often spent the cold months back in California.[77] By the end of the decade the colony had settled into being an artistic place, with several year-round residents, plus summer renters. The Whiteheads had a crisis in 1912, when Mrs. Whitehead became jealous of her husband's closeness to Misses Steele and Walker.[78] That year they sold Arcady, but rather than give up their California residence, they built a new house, Neroli, on their Montecito property. With its pitched roofs, stained wood façade, dark wood interiors, built-in furniture, large fireplaces, and plaster copies of Renaissance sculptures set into the wall, Neroli looks like a Byrdcliffe house (figs. 15 and 16).

The couple also continued their pursuit of crafts, turning to ceramics. They helped the virtuoso ceramist Frederick Hürten Rhead establish his own business in Santa Barbara. Rhead was a descendant of six generations of British ceramists, and had worked for several American Arts and Crafts pottery establishments.[79] Mrs. Whitehead studied with him in California, and soon the Whiteheads were making their own White Pines ceramics. They set up a ceramics studio on the top floor of White Pines and a kiln in an outbuilding. Rhead worked in both an

fig. 15 Unidentified photographer, *Neroli* (exterior). Winterthur Library, Downs Collection, 92x39.1140.336.

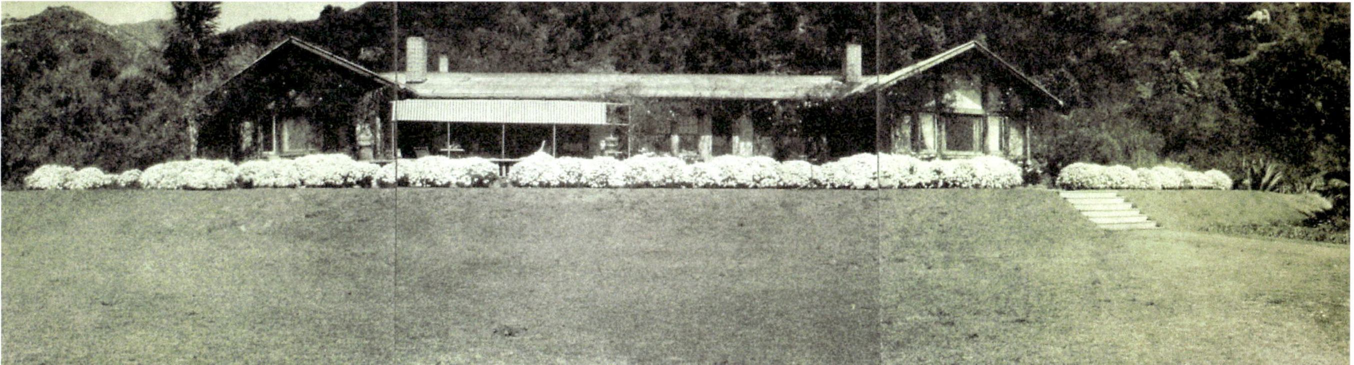

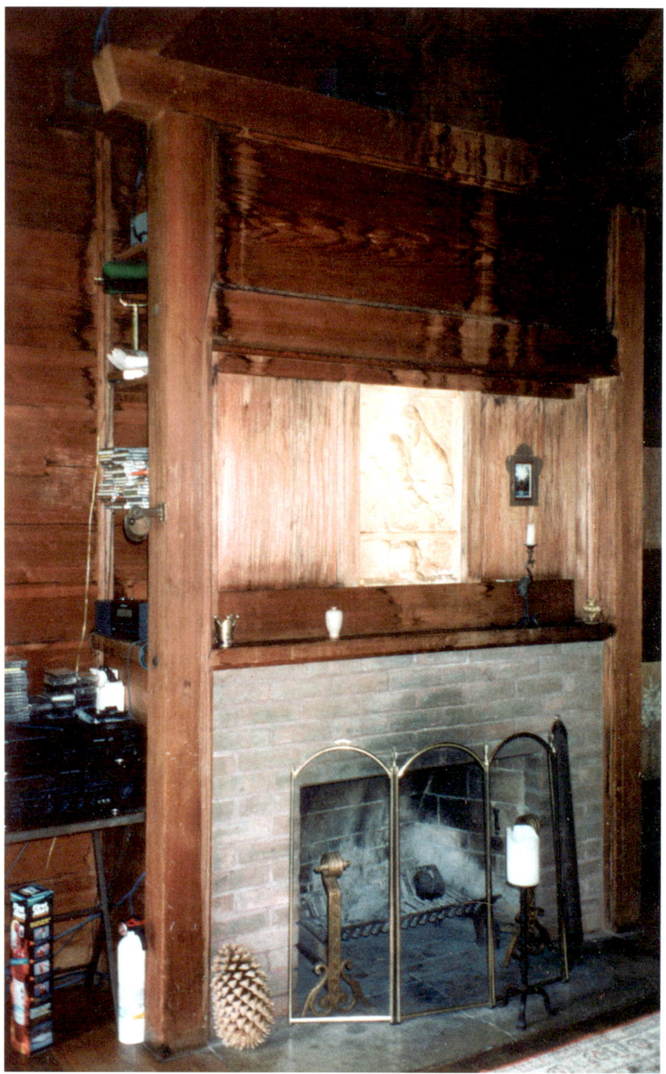

fig. 16 Tom Wolf, *Neroli* (interior).
Courtesy of the author.

elaborately decorated style with Art Nouveau ornament, and an austerely simple style derived from Chinese ceramics, which emphasized the beauty of the glaze (fig. 17). The Whiteheads emulated this purified style, casting simple forms in molds and then working carefully on their glazes, with some success. Sometimes they followed the Ruskinian practice of incorporating local flora into their designs, particularly the eucalyptus leaves which ornament many of their pots, and which refer to the trees they planted on their Montecito property (cat. 186). They showed their works in Santa Barbara and Boston, where they were well received. Finally they had found an outlet for their desires to live creative lives, but as Mrs. Whitehead wrote her eldest son, it came too late to be totally fulfilling.

While the Whiteheads worked on their ceramics, World War I made its stresses felt at Byrdcliffe, and Mr. Whitehead's income from English sources declined. Ralph Jr. joined the British army, and for a while in 1915 Mrs. Whitehead went to England to help the war-wounded. Zulma Steele was a nurse in France, and anti-German sentiment was felt in Woodstock. In a 1917 letter to her son Mrs. Whitehead wrote, "There is no pleasure in the human side of Byrdcliffe because one runs across pacifists or Germans so much. I wish not to go to a house where I am liable to meet such."[80] German professor Martin Schütze and his photographer wife, Eva, who were working with Jane Addams on a campaign for world peace, felt these tensions at Byrdcliffe; this was the period when the large two-story residence next to the Villetta in the colony had its name changed from the Germanic "Müllersruhe" to "Eastover," the name it bears today.

In the years following World War I, Byrdcliffe continued to be a place for summer residents, many of whom worked in the arts, as the Whiteheads encouraged. Meanwhile, with Hervey White's Maverick colony a mile away, and the summer school of the Art Students League also established in Woodstock, the town became one of the most prominent art colonies in the United States. The Whiteheads watched these developments with some ambivalence. They had accomplished a great deal, but it fell short of their original ambitions. Mr. Whitehead especially transferred his sense of his own unfulfilled accomplishments into lofty goals for his sons, and he was troubled when both of them turned out to be difficult boys, having disciplinary problems in school and little professional focus. By 1928 Ralph Jr., the older son, was maturing and developing a career for himself as an engineer when he booked passage to South America on the ship the SS *Vestris* which sank taking many of its passengers with it. His death devastated his father, who died within a year, in 1929. Mrs. Whitehead and her younger son, Peter, remained at Byrdcliffe, renting out buildings and favoring tenants with artistic inclinations. She died in 1955, and Peter continued to welcome artistic people to the colony; he is remembered as a man with no real professional identity and with a love of alcohol; he was generous with his inheritance, and always supportive of artists. When he died in 1975, he had willed most of the Byrdcliffe land and property to the Woodstock Guild of Craftsmen, an organization founded by artists in 1939, which continued the dedication to crafts that characterized the Byrdcliffe colony. Peter willed White Pines, the home of his parents, to Mark Willcox Jr., a great-nephew of Jane Whitehead. In 1999 New York State, through its Environmental Preservation Act, gave the Guild funds to help purchase White Pines from Mr. Willcox, uniting the Byrdcliffe colony once again, under the auspices of the Guild. The original students' dormitory, the Villetta, is available during summers to artists, who apply for residencies and receive housing and studio space at a modest cost, as the Guild continues to administer Byrdcliffe in accordance with its original dedication to artists. The former art studio and library are now the Byrdcliffe Theatre, rented by various theatre groups for summer productions, and since 2000 the Guild has sponsored annual summer exhibitions of sculpture projects sited on Byrdcliffe land.

With the purchase of White Pines by the Guild there is a new determination to publicize the colony, and to acknowledge its unique role in the Arts and Crafts movement in the United States. Not only is Byrdcliffe remarkable today, as twenty-eight of the original buildings are preserved in their original setting, but in the early years of the twentieth century it was a vital node in a system of Arts and Crafts organizations that shared many of the same personnel as they actively encouraged each other. With the interest in the American Arts and Crafts movement that has developed over the past several decades it is surprising that Byrdcliffe is not better known. This is in part due to the rhetoric of failure that has long surrounded it. As we have seen, Whitehead himself felt that his efforts failed—the theme occurs over and over in his letters. At the same time, he was not a foolish man, and before starting Byrdcliffe he studied and visited several other Arts and Crafts colonies. In 1897 he checked out a colony in Tennessee named Ruskin, and wrote to his wife:

> I don't think colonies can solve the social problems which are so urgently demanding solution, but they can make things better for a few people who are cooperating... you know colonies are always short-lived.[81]

He was aware that the odds were against a utopian colony surviving, and he had seen Ruskin's Guild of St. George and later Ashbee's colony decline. Nevertheless, he tended to stress the shortcomings of his own attempt, as opposed to its accomplishments. Hervey White seems to have shared his view, as he wrote, "Mr. Whitehead failed, Brown failed, and I failed. It was Birge [Harrison] who has the honor if not the glory...." And White explained, "better than building houses, he brought the Summer School of the Art Students League to Woodstock, which proved to be the true foundation of the Woodstock art colony."[82] He was too hard on himself; all the principal members of the colony accomplished a great deal. Whitehead was the stimulus, but his colleagues contributed to the idealistic endeavor that lured more and more artists to Woodstock. The uninhibited, bohemian Maverick festivals White held during the 1920s, with music and theatre entertaining hordes of spectators in wild costumes, furthered the image of Woodstock as an artistic place, as did the presence of Bob Dylan in the mid-1960s (cat. 191, see page 251). He lived in Byrdcliffe while he and the Band recorded the famous *Basement Tapes* in a house in neighboring Saugerties. Its reputation made Woodstock the logical locale for the rock festival in 1969 that made the small town, with its year-round population of about six thousand, famous around the world as a symbol of the 1960s generation.[83] In addition, over the years many accomplished visual artists made Woodstock their home, often originally attracted by the Art Students League summer school. They include Milton Avery, Alexander Archipenko, George Bellows, Andrew Dasburg, John Flannagan, Philip Guston, Yasuo Kuniyoshi, Doris Lee, and hundreds more. It is a rich legacy, all descending from the original Arts and Crafts colony founded by Whitehead and his small team in 1902. Bertha Thompson, the metal worker, summed it up nicely:

> Mr. Whitehead had dreamed of a community of workers in the arts and handicrafts, associated but independent, living a simple and satisfying life amid beautiful surroundings.... Many fine, sensitive spirits, in other times and other places, have dreamed this dream so impossible of full realization, forgetting that the human race has yet to learn the true meaning of cooperation in community living.... Who can say that Ralph Radcliffe Whitehead's dream has not been realized in this wider community as we know it today?[84]

Byrdcliffe turned out different than Whitehead hoped, but it played an important role in the arts of the United States. Its legacy today may be other than he imagined, but it is very much alive.

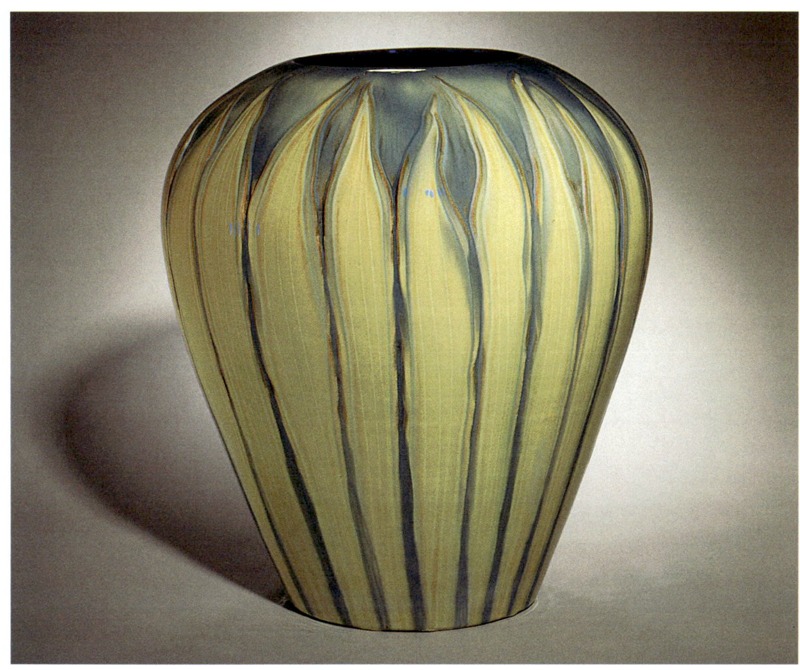

fig. 17 Frederick Hürten Rhead, *Vase*. Ceramic. Private collection.

Notes

1. According to Jane Whitehead's calendars in the Winterthur Museum Library, she first met Whitehead in 1885. This essay builds on a strong foundation of previous writings about Byrdcliffe. A pioneering study was Allen Staley's "Byrdcliffe and the Maverick, a Discursion in the Arts and Crafts," a master's thesis at Yale University, 1960. Following that are Karal Ann Marling's "Introduction" to *Woodstock, An American Art Colony*, 1902–1977 (Vassar College Art Gallery, 1977); *The Byrdcliffe Arts & Crafts Colony*, the catalog of an exhibition organized by Robert Edwards for the Delaware Art Museum in 1984 (which includes an essay by Edwards and one on ceramics by Jane Perkins Claney); and the writing of Woodstock historian Alf Evers in *The Catskills: From Wilderness to Woodstock* (Woodstock: The Overlook Press, 1972) and *Woodstock: History of an American Town* (Woodstock: The Overlook Press, 1987). Alf Evers has been unfailingly helpful, informative, and encouraging as work proceeded on this project, and I have greatly benefited from Nancy Green's and Cheryl Robertson's critical readings of my texts.

2. Typescript translation, by Berlitz Translation Service, of a letter from Marie Whitehead to Ralph Radcliffe Whitehead, 1894, "To be delivered after my death." Winterthur Library, Downs Collection.

3. RRW to Jane, Geneva, September 9, 1891. Winterthur Library, Downs Collection.

4. RRW to Jane, March 13, 1891. Winterthur Library, Downs Collection.

5. RRW to Jane, "Tuesday afternoon," probably August 4, 1891. Winterthur Library, Downs Collection.

6. Ralph Whitehead, *Grass of the Desert* (London: Chiswick Press, 1892). The Chiswick Press was run by Arts and Crafts artist and designer Walter Crane.

7. RRW to Jane, July 8, 1900: " 'Democracy' which however much I dislike its faults is after all what brought me west." June 4, 1891, from England: "The factories, I feel ashamed when I walk through them. I am living off the labor of these wretches at their weaving machines."

8. For example, RRW to Jane, Switzerland to Colorado, February 8, 1892: "Then again thy boy would fain begin his new life away from all old bad associations of Europe where till now all has been failure to him."

9. Jane Kimberly, nurse. Memoir collected by W. Edwin Gledhill, n.d., Santa Barbara Historical Society, and Jane Whitehead's calendars. Winterthur Library, Downs Collection.

10. Arthur Ogilvy. Memoir collected by W. Edwin Gledhill, n.d., Santa Barbara Historical Society.

11. Jane to her mother, February 23–March 2, probably 1895. Winterthur Library, Downs Collection.

12. Hervey White, *Man Overboard! A Naughty Novel* (Woodstock, NY: Maverick Press, 1922), 6–7, cited in Evers, *Woodstock*, 698.

13. RRW, "Pictures for Schools," *Arrows of the Dawn*, no. 3 (Montecito, 1901). Published by Stanley-Taylor Co., San Franciso.

14. Jane to her mother, February 23–March 2, probably 1895. Winterthur.

15. Otto Salomon, *The Theory of Educational Sloyd* (Chicago: Silver, Burdett & Co., 1896), 1. A copy of this book was in Whitehead's Byrdcliffe library.

16. African-American sculptor Meta Warrick Fuller became an artist thanks to her experience at Tadd's school.

17. The names of the students are listed on the back of the photograph Alf Evers Byrdcliffe collection of the Woodstock Guild of Craftsmen (fig. 4).

18. Edwards, 5f. In 1897 Whitehead attended a séance in Troy, New York, and reported on it for the Society—his report is in the Society's file, September 19, 1897.

19. Hervey White, *Autobiography*, 141. This unpublished, undated (probably early 1930s) manuscript in the Papers of Hervey White, Special Collections Department, University of Iowa, Iowa City, is an important source of information about the history of Woodstock as an artists' colony.

20. Jane to her mother, February 23–March 2, probably 1895. Winterthur Library, Downs Collection.

21. The Whiteheads owned a plaster cast version of a medieval *giglio*, now in the collection of the Woodstock Guild of Craftsmen, and adapted its form for bookplates and other Byrdcliffe imagery. For Eaton see Leslie Greene Bowman, "The Arts and Crafts Movement in the Southland," in Kenneth R. Trapp's *Living the Good Life: The Arts and Crafts Movement in California* (The Oakland Museum and Abbeville Press, 1993), 186–190, and Katherine Louise Smith, "A California Craftsman and His Work," *House and Garden*, vol. 9 (January 1906): 31–35.

22. Jane to her mother, April 20, 1896. Winterthur Library, Downs Collection.

23. Florence Thaw wrote to Mrs. Whitehead, "I have seen more reason... for making it necessary to decline having any calling acquaintance with you" (March 24, Winterthur), and, "It is a most dreadful thing for a young unmarried woman to have such remarks made about her as have naturally been made about Miss H.... I only wish we had not known about this painful thing. But I can assure you that our pain has been as sincere as our sympathy with and for you" (August 13 [1896?], Winterthur Library, Downs Collection). Evers, *Catskills*, 614; *Woodstock*, 412.

24. Jane to RRW, Santa Barbara, July 12, 1896: "This week has taught me much, taught me that whatever happens I must be with you... took sleeping pills, can't sleep.... Last night I came to the conclusion that nothing could take me to the East—that all I should demand of you was to be with you and that you should cease to see much of Miss Hart." Winterthur Library, Downs Collection.

25. RRW to Jane, June 21, 1901. Winterthur Library, Downs Collection.

26. The authoritative source of information about Brown is Clinton Adams's *Crayonstone: The Life and Work of Bolton Brown* (Albuquerque: University of New Mexico Press, 1993). A more recent publication is the catalogue of a Bolton Brown exhibition at the Samuel Dorsky Museum at the State University of New York at New Paltz, 2003.

27. Adams, *Crayonstone*, 50f.

28. The house is also known through an article by E. A. Needles, "Little House with Five Fireplaces," *The House Beautiful* (April 21, 1907): 23–24. (cat. 2)

29. White, *Autobiography*, 102.

30. For Hull House see Jane Addams, *Twenty Years at Hull-House* (Signet Classic, Macmillan Company, 1981) and Allen F. Davis and Mary Lynn McCree Bryan, eds., *One Hundred Years at Hull House* (Bloomington: Indiana University Press, 1990).

31. White, *Autobiography*, 101. Also quoted in Evers, *Catskills*, 611.

32. Among White's Chicago friends, most of who went on to spend time at Byrdcliffe, were lawyer Clarence Darrrow, illustrators Frank and Joe Leyendecker and their sister Augusta, sculptors Loredo Taft and Lou Wall Moore, Arts and Crafts theorist Oscar Lovell Triggs, and economist Thorstein Veblen.

The search for Byrdcliffe was preceded by a venture into Oregon in 1900. Whitehead bought some land in a forested part of Oregon, Alsea, and sent a trio of musicians to help erect cabins and rehearse their music for him and Hervey White; but when Whitehead and White arrived the musicians were feuding and little came of the experiment other than a pleasant stay. Evers (*Woodstock*, 411 ff.), Edwards (6), and Anita Smith (*Woodstock History and Hearsay*, Catskills Mountains Publishing Company, 1959, 55) see this as a failed attempt to establish a colony, but Hervey White in letters to Carl Lindin at the time described it simply as a camping trip: "Later on we will settle with our beautiful musicians in the pine woods and ride horses and lark for three weeks more then to part and face me toward Chicago." May 21, 1900, collection of Gregory Lindin.

33. Bolton Brown, "Early Days at Woodstock," *Publications of the Woodstock Historical Society* (August–September 1937): 5.

34. RRW to Bim (Ralph Jr.), Woodstock, June 2, 1902. Winterthur Library, Downs Collection.

35. *Ibid.*, June 4, 1902.

36. Hervey White, "Ralph Radcliffe Whitehead," *Publications of the Woodstock Historical Society* 10 (July 1933): 16, 20.

37. Ralph Radcliffe Whitehead, "Introduction," J. B. Radcliffe Whitehead, *Birds of God* (New York: R. H. Russell, 1902); RRW to Jane, August 20, 1902, from Woodstock. Winterthur Library, Downs Collection.

38. Of Zola he wrote to Jane from Florence on August 24, 1901, "in the Dreyfus affair he comes out boldly on the side of truth." Winterthur Library, Downs Collection.

39. Evers, *The Catskills*, 650 f. Anita Smith wrote that the Weyls, after living in Byrdcliffe for two years, "were not satisfied to buy any

of the Byrdcliffe land with its numerous restrictions" (*Woodstock History and Hearsay*, 42).

40. For Gilman's racism see Ann J. Lane, *To Herland and Beyond: The Life and Works of Charlotte Perkins Gilman* (Meridian, 1990), 255, 337. The only member of this circle of Chicago intellectuals that I have found who did not share this anti-Semitism was sociologist Thorstein Veblen, in his essay, "The Intellectual Pre-Eminence of Jews in Modern Europe," *The Political Science Quarterly*, XXXIV, March 1919, reprinted in Thorstein Veblen, *Essays in Our Changing Order*, Leon Ardzrooni, ed. (New York: Viking Press, 1954), 219–31.

41. Hervey White, "Our Jerusalem," *The Plowshare*, vol. 9, no. 1 (December 1919), n.p. In a related essay White wrote, "We may conquer and consume the black race, the red, the brown, and the yellow, but the Jews sit aloft on our backs, their blood-sucking trade-tentacles in our vitals, a glow of humble superiority in their guile" ("The Encroaching Race," *The Plowshare*, vol. 8, no. 12 [November 1919]). Alf Evers, describing White as "among the most tolerant Americans of his time," quotes an anti-Semitic passage in one of his poems written in the 1920s (*The Catskills*, 650).

42. RRW to Jane, New York, May 27, 1902. Winterthur Library, Downs Collection.

43. Evers, *Woodstock*, 490 f.

44. RRW to Bim, June 19, 1922. Winterthur Library, Downs Collection. My thanks to my Bard College colleague Joel Perlmann for his advice on this section, and to Nancy Green for this quotation.

45. Gene Patterson, in a memoir about staying at White Pines, recalled that in the early 1940s Mrs. Whitehead regularly entertained "refugee intellectuals. . . escaping Hitler's persecution" ("Dark Night at White Pines," *Woodstock Originals*, vol. II, Joseph Keefe, ed. [Woodstock: The Byrdcliffe Writers, 1987], 114). My thanks to Carla Smith for bringing this text to my attention.

46. RRW to Jane, Woodstock, October 23, 1902. Winterthur Library, Downs Collection. "In business matters Brown is a failure from overconfidence in his own ability to do things in five minutes."

47. *Ibid.*, December 11, 1902.

48. Alf Evers's "Walking Tour" of Byrdcliffe, in typescript at the Woodstock Guild of Craftsmen, is a valuable guide to the main buildings.

49. Brown, "Early Days," 11. Brown could not remember Duncan's name and thought it might be Cameron, but it is clear from other sources that he meant Duncan.

50. Evers, *Woodstock*, 424.

51. This design source for Byrdcliffe furniture, and the existence of copies of *The Studio Magazine* with images of furniture annotated by Whitehead, was pointed out by Robert Edwards in "Byrdcliffe: Life By Design" in *The Byrdcliffe Arts & Crafts Colony* (Delaware Art Museum, 1984), 10, fn. 39. In letters to his wife from early 1903 Whitehead repeatedly asked her to send him a special edition of *The Studio* titled "British Domestic Architecture and Decoration." RRW to Jane, January 22, 1903/February 1, 1903. Winterthur Library, Downs Collection.

52. RRW to Jane, Byrdcliffe, February 22, 1903. Winterthur Library, Downs Collection.

53. RRW to Jane, Woodstock, April 1, 1903. Winterthur Library, Downs Collection.

54. Brown, "Early Days," 13.

55. Wallace Stevens, letter to Harry Duncan, July 17, 1944. In his next letter to Duncan, the poet, who was also an executive in an insurance company, offered a pragmatic criticism of art pottery: "We still have a lot of things at home made by potters up there: in fact we started out to have them make a dinner set for us. The trouble with that sort of thing is that you have to wash the dishes yourself if you want to use the same dishes twice" (July 19, 1944. Wallace Stevens papers, The Huntington Library, San Marino, California, Box 69 [34]).

56. Alvan F. Sanborn, in "Leaders in American Arts and Crafts," *Good Housekeeping* (February 1907), wrote, "The relations of the Byrdcliffe resident and sojourner to Mr. Whitehead bear a striking resemblance to those of the vassal to his lord or, to use more modern terms, of the English tenant to his landlord, since the creator of Byrdcliffe retains the title to all the Byrdcliffe houses and lands and is the ultimate authority with regard to any and every question of policy and administration that may arise" (148). Poultney Bigelow's analysis was similar in "The Byrdcliffe Colony of Arts and Crafts," *American Homes and Gardens* (October 1909), part of which included, "The Byrdcliffe despot is the most gentle and admirable tyrant, for under him the colony knows no deficits, is never assessed!" (393)

57. John Ruskin, letter XXXVII, *Fors Clavigera, Letters to the Workmen and Labourers of Great Britain*, vol. 2, in *The Complete Works of John Ruskin in Twenty-Six Volumes* (New York: Brian, Taylor & Co., 1894), 135.

58. The playhouse today is, unfortunately, almost totally destroyed.

59. Brown, "Early Days," 13.

60. Bertha Thompson, "Recollections," n.d., n.p., "The Thompson Family Collection," Arthur and Elizabeth Schlesinger Library of Women's Studies, Radcliffe Institute, Harvard University; and the Woodstock Library.

61. RRW to Jane, Woodstock, January 16, 1908. Winterthur Library, Downs Collection.

62. A copy of the program exists at Winterthur.

63. For the British folk-music revival see Alan Crawford, C. R. Ashbee (Yale University Press, 1985), 121–24.

64. Jane Byrd McCall Whitehead, *The Morning Stars Sang Together: Folk-Songs and Other Songs for Children* (Boston: Oliver Ditson Company, 1903).

65. "Preface," Ralph Radcliffe Whitehead, ed., *Folk-Songs of Eastern Europe* (Boston, Oliver Ditson Company, 1912).

66. Evers, *Woodstock*, 447.

67. As with much in this essay, my discussion of metal working at Byrdcliffe builds on what has already been written by Alf Evers, *Woodstock: History of an American Town*, 429.

68. Sanborn, "Leaders in American Arts and Crafts," 148.

69 The drawings for a doorknob and for drawer pulls are at Winterthur; the jewelry sketch is in the Evers collection of the Woodstock Guild of Craftsmen.

70. Bolton Brown recorded an Ernest Chapman at Byrdcliffe in its early days who worked in brass and "made perforated objects out of sheet metal," which raises some questions about the attribution of the sconce to Thatcher (Brown, "Early Days at Woodstock," 12). The sconce belonged to the Lindin family.

71. Hervey White, "The Will to Live," in *Hue and Cry*, 1933. Thanks to Maribeth Harmes for information about her ancestor, Edmund Rolfe.

72. Ashbee, *The Ashbee Memoirs*, vol. 4 (June 1915): 227. My thanks to James Benjamin for supplying me with the source of this quote.

73. Bertha Thompson, "Recollections," Schlesinger Library, Radcliffe Institute, Harvard University.

74. Annie Thompson, "Bertha and Byrdcliffe," Schlesinger Library, Radcliffe Institute, Harvard University.

75. Diane Huneker, "Portrait Drawings by Dewing Woodward," *International Studio*, LXII, no. 245: 36–38.

76. Jane to RRW, July 11, 1910, Woodstock. Winterthur Library, Downs Collection.

77. Sanborn, 119.

78. In an undated (May 20) draft for a letter to her husband, Mrs. Whitehead likened his relationship with Steele and Walker to the one years ago with Miss Hart, who subsequently "was absolutely shunned and then took to opium." Mrs. Whitehead proposed a separation: "You and I and they cannot be at Byrdcliffe this summer together."

79. For Rhead, see Sharon Dale, *Frederick Hürten Rhead: An English Potter in America* (Erie Art Museum, 1986).

80. Jane to Ralph Jr., July 28, 1917. Winterthur. Anita Smith wrote about the German-Americans, "There was considerable friction between this group and the English during the war, but now all have become friends again" (*Woodstock History and Hearsay*, 45).

81. RRW to Jane, March 23, 1897. Winterthur Library, Downs Collection.

82. White, *Autobiography*, 173.

83. Although originally intended for Woodstock, the concert was actually held about forty miles from the town; Woodstock was the first choice because it was "a gathering place for singers, musicians, composers. . . . " Joel Rosenman, John Roberts, Robert Pilpel, *Young Men with Unlimited Capital: The Inside Story of the Legendary Woodstock Festival Told by the Two Who Paid for It* (New York: Harcourt Brace Jovanovich, Inc., 1974), 20.

84. Bertha Thompson, "The Craftsmen of Byrdcliffe," *Publications of the Woodstock Historical Society* 10 (July 1933): 11, 13.

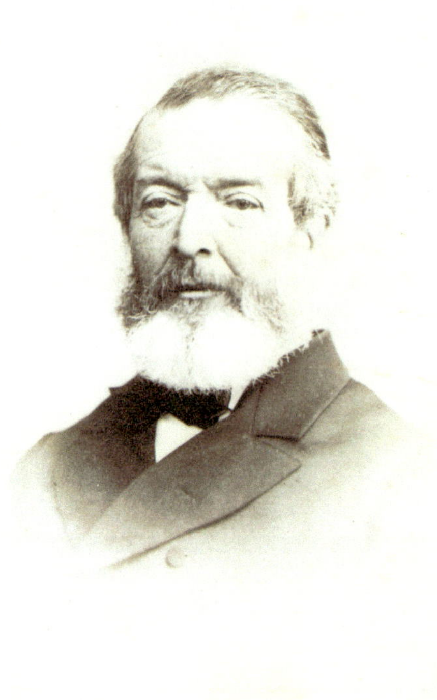

Left
fig. 1 Unidentified photographer, *Francis F. Whitehead*, ca. 1870. Albumen print. Collection of the Woodstock Guild

Right
fig. 2 Eugène-François-Marie Devéria, French, 1808–1865, *Isabella Dalglish*, ca. 1860. Oil on canvas. Collection of Jill and Mark Willcox Jr.

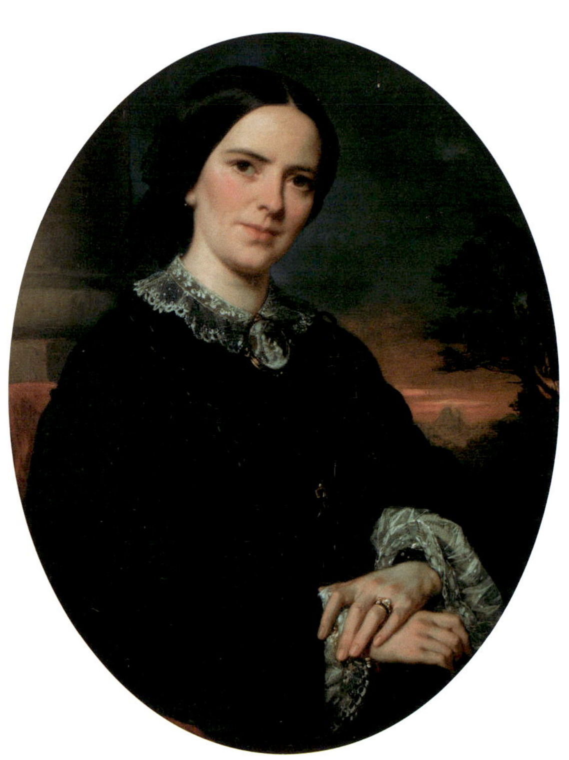

The Reality of Beauty

Ralph Whitehead and the Seeds of a Utopia in John Ruskin, William Morris, and Victorian England[1]

NANCY E. GREEN

Saddleworth on the River Tame, in the West Riding of Yorkshire, was the heart of England's woolen district when Ralph Radcliffe Whitehead was born there in 1854. His three uncles and father owned and operated the Royal George Mills, successful manufacturers of piano felts, and Ralph, as the only male heir, was raised in an atmosphere of wealth and prosperity. Named for his eldest uncle, Whitehead was the oldest and only surviving child[2] of Francis Frederick and his wife Isabella, née Dalglish (figs. 1 and 2). As he grew older, Ralph adopted the idealistic fervor of William Morris and John Ruskin, disdaining the source of his wealth though he never attempted to dispose of his money to humanitarian causes.[3] This was just one of the many contradictory impulses that would characterize his life and would, ultimately, affect the success of Byrdcliffe.

In the 1840s the Industrial Revolution fostered great changes in the woolen and cotton industry of Yorkshire. Earlier farming families had begun cottage industries of spinning and weaving to supplement their incomes, but by the late 1840s the mills were taking over this domestic industry. One observer described the area as it appeared in 1849: "The eye wanders... from cottage to cottage, and hamlet to hamlet, and mill to mill... the latter invariably nestled in the very bottom of the glen each beside its lakelet of clear water, dammed up from the rapid stream of the Tame."[4] The workers, often children, led a hard life. As an adult, Morgan Brierley remembered with irony, "Happy days of childhood... still happier days of boyhood. Twelve hours a day in a primitive woolen mill, learning the initiatory processes of cloth, flannel and shawl manufacture. The whole thing was brimming with poetry." He also described their education, or lack of it: "I was a short timer under the (1833) factory act when the hours of labour were ten and the school hours, two, or say, rather, should have been two, for the exigencies of the mill in which I worked were such that we children could not get so much, and if the inspector visited the mill in the hours when we ought to have been at school we were hidden under a skip of light wool, until he went away."[5]

The mills also provided an ever-present danger to the health of the local residents in the form of smoke and

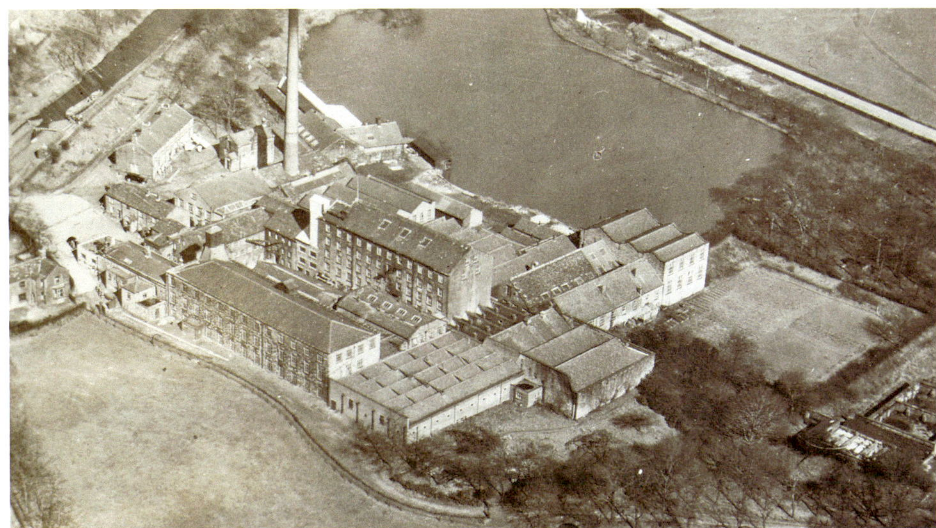

fig. 3 Unidentified photographer, *The Royal George Mill, Greenfield, Oldham*. Silver print. Winterthur Library, Downs Collection, 92x39.1140.634.

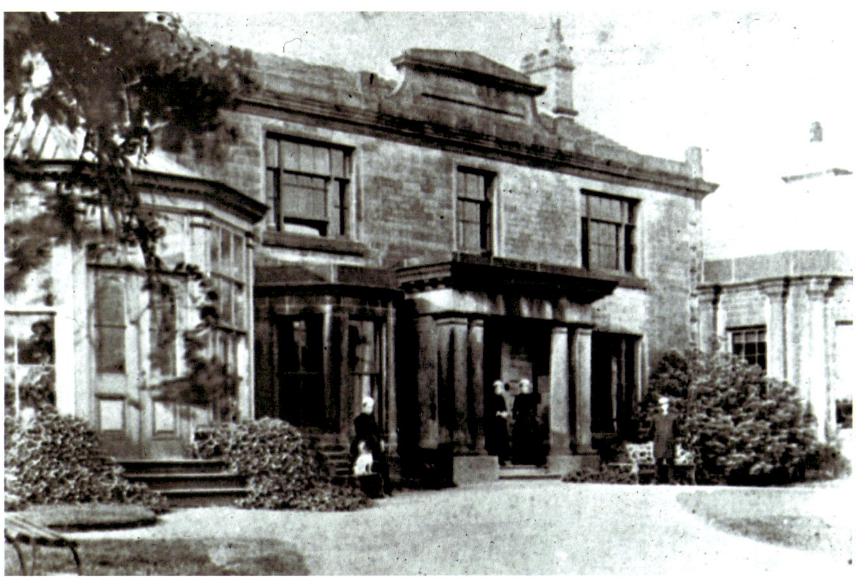

fig. 4 Unidentified photographer, *Beech Hill, the Whitehead Home, Oldham*, ca. 1865. Albumen print. Collection of the Saddleworth Historical Society.

black soot that infested the river and coated the buildings and the inhabitants' lungs. The mills' machinery periodically caused mishaps and, occasionally, death as recorded in the *Manchester Guardian* in 1843: "a youth in Saddleworth seized by a wheel and carried away with it... (he) died, utterly mangled."[6] On the night of May 16, 1864, a devastating accident at the Royal George killed eleven members of the Jeffrey family when a mill chimney collapsed and destroyed their home. It has been speculated that this may have been the catalyst that propelled Ralph into a more honest appraisal of the realities of mill workers' lives, sparking a concern for his family's employees that left him vulnerable to the social issues he would be exposed to by Ruskin.[7]

The Whiteheads came from a long line of wool manufacturers. Their ancestors had collected spun wool from neighboring cottages and smaller farms and then dyed and stored it until the time came for the trek over the Pennines by cart and packhorse to the center of the wool industry in Lancashire. Thus John Whitehead (1668–1752)[8] and his descendants entered the wool trade. In 1799 William Whitehead, Ralph's grandfather, bought the Oak View Mill and in 1838 his four sons bought a mill in Grasscroft, near Oldham, from the estate of Joseph Harrop, called the Royal George (fig. 3), so named in 1805 to honor King George III. Early on the mill was renowned for the flags produced there,[9] but the Whiteheads became interested in felt making, which, like wool dyeing, required access to an abundant water source, supplied by the River Tame. Prosperity followed and two more mills were acquired in the 1850s, the Throstle Nest Mill (for scribbling) and the Charlotte Mill (cotton manufacturing).

In 1843, as the Whiteheads' fortunes increased, the Harrop family home, Beech Hill, was purchased. The youngest of the four uncles, John Dicken, lived there for a number of years, but in 1861 he built a new residence, Wharmton Tower. His brother Francis Frederick then moved his family into Beech Hill[10] (fig. 4). This house, which still sits on the hill overlooking the Mill, was capacious, with plenty of room for the small family and their many servants. The lawns afforded space for tennis and other sports activities, and summer parties out-of-doors.

It was a genteel life, reflecting the status of the wealthy Victorian family. Ralph was indeed among the lucky ones. He learned to ride, fish, and shoot (his family kept a shooting lookout on the moors), and at a young age he was sent away to public school at Harrow, from where he wrote imperious letters home with strict instructions about food to be sent and visits to be made, early proof of his privileged upbringing[11] (fig. 5).

There is a delightful tale in Saddleworth folklore that tells of Captain Robert Radcliffe, an Elizabethan ancestor of Ralph's, who was stationed at Cadiz during the English occupation there. A Spanish lady fell in love with him, but he kindly told her of his sweet wife at home; for his honesty and fidelity, the señora sent a gift of jewelry to his wife.[12] This tale was turned into a popular ballad sung in the local alehouses in the 1820s and 1830s and the ballad itself is included in the *Oxford Book of Ballads*. It is perhaps not too fanciful to imagine that this song left an impression on the young Whitehead and contributed to his lifelong interest in the folksongs of Europe.[13]

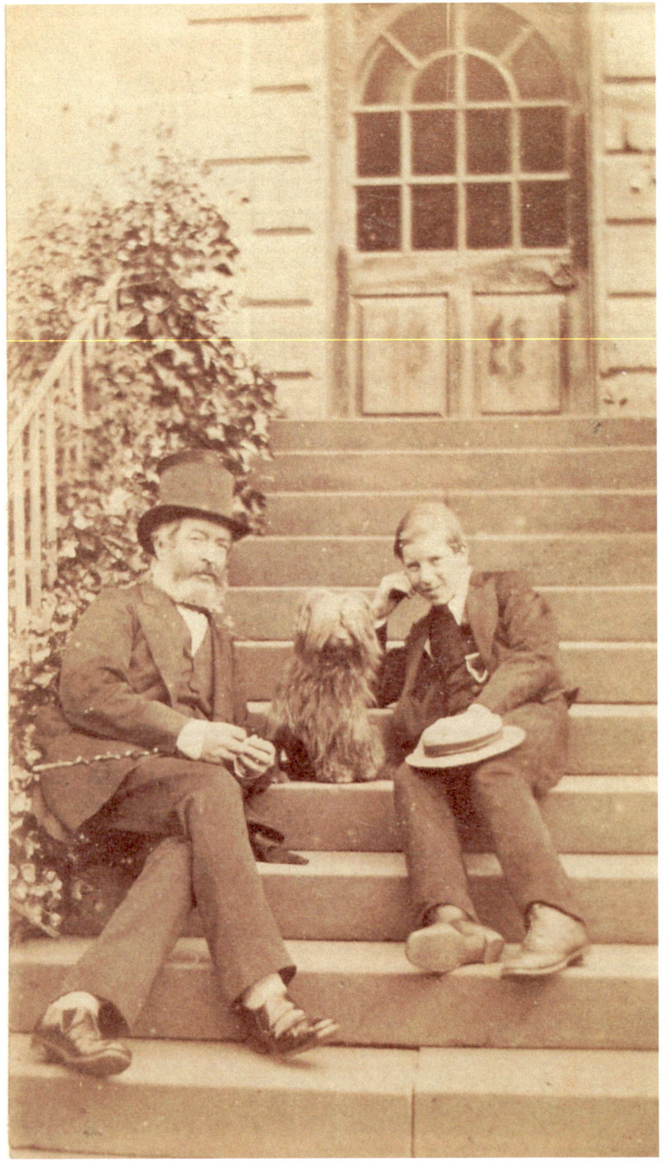

fig. 5 Scott & Son, photographers, Carlisle, *Francis and Ralph Whitehead*, ca. 1868. Albumen print. Winterthur Library, Downs Collection, 92 x 39.1140.353.

In 1873 Whitehead went to Oxford, entering Balliol College, where he met the man who would effectively change the course of his life. John Ruskin (fig. 6), who had been appointed Slade Professor at Oxford in 1869, was at the height of his influence though already suffering some of the indications of the madness that would haunt his later life. He was also a skilled artist, recording flora and fauna as well as architecturally detailed images to illustrate his own writings (fig. 7). Though Ruskin had no formal teaching schedule, he gave public lectures that were popularly attended by hundreds of undergraduates, and Whitehead rapidly succumbed to his spell. Like his student, Ruskin was born to wealth and he used this money for many worthy causes, most of which were of his own creation. In 1871 the germ of the plan for Ruskin's Guild of St. George was formed, his effort at a utopian community. It was to be a guild based on a medieval prototype in which people without independent means could acquire land, work toward a common good, and derive complete satisfaction from their chosen work. Each would pay a tithe to the common fund to buy land for farming, mills, and factories for the other workers. W. G. Collingwood, Ruskin's biographer, elaborated: "So far the plan was simple. It was not a *colony*—but merely the working of existing industries in a certain way. Anticipating further development of the scheme, Mr. Ruskin looked forward to a guild coinage, as pretty as the Florentines had; a costume as becoming as the Swiss; and other Platonically devised details, which were not the essentials of the proposal, and never came into operation. But some of the plans were actually realized."[14] Ultimately, the idea for the Guild was more a catalyst, inspiring other communal efforts rather than a powerful force, in and of itself.

Ruskin didn't stop there. He addressed many controversial issues of the day, including transportation (he loathed the railroad, feeling that it despoiled the landscape), women's employment, environmental pollution, and universal education. To someone of Whitehead's sheltered upbringing, Ruskin's words were enticingly inflammatory. When Ruskin looked for volunteers for his Hinksey Road project, Whitehead was purportedly among those who answered the call.[15] Other Balliol students, such as Arnold Toynbee, the historian and socialist (for whom the first settlement house, Toynbee Hall, was named), was also cited as a participant in the escapade. Oscar Wilde claimed to have been there as well, but this is totally fictitious as he did not come to Oxford until the fall of 1874. Ruskin's biographer, W. G. Collingwood, who was one of the diggers, recalled this memorable episode:

> He (Ruskin) had noticed a very bad bit of road on the Hinksey side, and heard that it was nobody's business to mend it: meanwhile the farmers' carts and casual pedestri-

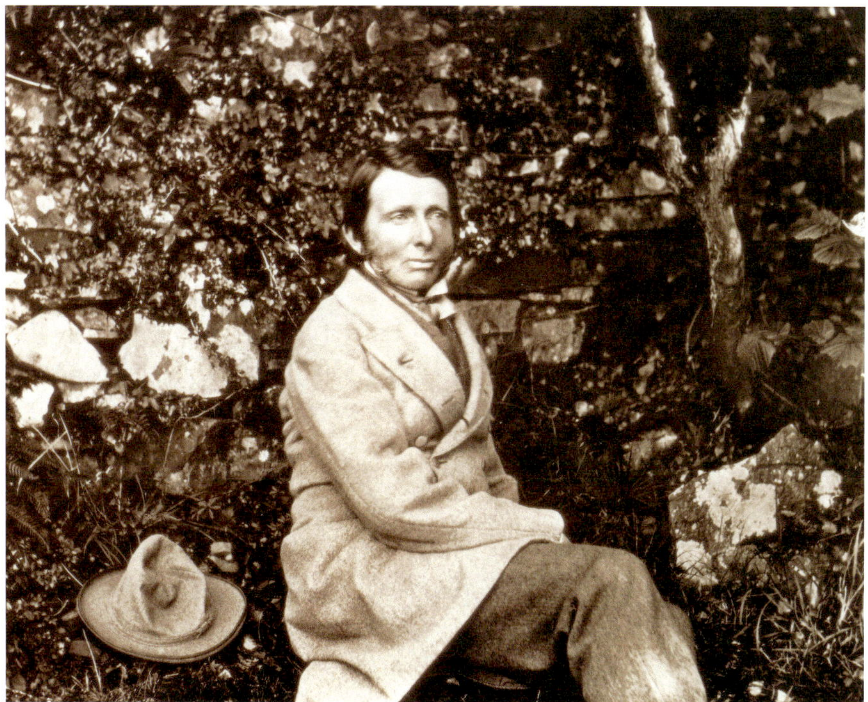

fig. 6 Frank Meadow Sutcliffe, British, 1853–1941, *John Ruskin*, ca. 1870. Albumen print. Courtesy of the Sutcliffe Gallery, Whitby.

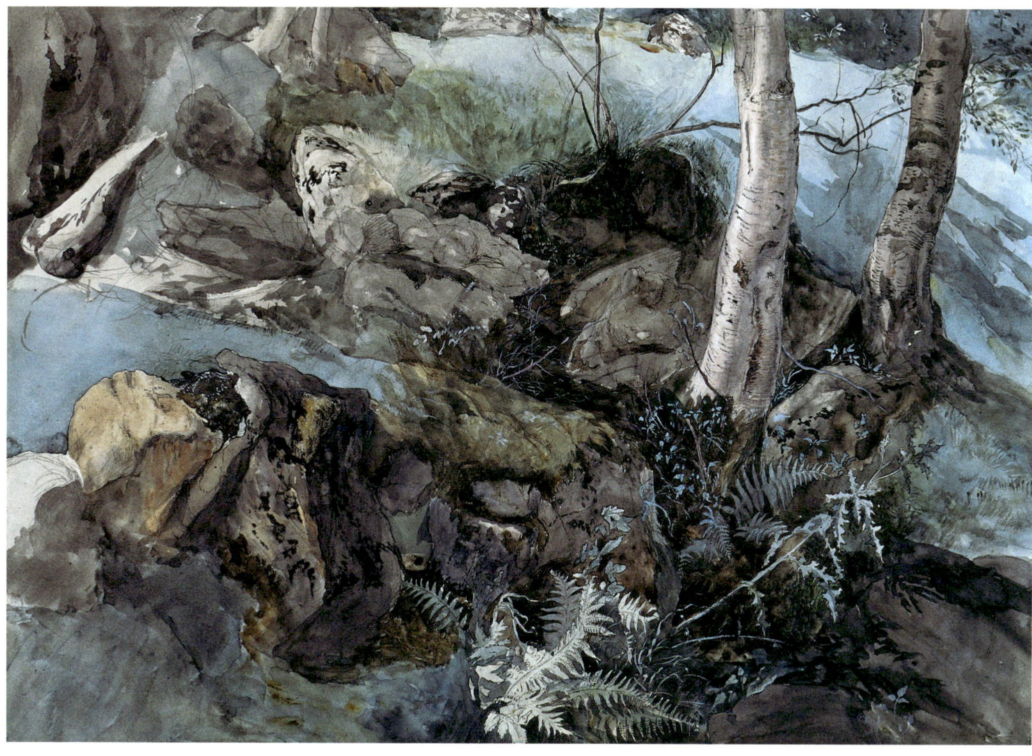

fig. 7 John Ruskin, *Rocks and Ferns in a Wood at Crossmount, Perthshire*, 1847. Watercolor. Courtesy of Abbot Hall Art Gallery, Kendal, Cumbria, England.

> ans were bemired. He sent for his gardener Downes... laid in a stock of picks and shovels, took lessons in stone-breaking himself, and called on his friends to spend their recreation times in doing something useful. In spite of a good deal of ridicule, something useful was actually done. More picks were broken and more time was lost than a regular business-contractor would have liked: but the men had their lesson and the cottagers their road.[16]

This strange and unusual event created quite a stir among the pundits of the day and Ruskin, ever a favorite for the cartoonists with his thin, aristocratic nose and long, lanky limbs, was shown overseeing the road construction as the "rustics" looked on, jeering (fig. 8). In reality, as Collingwood notes, "the Professor was absent."[17] In fact, he was far away, traveling in Italy.

When Jane Addams visited Toynbee Hall in the early 1880s, her reaction to the road-digging episode was initially uncomprehending. "Why should an American be lost in admiration of a group of Oxford students because they went out to mend a disused road, inspired thereto by Ruskin's teaching for the bettering of the common life, when all the country roads in America were mended each spring by self-

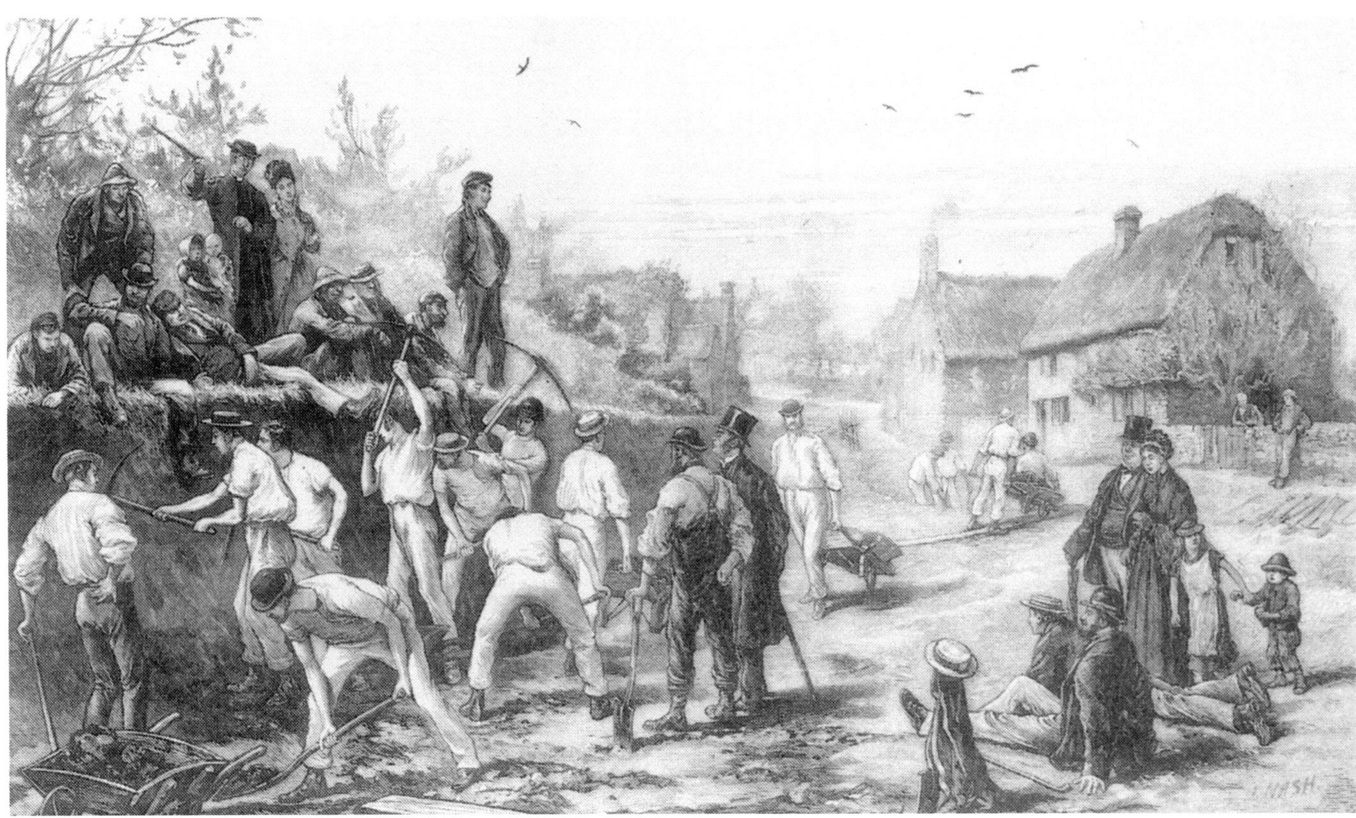

fig. 8 J. Nash, *Amateur Navvies at Oxford—Undergraduates making a road as suggested by Mr. Ruskin* from *The Graphic*, June 27, 1874 (pages 612–13). Courtesy of the University of Lancaster.

respecting citizens, who were thus carrying out the simple method devised by a democratic government for providing highways."[18] What Addams overlooked, but later came to realize, was that Ruskin was teaching stewardship to a class of students to whom such an idea might seem completely alien. Ruskin was never a socialist, as Morris was, but felt deeply that his wealth should be best used to improve the lives of those who had been born with less, and this obligation is one he tried to pass on to the undergraduates.

It is not really surprising that the shy young man from Yorkshire who had been raised in the expectation of his role in carrying on the family wool business was suddenly transformed. Fired by Ruskin's words, Whitehead returned home in the middle of his second year flush with new ideals. He told his father and uncles of his plans to turn the Royal George into a factory modeled on Ruskinian ideas. The workers' lives would be elevated as they participated in creating beautiful fabrics instead of continuing the tedious work of producing piano felts. They would be educated, work shorter hours—for which they would receive better pay—and the river and air would be cleansed of the polluting soot, smoke, and other deadly contaminants as steam power was relinquished. The family's consternation was palpable, and Ralph was quickly dispossessed of this fantasy and packed off to Paris where he would be away from Ruskin's influence.

Whitehead, however, was not to be so easily curtailed in his ambitions. He apprenticed himself to a carpenter believing, like his mentor, that working with one's hands was a spiritual endeavor, and one in which every man should be involved for several hours of each day. He later would recall this year as the happiest of his life.[19]

At Oxford, Whitehead had also developed a love of classical music under the guidance of the Reverend Sir Frederick Arthur Gore, professor of music. Music would remain an interest for the rest of Whitehead's life and would always be an important component in any of his plans for a colony.

After patching up the quarrel with his family, Whitehead returned to Oxford, though the year away had not disabused him of his admiration for Ruskin. In 1876 he traveled to Italy and visited his mentor (fig. 9). Collingwood makes note of this in the biography: "In August 1876 [Ruskin] left England for Italy. He traveled alone, accompanied only by his new servant Baxter, who had lately taken the place vacated by Crawley, Mr. Ruskin's former valet of twenty years' service. He crossed the Simplon to Venice, where he was welcomed by an old friend, Mr. Rawdon Brown, and a new friend, Prof. C. H. Moore of Harvard. He met two Oxford pupils, Mr. J. Reddie Anderson,[20] whom he set to work on Carpaccio; and Mr. Whitehead—'So much nicer they all are,' he wrote in a private letter, 'than I was at their age'—also his pupil Mr. Bunney, at work on copies of pictures and records of architecture, the legacy of St. Mark to St. George."[21]

Although never a true protégé of Ruskin's, Whitehead was a believer in many of the older man's doctrines and spent the remainder of his life attempting to fulfill the dream of communal living based on the ideals of the St. George Guild. Like Ruskin, he believed that "life without industry is guilt, and industry without art is brutality."[22] In a *Fors Clavigera* letter, Ruskin anoints Whitehead as "one of my own boys."[23] Many years later, Whitehead would write of the years wasted, when he should have followed Ruskin's lead.

In 1880 he graduated with a master's degree. Thus began a decade of mystery where the facts about his life are few and far between. He returned temporarily to Saddleworth for a short time, but such a sedentary life was not in his temperament. In the 1881 census, he is listed as living in London at 33A Crescent House, Kensington, with a twenty-four-year-old wife, Marie, who was Austrian, and four servants. He also maintained a large domicile in Sussex called Borden Wood, which he apparently owned from 1882 to 1890 (fig. 10). He is listed in Kelly's *Directory of Sussex* as justice of the peace there in 1882 and 1887.[24] It is not known exactly when his first marriage took place nor where the couple met, and Whitehead's second wife, Jane, is said to have disposed of any references to Marie among the papers left at her husband's death. There remains one sad, rather prescient letter, sent from Marie to Ralph several years after the divorce in which she warns him that "you will never find the blissfulness that you attempted to find. You request too much, you long for

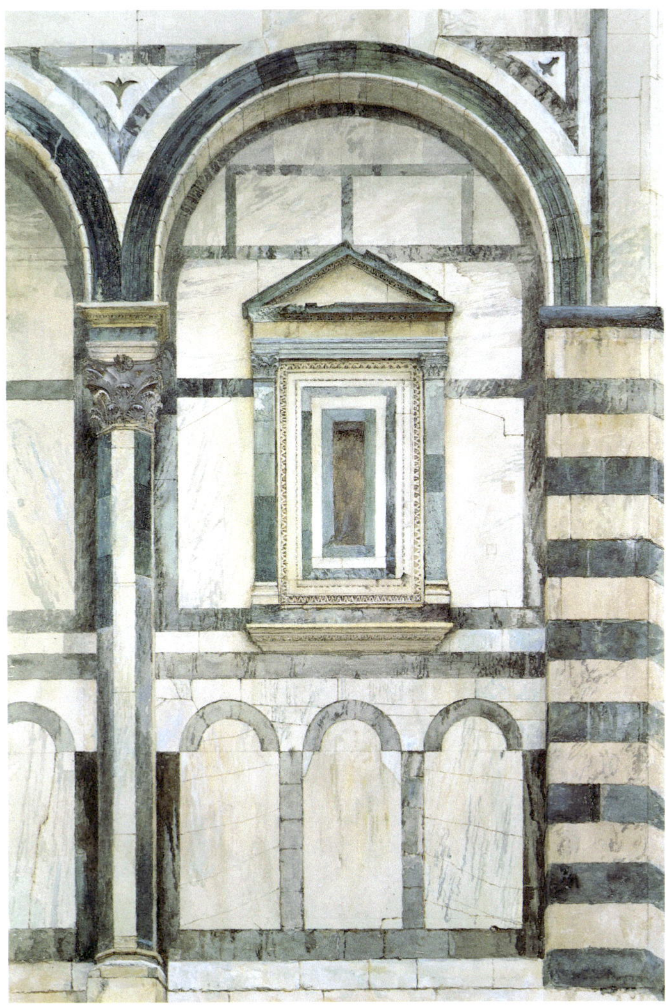

fig. 9 John Ruskin, *Exterior of the Ducal Palace, Venice*, 1852. Pencil and wash with some ink. Courtesy of the Ashmolean Museum, Oxford University.

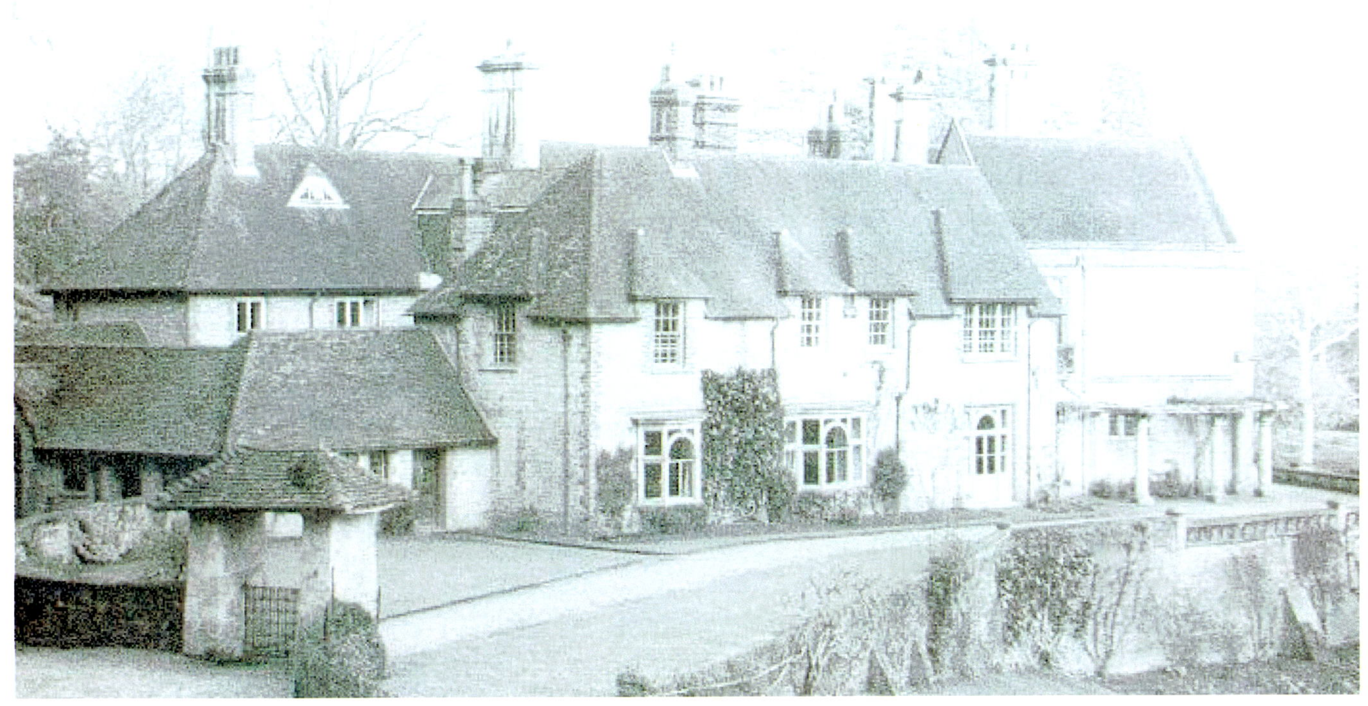

fig. 10 Unidentified photographer, *Borden Wood, Sussex*, ca. 1905. Albumen print. Photograph courtesy of Nick Marmont.

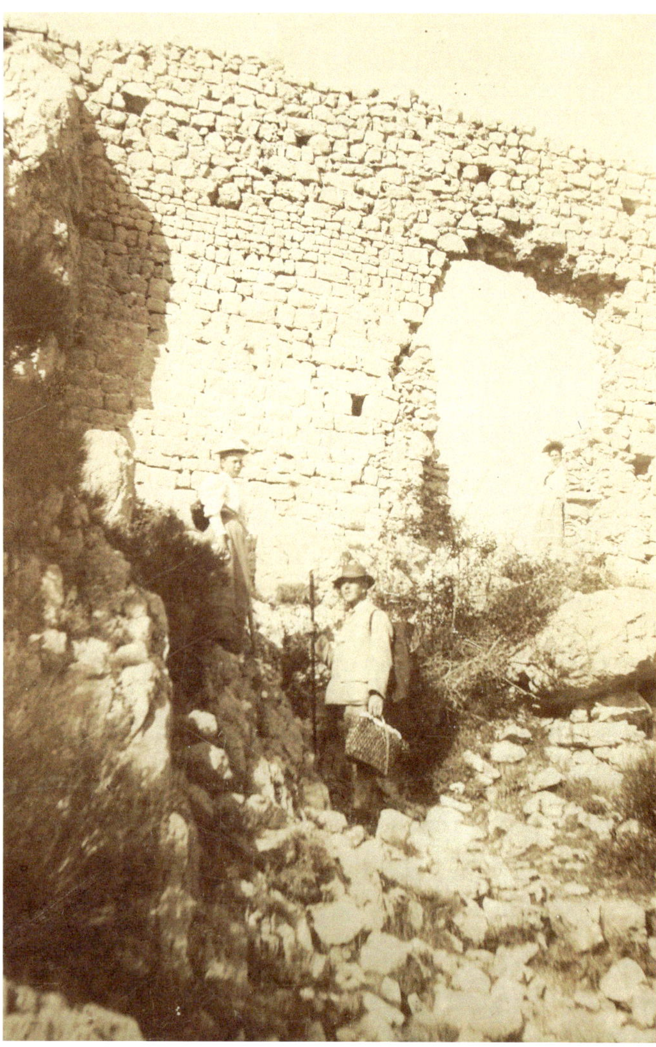

fig. 11 Unidentified photographer, *Ralph Whitehead and Friend Hiking* (possibly his first wife, Marie), ca. 1882. Albumen print. Winterthur Library, Downs Collection, 92x39.1140.83.

something impossible, and therefore, you must be discontented with reality. What occurred to me will have to occur to my rival, to you a life long. Your character is in one, your soul in another world."[25]

Although there is a dearth of information about Whitehead's life in the 1880s, we know that his wealth allowed him to travel extensively, to study whatever fired his imagination, indulge in the usual upper-class vices of extravagance, and lead a pretty much ordinary life for one who needn't work for his money[26] (fig. 11). His thoughts were certainly much taken up with the idea of a community or 'convent' where like-minded individuals could reside in harmony, working for the common good, isolated from the outside world. There is some indication that he and Marie attempted such a colony at Styria in Austria.[27] He also had a home in San Remo, on the Italian Riviera across the border from Nice, where Marie lived until early 1891.[28] In March of that year he wrote to his future wife, Jane Byrd McCall, of the past decade, lamenting the time lost in self-indulgence: "In the last days I have often considered how it is I do not surrender myself wholly to our master [Ruskin]. I had a chance once.... Anyhow, I should have saved ten years of wasted life; for from the time I saw him in Venice in 1876 till I came back to Italy two years ago I was dead to all that had moved me before. The failure to take such a chance when it is given seems to me to be the most base act which, alas, few can look back and fail to see what prevented my joining him was as much my own pleasure in lower things as his incapacity to be a leader."[29]

In 1885 Jane, who kept yearly diaries with one line allotted for each day's entry, noted tersely on January 14: "Whiteheads musicale."[30] This is the first mention of the Whiteheads and possibly the evening when Jane and Ralph met. It seems, however, that the attraction must have been immediate as more notations of just "Whitehead" appear sporadically over the next few months. Jane, too, like her future husband, was one of the lucky ones. Born to a wealthy Philadelphia family, she was raised in both America and Europe, traveling back and forth at regular intervals.

In the 1880s Jane, her mother, and her sister, Gertrude, seem to have spent most of their time in England, France, and Italy. For a time, they took a house near Oxford—Albury House—and became actively involved in the cultural and intellectual life of the town. In her scrapbook from this period, Jane accumulated many articles relating to social events the three had attended and many calling cards. Wedding invitations, including one to the wedding of Xie Kitchin, who had been made famous by Lewis Carroll's provocative photographs of her as a child, is also included, as well as an invitation to the nuptials of the daughter of philologist and Oxford don Max Müller. The Müllers would remain lifelong friends.[31]

Among the calling cards pasted into the scrapbook is that of John Ruskin. It is apparent that Jane met him sometime in 1882 or 1883 and, at some point, took a sketching lesson from him as there are two closely associated drawings of a branch with leaves (cats. 167 and 187), one signed by the master and one by Jane. This tie to Ruskin would have been an early area of interest shared with Whitehead.

In 1886 Jane and Gertrude were presented at court by Mrs. Phelps, wife of the United States Minister. The newspaper article detailing the spectacle made special note of the sisters: "The Misses McCall, two distinguished American ladies, attracted much notice by the simple elegance of their court gowns, the pearl embroideries being very beautiful"[32] (fig. 12). A month later they attended the State Ball at Buckingham Palace. This was the rather exalted circle in which the McCalls moved, and at the end of her scrapbook for the 1880s, Jane lists an impressive selection of celebrities she has met, including among them Oscar Wilde, Walter Pater, Longfellow, Gladstone, the Prince of Wales, Lord Tennyson, Oliver Wendell Holmes, President Garfield and several painters—Millais, Leighton, Burne-Jones, and Alma-Tadema. She and Whitehead were both familiar with the work of G. W. Watts, their favorite among the Pre-Raphaelites[33] (fig. 13).

Throughout the 1880s Jane, her sister Gerty, and their mother continued to travel in Europe, stopping for extended periods in England and Italy.[34] It was here, in 1890, that Jane began to see more of Ralph Whitehead, and to begin to "Dream of Somewhere."[35] By early 1891 they were arranging to meet frequently and were corresponding regularly.[36] On April 4, Ralph wrote, "the future is no longer in the hands of fate to make or mar us but it is in our own hands and our hands are strong when they are joined together, as thy soul and mine are joined till I hardly know what is mine and what is thine in our common life. Florence saw the birth and growth of our 'New Life,' but all the world shall be the scene of its fullness, for wherever life leads us we will no longer go out alone."[37]

Ralph was clearly thinking about this "convent" and settling in Italy. In a letter to Whitehead from J. N. Nettleship, his former tutor at Oxford congratulates him on his work on Dante,[38] saying, "I have often hoped that you would find some work of that kind." Later, in the same letter, he remarks, "I am glad you think of a Tuscan villa! It sounds the right thing."[39] In another letter, dated May 4 (no year), Nettleship thanks Whitehead for sending a check for Toynbee Hall.[40] "I can't say I feel much enthusiasm for the concern but I should like to see them try their experiment fairly. Nowadays the great thing seems to me to be to let anyone have their fling & trust that something straight will grow out of the many crookednesses."[41] The Nettleships would have a long friendship with the Whiteheads. Jane had her dresses made by Ada Nettleship, wife of the artist Jack Nettleship, J. N.'s brother,[42] and her own friendship most likely predates that of her meeting Whitehead.

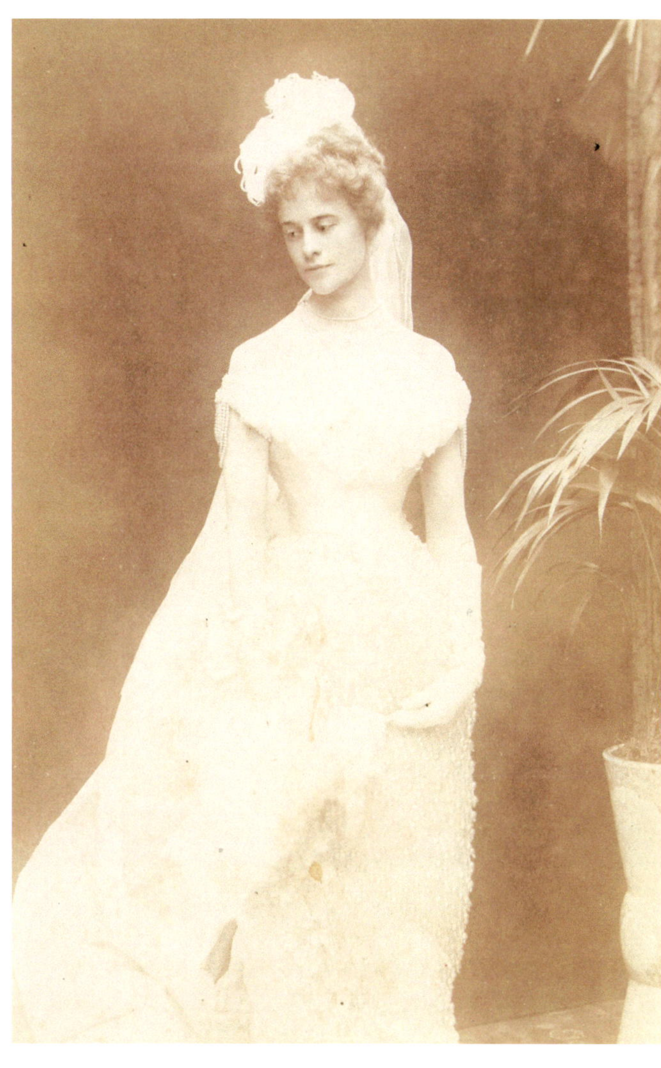

fig. 12 H. S. Mendelssohn, British, active ca. 1880s–1910s, *Jane Byrd McCall in Court Dress*, 1886. Albumen print. Winterthur Library, Downs Collection, 92x39.1140.49.

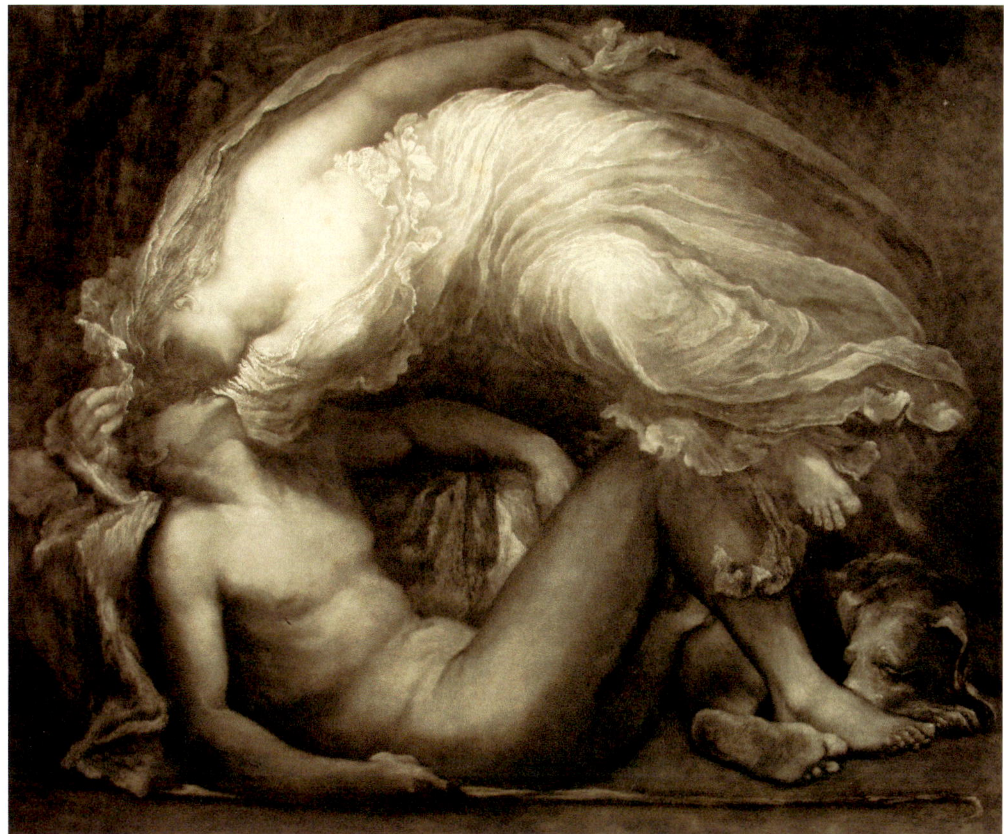

fig. 13 G. F. Watts, British, 1817–1904, *Diana and Endymion*. Mezzotint. Winterthur Library, Downs Collection, 92x39.504.

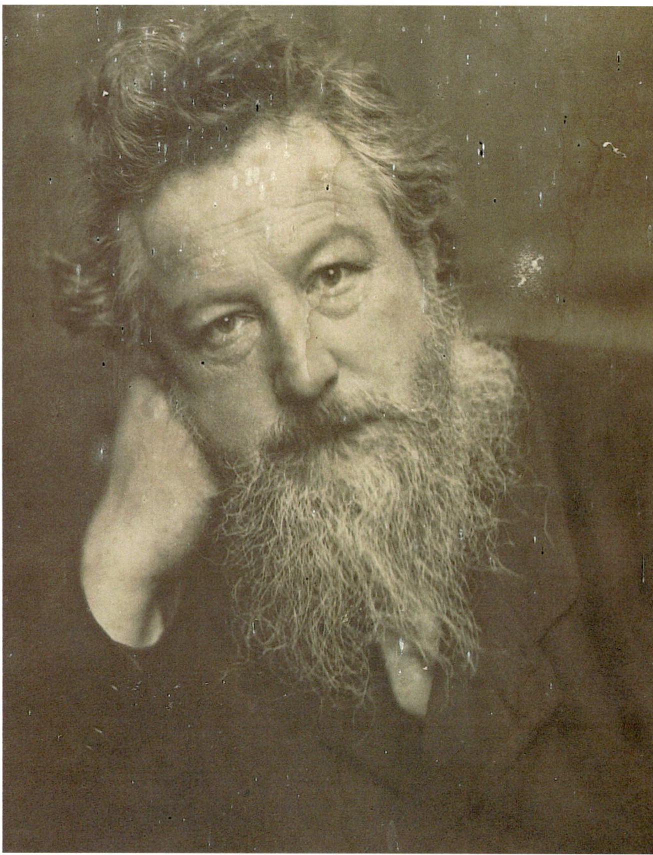

fig. 14 Frederick H. Hollyer, British, 1837–1933, *William Morris*, ca. 1880. Albumen print. Collection of the Woodstock Guild. Gift of Jill and Mark Willcox Jr.

At this time Whitehead was continuing his careful assimilation of the ideas of both Ruskin and Morris (fig. 14) into his own version of an ideal society or "convent," as he repeatedly referred to it.[43] Like Ruskin, he firmly believed that all men should put their hand to some sort of labor: "It would be well if all of us were good handicraftsmen in some kind, and the dishonour of manual labor done away with altogether."[44] Similarly for Whitehead:

> The only rational solution of the social problems of our time is the same which will give to the individual a fuller life, and is to be found in this: that each should do the work he is best fitted for; that all work well done deserves honour ; that no work which a rational being would demand of another, if well done, can be menial. . . . If all worked there would be less waste, for the rich now have to find an occupation in spending their money on mostly useless articles, whose only purpose is to show how rich they are.[45]

At this point Whitehead is following Ruskin's words closely; in one of his Slade lectures Ruskin notes, "The great arts can have but three principle directions of purpose. . . that of enforcing the religion of men, that of perfecting their ethical state, and that of doing them material justice."[46] Whitehead interprets these three basic points, laying them out in his notes for his 1892 book *Grass of the Desert*:

1. "The desire for ease and for greater material comfort."
2. "The ideal of Righteousness, or as Plato has called it, Justice."
3. "The love of Beauty, with its wide reaching associations. . ."[47]

Ultimately Ruskin's society would prove too utopian for Whitehead's ideal, as it had for Morris, whose socialist views were more robust than his mentor's. Like Whitehead, Morris had learned his lessons at the master's knee, while studying at Oxford in the 1850s. Ruskin, Morris noted, "before my days of practical Socialism, was my master towards the ideal. . . and, looking backward, I cannot help saying, by the way, how deadly dull the world would have been twenty years ago but for Ruskin! It was through him that I learned to give form to my discontent, which I must say was not by any means vague. Apart from the desire to produce beautiful things, the leading passion of my life has been and is hatred of modern civilization."[48] For all three men, the enemy to be combated was ugly utilitarianism, and the most logical way to do this was through the education of the masses in the training of visual perception. By developing one's discerning abilities, one would come to art and a sense of morality through nature and its ennobling features. In this way would ugliness and the resultant ennui be avoided. As D. H. Lawrence noted:

> The great crime which the moneyed classes and promoters of industry committed in the palmy Victorian days was the condemning of the workers to ugliness, ugliness, ugliness: meanness and formless and ugly surroundings, ugly ideals, ugly religion, ugly hope, ugly love, ugly clothes, ugly furniture, ugly houses, ugly relationships between workers and employers.[49]

To Whitehead's way of thinking, ugliness must be avoided at all costs, and this option was not just for the wealthy but should be for everyone. Complementing this was the urgent need for both a moral and physical healthfulness. Writing in *Grass of the Desert* he stated, "In time we shall have the education of children to look after. This will be very simple, if we are all living lives healthy in body and mind. Children learn more by example and association than by precept. The amount of education by books will be much smaller than is now required, for we wish our children to have healthy, active bodies, and bright, intelligent minds, to be able to appreciate all that is beautiful in nature and art; now, all that is to a high degree beautiful is simple."[50] For Whitehead this aesthetic appreciation was more intuitive than something to be learned by rote. As with Morris and Ruskin, it was about continuously being exposed to the aesthetically pleasing that would ultimately allow a person to make judgments about quality and beauty.

Americans inherited many of these Arts and Crafts precepts from their English counterparts. The furniture itself was "almost morality furniture: straight lines; honest joints; no paint; exposed grain; modest sheen." Its very qualities of plain sobriety, sturdiness, and sheer heft affirmed the continuance of hearth and family and restored man to a life of basics—"the outdoor life, vigor and health, crafts."[51] Whitehead followed this ideal up to a point but then returned to an aspect of English arts and crafts rarely found in this country: the surface decoration of the furniture, either with simple carving of naturalistic forms, or painted panels, that could be inserted into cupboard doors. This harks back to the Arts and Crafts work of Arthur Heygate Mackmurdo (1851–1942) (fig. 15) and Mackay Hugh Baillie Scott (1865–1945). Mackmurdo took drawing lessons at Ruskin's School of Drawing at Oxford and traveled with him to Italy in 1874. He founded the Century Guild in 1882. Some of his furniture has painted panels. Like his countrymen, Whitehead sought to meld simplicity with sophistication but without the overtones of Art Nouveau often seen in their work.

It was probably during the 1880s that Whitehead met and became good friends with the Arts and Crafts architect Halsey Ricardo.[52] He had set up his own practice in 1878, and in 1888 he went into business with William De Morgan, the tile manufacturer, a partnership that would last ten years (cats. 125 and 126). In the 1860s the interest in tile decoration had reached a fashionable apex in England, a reflection of the opulence found in the cultures of the Middle East, and De Morgan was the man who, above all others, oversaw this resurgence in the appreciation of artistic tiles. Halsey's best-known commission was for the Debenham House in London, decorated throughout with De Morgan's beautiful, richly colored tiles. Ricardo was not only an architect, but a teacher and writer as well, following the Morris/Ruskin tenet concerning the importance of work enjoyed: "If a man really likes what he has got to do, he will make great shifts to express and realise his pleasure; he will choose carefully his materials, and either in playfulness of fancy, or in grave renunciation of the garniture of his art, will put the stamp of his individuality on his work."[53]

Jane and Ralph shared many of the same ideas and interests as well as many of the same social contacts and mutual friends. Unlike Ralph's first wife, Jane moved in the same circles, and this may have been one of the initial attractions for them both. They were comfortable together and shared the same ideals. By 1891 it was obvious that they were planning a future life together, though Ralph was still legally married to Marie and Jane's family was determinedly disapproving.[54]

On April 12, as they prepared to separate as part of the initial step toward Ralph's divorce, Jane wrote to Ralph: "Do not think I shall fail to leave with thee when I go away a whole Gallery of my likenesses. Madeleine shall do a little pastel of me. She has done it before twice quite perfectly"[55] (cat. 161). Around the same time Jane, who hailed from a long line of Philadelphia politicians,

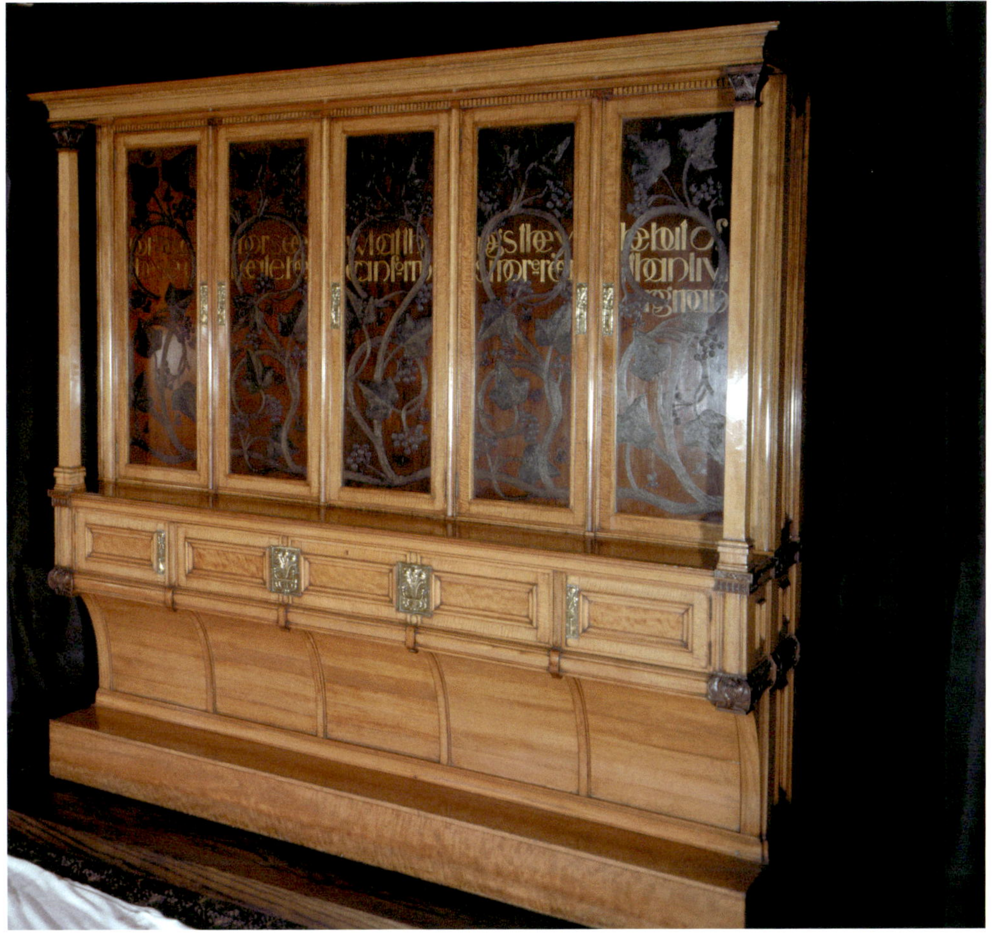

fig. 15 A. H. Mackmurdo & H. P. Horne, *Cabinet with Painted Doors*, for Century Guild made by Goodall & Co., Manchester, 1886. Courtesy of the William Morris Gallery, London.

proposed to Ralph that he might stand for Parliament. His response is tempered: "I am ready to be persuaded by thee to do anything, but I think Parliament is not for me. . . . Parliament would mean life in a big town. It is another life that I desire for thee and for me. . . . "[56] Jane quickly replies: "All one wants to be armed with is a little love & a little health—a little philosophy & a good deal of nature out of doors."[57]

In June 1891 Ralph was in England where, having spent an afternoon with William Morris, he sent off an enthusiastic missive to Jane:

> It was like a day in the century to be depicted. He took me over his works and drove back to Hammersmith with me . . . . W. M. showed me his dyeing & weaving and printing of cretonnes and tapestry making (figs. 16 and 17). He was frank & kind. . . . We should have to buy yarn, but to dye it ourselves and to weave it. Weaving on a hand loom is hard physical labor. Tapestry is made by knitting each stitch sitting the while on a bench. The same workman might do both with an advantage to himself. . . I still like the idea of this better than bookbinding."[58] Later, in the same letter, he makes a prescient statement about the possibility of setting up a woodworking shop: "Furniture making (with which some carving would be combined) I have still to enquire into & I think it would be more difficult." In August Ralph writes to Jane again about Morris: "Morris's foreman—Morris is away for his holiday & inaccessible till September—told me today that Morris would not take me for a pupil but would do all he could to help me by advice and letting me see his works & processes as often as I liked.[59]

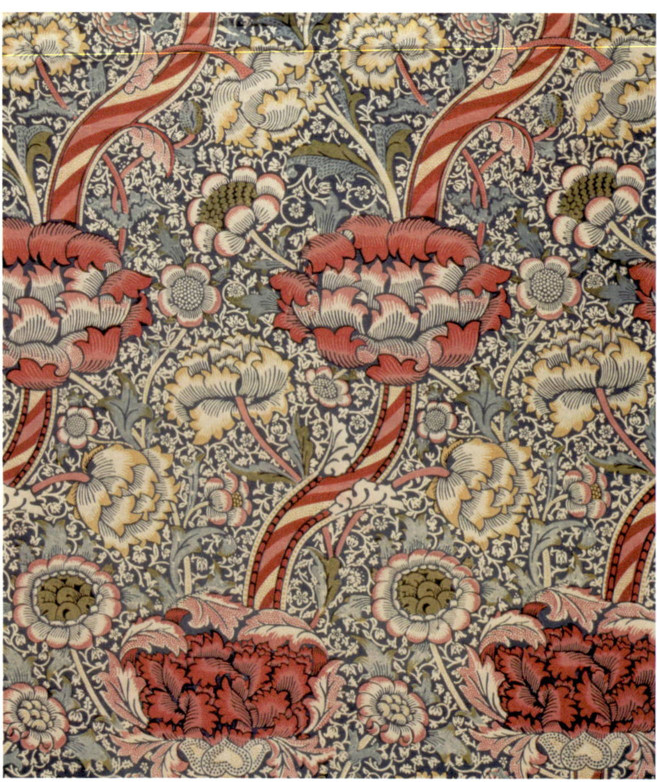

fig. 16 William Morris, *Wandle* textile design for Morris & Company, 1884. Courtesy of the William Morris Gallery, London.

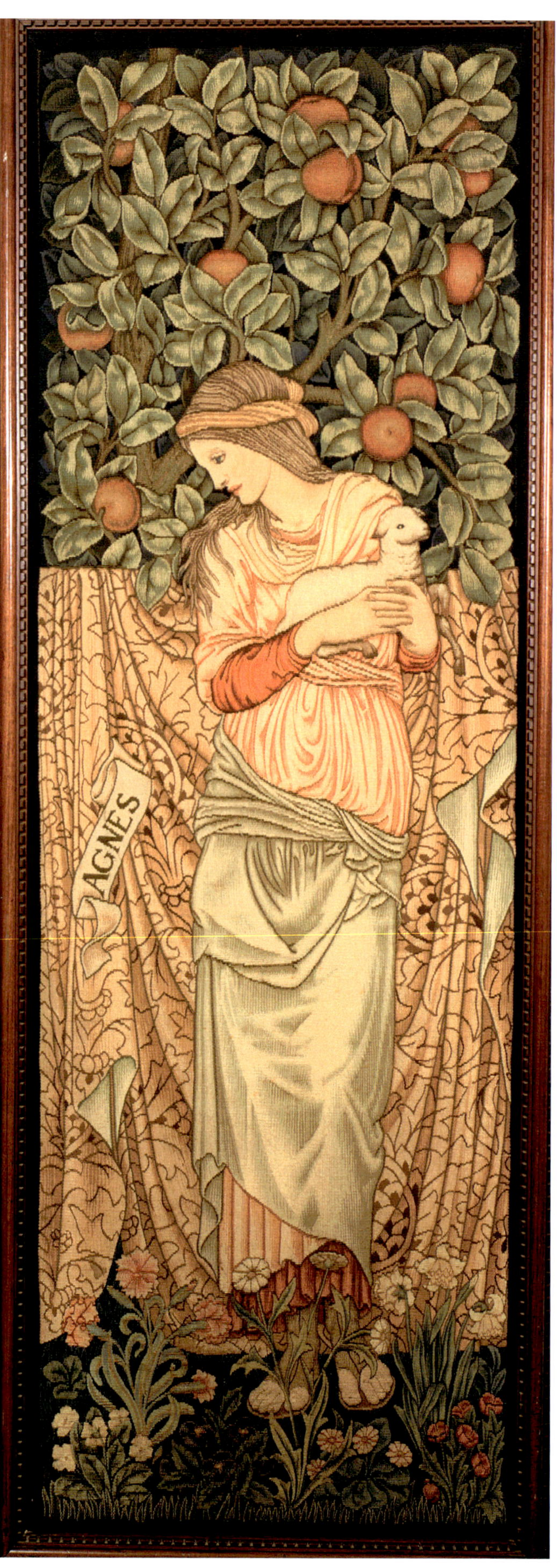

fig. 17 William Morris, *St. Agnes Tapestry*. Courtesy of the National Trust Photo Library.

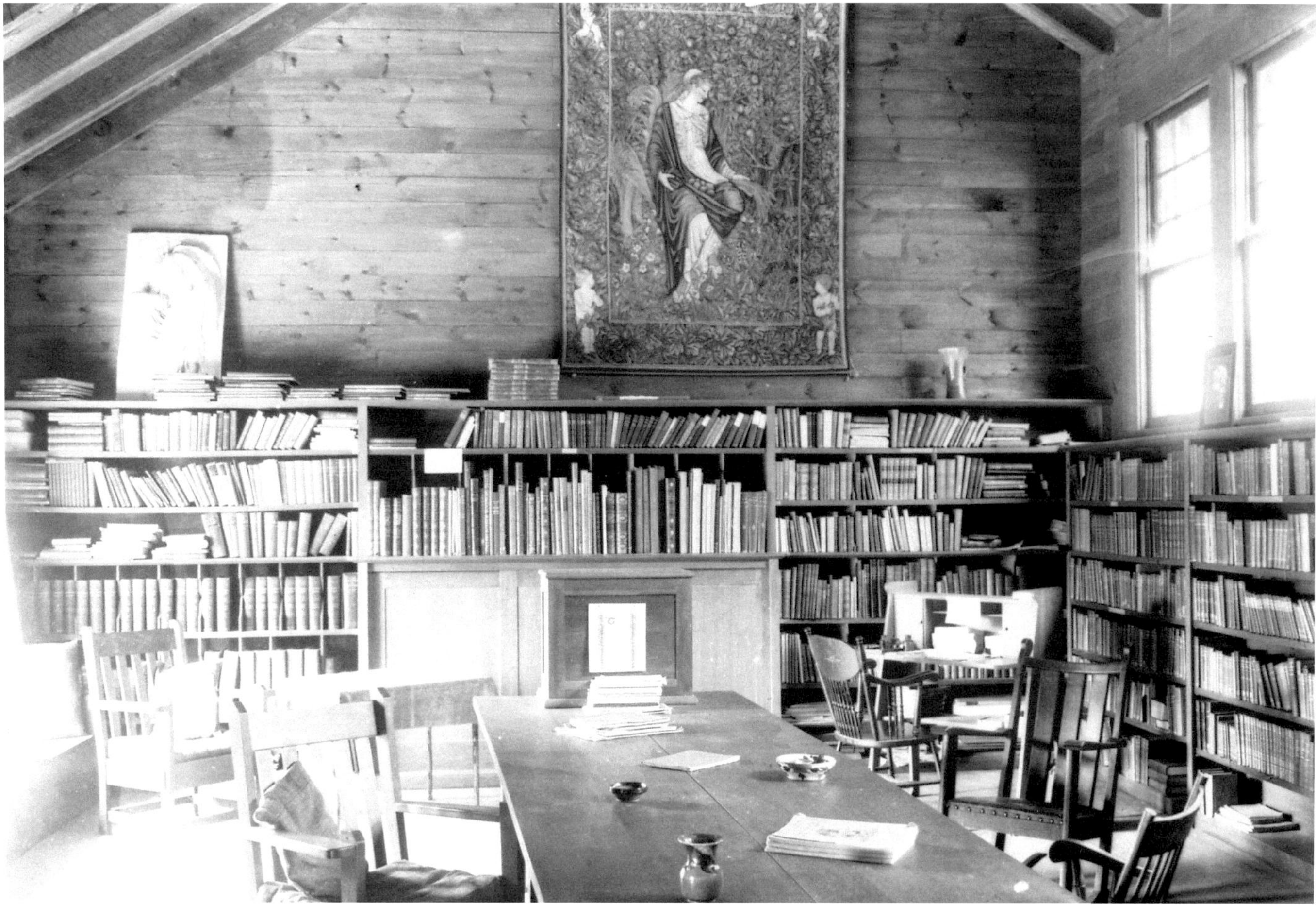

fig. 18 Jessie Tarbox Beals, *Library at Byrdcliffe*, 1908. Silver print. Collection of Winterthur Library, Downs Collection, 92x39.1140.253. The Morris tapestry hanging over the bookshelves was purchased by Whitehead in the 1890s.

Morris, while an inspiration, was also intimidating; described as "Irascible, impatient, visionary. . . [he] believed that almost everybody could and should do everything: he once said the man unable to compose an epic while weaving a tapestry might as well give up."[60] Whitehead, by his own admission, was not dexterous with his hands, and he must have questioned his own ability to rise to Morris's level.

While trying to gain sound advice and training that could be used toward his new life with Jane, Ralph was also pursuing practical investigations into obtaining a divorce. At first he had hoped that he could stay in England and apprentice himself to William Morris, but "Morris will not take me as a pupil—nor canst I go to him now—he thinks tapestry is too difficult for me which by my own confession I have no artistic faculty, I agree. Carpet making, such carpets as the East used to make would do perhaps—I incline to this—Byrd shall make the colours fit."[61] An English divorce would also be nearly impossible to obtain.

Several other ideas were considered before Ralph settled on what seemed the most expedient plan: to become a naturalized German citizen, which he did in February 1892.[62] This made the divorce much quicker than if he had tried to obtain it elsewhere. While residing in Germany, he wrote to Jane of his days, "I have arranged with one of the best cabinet makers here to learn his trade as far as may be. He is a man who only does good work and only employs a few men. I am to start next Tuesday. Every afternoon from two till six. I keep the mornings free, I shall get an hours ride, an hours gymnastics of some sort or other and a little carpentry at home."[63] He also described to Jane his new surroundings, which he decorated with curtains made of William Morris fabrics (fig. 18):

> I have chosen half a dozen designs of William Morris which Byrd is to have before long. For fun, I bought other patterns of chintz designs by some of the best English designers of today. What I expected happened, they are dull & wearisome after a week, while the beauty of W. M.'s designs grow daily. In my room where I am writing I have the honeysuckle on the blue ground. Dost remember thy running away & leaving me gaping at Morris's shop?[64]

In March 1892 Whitehead was granted his divorce and by April he was in New York, wiring Jane in Colorado of his arrival. They were married in Portsmouth,

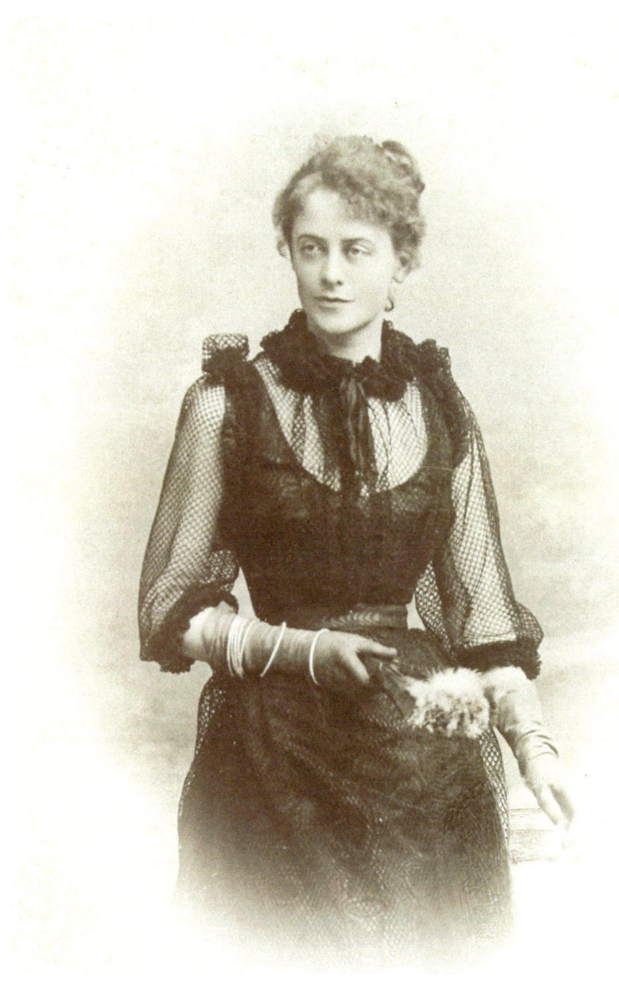

New Hampshire, in August[65] and then left for a year's honeymoon in Europe where they pursued their interests in art. In Paris, Jane took lessons at the Académie Julian where she had studied in 1886 and noted seeing Sarah Bernhardt perform *Phèdre*; Ralph left her there in November to look for a villa in which to live along the Riviera. But Jane was not alone; there are notations in her diary indicating that her mother and sister Gerty came along for part of the journey.

Almost fifty years later a German friend wrote to Jane of seeing her then and the impression she had made: "In fancy I see you always as you have been in Florence the first return of your wedding-day: young, lovely, with aureola of golden curls around your head and with the gracious movements of a fairy! Adorable garments from Paris, Ruskin jewels in your hair, the lute in your arm, old folksongs on your lips—I was perfectly drunk of so much perfection and shall never forget that"[66] (fig. 19). Small wonder that she appeared to Ralph at this time as the Pre-Raphaelite muse and emotional anchor of his fantasy, inspiring the chivalric and flowery language of their correspondence.[67]

Upon their return to the States, the Whiteheads decided to settle in Montecito, a suburb of Santa Barbara (fig. 20). It reminded them of their Italian idyll, and the mild weather would soothe the fragile health from which they both suffered. Here it was that they built their beautiful Tuscan villa, Arcady, and Ralph documented their

fig. 19 Flli. Alinari, Italian, 19th century, *Jane in Italy on Honeymoon*, 1892. Albumen print. Winterthur Library, Downs Collection, 92x39.1140.56b.

fig. 20 W. H. Rough, *Jane and Ralph Whitehead at Arcady*, ca. 1895. Albumen print. Winterthur Library, Downs Collection, 92x39.1140.301.

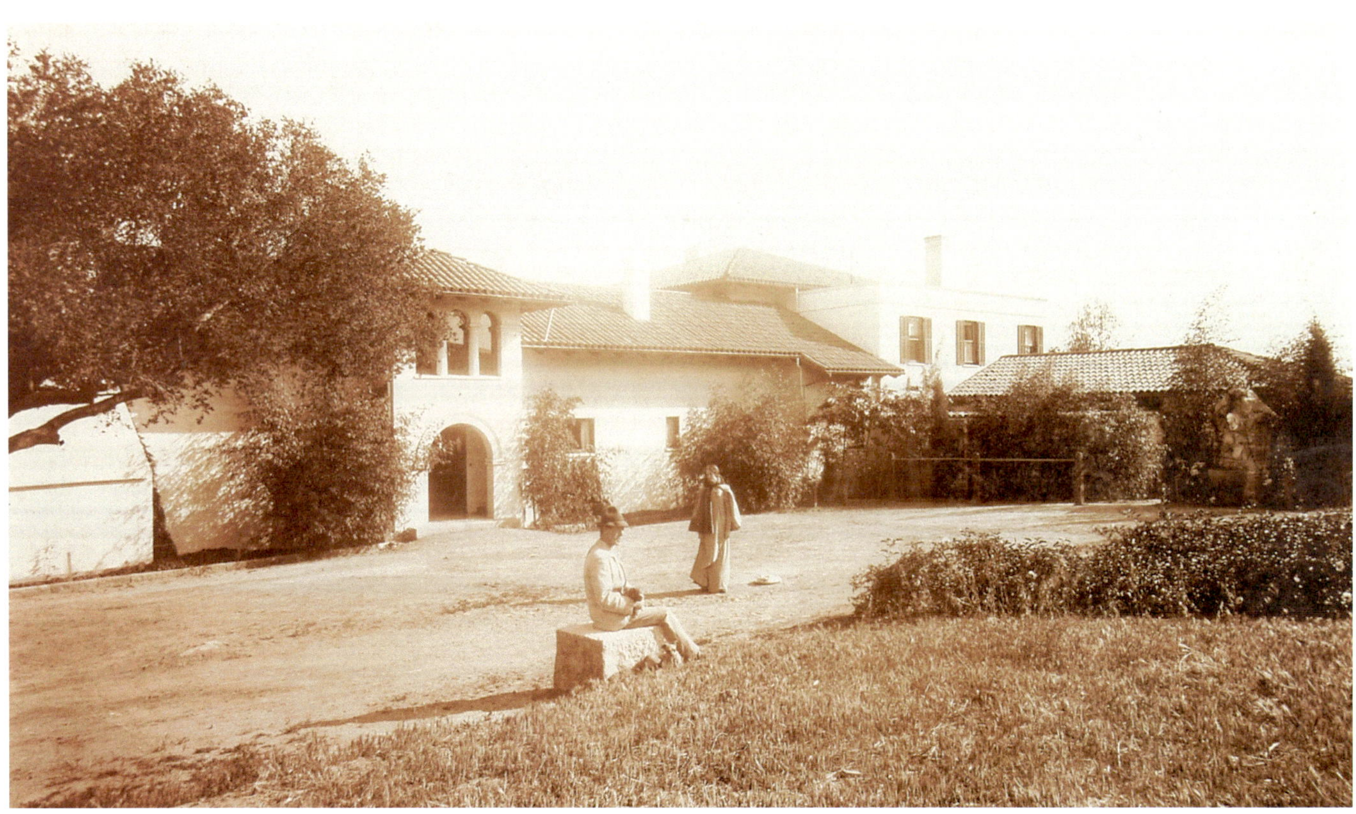

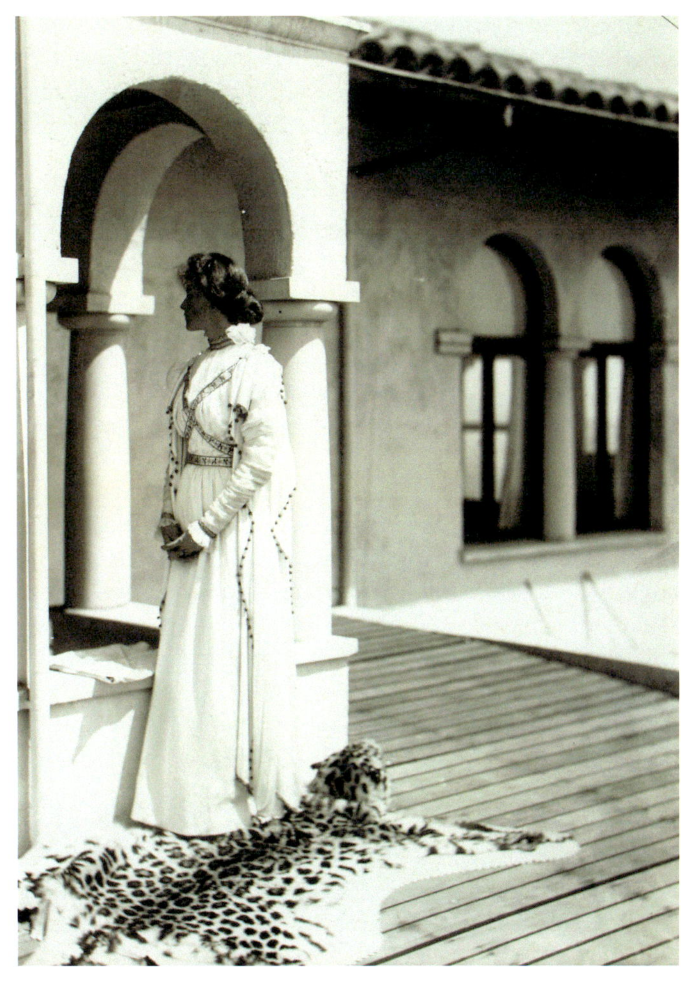

early years in lovely Pre-Raphaelite–inspired images (fig. 21). Here, too, was where they began to surround themselves with artists working in the area: Birge Harrison, Charles Stetson, Leonard Lester, and William Wendt. It was a leisurely life, filled with friends and culture, and it was here that Ralph put in his daily two hours of "work" establishing the lush gardens for which Arcady became known. Music was an important component of this life, and they lent space to the cellist Louis Opid, the nephew of the famous Polish actress Helena Modjewska, who in turn became a friend. They also sponsored a group of chamber musicians whom they sent out to play classical concerts in the Santa Barbara public schools.

Lovely and as aesthetically satisfying as this lifestyle proved, both of the Whiteheads became restless with its aimlessness. Jane took a few painting lessons with Birge Harrison (fig. 22), though her calendar entries reflect a more mundane life, with small, petty problems with the servants and day-to-day notations on her health. Ralph began to drift from the home, befriending a group of bohemian artists in Los Angeles and having a relationship with a Miss Louise Hart. There were separations and reunions and finally a conviction to make a change. Life seemed much improved in May 1896 when Jane gave birth to a son, but he only lived a day. In the fall, in what appears as an effort to reconcile again and escape some of the sadness of the loss of the baby, they traveled to Europe

fig. 21 Attributed to Ralph Whitehead, *Jane at Arcady*, ca. 1895. Silver print. Winterthur Library, Downs Collection, 92x39.1140.626.

fig. 22 Attributed to Ralph Whitehead, *Jane at her easel, Arcady*, ca. 1895. Silver print. Winterthur Library, Downs Collection, 92x39.1140.

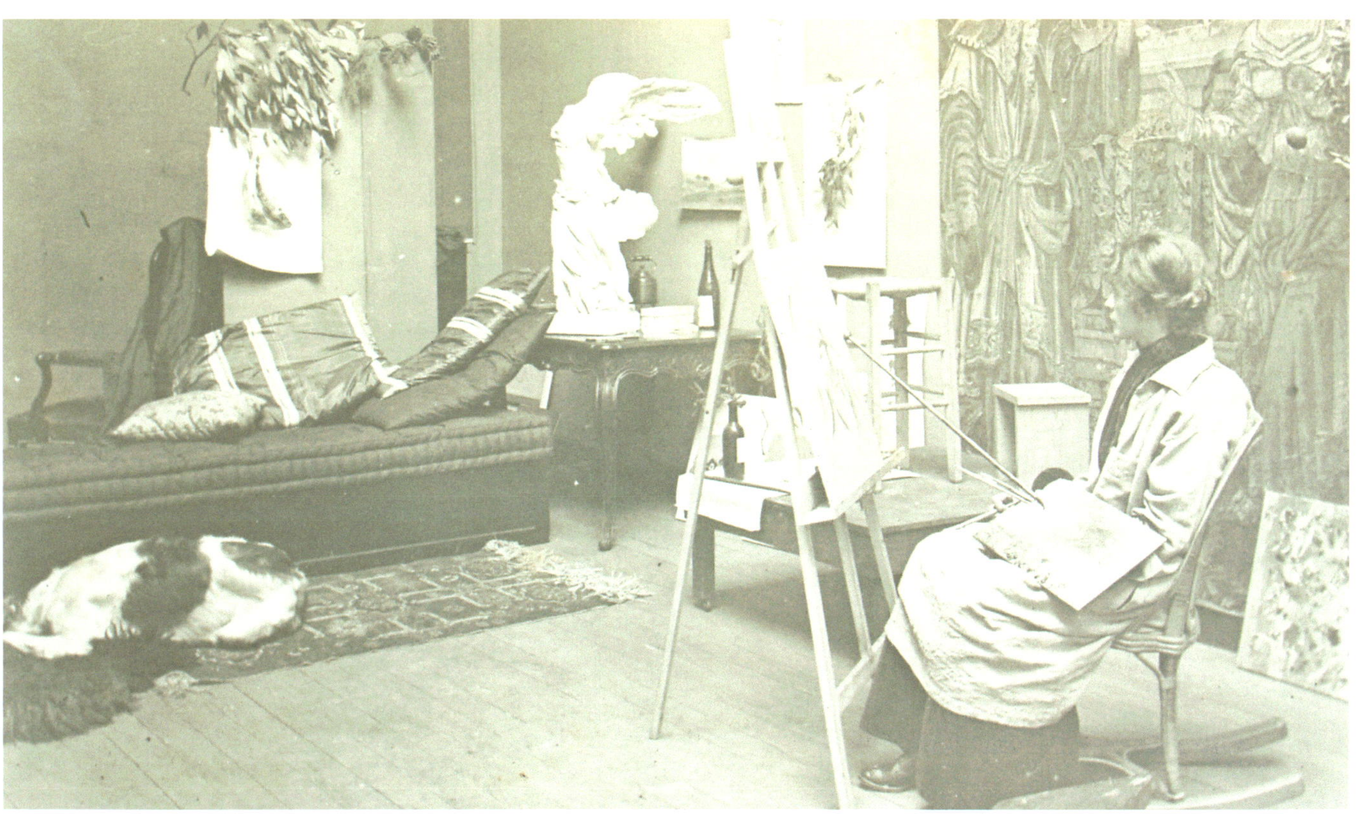

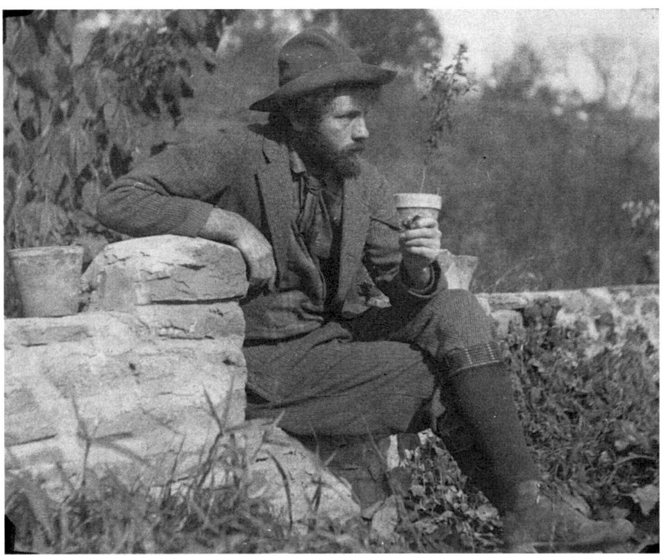

fig. 23 Unidentified photographer, *Hervey White*, ca. 1903. Silver print. Schlesinger Library, Radcliffe Institute, Harvard University.

where Jane again took formal art lessons, this time at the atelier of Edmond Aman-Jean. She also had corrections with J. P. Laurens and tried to revitalize her interest in painting.

They began again to talk of establishing the "convent" of their dreams. Ever cautious, Ralph decided to visit several such places first, before committing funds and energy to his own endeavor. Back in the States, he traveled east, visiting the Ruskin Colony in Tennessee, from where he wrote his impressions to Jane:

> "Ruskin" was very interesting to me. You know that I don't believe in "colonies" solving the social problem, which is to me an economic one. Nothing but capitalization of labor can do that and how much state interference will be necessary to attain to that is the crux of socialism.... "Ruskin" has been running for three years & has been through some hard times. There are sixty members each of whom has paid $500 per membership. They have bought land & farm it & besides this run some printing machines, make suspenders & chicory gum(!) They print their own paper and do job printing as well.... They work nine hours a day all with being paid equally![68]

But this was not the ideal toward which either of them was striving, despite the fact that Whitehead noted, "It is very well managed & the people are very intelligent as to economics & I hope they may succeed. Why it is that I & you too I suppose don't want to join them I can't tell. I suppose we require more of life's appliances than they have and more beauty of surroundings."[69]

That June Whitehead traveled to Glenmore in the Adirondacks, staying with the famed Fabian Thomas Davidson.[70] He also visited Summerbrook, Prestonia Mann's own Fabian experiment[71] only a stone's throw away.[72] Here he met Charlotte Perkins Stetson (cat. 99), author of the controversial *Women and Economics* (1898), who had divorced her artist husband in 1894 and would marry her second husband, George Houghton Gilman, in 1900. She would introduce him to her friends at Hull House and would later become a frequent visitor to Byrdcliffe with her second husband and her artist daughter, Katharine Beecher Stetson. Other new friends included Marie Little, who became the resident weaver at Byrdcliffe, and Katharine Babbitt, who became a friend of both the Whiteheads, and when visiting Byrdcliffe spent time in the woodworking shop. All are noted in Jane's calendar for this year as well as Mr. Hyslop, the famed spiritualist.[73] Ralph revisited Summerbrook in 1901 but wrote to Jane: "kind-hearted Miss Martin [Prestonia Mann married John Martin in 1900] is sincere; but somehow the reform atmosphere of Hull House & of Summerbrook doesn't suit me."[74]

In the fall of 1897 Jane and Whitehead were traveling together in the East and spent some time in Boston where they met with John Bowles, editor of the arts and crafts magazine *Modern Art*[75], and, through a meeting with Harvard professor and Orientalist Denman Ross, became acquainted with the painter Hermann Dudley Murphy, who would become the first painting instructor at Byrdcliffe.

They traveled separately back to Santa Barbara for the winter. Ralph broke his journey in Chicago where he went to Hull House and met Hervey White (fig. 23) for the first time. By way of introduction, Charlotte Perkins Stetson wrote to White, saying, "I am sending you a Yankeeized Englishman who is to spend a few days in Chicago. His name is Whitehead. Be nice to him, you may find him very interesting." White recorded his response to this letter: "'He will probably be hungry,' I thought, dropping the letter in the wastebasket."[76]

But when Whitehead arrived, Perkins's prediction proved correct and the two became friends. From then on, Whitehead usually stopped to see White when traveling through Chicago and White visited the Whiteheads in Santa Barbara, which is when White felt that he "got any perspective of the man. For the dominant characteristic of Mr. Whitehead was a modest, almost repellent reserve. We meet such quite often in Englishmen. We Americans are boys yet and speak a boy's language. Only at rare intervals usually when we're riding our horses over the trails of those delectable mountains, would he give me some glimpse of abashed intimacy from which I could construct a vague picture of his past."[77] This reserve is noted by most everyone who met Whitehead. Writing to her son Bim, who was stationed in London during the First World War, Jane, who certainly knew Ralph best, lamented this characteristic. "Do you suppose he will ever go back to his native land? He never gives himself a chance. I think the Ricardos thought he would come over at the beginning of the war—I certainly did—when I went, but he never expresses himself on the subject—that's where I find fault with English people—they're too darned reserved it's inhuman."[78] Jane was more emotional and must have frequently been frustrated by the lack of response in her more withdrawn husband.

In 1898 plans were made by the Whiteheads to establish a Sloyd school on their Santa Barbara property. Jane mentions in her diary "searching for site for school." In 1893 a wealthy Bostonian, Anna Blake, started the first Sloyd school in Santa Barbara, which provided free schooling for manual training and home economics to local elementary-school children. The Sloyd method evolved from the Swedish educator Uno Cygnaeus's efforts in developing handicraft teaching, and he is considered the father of educative handicraft. His ideas and methods appealed to Arts and Crafts practitioners worldwide, and in the United States schools cropped up in many cities. Annette Butler was hired by the Whiteheads to teach at the school the first year (she visited Byrdcliffe in 1903) and a Miss Tadd, daughter of the progressive Philadelphia educator, took over from Butler during the second season. Children here were taught lessons in weaving, wood carving, modeling, and other crafts.

In 1900 Ralph and Hervey White, known as "Nicolo"[79] to the Whiteheads, went to Alsea, Oregon, where they had planned for a community of musicians. Writing to Jane on July 15, Ralph noted:

> We have got to Alsea. It is a long, rough but very beautiful drive from Corvallis 25 miles, 7 of which are a bad mountain road with chuckholes deeper than the axles. But it is very beautiful country & the forests are magnificent. We have found the Reeds & the Opids & Mrs. Toles here & are right glad to have done with hotels for a time. They have built a room of logs with a fireplace and a shanty [...*unreadable*...] with a kitchen and several little huts of the most primitive kind nearby. They are primitive but they are sufficient for summer. . . . The air is very delightful, & I am in hopes that it will be summer while I stay here; for the rains would be unpleasant in such a shanty & we should drive each other crazy if we were all shut up in the log cabin for a few days, where the fire is. Opid & Miss Reed are impossibly nervous & make the rest have a rather bad time & that pretty constantly but Nicolo & Mrs. Toles & Ole Reed are all of a good sort & so balance the weakness of the others & keep things straight.[80]

The next day he wrote again: "One cannot have the greenery of this forest country & the luxury of Italian nights. The palm & the pine do not grow on one mountain. The forest country is magnificent and the days are beautiful, like June days in New England, but there are no Italian nights. The nights are damp."[81] Finally, on July 21, with the dream of Alsea slipping away, he wrote, "I wish you were here to see the magnificence of this forest country. You would love these woods, & the greenery of them. But the life is pretty rough, about what we had in that hut at Glenmore. It is certainly the best place we have found on our trip."[82] Upon his death, Whitehead still owned this land in Oregon.

Though the venture soon fell apart with the eruption of petty squabbles among the participants, Whitehead managed to see the humor in this endeavor and he left the Oregon venture without regrets. The following year he was in Europe with White, visiting places and people he thought might be useful toward planning his scheme. Before leaving the States, a letter arrived from Henry Rolfe, C. R. Ashbee's agent in America,[83] describing the Ashbees recent visit:

> I didn't manage to visit the Roycrofters, nor to see Liberty Tadd in the Adirondacks. I did, though, get a glimpse through Mrs. Ashbee's eyes. She and her husband, before they left us, read us their journals. From her I got a picture of a very honest simple affectionate man ruling his little community like a shrewd wise autocrat and coming as near to living happily and well as is possible just now. We must go there and see for ourselves. He and his people lack only the keen feeling for beauty, Mrs. Ashbee says. The longing is there, and she thinks they're learning. They know their weakness, and are looking for the man who will teach them.
>
> We enjoyed the Ashbees; everybody did. Ashbee has ripened greatly since he came in '96. His young wife is as clever and charming as he is. We did our best to send them to California. I wanted them especially to be with you and your wife a little while, and Joseph Worcester of the little Swedenborgian church in San Francisco. . . . Ashbee is living the life that you and I would lead if we could, more exactly than any one else I know. He is a good man to be with. Do not fail to see his book, *The Endeavor toward the Teaching of Ruskin and Morris*, which is coming out soon.[84]

In the spring of 1901, Whitehead went to England to see for himself whether something could be done about turning the Royal George into their colony, though this prospect seems to have quickly faded. Jane wrote from California, saying, "I have thought much about your letter which asked me to help you live a simpler life somewhere & to help you look for an occupation which could be fuller than that of a mere country gentleman. . . . It is a pity that we could not find the much desired industry in 'The Royal George.' It is a pity it is situated where it is & that it is not artistic. Everything has a 'but' & 'pity' about it. It is for us to make naught of such. I don't mean in this particular case that we should do so, but to get on, people must look beyond the obstacles."[85]

Looking at alternatives and fired by Rolfe's impressions, Ralph went to visit Ashbee himself and wrote to Jane describing their meeting: "At Essex House they do printing with Morris's old press & others. They make furniture which I don't like; & they work in gold & silver & copper & enamel (fig. 24). I have bought two silver cups one for Bimbi & one for Angelo & he is going to make a big buckle of your stone to wear with that Nettleship's brown dress."[86] Later in the month he tells her, "I have left your carnelians with Ashbee. He is going to make some sort of plaque to wear with a greek [*sic*] dress, a biggish ornament I have left entirely to him & have told him that I don't want to see the drawing. I think it is better to let any designer have his fling untrammeled by the criticism of those who don't realize as he does how things will look when it is carried out."[87]

Whitehead spent quite a bit of time with Ashbee on this trip:

> I went down to Chelsea on Wednesday to lunch with them; they have a charming house in what is always to me the prettiest part of London, near where Morris used to live. He has taste & a good deal of knowledge, but I find that Marshall & Ricardo both smile rather sardonically when he is mentioned. It seems he is rather a poseur & does a good deal of lecturing & making himself important... then again his furniture is not very good. But still he has absorbed some of Morris's view of life, & doing some fine work in metal & has forty men working for him at Essex House in Whitechapel where he spends two days each week ....[88]

On July 25 he went to Essex House, but

> Ashbee had not arrived so I had a long talk with White the pieceman & the metalworkers. He says that a man cannot learn much in less than five years & then wants several more to be a master. Of course he expects a workman to be able to draw and model (not the figure) without which he cannot carry out the feeling of a master designer. He thinks fifteen or sixteen early enough

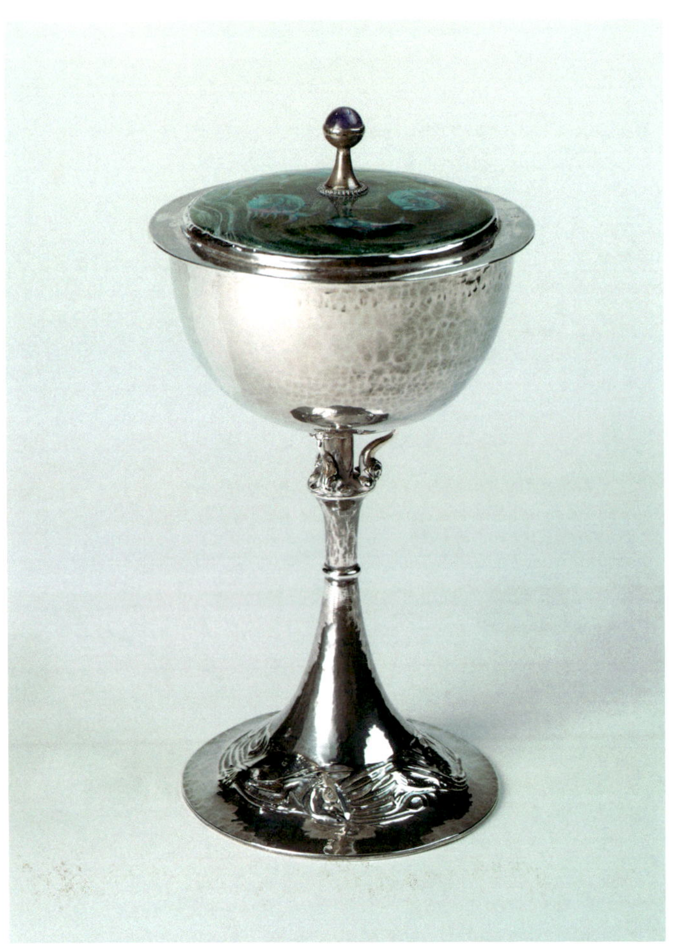

fig. 24 C. R. Ashbee, *Covered Goblet*, 1901. Silver, enamel, and amethyst. Herbert F. Johnson Museum of Art, Cornell University. Gift of Isabel and William Berley.

fig. 25 Unidentified photographer, *Byrdcliffe, looking towards the Barns*, ca. 1910. Silver print. Collection of the Woodstock Guild.

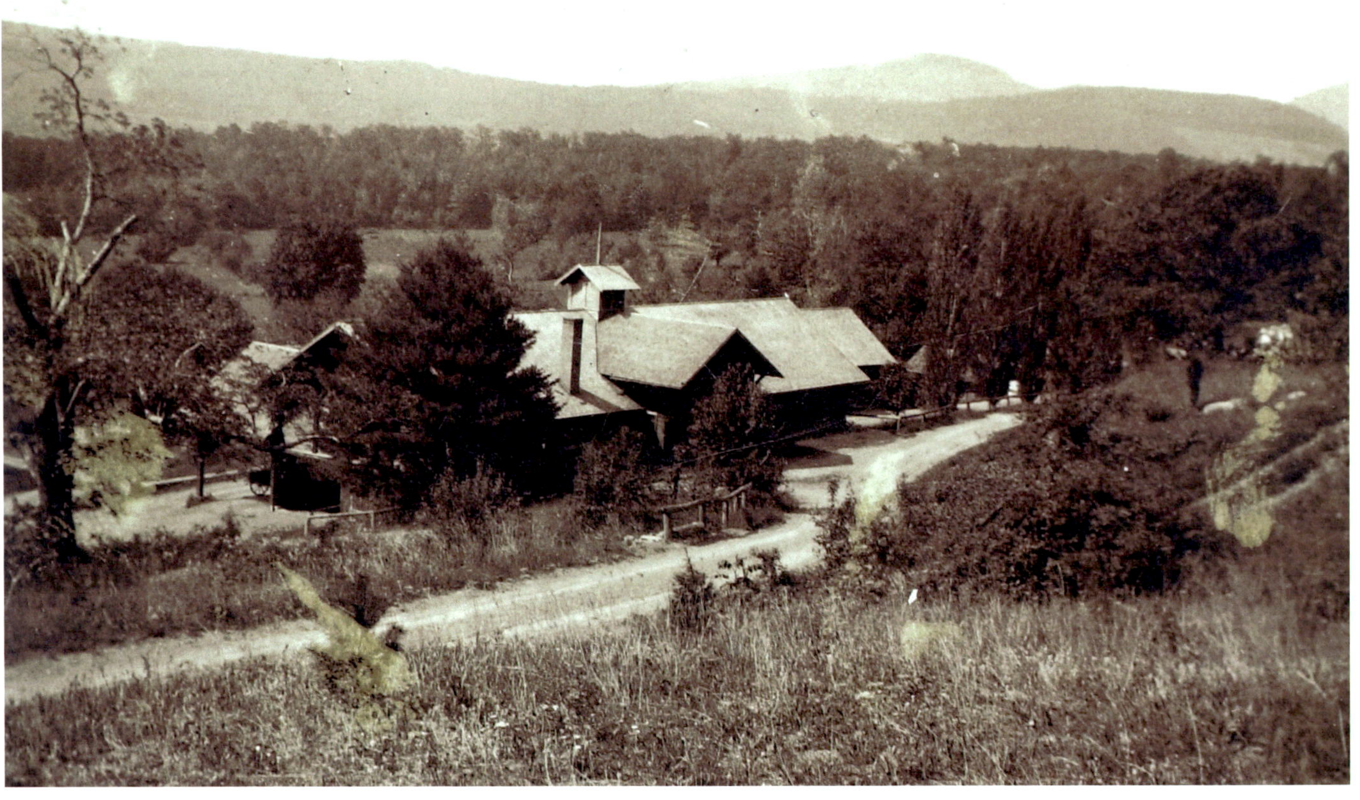

to begin metal work of any kind, & that begin fifteen carpentry, carving & clay modeling & drawing are the best means of educating the craftsman.[89]

For Whitehead, nearing fifty, the minimum of a five-year training for his artisans must have lent a discouraging note to his plans for Byrdcliffe.

Ricardo and Whitehead had continued to correspond sporadically over the years, and on this 1901 trip Whitehead mentions visiting the South Kensington Extension School and meeting with Lethaby and Ricardo.[90] Two years later, in the early days of Byrdcliffe, Ricardo wrote to Whitehead: "Don't be in despair about 'design'—Design comes by designing. And the designer, that is to be, has got to get first dexterity of hand & then knowledge of the capability of his materials—for it is out of the qualities of his material that his design should spring. . . design is the utterance of the material the mode of its expression; not always voluntary, for circumstances may dictate."[91] Their friendship continued until Ricardo's death in 1928; over the years, together and individually, Ralph, Jane, and their sons visited the Ricardos in London, though Ricardo's daughter recalls that the friendship was more between the two men than the families.[92]

The first notations of the appearance of Bolton Brown on the scene appear in Jane's calendar in the spring of 1902. He would become the third in the exploratory triumvirate, along with Whitehead and White, who would go eastward in May in search of a site for the colony. In the spring of 1902, the three set out on what would prove to be the final stage of his search. Meeting in Indianapolis at Brown's father-in-law's home, Whitehead met the artist Carl Lindin for the first time, coming away with a very favorable impression.[93] In the same letter he tells Jane, "If Nicolo & I get as far as Boston which is improbable we will go & see Dow's School at Ipswich."[94]

In June, summoned to Woodstock by an enthusiastic Brown, the men stood on Overlook Mountain and agreed that this would be the site of their "colony." For each of these men, that word meant something entirely different, but for Whitehead, it was the end of a long search (fig. 25). On June 5 he wrote enthusiastically to his son Bim: "Tell mother that Mr. Brown's country is much better than I expected & that the woods are fine tho [*sic*] the pines are few and that I will write her when we have seen some more of it. There is good water & fine air & painters country within five hours of New York."[95] To Jane he wrote, "We have hunted far you know dear & this place is on the whole by far the best, although it is not quite so high as I wanted to be nor has it a stream. But the air is very fine & smells of the mountains & the woods, the immediate surroundings are very beautiful & the distant landscape of exceeding beauty. My companions are both of them satisfied & I too."[96] In responding, Jane matched his enthusiasm, and the reality of Byrdcliffe began.

Notes

1. The title "Reality of Beauty" is derived from a December 1907 article Whitehead wrote for *The Education Bi-Monthly* in which he made a plea for "the validity of beauty as a too often neglected factor in our lives, and as an ideal to guide us amid the murky air of modern materialism."

2. Two other sons, Frederick James (1858–59) and William Frederic (1859–61), are buried in the vault of the Friezland Church in Grasscroft. The church, as well as a parsonage and school, were commissioned by the four elder Whitehead brothers, and designed by the eccentric Victorian architect, George Shaw, of Uppermill. The church was consecrated in 1850 by Ralph Radcliffe Whitehead, the eldest uncle.

3. "Six to six with half an hour for breakfast and one hour for dinner, and £1 or £1–10s per week for thirty years and some forty, they have been working in the factory, and you and I have been living in luxury. It makes me ashamed" (RRW to Jane, July 17, 1907, Winterthur Library, Downs Collection). Ralph remained dependent his whole life on the dividends provided by the Royal George Mills though he never lived in England again after the early 1890s. Byrdcliffe would not have been possible without this money, and, like Morris and Ruskin, who were also independently wealthy, he envisioned his financial position as a way to make things better for others, not as something to be rejected. Because it was his money that fully supported the continuing existence of Byrdcliffe, he considered the final say always to be his alone, not a very popular approach in a purportedly communal environment.

4. A. B. Reach, *Manchester and the Textile Districts in 1849*, C. Aspin, ed. (Helmshore Local History Society, 1972), 120–1, as quoted in Michael Fox and Peter Fox, *Victorian Saddleworth* (Uppermill, Lancashire: Taylor and Clifton, Ltd., n.d.), 5.

5. H. Bradley, "Morgan Brierley—A Memoir" (Rochdale, 1900), 6, as quoted in Michael Fox and Peter Fox, *Victorian Saddleworth*, 23–24.

6. *Manchester Guardian*, June 16, 1843, as quoted in Michael Fox and Peter Fox, *Victorian Saddleworth*, 23.

7. Alf Evers unpublished manuscript, HFJ files, 1.

8. John Whitehead married Ann Radcliffe (1667–1737), which began the merging of the names in many successive Whitehead generations.

9. This was done entirely by female labor: "they dye, spin and weave the bunting which is cut into the proper pattern and sewn together either in their mill or in the cottages around" (Anonymous unpublished paper, Saddleworth Historical Society, "R. R. Whitehead & Brothers Limited," n.d., 1).

10. Whitehead always retained fond memories of his childhood home. RRW to Ralph Jr. (called "Bim"), May 23, 1913: "I am so very glad that you write as you do with affection for Byrdcliffe. It has been a lovely home of your childhood & we shall have good times there yet. You will always have an affection for it as long as you live, just as I have for Beech Hill; and this will remain with you even if you are so situated that it no longer belongs to you, and you are at the other end of the earth." Winterthur Library, Downs Collection.

11. On April 29, 1869, RRW wrote to his mother, "The best things in a hamper would be cakes, jams, a small ham or fowls, or beef, or potted meet [*sic*]. It is best not to send a large one but to send small ones." Winterthur Library, Downs Collection. This is a rather remarkable letter in light of the fact that his mother died in early June 1869, at the age of forty-three. It seems from references in Ralph's letters home that the full extent of her illness was kept from the fifteen-year-old though he does mention her not feeling well.

12. Mary Hodge, et al., *The Saddleworth Story*, 4th ed. (Manchester: GM CVS Print Service, 1994), 41.

13. Both Whitehead and his second wife, Jane Byrd McCall, were interested in folksongs and published two books of them in the early 1900s. In 1908 Arnold Dolmetsch and his wife visited Byrdcliffe and gave a concert while there. Similarly, the famed English Arts and Crafts practitioner C. R. Ashbee and his wife Janet published *The Essex House Song Book* in 1903–4. Bertha Thompson, a Byrdcliffe metalworker, noted Whitehead's interest in folksongs in her diary: "I remember one time when he was gathering folk music for publication, he got a number of us together to sing the songs for him" (unpublished manuscript, Schlesinger Library, Thompson Family Papers).

14. W. G. Collingwood, *The Life of John Ruskin*, 6th ed. (London: Methuen & Co., 1905), 314.

15. Alf Evers, unpublished manuscript, 2. For more on the Hinksey Road digging, see Tim Hilton, "Road Digging and Aestheticism

Oxford 1875," *Studio International* 188, no. 972 (December 1974): 226–29.

16. Collingwood, *John Ruskin*, 308–9.

17. *Ibid.*, 309.

18. Jane Addams, *Twenty Years at Hull-House* (New York: The New American Library, 1960), 43. Like Ruskin, Addams believed in a social democracy that Whitehead ultimately would reject in his own venture, finding the subversion of the self for the greater good of all mankind a difficult road to follow.

19. Alf Evers, *The Catskills: From Wilderness to Woodstock* (Garden City, NY: Doubleday & Co., Inc., 1972), 604.

20. Also one of the Hinksey Road builders. See Hilton, "Road Digging....", 228.

21. Collingwood, *John Ruskin*, 323.

22. John Ruskin, *Works*. XXVII: 535.

23. E. T. Cook and Alexander Wedderburn, editors of the thirty-nine-volume *The Works of John Ruskin* (London: George Allen, 1907), cite Whitehead as the person described in this passage from Ruskin's *Fors Clavigera*, letter 72: "Here's one of my own boys getting up that lesson [on Adam Smith] beside me for his next Oxford examination," 28: 764. Special thanks to Stephen Wildman at the Ruskin Library, University of Lancaster, for his help with this notation.

24. I would like to thank Philip Gorton for sharing his information about Borden Wood with me.

25. Marie Whitehead to RRW, 1894. Winterthur Library, Downs Collection. This typed letter has a note at the bottom that reads, "To be delivered after my death," but it is not known when she died or when RRW was given this letter.

26. Hervey White, in his draft notes for a 1933 article on Whitehead for a Woodstock Historical Society publication, mentions, "he often spoke of some years spent in Styria where he bought an old castle and restored it purchasing the land around to add to the estate. One of his weaknesses was to want all the land that joined him. And when repulsed, he looked afield for new holdings.... Of the period in Italy that followed Styria, he gave me only a glimpse at rare intervals and always ugly ones when called to mind. A palace on the Tournabrioni, several servants, the extravagances and inanities of society life."

27. Apparently this lasted seven years, until the early 1890s. The name Styria provides an interesting link with Ruskin. In 1840 Ruskin wrote his only work of fiction, *The King of the Golden River*, for Effie Gray, whom he would marry in 1848. This story is a morality tale, describing justice and generosity in a make-believe land called Stiria.

28. RRW to Jane, January 28, 1891. RRW says that Marie has moved from San Remo to Klingenstein. Winterthur Library, Downs Collection.

29. RRW to Jane, March 13, 1891. Winterthur Library, Downs Collection.

30. Other notations of "Whitehead" are listed in Jane's 1885 calendar for February 25 and 27; March 4 and 8; and November 11. Other sources have cited their first meeting as late as 1890 but this clearly indicates an earlier acquaintance by five years.

31. The registry for the boarding house at Byrdcliffe, the Villetta, lists the Max Müllers as summer guests three consecutive years, 1916 to 1918; this is probably the son as Prof. Max Müller died in 1900. In a letter just dated *18th* (no year or month but most likely 1889) Jane notes: "Prof. Max Müller! What does the name mean?—a learned philologist—the possessor of more decorations than any man in England. An authority, a great man. Yes, but much more a dear, dear fellow for whom I have the tenderest reverence a spirit that scintillates a voice that moves & a smile that enraptures me. And Mrs. Max is worthy."

32. Newspaper clipping, unidentified newspaper, dated Wednesday, June 3, 1886, McCall Scrapbook, 1883–90. Winterthur Library, Downs Collection.

33. Among their extensive collection of reproductions, Rossetti, Burne-Jones, and Watts are the best represented (Winterthur Library, Downs Collection). Jane mentions visiting Watts's studio on March 23, 1890, and again, in Paris with Ralph on her honeymoon, October 10, 1892 (see 1891 and 1892 calendars series, Winterthur Archives, Downs Collection). On May 24, 1891, Ralph wrote to Jane from Paris: "Watts nearly comes up to what we feel." In his *Grass of the Desert* Whitehead goes further, stating, "the creators who give new life to the men of their time, and raise the beacon of man's noble aspirations once more to view when he is lost in a slough of commonplace vulgarity. To this group belong, in our day and country, Watts and Rossetti, and Millais in his landscapes" (Whitehead, *Grass of the Desert*, 157).

34. In 1882, after her father's death, Jane Addams and her stepmother had similarly traveled to Europe: "The two women had planned meticulously for their two-year venture. Addams wrote of the time-consuming process of assembling the necessary wardrobes, which included a number of fashionable dresses with massive mutton-sleeves. In Europe, Addams followed the routine that was customary for young Americans pursuing cultural refinement: she collected art reproductions, studied languages, worked her way through museums, and wrote up her impressions." From Jane Bethke Elshtain, *Jane Addams and the Dream of American Democracy* (New York: Basic Books, 2002), 67. Jane's experiences with her sister and mother would have been very similar.

35. Notes at the end of her 1891 calendar where she lists this "Dream" as a "Highlight" and yet Whitehead's name comes only under a list of "Acquaintances"—this, perhaps, to allay the fears of her family. "Somewhere" was the euphemism consistently used by Jane to refer to their planned community. On September 27, 1894, her calendar reads, "Great excitement about 'Somewhere.'" Interestingly, she refers to their "convent" as "somewhere;" Morris's *News from Nowhere* describes a utopia (nowhere) of the future.

36. RRW has several nicknames he uses to address Jane—"Suntreader," "Pauline," "Twin," and, most commonly, her middle name, "Byrd."

37. RRW to Jane, April 4, 1891. Winterthur Library, Downs Collection.

38. In the early 1890s Whitehead "compiled a volume on Dante in which the poet's ancient phraseology was annotated into modern Italian to enable the average reader to a better understanding of the masterpiece." See Anita M. Smith, *Woodstock History and Hearsay* (Woodstock, NY: Stonecrop, 1959), 40.

39. J. N. Nettleship to RRW, December 25, 1890. Private collection.

40. Toynbee Hall was started in 1884. Arnold Toynbee, who wrote *The Industrial Revolution in England* (published posthumously), was interested in developing a system that would improve conditions for working class people. He died at the age of thirty and Toynbee Hall was later founded in his memory.

41. J. N. Nettleship to RRW, May 4, no year. Private collection.

42. Ada Nettleship seems to have been more than a dressmaker to Jane. She is mentioned several times in Jane's calendars and in August Ralph is visiting with the Nettleships in Switzerland.

RRW to Jane, August 15, 1901, Lanx, Switzerland: "My darling Byrd, three charming days here with Mrs. Nettleship & her daughters. She is one of those rare women who as the years pass grow ever in grace & strength; and Ethel has grown & is a very beautiful character; she would like you & you her as you do Miss Babbitt [a friend of the Whiteheads whom they met at Summerbrook in the Adirondacks and who would become a frequent visitor to Byrdcliffe] of who she reminds me in temper. She is not so romantic as Ida, but she is a very perfect woman. It is a great thing we can pass on to the children, the friendship of five & twenty years. Ethel is still studying the cello in Berlin...Ursula is at the critical age of fifteen...I think she is very beautiful; she wants to sing. Truly a successful marriage in the children." Winterthur Library, Downs Collection.

Ethel, a cellist, drove an ambulance during WWI in Malta and Italy; Ida married the painter Augustus John and died in 1908 of puerperal fever and peritonitis after the birth of her fifth child; Ursula became a singer and teacher of singing as well as an accomplished skier and mountaineer.

43. See Ralph Whitehead, *Grass of the Desert* (London: Chiswick Press, 1892), 70–71.

44. Ruskin, Works, XXVII: 535; as quoted in Eileen Boris, *Art and Labor: Ruskin, Morris, and the Craftsman Ideal in America* (Philadelphia: Temple University Press, 1986), 5.

45. Whitehead, *Grass of the Desert*, 72.

46. David Gerard, *John Ruskin and William Morris: The Energies of Order and Love* (London: The Nine Elms Press, 1988), 6.

47. Typewritten manuscript titled "Obiter Dicta," n.d. Winterthur Library, Downs Collection.

48. R. D. MacLeod, *William Morris (As Seen by his Contemporaries)* (Glasgow: W. & R. Home [Books] Ltd., 1956), 34–35.

49. Gerard, *Energies of Order and Love*, 2.

50. Whitehead, *Grass of the Desert*, 70.

51. Joseph Giovannini, "Living with Mission Furniture on the East and West Coasts," *New York Times*, December 10, 1981: Home Section, C1 and C6.

52. Although it is not known exactly when and how they met, it

could have been through mutual friends, the Nettleships, or another friend, artist George Wilson (1843–90).

53. From *Arts and Crafts Essays*, preface by William Morris (New York and London: Garland Publishing, Inc., 1977), 278.

54. RRW to Jane, September 3, 1891: "We must be very careful now remember that all thy relatives are against me." In September 1891 Ralph received a discomfiting letter from Jane's mother asking him not to send any more books or to write again without her "express leave" (September 24, 1891, RRW to Jane, Geneva). He goes on to tell Jane, "it is obvious that she means us not to meet again...I cannot answer her letter at present for I cannot give her the promises she ask me for—not to write to thee again!"

55. Jane to RRW, April 12, 1891. Madeleine Fleury was an artist friend whom Jane probably met while studying at the Académie Julian in the 1880s. The following February Madelaine was painting a similar portrait of Ralph for Jane (cat. 162). See RRW to Jane, February 1892. Her brother was the artist Tony Robert-Fleury.

56. RRW to Jane, April 6, 1892. Winterthur Library, Downs Collection.

57. Jane to RRW, April 12, 1891. Winterthur Library, Downs Collection.

58. RRW to Jane, June 5, 1891. Winterthur Library, Downs Collection.

59. RRW to Jane, August 15, 1891. Winterthur Library, Downs Collection.

60. Fiona McCarthy, *The Beauty of the Earth*, 18.

61. RRW to Jane, September 22, 1891. Winterthur Library, Downs Collection.

62. Seven years later, in 1899, Whitehead became a naturalized American citizen.

63. RRW to Jane, November 25, 1891, Berlin. Winterthur Library, Downs Collection.

64. RRW to Jane, December 12, 1891. Winterthur Library, Downs Collection.

65. Although it seems that this is the fairy-tale ending to the long courtship, Jane's family was not sanguine about RRW's matrimonial history, and a Deed of Trust, dated August 23, 1892 (their wedding day), was drawn up giving Whitehead $125,000 upon their marriage; but in case of separation or divorce, the interest was to revert to Jane.

66. Toni Hendschel-Dracht to Jane, February 1, 1939. Winterthur Library, Downs Collection.

67. RRW to Jane, New Year's Eve, 1891: "What has failed me has been one whom I might serve; thou hast accepted my service and I am at peace. My life has little worth except such faithful service, but of that I am capable, dost believe me love?"

68. RRW to Jane, April 9, 1897. Winterthur Library, Downs Collection.

69. RRW to Jane, April 9, 1897. Winterthur Library, Downs Collection.

70. RRW to Jane, June 5, 1897: "I got here last evening. I had a long drive from Saranac where the big hotel & the society people nearly drove me into the Lake. In some ways it is nice to be here. Old Davidson is kind, but is rather too like a second rate Ruskin.... The water is good & so is the air.... There is a dining room & kitchen to accommodate twenty or thirty summer guests. D[avidson] gives courses here in July and August." Winterthur Library, Downs Collection.

71. Mann was a cousin of the educator Horace Mann and had attended Alcott's Concord Summer School of Philosophy and later, Glenmore, with her parents. Around 1895 she bought land from John Dewey's brother Davis on which to build her home, Summerbrook. (See Richard Plunz, ed., *Two Adirondack Hamlets in History: Keene and Keene Valley* [Keene Valley: Keene Valley Library Association, 1999] for a full account.) The educator John Dewey also owned land nearby to Glenmore and it may have been here, not in Chicago, that Whitehead first met him. Dewey was a visitor to Byrdcliffe in 1906, when he built a playhouse for his children there.

72. For further information on Summerbrook, see *The American Fabian* (Westport, CT: Greenwood Reprint Corp., 1970), 10.

73. There are other notations in the calendars and letters referring to visits with spiritualists, using a Ouija board, attending a séance, and other references to Hyslop. When Whitehead first arranged to meet Hervey White in Chicago, he was in that city to investigate certain spiritualist mediums for the Society of Psychical Research.

74. RRW to Jane, September 24, 1901. Winterthur Library, Downs Collection.

75. Ralph had met with Bowles earlier in the year and wrote to Jane about his meeting (June 1, 1897): "On Sunday afternoon I spent a couple of hours with the Bowles.... They neither of them draw but somehow they have got an appreciation of what is good in drawing & painting. They are very aesthetic without I think being aesthete & are not all a part of the cant of the aesthetic & literary class which flourishes in Boston." Winterthur Library, Downs Collection. Janet Bowles was a talented silversmith in her own right and was actively involved with the National Society of Craftsmen and the National League of Handicraft Societies.

76. From White's handwritten manuscript for a 1933 article on Whitehead. Collection of the Historical Society Woodstock (cat. 9).

77. *Ibid.*

78. Jane to Bim, August 8, 1917. Winterthur Library, Downs Collection.

79. Whitehead had a penchant for using Italian nicknames for friends and familiar. His sons came to be known as Bim (or Bimbo) and Angelo.

80. RRW to Jane, July 15, 1900. Winterthur Library, Downs Collection.

81. RRW to Jane, July 16, 1900. Winterthur Library, Downs Collection.

82. RRW to Jane, July 21, 1900. Winterthur Library, Downs Collection.

83. Trained as an architect, in the 1880s Ashbee resided at Toynbee Hall in the East End where he started a Ruskin reading class and began the nucleus of what was to become the Guild of Handicraft in 1888. In 1890 he acquired the lease of Essex house for the Guild and in 1902 he moved the Guild to Chipping Camden in the Cotswolds. Best known for his jewelry and metalwork, he returned to architecture after the Guild was liquidated in 1907.

84. Returning from Europe, Ralph made the trek to East Aurora himself to see what Elbert Hubbard was up to. RRW to Jane, September 17, 1901. Winterthur Library, Downs Collection.

85. Jane to RRW, July 9–11, 1901. Winterthur Library, Downs Collection.

86. RRW to Jane, July 12, 1901. Winterthur Library, Downs Collection.

87. RRW to Jane, July 25, 1901. Winterthur Library, Downs Collection.

88. RRW to Jane, July 12, 1901. Winterthur Library, Downs Collection.

89. RRW to Jane, July 25, 1901. Winterthur Library, Downs Collection.

90. Another artist teaching there at the time was Frank Morley Fletcher, who would come to Santa Barbara in 1923 at the invitation of his friend Albert Herter, to head the Santa Barbara College of Arts and Crafts. The Whiteheads probably met him again there; in an attic cupboard of White Pines is one of Fletcher's woodcuts, *The Waterway*, done around 1905. There is a notation in Jane's diary for 1933 of visiting the Morley Fletcher House. The Herters were neighbors in California and the Whiteheads frequently met with them socially at their house Mirasol. The Herters also ran the Herter Looms in New York where some Byrdcliffe participants, including Vivian Bevans White and Edna Walker, worked in the early days of its operation.

91. Ricardo to RRW, August 8, 1903. Winterthur Library, Downs Collection.

92. E-mail from Ricardo's great-great-grandson, March 19, 2003.

93. RRW to Jane, May 6, 1902. Winterthur Library, Downs Collection.

94. Arthur Wesley Dow was an important teacher at the turn of the century, first at the Pratt Institute and then at Columbia's Teachers College. He also taught classes at the Art Students League in New York and ran a summer school in Ipswich, Massachusetts, where students learned a variety of craft and fine-art skills. Many of his students from Pratt went to Byrdcliffe in the early years and several of them, including Bertha Thompson, Ned Thatcher, Vivian Bevans White, Zulma Steele, Olaf Westerling, and Edna Walker visited the Ipswich Summer School in 1907. (Schlesinger Library, Thompson Family Papers, handwritten notes by B. Thompson.)

95. RRW to Bim, June 2, 1902. Winterthur Library, Downs Collection.

96. RRW to Jane, June 5, 1902. Winterthur Library, Downs Collection.

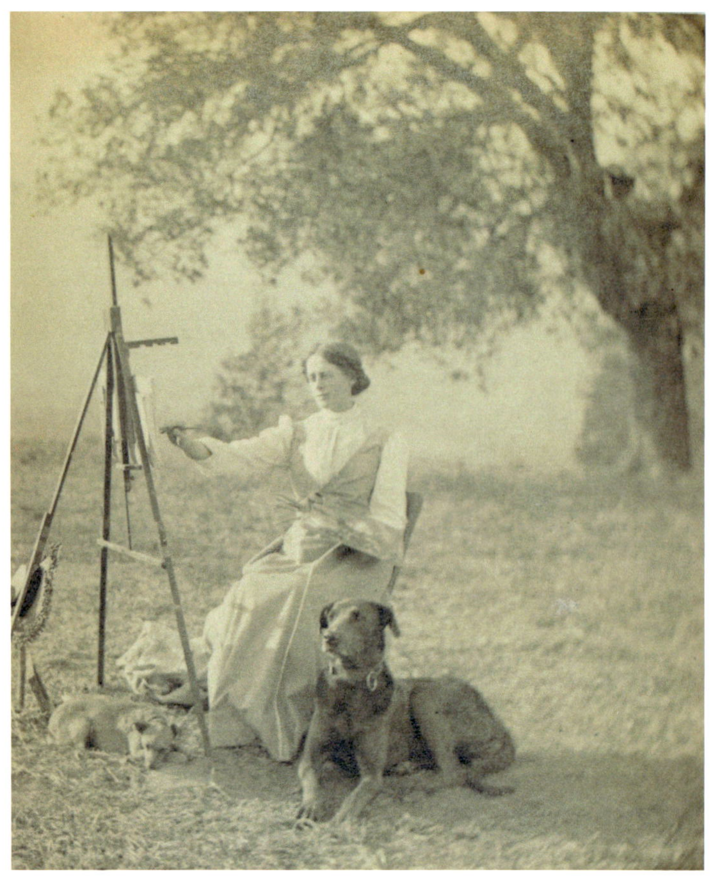

fig. 1 Attributed to Ralph Whitehead, *Byrd seated at easel painting outdoors.* Silver print. Winterthur Library, Downs Collection, 92x39.1140.575t.

Jane Byrd McCall Whitehead

Cofounder of the Byrdcliffe Art School

HEIDI NASSTROM EVANS

Jane Byrd McCall Whitehead (fig. 1) lived an extraordinary life. As an artist, she studied with some of the finest painters and craftspeople of her time and practiced in many diverse media, including painting, drawing, design, wood, textile, and ceramic. Heretofore her contribution to the conception and realization of the Byrdcliffe art school has been largely overlooked; nevertheless, her art and thinking were central to its establishment. Enriching our knowledge of the Arts and Crafts movement, Jane Whitehead's story also expands our understanding of what it means to be an artist.[1]

This essay is an overview of Jane Whitehead's life and artistic activity between the late 1870s and the end of the 1920s. Following a roughly chronological format, it connects the people and events that impacted her art, life, and work at Byrdcliffe; it also focuses on the reasons why she was largely omitted in previous Byrdcliffe scholarship.

Born in 1861 into a prominent family in Philadelphia, her elite place in society was defined by a distinguished family history. She was a descendant of Governor John Francis Mercer of Maryland, as well as George Mason and William Byrd. Her father, Peter McCall, was mayor of Philadelphia, and her mother was Jane Byrd Mercer McCall. Known as "Byrd" to family and friends, Jane Whitehead is referred to by this concise pet name throughout the remainder of this essay.

Little is known and nothing has been published about her early life between 1861 and circa 1876, the beginning date of records in the Joseph Downs Collection at Winterthur Museum, Garden, and Library—the primary repository of archival material on Byrdcliffe.[2] During this period, she developed interests in the arts while living in Philadelphia, and, in the 1880s, traveled overseas where she reportedly studied art with John Ruskin at Oxford University, and fine arts at the Académie Julian in Paris. There is some documentation suggesting that Byrd studied in Europe as a young child.[3] However, much more research needs to be done on the earliest years of her life.

At present, evidence of Byrd's activity in the arts begins in the late 1870s. An early scrapbook in the Joseph Downs Collection was compiled by Byrd on an extended trip abroad with her mother and sister Gertrude McCall (known as Gerty).[4] The beginning point of the scrapbook is circa 1876—the date of an included calling card. Given to Byrd by Mrs. Max Müller, this card was from the wife of the Orientalist and Oxford professor Max Müller, a life-

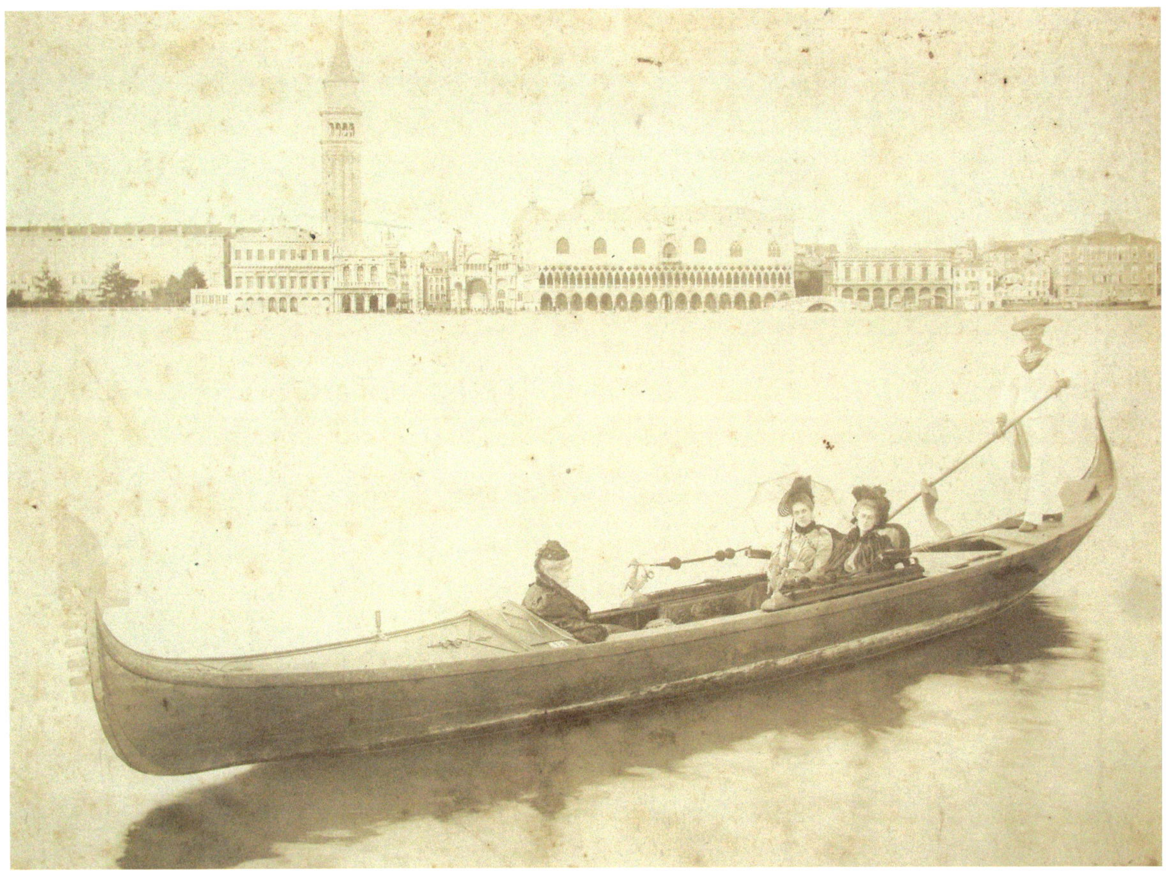

fig. 2 Unidentified photographer, *Mrs. Peter McCall (Jane Byrd Mercer McCall) with Byrd and Gerty in gondola in Venice*, ca. 1880s. Albumen print. Winterthur Library, Downs Collection, 92x39.1140.613.

fig. 3 H. S. Mendelssohn, *Jane Byrd McCall in Presentation Dress for Queen Victoria*, 1886. Albumen print. Winterthur Library, Downs Collection, 92x39.1140.49.

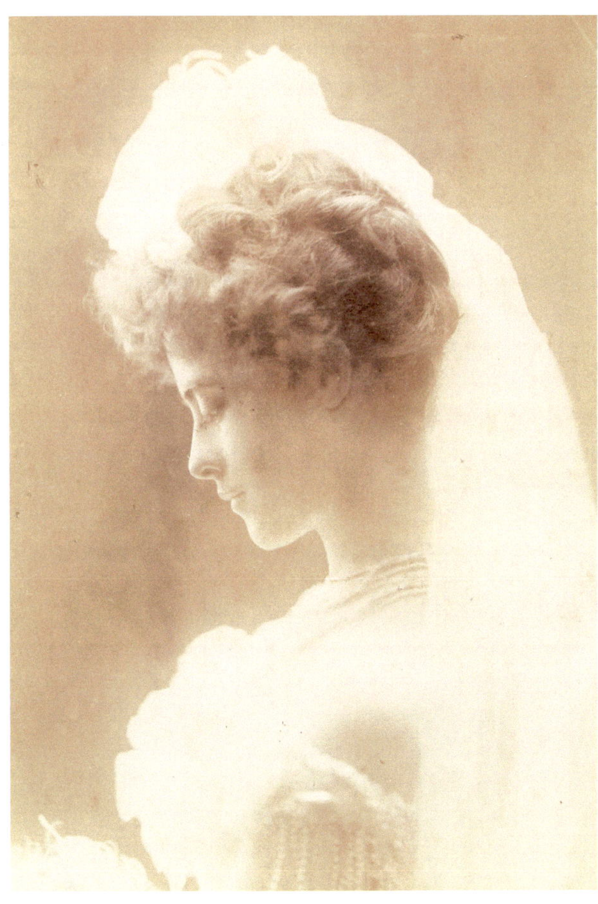

long friend of Byrd and her husband, Ralph Radcliffe Whitehead.[5]

The scrapbook is a marvelous conduit to the past life of an elite young American woman making her grand tour in the Victorian era. Among the recorded travels to England, France, Italy (fig. 2), and Turkey, the book commemorates her presentation to Queen Victoria in 1886 (fig. 3). A newspaper clipping dated Saturday, May 8, 1886, describes the court gowns that Byrd and her sister Gerty wore and the positive reception they received. It reads, "the Misses McCall, two distinguished American ladies, attracted much notice by the simple elegance of their Court gowns, the pearl embroideries being very beautiful."[6]

The scrapbook and Byrd's calendars from the period tell us that Byrd was a social success in Europe. She was invited to numerous functions hosted by Queen Victoria in England, and visited many of the country estates of England and France's landed gentry (fig. 4). Dukes, duchesses, ladies, lords, and counts are featured among the names of Byrd's friends and aquaintances. Since it was fashionable for wealthy American women to marry European noblemen, it is possible that Byrd's mother brought her daughters abroad to find them aristocratic

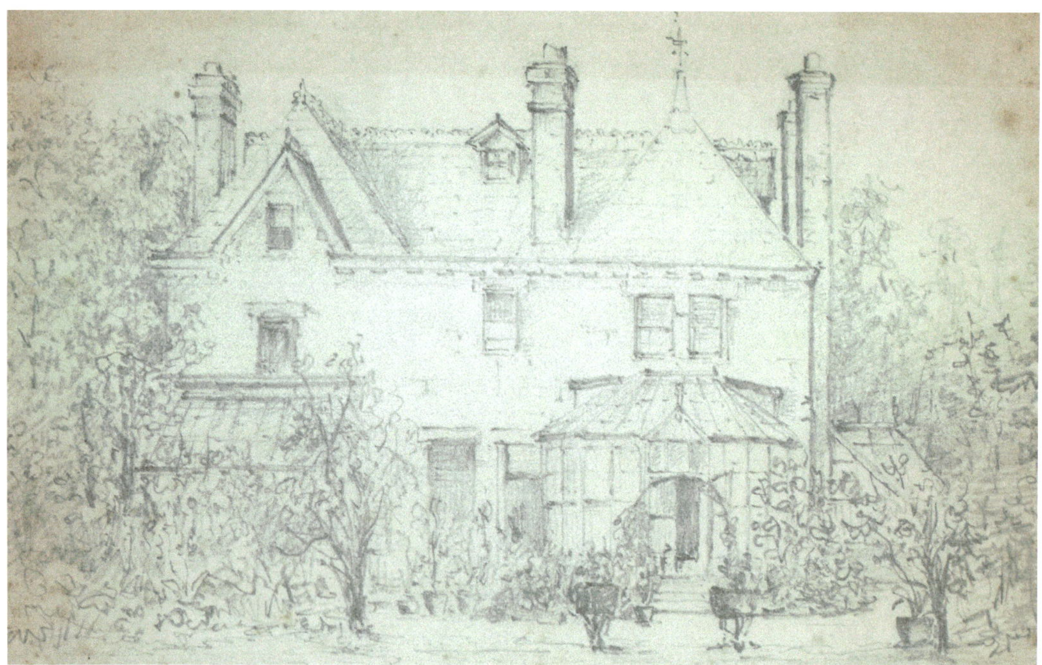

fig. 4 Attributed to Jane Byrd McCall Whitehead, *Albury Park, Guildford, House of Duchess of Northumberland*, 1888. Pencil. Winterthur Library, Downs Collection, 92x39.1538.

husbands.[7] This is only speculation; however, if it were the case, Mrs. McCall may not have been completely satisfied with the results of her efforts because Gerty never married, and Byrd married Ralph Radcliffe Whitehead. British, well-educated, and wealthy, Whitehead had two potential strikes against him in the late Victorian world of the elite social class in which Byrd lived: he was a recently divorced man, and his wealth was based on his family's fairly recent success in the textile manufacturing industry rather than on a distinguished lineage of family land holdings.[8]

It looks like Byrd may have first made Whitehead's acquaintance in 1885. A series of notations about a "Mr. Whitehead" and "RRW" (initials that correspond with Ralph Radcliffe Whitehead) appear between January 14 and November 11 in her calendar from that year.[9] Since the 1885 calendar is the earliest one known to exist, it is possible that Byrd and Whitehead met before that year. Curiously, no additional supporting evidence, such as correspondence or other personal ephemera, confirms their meeting prior to 1891—the date heretofore assigned to their meeting.[10]

At the same time Byrd was making a social splash throughout Europe, she was reportedly studying art with John Ruskin at Oxford (fig. 5), at the Académie Julian in Paris, and at other locations throughout Europe. The question remains, however, how and why did she develop an interest in art? Although not much is known about her early life in Philadelphia, it is easy to imagine that she was exposed to the arts in her hometown—a national art center of special prominence in those years. Philadelphia was the birthplace of a number of famous women artists, including Mary Cassatt (1844–1926), the only American to exhibit with the French Impressionists. The city was also the site of the Great International Philadelphia Centennial Exhibition in 1876, which introduced millions of Americans to avant-garde artistic trends from Great Britain and the Continent. Surely, artists like Cassatt and events such as the Centennial provided inspiration to young Byrd.

Furthermore, the fine arts were considered a suitably feminine activity for elite young women like Byrd. At this time, divisions between public and private spaces tended to be explicitly gendered male and female, respectively. Women of means who did not need or wish to transgress these boundaries or risk accusations of "gender inversion" found socially acceptable ways, spaces, and places in which to express their talents and accomplishments. Tamar Garb writes:

> For Léon Legrange, writing in the *Gazette des beaux-arts* in 1860, the woman artist, unlike the compromised figure of the actress, dancer, and musician, was potentially protected by her profession. In the seclusion of her studio she could preserve the purity of her person . . . . As a young woman, "she could be concealed, chaste and pure, in the corner of a solitary living room," married she would not have to disclose her smiles and affections to others, as a mother she would not bring shame to her offspring. On show in the public sphere would be her work rather than her body and as such both her modesty and her family's honor would be safeguarded.[11]

Evidence from Byrd's scrapbook suggests that she lived the gendered Victorian ideal at this moment in her life. Delicate, beautiful, charming, and in a constant battle with her health, Byrd's likeness brings to mind the ethereal, chaste, and untouchable beauty of women painted by the Pre-Raphaelite Brotherhood associated with her mentor, John Ruskin. Byrd's story, however, is not simply so one-dimensional. Like most people, she was a complex person with ideas about herself that were multifaceted and in constant evolution over the course of her life. Nevertheless, finding a socially acceptable way to express her abilities may have been another reason why Byrd chose to become an artist.

We know that she eventually traveled to Paris to study at the Académie Julian—one of the leading art schools in the Western world, and one of the few where women were permitted to get professional training studying with nude models.[12] The specific Académie Julian masters under whom Byrd studied remain uncertain. However, we do know that many of the gifted artists who taught and practiced at Byrdcliffe, and supplied students to the summer school, were in Paris and at the Académie Julian when Byrd was there. That she was the connection between these people and Byrdcliffe is not often acknowledged in scholarship. However, it is hard to discount her as a probable liaison.

Birge Harrison and Arthur Wesley Dow are two artists associated with Byrdcliffe. Their studies in Paris and Dow's at Académie Julian with Gustave Boulanger and Jules-Joseph Lefebvre are documented during Byrd's tenure there.[13] Harrison, who is best known for his moody tonalist landscapes, headed Byrdcliffe's art program the summer of 1904.[14] Byrd studied painting with him when she lived in Montecito, California (1894–1902), and later at Byrdcliffe in Woodstock, New York.[15]

Dow, a tonalist painter and printmaker, was inspired by Japanese art and aesthetics. He was an influential artist, educator, and author of *Composition: A Series of Exercises in Art Structure for the Use of Students and Teachers* (1899). According to Nancy Green, Dow acted as an advisor on the development of Byrdcliffe's curriculum.[16] Later, he reportedly sent students and colleagues to study and teach at Byrdcliffe; these people included the celebrated designers of conventionalized ornament Zulma Steele and Edna Walker, the metalworker Edward (Ned) Thatcher, and the Canadian artist Harry Stuart Michie.[17]

The cover of Byrd's 1903 publication *The Morning Stars Sang Together: Folk-Songs and Other Songs for Children* (Boston: Oliver Ditson Company) shows the influence of

fig. 5 Marsh Brothers, Henley on Thames, British, active 1870s–80s, *Byrd and Gerty McCall and friends including B. P. Lascelles at Oxford*, 1883. Albumen print. Winterthur Library, Downs Collection, 92x39.1140.558.

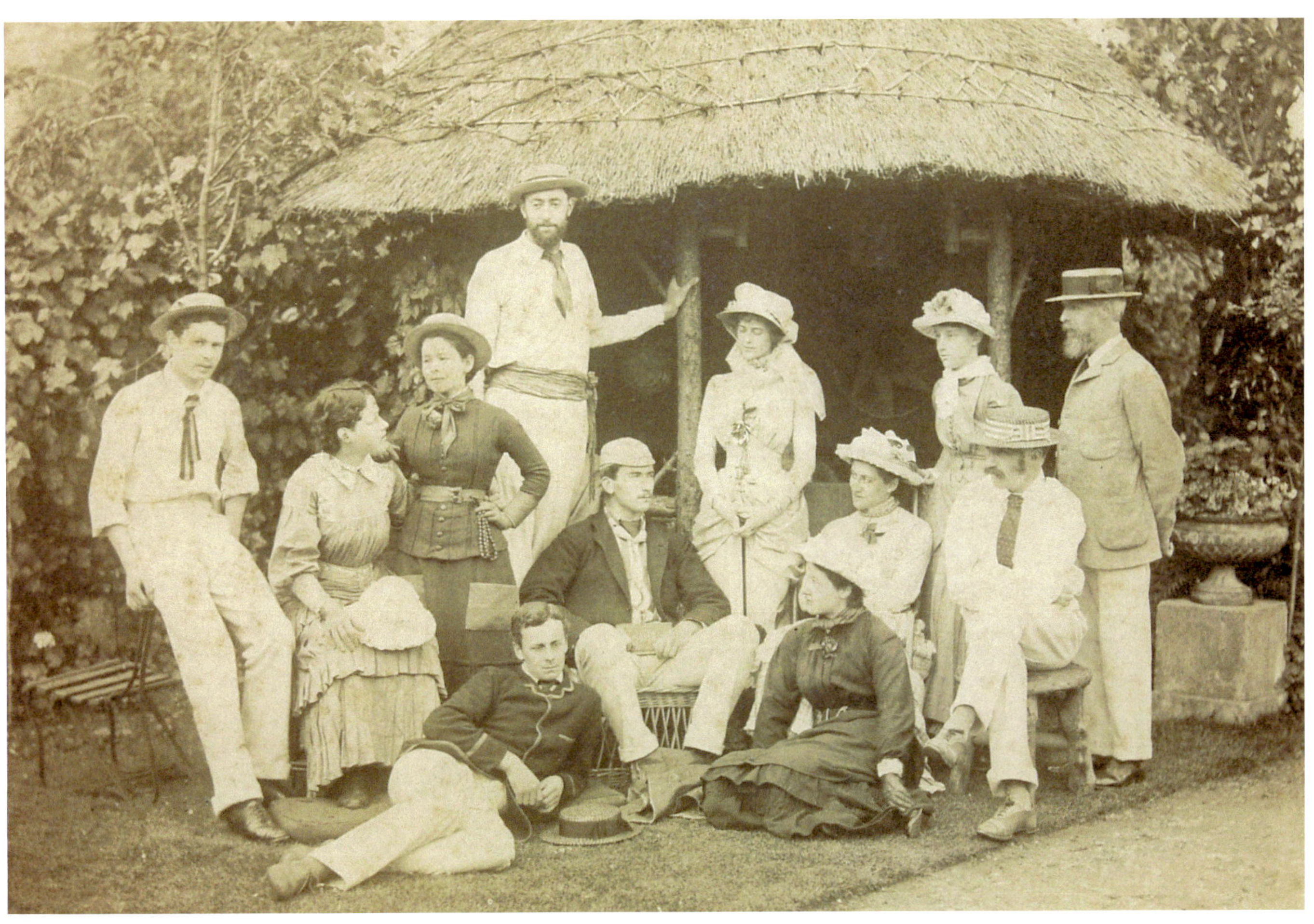

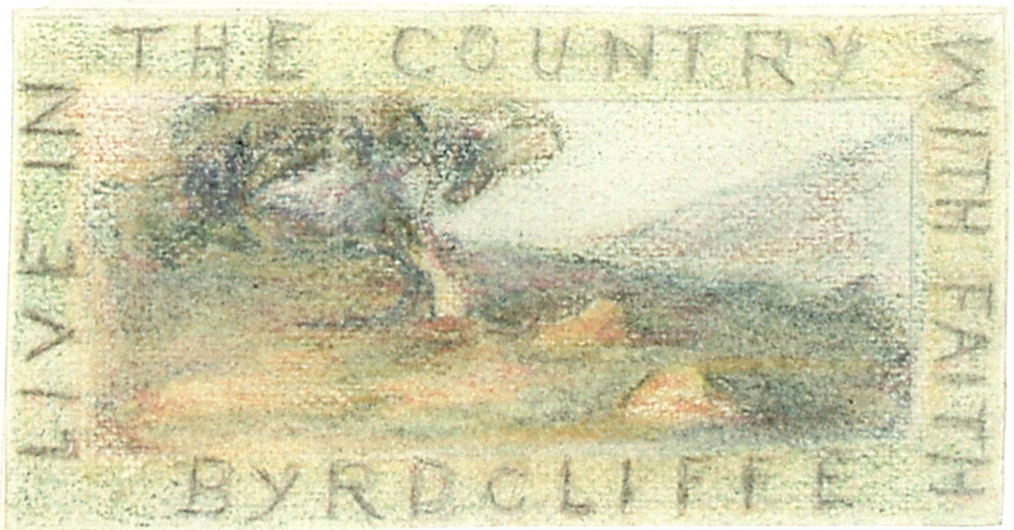

fig. 6 Attributed to Jane Byrd McCall Whitehead, *Landscape Sketch*. Watercolor from vellum-covered book, inscribed "Live in the country with Faith. Byrdcliffe." Winterthur Library, Downs Collection, 92x39.1546.

tonalist prints and compositions similar to those produced by Harrison and Dow (cat. 11) (figs. 6 and 7). It pictures a star-studded early morning landscape with mountains in the distance and tall cypresslike trees in the foreground, probably based on views of California. Typical of tonalist compositions is its low horizon line and heavily outlined, conventionalized motifs from nature. Bearing the stylized initials "JBRW," the design is most likely Byrd's. Evidence supporting this attribution includes similar, unsigned tonalist paintings in the Joseph Downs Collection, and references to Byrd's work on this project in her correspondence with Whitehead.[18] For example, one letter from Byrd noted, "I have been making a design for the cover of the song book and it has occupied me a good deal this week . . . ."[19]

fig. 7 Attributed to Jane Byrd McCall Whitehead. *Cover of vellum-covered book*. Winterthur Library, Downs Collection, 92x39.1546.

As one can see from the *Morning Stars* example, multiple forms of evidence are often needed to ascribe art to Byrd. In this case, the unsigned artwork, related unsigned artworks, and letters were consulted. Multiple sources are needed because she simply did not sign many things, and her artistic contributions are not recorded in publications from the period or in subsequent scholarship on Byrdcliffe. In the watershed book *Women Artists of the Arts and Crafts Movement, 1870–1914,* Anthea Callen wrote about anonymity among women of Byrd's social class:

> Anonymity was occasionally offered as a means of protecting the good name of a lady, indicating the extent to which paid work represented an embarrassing loss of status to be hidden at all costs . . . . For men, fame and ambition were taken for granted in the pursuit of their profession, but among women it was only the more socially progressive who were able to cope with the psychological and social conflicts created by stepping outside their traditionally defined feminine role . . . . Aside from the well-known few, the anonymity sought by many professional craftswomen has only served to speed their complete disappearance from the history of the movement, and to reinforce the common notion of the Arts and Crafts as a predominantly male arena.[20]

And so goes the story of Byrd. Like many women in the Arts and Crafts movement and especially like those from the upper class, Byrd's anonymity and her reluctance to sign her work and seek public recognition in her name have led to lack of recognition of her in the history of the movement.

Stepping back chronologically to reengage in Byrd's early life abroad, specifically, her study at the Académie Julian, we can look at her lifelong friend Madeleine Fleury.

Believed to be the sister of the internationally prominent painter and Académie Julian academician Tony Robert-Fleury,[21] Fleury executed several beautiful portraits of Byrd, her mother, and Whitehead and is often mentioned in Byrd's personal papers. Like Byrd, who is marginally known through her marriage to Whitehead, Fleury is another accomplished artist who is known in relation to a male figure, and has seemingly disappeared from the historical record.

One particularly striking portrait of Byrd by Fleury (fig. 8) is shown hanging in Arcady (fig. 9)—Byrd and Whitehead's home in Montecito, California. This photograph is a striking piece of documentation on a number of levels. It shows the now missing portrait by Fleury, and connects Byrd and Whitehead to proponents of the Arts and Crafts movement in England and to the Académie Julian in France. In it we see a Gothic Revival–style firescreen covered in William Morris–designed honeysuckle cretonne fabric. According to published scholarship and supporting evidence in the Joseph Downs Collection, Whitehead bought the fabric from the William Morris showroom in London while he was living in Berlin in 1891[22] (cat. 19).

The set of three framed tiles located on the ledge behind the firescreen was designed by the English architect Halsey Ricardo and produced by William De Morgan[23] (cats. 125 and 126). A longtime friend of Byrd and Whitehead, Ricardo is mentioned in their correspondence from 1891.[24] De Morgan is best known for the lusterware ceramics he produced in association with William Morris; he worked in partnership with Ricardo at Sands End in Fulham from 1888 to 1898.[25] It is likely that Byrd and Whitehead acquired the tile composition when they lived in Europe, prior to their move to California in 1894.

On the wall to the right of Byrd's head is a study of a nude boy playing a flute-like musical instrument. Today, this unsigned drawing is in the Joseph Downs Collection[26] (fig. 10). Entries in Byrd's November 1892 and February 1893 calendar include "Julian's studio Rue de Berr[i]," and notations about studies of a "Boy playing a flute."[27] Dating from a visit to Paris on a tour of Europe with Whitehead, these inscriptions strongly suggest the sketch is by Byrd and dates from a study at Académie Julian. Secondary evidence in Gabriel Weisberg's essay, "The Women of the Académie Julian: The Power of Professional Emulation,"

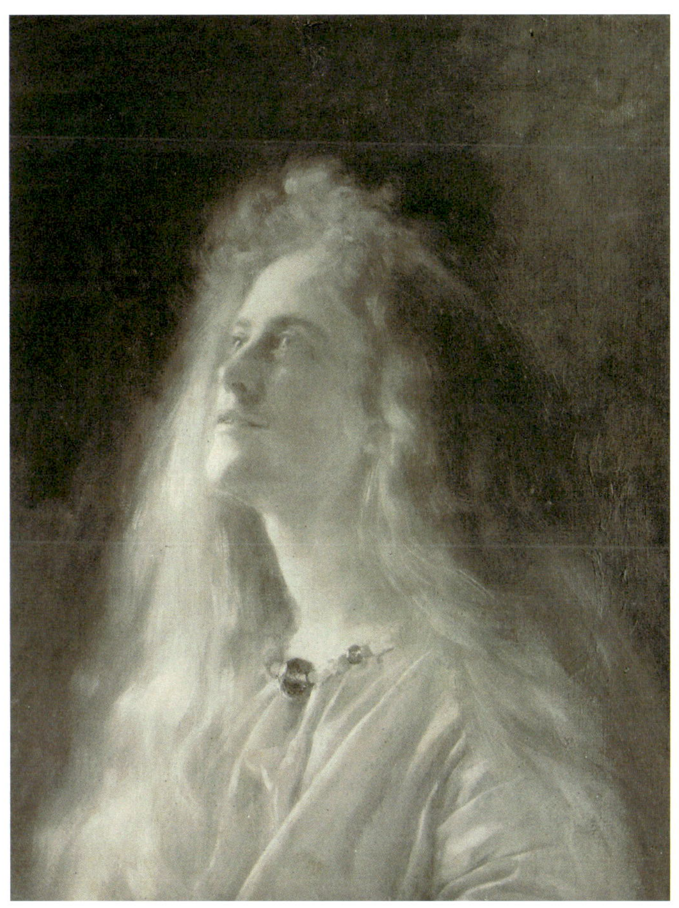

fig. 8 Photograph of missing portrait of Byrd by Madeleine Fleury. Inscribed "The Cameron Studio 70 Mortimer St. Regent So. W.", ca. late 1880s. Silver print. Winterthur Library, Downs Collection, 92x39.1140.72.

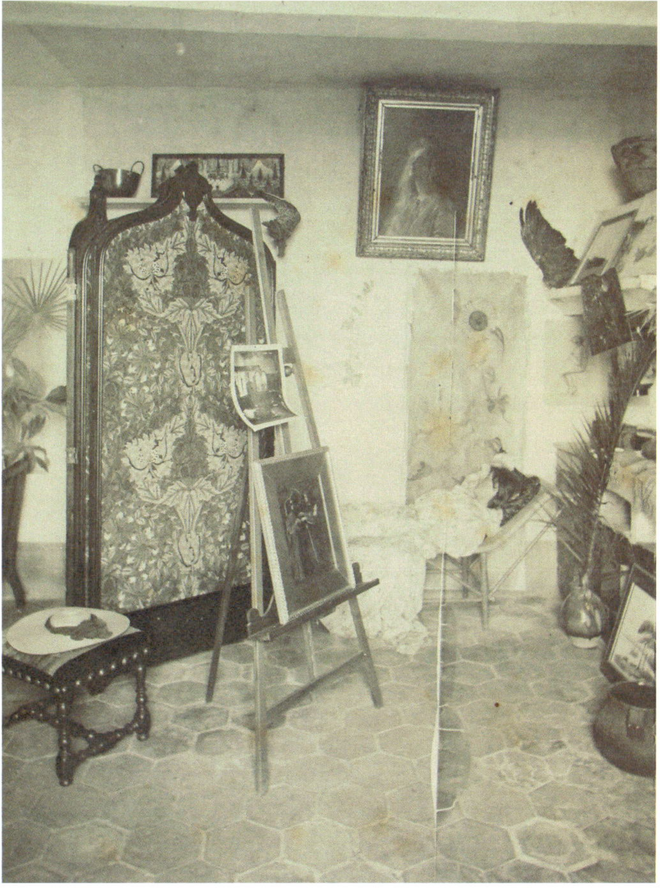

fig. 9 Ralph Whitehead, *Byrd reclining in Arcady studio.* Silver print. Winterthur Library, Downs Collection, 92x39.1140.329a.

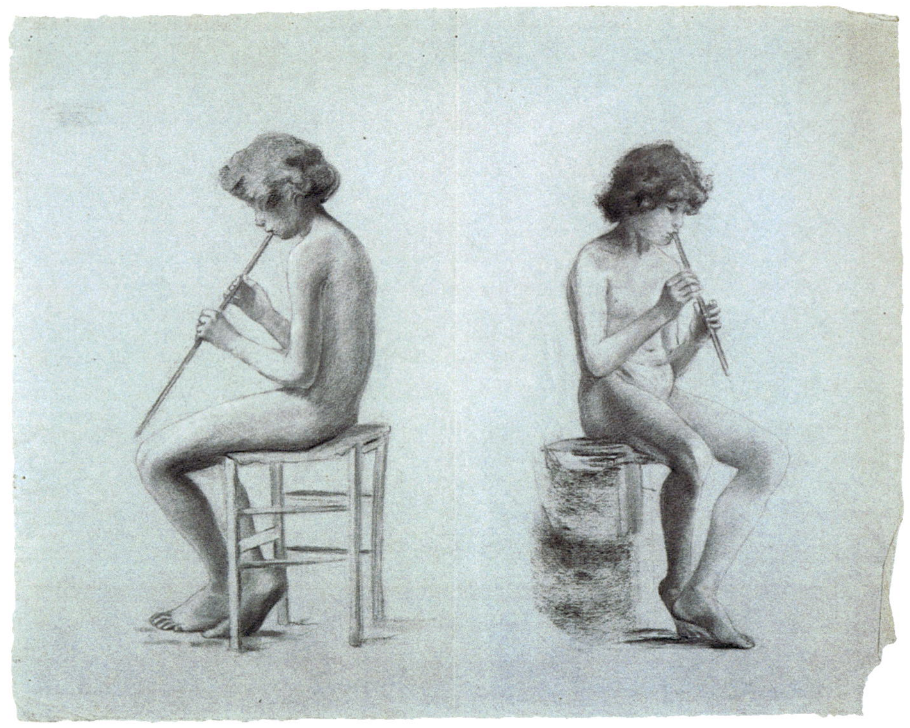

fig. 10 Attributed to Jane Byrd McCall Whitehead, *Two Nude Boys Playing Flute-like Musical Instruments*, ca. 1893. Pencil. Winterthur Library, Downs Collection, 92x39.280.

provides additional information supporting an Académie Julian association.[28] First, he notes that Julian had a branch of his atelier for female students at "5, rue de Berri," the address mentioned in Byrd's calendar entry.[29] Furthermore, similar boy models are shown in photographs and artwork picturing the Julian studios. For example, a comparable boy posing as a young Saint John the Baptist is pictured in Marie Bashkirtseff's painting of the Académie Julian called *In the Studio*.[30]

From the outset of Byrd and Whitehead's relationship in 1891, they planned to live a life in partnership, work collaboratively, and organize an environment similar to the one eventually realized at Byrdcliffe. Essays such as "Work" in the 1892 book *Grass of the Desert* (Chiswick Press, London) and "A Plea for Manual Work" in a 1903 Society of Arts and Crafts in Boston's edition of *Handicraft* (II, no. III, June 1903: 58–73) include the concepts that were the basis for Byrdcliffe. While they were published in Whitehead's name, they reflect the ideas that he and Byrd developed together.

Byrd's central involvement in the conception and realization of Byrdcliffe is often not acknowledged. In fact, she is more typically dismissed as a nonfactor or, in some cases, as a cause of failure. For example, Allen Staley's 1960 master's thesis says:

> Perhaps the chief reason for the decline was the atmosphere fostered at Byrdcliffe by Mrs. Whitehead. . . . "Poetic and sensitive," in Pre-Raphaelite robes, she completely denied the existence of the modern world. Following her lead, Byrdcliffe tended to become oblivious of anything but its own sensitivities.
>
> The most important figure at Byrdcliffe was, however, Ralph Radcliffe Whitehead.[31]

Many of Staley's ideas about Byrd are based on Anita Smith's 1959 publication *Woodstock History and Hearsay* and on a series of remembrances by Byrdcliffe artists, which date from the 1930s.[32] Following Staley's lead, subsequent writing on Byrdcliffe has often been equally dismissive of Byrd's contribution. Most of this scholarship ignores Byrd's activity, which is recorded in her and Whitehead's personal papers and artifacts. Analyzing these materials with attention to Byrd's perspective reveals a different history of Byrdcliffe—one in which Byrd and Whitehead were equal partners, working together to realize mutual goals.

Discussions of their joint plans in the arts are documented in their correspondence from the time of their meeting in 1891 and throughout their life together. For example, in April 1891, Byrd writes Whitehead:

> Yes, dear, a simple life is the best worth living. So few people understand even the idea of it. I am so glad we feel it in common. No matter how often I have strayed off to get new experiences I have come back to it as the mean. The center where dwells harmony. We are all groping. [What] do we ever find? All one wants to be armed with is a little love, a little health, a little philosophy, and a good deal of nature out of doors.[33]

Add to Byrd's prescription "a little art," and you have the foundation for what later became Byrdcliffe.

Evidence such as the 1891 letter quoted above and many other passionate letters from that year strongly support the idea that Byrd and Whitehead were very much in love while Byrd was studying art in Italy at the time.[34] Later that year, their courtship continued through the mail when Byrd moved back to the United States to live in Colorado Springs in an effort to improve her fragile health, and Whitehead moved to Germany to secure a divorce from his first wife.[35]

A rare signed and dated landscape painting by Byrd may document her 1891 stay in Colorado Springs (cat. 79). Depicting a vista of grasses with a view of mountains in the background, this delicate and subtle composition features soft hues of green, yellow ochre, and warm plum tones. Although the exact location it pictures is unknown, it appears to be a Western landscape, perhaps picturing an area near Colorado Springs.

Whitehead writes from Berlin to Byrd in Colorado Springs in December 1891:

> Byrd, don't talk of bookbinding, if painting is not enough for thou remember it is woodcarving that thou art to take to so we may work together.... That it shall be painting, someone is determined on that. Byrd shall be the poet-painter of whatever I and she lives in.[36]

In the year preceding their marriage in 1892, Byrd and Whitehead write back and forth about their plans for the future, and work together through the mail on Whitehead's 1892 publications, *The Vita Nuova of Dante* and *Grass of the Desert*. Letters record Byrd's role in these books, which were published in Whitehead's name. For example, a January 1892 letter from Whitehead stated he was "still hard at work at these essays" and he "would not do this writing unless thou hadn't demanded it .... I can no more write really well than that I can be a graceful skater! Byrd must take me as she found me!"[37] In turn, Whitehead asked Byrd to prepare engraved plates to ornament the books. He requested decorative initials "S, B, I, W, T, M," head and tailpieces for each chapter, and binding designs for both books.[38] Byrd writes back:

> I have accomplished two small designs on a steel plate for the back of your book .... I drew on a steel plate covered with dryish chalk, a design (the wing and arrow) .... All the drawings for the fleur-de-lys failed, I shall try again tomorrow. I will also do several Indian [*sic*] ink tailpieces.[39]

The "wing and arrow" and "fleur-de-lys" motifs described by Byrd were emblems they developed to symbolize their relationship; they were often used to identify their joint projects. Drawings of decorative initials in the Joseph Downs Collection are unsigned and undated[40] (fig. 11). Byrd and Whitehead's correspondence suggests that these initials were drawn by Byrd and that some of them may date to her work on the 1892 publications.

Later publishing efforts continue to show collaboration between Byrd and Whitehead. "Pictures for Schools" from 1901 features a frontispiece that was probably by Byrd—the wing and arrow flying over a sunset. This book is dedicated, "To my wife to whose knowledge of Art I am indebted for whatever is most useful in this lecture."[41] Here, Whitehead acknowledges his intellectual partnership with Byrd. Publishing projects, such as these, are cooperative efforts even though Whitehead is credited as the author.

An extended trip to Europe lasting well over a year followed Byrd and Whitehead's marriage in August 1892. After sailing from New York at the end of September, they arrived in Liverpool and left from London on October 12 to sail across the English Channel for Paris. In Byrd's calendars, Versailles, Cannes, and Rouen are among the places they visited before heading back to London to sail to New York at the end of April 1894. A honeymoon of this duration was not atypical for the time and for people of Byrd and Whitehead's social class. Also in keeping with the practices of the day, it appears that others, including Byrd's mother, were traveling with them.

During this trip, Byrd is painting and taking lessons with a teacher named Miss Mercier.[42] Her calendars record her working on an "Olive design for embroidery" in January 1893; "Painting cypress" on April 6; "Sunflowers" in Rouen on July 12; and "Bluebells," "Lavendar [*sic*]," and "Pine trees" throughout August.

By the end of May 1894, Byrd had sailed back to New York, visited her hometown of Philadelphia, departed for Chicago, and arrived in Las Vegas. She and Whitehead were rapidly making their way to Los Angeles and ultimately to Santa Barbara, where they would build their grand Mediterranean-style hillside villa Arcady in Montecito.

As the name suggests, Arcady—which refers to Arcadia, a district in ancient Greece whose people were noted for

fig. 11 Attributed to Jane Byrd McCall Whitehead, *Decorative initial "T" with woman playing a lute*, ca. 1892. Pen and ink.
Winterthur Library, Downs Collection, 92x39.1522.

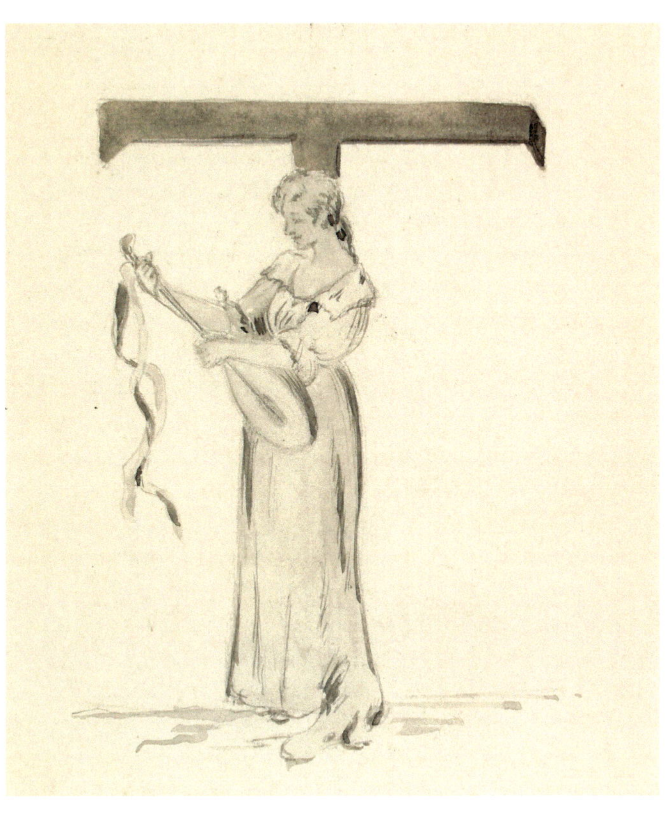

simplicity and contentment—was Byrd and Whitehead's vision of paradise on earth. In an earlier letter from their courtship, Byrd referred to Whitehead as her Arcadia: "Thou art Arcadia for me—the sweet country side, and a path that leads to a height."[43] Certainly this allusion was considered in the name they chose for their California home. Byrd and Whitehead lived at Arcady until they moved to Byrdcliffe in Woodstock, New York, in 1902–3. Even after she officially moved to the East Coast, Byrd continued to visit California in the winter months throughout the first quarter of the twentieth century.

As early as 1891, evidence suggests that Byrd and Whitehead were considering California as a site for their Arcadia. In a letter from January 1891, Whitehead writes to Byrd about his desire to travel to Colorado and California with her. He refers to the North American West as "wild country" and expresses an interest in riding horses, visiting Pikes Peak, and taking a cottage in California. In the same letter, he discusses his wish to move from the city, where it is an unhealthful environment full of anxiety, and to spend time in the "healthy outdoor life" like that lived in the North American West.[44]

Byrd and Whitehead's romance with the North American West was not an isolated case. By the 1890s, following the construction of a rail system that connected the East and West Coast and an aggressive advertising campaign promoted by the railways, tourism began to develop in earnest in the West. People were attracted by stories about the beauty of the landscape—the Grand Canyon, Yosemite, Pikes Peak, etc.—and the lure of vanishing and extinct peoples and their ways of life—Native Americans and Spanish missionaries in the Southwest and southern California, respectively. Byrd and Whitehead's attraction to southern California coincides with this tourist propaganda, and with their interest in the Arts and Crafts movement. In the United States, the Spanish mission and mission style was promoted as an indigenous, vernacular form. This was in keeping with romantic and nationalistic thinking associated with the movement. Here, advocates sought a return to highpoints in a culture's preindustrial past.

In Chris Wilson's *The Myth of Santa Fe*, he discusses the promotion of southern California as the land of sunshine and home of the Spanish mission culture. This campaign was spurred on by Charles F. Lummis,[45] who published extensively on the subject of the Southwest and West Coast from the 1880s through the early twentieth century. Lummis was an advocate of reform on Indian policy and the restoration of the California missions. As editor of *The Land of Sunshine* (renamed *Out West* in 1902), published by the Los Angeles Chamber of Commerce, he promoted a vision of the West that was very appealing to people like Byrd and Whitehead. It was Lummis's belief that in the West the Anglo-Saxon race could "thrive as never before, if they learned to temper the excesses of modern materialism and the Protestant work ethic with an outdoor life-style and the Spanish generosity of spirit, personal restraint, social purpose, and joy in life."[46] Lummis's description coincides closely with Byrd and Whitehead's lifestyle at Arcady. Even the Mediterranean origins of Arcady's name and its architectural style were in keeping with the thinking of the time. It was a commonly held belief that the North American West had a climate similar to the Mediterranean.

Life for Byrd at Arcady was certainly different from what she was used to. Given her exposure to refined environments and high society in the United States and Europe, it is hard to imagine the move to rural Montecito was made with no regrets. In her calendars there is evidence that Byrd's new "simple life" was not always the utopian dream she and Whitehead imagined. For example, in August 1894 she notes that it is "difficult to keep still," and in October there are passages about a drive into Santa Barbara, where it was "seedy."

At this time, Byrd "went in cottage hospital," where it appears she received some sort of treatment using ether. This may have been surgery following a miscarried pregnancy. On the days that follow, her diary says "hellfire," a possible reference to her reaction to the procedure. By the end of October things were getting "easier," and she got her "bandages off" in early November. Throughout December that year, Byrd writes about unhappiness, sickness, and boredom. Notably, the absence of references in her calendar to painting and artwork, or, for that matter, any activity seems to indicate that she was suffering quite a bit in her new environment, far away from her family and comforting surroundings.

While she would suffer through additional bouts of bad health in the years leading up to her move to Woodstock and the devastation of losing a baby in 1896, it appears that by January 1895, Byrd had fully recovered and was growing accustomed to her new life in California. In a letter from January, she tells her mother that she has "been up on the hill all morning painting. The heather has been divine."[47] The following years of her life are filled with artwork. As Whitehead fantasized in the early years of their courtship, Byrd became the "poet painter" of their world.[48]

In addition to her studies in California, Byrd made annual painting trips abroad in 1896–98. In 1896, she studied with Edmond Aman-Jean in Paris. Known for his association with the symbolist poets and for his paintings of women in languid profile poses, Aman-Jean seems to have been a popular teacher among upper-class American women painters.[49] Given the stylistic similarity to Aman-Jean's work, it is quite possible that several unsigned portraits of Byrd in profile may be by Aman-Jean[50] (fig. 12). Entries in Byrd's calendars from her study with Aman-Jean in November and December 1896 include numerous notations about dreams of birth, "prophecies by clairvoyants," and "presentiments." Undoubtedly, her dreams of birth refer to the recent and tragic loss of a baby, which was born alive and lived only thirty-two hours.[51] Notations about dreams, clairvoyants, and presentiments may reflect her exposure to symbolist interests in mysticism and the influence of Sigmund Freud, the father of psychoanalysis.

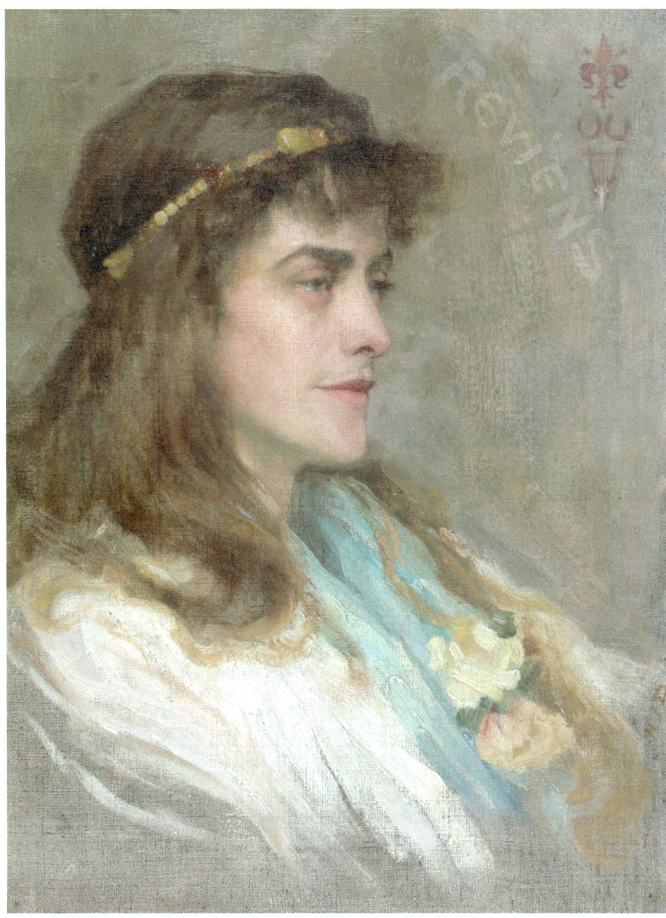

fig. 12 Unidentified artist, *Jane Byrd McCall*, inscribed "Reviens." Pastel. Private collection.

After the 1898 opening of a Sloyd school for manual arts training on the grounds at Arcady, the birth of her first son, Ralph Jr., in 1899, and second son, Peter, in 1901, Byrd remained closer to home. Still actively painting and involved in crafts and design, her calendars from those years are filled with references to her work at the Sloyd school, where she organized events and sales, and possibly taught. The responsibilities of parenting were cherished responsibilities to Byrd and Whitehead. In fact, their eventual decision to leave Montecito for Woodstock was based on their commitment to finding a suitable location in which to raise their sons.

Passages in her calendars and letters with Whitehead and her family document her role in the design of Arcady and its interiors. In a letter that is probably to her mother, Byrd asked, "Do you like the name 'Arcady'? . . . Illsley [*sic*] is extremely conciliatory for we took the entire plan into our own hands and simply left him proportions and interior comforts such as cupboard[s]."[52] Ilsley was the architect commissioned to design Arcady.[53] As one can surmise from Byrd's letter, his role was largely diminished in response to the Whiteheads's creative ideas about their new home. Another letter from Byrd was perhaps to her mother. It describes some of the grand interiors and fittings that Byrd and Whitehead designed:

> [Abalone shells] will be let into the chimney piece, all round probably there will be a border of "rough cast" outside the tiles, the chimney itself being of stone in Gothic shape, coming out into the room like the chimneys at Blois . . . . The chimney piece in the dining room took us ages to plan, but I think it will come out all right. It is very wide and has two seats inside it opposite each other of dark stained wood. The chimney breast projects into the room and has no mantel shelf on it, only built into it, is one large round Luca della Robbia Madonna of blue and white . . . . Canta Galli is sending it to us, with blue tiles to match around the hearth where the fire goes. The colouring of the room is the Morris blue and pink "honeysuckle" cretonne, like the big screen you know.[54]
>
> We are designing the end of this dining room with a view to your blue china . . . . There are cupboards in the wall with glass doors. I want it to have a worthy niche in which it will look to belong . . . . I want everything in the way of decoration to have a meaning and what has not a meaning, to be beautiful in the way of colour or form, and the forms of decoration I shall take as much as possible from the common things of the country, as in the case of the aboloni [*sic*] shells, Eucalyptus leaves, etc. I insist on Ilseley [*sic*] not giving us one commonplace stock machinery door and he complies very kindly.[55]

In this amazing letter, Byrd went on to describe their landscape design and plantings. She even included the names of specific plants. Byrd's description of interiors corresponds with period photographs of Arcady: the inset cabinets holding the blue china, and the chimney breast with the Luca della Robbia Madonna described in Byrd's letter (fig. 13).

Passages like this reveal a close relationship between the Arts and Crafts movement and Aesthetic movement. Often categorized as mutually exclusive by scholars today, these art movements were not segregated in the period. The Arts and Crafts movement is commonly identified with Will Price's phrase "the art that is life," which implies a desire for simplicity and morality in life, an appreciation for handcraftsmanship, and an avoidance of unnecessary or dishonest ornamentation. This corresponds with Byrd's wish to have "everything in the way of decoration to have a meaning and what has not a meaning, to be beautiful in the way of colour or form, and the forms of decoration I shall take as much as possible from the common things of the country."[56] On the other hand, the Aesthetic movement is related to Walter Pater's often quoted "art for art's sake"—an idea imbued with visions of rich interiors, exoticism, and even decadence. Byrd's description of period elements such as the Gothic shaped chimney and Renaissance Luca della Robbia rondelle alongside oriental-inspired blue and white ceramics and William Morris textiles evokes the artistic combinations associated with Aesthetic movement interiors. Byrd's words indicate that the Arts and Crafts movement and Aesthetic movement intertwined and overlapped in her lived experience—a view that corresponds with other writings from the period, such as the influential English illustrator, designer, and writer Walter Crane's passage on

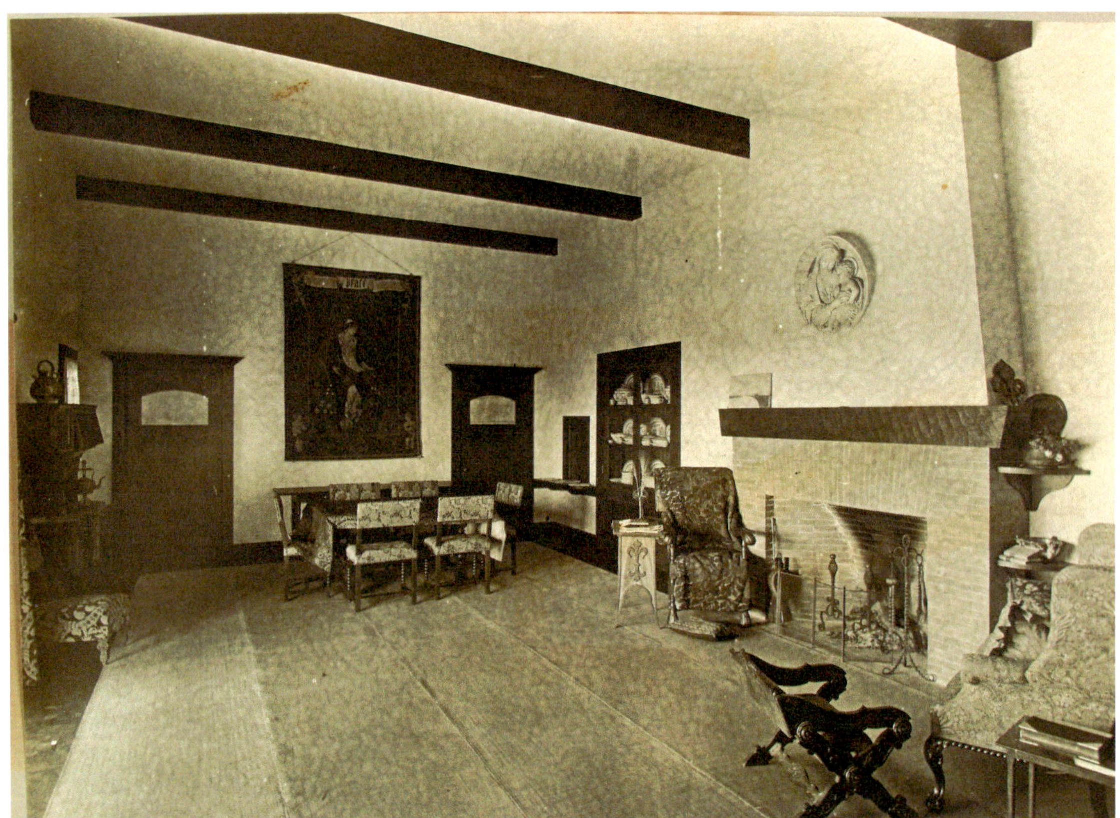

fig. 13 Ralph Whitehead, *Living Room at Arcady*, ca. 1895. Silver print. Winterthur Library, Downs Collection, 92x39.1140.327.

"simplicity and splendour" from his 1911 essay "The English Revival in the Decorative Arts." Crane wrote:

> The great advantage and charm of the Morrisian [reference to William Morris] method is that it lends itself to either simplicity or splendour. You might be almost plain enough to please Thoreau, with a rush-bottomed chair, piece of matting, and oaken trestle table, or you might have gold luster . . . gleaming from the sideboard, and jeweled light in your windows, and walls hung with rich arras tapestry.[57]

Period photographs illustrate that Arcady's interiors displayed both simplicity and splendor. Over time, Byrd and Whitehead's vision of what they called "the simple life" began to change, morphing from an image similar to that described by Crane, illustrated in the interiors at Arcady, into a more austere and rustic picture, which was realized at Byrdcliffe (fig. 14). In July 1900, Byrd wrote to Whitehead from Arcady:

> My dear Twin, Yes, let's talk about life. I think a good deal about the questions you have mentioned . . . . With [the occupation of writing] you can combine the principle of living like a peasant. Taken as we are at this time of life and in this house we could not carry it out very far but at any rate we can strive in that direction. Keeping early hours, eating simple food, and working the ground, as if it were someone else we were doing it for, which if done—without fretting—results in health.[58]

The "principle of living like a peasant" and the idea of "working the ground, as if it were someone else we were doing it for" seems humorous today, especially since it is coming from two people who enjoyed extremely sophisticated lives and never had to work for a living.[59] However, here we see early thinking about the rustic life that was realized at Byrdcliffe in the following two years.

As mentioned earlier, Byrd and Whitehead's eventual decision to leave Montecito and move to Woodstock was predicated on their wish to bring up their sons in a suitable location. In the same letter quoted above, Byrd goes on to say,

> After 6 or 8 or 10 years will come the other problem—I have to admit—Bimbi [Ralph Jr.] will then be beginning to feel the standards of life about him and be influenced by them. In the rare case of his being born an artist of some sort, there will be a quick and natural solution. We should take him to the old world where he could best develop and sacrifice our reasons for living here. But on the other hand he may not show any particular predilection for any one thing of that kind, and we wouldn't know what to do, because we would want to bring him up where he would eventually live and there is no career to be made in these parts in a business or professional way. We want to start him as a healthy animal for some years to come and this is in an ideal environment for that, but as there is a bare possibility that we may want to help him to become something more—a man and a soul—we shall have to keep in touch with Europe.
>
> I want to paint a little in the next few years. This and the housekeeping to say not of the boy and you, is as much as ever I can do, and I want to do it so that at the end—both at the end of the life phases, or at the end of life itself—I do not want to blush at the blank.[60]

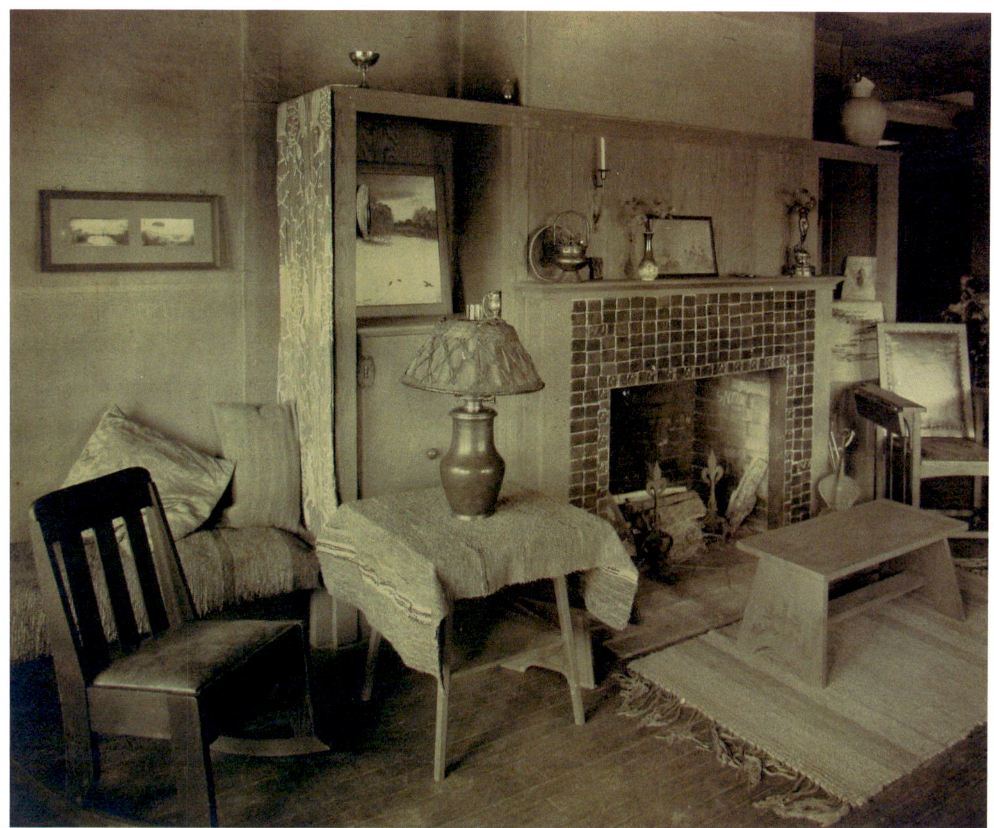

fig. 14 Jessie Tarbox Beals, *Living Hall at White Pines*, 1909. Silver print. Winterthur Library, Downs Collection, 92x39.1140.250.

The eloquent description in the above passage shows that Byrd was committed to three important aspects of her life: motherhood, her relationship with her husband, and her art. Amazingly, given the amount of energy it requires to do any one of these things, Byrd's tripartite focus on motherhood, being a wife, and art did not keep her from being a productive artist. Her desire to "not want to blush at the blank" is not typical of the stories of artists we are accustomed to. In the mind's eye, the term "artist" conjures an image of Leonardo da Vinci, Vincent van Gogh, Jackson Pollock—men with a devotion to their craft comparable to that of the relationship between a priest and God. In the case of van Gogh and Pollock, this devotion was so powerful that it was ultimately self-destructive. Even the few "great" women artists we read about in surveys of art in the Western world, people like Frida Kahlo or Georgia O'Keeffe, for example, are solitary figures. Both women were childless and maintained high levels of autonomy despite their marriages to the equally "great" artists Diego Rivera and Alfred Stieglitz, respectively.[61] Byrd's lived reality challenges our assumptions about artists. She helps us broaden our thinking about the lives they live and the art they produce.

During the Byrdcliffe years, Byrd worked in many diverse media, including weaving, basketry, furniture production, and pottery in addition to painting and design. Again, Byrd challenges our assumptions. Here, she problematizes hierarchies that privilege fine arts and relegate decorative art media, as well as those that showcase artists working in single media and a signature style. Her efforts in various art forms show the vital spirit of experimentation that is central to truly creative art. In order to give the reader a glimpse into the creative output of Byrd at Byrdcliffe, the remainder of this essay focuses on the art she made there through the end of the 1920s.

As at Arcady, Byrd played a significant role in the design and organization of the Byrdcliffe compound and art school. After leaving Montecito in October 1902, Byrd took up residence at a family camp in Aiken, South Carolina, before she moved to Byrdcliffe in February 1903.[62] In Aiken she started work on a frieze of pine trees for a pine tree room at Byrdcliffe. Her calendars and letters record her work on the frieze from December 10, 1902, to about February 27, 1903. In letters to Whitehead she described her preparation and execution of the frieze. In one letter, she wrote:

> I worked in pastel on a conventionalized frieze of pine trees. I found I cd. [could] get the result I was thinking of with [five] colours: 2 blues, 2 greens and a red brown. There is an upper sky, a lower sky, hills, near trees and far trees. Each mass of things having a flat tint and in some cases [*...unreadable...*] tints, one over another, for instance the lighter green of the farther trees coming down over the hills, under one tint of upper blue. The further trees having under their own tint a green one of the sky above. It was quite fun. The beauty of it will depend a good deal in the drawing.[63]

This letter and another description of the frieze, which mentions dye cards, seem to indicate that the frieze was meant to be a printed textile.[64] Byrd wrote that she was "sitting in pine tree room" at Byrdcliffe in April of her 1904 calendar. In October 1905, she recorded "Baskets at home in Pine tree room"; the room is mentioned two more times in December of that year. Unfortunately, the locations of the pine tree frieze and pine tree room are unknown.[65] If the frieze was printed on textile and applied to the burlap covered walls of White Pines—the Whitehead's home in Woodstock—or one of the other buildings at Byrdcliffe, it is no longer there or it remains undiscovered.

One of many additional references to Byrd's role in the design and decoration of Byrdcliffe was recorded in a February 1903 letter to Whitehead. In it she described a visit to her hometown of Philadelphia, where she met with her well-known cousin Henry Chapman Mercer, archaeologist, antiquarian, folklorist, and founder of the Moravian Tile Works in Doylestown, Pennsylvania.[66] Byrd's calendars, scrapbooks, and letters disclose that she had a close friendship with Mercer, and consulted him on design questions from time to time.[67] During her February 1903 visit to Mercer, she picked out tiles for a fireplace surround (fig. 15). Her letter to Whitehead describes the experience as follows:

> He [Mercer] had taken me all thro' his works in the afternoon and I had chosen a tile fire place of green blue oblong small bricks with occasional square tiles with a design on them. Two birds and a fleur-de-lys. I am almost certain you will like it and that I need not send you a sample.[68]

Apparently, Whitehead appreciated her choice, because the Mercer fireplace surround came to hold a prominent position in the living hall of their home White Pines, and it still stands there today. Slightly different in appearance from Byrd's description, the fireplace surround includes green-blue rectangular and square bricks rather than the oblong ones she mentions. The occasional tiles with designs she described picture the fleur-de-lys, as specified, and two rectangular bricks with "RW," Whitehead's initials[69] (fig. 16).

By December 1903, Byrd was busy on Byrdcliffe art projects. Her calendars record her staining "green furniture" and working on stained furniture between 1903 and 1905, the height of Byrdcliffe furniture production. Her participation on this project seemed to culminate in January and February 1905, when she wrote "staining sassafras," and "getting furniture ready." Based on her calendar notations, the furniture appears to have been exhibited February 7–9.[70] Pieces stained with a transparent green color and a cabinet with delicately carved panels featuring sassafras motifs are among the loveliest in the Byrdcliffe oeuvre (cat. 38). Here, Byrd's calendars provide evidence that she played an important role in the execution of the few pieces of furniture that were made at Byrdcliffe.

Weaving, basketry, painting, drawing, and design are other art forms in which Byrd engaged. Her 1906 calendar mentions weaving, working with "Miss Little" [Marie Little]—a notable textile artist employed at Byrdcliffe—and activity in the Loom Room. In fact, establishing the

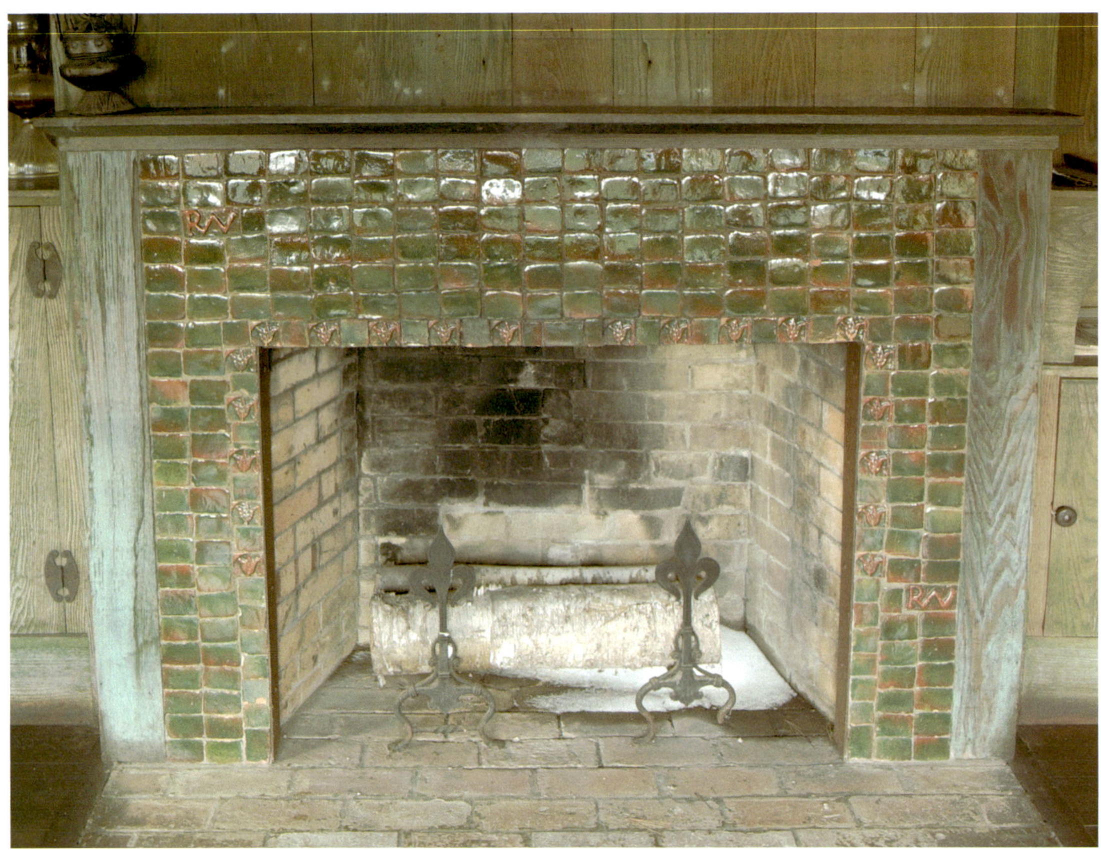

fig. 15 Henry Chapman Mercer, Moravian Tile Works, Fireplace surround, Living Hall, White Pines, 1903.

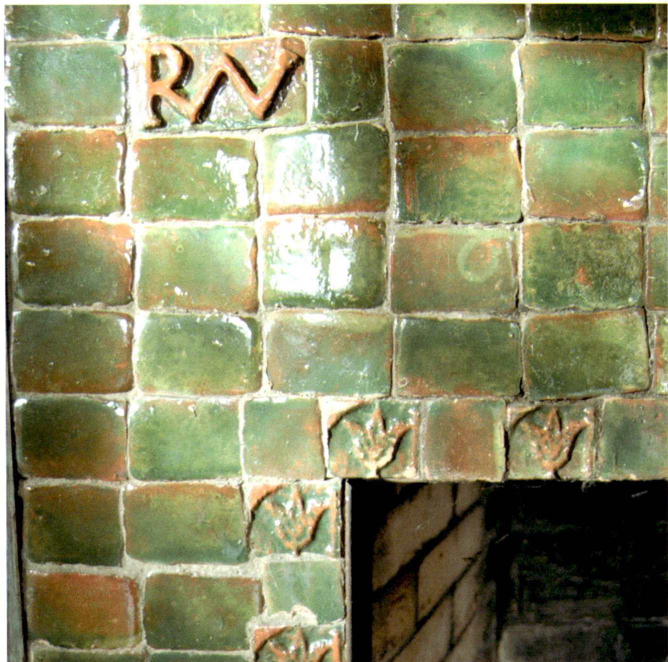

fig. 16 Henry Chapman Mercer, Moravian Tile Works. Fleur-de-lys and RW tile from fireplace surround (detail), Living Hall, White Pines, 1903.

loom room, and accomplishing "some good rugs and bags" are among the year's highlights listed at the end of the calendar. There are also notations about basket making, "arranging showrooms," "preparing for Onteora," and "ticketing weavings" that show Byrd's involvement went beyond craft practice to organization of exhibitions and sales.[71]

A letter from Byrd to Whitehead provides some information about her relationship to the weavings produced at Byrdcliffe:

> We had such a time with the blue warp on the little loom today! . . . Had to work for hours and when they were most confused, I had the lack of tact to give your message . . . saying that they might dye another warp if they got through with the one they had on. You can imagine that they felt a little pushed and I am telling you because you don't realize how long things take and how breathless it makes one to be told a shorter time rather than a longer time . . . for we think you expect so much more than you get.[72]

On one hand, we see Byrd working on the loom with Byrdcliffe craftspeople. She is very aware of the time considerations involved in weaving and dyeing. On the other hand, we see Whitehead removed from the scene; in this case, his request for faster production reveals little awareness of the craft itself.

Most Byrdcliffe scholarship describes weaving as the realm of Whitehead and Marie Little, with no mention of Byrd.[73] However, evidence in Byrd's personal papers leads one to speculate whether the award winning "finely coloured rugs and cushions" shown under Whitehead's name at the 1907 exhibition of the Society of Arts and Crafts in Boston were solely his work.[74] Perhaps Whitehead's name was attached to the weavings of other individuals or pieces prepared collaboratively with other people working in his studio. In this case, Whitehead's name may have been applied to weavings by his wife, and maybe even those by Marie Little.

While some women at Byrdcliffe and, more generally, women associated with the Arts and Crafts movement received published recognition for their work, it was not uncommon for women of Byrd's social status or women working in husband-and-wife teams to remain anonymous. Eileen Boris writes about this in her book *Art and Labor: Ruskin, Morris, and the Craftsman Ideal in America*:

> The arts and crafts movement provided some work for women although wives and daughters of craftsmen rarely gained individual recognition or their own wage. Uncredited female members of the Morris family and the Pre-Raphaelite circle executed much of the early needlework of the firm, and into the twentieth century, husband-wife teams would be known chiefly for the work of the man.[75]

With this in mind, it would not be surprising if some existing Byrdcliffe weavings may have been done by Byrd (cat. 158).

Pottery is first mentioned in Byrd's 1901 calendar, when she was still living in California. In 1908, she described a kiln on the grounds at Byrdcliffe. Slowly but steadily a growing passion for pottery is revealed in her calendars. By 1913, pottery appears to be her primary artistic occupation. From 1912 to 1914, she avidly worked on pottery and paintings for a eucalyptus collection, which seems to have been exhibited first in Woodstock in August 1913, and again in California in April 1914.[76]

It is fairly well known that Byrd was a student of the famous Arts and Crafts potter Frederick Hürten Rhead. Byrd's calendars suggest that she was studying with him by the end of 1913—a time when she was already fervently working on pottery and her eucalyptus series. Less well known are the connections between Byrd and other well known Arts and Crafts potters and potteries, which are documented in her calendars, correspondence, and business records. There are numerous entries discussing lessons with, and trips to Mrs. Warren at Dedham, Massachusetts (1904); Mrs. Crosse in Boston (1910); studies at Deerfield, Connecticut (1903); and pottery in New Orleans, including a visit to the Newcomb pottery at the women's division of Tulane University, the H. Sophie Newcomb Memorial College (1917).[77] Records of interaction with other individuals around the United States abound. This information is sure to intrigue scholars of Arts and Crafts ceramics.

Besides their interest value to people looking at individual potters and potteries, Byrd's records reveal a greater

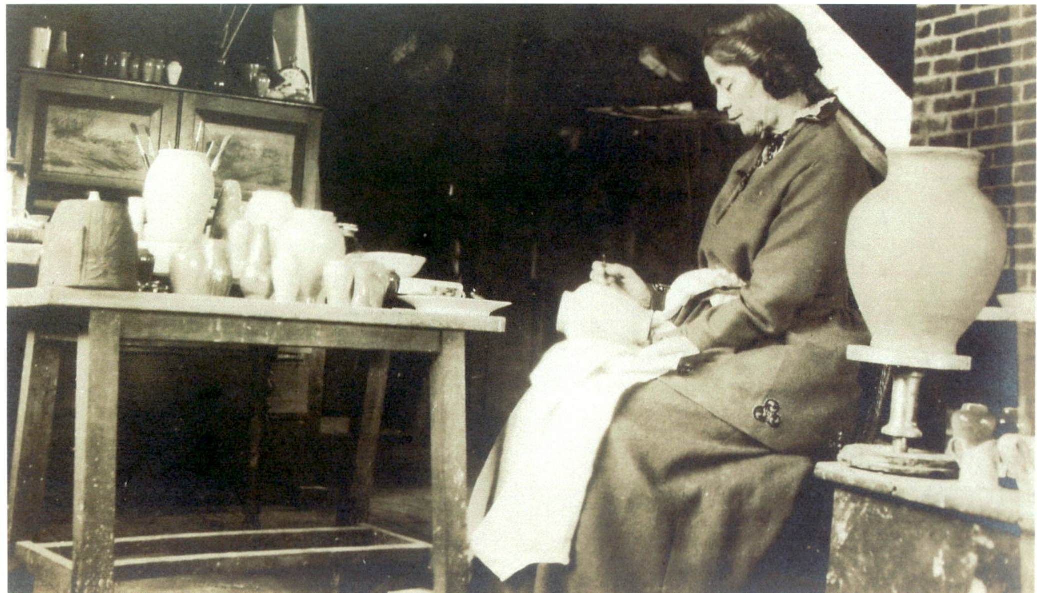

fig. 17 Attributed to Ralph Whitehead, *Byrd working on White Pines Pottery*, ca. 1913–25. Silver print. Winterthur Library, Downs Collection, 92x39.1140.233.

degree of interaction between regional Arts and Crafts potteries than is often recognized in scholarship from the present. This highlights a problem with traditional methods in art history which promote specialization and categorization of topics among experts, who are expected to be authorities on particular areas of knowledge. Consequently, we tend to see analyses of individuals or studies of distinct regional zones that often do not reflect attention to interaction, exchange, or joint efforts with other people and places. Byrd and Whitehead's pottery notes from 1921 to 1924 show that they consigned White Pines Pottery to galleries all over the United States, including the Woodstock Art Gallery, the galleries of the Society of Arts and Crafts in Boston, the Handicraft Club in Baltimore, the Crafter's Company in Cincinnati, the Pottery Shop on Madison Avenue in New York City, the Artist's Guild in Chicago, unnamed galleries in Cleveland, Ohio, and the Arden Gallery in Arden, Delaware.[78] In combination with information about her European contacts, Byrd's history underscores that a good number of people involved in the American Arts and Crafts movement were working closely with other advocates of Arts and Crafts around the United States and Europe.

fig. 18 Attributed to Jane Byrd McCall Whitehead, *Design Drawings of White Pines Pottery Markings*. Pencil. Winterthur Library, Downs Collection, 92x39.1505.

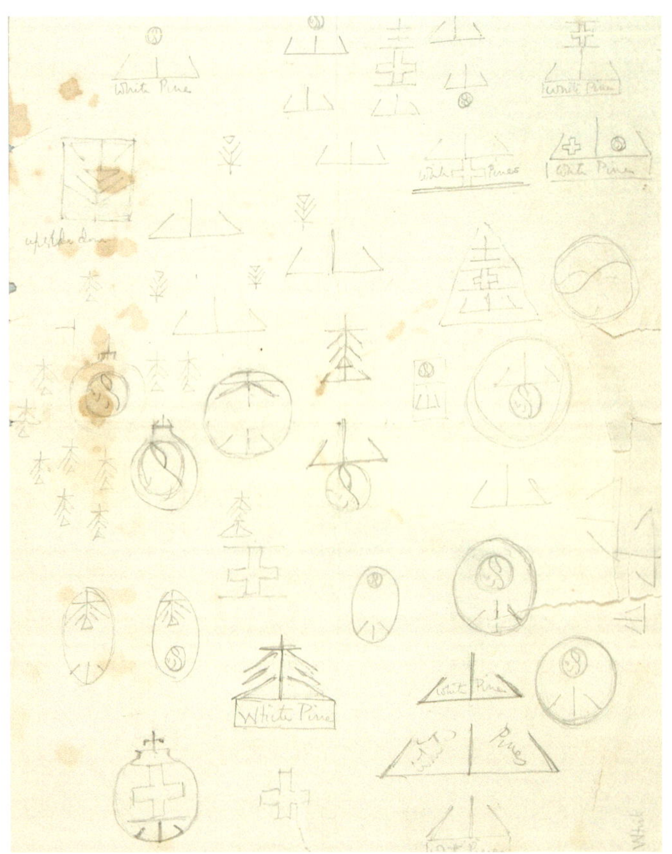

Byrd's efforts in ceramics are easier to document than the other media in which she worked. There are extensive records about her work as a potter in her calendars as well as in her correspondence. In addition, period photographs show her crafting in the pottery room she and Whitehead established in the attic of White Pines (fig. 17). A series of drawings for markings featured on White Pines Pottery are in Byrd's hand, indicating they are her designs[79] (fig. 18). Even secondary sources acknowledge her role in White Pines Pottery.[80]

Perhaps the most exciting piece of the "pottery by Byrd" story is the evidence that still exists in the pottery room at White Pines. In this room, one seems to have been transported back in time to the moment of the photograph. Shelves are loaded with pots; some are fired and glazed and appear to be finished works of art. The floor is covered with more pots, some unfired biscuit wares, and the plaster casts for molds. Jars of pigments, fluxes, and chemicals, along with rows of small tile glaze samples fill the room.

One pastel of eucalyptus leaves is still haphazardly tacked to the wall (fig. 19). While much has changed since the days when Byrd and Whitehead inhabited Byrdcliffe, the place still reflects their presence, helping one understand what they did there and the ways in which Byrdcliffe's art is tied to the location where it was made.

In 1929, her partner and husband Whitehead passed away shortly after the tragic death of their eldest son, Ralph Jr., in a shipwreck. Byrd continued to run Byrdcliffe until her death in 1955, when the property was left to her son Peter, and eventually to the Woodstock Guild. Some evidence suggests that Byrd added fine arts sculpture to her oeuvre in the 1930s.[81] However, this claim is merely speculative. As you can see from the sampling presented in this essay, Byrd's lifework in drawing, painting, design, woodwork, textile, and ceramic from the 1870s through the end of the twentieth century's first quarter is integral to the Byrdcliffe story. The challenges her life history presents to traditional Byrdcliffe history and that of the Arts and Crafts movement, as well as to our conception of what it means to be an artist, makes Byrd a figure from the past that resonates in the present.

fig. 19 Jane Byrd McCall Whitehead, Eucalyptus Image tacked to wall in White Pines Pottery Room, ca. 1913–14. Pastel.

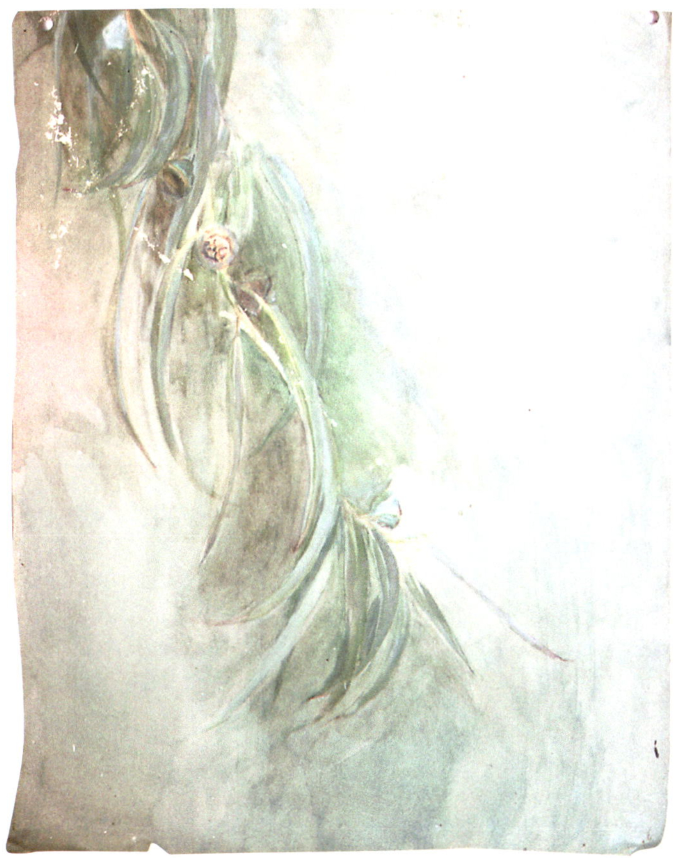

Notes

1. This essay is dedicated to the memory of my mentor and friend, Catherine Hoover Voorsanger, whose guidance, generosity, idealism, and high standards inspired me from the outset of our relationship. Many other generous individuals have aided the development of my work on Jane Byrd. I would especially like to acknowledge and thank Mark Willcox Jr., Jane Byrd's descendant; my mother and father, Marilyn and Sven-Åke Nässtrõm; my husband and daughter, Doug and Hanna Evans; my teacher and dissertation advisor, Mary Corbin Sies; Jeanne Solensky, Laura Parrish, and Rich McKinstry at the Joseph Downs Collection at Winterthur Museum, Garden & Library; Neville Thompson, Gretchen Buggeln, Pat Elliott, Gary Kulik and Lisa Lock also at Winterthur; Carla Smith at the Woodstock Guild; art historian Gabriel Weisberg; Nancy Green, who invited me to contribute to this catalogue; Cheryl Robertson, Robert Edwards, Tom Wolf, and Ellen Denker, colleagues on the Byrdcliffe Centenary exhibition project. Finally, thanks to Woodstock, whose natural beauty continues to inspire people and connect kindred spirits throughout the ages. For my additional thinking on Jane Byrd, see my forthcoming doctoral dissertation, which is being written in the American Studies Department at University of Maryland at College Park under the advisory of Dr. Mary Corbin Sies. For my other work on this topic, see "Rethinking the Arts and Crafts Movement in America: Substance and Method," comprehensive exam in material culture studies, Department of American Studies, University of Maryland at College Park (March 2002); "Feminist Art Criticism and Jane Byrd McCall Whitehead (1861–1955): A Conceptual Framework," research paper, Women's Studies 611, University of Maryland at College Park (May 2001); "Upper-Class American Women in the Arts, and Their Social Norms in the Late Nineteenth Century: An Annotated Bibliography Informing the Early Life of Jane Byrd McCall Whitehead," American Studies 602, University of Maryland at College Park (May 2001); "Jane Byrd McCall Whitehead, Byrdcliffe, and Arts and Crafts Movement Scholarship," review article, American Studies 628Q, University of Maryland at College Park (December 2000).
2. Research on the early years of Jane's life is included in my forthcoming doctoral dissertation.
3. A photograph of Jane as a young girl pictures her with the Alard children in Switzerland and a letter from Whitehead suggests that Jane was "brought up in Europe." See photograph of Jane, ca. early 1870s, inscribed on verso "Jeanie McCall/& the Alard children/Vevey Swiss," marked "Photographie/F. De Jongh/Entre dues villes/Vevey," Winterthur Library, Downs Collection, 92 x 39.1140.42; and letter, May 13, 1902, Winterthur Library, Downs Collection.
4. McCall Scrapbook 1883–90. Winterthur Library, Downs Collection 92 x 39.1158.
5. It appears that Jane befriended the Müllers before she met and married Whitehead. This is important because it means that Jane had connections to Oxford and its intellectual and artistic elite prior to her marriage.
6. Newspaper clipping, unidentified newspaper, Wednesday, June 3, 1886. McCall Scrapbook, 1883–90. Winterthur Library, Downs Collection 92 x 39.1158.
7. Maureen Montgomery writes about American women seeking aristocratic European husbands in *Gilded Prostitution: Status, Money, and Transatlantic Marriages, 1870–1914* (London and New York: Routledge, 1989) and *Displaying Women: Spectacle of Leisure in Edith Wharton's New York* (London and New York: Routledge, 1998).
8. For more on Whitehead's origins and life in Europe, see Nancy Green's essay in this exhibition catalogue.
9. These dates are based on Nancy Green's notes from Jane's 1885 calendar. Winterthur Library, Downs Collection.
10. In 1985, Robert Edwards wrote about Jane and Whitehead's meeting in Serbelloni, Italy in 1891. See Robert Edwards, "The Utopias of Ralph Radcliffe Whitehead," *Antiques* 127 (January 1985): 264.
11. Leon Legrange quoted in Tamar Garb, "'Men of Genius, Women of Taste': The Gendering of Art Education in Late Nineteenth-Century Paris," in Gabriel Weisberg and Jane Becker, eds., *Overcoming All Obstacles: The Women of the Académie Julian* (New York and New Brunswick, NJ: The Dahesh Museum and Rutgers University Press, 1999), 117–18.
12. For more on women's restricted access to professional arts education and the gendered nature of the education available to them at

the end of the nineteenth century, see Garb, "Men of Genius, Women of Taste: Gendering of Art Education," 115–33.

13. For more on Dow and his connections to Byrdcliffe, see Nancy Green and Jessie Poesch, *Arthur Wesley Dow and American Arts and Crafts* (New York: The American Federation of Art, 1999); Nancy Green's essay "Arthur Wesley Dow, Artist and Educator" (55–86) is especially recommended.

14. Alf Evers, *Woodstock: History of an American Town* (Woodstock, NY: The Overlook Press, 1987), 426, 429.

15. Jane's calendars from 1894–1906 include many references to lessons and corrections with Harrison. These took place in California and Woodstock. Winterthur Library, Downs Collection.

16. Nancy Green, "Arthur Wesley Dow, Artist and Educator," 70. See also Marilee Boyd, et al., *Inspiring Reform: Boston's Arts and Crafts Movement* (Wellesley, MA: Davis Museum and Cultural Center, 1997), 28. The letter inscribed "Indianapolis. May 6, 1902" from RRW to Jane mentions Dow's Ipswich Summer School. Winterthur Library, Downs Collection.

17. For more on Byrdcliffe students and teachers, see Alf Evers, *Woodstock*, 427–28, and Nancy Green, "Arthur Wesley Dow, Artist and Educator," 62, 65, 67, 71.

18. References to the *Morning Stars Sang Together* book are found in several dated and undated letters from Jane to RRW: letter inscribed "July 22nd. 11 a.m.," letter inscribed "Aug. 7th. Home," letter inscribed "August 12th. Arcady," 1900–01; letter inscribed "Arcady. 18th," letter inscribed "June 30th. Arcady. Sta. Barbara," no years given. Winterthur Library, Downs Collection. Related unsigned and undated paintings include: vellum covered book with landscape drawings (92x39.1546); oil painting of a landscape with a lone tree (92x39.269); oil painting on canvas of a sunset and a crescent moon (92x39.260); oil painting on canvas (mounted on cardboard) of a shore scene (92x39.268). Winterthur Library, Downs Collection.

19. Jane to RRW, "August 12, Arcady," 1900–01; Jane to RRW, April 2, 1902. Winterthur Library, Downs Collection.

20. Anthea Callen, *Women Artists of the Arts and Crafts Movement, 1870–1914* (New York: Pantheon Books, 1979), 9. For more on feminist interpretations of the Arts and Crafts movement, see Heidi Nasstrom Evans, "Feminist Art Criticism and Jane Byrd McCall Whitehead (1861–1955): A Conceptual Framework," and "Upper-Class American Women in the Arts, and Their Social Norms in the Late Nineteenth Century: An Annotated Bibliography Informing the Early Life of Jane Byrd McCall Whitehead."

21. Robert Edwards, conversation with author, Glen Mills, Pennsylvania (February 1, 2002).

22. The firescreen is documented in a letter from RRW to Jane, December 12, 1891; Jane to RRW, "23rd Feb.–March," 1902. Winterthur Library, Downs Collection. Also see Robert Edwards, "The Utopias of Ralph Radcliffe Whitehead," *Antiques* (January 1985): 270.

23. Mark Willcox Jr., telephone conversation with author, June 19, 2002. The tiles are currently in a private collection.

24. RRW to Jane, n.d. [January–February 1892]. Winterthur Library, Downs Collection.

25. Charlotte Gere and Michael Whiteway, *Nineteenth-Century Design: From Pugin to Mackintosh* (New York: Harry N. Abrams, 1994), 206.

26. Sketch of two boys sitting on stools playing flute-like musical instruments (92 x 39.280). Winterthur Library, Downs Collection.

27. Calendar entries from November 1, 1892, and February 12–18, 1893. Winterthur Library, Downs Collection.

28. Gabriel Weisberg, "The Women of the Académie Julian: The Power of Professional Emulation," in Weisberg and Becker, eds., *The Women of the Académie Julian*, 13–67.

29. *Ibid.*, 16. Two photographs of women in the 5, rue de Berri atelier are featured on page 17 of Weisberg's essay "The Women of the Académie Julian"—Jane is not visible in either picture.

30. This painting is pictured in Weisberg's essay, "Women of the Académie Julian," 18. Conversations with Robert Edwards helped me develop my thinking on the Académie Julian link to photographs of sketches of nude boy models in Jane's studio.

31. Allen Staley, "Byrdcliffe and the Maverick: A Discursion in the Arts and Crafts" (master's thesis, Yale University, 1960), 14. Staley drew the quoted passage about Jane from Anita Smith, *Woodstock History and Hearsay* (Saugerties, NY: Catskill Mountains Publishing Corporation, 1959), 46.

32. Lucy Brown, "The First Summer in Byrdcliffe," *Publications of the Woodstock Historical Society (PWHS)* 2 (August 1930): 16–17; Birge Harrison and Harry Leith-Ross, "Birge Harrison, 1855–1929," *PWHS* 4 (July 1931): 30–34; Carl Eric Lindin, "The Woodstock Landscape," *PWHS* 7 (July 1932): 14–25; Bertha Thompson, "The Craftsmen of Byrdcliffe" and Hervey White, "Ralph Radcliffe Whitehead," *PWHS* 10 (July 1933): 8–13, 14–29; Bolton Brown, "Early Days," and Carl Eric Lindin, "Bolton Brown," *PWHS* 13 (August–September 1937): 13–14, 15–16.

33. Jane to RRW, April 2–3, 1891. Winterthur Library, Downs Collection.

34. Calendar entries from January 1891 [located in 1889 calendar], and 1891 Highlights [located in 1886 calendar], Winterthur Library, Downs Collection; Jane to RRW, April 2–3, 1891. Winterthur Library, Downs Collection.

35. Jane's health was poor from the 1870s until her move with Whitehead to California in 1894, where it slowly improved.

36. RRW to Jane, December 6, 1892. Winterthur Library, Downs Collection.

37. RRW to Jane, January 3, 1892. Winterthur Library, Downs Collection.

38. RRW to Jane, n.d. [January–February 1892]. Winterthur Library, Downs Collection.

39. RRW to Jane, "Friday morning" [January–February 1892]. Winterthur Library, Downs Collection.

40. Drawings of decorative initials. Winterthur Library, Downs Collection, 92 x 39.1503 – .1534.

41. Ralph Radcliffe Whitehead, "Pictures for School," *Arrows of the Dawn*, no. 3 (Montecito, 1901): dedication page.

42. According to December 2, 2003, e-mail correspondence with art historian Gabriel Weisberg, Miss Mercier may have been related to the French academic painter named Mercie. In this case the spelling of Miss Mercier is incorrect in Jane's calendars.

43. Jane to RRW, April 2–3, 1891. Winterthur Library, Downs Collection.

44. RRW to Jane, January 25 [possibly 1891]. Winterthur Library, Downs Collection. Whitehead met Jane in Colorado in the spring of 1892. It appears they traveled to Colorado Springs, Aspen, Santa Barbara, and San Francisco through June 1892 when they headed back east to be married.

45. It is possible that Jane and Whitehead knew Lummis through Charles Eliot Norton, a Harvard professor and founding member of the Society of Arts and Crafts, Boston. Both Lummis and Hervey White, one of Byrdcliffe's founders, studied with Norton at Harvard. Another potential point of contact may have been through Norton and the Whiteheads' affiliation with the Society of Arts and Crafts, Boston. In addition, like Jane and Whitehead, Norton was a friend of Ruskin. For more on Norton, see Beverly Brandt's doctoral dissertation *Mutually Helpful Relations: Architects, Craftsmen, and The Society of Arts and Crafts, Boston, 1897–1917* (Boston University, 1985) and Edward S. Cooke Jr.'s "Talking and Working: The conundrum of Moral Aesthetics in Boston's Arts and Crafts Movement" in *Inspiring Reform: Boston's Arts and Crafts Movement* (Davis Museum and Cultural Center, 1997), 19–24.

46. Charles Lummis quoted in Chris Wilson, *The Myth of Santa Fe, Creating a Modern Regional Tradition* (Albuquerque: University of New Mexico Press, 1997), 87–89. The racist overtones of this passage correspond with pseudoscientific theories of the period, including social Darwinism. Although the racism implicit in these ideas is important to address, it is beyond the scope of this essay.

47. Jane to RRW, "Jan. 7–12, Montecito" [1891–95]. Winterthur Library, Downs Collection.

48. See the passage from Whitehead's December 1891 letter on page 63. Despite the numerous paintings and studies that are recorded in her personal papers, very few paintings by Jane are known to exist. Therefore, the recent discovery of her signed 1891 landscape mentioned is especially important (cat. 79).

49. The website Art.Magick mentions that Aman-Jean was known for languid profile poses of women (http://www.artmagick.com/artists/aman.aspx, accessed November 11, 2003). It has been my observation in studies of Jane and Alice Pike Barney, another wealthy American painter who studied in Paris, that Aman-Jean attracted wealthy American women as pupils. See Heidi Nasstrom Evans, "Cultural Landscape Study: Alice Pike Barney Studio House," research paper, American Studies 629L, University of Maryland at College Park (January 2000).

50. Art historian Gabriel Weisberg—an expert on French academic painting from the fin de siècle—did not see stylistic similarities

between the anonymous portraits of Jane and the work of Aman-Jean (Gabriel Weisberg, e-mail conversation with author, December 1, 2003).

51. Calendar entries from May 1896. Winterthur Library, Downs Collection.

52. Jane to RRW, n.d. ["Saturday 12th–19th"] Winterthur Library, Downs Collection. For more on the architecture Jane and Whitehead developed on the West and East Coasts, see Cheryl Robertson's essay in this catalogue.

53. According to Robert Edwards, Samuel Illsley is the spelling of the name of Arcady's architect. See Robert Edwards, "Byrdcliffe: Life by Design," in *Life by Design: The Byrdcliffe Arts and Crafts Colony* (Wilmington: Delaware Art Museum, 1984), 5.

54. This is the same screen pictured and described in figure 9; see also catalogue number 19.

55. Jane to RRW, "23rd Feb.–March" [1894?]. Winterthur Library, Downs Collection.

56. *Ibid.*

57. Walter Crane, "The English Revival in the Decorative Arts," in Walter Crane, *William Morris to Whistler: Papers and Addresses on Art and Craft and the Commonweal* (London: G. Bell, 1911). Anne O'Donnell shared Crane's passage with me.

58. Jane to RRW, July 14, 1900. Winterthur Library, Downs Collection.

59. *Ibid.*

60. *Ibid.*

61. Notably, both Diego Rivera and Alfred Stieglitz worked diligently to promote the artistic careers of their wives. One wonders whether Kahlo and O'Keeffe would be as well known today if it were not for the efforts of their husbands. Their example underscores the way many of the "great" women artists we read about today had important relationships with supportive male figures who handled the business end of their careers. In the case of Kahlo and O'Keeffe, their use of male promoters probably illustrates the lingering potency of gendered public and private spheres discussed earlier in this essay.

62. February 8, 1903, is the date of Jane's move to Woodstock. It is documented in her calendar from that year. See calendar 1903, Winterthur Library, Downs Collection.

63. Jane to RRW, undated letter with corresponding envelope postmarked January 21 and January 23, 1903, Aiken, South Carolina. Winterthur Library, Downs Collection.

64. Jane to RRW, "27th Feb." [1903–9]. Winterthur Library, Downs Collection.

65. Carla Smith, conversation with author, White Pines, Byrdcliffe, Woodstock, New York (June 13, 2002).

66. Bert and Ellen Denker describe Mercer's occupations in "Tile setting: The Arkansas Traveler," Catalogue 212, in Wendy Kaplan, et al., *"The Art That is Life": The Arts and Crafts Movement in America, 1875–1920* (Boston: Museum of Fine Arts Boston, 1987), 388–90.

67. An 1889 trip with Mercer through the Loire Valley is recorded in Jane's scrapbook and calendars. Also, in a passage in the 1892 letter discussed in endnote 33, Jane tells Whitehead she has heard from Mercer about some designs she requested from him. See McCall Scrapbook; calendar from 1889; and Jane to RRW, "Friday morning" [January–February 1892]. Winterthur Library, Downs Collection.

68. Jane to RRW, "23rd of Feb." [1903–9]. Winterthur Library, Downs Collection.

69. Thanks to Nancy Green for noticing the differences between the actual fireplace surround and the one described in Jane's letter.

70. Calendar from 1903 and 1905, Winterthur Library, Downs Collection. For more on Byrdcliffe furniture, see Robert Edwards's essay in this catalogue.

71. Calendar from 1906, Winterthur Library, Downs Collection. For references to Onteora, see calendar entries from August 14–15, 1906. Jane's 1907 calendar is missing from the Downs Collection. Its earliest entries may include some valuable insight into the authorship of the weavings shown under Whitehead's name at the Society of Arts and Crafts in Boston exhibition on February 5–26, 1907. Jane's mention of Onteora is one of many references of her interaction with Candace Wheeler and her daughter, who is described as "Miss Wheeler" in Jane's calendars. Miss Wheeler may be Wheeler's youngest daughter, Dora, who was a painter and designer of textiles. On Dora Wheeler, see Catherine Hoover Voorsanger, Candace Wheeler entry, "Dictionary of Architects, Artisans, Artists, and Manufacturers" in Doreen Bolger Burke, et al., *In Pursuit of Beauty: Americans and the Aesthetic Movement* (New York: The Metropolitan Museum of Art and Rizzoli, 1987), 482. Karal Ann Marling describes Onteora Park as "a cottage colony for city dwellers in comfortable circumstances with a desire to retreat to the woods to meditate on art, nature, and society" that was founded around 1883 ("Heavens on Earth," *Woodstock: An American Art Colony, 1902–1977,* Vassar College Art Gallery, 1977). For some of the latest thinking on Wheeler, see Amelia Peck and Carol Irish, *Candace Wheeler: The Art and Enterprise of American Design, 1875–1900* (New York: The Metropolitan Museum of Art, 2001).

72. Jane to RRW, n.d. ["Tuesday night"] Winterthur Library, Downs Collection.

73. For example, see Evers, *Woodstock*, 429; and Edwards, "The Utopias of Ralph Radcliffe Whitehead," 272.

74. See Eva Lovett, "The Exhibition of the Society of Arts and Crafts Boston," *The International Studio* 31 (March 1907): 29. Byrdcliffe business records document that weavings were sent to the Society of Arts and Crafts in Boston in 1907. For information on the weavings sent to Boston and other Arts and Crafts venues and individuals, see endnote 78 in this essay.

75. Eileen Boris, *Art and Labor: Ruskin, Morris, and the Craftsman Ideal in America* (Philadelphia: Temple University Press, 1986), 18.

76. See calendars from 1901, 1904, 1908, 1912–14. Winterthur Library, Downs Collection.

77. RRW to Ralph Jr., February 23, 1917, New Orleans. Winterthur Library, Downs Collection. "Mother came along here with me because she wanted to see the Newcomb Pottery which is in the University here. They do some very good work & mother is satisfied to have made the long journey, 22 hours for the purpose." Thanks to Nancy Green for sharing her notes about this letter.

78. Pottery Notes and Dyeing and Weaving Information, Box 2A, and Pottery Notes, 1921–23 (.1154), Winterthur Library, Downs Collection. Arden is a utopian community that was founded in 1900 by sculptor Frank Stephens and architect Will Price. For more information on Arden, see Mark Taylor, "Art, Craft and the Utopian Ideal: Arden, Delaware, 1900–35" (Wilmington: Delaware Art Museum, 2000). Byrdcliffe business records on the sale of weavings from 1905–21 include many additional Arts and Crafts venues and names of individuals with whom Jane and Whitehead were in contact. See Byrdcliffe business records, 1905–21, and Ledger of Weavings Sold, 1907–11, Winterthur Library, Downs Collection. The following names are in the same order they appear in the Byrdcliffe business records. Some entries incorporate addresses and dates, which are included here: Society of Arts and Crafts Detroit; National Society of Craftsmen, Art Club Studios, 119–121 East 19th Street, New York; Louise Garden Arts and Crafts Work, St. Louis; Arts and Crafts Studio, 811 Vermont Avenue, Washington, DC; The Arts and Crafts Society, Room 208, Altman Building, Kansas City; The Crafters Company Cincinnati, 142 Fourth Avenue, East; Boston Arts and Crafts (1907); Detroit Society of Arts and Crafts, 1 Knowlson Building, 22 Farmer Street (1907); Miss Katharine Dillon, Toledo, Ohio, (1907); National Society of Craftsmen, New York (9/19/1908, 11/13/1908, 11/24/1908); Mrs. F Guild, Santa Barbara (January 12, 1909); Mrs. Thayer, Boston (February 2, 1910); Mrs. John Cuyler, Princeton (May 19, 1910); W. M. R. French, Chicago Art Institute (October 1910); Edna Walker, Colony Club.

79. See Drawings for Logos for White Pines. Winterthur Library, Downs Collection 92x39.1505.

80. For secondary sources on pottery from Byrdcliffe, see Ellen Denker's essay in this exhibition catalogue, and Jane Perkins Claney, "White Pines Pottery: the continuing arts and crafts experiment," in *Life By Design*, 15–20.

81. A bust of a woman's head in a private collection is possibly from the 1930s. It is marked with the initials "JBMc." Because of the marking and its acquisition in the Woodstock area, it is tempting to consider an attribution to Jane.

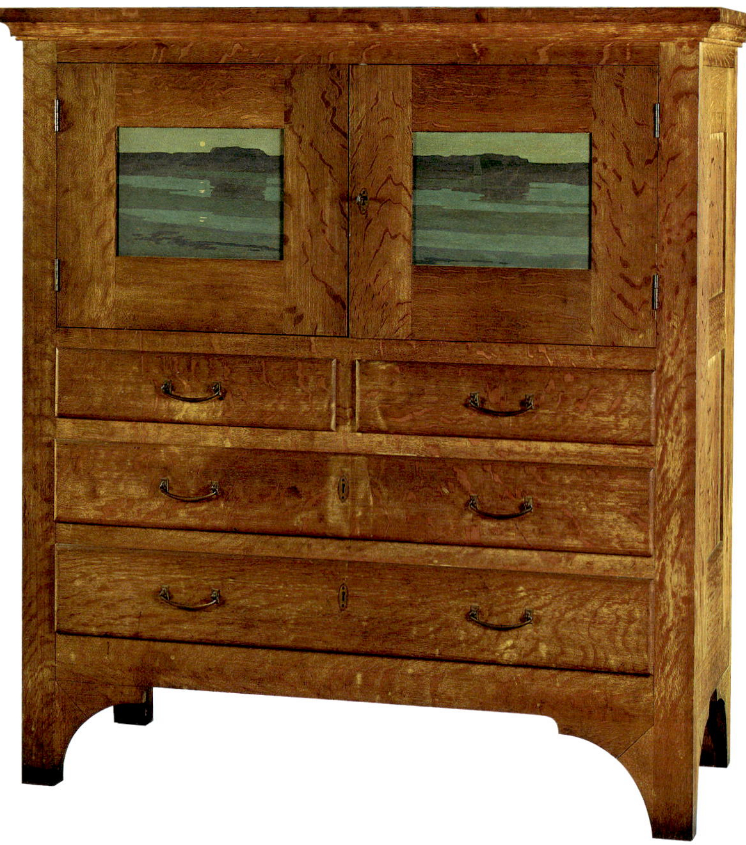

fig. 1 Linen Press. Oak with polychrome panels painted in the style of Dawson Dawson-Watson. Private collection. Courtesy of Christie's Images Limited.

Byrdcliffe Furniture

Imagination Versus Reality

ROBERT EDWARDS

The Arts and Crafts movement is generally conceded to have been spawned in Great Britain where it evolved from the thinking of people like Charles Eastlake (1836–1906) and A. W. N. Pugin (1812–1852) through the codifying theories of John Ruskin (1819–1900) and William Morris (1834–1896) into the later phase where designers like C. R. Ashbee and Earnest Gimson (1864–1919) tested their ideas with practical experimentation. The movement developed in the United States in a chronologically parallel sequence. Englishman Ruskin and American Walt Whitman (1819–93) were born in the same year and had a significant influence on Ralph Radcliffe Whitehead. There was much cross-fertilization as is evidenced by the Byrdcliffe Arts and Crafts colony and, most particularly, in the furniture made there.

It is estimated that fewer than fifty pieces of furniture were made at the woodworking shop of the Byrdcliffe Arts and Crafts colony (fig. 1). Most of it was produced in the short period of time between the fall of 1903 and the summer of 1905. This was a very small, short-lived enterprise that got little notice in its day, when ideologically similar furniture makers like Gustav Stickley (1858–1952) and Elbert Hubbard (1856–1915) were starting their grandiose promotional schemes.[1] Eventually Stickley and Hubbard would produce thousands of pieces of furniture, and smaller makers like Charles Rohlfs (1853–1936) would make hundreds. These American furniture makers espoused the Arts and Crafts version of the simple life as an aid to marketing just as they added symbols of Arts and Crafts construction, like the use of quartered oak and exposed mortise and tenons, so the consumer could easily identify their products. Their furniture was exhibited at world's fairs and expositions that were important advertising venues. It was featured in the showrooms of retail stores across the United States. Illustrations of their work salted dozens of magazines and books about interior decoration. They were even recognized in design books decades after their style was no longer popular. In contrast, Byrdcliffe furniture enjoyed no such fashion. A survey of hundreds of turn-of-the-century shelter and design periodicals and dozens of books about domestic design and taste turns up not a single reference to the furniture of

Byrdcliffe. Yet decades later, as we examine the Arts and Crafts movement, this ignored group of furniture provides much important information about decorative arts at the turn of the century, in particular the melding of the British and American versions of the Arts and Crafts movement as it happened at Byrdcliffe.

A moral tone saturates the theories of reform in the Arts and Crafts movement. Efforts to redefine beauty as an essential goodness that could transform one's life led directly to experiments in living such as the Byrdcliffe colony. The authors of nineteenth-century concepts of "reform," "beauty," and "goodness" were so convincing that their ideas are now often conflated with "progressive," "modern," or "high quality." In practice, reform usually results in mere change; there is no right or correct definition of beauty, and objects can't represent goodness. Still, by its very name, the Byrdcliffe Arts and Crafts colony purported to manifest these essentially romantic ideals.

Despite their high hopes, none of the Arts and Craftsmen, from William Morris to Gustav Stickley, managed to make their furniture meet their written ideals, yet their obsession with the potential saving grace of aesthetics did result in furniture that looked different from what was generally marketed at the time. By the late nineteenth century, there were many arbiters of taste, Arts and Crafts and otherwise, who railed against the "bad taste of the rich" and the dragon-carved, quartered-oak furniture that poured out of manufacturing centers like Grand Rapids to furnish the new houses of the middle class.[2] All attempted to guide consumers with a rigid code of beauty, yet their cry for good taste allowed for many styles, from American "Colonial" to eighteenth-century French. Therefore, analysis of Arts and Crafts concepts of beauty is not a particularly helpful way to understand the movement. An objective checklist of the ways the furniture of the Byrdcliffe Arts and Crafts colony relates to the principles of the movement provides better perspective and clarification.

Wordsmiths like John Ruskin, Frank Lloyd Wright (1867–1959), and Ralph Radcliffe Whitehead preached about the nature of Nature in design, but there was no difference in the way adherents to Arts and Crafts philosophy designed decorations for furniture and the way Persians designed patterns for tiles centuries before. Even such wildly stylized modes as Gothic or Rococo use the forms of nature in a way that is visually indistinguishable from the way of William Morris or Arthur Wesley Dow. Arts and Crafts proselytizers certainly influenced people who designed and made objects at the turn of the last century, but the philosophy's extreme idealization is seldom found in actual Arts and Crafts production. The romantic notion that wood should be used so as to recall nature and thus ought to be indigenous is not credible. Once a piece of wood is cut into the geometric shape of a board, its connection to the tree can only be intellectually understood and is not universally perceivable. A highly carved Rose Valley table designed by Philadelphia architect William Lightfoot Price (1861–1916) doesn't bring to mind the majestic oak from which its wood was harvested. However, if you read Price, you will learn that he thinks the table embodies many Arts and Crafts ideas: the Gothic style is supposed to remind one of days when handcraftsmanship was the only option. The dark stain also alludes to ancient oak—not as the tree grew, but as antique furniture would look hundreds of years after it was made. You would also have to read to know the table was made in an Arts and Crafts community founded by Price and it is held together with joinery that Price deemed honest because it wasn't dependent on modern factory technology.[3] The various Stickley brothers used quartered oak for most of their furniture as a way to meet Ruskin's call for indigenous materials, but the same wood had for decades before been so much used that it became synonymous with the cheapest furniture American factories had to offer.[4]

Ralph Radcliffe Whitehead was a fervent apostle of the word as written by Ruskin and Morris, but he does not seem to have insisted on a purely Arts and Crafts language for Byrdcliffe furniture. Most Arts and Craftsmen sought to place craft and fine art on the same level. As early as 1892, Whitehead made it clear that he didn't have the same esteem for the mere craftsmen who would make the furniture as he did for the artist who would design it. When describing his dreamed-of Arts and Crafts colony he wrote, "*Now*, in order to have anything good made in stuff, or in hard material, we must seek out the artist to provide us with a design, and then a workman to carry it out as mechanically as possible, because we know that if he puts any of his coarser self into it he will spoil it."[5] The furniture was eventually made at Byrdcliffe just as Whitehead wanted. The emphasis on the artist/designer is evident in a chiffonier with door panels painted by Hermann Dudley Murphy (cat. 20). This little cabinet has been exhibited and published so much during the past two decades that many consider it to be the masterpiece of Byrdcliffe furniture production. Yet this is due to Murphy's fame beyond Byrdcliffe and the beauty of his easel paintings[6] (cats. 67 and 68). The "workman" who built the cabinet remains unknown. It is not likely that the oak used in Byrdcliffe furniture came from the hills around Woodstock. Theorists like Ruskin, Stickley, and Price wrote much about "honest" joinery by which they meant that the way furniture was constructed should be obvious and "structural." The only such detail on the Murphy chiffonier is the hand-cut dovetails hidden in the drawers. The once vibrant green stain of the case and the oil paintings on wooden panels are fragile and vulnerable, rendering it less useful than the Morris edict "Have nothing in your house that you do not know to be useful or believe to be beautiful"[7] demanded. The obvious defense would be the chiffonier is beautiful, but I interpret Morris to mean that furnishings must be *both* useful and beautiful. Most Arts and Crafts theorists wanted an object to be handmade by a single craftsman, but the graceful hardware on this piece was not handmade in the Byrdcliffe metal shop. The paintings as used violate a basic principle established by Pugin and espoused by William Morris himself. They thought two-dimensional patterns were the only type appropriate

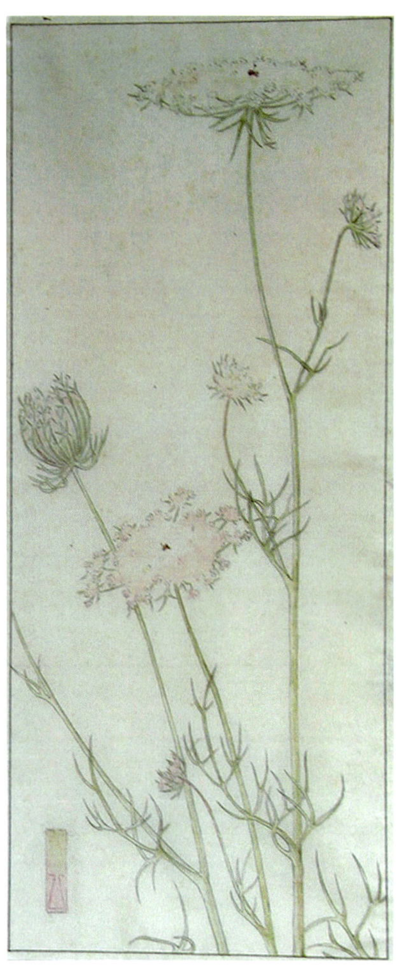

fig. 2 Zulma Steele, Rendering of "Wild Carrot" cabinet. Graphite and watercolor. Private collection. Courtesy of the author.

for application to decorative arts.[8] Murphy conceived the two panels as one composition—a river runs through it, apparently right behind the door frames and into a faraway horizon, which belies the utilitarian storage space concealed behind the doors (see fig. 16).

At first glance, atmospheric blue landscapes like Murphy's that were set into some Byrdcliffe cabinets (fig. 2) might seem to be the result of Arthur Wesley Dow's teachings. In fact, blue, moonlit landscapes had been fashionable among a certain circle of artists for at least a decade before Dow's book *Composition* was first published in 1899. Jane Whitehead bought a blue, nocturnal seascape from Birge Harrison (cat. 63) as a birthday surprise for her husband while they were still living in California. Later the same painting was hung in a prominent spot in the first floor hall of White Pines. Harrison was Dow's contemporary. His taste for nocturnes would not have come from Dow even though he made at least one woodcut of a blue, moonlit river while in Woodstock (cat. 163). The inspiration for such artworks could have as easily been the work of artists like Henri Rivière, whose prints the Whiteheads owned.[9] Bolton Brown, Hermann Dudley Murphy, and Dawson Dawson-Watson had all studied in France and were painting with moody blues before they painted panels for Byrdcliffe furniture. Similarly atmospheric studies in blue by James McNeill Whistler (1834–1903), Dwight William Tryon (1849–1925), and Thomas Wilmer Dewing (1851–1938) were collected by American tastemaker

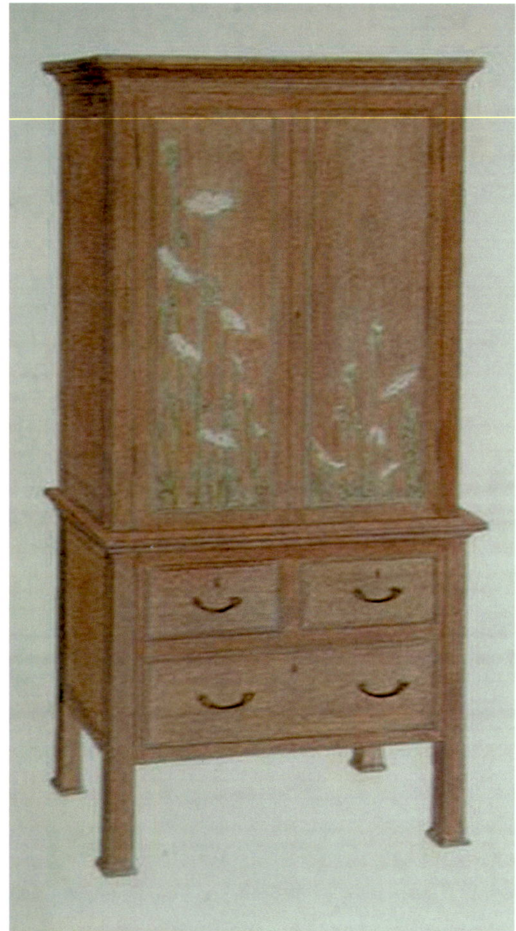

Left
fig. 3 Zulma Steele, Study for "Wild Carrot" cabinet panel. Graphite and watercolor. Private collection. Courtesy of the author.

Right
fig. 4 Zulma Steele, designer, "Wild Carrot" cabinet. Mahogany with polychrome panels. Private collection. Courtesy of the author.

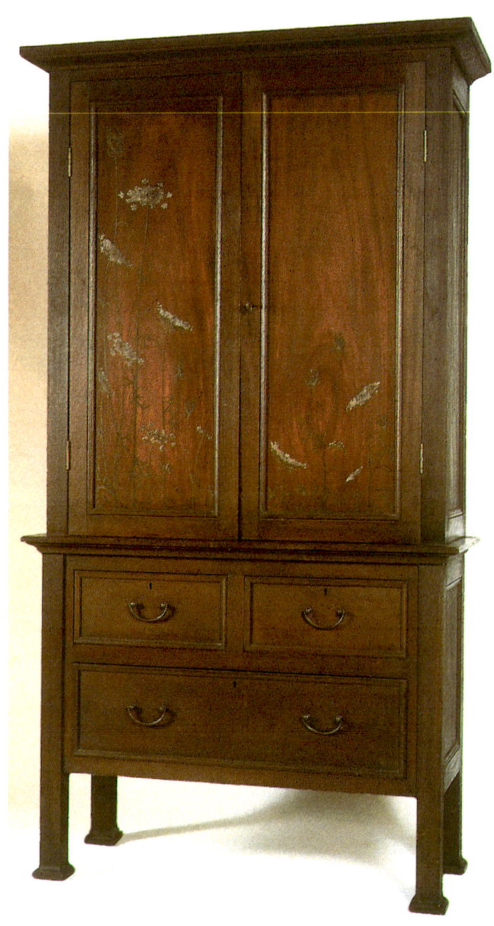

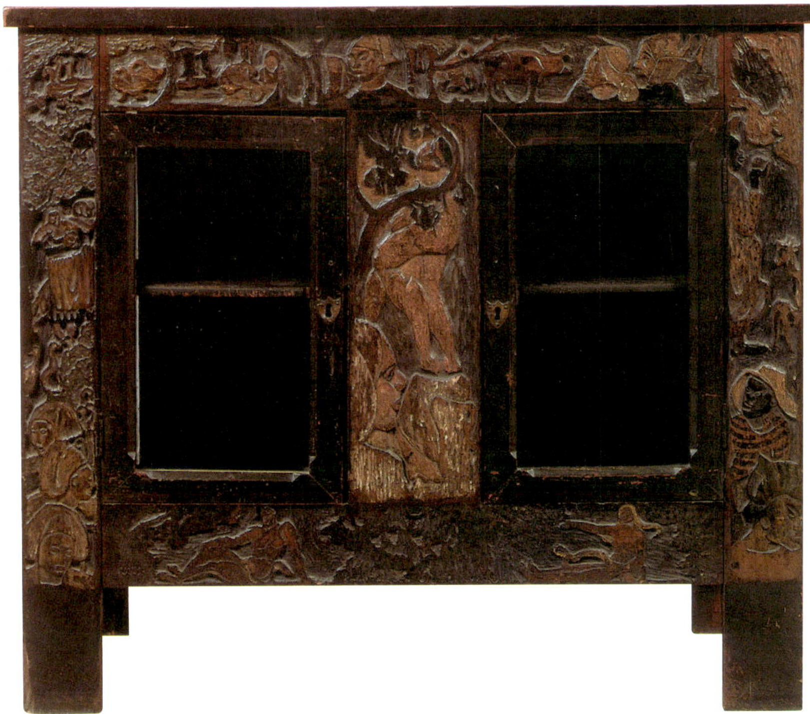

fig. 5 Paul Gauguin (1848) and Emile Bernard (1868–1941), *Le Paridis Terrestre*, 1888. Chestnut. Courtesy of Tajan Commissaires-Priseurs, Paris.

Charles Langford Freer (1854–1919), who made his collections available to the public.[10]

Dow published his theories just as Arts and Crafts reached full bloom in the United States. He reiterated already current methods of conventionalization and described already fashionable Japanese formulas of composition. Dow's books about design were therefore of their time without being progressive or innovative. His influence on American Arts and Crafts and Byrdcliffe furniture should not be overestimated because the overall plan for the colony was formed years before it was actually built in Woodstock.[11] To be sure, Zulma Steele and Edna Walker trained at Pratt when Dow was teaching there, but once at Woodstock, they had access to Whitehead's extensive design library. Steele designed Byrdcliffe furniture decorations using many styles that ranged from realistic to highly stylized. It is not known if one of her most radical and atypical designs was executed: a desk was planned to have a huge black raven dropping into the upper panel of a desk like an ominous shadow. The composition was almost certainly inspired by a strikingly similar print made by Shibata Zeshin.[12] Birds were important symbolically to Ralph Whitehead, who approved the designs used on Byrdcliffe furniture, but this dramatic, foreboding image may not have appealed to his conservative nature. The panels she painted for the "wild carrot" cabinet are also Japanese in composition, but the flowers are rendered in a highly realistic manner (figs. 2, 3, and 4). She used brushstrokes to imitate the hundreds of tiny, fragile florets that characterize this plant. On the other hand, the lily she designed to be painted on the sides of a lamp stand and to be carved in panels on chests (see cat. 23) and chairs was reduced to a flat, symmetrical motif. Even that lily can be traced to a plate in the 1856 Owen Jones *The Grammar of Ornament*.[13]

It is not yet known who developed the distinctive way Walker's and Steele's designs were carved into the panels. They are very similar to the woodblocks carved for making prints on paper and might have been the result of the women's earlier training in printmaking at Pratt. Birge Harrison and Vivian Bevans were carving blocks for printing at a studio below the Byrdcliffe shops.[14] However, there are only two instances I know of when Steele experimented with adapting one of her nature drawings for a wood-block print. One is a realistic black-line rendering of a columbine plant (cats. 169 and 174) that virtually reproduces her original drawing and has none of the bold, flat planes of her chestnut design (cat. 34) or Walker's tulip poplar panels (cat. 39).

Despite the British roots of Ralph Whitehead's ideas about furniture design, the term chosen for the distinctive low cabinet made in several variations at Byrdcliffe was "chiffonier," making a French connection. The term *was* current among American furniture manufacturers, but it described a tall chest of drawers usually with a mirror and usually used in a bedroom. The Byrdcliffe version was strikingly similar to the *buffet bas* that had been produced in rural France for centuries. While the form was made in America as early as the seventeenth century and as late as 1901, it is more likely, given Whitehead's training in Paris and the many Byrdcliffe connections to the Académie Julian, that the idea came directly from France.[15] Paul Gauguin (1848–1903) and Emile Bernard (1868–1941) decorated a low cabinet with polychromed relief carving in 1888. This cabinet exhibits many characteristics of Arts and Crafts style, including a rustic finish seldom found in

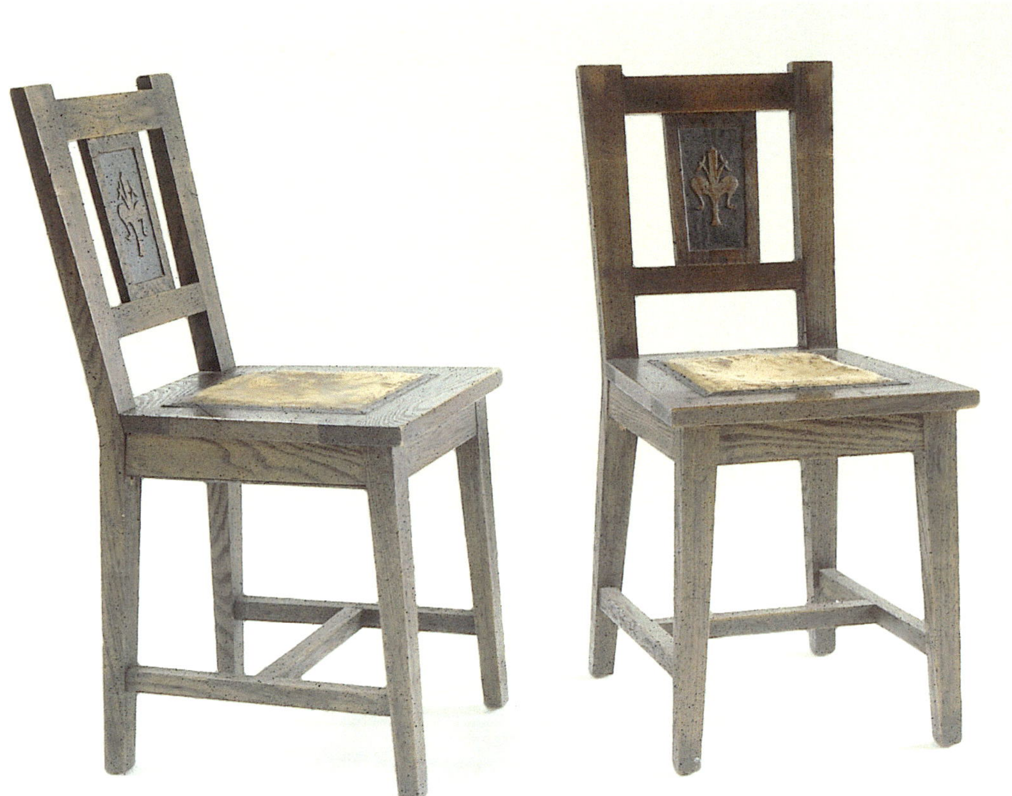

fig. 6 Dining chairs for White Pines. Oak. Collection of the Woodstock Guild. Gift of Jill and Mark Willcox Jr.

the Art Nouveau style, which dominated French decorative arts at that time[16] (fig. 5).

The furniture forms Whitehead chose are unusual in American Arts and Crafts production. While tall, tapering shelves do appear in Roycroft and Stickley, they were called bookstands. At Byrdcliffe such stands were called lamp stands and were offered in various heights to allow for optimum placement of the fluid lamps that were still much in use despite the increasing availability of electricity. The way a raised shelf is mounted to one side of the main work surface of a 1904 Byrdcliffe mission-style desk is similar to the arrangement of lighting on a table designed for Frank Lloyd Wright's 1909 Irving house. Wright's design is considered progressive while the modern aspects of Byrdcliffe designs have, until now, not been considered at all.

The large Byrdcliffe cabinets having a decorated two-door compartment above two side by side drawers above two cabinet-wide drawers are identical to M. H. Baillie Scott's "clothes press" published in *International Studio* for September 1898 (see page 26). Armoires were used in the United States throughout most of the nineteenth century, and they are still much used in Europe because British and Continental houses were seldom built with closets for clothing storage. American houses were just beginning to be constructed with enough built-in space near each bedroom to dispense with large, freestanding cabinets. White Pines had a large linen closet, and the principal bedrooms had built-in drawers and enough hanging space for seasonal clothing, but such planning was unusual except in the grandest houses where whole rooms could be given over to clothing storage.

No designs for the then-popular Morris chairs or any kind of easy chair have been found, but side chairs were made at Byrdcliffe, usually as part of dining suites. Although no complete dining suites are known, designs and inventory lists indicate that at least two were made: a lily-decorated group made for Bolton Brown's Byrdcliffe house, Carniola (cats. 23 and 24); and a tulip-poplar decorated suite that included a sideboard, a "service table," and an extension dining table. The dining table and chairs made for White Pines are unique among Byrdcliffe designs. The form of the table and the awkward chair design appear in drawings with Steele decorations, but the White Pines suite is embellished with a stilted fleur-de-lys motif suggesting the hand of Ralph Whitehead, who claimed to be "without any creative power at all"[17] (fig. 6).

No Byrdcliffe beds are known today, but a fascinating design for a bed for "Mrs. Whitehead" survives (fig. 7). This drawing has more extensive notes written on it than any other drawing in the Byrdcliffe archive. This is an indication of the importance a piece specifically made for the founding family had. At the time, Whitehead was trying to lure Jane from Arcady with descriptions of the delicately colored bedroom he intended to provide for her. Her bedroom seems not to have been completed as planned, but her bed might have been finished. The notations include detailed instructions about the proper way to set nails, a process so basic to cabinetmaking that one is led to believe the workmen Whitehead employed had few

fig. 7 Bolton Brown, Design for Jane Byrd McCall Whitehead's White Pines Bed. Pencil. Winterthur Library, Downs Collection, 92x39.409.

skills in woodworking. The instructions as to finish would have produced a unique and uncharacteristic Byrdcliffe piece: "Wood surface to be sized & design solidly painted on flat dark-brown tint that shall dry shining like lacquer." This drawing also notes (in Whitehead's hand) "designed by B. C. Brown [Bolton Coit Brown]," but there is little to indicate if the reference is to the decorations, the bed itself or to both.

The designers of Byrdcliffe furniture did not adhere to the American version of Arts and Crafts construction. Details like exposed tenons and loose-pin joinery, even when fake or nonfunctional, were essential to the

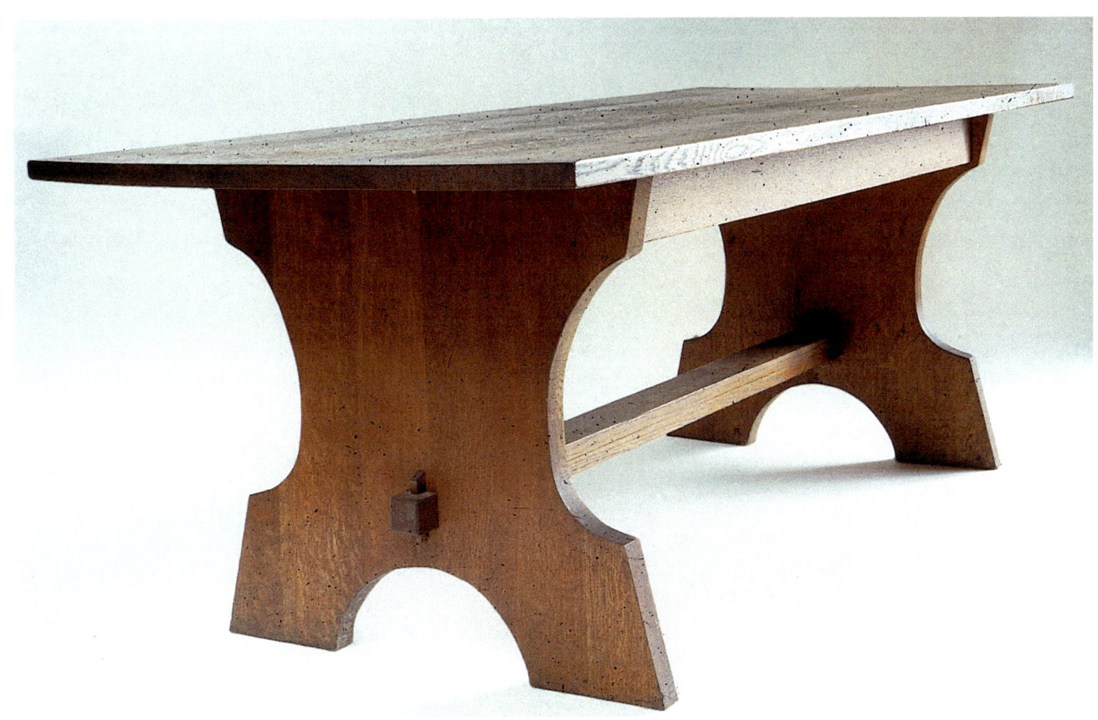

fig. 8 Byrdcliffe trestle table with exposed, loose-pinned tenons. Oak. Collection of Jill and Mark Willcox Jr.

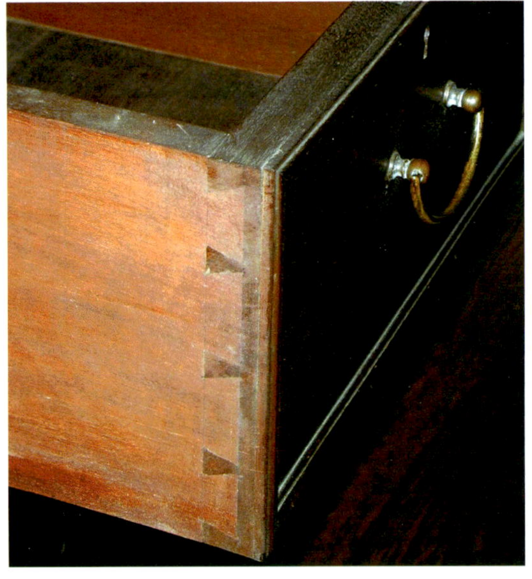

Left
fig. 9a Dove tails on drawer of "Wild Carrot" cabinet. Private collection. Courtesy of the author.

Right
fig. 9b Nailed drawer on linen press with Edna Walker tulip designs. Poplar. Collection of Jill and Mark Willcox Jr. Courtesy of the author.

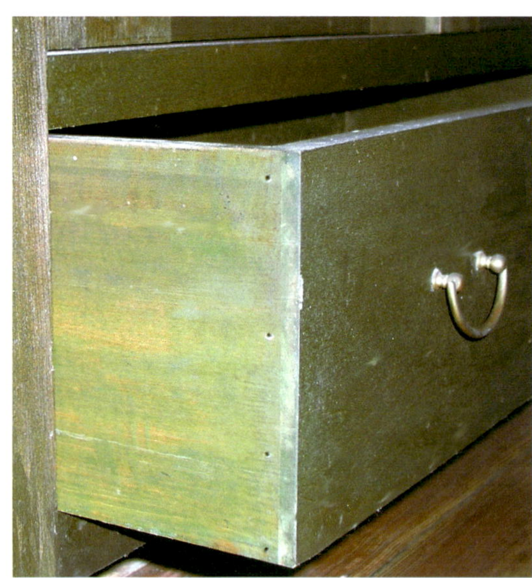

promotion of Craftsman, Roycroft, and Rose Valley furniture. There are only two or three known Byrdcliffe pieces that incorporate through tenons, and these are incidental to the furniture's overall design (fig. 8). Working drawings for Byrdcliffe furniture often have precise templates for creating moldings, but they show few construction instructions. As a result, the quality of construction varies. Some drawers are joined with refined dovetails, on others, the dovetails are crude, and some have no dovetails at all, being held together with glue and nails (figs. 9a and 9b).

The workshops and dwellings on the Byrdcliffe campus sprung up fully equipped, but, though they were operational by 1903, Byrdcliffe stationery and sales receipts for that year list only weaving, pottery, metalwork, and frames as products of the colony. It is strange that furniture was omitted since Whitehead studied woodworking,

fig. 10 Unidentified photographer. *Byrdcliffe Woodworking Shop*, ca. 1904. Silver print. Winterthur Library, Downs Collection. 92x39.1140.19b.

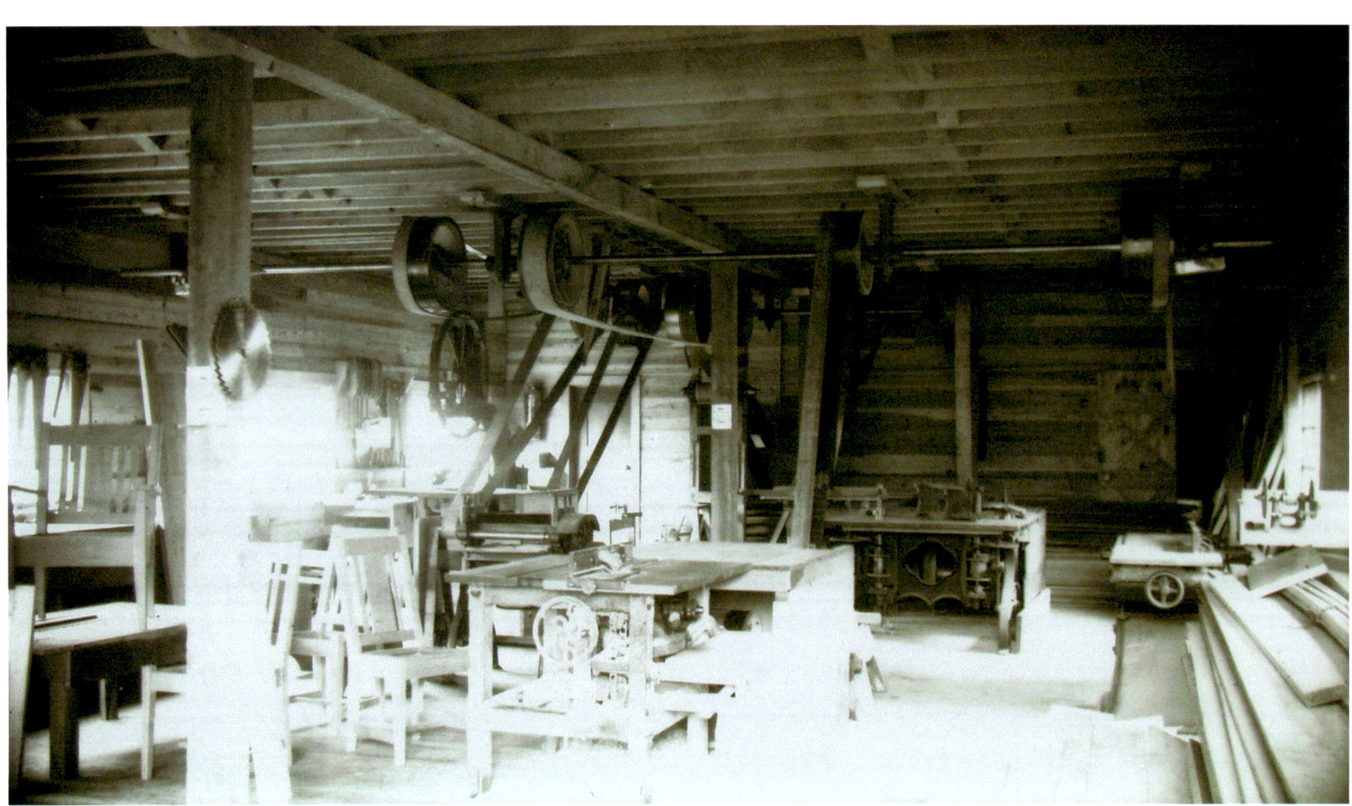

and furniture making was a part of his original plan.[18] A contemporary photograph of the woodworking shop shows a number of chairs in various stages of production (fig. 10). Many of the designs for Byrdcliffe furniture were made before 1904, the date that is on all signed examples (fig. 11). Some furniture drawings are dated December 1904, so that furniture could not have been completed until 1905. There is no guiding aesthetic evident in the heavy linen presses or the more delicate lamp stands. The melon turnings of handmade tables used at Arcady and later at White Pines probably refer to fifteenth-century British furniture, but the designer of Byrdcliffe furniture seldom went more than a decade back in history for inspiration. Whitehead's vast library included many volumes about contemporary decorative arts. He also subscribed to *The Studio* and his many notations on these magazines suggest that they were a primary inspiration. The design for Baillie Scott's clothespress mentioned above, for example, was marked with Whitehead's penciled notes. Moreover, a tiny sketch of a stool appears on the corner of a magazine page (fig. 12). An exact duplication of that stool was eventually made at Byrdcliffe (fig. 13) and the drawings for it signed by Zulma Steele remain in the Byrdcliffe archive.[19] The stool is decorated with Steele's tiger lily but she and Walker also made drawings of furniture with decorations they did not design. It seems as if Whitehead was browsing through design sources and picking whatever suited his fancy or particular need. White Pines was built with shelves on the walls to accommodate the fluid lamps since they did not need to be tethered to an electric or gas outlet. Early photographs of the interior of White Pines show a fluid lamp on a tall Byrdcliffe stand placed where it could illuminate the piano.

It is difficult to determine why Whitehead abandoned the furniture shop in such short order. Bertha Thompson, who lived at Byrdcliffe and knew the Whiteheads, hypothesized that the furniture enterprise failed "because it did not produce furniture that could compete in price with other handmade furniture on the market—an inability which is more than half due to an unwillingness to advertise."[20] Thompson's theory is faulty because whatever the furniture cost to make, it was competitively priced. The furniture inventories give prices of each piece of furniture. As might be expected the large maple-leaf cabinets were the most expensive at $160 (cats. 30 and 35). Dawson-Watson's "Tirol" cabinet evidently sold at $130. A comparable Rose Valley piece, a table having much intricate carving, sold for $150. These prices might seem high when compared to large pieces mass-produced by Gustav Stickley that sold for well under $100. Stickley, of course, made very few unique or custom pieces and was targeting a middle-class clientele. Virtually all Byrdcliffe and Rose Valley pieces were unique. Some were made or finished to order.[21] Will Price did try to convince consumers for whom cost might be an issue that they would be better off to find a way to afford his furniture than to settle for the lesser factory-made product. Whitehead didn't dwell on such democratic issues when he wrote about Arts and Crafts.

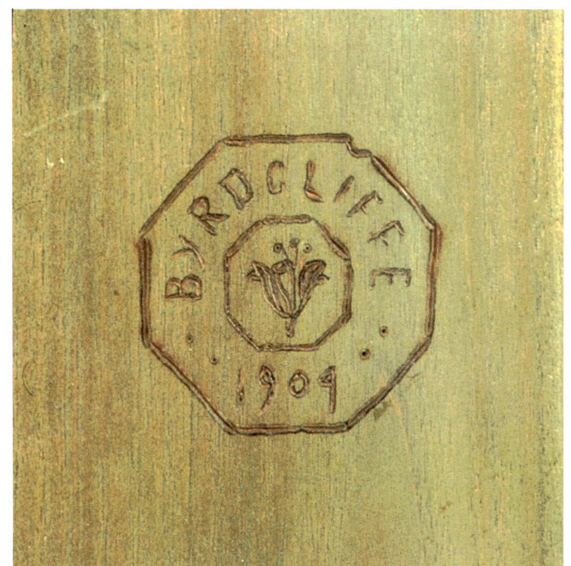

fig. 11 Byrdcliffe furniture mark.

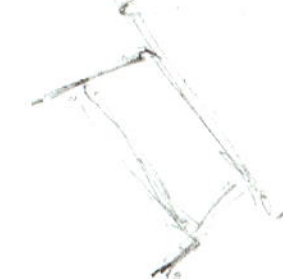

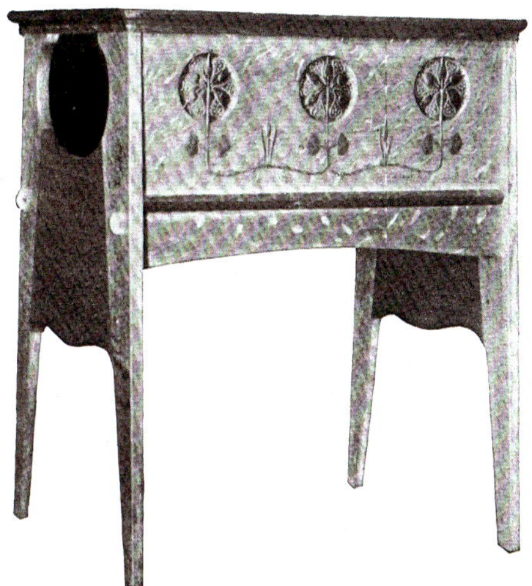

fig. 12 Page from *The Studio*, September 1898, with Ralph Whitehead's notations. Photocopy. Author's collection.

fig. 13 Zulma Steele, designer. *Stool.* Cherry with polychromed panels. Woodstock Artists Association. Gift of Jill and Mark Willcox Jr.

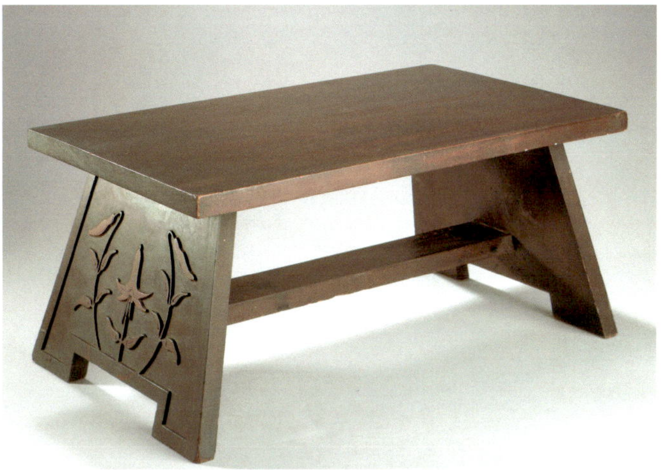

He chose the role of an arbiter of taste whose responsibility was to define what others ought to believe. It was enough that Byrdcliffe furniture existed as an oasis in the desert of inartistic household objects. He was not about to lead the public to the water or to make them drink it.

The inventory list, when compared to period photographs and colored renderings, indicates that a number of the pieces that were made and sold are now lost. In addition to the Tirol cabinet, a bookcase with chestnut decorations appears in a photograph. A large dining-room suite with tulip poplar decorations was also likely made and sold. A cabinet now in the collection of the Woodstock Guild of Craftsmen can be identified as "Cabinet, same shape as sassafras, but with two painted panels, [Bolton] Brown." Not enough information is given to identify "fumed oak cabinet (George Eggers panels)" although it could be a cabinet with paintings of a tree that is also in the Woodstock Guild collection (cats. 17 and 18). The list notes that $125 had been offered against the list price of $125 so the Eggers cabinet could have been sold, but other pieces with offer notations remained at White Pines.[22]

A railroad serviced Woodstock, and carting unwieldy objects from remote locations to retail outlets in urban centers did not daunt a population still using oxen and cheap, plentiful manpower. Huge pieces of furniture made by Charles Rohlfs, Gustav Stickley, and Joseph McHugh made it from New York cities to Adirondack camps, many of which had their own railroad sidings. It is apparent that the relatively rich Whiteheads were enthralled with the creative process and had neither need nor interest in drumming up business beyond having little shows and sales in Woodstock. The archives of the New York City studios of Edna Walker and Zulma Steele suggest that these women were more aggressive about selling. They ran an interior decorating business for the studio, which would have allowed them to specify particular Brydcliffe pieces for clients. Many of their drawings of furnishings have notations with clients' names. They made the color

fig. 14 Group of "Tirol" furniture with Dawson Dawson-Watson decorations in a showroom at Byrdcliffe, ca. 1904 (see cats. 14 and 31). Winterthur Library, Downs Collection, 92x39.1140.280.

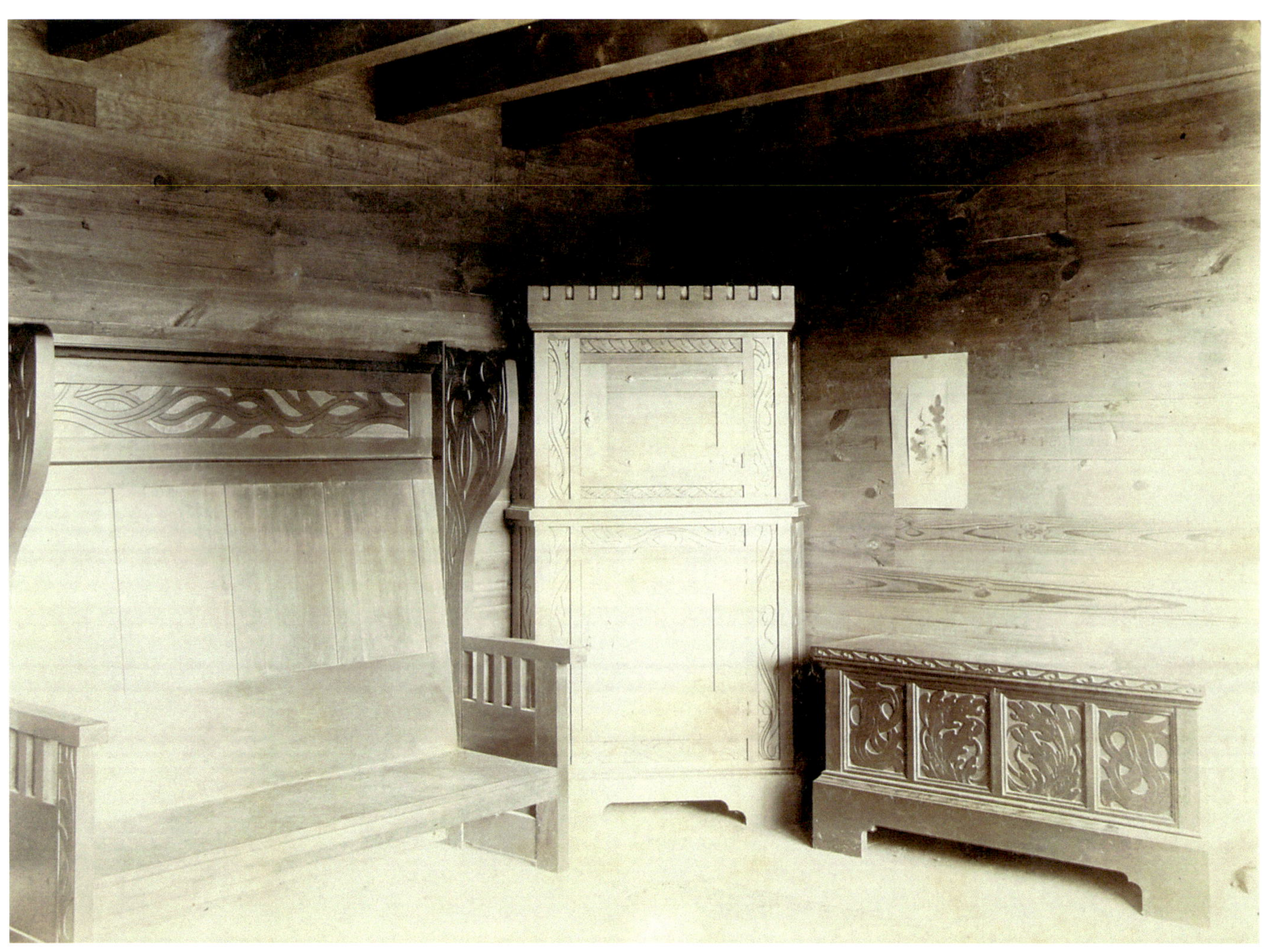

renderings showing the furniture in a finished state and often offered multiple color schemes. These were evidently used not only for their own clients, but also as a way for customers at McCreery's, a New York City furniture retailer, to place custom orders without having the actual furniture on the premises. As Jane Whitehead's diaries prove, the final coloring did not take place until well after the furniture was finished so the customer could specify a color scheme.[23]

A considerable number of Byrdcliffe pieces were sold despite Whitehead's lack of interest in marketing, and it cannot be said that the style of the furniture was not up-to-date. This was the time when Gustav Stickley was producing designs that ranged from the flimsy "India stool" and "celandine tea table" to the uncompromisingly ponderous eight-legged sideboard and "Eastwood" chair. American Arts and Crafts furniture had not yet acquired the homogenized look that was soon to characterize mission style. A few American craftsmen like Charles Rohlfs decorated their essentially mission designs with high-style Art Nouveau carving and some furniture factories like Tobey and Karpen offered designs awash with swirling flora along with their more sedate mission-style offerings. But Art Nouveau in its French guise was not much liked or used in America.[24] Even the Art Nouveau glassware of Louis Comfort Tiffany was more often incorporated into Colonial Revival interiors than into exotic schemes like those he designed for the H. O. Havemeyer house. The Whiteheads owned inlaid furniture by Emile Gallé, and there are Art Nouveau elements to be found in Byrdcliffe designs. They appear most obviously in the designs of Dawson Dawson-Watson, but they are also evident in the whiplash poppy stem Zulma Steele placed in the panels of a small cabinet now at Winterthur (cats. 14 and 31).

Dawson-Watson's broad swirling leaves may not have been perceived as Art Nouveau, however. His large settle, library table, chest, and cabinet are called "Tirol" on inventory lists[25] (fig. 14). Just as Swiss chalets inspired much American turn-of-the-century architecture, Tyrolean decorative arts provided motifs for craftsmen who saw a connection to the imaginary simple life of Alpine shepherds. Gustav Stickley offered a "chalet" stand and desk. Dawson-Watson was the only Byrdcliffe designer who looked to sources earlier than the contemporary designs found in publications like *Studio*. His "Tirol" cabinet is a virtual copy of fifteenth-century models, down to the crenelations and strap hinges. Even its convoluted "Art Nouveau" leaves can be found on the antique versions. Several books by Lewis F. Day were in the Whitehead library. In them are pages of illustrations and design suggestions that are strikingly similar to the carved panels used on Byrdcliffe cabinets. These books were published before 1892 and were in Whitehead's library so Dawson-Watson's designs seem to generate more from Day's aesthetic than from Dow's[26] (fig. 15).

Another influence on at least one of Dawson-Watson's designs was William Morris. The Whiteheads used Morris and Company furnishings in both Arcady and White Pines. However, these objects were in the highly decorated, formal style of Morris & Company designer George B. Jack.[27] They were made of exotic materials and elaborate inlays that had little to do with earlier, simple Morris designs. Dawson-Watson's lift-lid chest appears to be a simplified version of a Morris & Co. piece (cats. 15 and 16).

While Steele and Walker are not known to have been trained in the design and construction of furniture, Whitehead presumably was since he studied cabinetmaking in Germany and Paris as preparation for the planned craft community.[28] No documented results of these studies are known although there are several pieces of furniture that are obviously handmade and can be seen in photographs of interiors where the Whiteheads lived before

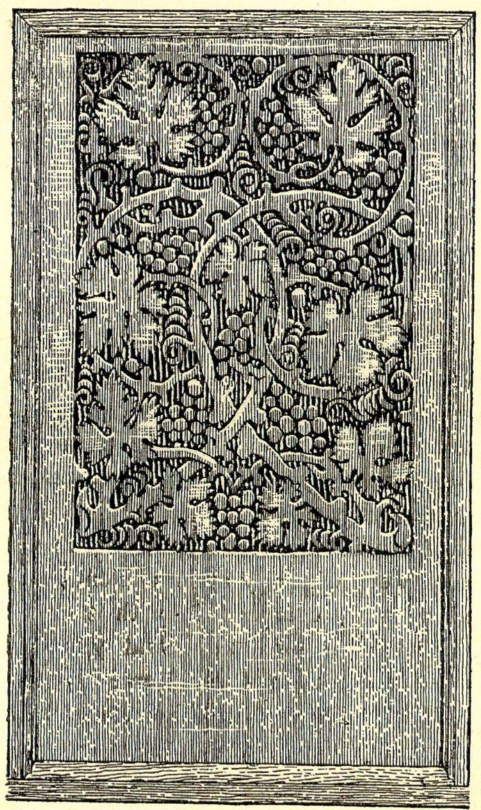

The Workman and his Tools. 103

the resemblance of the forms which grew under his hand to the honeysuckle may eventually have struck

50. Direct and workmanlike flat carving—Old German.

the painter (as it strikes us) is likely enough; and, having perceived that likeness, he may have empha-

fig. 15 Low-relief, flat carving similar to that done on Byrdcliffe furniture was recommended in 1894 by Lewis F. Day in *Some Principles of Every-day Art: Introductory Chapters on the Arts Not Fine.*

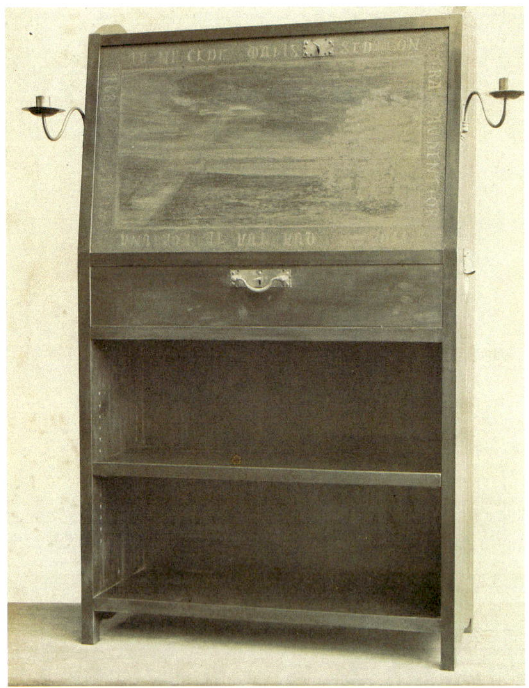

fig. 16 Desk with panel that is a reproduction of one made by Jane and Ralph Whitehead in Italy. Whereabouts unknown. Photograph in Winterthur Library, Downs Collection, 92x39.1140.281.

starting Byrdcliffe. A sturdy if inelegant lounge and several tables with legs having curious bulbous turnings appear in pictures that could be their studio in Europe, then at Arcady, and finally, at Byrdcliffe. Another piece either made or commissioned by Whitehead before Byrdcliffe was established is known only from a photograph. It is worth describing because it undoubtedly had great significance for the Whiteheads. At first glance this oak, drop-front desk looks like a Gustav Stickley design. Closer inspection reveals brass-candle arms mounted on the sides, and further study brings the drop front into focus. That panel recreates the "marriage contract" Ralph and Jane made on the hillside in Serbelloni[29] (fig. 16).

Before coming to Woodstock from Chicago, Hervey White, artist Carl Lindin, and others formed a craft cooperative called the Krayle Company (fig. 17).[30] Among the products the company offered were tooled leather objects (Lindin continued binding books in Woodstock) and

fig. 17 The decorations on the edges of a hall-seat by Miss Bracken visible in a photograph of the Krayle showroom relates to carving designed by Dawson Dawson-Watson for Byrdcliffe furniture. "Holiday Gifts," *The House Beautiful*, December 1900: 5.

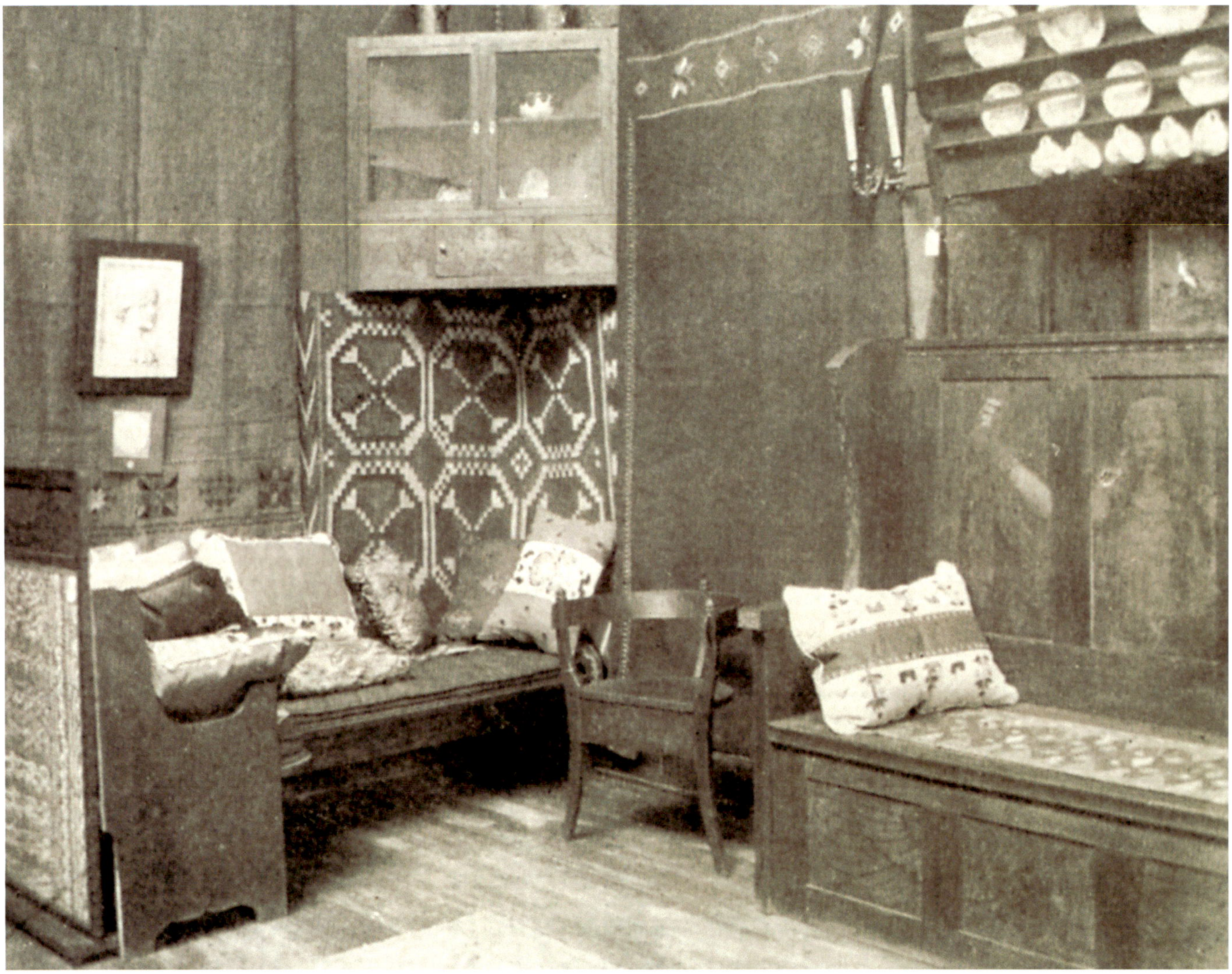

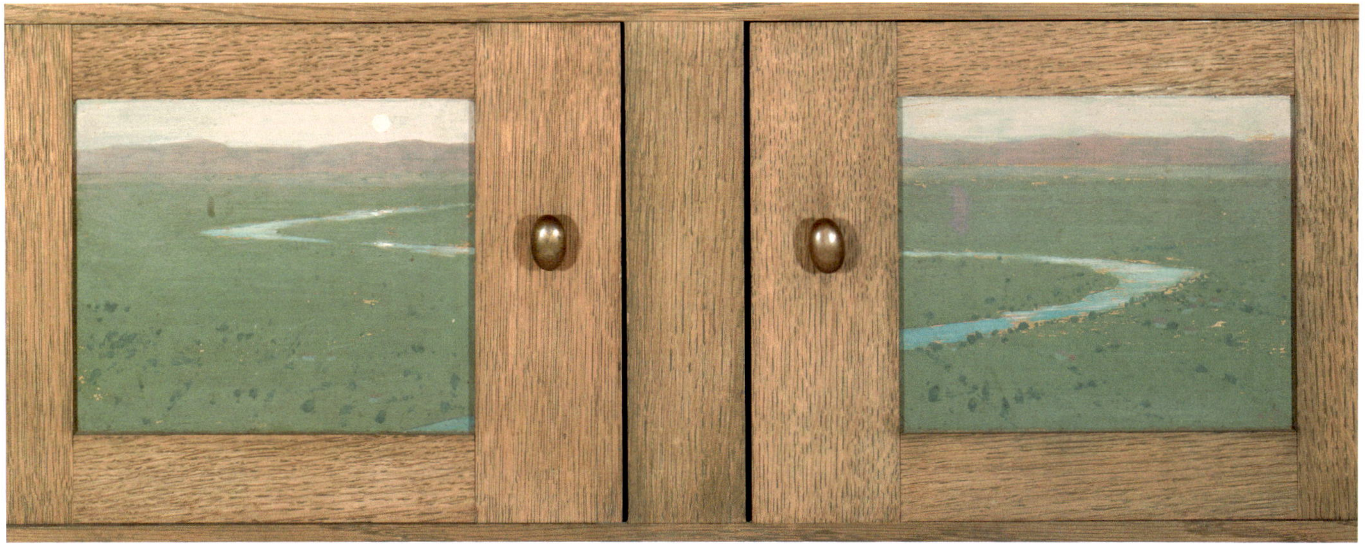

fig. 18a Detail of chiffonier with landscape painted by Hermann Dudley Murphy (see cat. 20).

furniture. Period photographs show that there were some ornamental devices, such as meandering leaves carved along the edges of the boards forming settle arms and ends, that were comparable to those Dawson-Watson used on Byrdcliffe designs. White's role at the Krayle Company is unknown and there is no documentation of his participation in any aspect of craft design at Byrdcliffe. Writing was Hervey White's primary form of creative expression, and music was the essential core of the Maverick Community he formed after leaving the Whiteheads, so it may be that his interest in art and craft making was the fellowship of artists.

Ever the scientist, Whitehead also researched finishes. Interestingly, he looked again to France and took notes about centuries-old techniques. However, no consistent formula for finishing Byrdcliffe furniture resulted. Against Ruskin's dictates, mahogany pieces were stained and varnished in a manner similar to formal English furniture and some pieces, as we have seen, were intended to look like lacquer (see fig. 4). The natural color of oak was changed to the moody blue/green color so beloved by the Whiteheads. Some pieces have a fragile water-based wash of color, while others have been coated with more durable oil-based colors and varnishes. The only constant is the transparency of the stains, which allows the character of the wood grain to show through, making it an integral part of the decorating scheme.

The variance in the way furniture was finished may have resulted from the fact that most pieces were not colored when construction was completed. Several color schemes were offered for some pieces and cabinets that had unique decorations like those with artist-painted landscapes were finished after the panels were installed (figs. 18a and 18b). The December 16 entry in Jane Whitehead's 1903 diary reads, "stained green furniture." Her references to staining furniture continue until April of 1905 and included the information that she stained the sassafras cabinet on January 2, 1905 (cat. 38). These notations suggest that Jane was responsible for the subtle, shaded

fig. 18b Rendering of completed Murphy chiffonier showing original green stain. The price was $60. Although the landscape is quite realistic by modern standards, it is here referred to as a "conventionalized landscape. (Sunset. River. Mountains)." The handwriting appears to be Ralph Whitehead's. Pencil and watercolor. Collection of Jill and Mark Willcox Jr. Courtesy of the author.

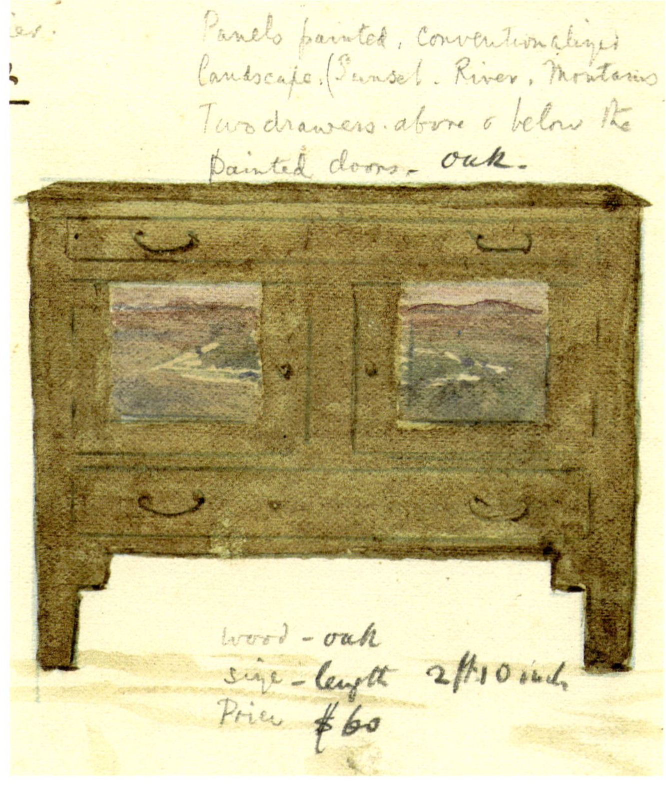

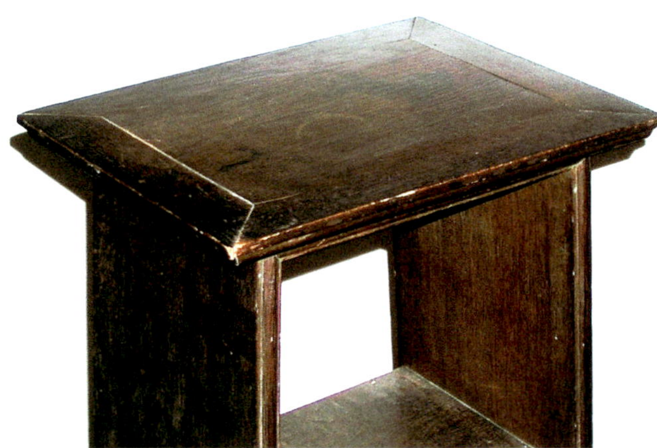

fig. 19a Detail of lampstand showing mitered moldings on two sides of top. Cherry. Collection of Jill and Mark Willcox Jr. Courtesy of the author.

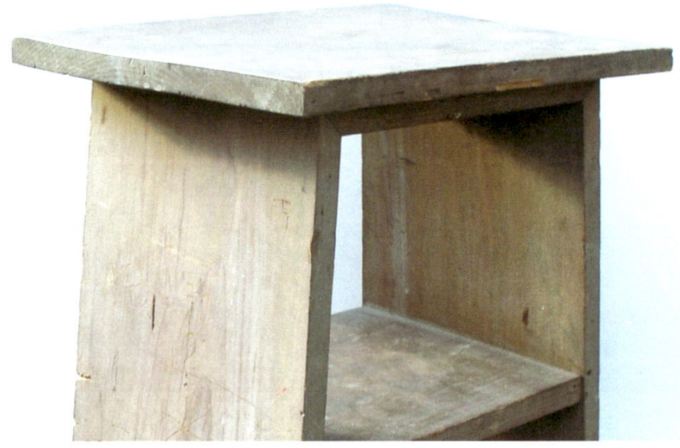

fig. 19b Detail of lampstand with top made of a single board. Poplar. Collection of Jill and Mark Willcox Jr. Courtesy of the author.

colorings on furniture with flat carving. The decorations on pieces like the "ampelopsis" (woodbine) desk required more sophisticated skills. The colored drawings for vines and berries used on that desk remained among Zulma Steele's papers, and she certainly had talent enough to have created the panel (cat. 175). Some pieces remained in an unfinished state at White Pines, where the beautiful quartered oak aged to the mellow shimmering surface that we see today. Now that the acids in the wood have darkened, it is as difficult to imagine how the Byrdcliffe furniture was supposed to look when it was new as it is to imagine how the white marble of a Greek temple looked when it was still painted with vivid colors.

It is problematic to assign specific designs for Byrdcliffe furniture to specific people because their modular concept involved more than one artisan. Most furniture was designed so panels decorated differently but of identical dimensions could be used on more than one piece. For example, the panels on chiffoniers were usually 9 ½ x 5 ½ inches. This allowed oil paintings done by Jane and Leonard Lester in California before the founding of Byrdcliffe to be incorporated into marked Byrdcliffe furniture. Except in the case of the panels on which landscapes or flowers were painted directly, the designers did not carve or color the decorations. A cabinet could be fitted with a pair of panels with Steele's maple-leaf pattern realistically molded by Giovanni Battista Troccoli or flat carved by an unknown craftsman. Although most drawings for the furniture are signed by Zulma Steele, the price lists designate pieces by the artist who designed the inserted panels. In some cases Steele has signed drawings of pieces documented as designed by Dawson Dawson-Watson, so it must be assumed that she was responsible for the drawings only (cat. 21).

There is great variation in the method of joining the door frames that hold decorated panels. Some vertical members have long tenons that have been securely embedded in the corresponding horizontal boards. These joints have held together for nearly one hundred years, while more shallow joints on other pieces have not. Some tops of lamp stands have molding strips on two ends that are mitered into corresponding molded edges, which are part of the center panel, while other stands have molding strips tacked on to all four sides (fig. 19a). A few are finished with no molding at all leaving the end grain of the top board exposed and susceptible to warping (fig. 19b). The discrepancy in production technique does not seem to be the result of student participation. All but the crudest lamp stands seem to be the work of hired, trained woodworkers.

All the flat carving was probably the work of one craftsman whose skills were developed before coming to Byrdcliffe. The patterns are outlined with a bevel having an unwavering angle and the backgrounds have been almost perfectly flattened with only a chisel. Troccoli could easily have accomplished this, but such was not his style. Women in Cincinnati developed amazing carving skill in a relatively short period of time under the tutelage of Benn Piton and Henry Fry.[31] However, it is unlikely that Steele, Walker, or Dawson-Watson could have mastered the Byrdcliffe technique enough to be producing finished panels as early as 1903.

Marketing was key to the success of Gustav Stickley's Craftsman Company and Elbert Hubbard's Roycroft. The style of their production was distilled so that consumers would immediately associate it with their companies. Even smaller operations like Rohlfs in New York, Price in Pennsylvania, and the Greene brothers in California were known by their distinctive styles. But there was no permanent work force at Byrdcliffe. Artists and students came and went with the seasons. The school did not teach to sustain craft production at the colony. The involvement of so many designers in craft production meant that there was no single style associated with Byrdcliffe products. Whitehead's published writings did not promote Byrdcliffe crafts as the Stickley, Price, and Hubbard publications promoted their furniture. If Byrdcliffe stationery and receipts are any indication, Whitehead was not particularly

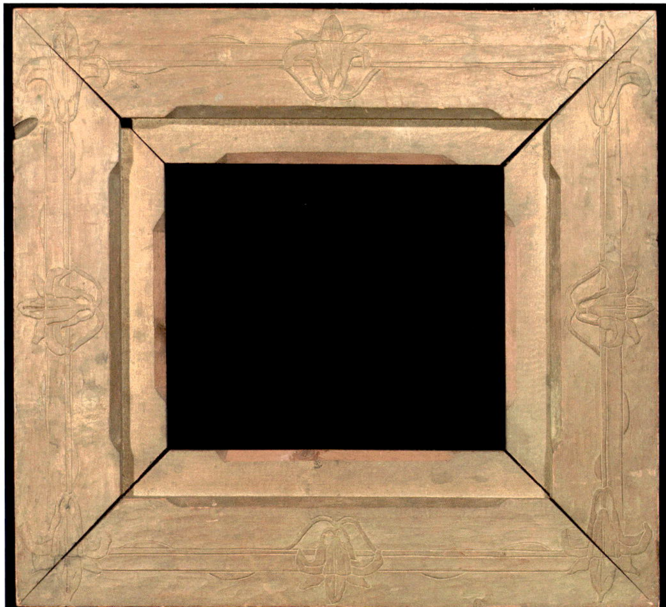

fig. 20a Frame attributed to Zulma Steele. Pine or poplar with bronze powder paint. Collection of the Woodstock Artists Association.

fig. 20b Frame attributed to Carrig-Rohane Shop. Gold leaf and gesso on wood. Collection of the Byrdcliffe Art Colony of the Woodstock Guild, Alf Evers Collection. Gift of the Douglas C. James Charitable Trust.

fig. 20c Frame. Cherry. Collection of the Byrdcliffe Art Colony of the Woodstock Guild.

interested in making anonymous consumers aware of his colony and crafts. Tellingly, he wanted "checks payable to R. Radcliffe Whitehead," not the Byrdcliffe Arts and Crafts colony.

Hermann Dudley Murphy visited the Whiteheads in Santa Barbara in 1897. He later came to Byrdcliffe from Boston to teach the making of picture frames as well as painting. As early as 1903, Whitehead was listing frames on the colony letterhead, but there is little evidence of a sophisticated product like those Murphy designed for Carrig-Rohane (see cat. 56). Murphy's designs required very advanced skills in carving, application of gesso, and gilding. There is a charming frame in the collection of the Woodstock Art Association that was found in White Pines (fig. 20a). It is decorated with Zulma Steele's lily motif and gilded with bronze powder, but it has no relationship to Murphy's sophisticated designs or techniques. Steele owned a tiny gold-leaf frame she claimed to have made at Byrdcliffe, but this frame is not the work of an amateur and was probably the product of the Carrig-Rohane shop[32] (fig. 20b). The Whiteheads owned several carved frames from Morris & Company. Some have mistaken these frames for Byrdcliffe productions. Birge Harrison and George Eggers may also have made frames, but nothing remains to verify their activity in this craft. The frames most likely to have been made at Byrdcliffe are those Whitehead used to frame his large collection of reproductions of European masterpieces. These were made up of very plain mouldings usually of quartered oak sometimes left in its natural color and sometimes given a very dark brown stain. Dozens of these empty frames remained in the attic of White Pines until 1998 (fig. 20c).

A well-equipped metalworking shop was part of the Byrdcliffe campus, but too little evidence remains to accurately assess the products promised by the Byrdcliffe letterhead. A few pieces of furniture have handwrought handles on cabinet drawers and a door in the living hall

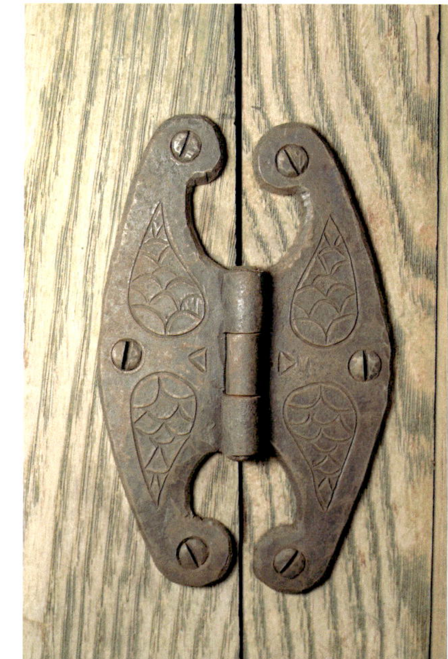

fig. 21 Iron hinge in the shape of wings used on cabinet door built into the side of the fireplace in the living room of White Pines.

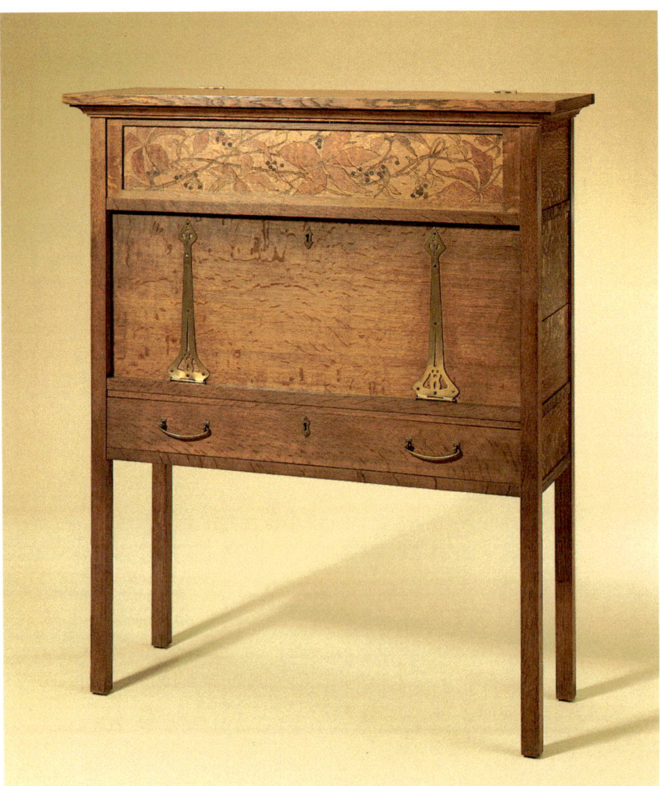

fig. 22 Zulma Steele, designer, "Ampelopsis" desk (also known as Woodbine Desk). Oak with painted panel and brass hardware. Collection of the Los Angeles County Museum of Art. Gift of Max Palevsky.

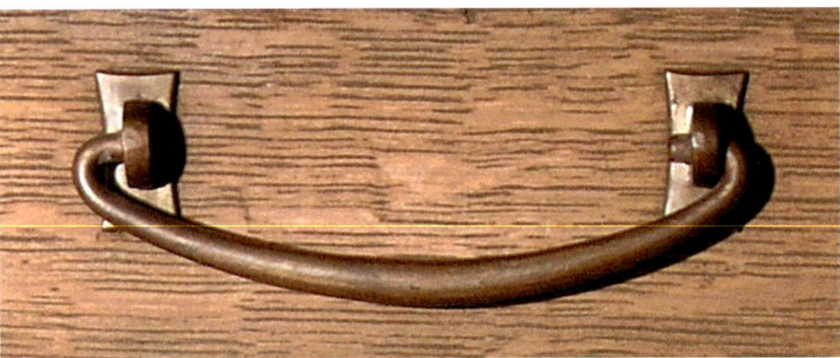

fig. 23a Drawer pull from H. D. Murphy chiffonier made by Reading Hardware Co. or G. Bayer Co. Bronze (see cat. 20).

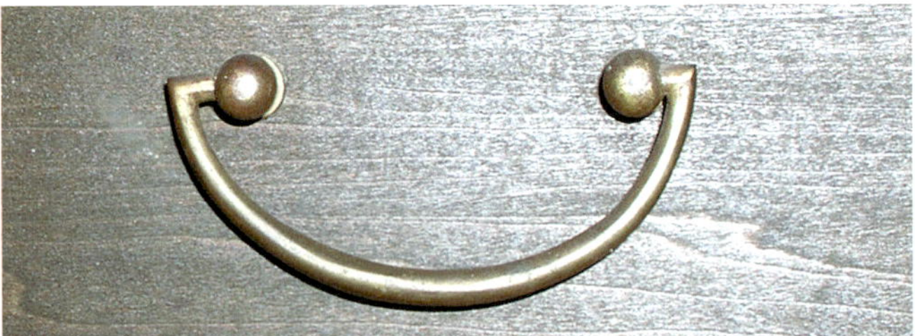

fig. 23b Drawer pull from "Wild Carrot" cabinet made by Reading Hardware Co. or G. Bayer Co. Bronze. Private collection.

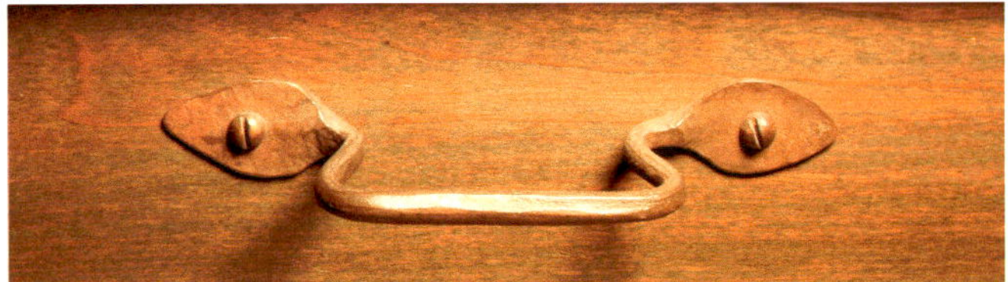

fig. 23c Drawer pull from chestnut chiffonier (see cat. 25). Iron. Collection of the Milwaukee Art Museum.

of White Pines has iron hinges made in the form of wings (fig. 21) (see also cat. 49). Only four of the known examples of Byrdcliffe furniture have hardware that might have been made in the Colony forge. Of those, three have drawer handles that could have been made by a craftsman with only rudimentary skills. The fourth piece (the "ampelopsis" or woodbine desk) (fig. 22) has hand-cut brass hinge straps for which the drawings still exist.[33] This adds up to fewer than a dozen pieces of handmade hardware. Otherwise the hardware used in the house and on the furniture was a commercial product. Locks, knobs, hinges, and handles were ordered in bulk from either the Reading Hardware Company of Pennsylvania or G. Bayer of New York (figs. 23a, b, and c). Metalworking seems to have been relegated to summer-school activities. Ned Thatcher is the craftsman most associated with Byrdcliffe. Bertha Thompson says he "forged the red-hot iron and steel into hinges, lock plates, and drawer pulls for the furniture being made in the carpenter shop. . . ."[34] I have seen no handmade lock plates or hinges on Byrdcliffe furniture, and the straps on the ampelopsis desk are only decorative. These straps are not functional parts of the factory-made hinges. Thatcher was an instructor in decorative metalwork at the Teachers College at Columbia University and ran his own summer school with his own facility in Woodstock. Some existing examples of Thatcher's work, like the brass dolphin sconce, were used to illustrate ads for his school and were probably made in his own shop away from the Byrdcliffe campus (see page 29). Laurin Martin taught at Byrdcliffe, but nothing of his accomplished craftwork remains at Byrdcliffe (see cat. 40). Martin's friend Harry Stuart Michie visited and even brought examples of his work to display (cats. 41, 42, and 85), but there is no evidence to suggest that he produced anything while at Byrdcliffe.[35]

Bertha Thompson, by her own account, was highly trained in metalwork and her recollections provide most of what we know about Byrdcliffe metalwork. She wrote about her summer taking courses at Byrdcliffe and later built a house above White Pines. She and Bolton Brown's wife Lucy both recalled Ernest Chapman, who was called the "brassbeater." Edmund B. Rolfe (1877–1917) replaced Laurin Martin as a teacher at the metal shop in 1905.[36]

Among the extant designs for hardware is a bail handle comprised of entwined serpents. Two such wrought-iron handles are mounted on a blanket chest decorated for Jane Whitehead by her cousin William Mercer (fig. 24). It was impossible to determine if the drawing was made before the handles were forged or if it was made after the chest was presented to Jane with the idea that they might be reproduced at the Byrdcliffe forge (fig. 25). The latter seems most plausible because the chest decorations were designed to surround these handles, and the snakes do not relate in style to examples thought to have been made at the colony. This little drawing is executed on a woven drafting material that is not typical of the hundreds of other drawings relating to Byrdcliffe furniture.[37]

William Hunt Diederich is best known for his metalwork. He stayed with the Whiteheads for a time and several weather vanes (fig. 26) as well as unfinished ceramic chargers were found at White Pines in 1976. But, as with the other metalworkers, there is nothing to indicate that he used Byrdcliffe facilities to make these examples of his craft.[38] It seems that metalworking, like frame making, never amounted to much at Byrdcliffe. This could be due to the fact that most of the metalworkers were teaching. Their reputations were already established and they had their own studios away from the Byrdcliffe campus. Their students would have taken their handiwork away with them at the end of the summer. There was neither permanent metal production nor a retail outlet.

Byrdcliffe furniture measured up to the prevailing Arts and Crafts standard in that it was made at a community of artisans who in many ways attempted to live the "simple life," which was to be enhanced by art and appreciation of beauty. It was expected that the use of such furniture would improve the quality of life whether or not its owners professed an Arts and Crafts philosophy. Whitehead was not an entrepreneur like Elbert Hubbard or Gustav Stickley, so he had furniture made at his colony because it was part of his design for living and not because he intended to profit from the project. The overall design of the furniture may have been copied directly from British prototypes, but the carved panels were, in 1904, distinctive, especially in America. Examples of comparable woodwork were made earlier, but most furniture with similar inset carved panels like that designed by Margery Wheelock (ca. 1890–ca. 1967), Arthur (1860–1945) and Lucia Klienhans (1870–1955) Matthews, and William Templeton Johnson didn't appear until a few years after

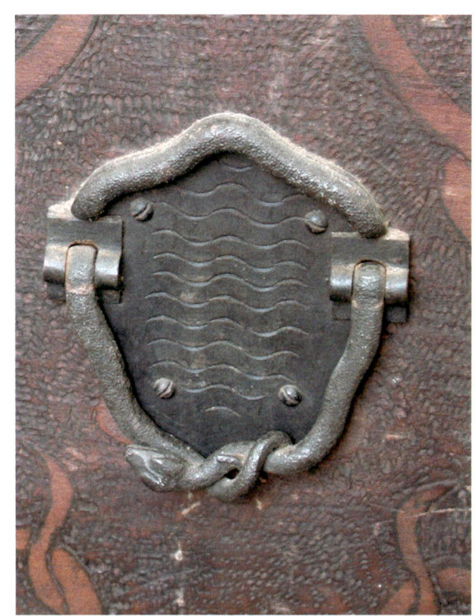

fig. 24 Hardware from Mercer decorated chest. Iron. Collection of Jill and Mark Willcox Jr.

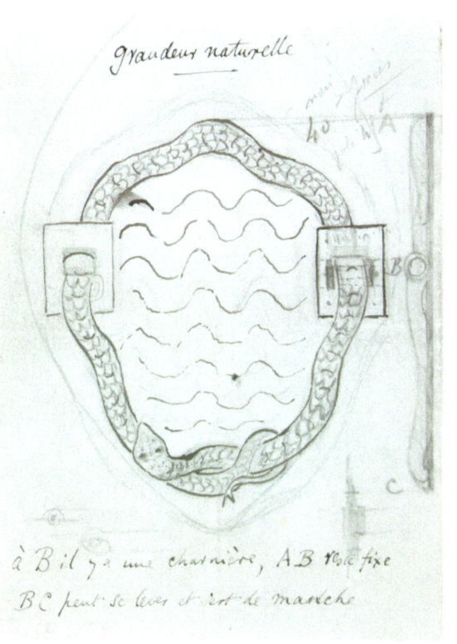

fig. 25 Sketch for iron hardware. Graphite. Winterthur Library, Downs Collection, 92x39.231.

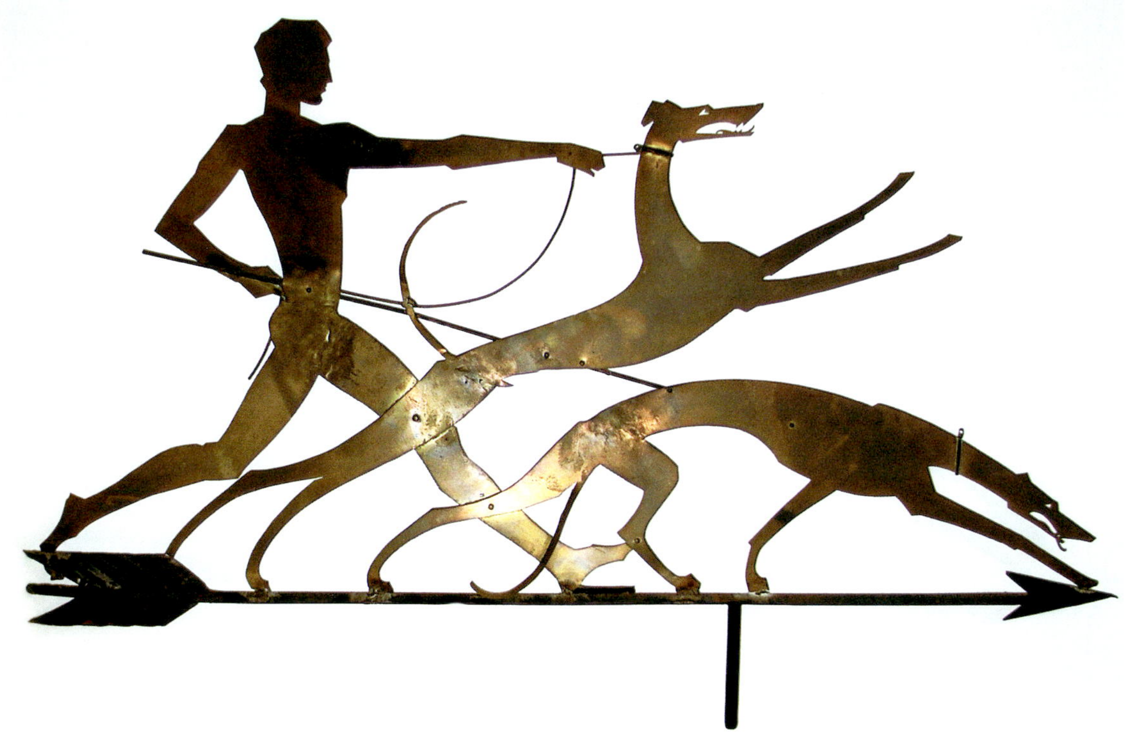

fig. 26 Hunt Diederich. Weathervane, ca. 1925. Iron and sheet brass. Collection of Jill and Mark Willcox Jr. Courtesy of the author.

the Byrdcliffe wood shops ceased production in 1905.[39] The craft classes at Byrdcliffe were certainly in the spirit of the movement even if they had little influence on later furniture design.

If the style the designers of Byrdcliffe furniture used was consistent with then current Arts and Crafts ideas, the details of construction were not. Like most of the proponents of the Arts and Crafts version of democracy, Whitehead was unable to make Byrdcliffe furniture available to people outside America's cultural elite.[40] This was not just because the furniture was expensive; it was also due to Whitehead's attitude of superiority. Then, as now, very few consumers cared what high-class taste pundits thought of the kind of furniture they liked or could afford to buy. Ultimately Byrdcliffe furniture, as beautiful as it is, was only art furniture and not Arts and Crafts furniture—it changed no one's way of life. The people who designed and made it moved beyond Arts and Crafts to work in other fields.[41] The pieces that got away either by purchase or gift were soon lost in fires, abused by neglect, or spiffed up with white paint or bright varnish.

We are fortunate to have so many details of furniture production at Byrdcliffe: the working drawings, the colored renderings, photographs of the workshop, partially finished pieces, and a large collection of the finished product. From these remnants we have gained insight into the workings of an American Arts and Crafts colony.

Notes

1. The first issue of Gustav Stickley's *Craftsman* magazine came out in 1901. It was a vehicle by which he marketed not just the furnishings he thought were needed in order to live the Arts ands Crafts life, but also plans for the kinds of buildings he wanted to house his products. *The Roycrofter, Fra Elbertus*, and *The Philistine* were among the several magazines Elbert Hubbard used for marketing Roycroft products.

2. In 1904 and 1905, *House Beautiful* published essays under the general title "The Poor Taste of the Rich: A Series of Articles Which Show That Wealth is Not Essential to the Decoration of a House, And That the Homes of Many of Our Richest Citizens Are Furnished in Execrable Taste." Similarly, in her article "Principles of Home Decoration" in the July 1905 issue of *American Homes and Gardens* Joy Wheeler Dow opined, "Fully three-quarters of the household furniture that is offered for sale in the huge furniture warerooms and department stores of this city [New York] is hopelessly bad in design," (35–36) and "Now, rich people sometimes have extremely poor taste" (36).

3. William L. Price, "The Building of a Chair," *The Artsman* (May 1904): 283.

4. For a discussion of the use of quartered oak in Grand Rapids, see Jane Perkins Claney and Robert Edwards, "Progressive Design in Grand Rapids," *TILLER* (September–October, 1983) and Frank E. Ransom, *The City Built of Wood: A History of the Furniture Industry in Grand Rapids, Michigan, 1850–1950* (Ann Arbor: Edwards Brothers, 1955).

5. Ralph Radcliffe Whitehead, *Grass of the Desert* (London: Chiswick Press, 1892), 63.

6. By 1903, when Murphy first signed the register at Byrdcliffe, he had already won four prizes in composition from the Académie Julian where he studied, as had Arthur Wesley Dow and Jane Byrd McCall, and a bronze medal from the Pan-American Exposition, Buffalo, 1901. He exhibited twice in Paris at the Exposition Nationales des Beaux-Arts and many times in Philadelphia at the Pennsylvania Academy of Fine Arts. In 1903, he opened a frame shop in Boston, Carrig-Rohane, with Charles Prendergast, and from 1902 until 1937 he taught life drawing at the Harvard University School of Architecture.

7. William Morris, "Labour and Pleasure *Versus* Labour and Sorrow, An Address" (reprinted with the title "The Beauty of Art" in "Hopes and Fears for the Arts," London, 1880).

8. "Nothing can be more ridiculous than an apparently reversed graining to walk upon, or highly relieved foliage and perforated tracery for the decoration of a floor." A. W. N. Pugin, *True Principles of Pointed or Christian Architecture*, 1841. The furniture Morris and Rossetti made for Morris's Red Lion Square lodgings and other furniture Morris made or decorated in the 1860s were virtually covered with illustrations of medieval myths. By 1899 when Morris & Co. was printing wallpapers, weaving rugs, and making furniture, Morris wrote in "Textiles," *Arts and Crafts Essays* that patterns should be "absolutely flat." He was writing specifically about carpets, but the patterns on his ceiling papers and the inlaid patterns on his furniture were also flat.

9. The author inventoried the Whitehead family home at Byrdcliffe, White Pines, in 1976 after the death of the Whiteheads' youngest son, Peter. Much of the contents remained untouched and as it had been before 1928 when both of Peter's parents were alive. A large lithographic reproduction of a Rivière print was found in the attic along with other art reproductions evidently used by the Whiteheads as educational aids. An oak frame (possibly Byrdcliffe-made) with an original Rivière woodblock print was hanging in the upstairs hall. Postcard reproductions of Rivière's series *La Marche l'Etoile* were found in a desk drawer along with Whitehead stationery. Since Peter Whitehead is not known to have knowledge of or interest in European art, it is probably safe to assume that these Rivière works were acquired by his parents.

10. Among the well-known Whistler nocturnes owned by Freer and in the United States before 1903 were *Nocturne: Blue and Silver—Battersea Reach, Nocturne: Silver and Opal—Chelsea, Nocturne: Blue and Gold—Valparaiso*. In 1904, Freer also purchased Whistler's sensational "Peacock Room," which was installed in his Detroit home. All these works were offered to the Smithsonian Institution in 1904 and so were then much in art-world news.

11. Ralph Radcliffe Whitehead, *Grass of the Desert*, 59–74.

12. Drawings for the blackbird desk are now among the collection of papers retrieved from Steele's studio and given by Alf Evers to the Woodstock Guild of Craftsmen. Zeshin's woodblock print was well known among Western collectors at the turn of the last century.

13. Plate 28, "Leaves and Flowers from Nature, No. 8." Christopher Dresser. Owen Jones, *The Grammar of Ornament* (London, 1856), unpaginated.

14. Bertha Thompson, "The Craftsmen of Byrdcliffe," *Publications of the Woodstock Historical Society* (July 1933): 10.

15. In 1901, Deerfield Society of Arts and Crafts members Dr. Edward C. Thorn (1874–1920) and Caleb Allen (1861–1927) designed and made a cabinet based on seventeenth-century "Hadley" chests. Their chest (cat. 62 in *"The Art That is Life": The Arts and Crafts Movement in America, 1875–1920* [Boston: Museum of Fine Arts, 1987], 176) has wrought-iron hardware that is very similar to copper handles on a Byrdcliffe "chiffonier" that is now in the Milwaukee Museum of Art (cat. 25).

16. This cabinet was offered at auction in "Tableaux & Sculptures Des XIX et XX Siècles" December 19, 2001, A 20 H-No 11 du Catalogue, Tajan Commissaires—Priseurs.

17. Ralph Radcliffe Whitehead, *Grass of the Desert*, 63.

18. *Ibid.*, 59–74.

19. The stool sketch was on page 57 of Whitehead's copy of *The Studio*, vol. 14, no. 63. The Baillie Scott "clothes press" was reproduced in "The Choice of Simple Furniture" (see page 26, fig. 10).

20. Bertha Thompson, "Personal History," Thompson Family Papers 1887–1947 (inclusive), The Thompson Family Collections, Schlesinger Library, Radcliffe Institute for Advanced Study, Harvard University.

21. Two tulip poplar–decorated cabinets are known. They are of different woods and are colored in different ways (see cat. 39). Three lamp stands with hollyhock decorations are known. Two have carved sides and one has painted panels (see cat. 37). Two chiffoniers with chestnut carvings are known (see cat. 25). They have identical coloring, but differing hardware. Four blanket chests with carved lily panels are known (see cat. 22). Three of these are of light-colored oak. One is dark-stained wood. Two identical large tables with lily carved panels are known. The original handwritten sales inven-

tories are now lost and exist only in electronic copy form in the author's collection.

22. George Eggers, Riulf Erlenson, Fordyce Herrick, and Olaf Westerling were hired as woodworkers. *Who Was Who in American Art* lists Eggers (1883–1958) as an artist who studied with Hermann Dudley Murphy, Birge Harrison, and Bolton Brown. He later became director of the Denver Art Museum and the Worcester Museum of Art. He was teaching industrial arts in 1923. Riulf Erlandson is listed in *Who Was Who in American Art* (1055) as a painter. No more information is provided. There is a drawing of a "yellow pine or cypress" cabinet (Winterthur Library, Downs Collection, 92x39.394) with Erlandson's name incorrectly spelled on it, indicating that he did not sign it. The cabinet is not known to exist and there is not yet any information regarding Erlandson's other activities at Byrdcliffe.

23. Series IX, Winterthur Library, Downs Collection.

24. *Art Nouveau: 1890–1914* (London, V&A Publications, 2000) is an exhaustive study which argues that all decorative arts produced anywhere in the world during the years 1890 to 1914 may be considered Art Nouveau. This premise necessarily includes the furniture designs of George Grant Elmslie, George Washington Maher, and Frank Lloyd Wright, traditionally among the Prairie School architects who have only recently been ensconced as heavyweights in the American Arts and Crafts movement. Accepting such an all-inclusive definition of Art Nouveau does not mean that the style was popular in the United States. The work of Prairie School architects was too radical. Factories like Tobey gave American consumers a tepid version of the Continental style by slipcovering old-fashioned forms with new swirls (for example, see cat. 100 in *"The Art That is Life": The Arts and Crafts Movement in America, 1875–1920* [Boston: Museum of Fine Arts, 1987], 242).

25. The whereabouts of the original lists are presently unknown. They exist in copy form in the author's collection.

26. While Day's *Nature in Ornament* (London: R.T. Batsford, 1892) is filled with illustrations of "simplified" and "quasi realistic" plant forms that obviously relate to Byrdcliffe designs, the closest analogies are to be found in *Some Principles of Everyday Art* (London, R.T. Batsford, 1894) particularly plate 29 and the "workmanlike flat carving" on page 103.

27. The Whiteheads' Morris & Co. desk is now in the Philadelphia Museum of Art.

28. Hervey White, "Ralph Radcliffe Whitehead," *Publications of the Woodstock Historical Society* (1933): 19.

29. Robert Edwards with Jane Perkins Claney, "Byrdcliffe: Life By Design" in *The Byrdcliffe Arts and Crafts Colony: Life by Design* (Wilmington: Delaware Art Museum, 1984), 4. The panel used on the desk (Winterthur Library, Downs Collection, photographs 92x39.1140.282 and .281) appears to be the piece that appears on an easel in an earlier photograph of Jane in an unknown studio, but the desk panel has a keyhole in the upper edge. The panel that survives in the collections of the Woodstock Guild of Craftsmen has no indication of a keyhole although it does have cutouts for two hinges along the bottom edge.

30. Sharon Darling, *Chicago Furniture: Art, Craft, & Industry, 1833–1933* (New York: The Chicago Historical Society in association with W. Norton & Company, 1984), 225.

31. Henry and William H. Fry and Benn Pitman founded the McMicken School of Design in Cincinnati, Ohio. There female students learned to carve furniture that had been constructed by male students.

32. This tiny gesso and gold-leaf frame has distinctive carved flowers in each corner that are almost a trademark of the Carrig-Rohane shop. The art of carving a frame, applying and preparing a gesso ground, and laying gold leaf requires intense training and could not be mastered in a few summer classes.

33. Drawing 92x39.237, Winterthur Library, Downs Collection, is of one of the commercially cast brass handles ordered in bulk for use on Byrdcliffe furniture drawers. The details of measurements were probably done to facilitate the drilling of holes on the cabinets for which this particular design was specified. Drawings 92x39.218, .217, and .215 describe hinges that were made at the Byrdcliffe forge for one of Dawson-Watson's now lost "Tirol" cabinets.

34. Bertha Thompson, "The Craftsmen of Byrdcliffe," 9.

35. H. Stuart Michie's pocket diary for June 29, 1906, notes, "Went down to Camberwell with Miss Woolrich, finished tray and large bowl." He accepted "Handicraft Guild of Minneapolis offer" that same year. He signed the Byrdcliffe register in the summer of 1907 (his friend Laurin Martin first signed the register in 1904). The metal pieces made at Camberwell are those that are shown in a photograph taken at Byrdcliffe and reproduced in *Inspiring Reform: Boston's Arts and Crafts Movement* (Wellesley, MA: The Davis Museum and Cultural Center, 1997), 83. (See also cat. 85, page 189.)

36. Bertha Thompson, "Personal History," Thompson Family Papers 1887–1947; and Lucy Brown, "The First Summer at Byrdcliffe," 18.

37. William Robert Mercer, Jr. was Henry Chapman Mercer's brother and Jane Byrd McCall Whitehead's cousin. He studied at the Académie Julian in 1895. He later built a house and studio near his brother in Doylestown, Pennsylvania, and became known for his plaster casts and concrete garden furnishings (Winterthur Library, Downs Collection, Drawing 92x39.231). The inscription "Grandeur Naturelle" could refer to the source for the design. As executed on Jane Whitehead's chest, the hardware is more oval than round as in the drawing. It is possible that the drawing was made while either Ralph or Jane was studying in Paris.

38. According to *Who Was Who in American Art* (914), Diederich studied at the Académie Julian (1904–5) and at the Pennsylvania Academy of Fine Arts. His reputation as a decorative sculptor was already established by the time he visited the Whiteheads in the 1920s (his name does not appear in the Byrdcliffe register, which most of the artists and craftsmen signed). As with the other metalworkers associated with Byrdcliffe, there is nothing to indicate that he used Byrdcliffe facilities. Diederich had artist friends in the town of Woodstock, among them the decorative painter Robert Chanler (another student of the Académie Julian). Konrad Cramer had a Diederich rooster weather vane, and other denizens of the town had examples of his ceramics and metalwork. He did not make the ceramic forms he decorated and many of his vane designs were made in multiples and executed in several mediums at factories nowhere near Woodstock.

39. Illustrations of pieces by Wheelock and Matthews may be found in *"The Art That is Life:" The Arts & Crafts Movement in America, 1875–1920*, cat. 80 and 175. Templeton's desk and chest are shown in *The Arts and Crafts Movement in California: Living the Good Life* (The Oakland Museum, 1993), cat. 183 and 184.

40. For the most part it was the rich who had the means and art education to acquire the Arts and Crafts furniture of the Greene Brothers, Will Price, Frank Lloyd Wright, and Ralph Radcliffe Whitehead. Arts and Crafts–style furnishings constituted but a small part of what was available to the rich and cultured at the turn of the last century in the United States. This class of consumer much preferred designs like those of the architectural firm of McKim, Mead, and White for their grand Beaux Arts mansions.

41. Bertha Thompson claimed that Edna Walker moved to New York City where she was director of American weaving at the famous Herter Looms. She then moved to Scotland and was not heard from again. Zulma Steele moved away from Byrdcliffe and is now best known for her excellent paintings. Byrdcliffe was but a blip in Murphy's illustrious career.

Art at Byrdcliffe

TOM WOLF

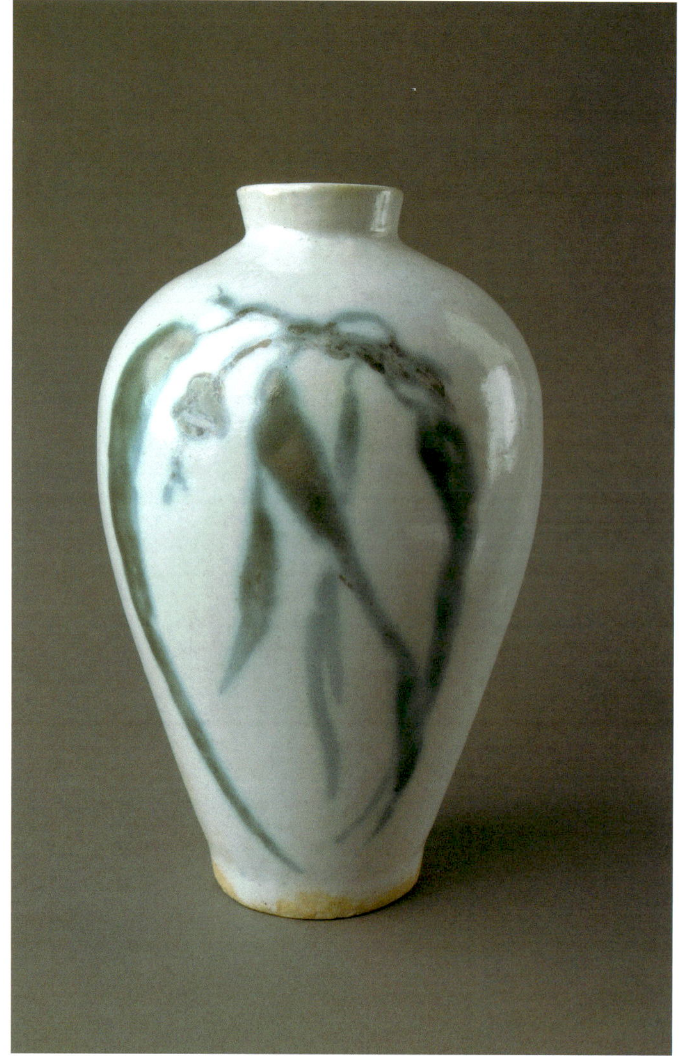

fig. 1 White Pines Pottery, *Eucalyptus pot*. Glazed ceramic. Woodstock Artists Association.

The Byrdcliffe colony was different from most Arts and Crafts colonies because, from its inception, the fine arts were incorporated as a central part of its identity. Its founder, Ralph Radcliffe Whitehead, was inspired by the Arts and Crafts movement in England, his native country, and that movement was closely allied with a group of painters, the Pre-Raphaelites. Whitehead's appreciation of painting and sculpture was part of his lifestyle, and from the start he planned Byrdcliffe as a place for artists to do their work, and to teach their skills to students.

Long before starting the colony, he and his wife, Jane McCall, had been immersed in the arts, and the prologue to the history of art at Byrdcliffe begins with the Whiteheads' encounters with art in England and Italy in the 1890s. After they moved to Santa Barbara in 1894 they associated with some of the most progressive painters in California at the time. Two of these, Bolton Brown and Birge Harrison, went on to Byrdcliffe.

At Byrdcliffe, the studio building was dominated by a spacious room specifically designed for painting classes, and senior artists had individual studios. The colony included many women artists, but only men taught in the school; most of them specialized in landscape painting, and several were members of the National Academy. Many of Byrdcliffe's painters had spent time in French art colonies; they generally worked in a textured, painterly manner related to Impressionism and leaning toward Tonalism, the American style of painting poetic subjects with muted colors.[1] The Tonalist aesthetic coexisted at Byrdcliffe with paintings composed of flat colors, one next to the other like pieces of a jigsaw puzzle. This mode derived from Japanese prints and French Post-Impressionist art, and was popularized in the United States by Arthur Wesley Dow, who sent several of his students to Byrdcliffe.

The artists of Byrdcliffe practiced the most popular and accepted styles of the early twentieth century, and it is striking to see a sudden change around the time of the 1913 Armory Show, which explosively introduced the radical innovations of European modernists to the American public. Early in the second decade of the twentieth century we find some of Byrdcliffe's artists, who had previ-

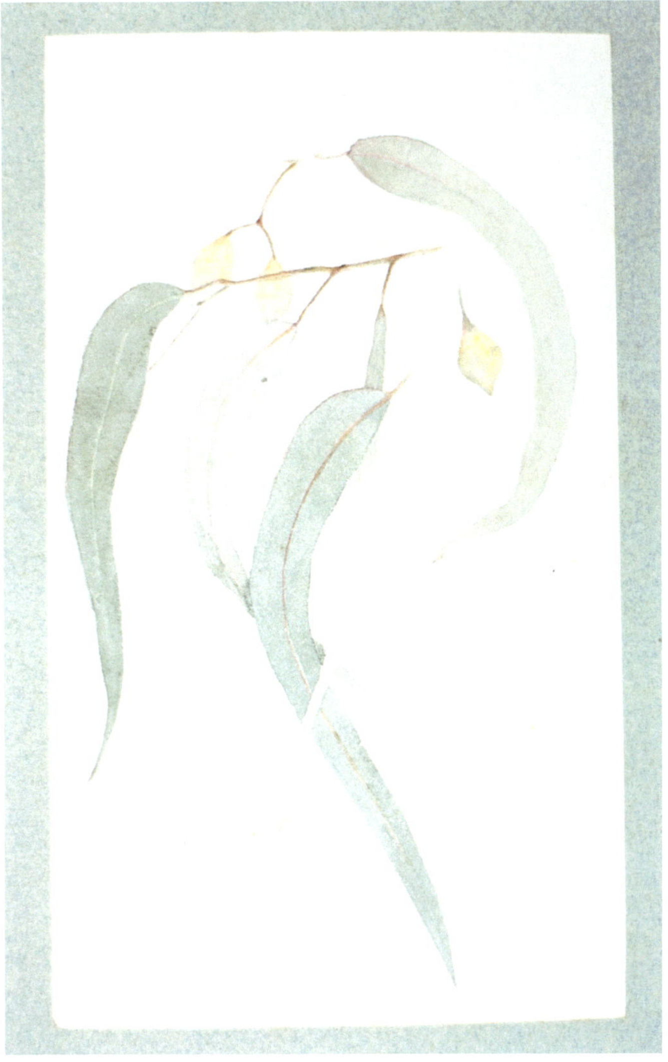

fig. 2 Jane Byrd Whitehead, *Eucalyptus*. Watercolor on paper. Private collection.

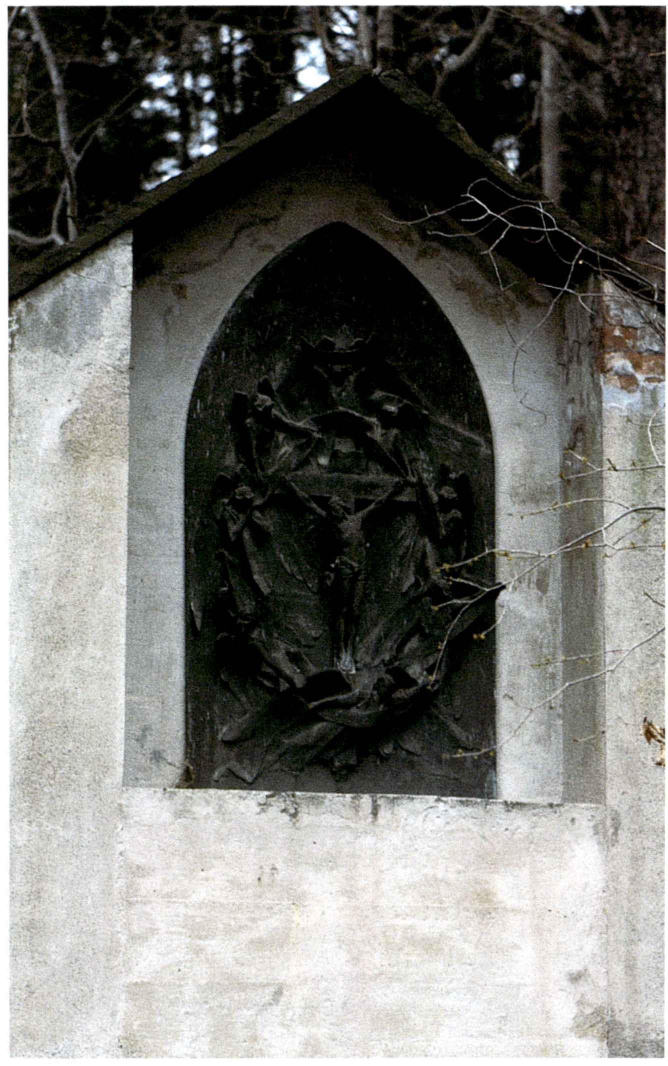

fig. 3 Rinaldo Carnielo, *Christ on the Cross with Angels*. Bronze. Woodstock Guild of Craftsmen.

ously worked in a Tonalist mode, building their paintings with slabs of bright color, a technique that descends from the dab-like brushstrokes of the Impressionists but, by enlarging them, incorporates the geometry and the abstraction of the new modernism.

Painting was the dominant fine art at Byrdcliffe, and in some instances it was integrated with furniture and frame making in ways that effectively realized the ideals of the Arts and Crafts movement. The painters at the colony were ambitious and willing to experiment with different media—besides painting, they worked in crafts, printmaking, and photography. Most of Byrdcliffe's artists are not well known today, and in several cases significant bodies of their works have disappeared; some of their careers are currently in the process of being retrieved, and examining them now opens up a fascinating chapter of the history of art in the United States.

Both Jane and Ralph Whitehead loved the art of Italy, the country where their courtship took place. She worked as an artist while also making many of the aesthetic decisions involving the décor of their homes in California and at Byrdcliffe. Through much of her life she would struggle to produce paintings despite the distractions of being a mother, suffering from ill health, and running a colony. Following the precepts of her mentor, John Ruskin, she made close studies from nature—on one occasion Ruskin was apparently by her side, drawing the same plant.[2] Along with painting, she designed occasional invitations and book covers, and when the Whiteheads turned to making ceramics, she adapted some of her floral watercolors for decoration on their pots (figs. 1 and 2).

During the early years of their relationship, the Whiteheads were immersed in the European art world. They saw exhibitions in London of the Pre-Raphaelites, and Whitehead contemplated buying paintings by Rossetti and Burne-Jones. He visited the studio of George Frederick Watts, a member of the Pre-Raphaelite circle, and proclaimed the artist's *Orpheus and Euridice* "the first design of our day or for that matter since Michelangelo."[3] It was not available for sale, but Whitehead did end up owning a splendid engraving of Watts's *Diana and Endymion* (see page 43). In 1893 the Whiteheads were in Paris, where Jane

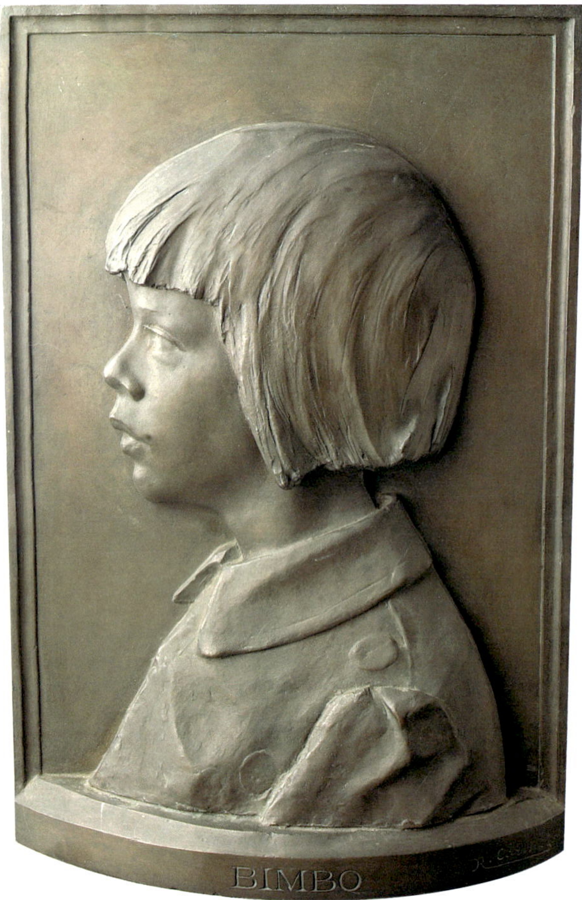

fig. 4 Rinaldo Carnielo, *Bimbo*, 1904. Bronze relief. Collection of the Woodstock Artists Association.

studied at the Académie Julian. On later visits to Florence they went to the studio of the painter Giovanni Segantini and spent time with art historian Bernard Berenson.[4] In 1889 Whitehead had befriended the Florentine sculptor Rinaldo Carnielo, whose bronze *Christ on the Cross with Angels* is still displayed in a shrine in front of White Pines at Byrdcliffe (fig. 3). Carnielo had achieved early success with his *Dying Mozart* of 1878, and he produced a wide range of work, from virtuoso, melodramatic monuments to functional objects. Carnielo struggled financially in his later years, and Whitehead attempted to help him by buying his works and trying to get them exhibited in London and the United States.[5] The sculptor was steeped in the Italian tradition, and his bronze relief bust of the Whiteheads' older son, from 1904, is modeled in pure profile, evoking early Renaissance portraits (fig. 4).

Once they came to the United States and settled in Montecito in 1894, the Whiteheads fraternized with a group of ambitious California painters, including landscapist Birge Harrison, who had a studio adjacent to their Arcady estate and who would become an influential art teacher in Woodstock. Whitehead also befriended a trio of painters based in Pasadena: Charles Walter Stetson, William Wendt, and Leonard Lester. Stetson was recently divorced from feminist author Charlotte Perkins, whom Whitehead had met in Chicago. After the divorce Stetson married his wife's good friend Grace Channing, and they raised his and Perkins's daughter with Perkins's approval in Channing's father's house in Pasadena. Stetson was a versatile and well-respected artist who nevertheless had difficulties supporting himself; he wanted to paint ambitious literary paintings and mythological fantasies while the market preferred portraits and still lifes. After Whitehead visited Stetson's studio in 1899 he wrote, "He's an artist alright, though he is not a great painter. He has color and imagination," which from Whitehead was high praise for a living artist.[6] In March 1900 Stetson executed several decorative paintings for one of Whitehead's outbuildings at Arcady, including a panel of Tuscan fleurs-de-lys that the artist described as "Very directly painted but about as good as any thing I've done."[7] Both men admired Watts, and the British painter's range, from ambitious mythological paintings to dramatic landscapes, combined with his fascination with the female nude, served as a model for Stetson, who wrote in 1885 that Watts's paintings were "nearer like what I have dreams of doing than any I have seen."[8] In Pasadena, Stetson painted pagan fantasies executed with daringly loose brushwork and rich color, as well as more subdued scenes like *Under the*

fig. 5 Charles Walter Stetson, *Under the Oleander*, 1896. Oil on canvas. Courtesy of William Vareika Fine Arts, Newport, RI.

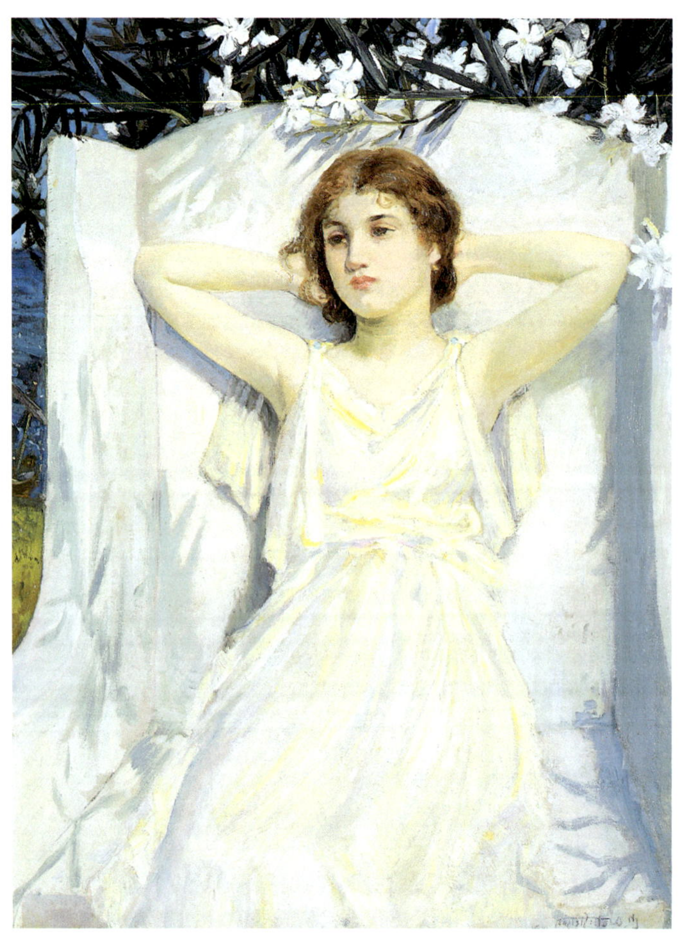

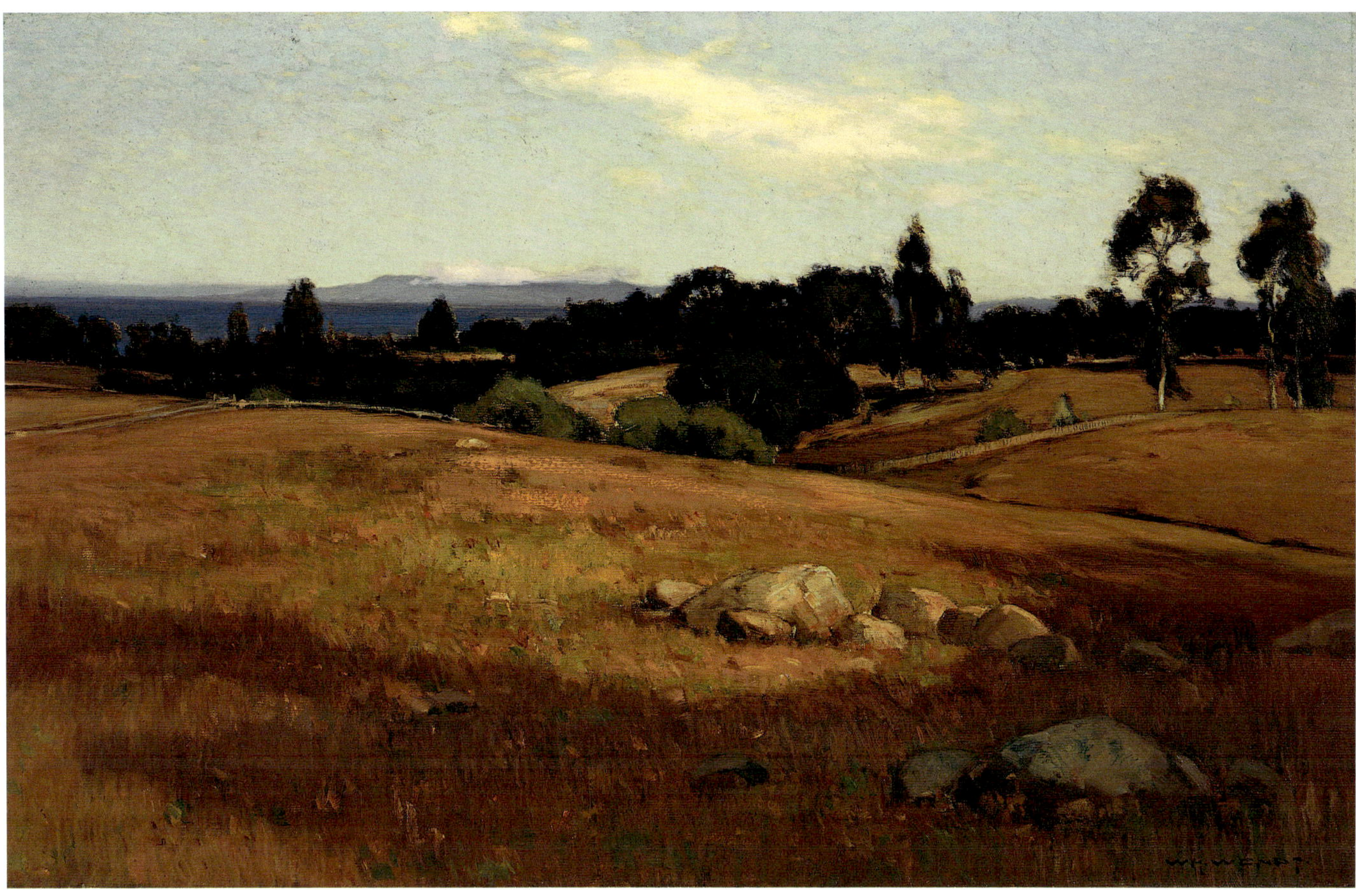

fig. 6 William Wendt, *Distant Coast*, ca. 1905. Oil on canvas.
Courtesy of William A. Karges Fine Art.

Oleander, which is still sensual in its image of a pensive young woman, its painterly touch, and its subtle harmonies of off-whites (fig. 5).

The painters who would be associated with Byrdcliffe shared Stetson's fondness for moonlit landscapes. The mood of Romantic mystery evoked by such scenes was characteristic of American Symbolist tendencies of the late nineteenth century inspired in part by the nocturnes of James McNeill Whistler.[9] Whitehead considered Whistler "the greatest best painter whom America has produced," an opinion shared by most of the artists at Byrdcliffe.[10]

William Wendt also painted moonlit scenes around the turn of the century, though he would develop an individualistic style of painting, with firm compositions and broad, tactile strokes, that led to his being considered one of the major early twentieth-century painters in California.[11] German-born, he came to Chicago when he was fifteen and developed into an artist there; in the 1890s he began taking extended painting trips to California. Carl Eric Lindin, who would be one of the first painters at Byrdcliffe, knew Wendt in Chicago, and introduced him to writer Hervey White and Whitehead's California circle around 1900.[12] It was in Santa Barbara that Wendt excitedly warned White that Whitehead was just a dilettante amusing himself with artists:

> To which I replied naturally that I was willing to be his buffoon if he took me places I wanted to go. . . . He is familiar with a life that I know nothing of, and as a novelist if not as a friend, I can gain great advantage by being with him. Wendt usually relented after his outbursts and wound up with, "After all, I am rather fond of old papa."[13]

Wendt's skepticism about Whitehead did not prevent him from accepting the use of studio space near Arcady, in a converted barn he shared for a time with White and Leonard Lester. Wendt's *Distant Coast* has tentatively been dated circa 1905 because it has elements of his firmed-up later style; but the Channel Islands on the horizon define it as being a view from Santa Barbara, and the sweeping vista, with the boulders in the foreground and the ocean beyond, have some of the feeling of the view from Arcady[14] (fig. 6).

Lester was a British painter who, like Wendt, made his career in California. He eventually settled in San Diego, where he married artist Miriam Butler. The mural of the California coast Lester painted for Whitehead's manual training school at Arcady is almost twenty feet long (fig. 7). Its light-infused colors, glowing pink at the horizon, give the panoramic scene a mystical effect related to the landscapes painted by members of the Point Loma Theosophical group, with whom Lester would associate in his San Diego days.[15]

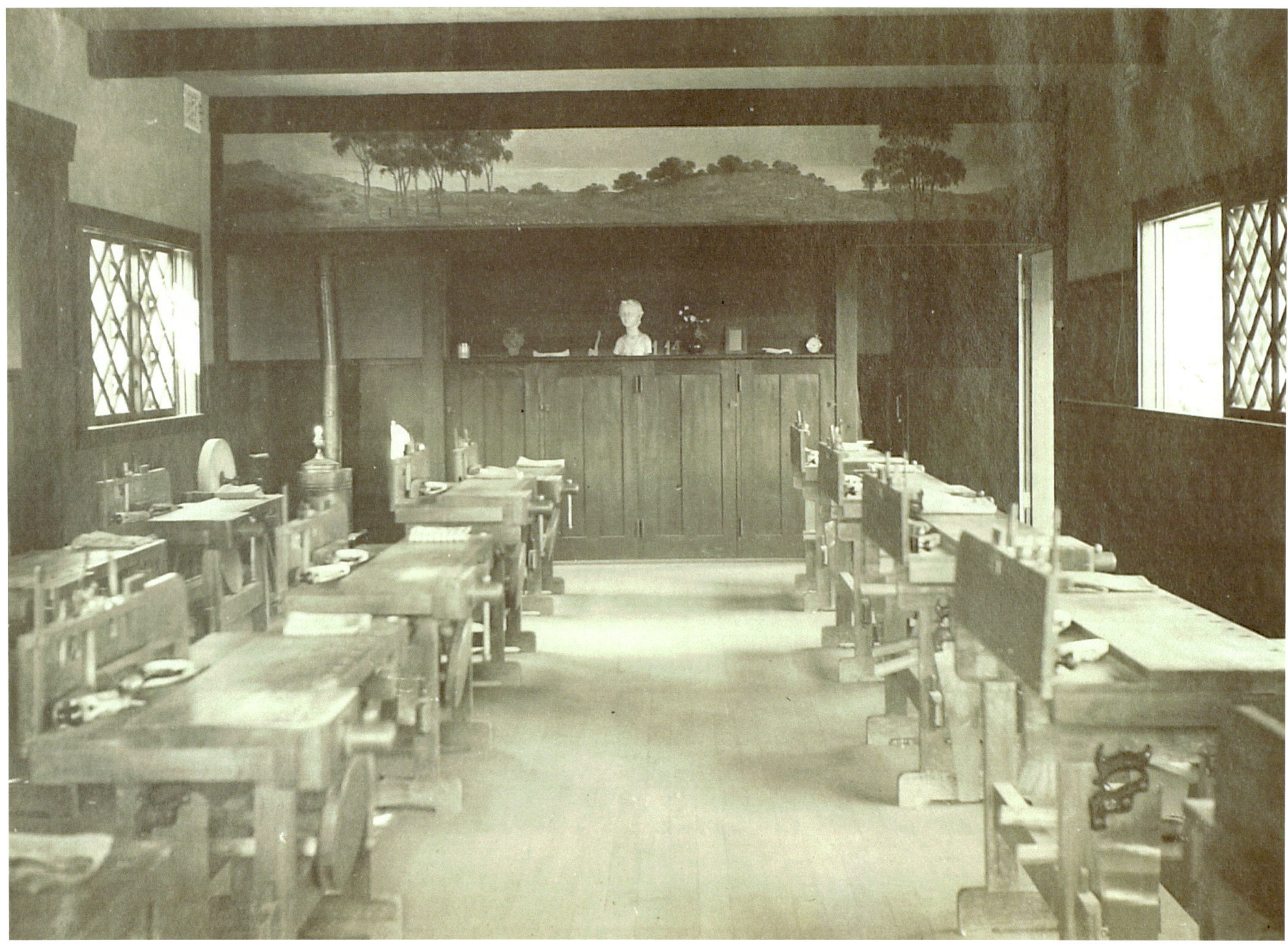

fig. 7 Unidentified photographer, *Leonard Lester's Montecito School Mural*, ca. 1895. Winterthur Library, Downs Collection, 92x39.1140.603.

In 1900 Lester took a tour of Europe financed by Hervey White, who, with typical generosity, gave Lester royalties from his novel *Differences*. "I still held to my idea that I had no right to any profit from my art," White later recalled[16] In the same year, the writer accompanied Stetson to Europe, serving as an aide to the artist, who was in poor mental shape, drinking too much and in need of a change of scene.[17] On this trip White and Whitehead got together in Paris, where they agreed to develop their plans for an Arts and Crafts colony when back in the United States. They met again in Indianapolis with Bolton Brown, the third member of their group, and by 1902 they had decided on Woodstock as the site for their colony. Whitehead purchased the land, and White and Brown supervised the construction of the buildings that would house the artists and students in 1903, when the colony began functioning.

Brown was the first painter at Byrdcliffe, as he discovered the site. Born in Dresden, New York, he fell under the spell of Ruskin and made thousands of drawings from nature before turning to etching and then painting. He was the first professor of art at Stanford University, and encountered Whitehead in California as a customer for the Japanese prints he dealt in on the side. During Brown's first year at Byrdcliffe he made designs for furniture, trays, lampshades, and other functional objects, as well as paintings. The mystery is why so few of his paintings are known today, given that he was a compulsively energetic and organized man who devoted several decades of his life to being a painter.[18] Of those that do exist, several are landscapes strikingly simplified in form, with precisely attuned colors that convey the artist's spiritual feeling for nature (cat. 56). In the Tonalist *Sifting Shadows*, Brown delineated another of his favorite subjects, a demure idealized nude surrounded by trees, painted in subdued but radiant hues (cat. 57).

The Byrdcliffe Art School was intended to be a "year around school of painting, decoration and handicraft."[19] The instructors for its first term were two painters to teach art, Brown and Hermann Dudley Murphy, plus Dawson Dawson-Watson to teach decorative design and Giovanni Troccoli to teach woodcarving. The art students worked directly from the landscape outdoors and from the model in the studio; the instructors gave one public criticism and one individual instruction at the easel each week. Whitehead had hired Brown to direct the school but became disillusioned with him and demoted him to drawing instructor. Disappointed, and critical of what he felt was undisciplined art instruction, Brown left, although Whitehead amicably allowed him to buy some property nearby at a low price, providing the artist with a home in the Woodstock area for the rest of his career.

In 1915 Brown shifted his interest to lithography, which he pursued with characteristic fervor for the next decade. He became a major force in the popularization of that medium, writing extensively and working as a printer for artists such as George Bellows and Arthur B. Davies. His own prints were characterized by their technical excellence and silvery tones. Brown was an artist who constantly turned back on himself: some of his lithographs were based on drawings he had made over two decades before, in California, and many of his prints from the early stages of his career as a lithographer, such as *Cloudy Dawn*, revert back to the subdued, nearly abstract values of his Tonalist paintings (fig. 8). After 1925 Brown's interests turned from lithography to ceramics. He made small, thick-walled bowls with graceful decorations in earth-colored glazes, that recall his early interest in Japanese art (cat. 109). Like many Byrdcliffe artists, Brown moved easily between fine arts and crafts.

If Brown was the first artist in Byrdcliffe, Carl Eric Lindin was close on his heels. Born in Sweden, Lindin moved to Chicago as a teenager, became part of the Hull House community, and befriended Hervey White. In the late 1890s a collector financed Lindin's studies at the Académie Julian in Paris, after which he returned to Chicago, exhibiting ten paintings at the Art Institute in 1897. When Byrdcliffe's founders started developing the colony, in the summer of 1902, Lindin was there, sharing an abandoned Lutheran church with White and Captain Fritz Van der Loo, another friend of White's. Lindin made Woodstock his home for the next forty years; in 1911 he and his wife bought the church and turned it into their residence, complete with his paintings set into the dark wood walls, and tiles by him and his wife decorating the premises (fig. 9). Lindin described himself in his Chicago years as a "painter of moonlight and night."[20] His *Landscape*, with its deep blue tones ignited by the central orb of the moon typifies his early style, and its suggestive, veiled quality is typically Tonalist (cat. 65).

Painter Hermann Dudley Murphy greatly impressed Whitehead in early 1903, when the Englishman visited Boston looking for artists to work at Byrdcliffe. Murphy had studied at the Académie Julian in Paris, as had Mrs. Whitehead and Lindin, and back in the U.S. his career was on a roll—he won a bronze medal at the Pan American Exposition in Buffalo in 1901 and in 1902 he began teaching art at Harvard University, where he would work for thirty-five years. He also began teaching at the Worcester Museum School in 1903, and founded the Carrig-Rohane framing business with his friend Charles Prendergast.

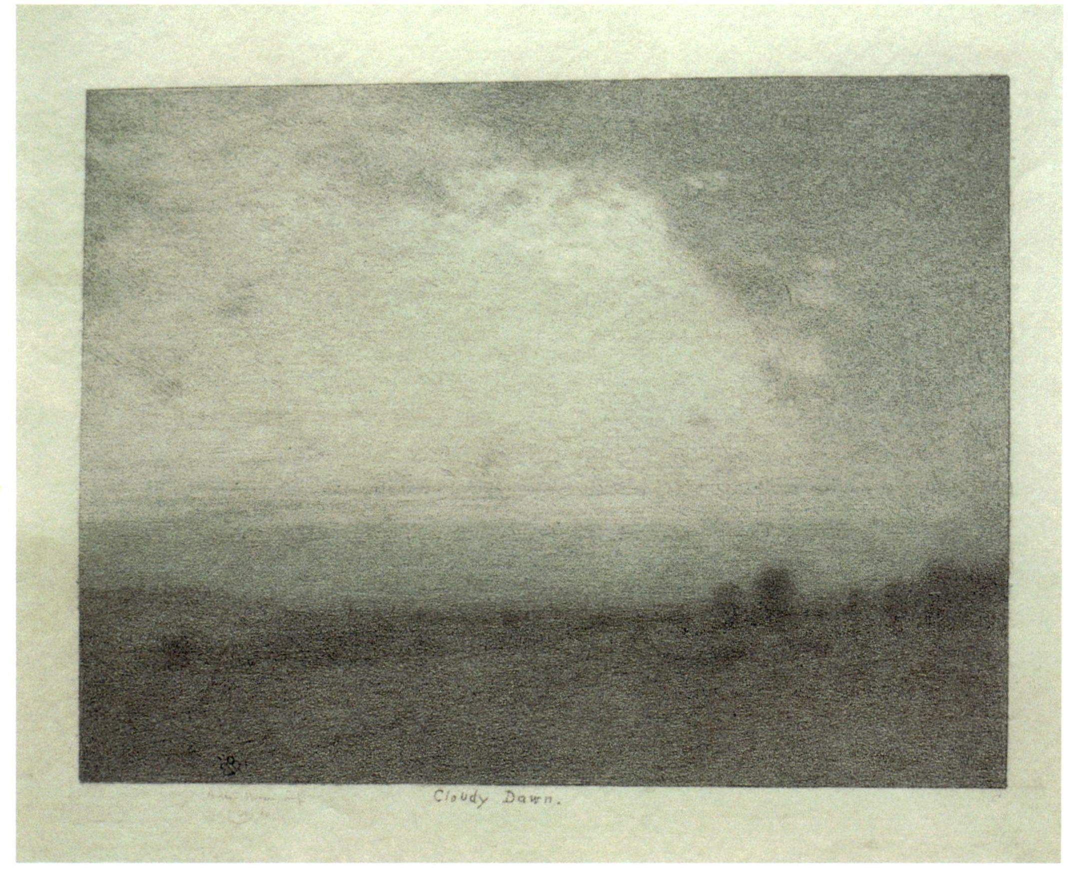

fig. 8 Bolton Brown, *Cloudy Dawn*, 1916. Lithograph. Courtesy of the author.

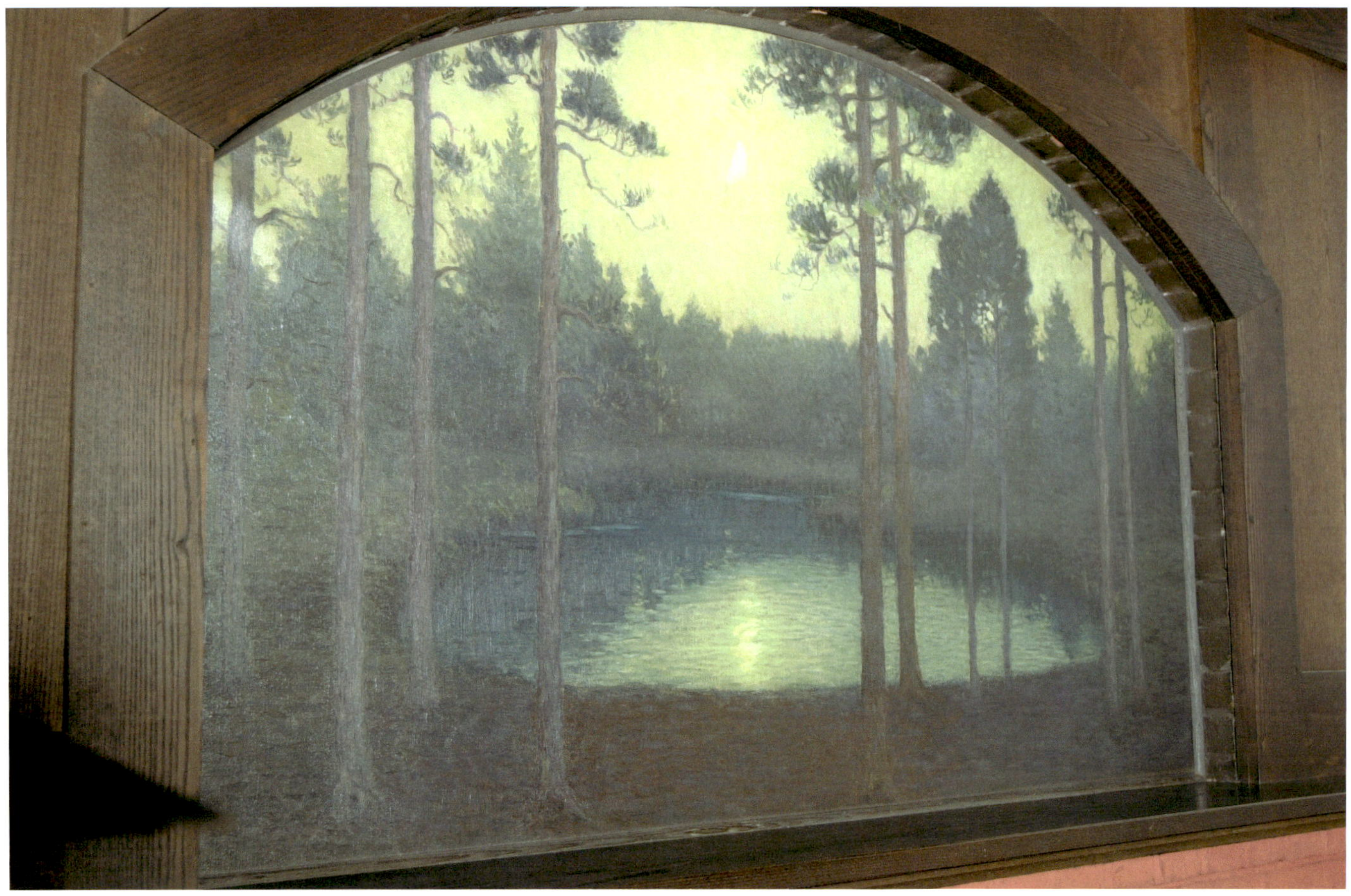

fig. 9 Interior of *Talledungen*, Carl Eric Lindin and Louise Hastings Lindin's house in Woodstock, with mantel painting by Lindin.

In the midst of all this activity, he spent the summers from 1903 to 1905 at Byrdcliffe, painting, teaching, and making frames.[21] He received acclaim for his portraits, but he preferred landscapes, and painted some marvelously delicate and atmospheric Woodstock views. Although in his later years he became an opponent of modernism, some of his little landscapes painted at Byrdcliffe are remarkably abstract: views of the sky, or a mountain's face that takes up most of the canvas with only a little slice of sky in a top corner.

One of the most distinctive Byrdcliffe objects is a small rectangular cabinet with two panels of a landscape by Murphy set into it (cat. 20). Murphy's experience with frame making, which includes preparing wood for gilding or painting, may explain why this landscape is one of the best preserved of the Byrdcliffe paintings on furniture. The two panels depict one continuous vista divided in half by the frames of the doors. Murphy unified the scene by composing the landscape of three horizontal bands: the meadow, the mountain range, and the sky—flat units which are pushed into deep space by the glistening river which curls into depth, winding back from the foreground of the right panel to the background of the left. The result is a tour-de-force actualization of the Arts and Crafts ideal of uniting fine art with craft. Murphy was well suited to accomplish this feat—some of his landscapes from this period were remarkably horizontal in proportion, and lent themselves to being divided in such a fashion. For example, his *Landscape* (ca. 1903), probably a Woodstock view, is more than twice as long as it is wide (cat. 67). Murphy's stretched-out formats can be related to Asian scroll paintings, a translation of Asian ink technique into European oil painting that is typical of turn of the century *Japonisme*, while his splitting of a unified landscape space has something in common with Japanese screens.[22]

A multitalented British artist, Dawson Dawson-Watson made a substantial contribution to Byrdcliffe during the summer of 1903, both as a painter and a furniture designer. Dawson-Watson's father was an illustrator and painter, and the son was raised in an artistic milieu where he learned design and the decorative arts as well as painting and printmaking. A patron financed his studies in Paris, and in 1888 he began frequenting the artists' colony that formed around the home of Claude Monet at Giverny. That colony included many American artists, and Dawson-Watson was encouraged to relocate to the United States in 1897. After several years in Connecticut he moved to Quebec, where he met the Whiteheads' painter friend Birge Harrison, a fellow veteran of French art colonies. Harrison, who was painting snow scenes in Canada, recommended him to Whitehead.[23]

During his summer at Byrdcliffe, Dawson-Watson designed furniture, including a dramatic settle with scalloped side wings filled with interlacing floral ornament (cat. 14). Unlike most of the furniture made at the colony, it echoes the French Art Nouveau style, popular at the turn of the century, although its massiveness is typical of Byrdcliffe. In his remarkable 1903 painting *Aster, Mullein, Burgloss, Bergamot*, Dawson-Watson depicted a Hudson Valley landscape with a palette of delicately varied blues, harnessed by thin pencil lines (cat. 60). This is a departure from his earlier works, which were painted in a thickly textured, Impressionist style, and it reflects the Japanese-influenced style of Dow. Back in France in 1893, Dawson-Watson had exhibited with pioneers of the modern, flat style, including Paul Gauguin, Pierre Bonnard, and Edouard Vuillard.[24] This painting, and a few small studies related to it, suggests that at Byrdcliffe the artist adopted the decorative style he saw early on in France and experienced again in its American manifestation at Byrdcliffe. The painting is exhibited in a custom-made frame that has the names of the local plants in the landscape carved into it. Together frame and painting make a quintessential Arts and Crafts object, its imagery based on local flora, with fine art (painting) inextricably united with craft (the frame) into total unity. A similar fusion of art and craft is found in a Byrdcliffe chest (see page 74) that includes landscape paintings that are attributed to Dawson-Watson because they share a vocabulary of flat, blue, outlined shapes with *Aster, Mullein, Burgloss, Bergamot* (see cat. 60). Information about Dawson-Watson's summer at Byrdcliffe is scant, and more needs to be known; after 1903 he went on to pursue a career as an artist in St. Louis and then in San Antonio, Texas. While most of Byrdcliffe's artists favored the Tonalist style, another example of the flat style can be found in the striking book cover Jane Whitehead designed for one of the Whiteheads' musical anthologies, *The Morning Stars Sang Together: Folk-Songs and Other Songs for Children*, published in 1903 (cat. 11).[25]

After he met the Hermann Dudley Murphys in Boston in 1903, Whitehead wrote, "Someday perhaps they will come to Woodstock for the summer to do color prints, at least so I fondly imagine!"[26] He wanted printmaking in his colony because of its democratic nature—prints, since they are produced in multiple copies, are more affordable than paintings, which are unique. Brown was selling Japanese prints when he met Whitehead in California, and wood-block printing is what the Englishman encouraged in his colony. He brought young Vivian Bevans from Chicago, where she had studied with the respected Norwegian artist B. J. O. Nordfeldt, a Japanese-art enthusiast who was known for his wood-block prints. Bertha Thompson recalled, "On the strength of her work with Nordfeldt (and her unusual beauty and charm)—Mr. Whitehead invited Vivian to 'Byrdcliffe' to teach wood-block printing."[27] Soon Bevans would marry Hervey White. Apparently she was a serious, active Byrdcliffe artist, but her art has almost totally disappeared, including her ceramics as well as her prints. One of the few pieces known by her is a small but impressive block print of a city at dusk (cat. 159).[28] The luminous little print, with dark blue silhouettes of buildings printed over the glowing orange and yellow rectangles that represent lit windows, was made by an artist of considerable promise.

In the print shop, Bevans helped Birge Harrison with his unusual technique of combining block printing and pastel. Harrison believed that pastel could be superior to oil on canvas, since the latter was customarily varnished, producing a glossy, reflective surface which made it less atmospheric than the grainy, matte surface of a pastel. The pastel chalk needed to be rubbed into heavy, porous paper so it would not smear or flake off.[29] He published these observations a decade after working with Bevans at Byrdcliffe, when a severe attack of lead poisoning forced him to abandon oil paint and turn to pastel, but his involvement with the medium dates back to those days in 1904. One work that features woodblock and pastel in combination is a lyrical view of a quiet river under a glowing moon (cat. 163).[30] The contours of the scene were printed in woodblock and then colored with cool blue hues that dominate the landscape, complemented by the yellow moon and its flickering reflection. The serenely moored rowboat recalls Arthur Wesley Dow's use of the same calm motif in his wood-block prints, while the meditative mood and the delicately varied colors are typical of Harrison's paintings.

Zulma Steele and Edna Walker, roommates who had studied with Dow at the Pratt Institute in Brooklyn before coming to Byrdcliffe, also made wood-block prints, as well as drawings for Byrdcliffe furniture under Whitehead's supervision. These two young women designed the floral carvings that decorate some of Byrdcliffe's finest pieces. In the manner of Ruskin and Dow, they made detailed studies from nature, which they then stylized into ornamental drawings; these drawings were guides for the craftsmen who carved the panels for the furniture. A page of drawings by Steele includes a realistic study of a day lily and some orange flower petals next to a design for a decorative spoon derived from those details (cat. 179). A study of a flowering plant becomes an Arts and Crafts furniture panel when slightly recomposed and intersected by framing units (cat. 177). Steele and Walker also made lovely block prints of floral subjects on delicate, translucent paper, often including their initials enclosed in floating rectangles, emulating the seal of Japanese printmakers. Steele's sensitively rendered *Lily*, which represents one of the symbols of Byrdcliffe, was hand colored after it was printed (cat. 172). When she adapted the flower for a carved relief to ornament bulky pieces of furniture, such as a blanket chest, she stiffened the flower's delicate sway into a pure vertical to echo the chest's geometry (cat. 22).

In their willingness to move from one medium to another, Steele and Walker were typical Byrdcliffe artists.

Walker made prints and designs for furniture, and then helped Whitehead when he began handweaving; eventually she left the colony to direct weaving at Herter Looms. Steele, whose brother, Frederick Dorr Steele, was a well-known illustrator of Sherlock Holmes novels, lived in Woodstock for most of her productive life. From the start she was ambitious to paint; her 1904 *Summer*, with its misty blue-gray color scheme, is a fine example of Byrdcliffe Tonalism, and the fact that it features three women and one man relaxing in an unspoiled landscape indicates how women outnumbered men at the colony (cat. 76). Her monumental drawing *Crows*, over five feet long, is a study for three panels to be set into a piece of furniture (cat. 171). Steele arranged the dramatic silhouettes of the black birds in flight across the panels in an asymmetrical image that recalls Japanese prints and screens.

While Whitehead encouraged block prints, lithography was a source of controversy. The artists wanted Whitehead to include a lithographic press among the facilities at the colony, but he refused. White and Lindin supported the idea, which would seem in line with Whitehead's desire for a democratic art, but he apparently thought lithography, which was associated with advertising and commerce, not artistic enough.[31] White later referred to this episode as "our great disappointment," and felt it gave him insight into the central problem of the colony: Whitehead "would only employ people he could dictate to, and no self-respecting artist would ever stand for his dictation."[32] It would be left for Bolton Brown, a decade later, to become an important popularizer of lithography. The controversy was at the center of artist John Duncan's brief involvement with Byrdcliffe. Duncan spent three years teaching in Chicago, visiting from his native Scotland; Vivian Bevans was one of his students. In his paintings he illustrated Celtic, Greco-Roman, and Christian subjects and rendered them in a linear style that owed a lot to the Pre-Raphaelites—art that Whitehead could instantly appreciate. Whitehead enlisted Duncan to teach printmaking at Byrdcliffe, but after spending part of the summer there in 1903 the artist apparently withdrew once it became clear that no lithographic press would be available.[33] A small plaster relief of *St. Francis and the Birds*, designed by Duncan and modeled by Bevans, features the dry, precise contours and traditional subject matter that characterized Duncan's style after he returned to Scotland in 1903 (cat. 124).

By the second summer of the Colony, Brown had moved on, and Lowell Birge Harrison came to teach painting. Harrison was an old friend of the Whiteheads'; in the 1890s he lived next to their estate in Montecito, painting with Jane, critiquing her work, and taking camping trips with Whitehead. Harrison was born in Pennsylvania, and studied with Thomas Eakins before moving to Paris in 1876 for almost a decade, at the suggestion of John Singer

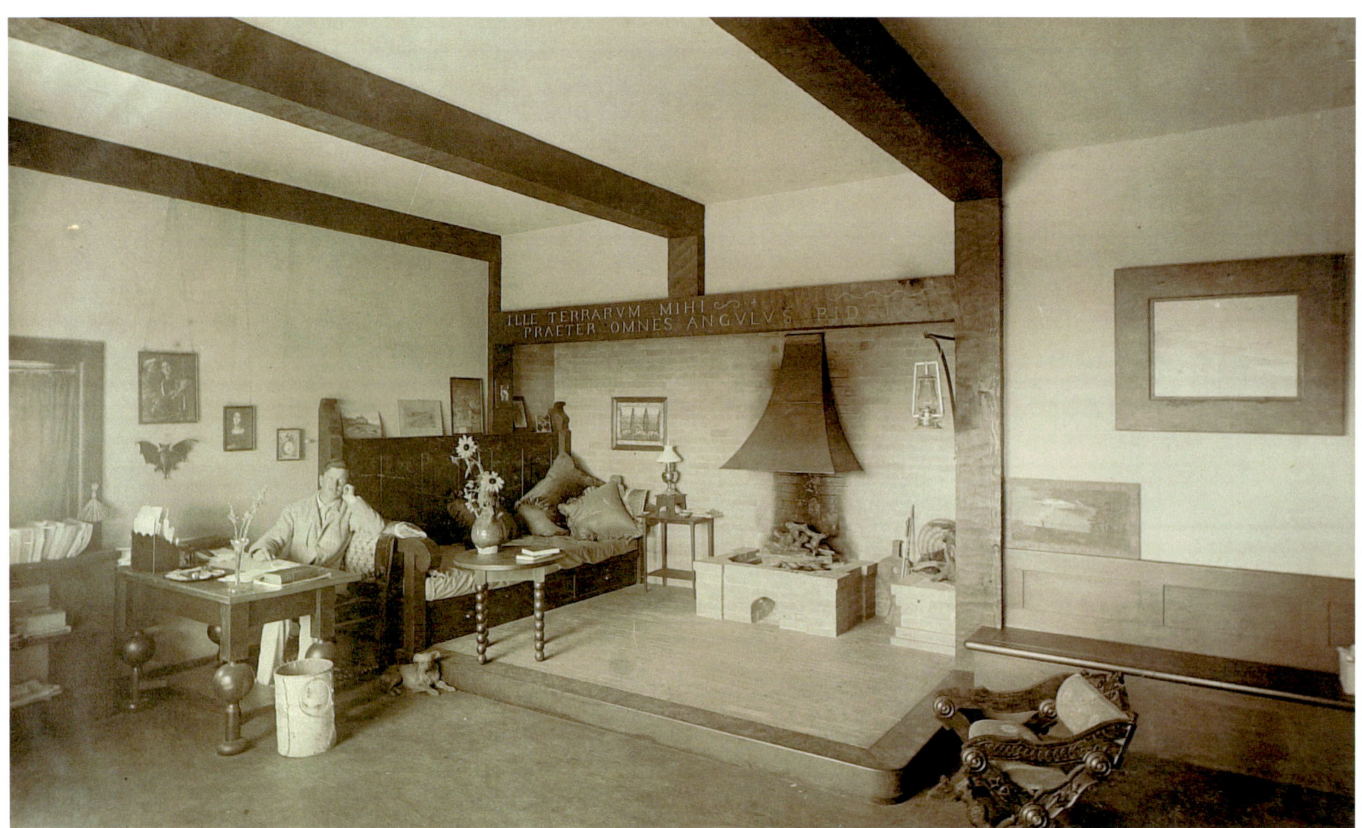

fig. 10 Unidentified photographer, *Arcady Interior with Birge Harrison's painting* Serenity on the Pacific *at right*, ca. 1895. Winterthur Library, Downs Collection, 92x39.1140.28.

Sargent. His older brother, Alexander, was an esteemed marine painter who lived in Paris and was a friend of Arthur Wesley Dow. In France Harrison studied at the Ecole des Beaux-Arts for six years, during which he saw the Impressionists' early exhibitions. While he admired their accomplishments, his heart was really with the preceding generation of Corot and Millet, and in France he made paintings of peasant laborers in rural landscapes that recall Millet. After a decade Harrison left France because of health reasons and traveled around the world, visiting India, Ceylon, Africa, South America, and Australia, in addition to living with Native American tribes in Arizona. He painted little, but wrote and illustrated travel articles for *Scribners Magazine*.

In mid career, Harrison decided to become a landscape painter rather than a figure painter, and he developed a delicate, richly colored style related to Tonalism. Like the late nineteenth-century Symbolist painters, he felt it crucial to go beyond realism to something more poetic: the highest form of art "should stimulate the imagination and suggest more than it expresses."[34] In a knowing critique of the Impressionist credo, he wrote:

> I believe that the final picture must always be painted from *memory*; and I seriously question whether any really great landscape was ever wholly painted in the open .... Of course one must paint what one sees, but one must see through the mind as well as through the eye.[35]

In typical Tonalist fashion he avoided mundane realism by painting scenes set at night, dawn, or dusk, and snow landscapes where the contours of objects were suggestively veiled.

Harrison's *Serenity on the Pacific*, with a mother-of-pearl color scheme and simple but vast composition, was owned by the Whiteheads in California (fig. 10) (cat. 64). His *Woodstock Meadows in Winter* (cat. 62), with its receding river opening up the space and leading to a rural farmhouse, set a type for Woodstock scenes that was followed by many of Harrison's students. When Whitehead first saw Woodstock he described it as "painters country"; the well-traveled Harrison, a connoisseur of landscapes, wrote an insightful analysis of Woodstock's topography.[36] He pointed out that the area is partly a valley, framed by mountains on three sides, but it develops into a plain to the east, which culminates in the Hudson River. Mountains, rivers, and flatlands are available to the landscape painter, as well as snowy winters, quiet ponds, and exuberant falls:

> The close juxtaposition of the mountains and the plains made possible many beautiful picture motives which could have existed under no other conditions, for the low-lying country to the east, with its long, level horizon, furnished just the ideal landscape over which to paint the clouds which had been tossed into racks of magnificent and dramatic beauty by the towering mountain peaks to the west.[37]

Harrison painted a series of nocturnal skies that combine realism with abstraction in a way so reductive that they seem to make the next generation's movement into pure abstraction inevitable (fig. 11). Brown and Murphy painted comparable scenes, dominated by sky, that occupy an art-historical position between John Constable's cloud studies of the 1820s and Alfred Stieglitz's *Equivalents* photographs of the 1920s, as these traditionally minded Byrdcliffe artists inadvertently made some quite modern paintings.

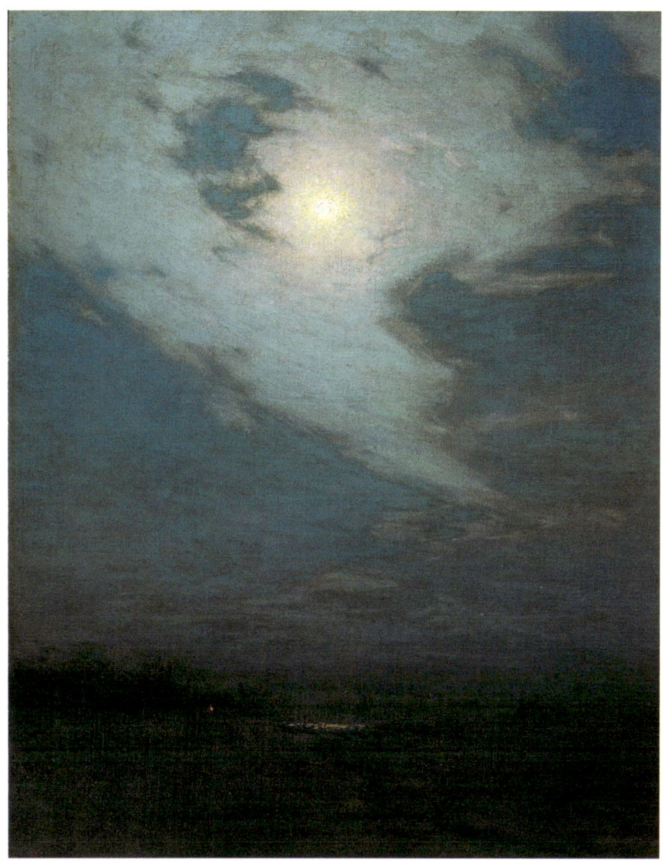

fig. 11 Birge Harrison, *Soaring Cloud*, ca. 1910. Oil on canvas.
Courtesy of the National Arts Club.

Following Harrison's retirement from teaching at Byrdcliffe in 1905, painting was taught by Leonard Ochtman, an accomplished landscape painter from the Cos Cob artists' colony in Connecticut. Born in Holland, Ochtman spent his youth in Albany. He developed a style of loosely painted, serene landscape subjects that allied him with Hermann Dudley Murphy and with Birge Harrison (who reproduced Ochtman's paintings in several of his essays).[38] Critic Charles Caffin honored Ochtman by including one of his paintings in his 1907 book, *The Story of American Painting*, and writing, "Among the artists of this country who have taken the lead in studying nature in the light of the open air, Ochtman has won a foremost position.... Few canvases equal his in refinement of observation and delicate tonality."[39] Ochtman shared Bolton Brown's and Harrison's belief in the importance of memory in painting: "I find that in painting my pictures away from nature I get better results, for, after all, we want the effect of the day, hour or moment, the mood and not a transcript of the place."[40] He reproduced *In May* to

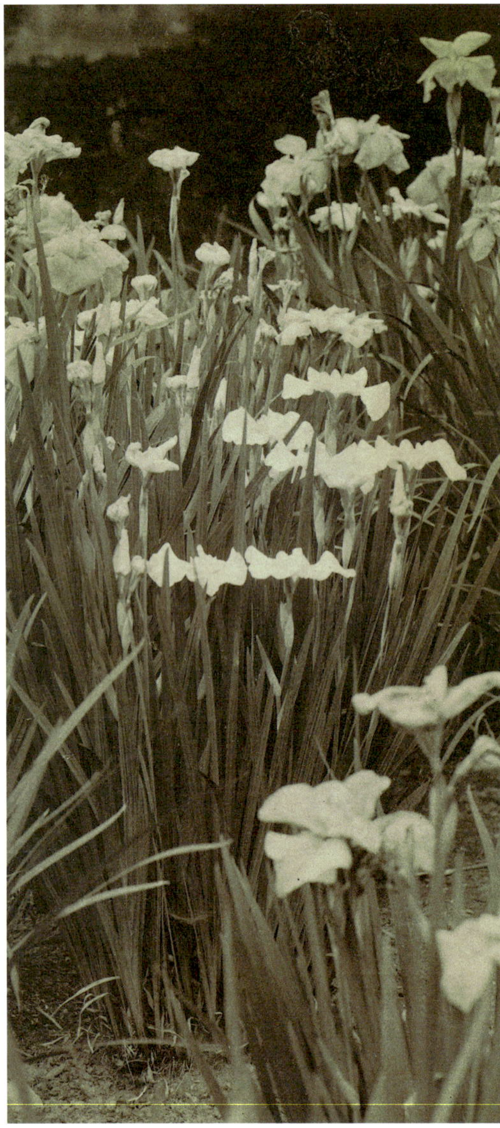

fig. 12 Eva Watson-Schütze, *Irises*. Platinum print. Courtesy of the Howard Greenberg Gallery, New York.

accompany the essay just quoted; it shares a serene mood with most of his paintings. It is gently brushed with colors that glow, thanks to some warm underpainting that shows through. As he desired, because of its lack of detail the lone house behind the screen of trees has the softness of a memory (cat. 69). By the time he came to Byrdcliffe, Ochtman had won several prestigious prizes and was elected to the National Academy, where he showed *Sunrise at Byrdcliffe* in 1906, after ending his summer at the colony with an exhibition in his studio.[41]

The Byrdcliffe painters' muted, sensuously painted landscapes parallel the soft-focus style of the Pictorialist photographers, who campaigned at the turn of the century for photography to have the status of a fine art.[42] Eva Watson-Schütze was one of the founders of the Photo-Secession, with Alfred Stieglitz and others, before she became the most important photographer at Byrdcliffe. Like Birge Harrison, she studied painting at the Pennsylvania Academy with Thomas Eakins. Eakins's example, as a painter of portraits who was seriously involved with photography, had a lasting influence on his student.[43] She was active both as a painter and a photographer, although few of her paintings are known today and her reputation rests on her photographs.[44] After leaving the Pennsylvania Academy she worked in a commercial printing outfit, and then opened a photographic portrait studio with Amelia van Buren. Soon she became involved with Stieglitz's group. Most of her surviving photographs are portraits, but a variety of subjects are reproduced in the pages of Stieglitz's photo magazines, including a moody landscape and a tall, vertical panel of flowers illustrated in a 1900 issue of *Camera Notes*.[45] In that photograph, as well as in the delicate little *Irises* (fig. 12), she combined the natural irregularity of the flowers with a format that recalls Japanese pillar prints. The effect, of nature's randomness harnessed by the right angles of human structure, looks forward to the panels of dynamic floral ornament included in pieces of Byrdcliffe furniture.

In the early years of the twentieth century Watson-Schütze was working in Philadelphia with the most advanced exponents of art photography in the United States, and in 1901 she was elected a member of the progressive Linked Ring society in England. But she fell in love with Martin Schütze, who taught German studies at the University of Chicago. After they married in 1901 and moved to Chicago, her connections with the Photo-Secession group waned away from Stieglitz's group in New York, and she became involved with the social progressives affiliated with the University and with Hull House. Soon she and her husband, who was active in Chicago's Morris Society, were spending nearly half of every year at Byrdcliffe.[46] She pursued her art as a photographer, making soft-focus platinum prints with the people around her as subjects: the educated, liberal individuals who were her friends, children, and mothers with children, a subject she described as "a great theme, never exhausted."[47]

Following the tradition of Eakins, her portraits communicate a sense of human dignity, intellectual aliveness, and individuality on the part of her sitters. Her photograph of John Dewey (cat. 87) depicts him in profile, his hands on an open book, his head the apex of a mass of dark, academic robes, with her stylized butterfly monogram animating some of the space left void by his asymmetrical placement (fig. 13). Watson-Schütze composed her portrait of Jane Addams with the sitter's head way off-center. Addams, a writer at work, pauses for a moment to contemplate the next words of her text (cat. 100). Watson-Schütze did a series of studies of painter Carl Lindin, a handsome ladies' man, in romantic nineteenth-century costume. Less contemplative than Dewey and Addams, he stares at the viewer as his arms angle across the scene, his hands tensely poised (cat. 96). Feminist Charlotte Perkins Gilman, an enormously productive writer famed for her dramatic lectures, was photographed by Watson-Schütze seated half in shadow in a moment of reverie, her hand awkwardly supporting her listless head. The photograph suggests the psychological depths of this celebrated public woman, who was the author of the disturbing short story "The Yellow Wallpaper," about a wife held in confinement and almost driven to insanity by her well-meaning husband (cat. 99).

Jessie Tarbox Beals's series of photographs of the colony's buildings complements Watson-Schütze's portraits of Byrdcliffe's artists and intellectuals. Beals, a New York City resident who has been called the "first woman news photographer," came to Byrdcliffe on an assignment to illustrate an article about the colony by Poultney Bigelow.[48] Her handsome, straightforward prints depict an idyllic environment of Arts and Crafts buildings nestled in a sylvan setting (fig. 14). They include an image of a group of children doing exercises on a field in front of the Byrdcliffe house Carniola that illustrates the Whiteheads' desire to make the colony a center for physical fitness as well as mental and artistic health (cat. 81).

The third of Byrdcliffe's photographers was, surprisingly, Ralph Whitehead. This is unexpected because there is no evidence that he thought of himself as a photographer—

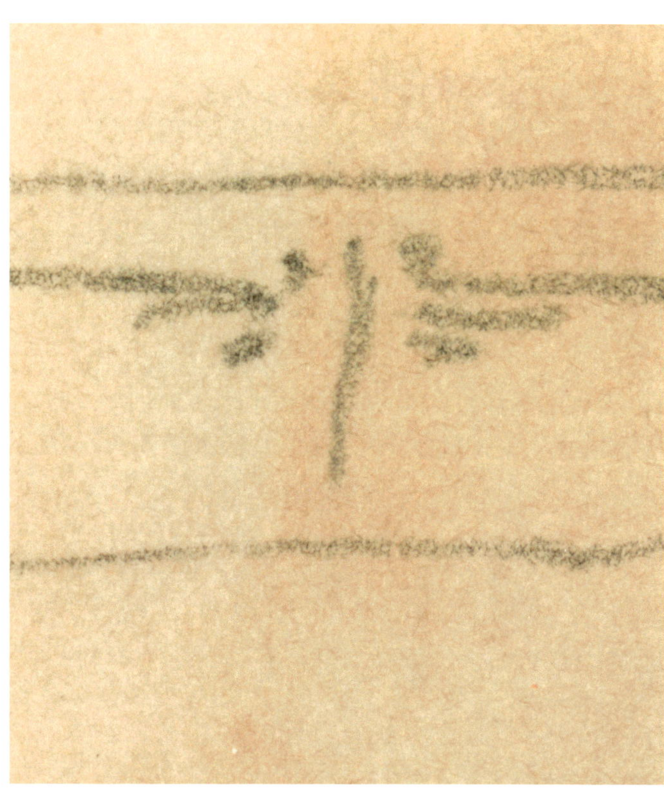

fig. 13 Eva Watson-Schütze's distinctive butterfly signature used on many of her photographs.

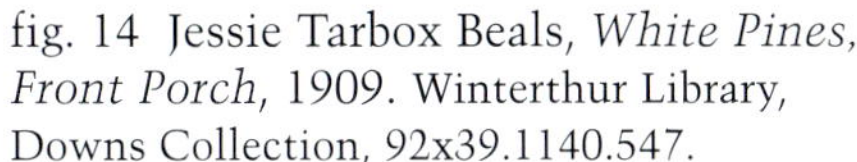

fig. 14 Jessie Tarbox Beals, *White Pines, Front Porch*, 1909. Winterthur Library, Downs Collection, 92x39.1140.547.

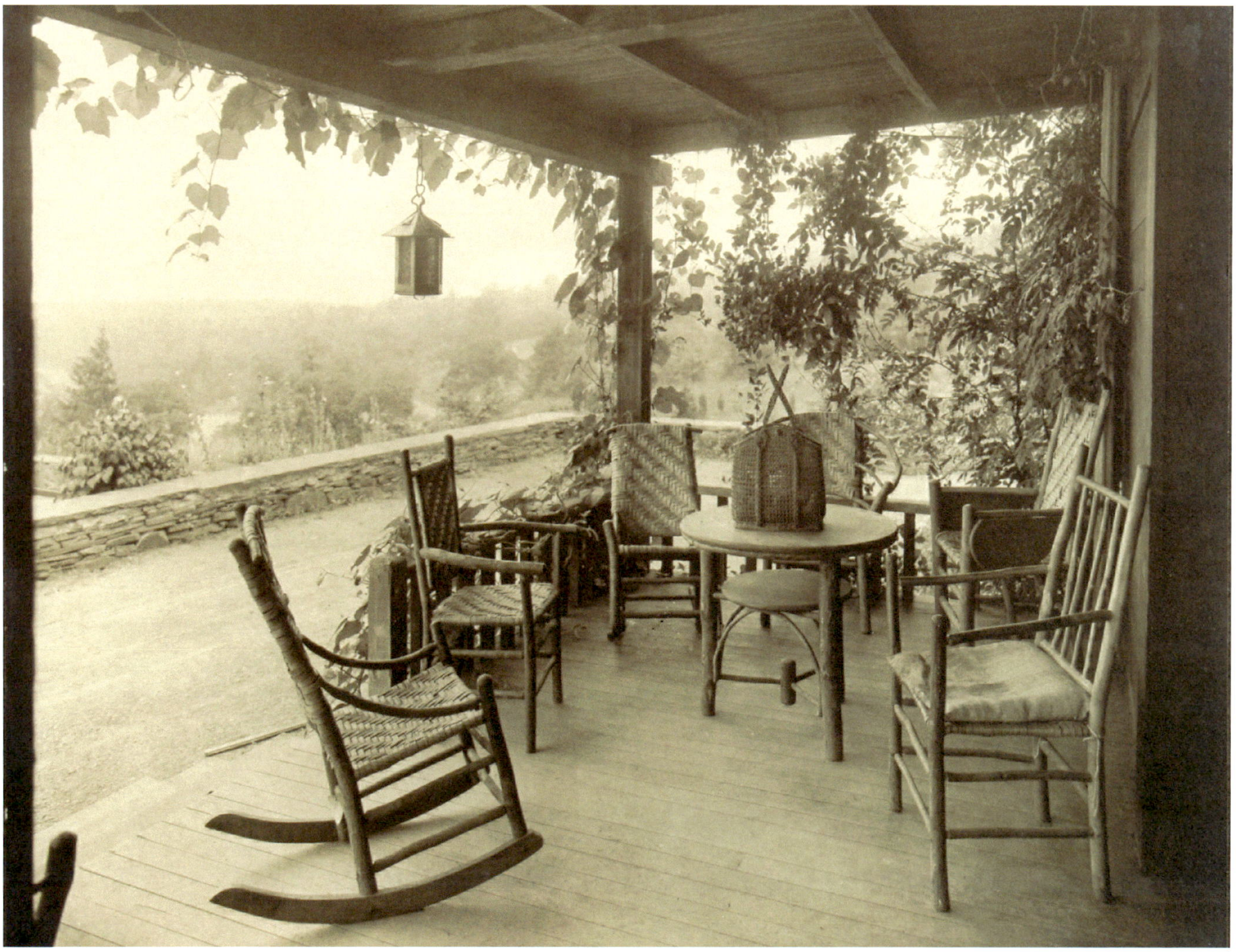

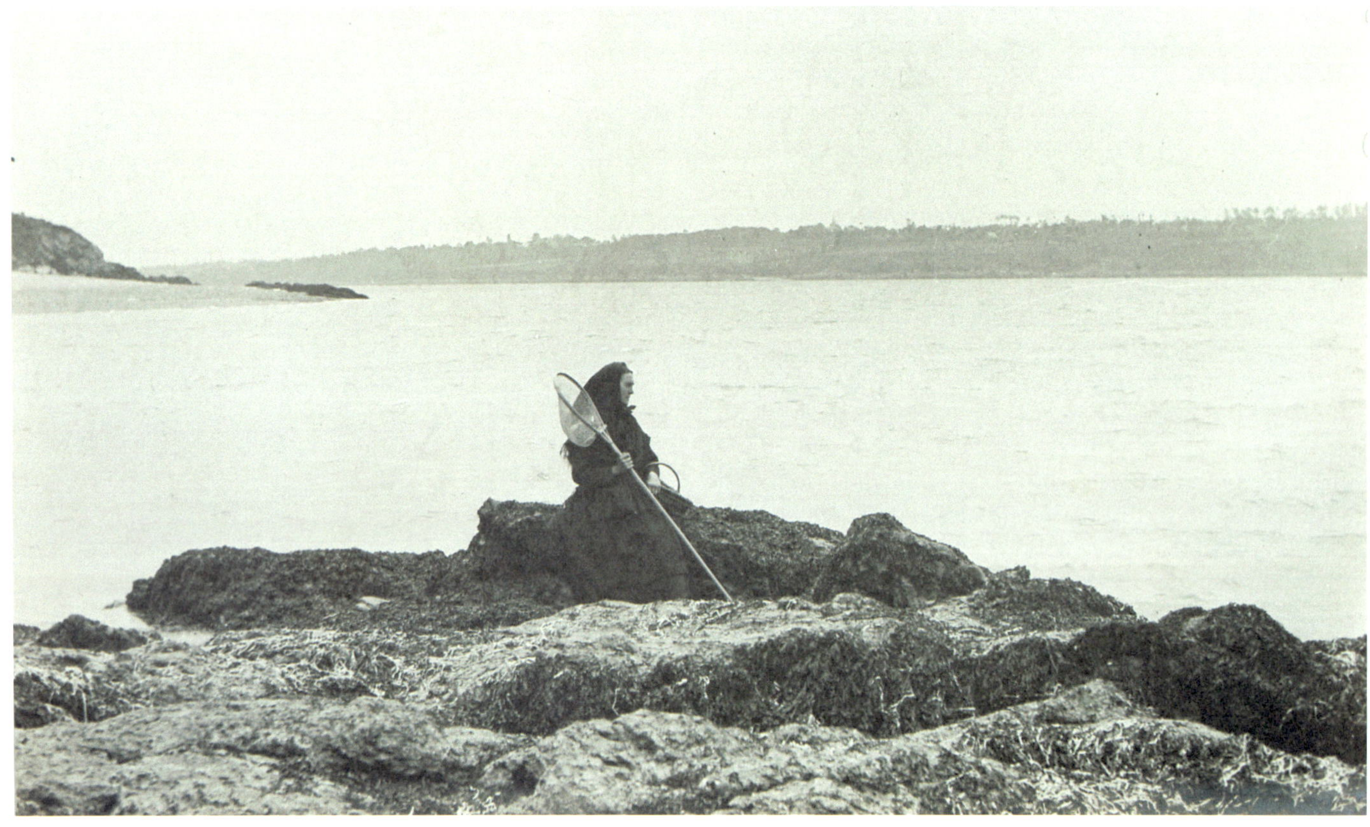

fig. 15 Ralph Radcliffe Whitehead, *Fisherwoman*, 1890s. Winterthur Library, Downs Collection, 92x39.1140.668.

fig. 16 Ralph Radcliffe Whitehead, *Peasant Women*, 1890s. Winterthur Library, Downs Collection, 92x39.1140.668.

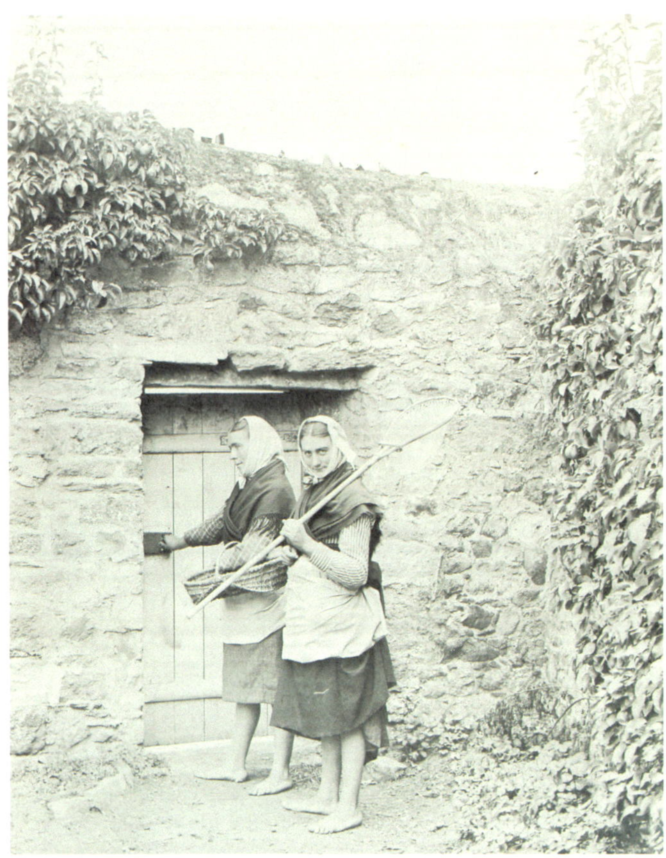

he just made photographs. Like his wife, who painted most of her life but never signed her paintings, he took and printed photographs but did not sign them, nor did he write about them. Perhaps this aesthete, who felt lithography was tainted by commercialism, did not consider photography an art form. Like other gentlemen of the time, he was an enlightened amateur, with a dark room in the basement of Arcady in California and one in White Pines, and he had years of experience looking at art to guide his aesthetic decisions. Many of the pictures we have of Arcady and of Byrdcliffe are by him, as are some striking travel photographs of exotic views, European towns, and rural laborers (figs. 15 and 16). Except for his immediate family, Whitehead did not photograph the members of his cultural or intellectual circle—that was Eva Watson-Schütze's territory. But out of his Ruskinian love of nature he made many photographs of flora and of richly vegetated landscapes. Some of these he printed in sizes unusually large for the time, and since he seemed to care little about refined printing techniques they often have a scale and a spontaneity that look very modern (cats. 106, 107, and 108). Arguably, Whitehead's greatest artistic successes came as a photographer, not as a weaver or a ceramist, perhaps because here he was least self-conscious of himself as an artist.

There is little information about what happened with painting classes at Byrdcliffe following the summer of 1907, when Leonard Ochtman was the painting instructor. The Whiteheads' correspondence is scanty for the next years, and other documentation is sparse. Artists in the colony, like Zulma Steele, continued to paint, but the fate of the art classes in the Byrdcliffe studio is unclear. Birge Harrison maintained his long-standing friendship with the Whiteheads, and his Art Students League Summer School in Woodstock was a success, drawing scores of young art students to the town. They came up to Byrdcliffe for parties, but increasingly the colony and its artists looked dated and old-fashioned to the students who enlivened the Woodstock milieu. Some of the younger generation, like Andrew Dasburg and Konrad Cramer, had firsthand experience of the new European modernism, and experimented with it in their art. When Harrison retired after five years at the League he was succeed by John Carlson, a landscape painter who was a student at Byrdcliffe in its first year. In his early works Carlson painted local scenery in the gentle Harrison mode; then he gradually broadened his technique to paint the landscapes with broad, thick strokes (cat. 59). He also became the voice of antimodernism in the colony, although his technique of slablike brushstrokes can suggest an early modernist like Cézanne. One of Carlson's accomplishments was that he wrote *Carlson's Guide to Landscape Painting,* a book that stayed in print for over fifty years.

During the second decade of the twentieth century, painting and the teaching of painting continued in Byrdcliffe thanks to William Emile Schumacher, who summered there and who brought a modernist style to the colony. Eva Watson-Schütze was one of his students; she increasingly devoted her time to painting rather than making photographs and felt that Schumacher, in 1912, brought back from France "a new and living conception of form and color."[49] Born in 1870, Schumacher, like many of Byrdcliffe's artists, had studied at the Académie Julian before he came to the United States in 1912. He showed two paintings at the Armory Show and had an exhibition at the Daniel Gallery in 1913. He painted his most striking works during this period, when, leaving his academic training behind, he developed a style of flat areas of intense color. In his *Floral Landscape* from 1916 he reduced the carnations into serrated red, yellow, and white ovals set against a dark blue hillside and a pastel sky (cat. 75). The stretched-out vertical format, filled with decorative floral elements, recalls Watson-Schütze's earlier floral photograph, and suggests a sympathy of spirit that explains why she was one of his most enthusiastic painting students. Another of his students was Blanche Lazzell, who went on to become a noted printmaker at the Provincetown art colony, where she made woodcuts with blocks of flat color adjacent to each other reminiscent of her teacher's style (cat. 164). This, her first print, was made at Byrdcliffe under Schumacher's supervision.

In his *Cows and Pasture,* Schumacher set the simplified black-and-white animals against a lime-green field filled with flat patches of golden paint, overlapped by irregular bands of plant life (cat. 74). He turned a bucolic country scene, worthy of a traditional Woodstock landscape painter, into a bright, jazzy modernist composition.

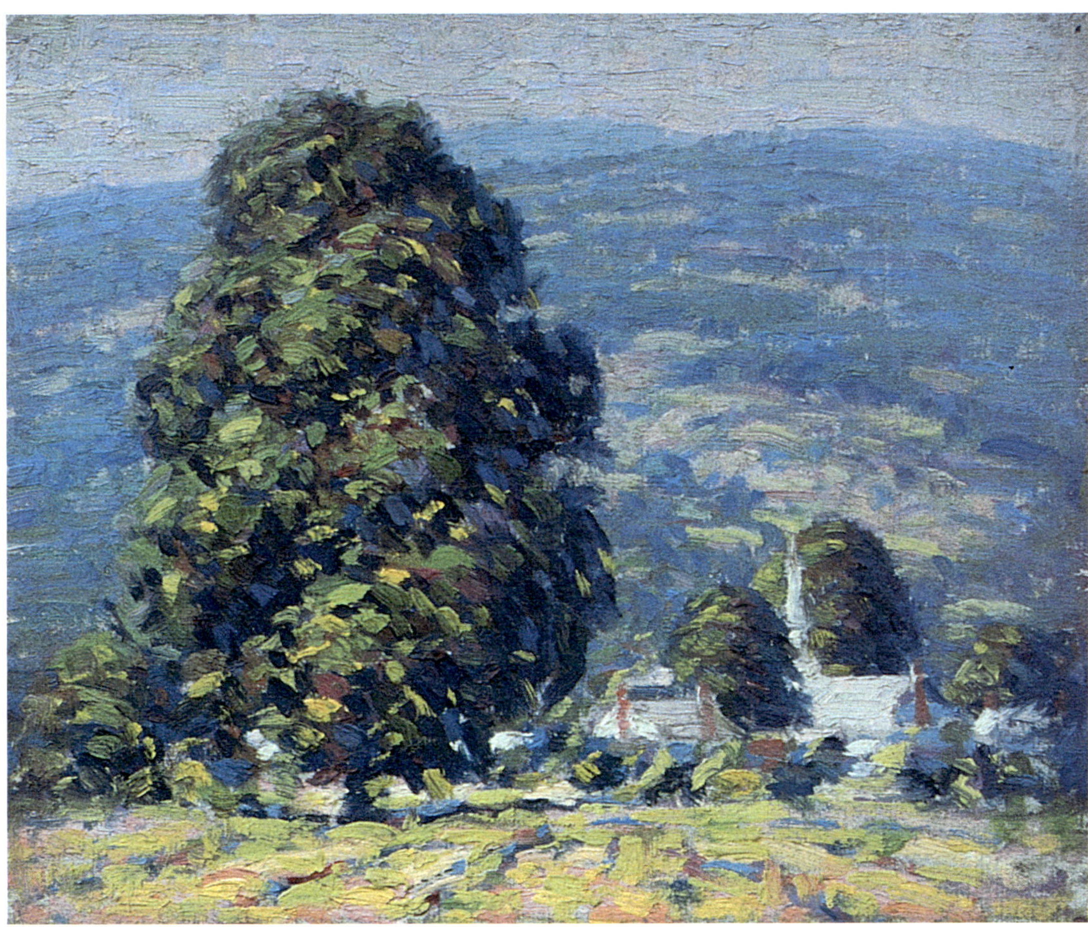

fig. 17 Bolton Brown, *Landscape with Steeple,* ca. 1914. Oil on canvas board. Courtesy of the author.

Other of Byrdcliffe's painters adopted similar modernist styles in reaction to the Armory Show. A good example of the attitude change that came about in 1913 can be seen in the work of Gino Perera, an Italian-born student of Murphy and Harrison who was a regular summer resident at the colony beginning in 1905, and as a friend of the Whiteheads enlivened many of their gatherings with his classical mandolin playing. In his 1911 *Catskill Valley* (also known as *Moonlight*), Perera continued the Harrison-like play of muted blues in the mountain range and the sky that towers above it (cat. 70). But two years later, in his *Study* for a still life, he was painting in an aggressively modernist mode, with rectangular patches of contrasting color that jangle and vibrate against each other (cat. 71).[50] Perera could have been aware of modernist developments from his frequent trips to Europe. In addition, his friend Jane Whitehead had studied with Edmond Aman-Jean, a friend of Post-Impressionist Georges Seurat, on a Paris visit in 1896, and might well have been exposed to Seurat's pointillism at that early date.[51] Dawson-Watson, as mentioned already, had exhibited with Gauguin and his followers in 1893.

Bolton Brown, before turning to lithography around 1915, was intensely involved with painting; he made a systematic study of color theory and published a small book about it in 1913.[52] Like Schumacher, Brown exhibited in the American section of the Armory Show, and a group of small paintings by him from around 1914 show that he rejected his muted Tonalist mode and put his color theories to work in landscapes built up from strokes of bright color (fig. 17). Other Byrdcliffe artists adopted similar styles that negotiated a compromise between traditional landscape painting and advanced modernist abstraction, as can be seen in Zulma Steele's patchwork application of paint in *Autumn Landscape*, ca. 1914 (cat. 78). These artists were taking the Impressionist idea of building a painting up from individual marks and broadening the scale of the marks so that they functioned as abstract entities as well as blocks that created a mosaiclike image.

A similar effect can be found in one of the only known paintings by Dewing Woodward, another product of the Académie Julian, where she studied for ten years. Woodward, who lost much of her work in a studio fire in 1911, is almost totally forgotten today, but she lived and worked in Woodstock in the second decade of the twentieth century, and made portrait drawings of some of the key members of the Byrdcliffe community, including Hervey White and Birge Harrison.[53] She organized the Blue Dome Fraternity, dedicated to painting the nude outdoors, and held several exhibitions of the group, which included Edmund Rolfe, the Byrdcliffe jeweler who also painted (cats. 72 and 73). Woodward's *Listening to the Footsteps of Autumn*, which was exhibited in New York in 1914, features an idealized, academically drawn nude woman with pale blue shadows modeling her form, standing in a forest and surrounded by leaves made of abstract patches of paint—another example of a painter modernizing her style after the Armory Show (cat. 80).

Woodward lived with her companion, Louise Johnson, in Woodstock, where her gregarious sociability made her popular. She and Johnson were among several single women or women couples who lived in the Byrdcliffe milieu. The early presence there of feminist Charlotte Perkins Gilman and other women from Hull House may have encouraged them, as Byrdcliffe nurtured a group of women who wanted independence from traditional wifely roles so they could live as artists.[54] Abastenia St. Leger Eberle, an innovative realist sculptor who spent her life mostly in the company of women, spent three or four summers in Woodstock.[55] Why did she leave the Lower East Side, where she had moved to be close to the immigrants who were the subjects of most of her sculptures? Certainly Woodstock offered a more pleasant, comfortable summer environment, and the Byrdcliffe-inspired community of unmarried, artistic women would have made her feel welcome.

Five or six years after its founding, artistic activity tapered off at Byrdcliffe, but the colony was far from moribund. The Whiteheads continued to sponsor musical entertainments, and they turned to making ceramics with some success. Original settlers like Bolton Brown and Hervey White had left the colony but remained in Woodstock, as did Lindin, Harrison, Steele, Bertha Thompson, Marie Little, and others. The Art Students League established its summer school in Woodstock in 1906, and at the recommendation of John Carlson appointed Birge Harrison its first teacher; hundreds of young aspiring artists were drawn to the town, and some stayed and made Woodstock their home. The impulse toward making art in this lovely rural setting within an easy commute from the galleries and museums of New York City flourished and spread. Scores of artists, unknown and famous, from George Bellows and John Flannagan to Philip Guston and Eva Hesse, spent crucial and productive parts of their careers in this artistic community that grew from the idealistic experiment that was Byrdcliffe.

Notes

1. For Tonalism see Wanda Corn's classic catalogue, *The Color of Mood: American Tonalism, 1880–1910* (The M.H. de Young Museum and the California Legion of Honor, 1972).
2. Robert Edwards, "Byrdcliffe: Life by Design," *The Byrdcliffe Arts and Crafts Colony*, (Delaware Art Museum, 1984), 3.
3. RRW to Jane, May 3, 1891. Winterthur Library, Downs Collection.
4. RRW to Jane, June 22, 1899. Winterthur Library, Downs Collection. Berenson appears several times in Mrs. Whitehead's diaries from March and April 1904, when the Whiteheads were in Italy.
5. The Galleria Rinaldo Carnielo can be found at 3 Piazza Savonarola in Florence. Also see Helen Zimmern, "An Italian Sculptor: Rinaldo Carnielo," *The Art Journal* (1893): 287–92; helpful to me was a letter from Elisabetha Palminteri Manteucci to Mark Willcox concerning her thesis about Carnielo's collection of paintings; July 5, 2000, Willcox collection. See also Laura Lucchesi, "Uno studio d'artista: la galleria Carnielo a Fierenze," in *Le Gipsoteche in Toscana* (Commune di Pescia, 2001), 101–12.
6. RRW to Jane, Los Angeles, January 29, 1899. Winterthur Library, Downs Collection.

7. Charles Walter Stetson, in a record book of his paintings, Archives of American Art, Roll 3211, frames 285–86. He also describes painting an "orange tree, anemones under it, mts. & bay beyond," and "some slight scaffitto work in the gables . . . ."

8. Charles Walter Stetson, in his Diary for January 18, 1885, quoted by Charles Eldredge in *Charles Walter Stetson, Color and Fantasy* (Lawrence, KS: Spencer Museum of Art, 1982), 36.

9. For American Symbolists see Charles Eldredge, *American Imagination and Symbolist Painting* (Grey Art Gallery and Study Center, New York University, 1979).

10. RRW, "Pictures for Schools," *Arrows of the Dawn*, no. 3 (Montecito, 1901): 42.

11. Nancy Dustin Wall Moure, *William Wendt, 1865–1946* (Laguna Museum of Art, 1977), 27.

12. Hervey White, *Autobiography*, 118f.

13. *Ibid*., 125.

14. My thanks to Whitney Ganz for finding this painting for me, and to Franklin Riehlman for putting me in touch with him.

15. Bruce Kamerling, "The Arts and Crafts Movement in San Diego," *The Arts and Crafts Movement in California*, Kenneth R. Trapp, ed. (The Oakland Museum and Abbeville Press, 1993), 209–12.

16. White, *Autobiography*, 124; White's letters to Lindin, April 16, 1900, and May 21, 1900. Collection Gregory Lindin.

17. White, *Autobiography*, 133.

18. Clinton Adams, the author of the definitive book about Brown, *Crayonstone* (University of New Mexico Press, 1993), agreed that this was an enigma when I raised the issue during a meeting with him in 1998. For Brown see also *Bolton Coit Brown, A Retrospective* (Samuel Dorsky Museum of Art, State University of New York, New Paltz, 2003).

19. Prospectus for the 1903 Byrdcliffe Art School, copy at the Woodstock Guild of Craftsmen.

20. Carl Eric Lindin, "The Woodstock Landscape," in *Fallen Leaves*, n.d., n.p., and in *Publications of the Woodstock Historical Society* 7 (July 1932): 20.

21. These dates are based on Murphy's papers in the Archives of American Art; his ledger listing his paintings includes several Byrdcliffe scenes from 1903, 1904, and 1905; reel 4038, frames 0491–0495.

22. William A. Coles related Murphy's *Coyote Point, Salt Flats, California*, ca. 1916–17, an extremely horizontal landscape divided into a triptych, to scroll painting. *Hermann Dudley Murphy* (Graham Gallery, New York, 1982), 25.

23. RRW to Jane, February 22, 1903: "Harrison writes me about a painter who is in Quebec whom he most strongly recommends as a decorator and a designer of woodwork." Winterthur Library, Downs Collection.

24. *Troisième Exposition des Peintres Impressionistes et Symbolistes* (Chez le Banc de Boutteville, 1893). My thanks to William Gerdts for letting me study his files on Dawson-Watson, which include a copy of the brochure for this exhibition.

25. Jane Byrd McCall Whitehead, *The Morning Stars Sang Together: Folk-Songs and Other Songs for Children* (Boston: Oliver Ditson, 1903).

26. RRW to Jane, January 24, 1903. Winterthur Library, Downs Collection.

27. Bertha Thompson, "Recollections," n.d., n.p., "The Thompson Family Collection," Arthur and Elizabeth Schlesinger Library of Women's Studies, Harvard University, and the Woodstock Library.

28. The print measures 7 x 9 3/4 inches. It is attributed to Bevans because it is a block print, and because of its monogram, which looks like a "W" with a "B" attached to its right-most line, a monogram also found on two small watercolors also in the Alf Evers Collection of the Woodstock Guild of Craftsmen (see cat. 159).

29. Birge Harrison, "The Case of Pastel," *Art and Progress*, vol. 6, no. 5 (March 1915): 155f.

30. A second version of this print is in the Mark Willcox collection.

31. The lithography debate is summarized in Evers, *Woodstock*, 425, and most specifically in a letter from Evers to Clinton Adams (February 18, 1980), a copy of which is in the Bolton Brown files at the Woodstock Artists Association.

32. White, *Autobiography*, 161.

33. John Kemplay, in *The Paintings of John Duncan, a Scottish Symbolist* (San Francisco: Pomegranate Artbooks, 1994), includes a short chapter about Duncan's period in Chicago, but no mention of Byrdcliffe.

34. Birge Harrison, *Landscape Painting* (New York: Scribner's Sons, 1909), 21.

35. *Ibid*., 171–72.

36. RRW to Jane, June 2, 1902. Winterthur Library, Downs Collection.

37. Birge Harrison, "Painting at Woodstock; the Work of a Group of American Landscape Painters," *Arts and Decoration* (May 1912): 248.

38. Harrison reproduced Ochtman's *November Sunrise* in "The Mood in Modern Painting," *Art and Progress*, vol. IV, no. 9 (July 1913): 1019, and his *Moonlit Pasture* in "Painting at Woodstock," *Arts and Decoration*, vol. II, no. 7 (May 1912): 245.

39. Charles Caffin, *The Story of American Painting* (New York: Frederick A. Stokes Company, 1907), 345.

40. Leonard Ochtman, "A Few Suggestions to Beginners in Landscape Painting—Concluded," *Palette and Bench* (August 1909): 243.

41. The main source of information about Ochtman is Susan G. Larkin's *The Ochtmans of Cos Cob* (Greenwich, CT: The Bruce Museum, 1989). The reference to Ochtman's Byrdcliffe studio exhibition is from Jane Whitehead's calendar entry, August 19, 1906. Winterthur Library, Downs Collection. Ochtman is listed as the painting instructor in the Byrdcliffe pamphlet from 1907, copy in the Woodstock Library.

42. The parallel between Tonalism and Pictorialist photography has been often observed, most influentially by Wanda Corn in *Color of Mood*, where she juxtaposes Birge Harrison's *Fifth Avenue Nocturne* with Edward Steichen's *The Flatiron—Evening* (plates 6 and 7).

43. Elizabeth Johns has suggested that most of Eakins's paintings can be considered portraits, as he "was passionately devoted to the portrait." *Thomas Eakins: The Heroism of Modern Life* (Princeton University Press, 1983) 3.

44. Watson-Schütze's oil painting *Portrait* is in the collection of the Woodstock Artists Association, and black-and-white photographs of several of her paintings are in the archives of that organization. The main study of the photographer is Jean F. Block's *Eva Watson Schütze, Chicago Photo-Secessionist* (The University of Chicago Library, 1985).

45. "Maker and Critic," *Camera Notes*, vol. IV, no. 2 (October 1901): 81.

46. The Morris Society was founded in Chicago in 1903 and discontinued in February 1905. Its leader was Arts and Crafts writer Oscar Lovell Triggs. In 1904 the Society circulated "A Program for the Study of the Life of William Morris" by Martin Schütze. Bruce Kahler, *Art and Life: The Arts & Crafts Movement in Chicago, 1897-1910* (PhD dissertation, Purdue University, 1986), 90, 92, 95. My thanks to Cheryl Robertson for this information.

47. Eva Lawrence Watson, "Gertrude Käsebier," *The American Amateur Photographer*, (May 1900): 220.

48. Alexander Alland Sr., *Jessie Tarbox Beals: First Woman News Photographer* (New York: Camera/Graphic Press Ltd., 1978). Poultney Bigelow, "Byrdcliffe Colony of Arts and Crafts," *American House and Gardens* (October 1909): 389–93.

49. Eva Watson-Schütze, "Eva Watson-Schütze" in J. Z. Jacobson, *Art of Today* (Chicago: L. M. Stein, 1932), 119.

50. Three other Perera paintings in this style exist, two of them in Carrig-Rohane frames that are dated 1913.

51. Jane Whitehead's calendars have several references to Aman-Jean in November and December 1896. Winterthur Library, Downs Collection.

52. Bolton Brown, *The Painter's Palette and How to Master It* (New York: The Baker and Taylor Co., 1913).

53. These drawings are reproduced in Diana Huneker's "Portrait Drawings by Dewing Woodward," *International Studio*, vol. LXII, no. 245 (July 1917): 36–38.

54. These women included Zulma Steele and Edna Walker; Edith Penman and Elizabeth Hardenbergh; Marie Little; Bertha Thompson, who sometimes lived with her sister, Annie; and regular visitors like Ellen Gates Starr.

55. Louise R. Noun, *Abastenia St. Leger Eberle, Sculptor* (Des Moines, IA: Des Moines Art Center, 1980), 8. Eberle and Woodward both showed at the Macbeth Gallery in New York City.

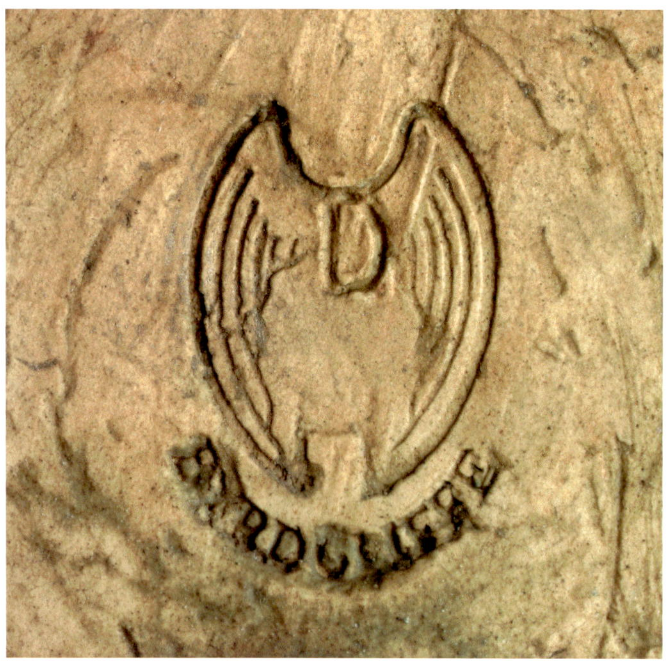

fig. 1 Byrdcliffe Pottery Marking, ca. 1907. Private collection.

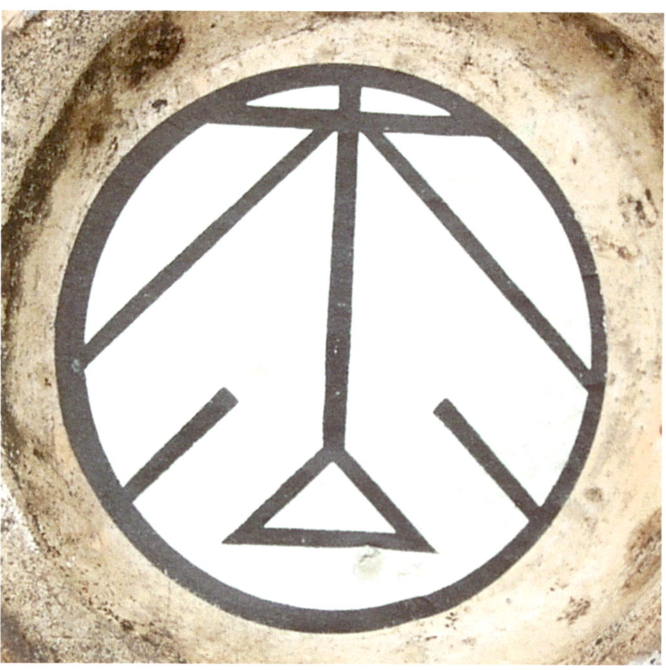

fig. 2 White Pines Paper Label, ca. 1915. Woodstock Guild of Craftsmen.

Purely for Pleasure

Ceramics at Byrdcliffe

ELLEN PAUL DENKER

Several potters worked in and around Woodstock, New York, during the first quarter of the twentieth century; however, only two potteries can be associated with the Byrdcliffe colony specifically. The earliest was the Byrdcliffe Pottery started by Edith Penman and Elizabeth Hardenbergh in 1903 in a building constructed by Ralph and Jane Whitehead as one of several devoted to the crafts they hoped to develop in order to make the colony self-sufficient. Pottery continued to be made in this facility by Penman and Hardenbergh under the Byrdcliffe Pottery name until about 1922. Byrdcliffe Pottery wares are marked with a distinctive impressed device of two bird wings folded in a vertically oriented oval with the word "BYRDCLIFFE" below (fig. 1). The second pottery was the one developed by Mr. and Mrs. Whitehead in 1915 as the White Pines Pottery. The ware associated with this operation was produced in a small building near White Pines, the Whiteheads' home. Ware, mostly vases, continued to be made intermittently in this facility until about 1926. These wares were marked with a variety of initials and numbers. Some examples that survive feature a paper label with an engraving of the stylized White Pines logo developed by the Whiteheads (fig. 2).

Other potters worked in the facilities where Penman and Hardenbergh made the Byrdcliffe Pottery after their departure. The later artists, however, did not mark their wares with the Byrdcliffe Pottery insignia, as did Penman and Hardenbergh. Therefore, the history of these potters, including Zulma Steele (who called her pottery "Zedware") (cats. 127, 128, and 129), Bolton Brown (cat. 109), Hunt Diederich, and Alexander Archipenko, has not been included in this essay.

The goals of Byrdcliffe Pottery and White Pines Pottery were similar, although the wares were quite different. For both potteries, the integration of process into daily life seems to have been far more important to the potters than commercial product.

Byrdcliffe Pottery

"Misses Penman and Hardenbergh showed a number of their hand built pieces, which are ever interesting and show much appreciation of fine color, textures and form," remarked a *Keramic Studio* reporter about the work shown by these two potters at the annual exhibition of the New York Society of Keramic Arts in 1911[1] (figs. 3 and 4).

Relatively few women were getting dirty in the clay studio in 1903 when Edith Penman and Elizabeth Hardenbergh began making pottery at the Byrdcliffe colony. Although pottery making as a craft goes back to the beginning of mankind, it was usually an activity of artisans whose livelihood depended on their making a limited range of useful forms on a regular basis. The notion of women in America making pots simply for their beauty had been tried by very few and usually with limited financial success. Susan Frackelton, Mary Louise McLaughlin, and Adelaide Robineau are among the few prominent women potters from this era.[2] However, industry observers would have considered it risky, if not downright subversive, for women to make pots. Most women who were associated creatively with ceramics in this period were decorating ware in factories and studios (at the Rookwood Pottery, for example), but not turning them on a potter's wheel.[3] Penman and Hardenbergh, however, had no qualms about indulging their creative spirits in the making of pots.

How Penman and Hardenbergh became involved with pottery making is a mystery at present. They may already have been making ceramics when they ventured north, perhaps from Philadelphia, to the Byrdcliffe colony in the summer of 1903. In the early 1900s, both women were known principally as painters and only secondarily as potters. Edith Penman was born in London, England, in 1860 and studied painting there with R. Swain Gifford. Later, in America, she studied painting with Henry B. Snell and also studied at the Cooper Union School of Design for Women in 1879–80.[4] Elizabeth Rutgers Hardenbergh was born in New Brunswick, New Jersey.[5] She studied with Mrs. E. M. Scott and Henry B. Snell. Perhaps the women met in Snell's studio. Or, just as likely, they may have become acquainted through one of the many artists' organizations to which they both belonged, including (but not limited to) the National Association of Women Painters and Sculptors and the New York Watercolor Club.[6] Later, they both joined the New York Society of Keramic Arts, the Society of Arts and Crafts in Boston (entered as Craftsmen in 1907; both designated Masters in 1915), the Allied Artists of America, and the New York Society of Painters (the latter two organizations established in 1916).

Perhaps the earliest mention of Penman and Hardenbergh in the Whiteheads' papers preserved in the Winterthur Library is in the correspondence of Ralph Radcliffe Whitehead with his wife, Jane. In a letter dated January 14, 1903, and written from Philadelphia, Ralph referred to the two women as "Edie" and "Betty." "Edie" was apparently the one who was best known to the Whiteheads. Ralph was planning to see Edie on January 14 when he wrote initially. Afterward, he reports in his postscript: "I have seen Edie. . . . I think perhaps she would like to come in March & certainly it will be good for her. I said nothing about Betty."[7] The origins of Whitehead's desire to have a pottery as part of his financial plan for the Byrdcliffe colony can be seen in the same letter to Jane. Referring to his meeting with Henry Chapman Mercer, one of Jane's cousins, Ralph noted that Mercer was "very happy about his tiles & has lots of orders. . . . Says he makes eight or nine thousand dollars a year. I don't quite understand this but take it for gospel & hope it is so."[8] Mercer had established the Moravian Pottery and Tile Works at Doylestown, Pennsylvania, north of

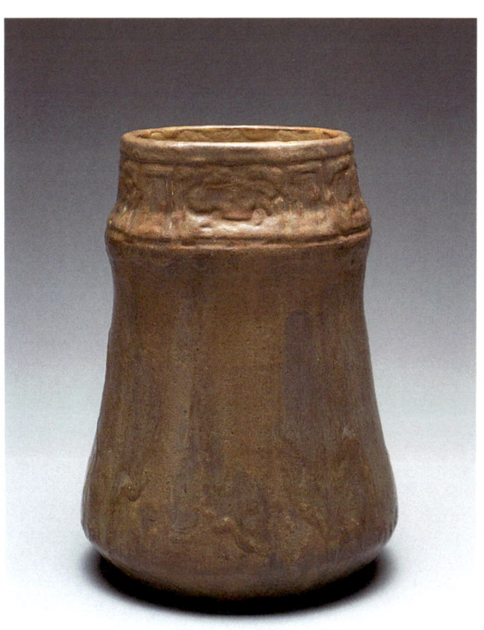

fig. 3 Byrdcliffe Pottery, 1903–22. Edith Penman and Elizabeth Hardenbergh, *Vase*. Ceramic. Collection of Robert Ellison.

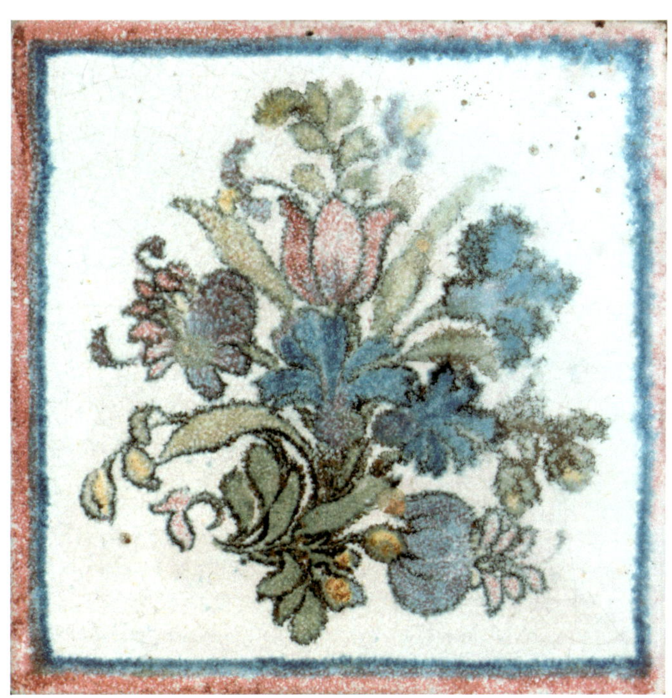

fig. 4 Byrdcliffe Pottery, 1903–22. Edith Penman and Elizabeth Hardenbergh, *Tile*, ca. 1920, Ceramic. Collection of Greg and Kathleen Eagen Johnson.

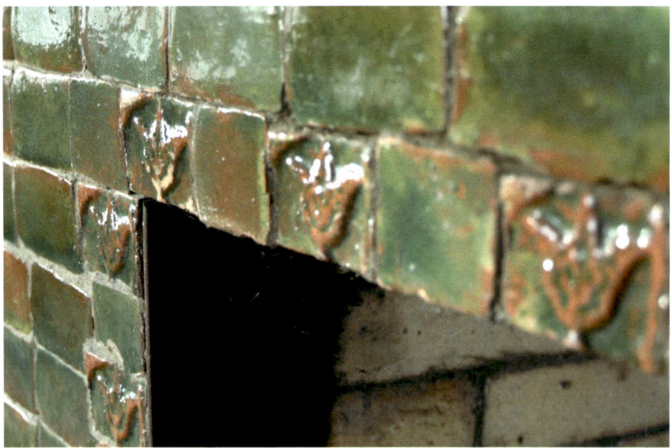

fig. 5 Moravian Tile Fireplace at White Pines (detail).

Philadelphia, in 1898. His pottery made the tiles that surround the fireplace in White Pines (fig. 5).

The pottery at the Byrdcliffe colony seems to have been established in that summer of 1903, perhaps by Penman and Hardenbergh on their first visit to the area. Following that first summer, they also may have decided to move from Philadelphia to New York City. Although the women were closely associated with the art scene in New York City during the early 1900s, their names are not shown in that city's directory until 1904–5, when they are listed as residing together in the Van Dyck Building at 939 Eighth Avenue. The Van Dyck Building was an artists' studio and residence constructed about 1895.[9] There is no evidence that the women made pottery during the fall and winter months of residence in New York City, when they were likely painting and exhibiting. However, they were probably sketching and painting as well as making pottery during their summers in upstate New York.

According to tradition, well-known art potter Charles Volkmar helped fire the kiln in the earliest days of the Byrdcliffe Pottery's operation.[10] Penman and Hardenbergh, however, must have been quick learners. Bertha Thompson, who worked for a while in the pottery, remembered that the potter's kiln was often "the rallying point for gay spirits bent on pleasure. I could tell you of many a merry midnight hour spent with them as we watched the pots glow to a white heat."[11] Charles Volkmar was, like the women, a painter turned potter. During his long career, he operated potteries in various locations in New York (Greenpoint, Tremont, and Corona) and New Jersey (Menlo Park and Metuchen) beginning in 1879. Because of his early work as a painter, he was well-known in New York City art circles and was closely involved with the Salmagundi Club as early as 1880, helping members with their tile- and mug-decorating projects. His association with the Byrdcliffe Pottery may well have come through his connections to New York City painters.

Penman and Hardenbergh decided to hand build their ware instead of turning it on a potter's wheel. This was an unusual choice for the period in which art potteries were routinely making ware by turning it on a potter's wheel or by using molds for pressing or slip-casting. Perhaps the option to hand build was chosen out of expediency. If Penman and Hardenbergh were not already proficient at wheel turning, they may have chosen hand building as the easiest entry point for starting up the pottery operation. Furthermore, the long skirts that women wore during this period were a hindrance to making pottery on a kick wheel and were dangerous to use with a belt-driven electric wheel, which could easily catch a lady's skirt and injure all concerned. Hand building was the safer alternative. In addition, they may have wanted to invoke the earliest methods of pottery making in America as a philosophical statement typical of the Colonial Revival mentality. Native Americans had not made their pots on a wheel, which would not have been available to them until the arrival of skilled European potters. Penman and Hardenbergh may have considered this historical situation in their choice of which pottery-making skills to employ.[12] Although hand-building methods are time-consuming and hardly competitive in a commercial sense, the initial desire of the Whiteheads to make their colony financially self-sufficient does not seem to have been a factor in

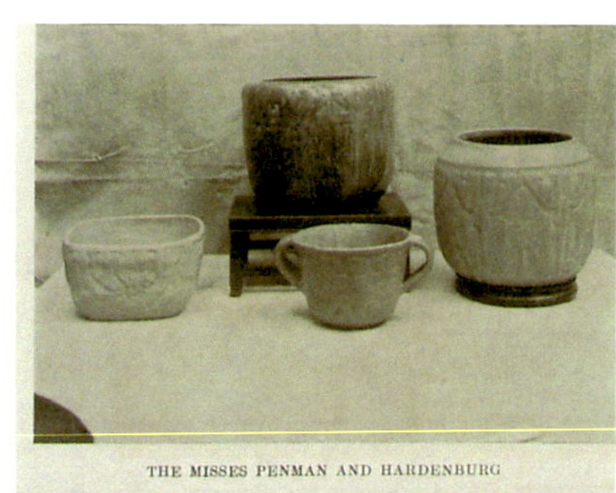

THE MISSES PENMAN AND HARDENBURG

fig. 6 *Keramic Studio*, vol. 11, no. 2 (June 1909): 39 (detail). Winterthur Library.

fig. 7 *Keramic Studio*, vol. 10, no. 2 (June 1908): 41. Winterthur Library.

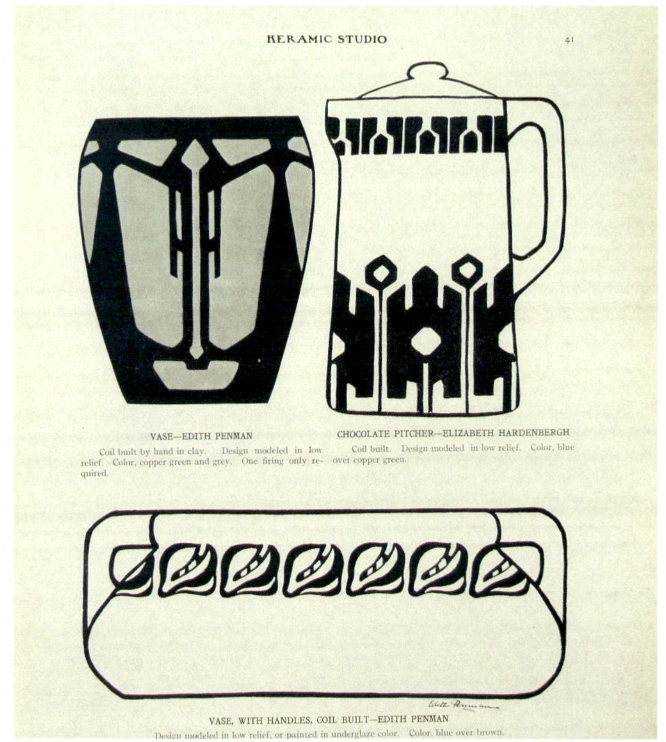

KERAMIC STUDIO 41

VASE—EDITH PENMAN

Coil built by hand in clay. Design modeled in low relief. Color, copper green and grey. One firing only required.

CHOCOLATE PITCHER—ELIZABETH HARDENBERGH

Coil built. Design modeled in low relief. Color, blue over copper green.

Edith Penman

VASE, WITH HANDLES, COIL BUILT—EDITH PENMAN

Design modeled in low relief, or painted in underglaze color. Color, blue over brown.

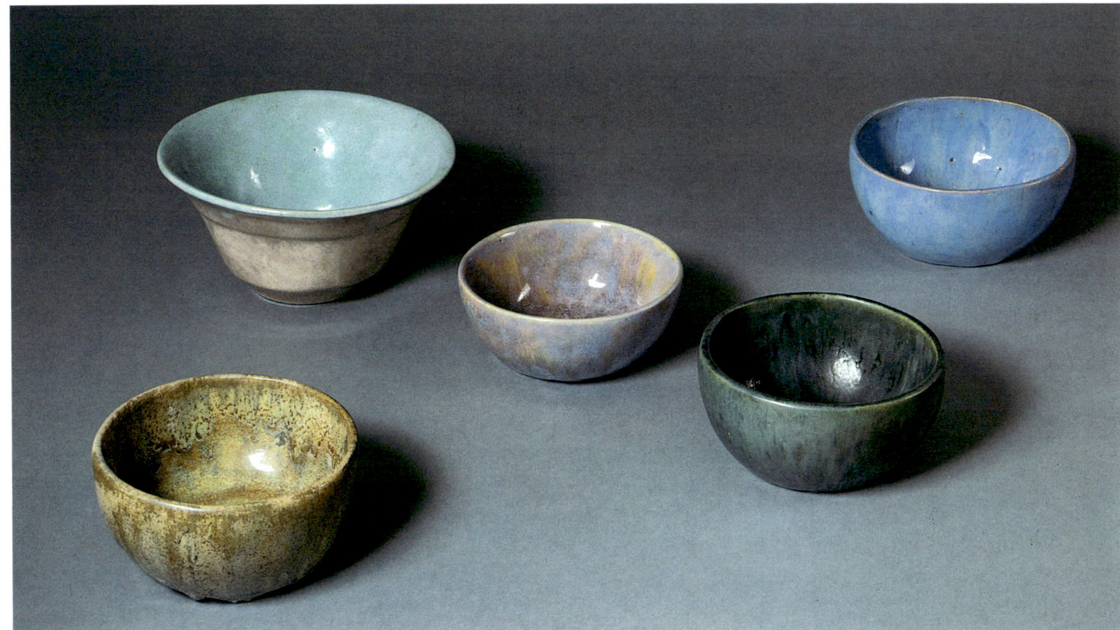

fig. 8 *Byrdcliffe Pottery*. Ceramic. Collection of the Newark Museum. (See also cats. 118, 119, and 120.)

production at the Byrdcliffe Pottery. Hardly any ware and no business papers survive today on which to judge the financial success of the operation.

Byrdcliffe Pottery wares were publicly exhibited at least as early as 1906 when they were shown at the first exhibition of the National Society of Craftsmen, held in December in New York City. A tall green vase, which appears to have sweeping organic ornament in low relief, was illustrated in an article in *Keramic Studio* describing the exhibition.[13] The accompanying article gave "special mention...[to] the work of Misses Penman and Hardenburgh [*sic*]. . . ." The Society had been organized earlier that year through the efforts of the National Arts Club and shared the Club's facilities initially on West 34th Street and later in the year when the Club took possession of the old Tilden mansion on Gramercy Park, where the National Arts Club remains today.[14] Spencer Trask, president of the National Arts Club, became first president of the Society, while Arthur Wesley Dow was elected vice president. The first directors included art potter Charles Volkmar and china painter Anna B. Leonard, among others.

Ware by Penman and Hardenbergh was also included in the regular annual exhibitions of the New York Society of Keramic Arts (NYSKA) as early as the spring of 1907. Over the next few years, illustrations of their exhibited work included a limited variety of useful and ornamental wares with low relief decoration. A covered jar, chocolate pot, bowl, two-handled cup, and various vases, low dishes, and holders for floral arrangements are shown in reports of NYSKA's exhibitions (figs. 6 and 7).[15] NYSKA was founded originally to exhibit the work of china painters in the greater New York area, but the organization was national in scope by 1907 and had expanded its exhibitions to include potters and tile makers. Exhibitions were significant events in the New York Arts and Crafts scene of the time. For example, the many attendees at the opening banquet for the 1911 NYSKA exhibition included the painter Henry B. Snell, with whom both women had studied; Edward Robinson, director of the Metropolitan Museum; potter Leon Volkmar, Charles's son; and Charles F. Binns, director of the New York School of Clayworking and Ceramics at Alfred, New York.

Both Penman and Hardenbergh were NYSKA members and Penman was listed as Chairman of Art in 1908.[16] As a national organization, NYSKA was much concerned with setting artistic standards by this time. Members were no longer exhibiting naturalistic china painting because the juries "considered such naturalistic pieces...as not of sufficient excellence for the purpose" of exhibition. Although NYSKA did not bar naturalistic china painting outright (as some china painting organizations were doing), they refused to show objects with "naturalistic painting of flowers or figures on objects of utility, such as tableware, vases, etc."[17] During this period, Byrdcliffe Pottery was also exhibited at the Society of Arts and Crafts in Boston where the women received mention in the pamphlet issued for the 1907 exhibition.

The few examples of Byrdcliffe Pottery that survive from this early period exhibit similar characteristics of form and decoration. The forms are simple, rather heavily potted, and typically embellished with carved bands of low relief decoration. The whole is then covered with a flowing matte glaze in earthy colors, including browns, greens, grays, and blues (cats. 110, 111, and 113).

By 1917, however, their work was decidedly different. Although the forms appear to be hand built in this middle period, as in their earlier work, the potters were no longer using low relief decoration and the glazes were glossy rather than matte. This is the general character of the five bowls acquired by the Newark Museum in 1918, which are relatively small and built in plain shapes[18] (fig. 8) (cats. 118, 119, and 120). The visual interest of these five bowls is provided by the accidental character of the glossy flowing glazes. Indeed, the atmosphere of the kiln was as much a partner in this creative process as the potters themselves. The glazes took on subtle variations in color and texture as they flowed and matured in the kiln at its highest temperatures.

By 1915, the Byrdcliffe colony would have been abuzz with the results of glaze experiments conducted by Ralph Whitehead as he and Jane pursued their new dream of becoming potters. Although the working methods and shapes of the White Pines Pottery are quite different from those of the Byrdcliffe Pottery, there is some evidence in the glazes that there was conversation among all concerned. In addition to the glossy nature of the glazes in this second period, the Byrdcliffe Pottery palette is somewhat lighter and more colorful. It shows more consistent use of a pale, robin's-egg blue that is often called "Byrdcliffe blue."

Finally, there is a curious group of delftlike examples that survive today. These may have been among the last wares made by Penman and Hardenbergh at the Byrdcliffe Pottery. Several tiles, a bowl, and a small plate share a white ground with plain blue border enclosing polychrome clusters or bouquets of flowers[19] (cats. 112, 115, 116, and 117). The emphasis on white and blue suggests analogy to traditional delftware, generically called tin-glazed earthenware, which has been popular in Europe and America almost continually since the seventeenth century.

fig. 9 White Pines Pottery, *Eucalyptus Vase*. Cream-glazed vase with painted design. Collection of the Byrdcliffe Colony of the Woodstock Guild.

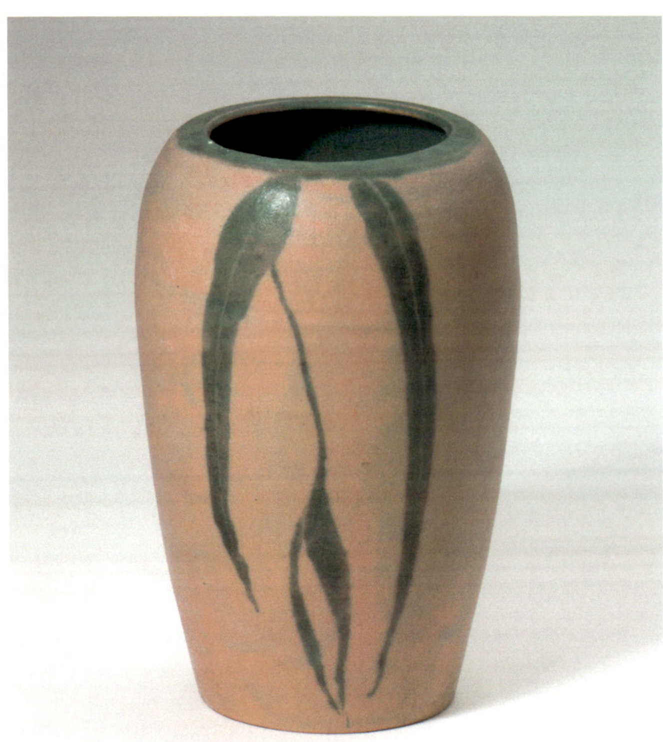

However, Penman and Hardenbergh were probably not using the classic tin-glaze recipe, which provides a white, stable background for painting with colored glazes. The surface irregularities and flowing nature of the decoration on the finished pieces suggests use of some other ingredients to achieve the decorative effects they desired. The last showing of Byrdcliffe Pottery with the New York Society of Keramic Art in 1922 describes the wares of this last phase as well. "The Misses Penman and Hardenberg [*sic*]," reported *Keramic Studio*, "who many of us have watched as they built up one interesting shape after another at their pottery at Byrdcliffe in the Catskill mountains, exhibited a water jug and several bowls with colorful underglaze decorations."[20] Use of the last three words in describing their work certainly suggests this cluster of delftlike wares.

Most sources identify a change in personnel in the Byrdcliffe Pottery facilities about 1922–23. This is mirrored in the New York City directories as well. Hardenbergh, who lived until at least 1940, is not listed in the city's directories after 1921. On the other hand, Penman continues to live at the Van Dyck Building through the mid-1920s, listing herself as treasurer of the National Association of Women Painters and Sculptors. When she died early in 1929, at the age of sixty-nine, she was living on East 62nd Street. A memorial exhibition of her work was mounted at the National Association of Women Painters and Sculptors the following March. The *New York Times* characterized the exhibit as "largely flower subjects...simple and unforced in style...[with] a great deal of quiet charm."[21]

The pottery work of these two women was always considered secondary to their painting in oils and watercolors. In Penman's *New York Times* obituary, for example, she was described as a "painter . . . known especially for her pictures of flowers." Almost as an afterthought, the reporter noted that "she also made pottery at her summer home in Woodstock, N.Y." Their pottery was only one of the many ways they expressed themselves as artists. The ware was not calculated to be salable so much as to be exhibitable. Their point of view as potters, that is embracing the old-fashioned hand methods, was always noted in the reviews, though there was little real enthusiasm for what they achieved as relative amateurs. Novelty and curiosity are the principal critical assessments that are expressed by reviewers. Of course, the reviewers at this time were much more focused on the latest work of the well-known commercial art potteries, such as Rookwood and Grueby, or the achievements of recognized masters such as Binns and Robineau. With limited interest in production, marketing or promotion, Penman and Hardenbergh were not so much making pottery for public consumption as for their own personal goals.

White Pines Pottery

The genesis of the White Pines Pottery was quite different from the Byrdcliffe Pottery. Whereas the Byrdcliffe Pottery was started as one of the income ventures for the

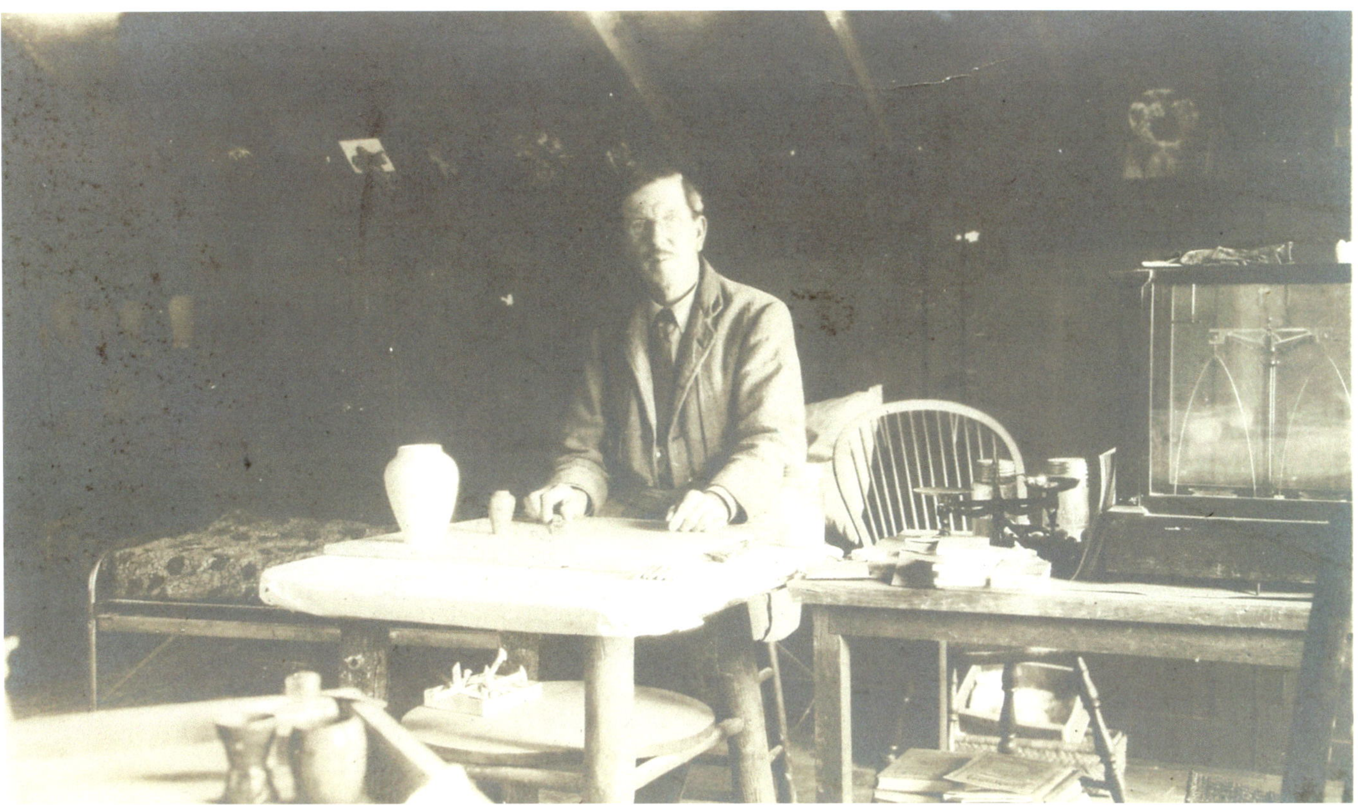

fig. 10 Unidentified photographer, *Ralph Whitehead in Pottery Studio, Byrdcliffe*, ca. 1920. Winterthur Library, Downs Collection, 92x39.1140.235.

colony, the White Pines Pottery began as a personal interest of Jane Whitehead that was later expanded and partially developed as a commercial enterprise.

By 1913, Jane Whitehead's interest in pottery making was aroused and she decided to learn at least the rudiments of the potter's art from Edith Penman and Elizabeth Hardenbergh. For many years, Jane's artistic interests had been in weaving and painting watercolors. On June 12, however, she unpacked after her annual trek eastward from California and the very same day had her "First lesson in Pottery."[22] In the fall, when she returned to Arcady in California, she sought out Frederick Rhead (see page 33), who was just moving to Santa Barbara to set up his own pottery after several difficult years at the Arequipa sanitarium in northern California and a short stint designing garden pottery in San Francisco for the Steiger Pottery. An Englishman by birth, Rhead had been in America since 1902 and had worked in significant enterprises during the intervening years. Of special note for the White Pines Pottery story were his few years as the pottery instructor for the People's University of the American Woman's League, a correspondence program developed by a magazine publisher and distributor in University City, Missouri, near St. Louis. Rhead's association with Jane Whitehead also proved to be useful to him. Ralph Whitehead took a small financial interest in Rhead's Santa Barbara venture in January 1914.[23]

Through the winter of 1913–14 and early spring of 1914, Jane was intent on developing her pottery-making skills (fig. 9). She spent much time at Rhead's pottery, even enticing Ralph to join her on at least one occasion. She noted, however, in March that her "Pottery kiln [was] a failure." Undeterred, she had her "First lesson in throwing on my own wheel" on May 23, leaving on her annual eastward trek in early June. That year she decided to spend much of the summer in Chicago for some serious study through a course taught by William Whitford, a potter and educator teaching under the auspices of the University of Chicago.[24]

By the fall of 1914, Ralph, too, had taken a serious interest in learning ceramic processes, and the Whiteheads were working together to set up their own clay studio at White Pines (fig. 10). A potter's wheel arrived in early October and by early November Jane had written to their son, Peter, about Ralph's involvement: "You can't think how dear & nice father is, & how hard he is trying to help me with the pottery."[25] The more Ralph worked with Jane, the more interested he became in the whole subject. "He has been helping me daily in the pottery work, & I am very grateful." Jane wrote to their son Ralph Jr., "I really think it must interest him a bit."[26] Indeed, Ralph became so engrossed in the whole process that he was moved to comment on the effort himself early in 1915. In a letter to Ralph Jr., he mentioned that "Mother and I have burnt the

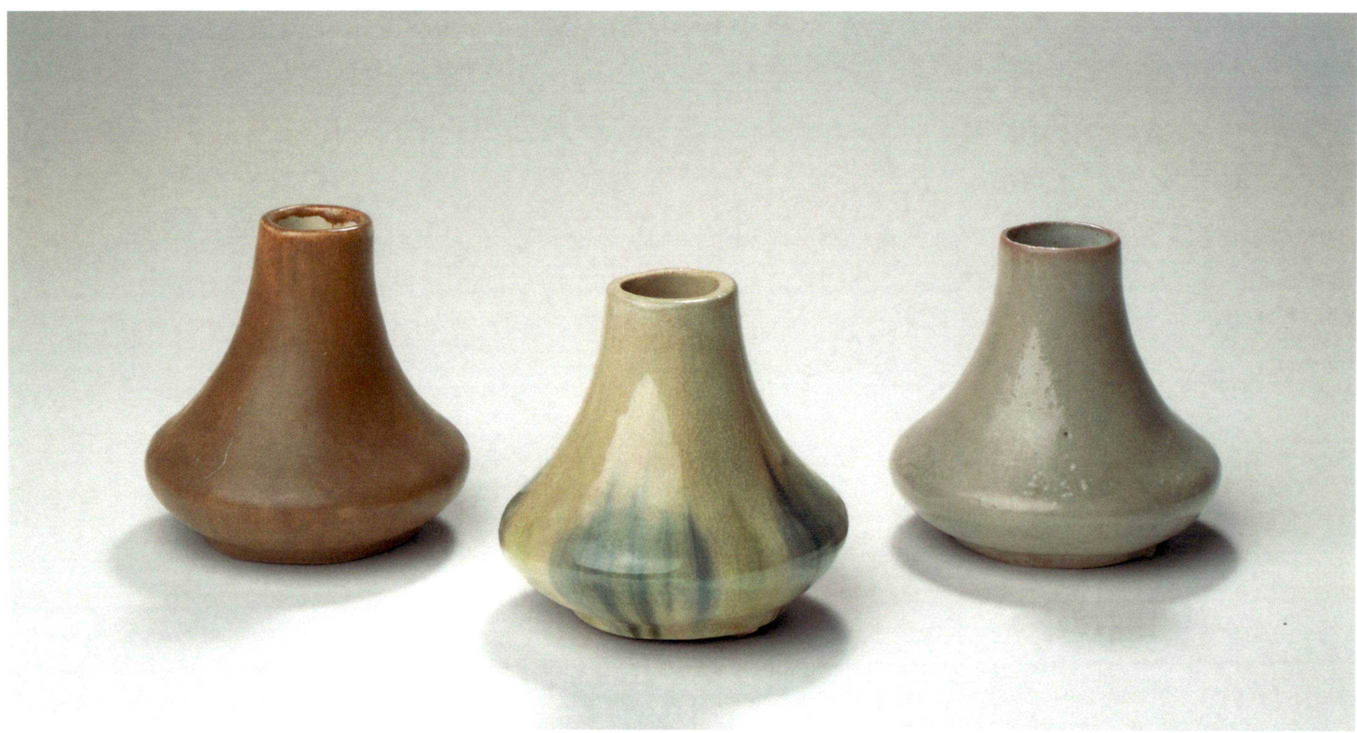

fig. 11 White Pine Pottery, *Three Sample Vases*. Ceramic, various glazes. Private collection.

pottery today. I think we can find out some of the processes of pottery in the next two months. But you cannot learn much about a craft like pottery unless you work at it daily for a couple of years. Anything else is merely amateurish!"[27]

Despite their best efforts, however, the Whiteheads had great difficulty understanding the chemistry of clay and glazes. They were still fussing over these issues in the fall of 1915. Their frustration is revealed in a series of notes from Ralph to Jane in October. He had learned to handle plaster of paris and was excited by the prospect of producing a group of small test vases (fig. 11) using her originals as models for the molds when he wrote on October 29: "I have made about two dozen slip casts of your pots & shall fire them tomorrow, along with some little tiles for more experiments...I am quite charmed with some of your pots [from] which I have made plaster moulds; seven of them. I think some of your pots are little poems."[28] By the next day, however, he was discouraged yet again: "The biscuit firing goes all right but alas, as to glazes & what they will do & what can reasonably be attempted with them all is still to learn"[29] (cats. 133 and 134).

For two novices who had not grown up in the pottery business or served apprenticeships of several years, as so many potters had in those days, the amount of mechanical and technical knowledge necessary to combine clay, glaze and fire into something they considered beautiful was truly overwhelming. Yet they both kept at the quest doggedly. Ralph had begun keeping copious notes in January 1915 and his little books of production tips and glaze formulas gleaned from reading countless books and asking many experts show that the Whiteheads were clearly in over their heads. They had access to some of the best and most inventive potters working in America at the time.[30] Frederick Rhead, Adelaide Robineau, Arthur Baggs, William Jervis, and Charles Binns had long been teachers as well as practical potters, and their advice was invaluable to the Whiteheads though often beyond their scope. Maud Mason, the noted ceramicist, was at Byrdcliffe in 1916 and 1920 and seems to have worked with Jane in the pottery. Mary Sheerer, director of the Newcomb Pottery, visited Byrdcliffe in the summer of 1917, after the Whiteheads' visit to Newcomb. Dr. Herbert J. Hall, founder of the Marblehead Pottery, came in 1920. A thorough man, Ralph continued to collect books on materials and processes and seek advice from experts well into the 1920s.[31]

The working method developed by the Whiteheads suggests that they may well have sought to bypass some of their apparent shortcomings by taking advantage of processes they already understood: photography and woodworking. Instead of inventing new shapes by hand building clay or turning it on a potter's wheel, they came to rely on books that illustrated the ancient Asian wares they considered desirable. Many photographs survive, probably taken by Ralph Whitehead, that are copies of photographic illustrations from Robert Lockhart Hobson's *Chinese Pottery and Porcelain* (1915) and Garret Chatfield Pier's

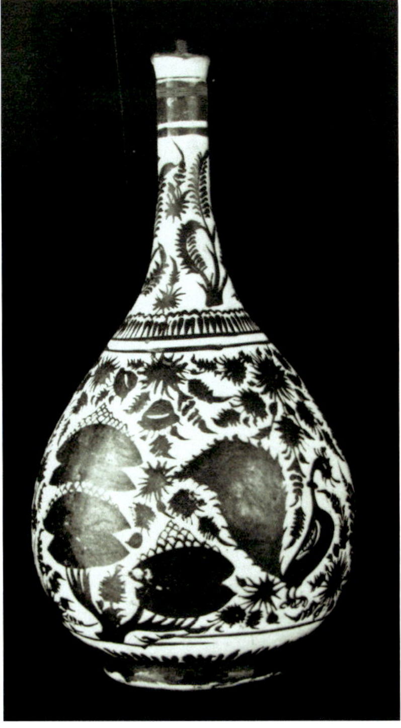

fig. 12 Ralph Whitehead's photographic copy of illustration from Robert Lockhart Hobson's *Chinese Pottery and Porcelain* (1915).

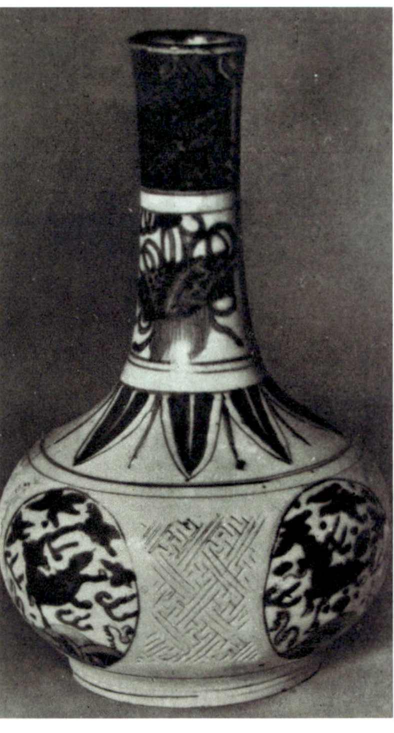

fig. 13 Ralph Whitehead's photographic copy of illustration from Garret Chatfield Pier's *Pottery of the Near East* (1909).

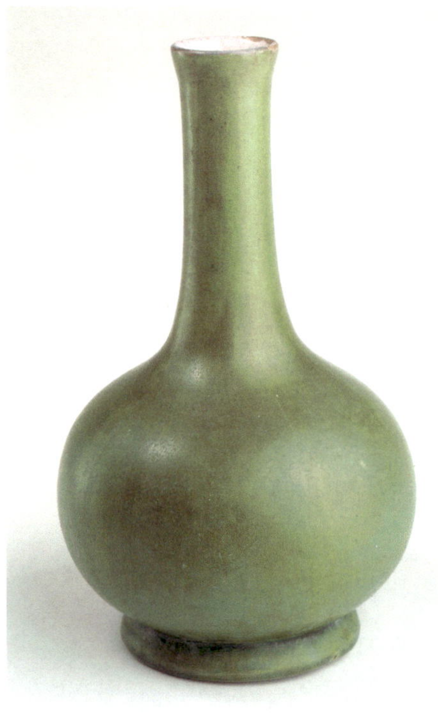

fig. 14 White Pines Pottery, *Vase, Persian Bottle Shape.* Glazed ceramic. Collection of Lawrence Webster.

Pottery of the Near East (1909) (figs. 12 and 13). Prints from the copy negatives were enlarged to take into account the final size desired as well as the fifteen percent shrinkage that could be expected from firing the clay vessels. In some cases, pencil additions further defined the shape of a vase's foot when the information in the photograph was ambiguous. The photographs were then supplied to a wood turner, who translated them into three-dimensional shapes (cats. 132, 148, 149, and 150). These turned wooden forms became the models for the plaster of paris molds. Many of the wooden models survive from the White Pines Pottery, and most are identified as to their culture of origin or classification by Hobson. "Chinese" and "Persian" shapes were favored by the Whiteheads (fig. 14). Many of the working plaster molds also survive. The small pottery building near White Pines still survives (fig. 15).

Ware made from the models and molds was biscuit fired first, that is, burned in the kiln without glaze. After biscuit firing, a wide variety of glazes were applied. The effects on finished wares range from a quiet, poetic pale mauve-gray, reminiscent of the sky at sunset (fig. 16), to a brash pumpkin orange (once likened to the fall color of the eastern sumac) (fig. 17) along with every color in between these two extremes. Although most of the vases that survive today have glazes of a single overall color effect, a few were decorated by painting and some others carried low-relief decoration that was suggested in the plaster mold and further worked by hand (fig. 18). All of the decorated vases—whether painted or modeled—feature the leaves and berries of the eucalyptus tree. In spite of the diversity of glazes employed on the exterior of the ware, the insides of many vases carry the distinctive robin's-egg blue that was a signature color for the Byrdcliffe colony.

There are two kilns that survive in the pottery shed at White Pines today, and they are probably all the clay-burning equipment that was ever employed. The larger of the two was likely used for biscuit firing at a fairly high temperature, while the smaller one was apparently intended for glaze firing at a lower temperature. Both were fueled by gas. In 1917, Jane Whitehead complained to their son Ralph Jr. that they might have made bigger plans if they had understood all the elements necessary to make a pottery operation successful: "You were right in what you said—the only way to make it pay is to have a brick kiln etc., but—we are too old darling, I'm afraid it must just be an amusement, if we had found this out 6 or 8 years ago, perhaps we might have made it go, but you know Father with all his shrewdness & intelligence is not practical."[32] The brick kiln would have given them more space for processing larger numbers of pieces in a single firing. What they made in the smaller kilns sometimes came out warped and sagged in the biscuit fire and glazes often crawled and curdled uncontrollably in the smaller muffle kiln. If the Whiteheads had truly hoped to put the pottery operation on a paying basis, they would have hired trained potters to carry out their designs, but this was probably never their intention. Ralph wrote to his wife from Woodstock in July 1917 that he was "going to let pots go & have a rest" the next week. He complained about being too busy and noted that "for one week I shall do no pots in the morning. One should enjoy summer before it passes, & one can enjoy nothing when one is too tired."[33] Clearly, the pottery operation was meant to fit into their lifestyle at Byrdcliffe, not determine it.

Hundreds of small glaze-test tiles, one by two inches (cat. 147), survive as well as a large group of small vases, two to three inches in height, which may also have been used for testing glaze formulas (see fig. 11). While many glaze formulas are transcribed in Ralph Whitehead's notebooks, notes referring to specific test tiles do not survive, if there ever were any. Instead of a paper system, the Whiteheads probably employed a visual system. Most of the tiles are identified on the reverse with idiosyncratic notations that seem to refer to glaze mixtures.

In addition to the test tiles and his glaze formula book, Whitehead seems to have kept a record of every vase they made. Although the sequence of these records is incomplete, it appears that vases were numbered consecutively beginning with one and going up to 999. At that point the consecutive numbering began with one again, but with a capital "A" appended to the number. When 999A was reached, the numbering system started from one again, but with a B added to the number. Records go up to 802B, suggesting that a total of about 2800 pieces was entered into his system. The number may also represent the extent of the White Pines Pottery's total output. Some vases survive with these numbers visible on the bottom either incised or painted in black (fig. 18) (bottom of cat. 130). However, since glazes often flowed during firing, the bottoms of many vases are completely coated and the numbers and other identifying notations are not readable. The numbering system continued to be used in tracking the ware during marketing. Among the many small notebooks kept by Ralph there is one entitled only "Pottery" that contains notes on the consignment of White Pines Pottery wares. Each entry in the lists of consignment accounts carries a number that corresponds to the assigned production number that is recorded in the other notebooks.

Although there were some inquiries made in New York City as early as 1917, marketing efforts for White Pines Pottery began in earnest almost two years later. In January 1917, Jane Whitehead complained to their son Ralph Jr. that "the way we do things does not succeed, the furniture failed, the weaving failed, & now the pottery looks to me to be going to fail because Ralph won't have an expert here

fig. 15 White Pines and Pottery Studio (seen to the right, at back), 2003.

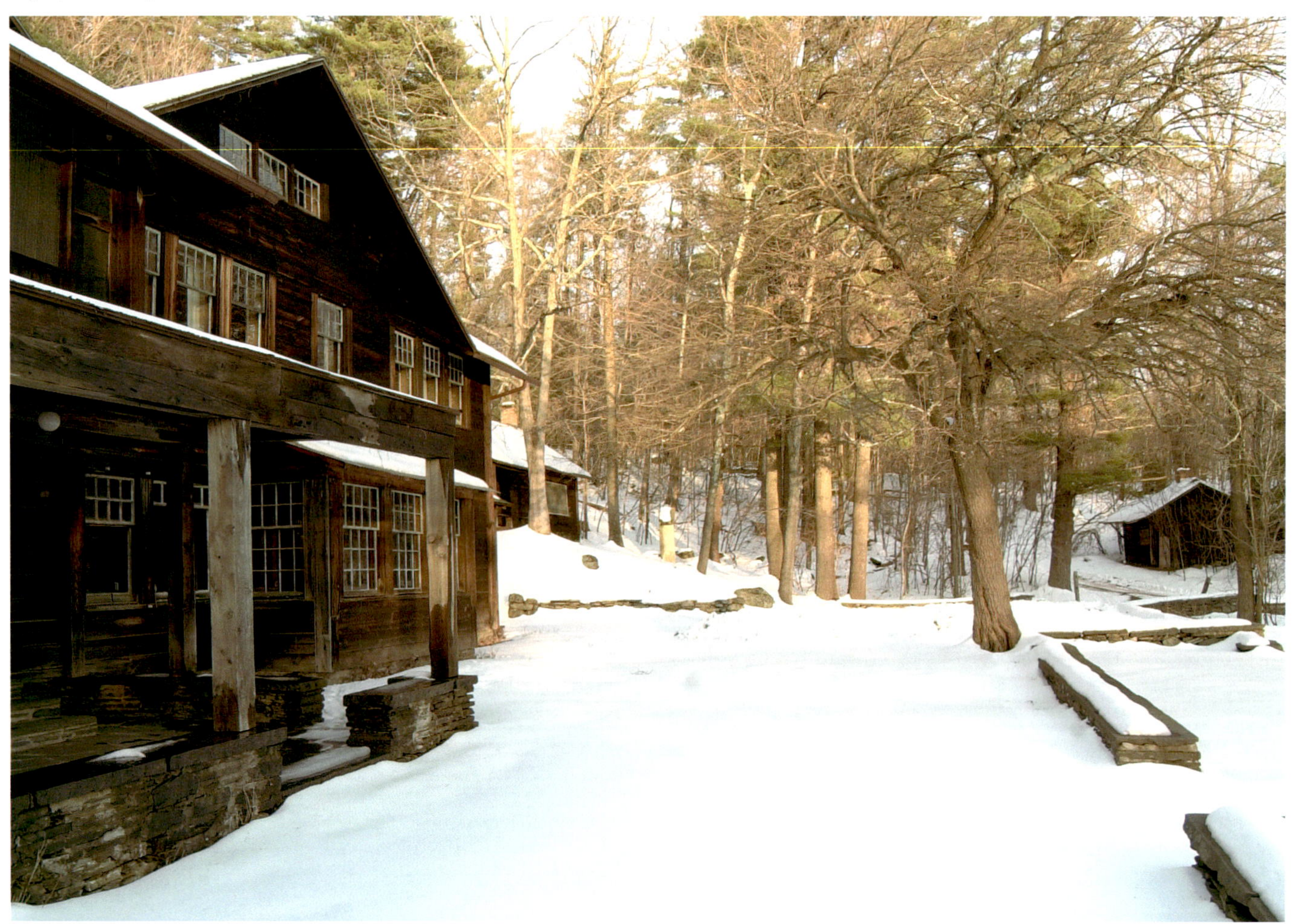

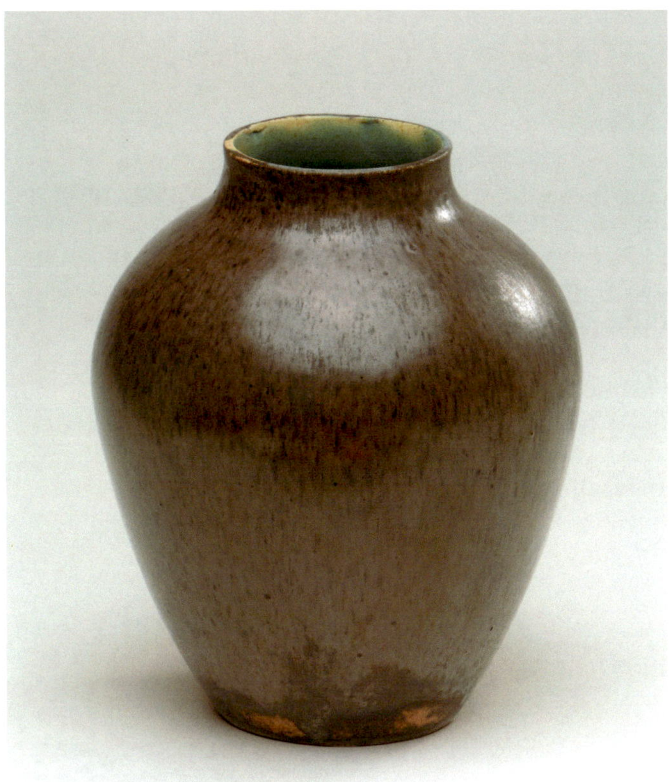

fig. 16 White Pines Pottery, *Vase with Purple-gray Glaze*. Ceramic. Collection of the Byrdcliffe Art Colony of the Woodstock Guild. Gift of the Douglas C. James Charitable Trust in honor of Carla Smith.

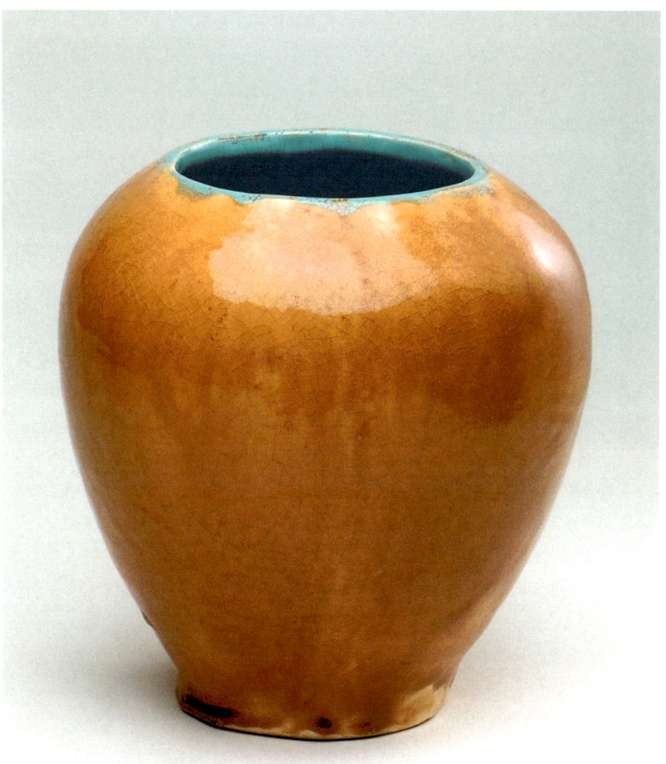

fig. 17 White Pines Pottery, *Vase with Sumac Glaze*. Ceramic. Collection of the Byrdcliffe Art Colony of the Woodstock Guild. Gift of the Douglas C. James Charitable Trust in honor of Carla Smith.

to show him the way, & an outlet in New York to get rid of what he makes."[34] In her agitated state, Jane "tackled" Phillip Chase, a family friend, and turned him into the pottery's "promoter" in New York City: "I want to have our pottery—what is already made—shown in N.Y. this Spring before it is placed at a shop for sale. All that entails much work—work which cannot be done by correspondence. Phillip will do this professionally—see the gallery agent & do the advertising—attend to the exhibition—tote around the pots which I left at Anne Moore's to shop & interest them in taking it for sale."[35] Chase reported quickly that a visit to the Montross Gallery had not been successful: "They could not do anything for us because they handle the old Chinese pottery. The White Pines pottery resembles and is very much like the old Chinese so they said, and they also said that the public could not tell the difference. This I thought quite a compliment."[36] From a vantage point in the early twenty-first century, when connoisseurship of ceramics is perhaps further advanced than in 1917, the gallery's assessment of the ware appears quaint. His visit to the MacBeth Gallery yielded similar results.

That same year, en route to California for the winter months, the Whiteheads made a detour to New Orleans so they could visit the famed Newcomb Pottery at Tulane University, which had been producing Arts and Crafts ceramics since the 1890s.

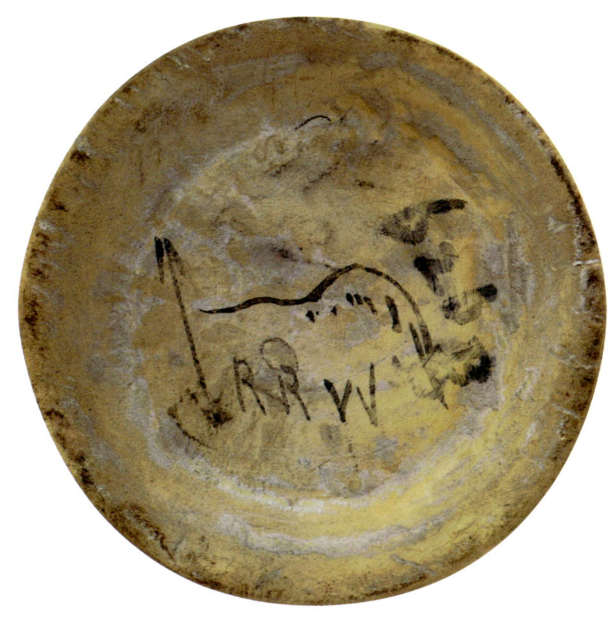

fig. 18 White Pines Pottery. RRW notation (bottom of cat. 130). Private collection.

Marketing efforts became more methodical early in 1919. Ralph Whitehead put many pieces on consignment in shops across the country and a sale of the pottery was arranged in Santa Barbara. The latter event was apparently considered successful by the Whiteheads. Jane wrote to their son Peter in May of that year: "Were you ever told how very successful the pottery sale was? Two hundred and fifty pots sold—bringing $450.00. Clearing $300. Some pots sold for $25, $20 and $15 a piece—and down to $1. A few of the best judges of art in Santa Barbara said it was the best pottery made in America."[37] A second exhibition in Santa Barbara the following January was noted by the local press.[38] On the other hand, consignment sales must have been a disappointment if the notes in Ralph's "Pottery" record book are any indication of the outcome of this activity. The shops stretched from Boston to Chicago and Santa Barbara to Baltimore, including addresses in Cleveland, Philadelphia, Woodstock, Cincinnati, and several in New York City.[39] Brisk sales through the Society of Arts and Crafts shop in Boston were recorded, although most ware was returned to Whitehead from other vendors after a year or two. Three barrels, containing nineteen pieces, were shipped to Santa Barbara in January 1920. Although this may have been intended for the above-mentioned exhibit, Ralph noted in his records that these pieces were "to keep." Today, most White Pines pottery that survives is either held in the family or can be traced through family friends who purchased vases directly from the Whiteheads or received them as gifts.

Conclusion

If the work of the Byrdcliffe Pottery and White Pines Pottery is compared to other art and studio potteries of the early twentieth century, Penman, Hardenbergh and Jane and Ralph Whitehead would likely be seen as amateurs. Technically, their work does not match the general high standards of the American studio and factory ware of the period. Although the glazes are endlessly interesting in their variety, the shapes of the hand-built Byrdcliffe Pottery are clumsy and those of White Pines Pottery are almost totally derivative. But comparison of Byrdcliffe productions to the commercial art potteries, such as Rookwood or Grueby, is unreasonable. These potteries were large affairs with many skilled workers, each concerned with a small part of the overall operation (like turning, firing, or glazing) rather than the total process. Furthermore, studio potters of this early era, such as Binns, Volkmar, or Robineau, had spent many years in apprenticeship before producing the work for which they are best known today.

On the other hand, the four potters of Byrdcliffe colony were living in the moment of the Arts and Crafts movement. They were getting dirty, using their hearts, hands, and minds to create something from common earth and a few minerals, and gaining a fair amount of satisfaction from the process. Collectively, their work provides a stark and instructive contrast to the output of professional potteries and potters of the era. The Byrdcliffe wares are not so much work for sale as pottery created out of the artists's desire to express themselves. For Penman and Hardenbergh, being involved in the vitality of the New York City art scene must have been exhilarating, participating in exhibition openings, sharing insights and information with their colleagues, and integrating all of the visual arts into their lives every day in the city as well as the country.

The life goals for the Whiteheads may have been a bit different, but they were no less successful in meeting them. Jane and Ralph both yearned to "evolve something worthwhile"[40] by creating a lifestyle in the arts. "I spent all morning doing pots up in the workroom," Jane wrote to their son Peter in 1916. "It is good to have a comfortable house & some hand work, I ask nothing better."[41]

Notes

1. *Keramic Studio*, vol. 13, no. 1 (May 1911): 10.
2. For examples of the work of these women potters, see pertinent entries in Wendy Kaplan, et al., *"The Art that is Life": The Arts & Crafts Movement in America, 1875–1920* (Boston: Museum of Fine Arts, 1987).
3. See, for example, the work of women at the Rookwood Pottery in Cincinnati or Grueby Pottery in Boston and compare that with the work of independent women china painters. Anita J. Ellis, *Rookwood Pottery: The Glorious Gamble* (Cincinnati: Cincinnati Art Museum and Rizzoli, 1992); Susan J. Montgomery, *The Ceramics of William H. Grueby: The Spirit of the New Idea in Artistic Handicraft* (Lambertville, NJ: Arts & Crafts Quarterly Press, 1993); Ellen Paul Denker, "The Grammar of Nature: Arts and Crafts China Painting" in Bert R. Denker, ed., *The Substance of Style: New Perspectives on the American Arts and Crafts Movement* (Winterthur, Delaware: The H. F. du Pont Winterthur Museum, 1996), 281–300. Penman and Hardenbergh were first mentioned by Paul Evans in *Art Pottery of the United States: An Encyclopedia of Producers and Their Marks* (New York: Charles Scribner's Sons, 1974), 38–39.
4. *Who Was Who in American Art*, 2567.
5. *Who Was Who in American Art*, 1453. Hardenbergh may have died about 1940, after which year her name no longer appears in the *Who's Who in American Art* annual series. Although Hardenbergh's life dates are not presently known, she may have been ten or fifteen years younger than Penman, judging by their histories of exhibiting in New York and Philadelphia. Penman's earliest known exhibition date is 1886 at the National Academy of Design, while Hardenbergh's earliest exhibition date is 1901 at the Pennsylvania Academy of the Fine Arts.
6. The National Association of Women Painters and Sculptors (later the National Association of Women Artists) was established in 1889 in New York City as the New York Woman's Art Club; the New York Watercolor Club was established in New York City in 1890.
7. RRW to Jane, January 14, 1903. Winterthur Library, Downs Collection.
8. *Ibid.*
9. Penman and Hardenbergh probably lived there together because there is no other residence noted for either of them and the same room number is listed for both consistently from 1904–5 through 1920–21, when Hardenbergh's name appears for the last time in the directory. The Van Dyck Building is first listed in the 1895–96 directory for New York City. The address is on the west side of the block between 55th and 56th Streets.
10. Paul Evans, *Art Pottery of the United States*, 2nd ed. (New York: Feingold & Lewis Publishing Corp., 1987), 38. For more on Volkmar, see Evans, *Art Pottery*, 2nd ed., 307–15.
11. Alf Evers quoting Bertha Thompson, "The Craftsmen of Byrdcliffe," *Publications of the Woodstock Historical Society* 10 (July 1933): 8–13; this quotation on page 12.

12. For an investigation of these philosophical issues, see Ulysses Grant Dietz, "Paul St. Gaudens and the Emerging Studio Pottery Movement" in Henry J. Duffy, ed., *Paul St. Gaudens (1900–1954) Ceramic Artist* (Cornish, NH: Saint-Gaudens National Historic Site, 2001), 27–35. In 1926, Paul St. Gaudens, nephew of the sculptor Augustus Saint-Gaudens, wrote that "pottery is a craft that can be raised to the level of an art, and is a legitimate means of artistic expression, which can be freed from the stigma of quantity production by returning to the old crude hand methods of production" (30).

13. *Keramic Studio*, vol. 8, no. 10 (February 1907): 234.

14. *Keramic Studio*, vol. 8, no. 3 (July 1906): 69.

15. *Keramic Studio*, vol. 9, no. 2 (June 1907): 39; vol. 10, no. 2 (June 1908): 41; vol. 11, no. 2 (June 1909): 39; vol. 13, no. 1 (May 1911): 10.

16. *Keramic Studio*, vol. 10, no. 2 (June 1908): 45.

17. *Keramic Studio*, vol. 10, no. 2 (June 1908): 25.

18. For information on these five bowls, see Ulysses G. Dietz, *The Newark Museum Collection of American Art Pottery* (Newark, NJ: The Newark Museum, 1984), 22–23.

19. For examples, see Norman Karlson, *American Art Tile, 1876–1941* (New York: Rizzoli, 1998), 37; and Nancy E. Green, et al., *Arthur Wesley Dow (1857–1922): His Art and His Influence* (New York: Spanierman Gallery, 1999), 229. The small plate decorated with what may be yellow primroses is in a private collection in Woodstock, New York.

20. *Keramic Studio* (June 1922): 22.

21. Obituary, *New York Times*, January 16, 1929: 25; review of memorial exhibition, *New York Times*, March 24, 1929: Section X, 13.

22. Jane Whitehead, calendar for June 12, 1913. Winterthur Library, Downs Collection. The White Pines Pottery was first discussed in detail by Jane Perkens Claney using many of the same documents noted here. See Jane Perkins Claney, "White Pines Pottery; the continuing arts and crafts experiment" in *Life by Design: The Byrdcliffe Arts and Crafts Colony* (Wilmington: Delaware Art Museum, 1984), 15–20.

23. For more information on Rhead's career, see Sharon Dale, *Frederick Hürten Rhead: An English Potter in America* (Erie, PA: Erie Art Museum, 1986). The White Pines library included Rhead's instruction book *Studio Pottery* (University City, MO: People's University Press, 1910). Winterthur Library, Downs Collection.

24. Jane Whitehead, calendar for 1913. Winterthur Library, Downs Collection.

25. Regarding kiln, see Jane Whitehead, calendar for 1914; for quotation, see Jane to Peter Whitehead, November 8, 1914. Winterthur Library, Downs Collection.

26. Jane to RRW, November 19, 1914. Winterthur Library, Downs Collection.

27. RRW to Ralph Jr., January 19, 1915. Winterthur Library, Downs Collection.

28. RRW to Jane, October 29, 1915. Winterthur Library, Downs Collection. Plaster of paris was developed in the mid-eighteenth century in France and England for use in press-molding and slip-casting vessels of clay. Press-molding involved pressing pancakes of damp clay into molds made from original models. The parts of a vessel made in this way were later joined using a mixture of clay and water as a kind of cement; then the whole piece was hardened in a kiln firing. Slip-casting involves creating a hollow plaster of paris mold from a model and filling the mold with slip, a mixture of clay and water having the consistency of cream. A deflocculant is added to the slip to hold the clay particles in suspension while the plaster is absorbing water from the slip. As the water is absorbed, the particles are deposited against the wall of the mold and a thin layer of clay develops. This layer will become the wall of the vessel. After a short period of time, the excess slip is poured off. The clay left behind has formed the vessel, which will be hardened in a kiln firing. For a detailed discussion of these processes, see Donald E. Frith, *Mold Making for Ceramics* (Radnor, PA: Chilton Book Company, 1985). The text used by Ralph Whitehead was likely Frank Forrest Frederick, *Plaster Casts and How They Are Made.* 3rd ed. (New York: William T. Comstock Co., 1911) which survives in the Winterthur Library, Downs Collection.

29. RRW to Jane, October 30, 1915. Winterthur Library, Downs Collection.

30. Ralph Whitehead's notebook entitled "Pottery Collected Notes Dec 1915," which actually covers the years 1915 to 1922, includes references to clays and glazes from Binns, Rhead, Robineau, and Whitford. In addition, he lists Baggs and Jervis, along with Rhead, Whitford, and others under "Potters" in the same notebook. Winterthur Library, Downs Collection. The White Pines library also included books by many of these potters.

31. Jane Whitehead, calendar for 1923, notes "R at School of Mines" on January 1. Ralph would likely have been investigating clays and their properties. Likewise, books and pamphlets surviving from White Pines includes an offprint of an article by Dr. M. W. Twitchell entitled "The Geology of Clay Deposits: With Particular Reference to those of New Jersey" that was originally published in *The Ceramist*, vol. 4, no. 4 (July 1924). Winterthur Library, Downs Collection.

32. Jane to Ralph Jr., January 19, 1917. Winterthur Library, Downs Collection.

33. RRW to Jane, July 7, 1917. Winterthur Library, Downs Collection.

34. Jane to Ralph Jr., January 6, 1917. Winterthur Library, Downs Collection.

35. Jane to Ralph Jr., January 14, 1917. Winterthur Library, Downs Collection. Anne Moore was a noted children's book reviewer and librarian at the Pratt Institute who spent many summers at Byrdcliffe.

36. Phillip Chase, letter to Jane Whitehead, January 17, 1917. Winterthur Library, Downs Collection.

37. Jane to Peter, May 7, 1919. Winterthur Library, Downs Collection.

38. "White Pines Pottery is Placed on View," clipping from unidentified newspaper, January 10, 1920, n.p. Winterthur Library, Downs Collection.

39. Ralph Whitehead, "Pottery," Winterthur Library, Downs Collection. From the total of 355 pieces listed for sale at the various commercial venues in this notebook, only fifty-nine appear to have been sold. These records were rather haphazardly kept and are probably incomplete; however, the existing notes suggest an overall lack of significant pottery sales by Whitehead.

40. Jane to RRW, October 25, 1915. Winterthur Library, Downs Collection.

41. Jane to Peter, January 13, 1916. Winterthur Library, Downs Collection.

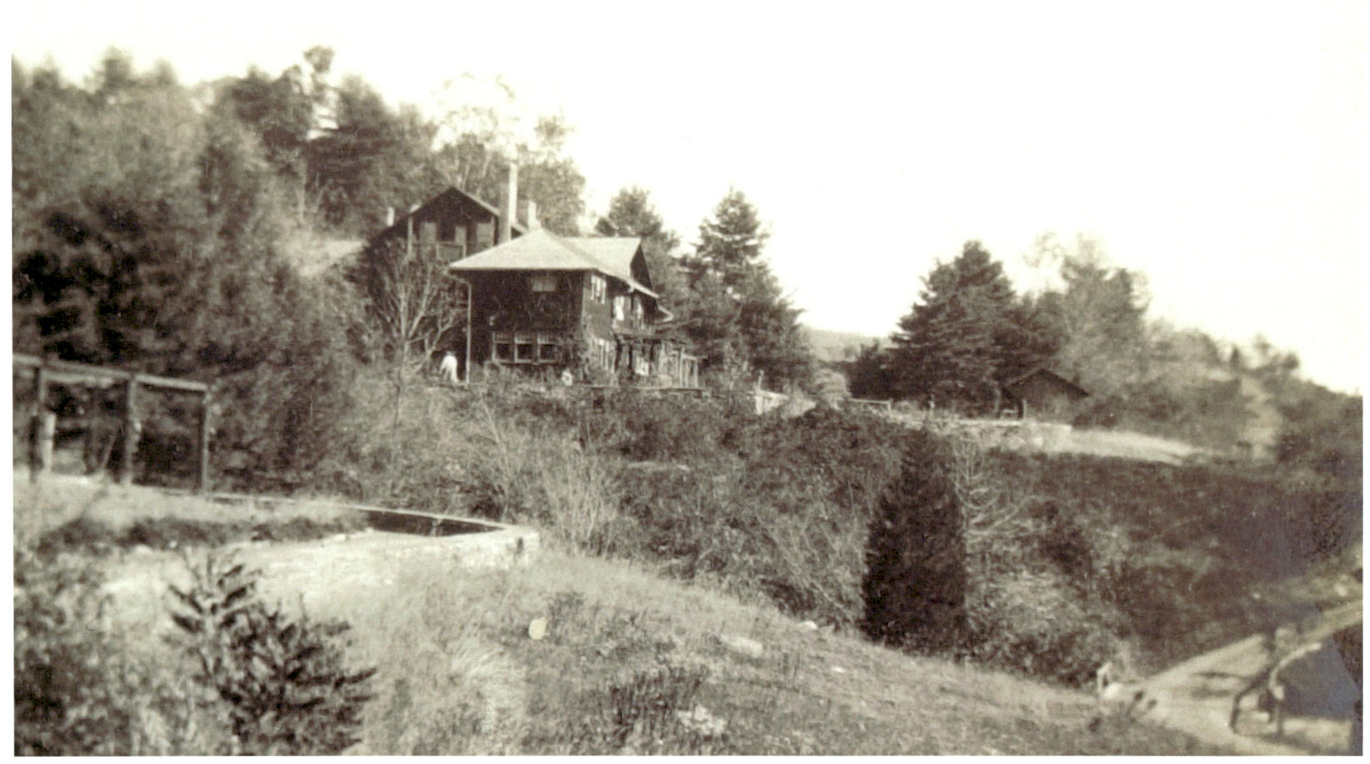

fig. 1 View from the southwest of White Pines, the Whiteheads' Byrdcliffe home. Webster family photograph, ca. 1907. Woodstock Guild.

Nature and Artifice in the Architecture of Byrdcliffe

CHERYL ROBERTSON

Ralph Whitehead had specific climatic qualities, scenic preferences, and site requirements in mind for the Arts and Crafts colony he was eager to establish by 1902.[1] He spelled out the three principal criteria—healthfulness, beauty, and accessibility—in "A Plea for Manual Work" for the magazine *Handicraft* in June 1903; they were reprinted in Byrdcliffe's 1907 prospectus. Comrades Hervey White and Bolton Brown had impressed on him the importance of acquiring land accessible to a large city and to reliable transportation for cultural and marketing reasons.[2] Left to his own devices, Whitehead's deep-seated urge to transcend both the physical and moral pollution of the industrial landscape might well have driven him deeper into rural America than Woodstock. After all, it was only a few miles from the railway station at West Hurley, which was but a ten-minute train ride from Kingston, served daily by trains and boats from New York City.

Concern for the well-being of his two very young sons had been key in propelling Whitehead eastward from Arcady, the Italianate home he and wife Jane had constructed in the Mediterranean-like Montecito environs of Santa Barbara in 1894 (see page 16).[3] They now aspired to rear their offspring in an invigorating locale away from the noxious influence of the idle rich. Whitehead, who spoke and wrote often of the benefits of physical culture and the need for useful work, dismissed most of Montecito's inhabitants as leisured, dissolute denizens of stately mansions.[4]

Jane Whitehead herself testified to her husband's profound desire to "live like a peasant," and his "Plea" emphasized the importance of mingling with rustic people and engaging in muscular contact with the soil to ensure both individual and national health.[5] Ralph asserted:

> It is a commonplace of modern scientific observation that the towns have to be recruited by a constant influx of healthier blood from the country . . . the people who have lived for centuries in one countryside, who have seen their fathers die and their children born and the seasons come round in one place, seem to possess qualities which cannot be otherwise acquired.[6]

Woodstock still retained descendants of its eighteenth-century farmers, like the Lasher family with whom Brown and Whitehead boarded before their respective residences at Byrdcliffe were completed. As late as 1924, the *Christian Science Monitor* described Cane Lasher as a wrinkled plowman plucked from picturesque Brittany or Normandy. The reporter concluded:

> The Lashers and the Elwyns and the Snyders and the Schoonmakers have farmed hereabouts since Rip Van Winkle Days and not all the pictures made by all the artists that have ever lived would be considered fair exchange by Cane for that old ox that moves so slow and looks so sleek and fat and philosophic. Thus Woodstock has its rustic charms.[7]

For Whitehead, an alpine atmosphere, along with agriculture, gardening, and other country pursuits, was essential for healthfulness. Fresh, clear air was generally prescribed as a preventative and cure for tuberculosis. Mountain-fed streams and springs promised unpolluted, microbe-free water, which Ralph intended to pipe into bathrooms at the boarding houses and studios.[8] A mountain prospect was also fundamental to the pursuit of beauty, which Whitehead, in common with other Victorian-era aesthetes, considered synonymous with moral health. The first circular printed to promote the Summer Art School at Byrdcliffe, in 1903, stressed "the paintable quality of its beauty," situated as it was on "the whole of the southern as well as a part of the northern side of a mountain [ranging] in altitude from six hundred feet, where, along the base, the agricultural land lies, to twenty-two hundred feet, where crags and forest fret the sky."

Shaping the Communal Landscape: Ruskinian Ideology Incarnate

Whitehead's fixation on an ideal mountainside location of one thousand to fifteen hundred feet above sea level, with stalwart pines overlooking cultivated fields and edged by rocky precipices, came directly from the reverential musings on mountain beauty penned by his Oxford mentor, John Ruskin. He maintained in *Modern Painters* that flat land was like a prison to him; whereas even the suggestion of hilly terrain, with a bit of ferny undergrowth and a fir or two, instantly raised his spirits.[9] Whitehead actually likened comprehension of Ruskin to scaling the heights. During his courtship of Jane, he wrote from Europe in early August 1891, "I have analyzed a difficult bit of Ruskin and this has given me a feeling like one has after climbing a bit, the blood circulates better and 'the blues' are dispelled." For Ruskin, mountains equated with energy, passion, and endurance, as opposed to lowlands repose, the inactivity of plains dwellers, and the enervating influence of the seashore.[10] Ralph reprised these notions in a letter to Jane from Byrdcliffe on October 29, 1902, during construction of their new abode:

> For the boys' sake we will overcome our restless nervousness and here in this more vigorous climate we may hope to do so more easily than where we were. And you must not forget that my choice of hill side was guided by the desire for a certain altitude, knowing as I do how much better physically and in every way I am and you too will be in bracing air which the valleys never give. Even in Florence they talk of "aria di Fiesole."

Whitehead owned a copy of the "Inaugural Address at the Cambridge School of Art" (1858), wherein Ruskin waxed poetic about the placement of a ruined Savoyard villa.[11] It had been built on the slope of a pretty hill to command the view of Turin, which, Ruskin enthused, lay at the center of a crescent formed by the Alps round the basin of the Piedmont. Bolton Brown was similarly awed by his first glimpse of Woodstock and the future Byrdcliffe realm, in May 1902, from the notch at Mead's House atop Overlook Mountain:

> Wide and almost as blue as the sea, that extraordinarily beautiful view [was] amazing in extent, the silver Hudson losing itself in remote haze, those farthest and faintest humps along the horizon being the Shawangunk Mountains. I walked slowly along the highway facing this panorama...and a little down the road came upon an old man. . . . Pointing down to what seemed an earthly paradise, stretched at our feet, I asked [Mr. Mead]: "What is the name of that place down there?" He replied: "That is Woodstock Village."[12]

In addition to the physical site, the social landscape of the Byrdcliffe colony was indebted to Ruskin. His championing of medieval art and life as a golden age, worthy of resurrection through his St. George's Guild, influenced Whitehead's' preference for the terms "art village" or "convent" to characterize the craft-based settlement he wanted to found.[13] The dormitory built in 1902–3 was called "Villetta," or "little village" (see page 12). It was at the heart of the colony's educational and craft-shop zone (fig. 2, no. 2). There were also residential studio-cottage and farming zones, between which stood the Whitehead family domicile (see fig. 2, no. 1) in the "West Riding" on Mount Guardian. Ralph Whitehead hailed from Yorkshire, which had been the center of English monastic life in the later Middle Ages, before Henry VIII dismembered all the church-owned communal estates. Whitehead's ancestral manse was at Saddleworth in the West Riding—Yorkshire having been divided into North, East, and West Ridings since the days of Norse occupation in the ninth to eleventh centuries. In fact, the designation "riding," meaning "a third part," was of Viking origin.

In his "General Statement Explaining the Nature and Purpose of St. George's Guild" (1882), Ruskin had revealed a particular fondness for the north of England and its largest county, Yorkshire, "[still] in the main temper of its inhabitants, old England, and capable therefore yet of the ideas of Honesty and Piety by which old England lived."[14] He linked the mountain-loving pine tree with the steadfastness and warrior strength he admired in "the Northern peoples . . . the Norwegian and the Goth . . . taught under the green roofs and wild penetralia of the pine."[15] Thus

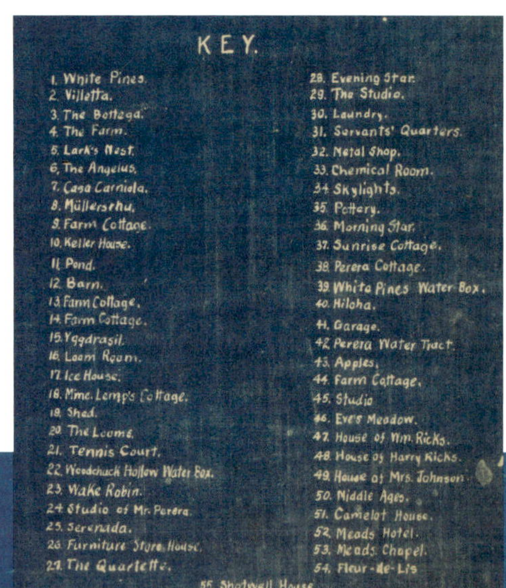

fig. 2 *Map of Byrdcliffe*, dated September 1910. Historical Society of Woodstock.

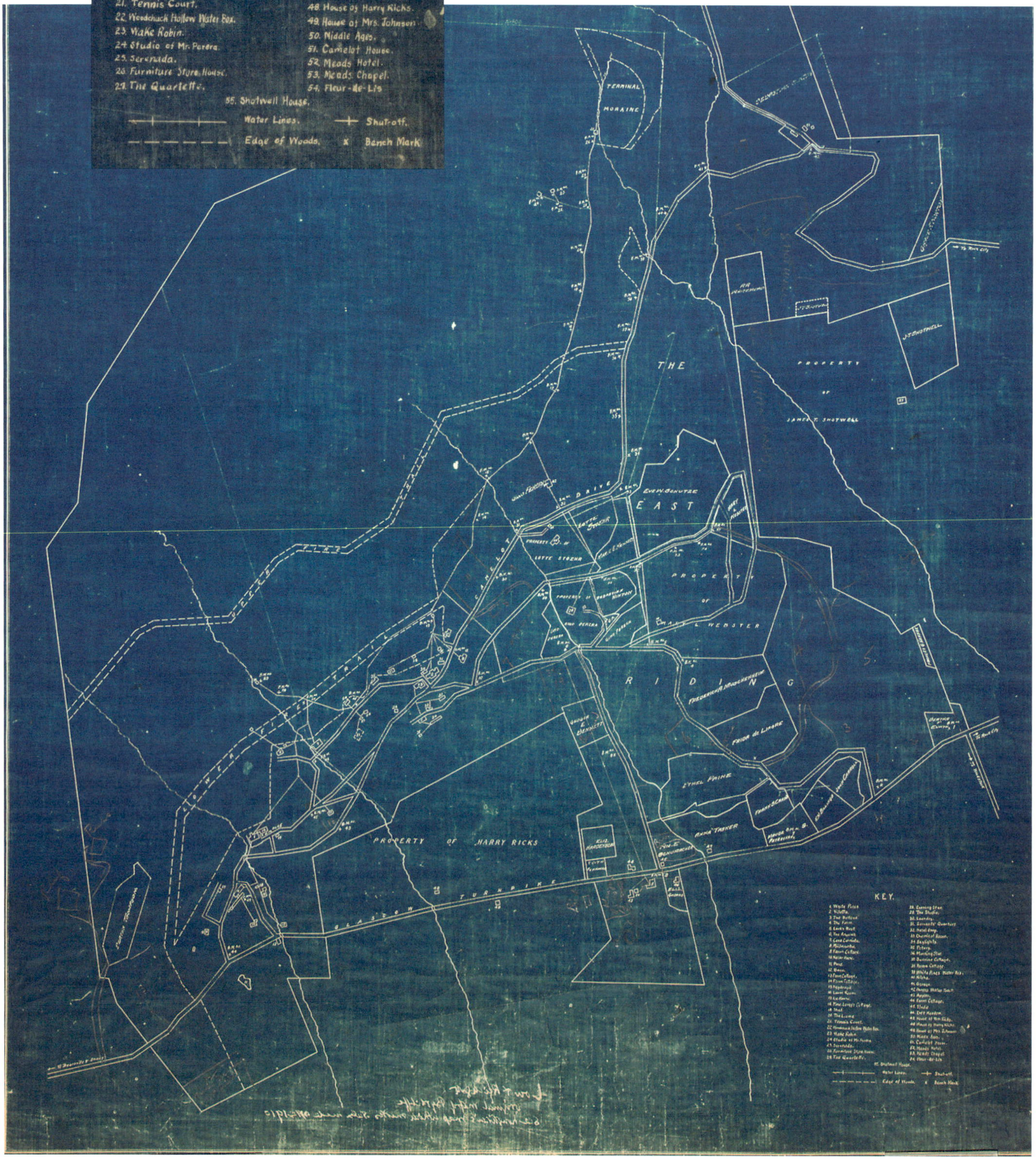

Whitehead christened his family's Byrdcliffe home "White Pines," as much for its Ruskinian/Yorkshire associations as for the conifers indigenous to the Catskills. On his first foray to the Woodstock region, Ralph had painted a word picture for Jane of the natural surroundings:

> I have picked out a couple of little farms with real woods on the hillside, which can be had for a small price[,] about ten dollar[s] per acre. You have the wooded hills behind you & to the South and the South East a distant horizon of blue wooded country sixty miles away, then to the S.W. and W. some mountains, not like the Alps but like the Scotch hills, and at one place at the edge of the woods a clump of pines for Bimbi [Ralph Jr.] and me, and for you too, dear, for they are our own white pines, though not such ancient trees as those we photographed and drew at York. Shall we call it "White Pines" for the sake of York?[16]

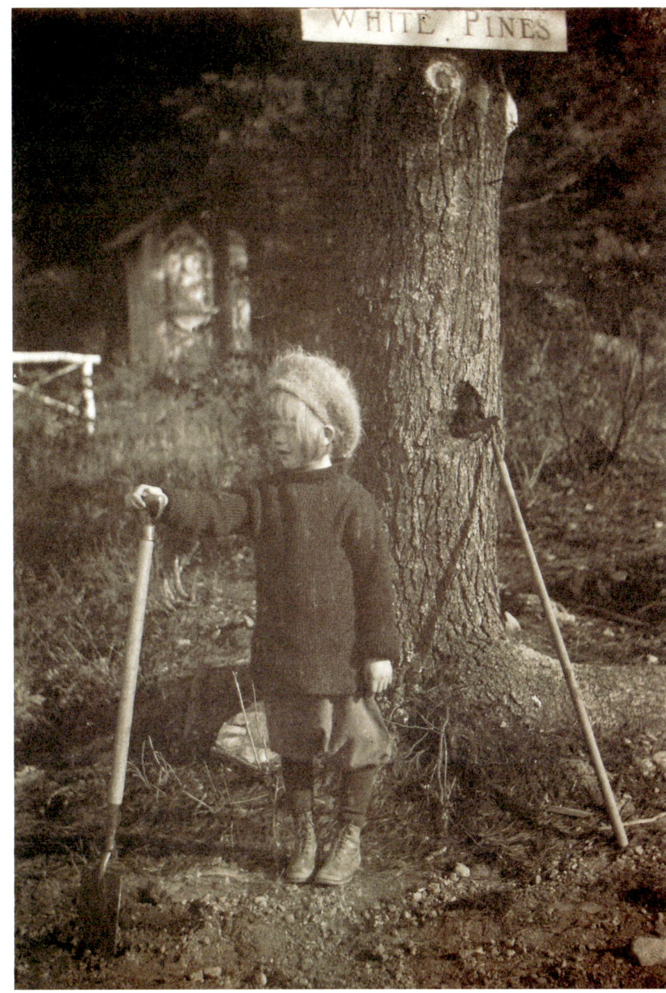

fig. 3 Ralph Whitehead Jr., at the "White Pines" marker, ca. 1905.
Winterthur Library, Downs Collection, 92x39.1140.647a

The rustic White Pines sign (fig. 3) marked not only the aforementioned clump of pines but also the path to a wayside shrine featuring a Renaissance-style della Robbia image of the Madonna and Child. The same icon provided a focal point in Ruskin's study at Brantwood, his rural retreat at Coniston in the Lake District of northern England.[17] Like Whitehead, Ruskin had purchased his property for the views above all. Brantwood and White Pines (fig. 1) were similarly sited: that is, backed by a sheltering mountain; with terraced, but naturalistic, rock-accented gardens alongside; and, stretching away from the front side, a pastoral expanse of valley, village, and viniculture amidst mountainous scenery.[18] The Whiteheads literally wedded house and vine, for the latter were trained up along porch balustrades and pergola extensions at White Pines and other large colony residences, notably the Villetta and nearby Müllersruhe (later called Eastover), where art-school faculty were once housed.[19]

The love of scenery was the wellspring of Ruskin's admiration for art, especially the fine draftsmanship and "tender" color he taught devotees like Whitehead to revere. Without mountainscapes, Ruskin claimed, one could not know what tenderness in color meant, for that lesson was learned in lofty reaches through personal experience of the subtle blues, azures, purples, and rosy rays tinting skies and summits.[20] Whitehead was paraphrasing Ruskin when he sent an enthusiastic missive to Jane, "my painter," on June 5, 1902, about Woodstock's transparent sky and its gradations, plus the beauty of the cloud forms backed by the distant blue landscape. According to Ruskin's biographer and former secretary, W. G. Collingwood, the master's precepts regarding artistic composition and appreciation constituted only the first "leg" of four supporting his conception of "the metaphorical chair professors are supposed to fill at the University."[21] The other legs stood for literature, nature study, and the dignity of labor—Ruskinian fundamentals that also underpinned the conceptualization of the Byrdcliffe colony and the forty-some buildings in place there by 1910.

Literary allusions and symbolism abounded in the Whiteheads' correspondence during 1902–3, when Byrdcliffe was under design. For instance, Ralph mused about the name "White Pines" in relation to the Aesthetic treatise *Marius the Epicurean* (1885) by Oxford scholar Walter Pater. Whitehead had sent Jane a copy of *Marius* when she was undergoing a rest cure back home in Pennsylvania in May–June 1897. He invoked it five years later from Woodstock: "I like the 'White,' it reminds me of 'white nights'—you remember in 'Marius' the Umbrian farm where he spent the happy days when his faith in Beauty was unshaken. Our house then 'White Pines'!"[22]

Marius's quest was a philosophical journey that took him through stoicism as well as hedonism, and after paganism to life in a Christian community. On July 12, 1900, Ralph had written to Jane of his longing for some way to express "the truths and the realities of the higher world which we touch sometimes"; he despaired that the language of neither the "old Pagan gods" nor "the Judeo-Christian scriptures" might avail any longer. Nevertheless such archaic sources were tapped for names of various buildings in "Atlantis," as he termed Byrdcliffe in another letter to his wife (February 1, 1903) before the Colony's designation had been settled. The cottage Zulma Steele

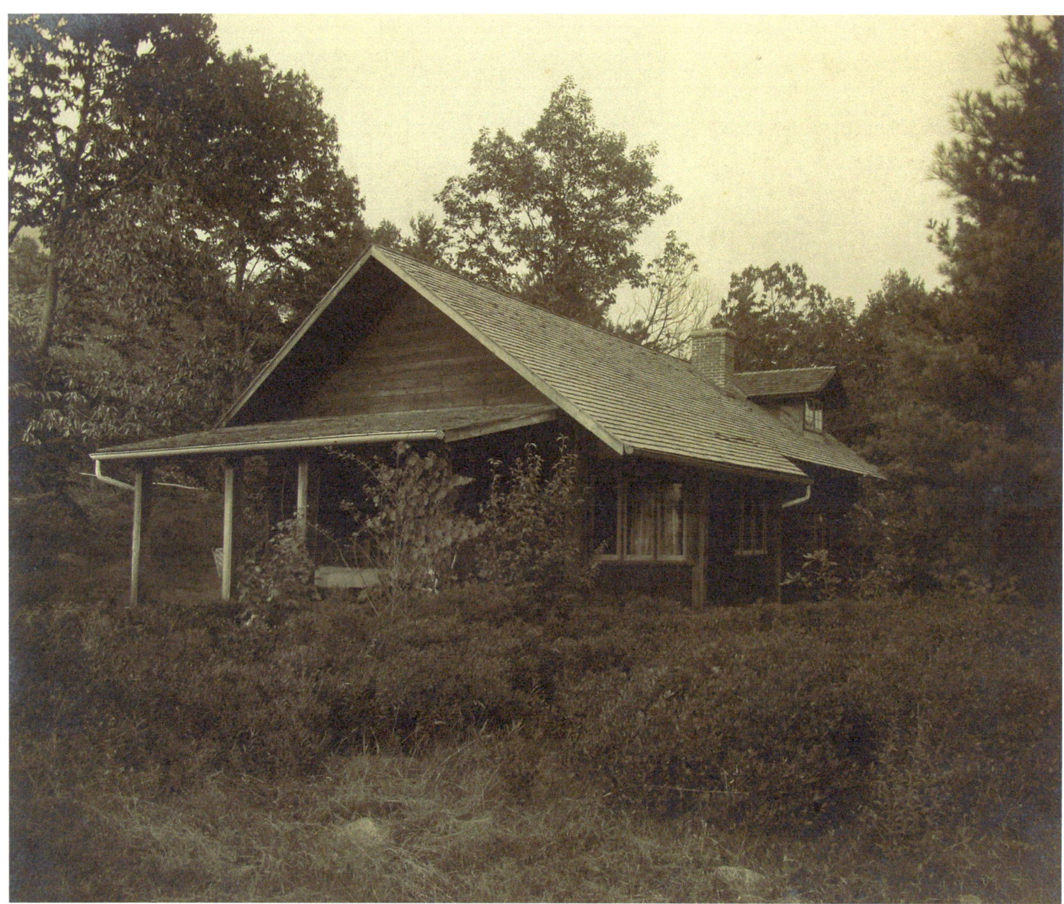

fig. 4 The Angelus, photographed by Jessie Tarbox Beals, ca. 1908. Winterthur Library, Downs Collection, 92x39.1140.556.

and Edna Walker initially occupied was baptized "Angelus" (fig. 4), signifying a Roman Catholic prayer said three times a day in memory of the Annunciation. A dwelling with a big open-raftered room graced by a balcony at one end—not unlike Jane's Arcady studio (fig. 7)—became "Yggdrasil," in honor of the tree of life in the Norse sagas translated by William Morris. Situated below White Pines near the barn compound (see fig. 2, no. 15), its interior became a model for studios later built all over Woodstock.[23]

Jane had promoted "Yggdrasil" as an alternative to both the monikers "Byrdcliffe" and "White Pines." " 'Yggdrasil' our house might be," she opined to Ralph on January 21, 1903, " 'Ye House of Yggdrasil,' and the company 'The Looms of Yggdrasil.' I like looms very much, and am quite willing to give up 'Byrdcliffe.'" "Yggdrasil" had the advantages of catalyzing artistic imagination and being directly tied to Ruskin. He wrote in the first volume of *The Laws of Fiesole* (1877): "The fair tree Igdrasil of Human Art can only flourish when its dew is Affection, its air Devotion; the rock of its roots, Patience, and its sunshine, God."[24]

Ralph liked the word "looms" for its literary appeal. He commented in his letter of January 18, immediately preceding Jane's:

> The poetic connotation of "looms" is good; you know Goethe's famous lines about the weaving of nature's garments, lines from Wilhelm Meister, translated by Carlisle, and I personally should not mind that "the looms" to outsiders would be too specific. To us they would stand for "arts and crafts."

"The Looms" became the label for Marie Little's quarters, the closest dwelling to White Pines after Yggdrasil (see fig. 2, no. 20, also fig. 17). She was Byrdcliffe's year-round resident weaver, specializing in cotton-strip rugs dyed by hand "from barks and berries which gave her materials the tones of the woods and fields."[25]

Whitehead chose "Loom Room" as the designation, at once literal and poetic, for the workspace he appended to White Pines in 1906 (figs. 5 and 6), in order to conduct experiments with subtly colored handwoven silk. The term was emblematic of the larger joint venture on which he and Jane had embarked. When she separated from him in 1912 over disagreements concerning Steele, Walker, and Little, among other grievances, he urged her not to forget "our loom room motto," taken from Sophocles's *Ajax.* Ralph spelled out the quotation in Greek, which translates as "It is grace that always gives birth to grace."[26]

Having first vowed their love in Italy and there dreamed of building an Arts and Crafts utopia, Jane and Ralph called Hervey "Nicolo" White's Byrdcliffe farming domain "Sabine"—after central Italy's ancient people.[27] The word's botanical denotation as red cedar or the coniferous shrub *Juniperus sabina* was probably not lost on

fig. 5 View from the southeast of White Pines and the covered bridge connecting with the Loom Room, ca. 1907. Winterthur Library, Downs Collection, 92x39.1140.10b.

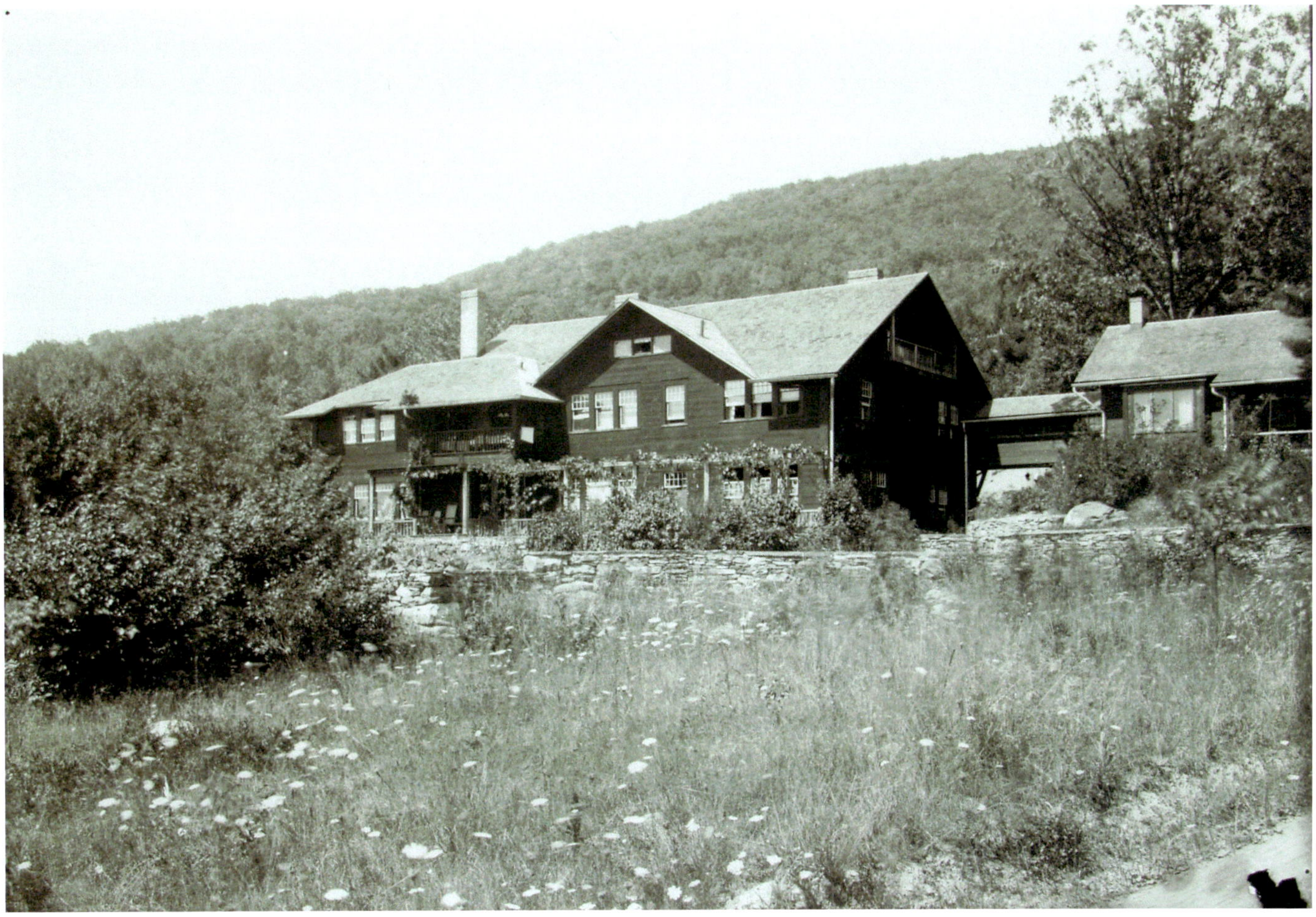

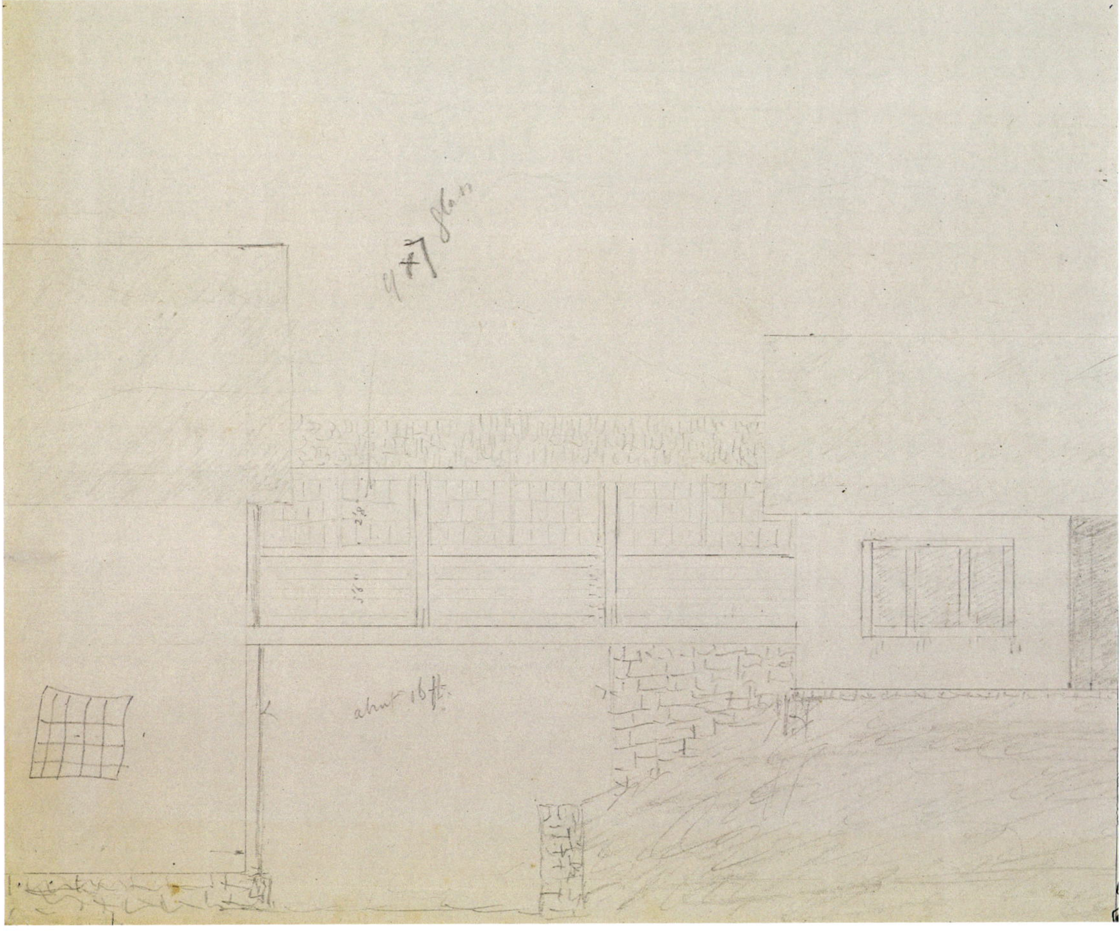

fig. 6 South elevation of the Loom Room (western portion) and bridge connection to White Pines, ca. 1906. Pencil drawing attributed to Ralph Whitehead. Winterthur Library, Downs Collection, 92x39.77a.

the denizens of White Pines, either. Other appellations for artists' accommodations, such as "Morning Glories" and "Fleur de Lys," illustrated more directly the Whiteheads' cultivation of a language of flowers.[28] They selected the Florentine lily (actually an iris) for their personal crest, bookplate, and Byrdcliffe's logo. A stylized version of the flower had been affixed to the door of the "Giglio" ("lily" in Italian), a bark-covered outbuilding at Arcady (see fig. 25). Orange lilies appear in two surviving drawings of proposed decoration for the dining-room inglenook at White Pines. Discrete blooms dot the back of the built-in settle, topped by a series of long-stemmed lilies painted on green-stained wainscoting that extends across the chimneypiece; the suggested frieze seems to be a motto.[29]

What plants were in season, their appearance, fragrance, and the thoughts or memories they occasioned figured prominently in letters between Ralph, Jane, and their sons. One of Ralph's early communiqués from the Catskills, ostensibly intended for his toddler son, detailed among the hillside flora, "purple giglias [*sic*] in the gardens, and in the low field in the valleys a wild giglio." He enclosed for Ralph Jr. on June 2, 1902, a real spray of spruce, some fern, and bluegrass flowers. Likewise, he had sent to baby Peter the year before, from the Swiss Alps, "some leaves of the little wood geranium which I knew and loved as a child and which Ruskin loved, too."[30]

Whitehead considered the close study of nature—one of the "legs" supporting Ruskin's "metaphorical chair"—as a means for developing an exemplary architecture.[31] "'Tis a real city of the forest," Poultney Bigelow said of Byrdcliffe in 1909, and White Pines was "a nature lover's home."[32] He described the Angelus (fig. 4) as "tinted the color of a partridge"; in fact, all Byrdcliffe buildings were akin in coloring and design. They were not painted but stained "to preserve the wood in its natural beauty of color." Corroborating testimony appeared in the journal of one-time Angelus resident Annie Thompson: "So many things arrested my attention; the brown houses that faded into the scenery because of their color or shape. . . ."[33] Still extant is Whitehead's notebook wherein he copied various French *ébénistes'* recipes for wood varnishes and stains

fig. 7 South façade of White Pines, photographed by Jessie Tarbox Beals. Winterthur Library, Downs Collection, 92x39.1140.602. Published in *American Homes and Gardens* (October 1909), and *House and Garden* (January 1910; June 1914).

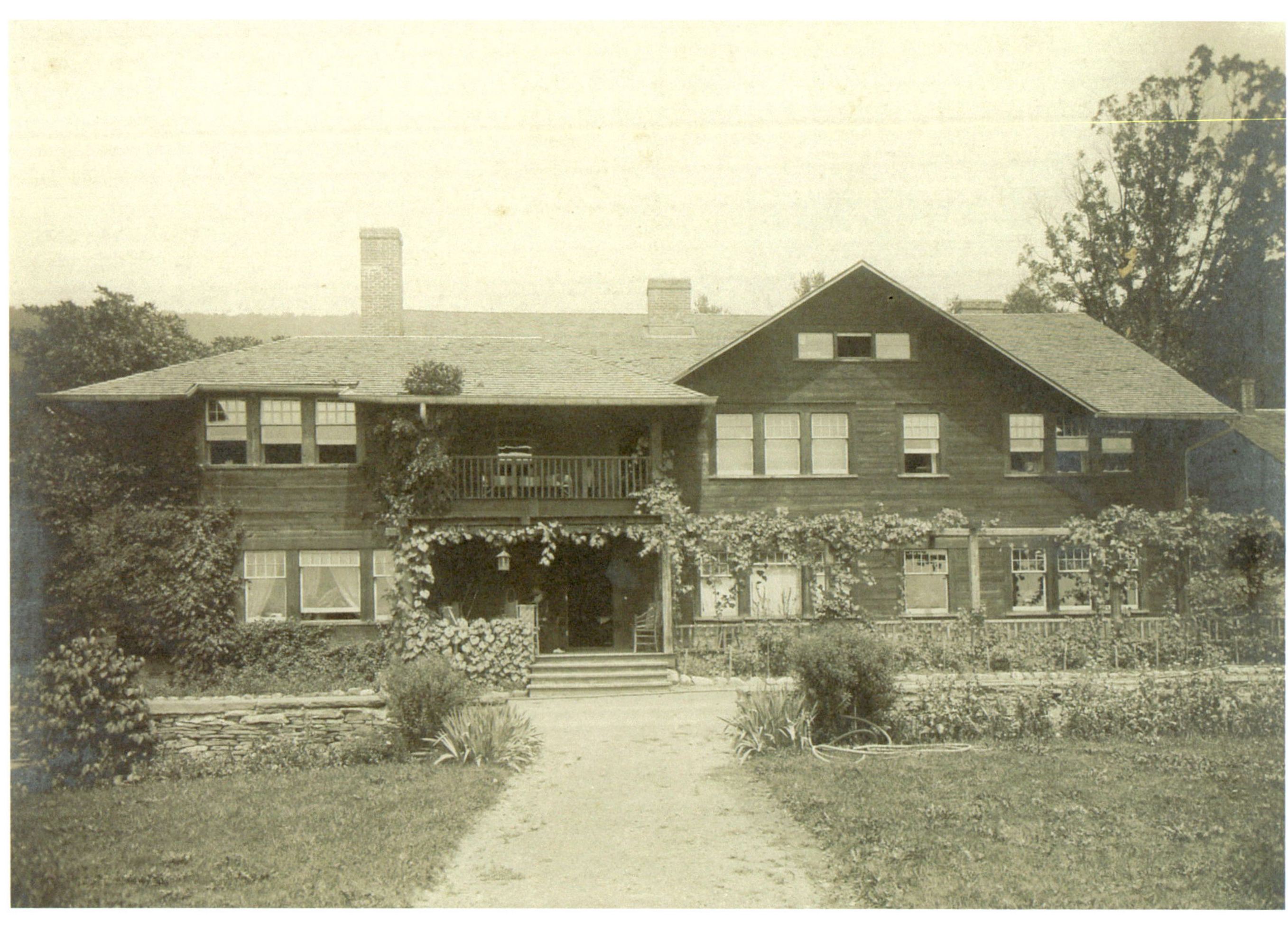

made from natural ingredients and concocted outdoors in sunlight.[34]

Whitehead's adoption of unpretentious finishes to link the simple wood-boarded colony structures to one another and the adjacent forest—the cottages were grouped along the edge of the woods, as indicated by a dotted line on the map (fig. 2)—conformed with Ruskin's view that architecture should found itself entirely on knowledge of, and fealty to, nature. He had set forth his opinions in *Seven Lamps of Architecture* (1849) regarding the proper aesthetic expression of nature's qualities in the man-made environment. Each "lamp" stood for a spirit, or attitude, which helped give meaning to buildings. In 1851–53, he elaborated upon these precepts in *Stones of Venice*. Whitehead referenced the "wonderful chapters in the *Stones of Venice* . . . on the *Nature of Gothic* and on *The Grotesque*" in his own publication titled *Grass of the Desert*.[35] He assiduously followed the path "lit" by Ruskin to create "Gothic" structures at Byrdcliffe, though these were not Gothic imitations with pointed arches, vaulted roofs, or flying buttresses. Rather, as Ruskin advised, they were Gothic in spirit; that is, illuminated by the "Lamp of Life," ennobled by bold, irregular forms and rough surfaces reminiscent of medieval hand craftsmanship—and of Nature herself.[36]

The Gothic characteristics Ruskin dubbed "Changefulness," "Imperfection," and "Savageness" were well represented at White Pines (fig. 7) in the asymmetrical plan and fenestration, rough wood-shingle roofing (now replaced), and nailed pine façades bounded by dry-laid stone walls.[37] The house plan was a large rectangle overlapping a smaller rectangle to the southwest, with a perpendicular service wing attached off-center at the back in a northerly direction (see fig. 2, no. 1, for the building's footprint). The entrance porch on the south façade was also off-center; furthermore, the interior stair hall was off-axis vis-à-vis the front door. The irregular roofline was comprised of an expansive gable roof pierced, on the north elevation, by multiple, variously sized dormers and punctuated, on the south side, by an imposing cross gable. Contrary to expectation, this cross gable did not serve a centralizing, ceremonial function to highlight the principal doorway for the house. Instead the entry was to the left of it and crowned by an open balcony.

In keeping with Whitehead's specification of a "picturesque detail at one corner" of White Pines, the southwestern appendage featured visible roof-rafter tails in contrast to the enclosed eaves elsewhere.[38] Over the south-facing windows of Jane's bedroom, the roof was cut back in the manner of thatched roofs on old English cottages.[39] The windows themselves were double-hung in the same pattern of 8/1 panes used for the rest of the fenestration in first- and second-floor rooms. Changefulness, besides picturesqueness, resulted from sliding the top and bottom sections of the windows at different intervals to regulate ventilation. In the process, the grid patterns formed by the wood mullions were modulated as well. Whitehead's antipathy for regularity extended even to the sizing of the window sash; the lower single-light sections were taller than the multipaned upper portions. These "guillotine" windows, as he labeled them, contrasted with the eight-light casements found in the cross gable and the big single-pane window on the west side of Jane's bedroom.[40] The latter, with no intervening muntins, was a picture window framing nature. This end of White Pines originally sported an arbor as did the main south façade of the building. Poultney Bigelow testified to Whitehead's fluency in Ruskin's Gothic doctrine of Naturalism when he depicted the Whitehead domicile as a "house of massive timber, the interior made by artists in woodwork, the whole a thing which appears to have grown out of its happy environment."[41]

Ruskin's lexicon of architecture defined naturalism and truthfulness as practically synonymous. In "The Nature of Gothic" he contended:

> For, so soon as the workman is left free to represent what subjects he chooses, he must look to the nature that is round him for material, and will endeavor to represent it as he sees it. . . . I say first, that the Gothic builders were of that central class which unites fact with design; but that part of the work which was more especially their own was the truthfulness. . . . Gothic work, when referred to the arrangement of all art, as purist, naturalist, or sensualist, was naturalist. This character follows necessarily on its extreme love of truth.[42]

What Ruskin called the "Lamp of Truth," with subdivisions for structural, surface, and operative deceits to be avoided, sheds light on Ralph Whitehead's scheme for Fleur de Lys (fig. 8). In conformity with Ruskin's dictum to build with materials readily available from the earth, Fleur de Lys as erected sits on a bluestone drywall foundation. During the second half of the nineteenth century, commercial quarrying of bluestone had been a significant source of income for Woodstock, but competition from the Portland cement industry rendered the quarries a losing proposition by 1900.[43] For the walls Whitehead suggested shiplap siding out-of-doors and planed upright boards indoors.[44] He literally followed Ruskin's admonition to "Leave your walls as bare as a planed board . . . do not rough-cast them with falsehood."[45] The built-in seats, extant but now painted, partake of a planar constructional aesthetic. They are straightforward, horizontally boarded benches with hinged seats, plank armrests, square underarm spindles, and canted butted-board back rests. In general at Fleur de Lys, structure was revealed, not obscured by decorative moldings or facings. Whitehead underscored that point in several notes on his building sketch concerning "rafters showing" and "cross rafters showing." The rafter ends are still visible under the eaves on the principal façade. The eaves turn up slightly at the corners, as indicated in Ralph's gable-end elevation at the far left side of his drawing. Calculations for the cost of wood shingles are at the upper right. Throughout the 1800s, making shingles from trees felled in Woodstock's ample forests had been a traditional winter activity of the local farmer-craftsmen.[46]

Surface enrichment was achieved in the doors at Fleur de Lys via the interplay of wide horizontal and vertical framing members with recessed panels made up of narrower planks.[47] The fenestration was enlivened by mixing 8/8 double-hung sash with four- and six-light inward-swinging windows. Whitehead's proposed twelve-pane windows, which slid side to side, were not carried out here; they were instituted later for the glazing of the covered bridge linking White Pines to the Loom Room[48] (see figs. 5 and 6).

Whitehead evidently took to heart the advice given in *Stones of Venice* that there is no connection between delight in ornament and the delight of construction or usefulness.[49] Ruskin castigated machine-made ornament as operative deceit and considered morally reprehensible the substitution of cast iron for handwork. Metal was only admissible in support of structure, as in nails to secure wood and bars to stabilize diamond-paned casements. Whitehead's wood-muntin windows were both operatively honest and operationally simple. They were placed strategically to accord with the functions of particular interior spaces and elements. Thus windows appeared above Fleur de Lys' wall benches and in the paired closets to supply ventilation along with illumination. Such usefulness was born of necessity in a community where no gas or electrical lighting was provided, as prescribed in the General Statement of St. George's Guild.[50]

Ruskin explained the Guild's interdiction of power machinery in terms of the tendency for machines to supersede "healthy bodily exercise, or the art and precision of manual labor"; in other words "the dignity of labour," constituting one of "Ruskin's chair" legs described by Collingwood.[51] The master himself had urged his acolytes to judge the appearance of a building, first, by whether it looked like strong men built it.[52] Poet-naturalist John Burroughs, a Catskills neighbor and welcome visitor at Byrdcliffe, paid the highest compliment to the Colony's architecture in likening it to the rugged Slabsides mountain cabin he built by hand in 1895–96: "The various cottages & buildings are as picturesque as 'Slabsides' both outside and in; low & rambling[,] of undressed boards and timbers. . . ." He continued, "And the people, upwards of fifty of them, go with this kind of background . . . thoroughly serious & earnest, each one with some work or pursuit that occupies the greater part of each day."[53]

fig. 8 Plan and elevations for a cottage resembling Fleur de Lys. Undated pencil drawing attributed to Ralph Whitehead. Winterthur Library, Downs Collection, 92x39.92a.

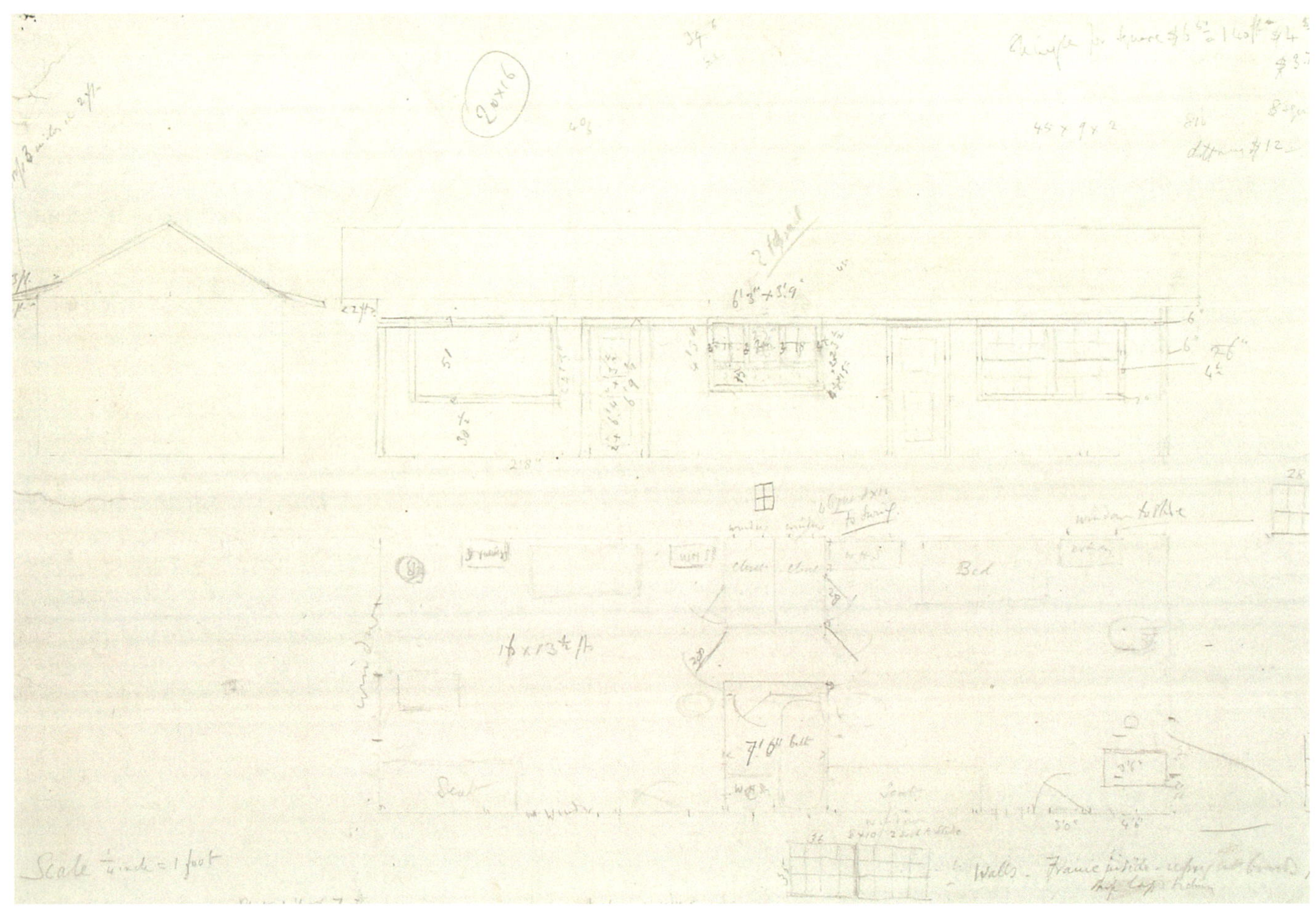

In the beginning Byrdcliffe had but three denizens—Whitehead, Brown, and White—joined shortly by White's comrades, Boer War veteran Fritz Van der Loo and the Chicago painter Carl Lindin. As soon as Brown had purchased the seven farms that were to make up the colony, Ralph put his cohorts to work digging cellars and laying out roads in the late summer of 1902.[54] At Arcady, Whitehead had been a hands-on landscape architect, carving out pathways and carriage roads, and tending to ornamental plantings with painstaking respect for the geology, native flora, and topographical features of the site. Hervey White testified:

> I visited Mr. and Mrs. Whitehead at their home near Santa Barbara. . . . The work of the garden was still going on. Mr. Whitehead was out digging for a terrace wall two hours a day. I was to learn then the importance of a curve that would bear out the contour of a hill. . . . He thought nothing of taking out a terrace wall and moving it a foot or two to right or left to change the curve, but the final result was right.[55]

Whitehead was following the example set by Ruskin, who had put his intellectual, artistically inclined students to constructing roads at Oxford. Later, he had drawn his disciples into harbor improvements and the reclaiming of moorland for terraced gardens at Coniston. In addition, he had urged his "youthful visitors" to dig a tennis lawn from a glade; Whitehead did likewise at Byrdcliffe (see fig. 2, no. 21). Digging, Collingwood maintained, was a Ruskin "object lesson in ethics, the first rudiments of human fellowship, which branched upward into all the moralities."[56]

White remembered that, initially, he was put in charge of road making; whereas Brown oversaw the gathering of materials and the laying of foundations for four buildings—the school with a large studio space and an adjoining library (Studio), the student dormitory (Villetta), and the residences for the Whiteheads (White Pines) and his own family (Carniola).[57] Brown himself selected, hauled, and set in place the boulders composing the main sitting-room fireplace at Carniola. He had originally planned an all-stone house but, as winter set in, the freezing of the mortar became a major impediment, as did Whitehead's objections to the cost of a masonry edifice.[58] It was Brown, too, who scoured the local sawmills for timber and went into the woods to "hunt out and mark, one by one, the chestnut and oak trees that would yield the beams we wanted."[59]

Brown and White both hired work crews. Skilled labor was readily available since rock cutting and excavating had been a mainstay of Victorian-era Woodstock, and lumbering was implied in the town name. *Wodstoc* in Saxon meant a "clearing in the wood," or "a woody place."[60] Carl Lindin reminisced fondly, in 1932, about the carpenter-foreman for White Pines: "When I think of the Woodstock landscape, certain figures at once also come into it—old Ford Herrick, who built so many of our houses, [was] sturdy, temperamental, telling a good story while he made his men work at full speed."[61] Herrick was the builder as well for Bertha Thompson's 1913 Hillside home and studio, but Whitehead "made the road past the farmhouse up to where her latest workshop was put," her sister Annie reported.[62] When Bertha subsequently added a terrace, she benefited from Whitehead's "cutting a road at the time." He sent up load after load of earth to pack atop the foundation, itself the product of "many supper parties of friends who pitched in and laid stone for awhile."[63]

Did Whitehead, in fact, put his own shoulder and hand to pick and shovel? The Thompson sisters' accounts are ambiguous, but Ralph's correspondence with Jane clarifies his practice of Ruskin's preaching that the glory of living lay in the wielding of ploughshare and spade—or of "the road level machine" he asked to have sent from Arcady.[64] Five months later he told her, "I don't think I can get away for three weeks holiday...till the middle of February. Too many things go wrong when I am long away especially as to finishing. Cannot settle dates yet. It depends on when I get chestnut wood dry and when I get to put it up."[65] On February 27, 1903, he wrote to his "dearest Wife":

> I am going out with Will—Will Wolven who is my head man for outside work—to tidy up the ground round the house and build a limit line of wall between the ground belonging to the house & the sweet fern beyond. . . . Tell Bimbi I am coming to see him & that someday he shall help me in place of these strangers to do my work here, as he used to go with me to make those paths at Arcady. Those were sweet morning hours last spring when he went with me every morning under the trees "digging"! Remind him of them.

Back in October, Whitehead had lost confidence in Brown's ability to accomplish the building tasks in an orderly and timely fashion. After six weeks away, Ralph had returned to Woodstock to discover "Brown had most things in a muddle."[66] For example, no access had been provided to the basement at White Pines when the first-story flooring was installed. Even when a hole was cut for a stairway, he could not inspect the cellar since Brown had not specified any windows.[67] Whitehead then transferred homebuilding responsibilities to White although he himself functioned as a cosupervisor and chief engineer. Meanwhile, Brown focused on interior details. Whitehead provided particulars to Jane, on November 20 and 23, concerning the division of labor:

> Brown has been very nice the last few days & I have got him to draw me some doors & to criticize my plans of fireplaces.[69] I think in another fortnight we can begin to make tables, but I am not sure that we shall get to work till after the turn of the year.
>
> We have been working hard, both Nicolo & I; I begin at seven to write letters & make plan[s]. Then we go for the mail & up to the Sabine Farm. And there we are kept busy till the men stop at half past four & we get back there just as the daylight goes. I am enjoying it and am getting things put straight.

What plans was Whitehead committing to paper? He had a talent for the civil engineering Ruskin admired and

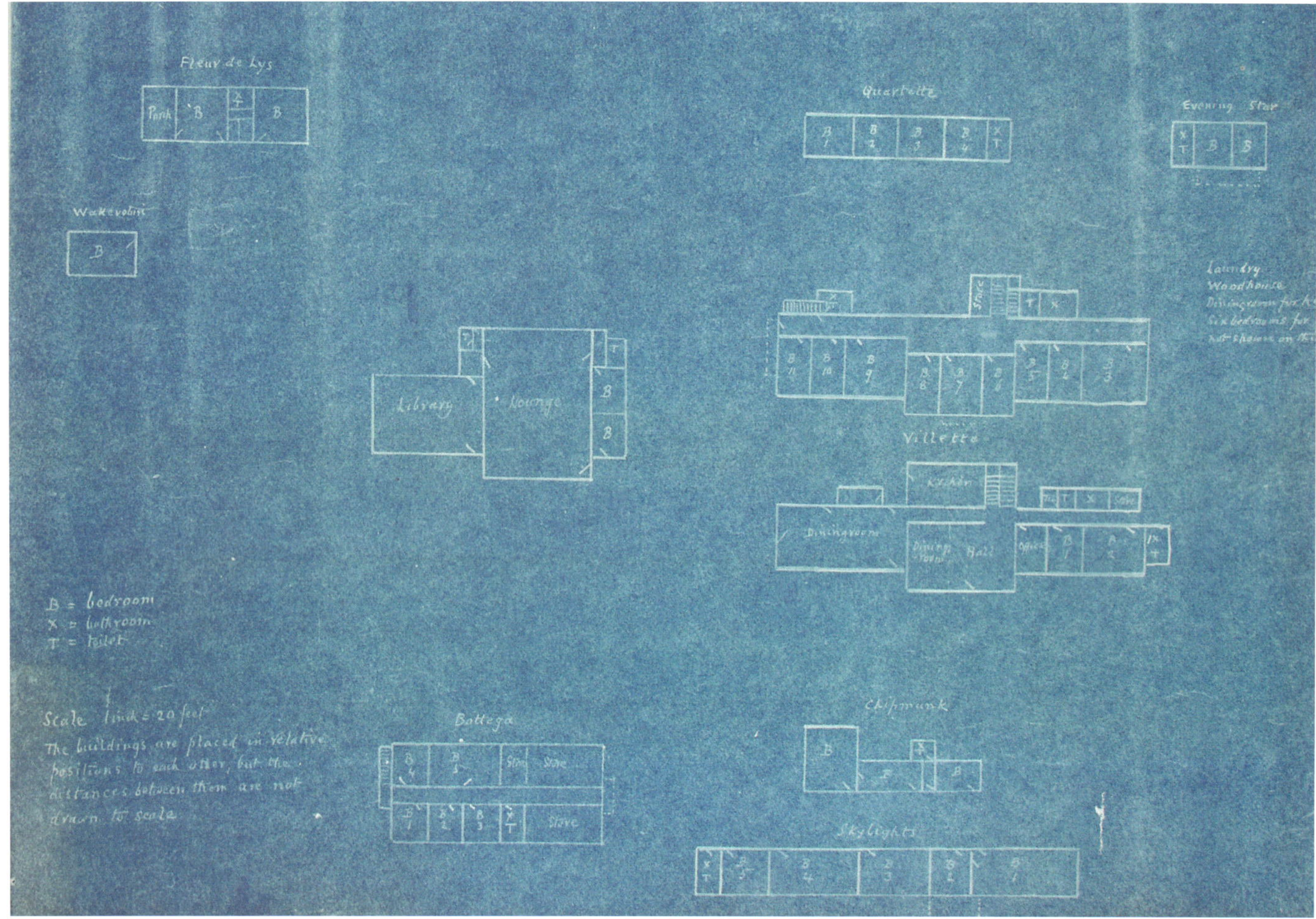

fig. 9 Layout of selected Byrdcliffe buildings, with bedrooms, bathrooms, and toilets specified. Probably drafted by Bolton Brown, ca. 1902. Winterthur Library, Downs Collection, 92x39.1140.1262b. The central structures are the two-story Villetta and the Studio. The latter, here labeled "Lounge," was also referred to as a dance hall.

promoted in his waterwork "digs" to make dams, reservoirs, and sluices at Brantwood.[70] Ralph had masterminded an irrigation system in Montecito, known as "Whitehead's tunnels," to transport water to Arcady and the surrounding orchards.[71] At Byrdcliffe he anticipated construction of a reservoir and also took the unusual step of equipping White Pines with a standpipe system to fight fires.[72] White noted, "water [was] piped a mile down the mountain and leads branch[ed] off to every structure. . . ."[73] Indeed, a principal purpose of the 1910 Byrdcliffe map illustrated in figure 2 was to delineate the water lines and shut-offs at the colony.

Whitehead had a flair for mapping space and proportional relationships, but he lacked fine drafting skills. He complained to Jane, "Only one thing gives me trouble & that is my incapacity to draw. I know what is good when I see it, but I can't visualize a piece of paneling or furniture & can't sketch it to see the effect."[74] Hence, early on, Whitehead looked to the "drawing teacher" Bolton Brown as his architect.[75] The latter reminisced about setting up Woodstock's first studio in a local barn, where,

> at a draughtsman's table, I, jack of all trades, was transformed from a go-getter to an architect. I planned Whitehead a house and one for me. . . . We decided other building sites [see fig. 9]—that of the library and dance hall, the eating house, a studio or two, a barn and so on—and vaguely, the lay out of the roads to serve them.[76]

Brown, unfortunately, failed to meet deadlines, so Whitehead relieved him and took charge. Writing from New York City on January 19, 1903, he informed Jane, who was in Aiken, South Carolina, where they had celebrated Christmas:

> Unless I hire an architect which I won't do I have got piles of work when I get back to Woodstock, specifying before hand every detail of a small students boarding house, and of the alterations to the farmhouse which will have a dining room built on to it for the boarders, and then the barn.

> It is necessary in building to have every detail worked out before breaking the ground. I have lost much time and hundred[s of] dollars owing to not having done this last autumn . . . I spent hours yesterday afternoon calculating and specifying the wood for the wainscots and cupboards in the rooms which we designed together [for White Pines].[77]

The postscript asked Jane to send on to him at Woodstock a parcel of drawing instruments, T square, roll of paper, etc.

Many years later, Anita Smith recorded Whitehead's claim that his greatest ability might have been as an architect.[78] Clearly, he had gained confidence from his forays into the field in 1902–3, and from devising his own plans for the Loom Room addition to White Pines in 1906.[79] He may have been defining architecture in the collaborative, albeit feudal, way set forth by British architect J. D. Sedding, whose *Art and Handicraft* (1893) was ensconced in the Byrdcliffe library:

> Naturally, the architect can never say of any building "This is my work," remembering by whose toil and handicraft it was reared, any more than the general of a victorious army can say, "I won the battle," or the composer of an oratorio that has been orchestrally rendered, "I made the music." Yet, whether the mason, the carpenter, and other of the building trades have alone helped him, or whether he have likewise engaged the highest powers of the finest natures in the kingdom, the triumph that has been won in the building comes of his generalship; his hand held the hazards of the lines of the structure, and made of it an organic whole; his mind conferred unity of impression, his thought anticipated every stroke that is there.[80]

Whitehead could have been thinking, too, about architectural aptitude as a traditional signifier of elite status in England. Despite certain democratic leanings, he remained, as C. R. Ashbee—a fellow English Arts and Crafts adherent and founder of the Guild of Handicraft—put it, "an English gentleman transplanted to the Catskills."[81]

Styling a Rustic Community: Design Traditions and Sources

Ralph Whitehead had been reared to aspire to the leadership roles and attributes of aristocratic landowners; he, along with Ashbee and Morris, was thoroughly schooled in the tried-and-true mores of British country life.[82] Hermann Multhesius asserted in *The English House*, "no one doubts for a single moment that city-dwelling can never be more than a mere makeshift, an enforced substitute for the ideal of the freehold, free standing country house."[83] Byrdcliffe was the last of a series of attempts Whitehead made to find enough of the right kind of land to satisfy his estate criteria. White recorded Ralph's complaining, humorously,

> I never get what I want. Once I decided to buy an estate in England. I was completely unhampered, and I said I desired only three things. Pines, hills, a view of the sea. Surely not difficult in England. Do you know what I finally secured? A tract of flat swamp land, a hundred miles from the sea. No pines, no hills in my range of vision.[84]

White went on to describe the Whiteheads' routine at Arcady, marked by issuing invitations, receiving, making detailed arrangements for both business and "trivial pleasures," and setting schedules like those prevailing at British country houses.[85] Yet Ralph was unable to realize at Montecito the kind of self-sustaining community traditionally connected to a manor in the English countryside. Byrdcliffe came much closer to the ideal with its tenant-craftsmen and handpicked cottager-yeomen. The latter were allowed to buy lots ranging from two to five acres in the East Riding (see fig. 2), provided they contracted to build but one residence with "proper and necessary" outbuildings and gave Whitehead a repurchase option.[86] These stipulations buttressed Alvan Sanborn's conclusion that Byrdcliffe's organization was feudal:

> The relations of the Byrdcliffe resident and sojourner to Mr. Whitehead bear a striking resemblance to those of the vassal to his lord or, to use more modern terms, of the English tenant to his landlord, since the creator of Byrdcliffe retains the title to all the Byrdcliffe houses and lands and is the ultimate authority with regard to any and every question of policy and administration that may arise.[87]

Byrdcliffe structures like the four-unit Quartette and the five-studio Skylights (fig. 9) followed the centuries-old British model of clustering rural laborers in rows of one-storied terrace lodgings under a common roof. English Arts and Crafts designers praised modest, timeworn vernacular housing as a wholesome domestic architecture, refined through eons of use and exhibiting great pictorial appeal.[88] Whitehead was sensitive to the "artistic value of grouping" cottages, a chapter subheading in *Country Life*'s book of modern cottages.[89] Paired Byrdcliffe cottages of the ilk of Sunrise and Serenata (fig. 10)—"a double house of cozy build"—were distinguished by twin gables, multiple entrances, and a layout emphasizing a common living room.[90] Such "collegiate" planning had been outlined in a March 1901 essay on modern cottages by Esther Wood for *The Studio* magazine.

The various Byrdcliffe habitations possessed an aura of community due, in part, to Whitehead's penchant for standardization. He developed patterns for doors, windows, fireplaces, and even the stairways installed at White Pines, Villetta, and Eastover. Similarly, the Arts and Crafts architect Halsey Ricardo, Ralph's longtime friend, devised three kinds of windows and two types of doors for the coupled, semidetached cottages at a new estate village he orchestrated in Dorsetshire. Standardized architectural elements reduced costs while imparting visual unity. His whole village-building endeavor, Ricardo explained in a letter to Whitehead, was an experiment in employment of local materials and labor, preservation of local processes and traditions, and creation of a school of craftsmen competent in the construction trades. Furthermore, the venture was intended to demonstrate that these building practices were economically viable for both proprietors and tenants.[91]

Bolton Brown, for his part, was less than sanguine about Whitehead's rural village-building motivations at Byrdcliffe:

> Whitehead was all for "democracy," in theory; but down in his British subconscious class consciousness was an influential ghost of medieval social arrangements—in scales with steps up and steps down, and a central court and so forth and so on. The idea implied something like a benign reign over gracious and grateful dependents.[92]

The locus of the "central court" was the "sprawling manor house" of White Pines.[93] It was indeed a seat of power in the English manner, with almost half the floor plan of the first and second stories devoted to live-in servants and the functions they performed for the family. By comparison, American country houses normally reserved a fourth to a third the total area of the first floor for service.[94]

Vis-à-vis their in-house dependents, the Whiteheads did align themselves with the patrons of progressive Arts and Crafts architects, who sought to reduce the differentiation between family and servant domains in matters of taste as well as health. Mrs. Wyndham remarked of her Philip Webb–designed manse, Clouds (1886), after the principal block burned in 1889: "It is a good thing that our architect was a Socialist because we find ourselves just as comfortable in the servants' quarters as we were in our own."[95] Jane registered concern for the physical and emotional comfort of future White Pines servants in her letter to Ralph on June 13, 1902: "I want to try some rather advanced lines. Make them a fine sitting room and let them have all the company they want, or rather can get. They must have a chance of getting married. . . ."

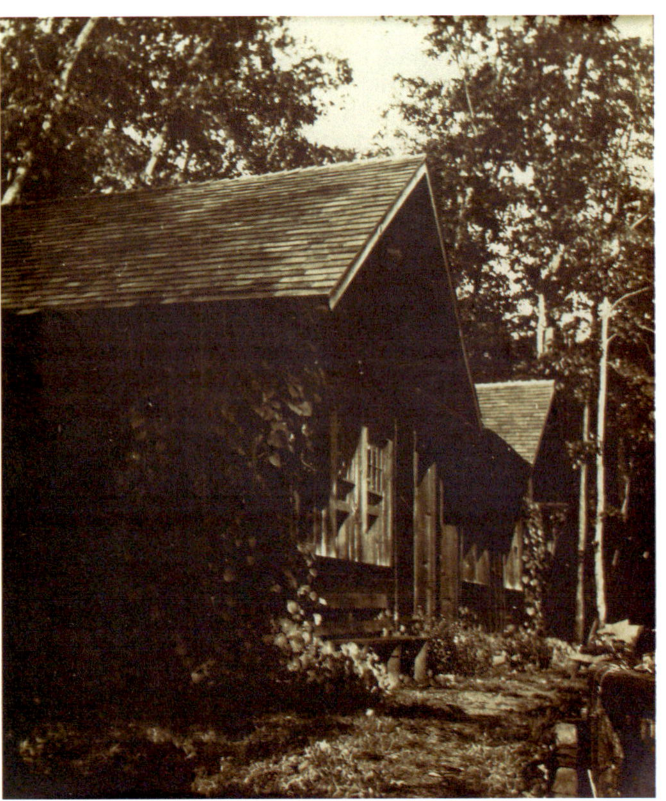

fig. 10 View from the southwest of Serenata, ca. 1907. Winterthur Library, Downs Collection, 92x39.1140.266.

The Whiteheads did not banish the help to the basement, attic, or a conspicuously segregated wing, as had been common in Victorian-era country houses. Instead, they were quartered in the main house immediately behind the family bedrooms, and the same central hall served both ranges of rooms on the second floor. Downstairs, the servants' eating and gathering place was right behind the family's dining room. Unrealized White Pines alterations drafted by Addison Le Boutillier (ca. 1905), called for an eastward extension of this space and an adjoining porch.[96]

There were noticeable but not remarkably different gradations in the finish of the family versus servant rooms. Wider softwood boards for walls, floors, and ceilings were found in the rear portions of the house, in contrast to narrower hardwood flooring, wainscoting, and fabric or burlap for wall and ceiling coverings in the Whiteheads' rooms.[97] Ralph was concerned about harmonizing the color scheme in Mackie's (the nanny's) room; as a matter of fact, this was his first query to Jane in a long communication, dated February 22, 1903, regarding the house-under-construction:

> Today I have at last time to sit down and ask you some questions about the house. Here they are: 1. Mackie's room—what color are the curtains? I am going to put burlap on the floor & can either have it the undyed neutral grey, or I can choose a tint to go with your curtains.

Mackie's chamber at the northeast corner of White Pines had been planned as a guest room at first. A hand-colored elevation labeled "meant for guest room 2nd floor now Mackie's room" (fig. 11) depicts built-in closets and cabinets backed by a floral-sprigged wall. C. F. A. Voysey, the most successful country-house designer among the core English Arts and Crafts architects, went so far as to allot interchangeable built-in furniture to guest and servant bedrooms at the Homestead (1905–6).[98] Typically there was a hierarchy of finishes in his commissions, yet he argued for attention to quality as a worthy criterion in every aspect of a building.

In a similar vein, Ralph Whitehead strove for consistent quality construction, be it in domestic or farm structures. Byrdcliffe's barn was a tour de force of post-and-beam joinery, with rafter projections and bracing conspicuously displayed as structural ornamentation on the exterior (fig. 12). In keeping with English tradition, grain storage, livestock, the forge, and creamery were segregated from one another.[99] The lower portion of the barn complex (fig. 13) was subdivided into a twin-chimneyed eastern flank accommodating the dairy and a tack room, set apart by a dogtrot from the enclosures for cows, pigs, and chickens. A small smithy stood to the west. Historically, estate plans situated the ruder operations of animal husbandry, blacksmithing, and various workshops out of sight of

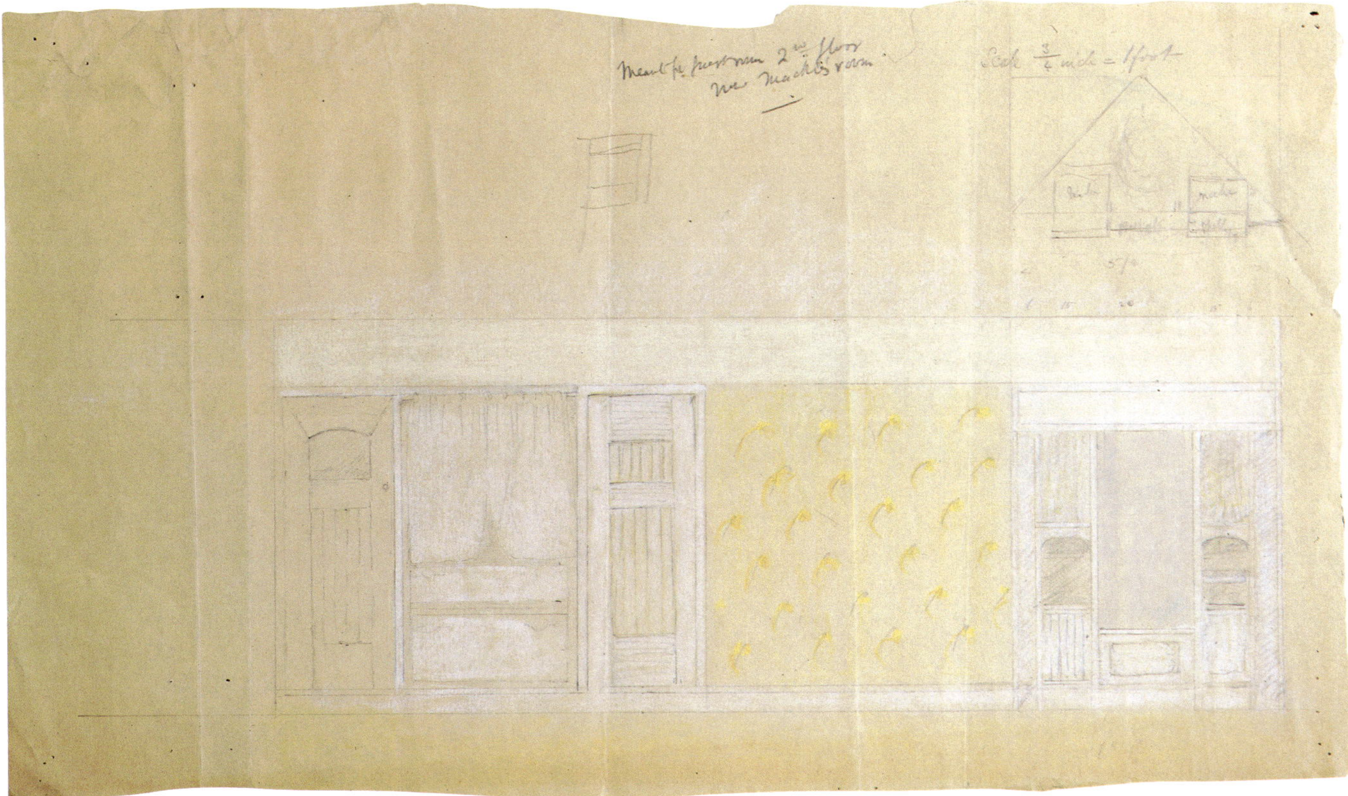

fig. 11 Decorative scheme for guest/ Mackie's room at White Pines. Hand-colored pencil drawing attributed to Ralph and Jane Whitehead, ca. 1903. Winterthur Library, Downs Collection, 02x170.127.

the master's mansion. So, too, the pottery, metal, and furniture craft shops at Byrdcliffe were placed below the brow of the hill and across the road from the Villetta boarding house.

Jane had written to Ralph, in June 1902, about the pleasurable prospect of living on a real farm—something lacking at Arcady, which had been developed on a portion of the seventy acres Whitehead acquired in Montecito in the fall of 1894.[100] What distinguished a true English country house from a mere wealthy man's house in the country was a large tract of land with attendant agricultural enterprises, represented by the divisions of farmyard, vegetable garden, and fields and orchards.[101] The other requisites of the landed estate were, of course, the owner's residence and its adjacent ornamental garden.

The Whiteheads assembled these components at Byrdcliffe, plus a library and art collection that were portable, highly personal signifiers of gentility. The Studio/Lounge included a room for Ralph's books, available to all Byrdcliffe denizens (fig. 14, see also fig. 9):

> The library, which already contains about five thousand volumes and which is simply and tastefully decorated with sculptures, potteries, tapestries and paintings, is a delectable retreat well worth by itself the trip from New York to a person of bookish habit, if only by reason of its freedom from the slightest taint of institutionalism. In fact, it might readily be mistaken for the library of a private individual with a bias artward.[102]

Author John Burroughs considered the Colony's library to be better than most colleges could offer.[103]

Still, a grand barn was the most potent emblem of landed aristocracy. Whitehead made the top tier of his barn, used for hay, the focal point of the vista from the porch at White Pines. The edifice paid homage to medieval English timber-framed, weather-boarded manor or tithe barns. In accord with those prototypes, it featured a central nave-like hall and side aisles, with wagon doors positioned in a projecting porch entry on the broad northern side visible from White Pines (see fig. 12). Due to the inclined site, the upper component of the Byrdcliffe barn actually had two stories. Its total area of 6200 square feet rivaled the capacity of the monastic barn at Great Coxwell, Berkshire, which William Morris once called the greatest piece of architecture in England.[104]

Making hay was one of the aspects of Byrdcliffe that induced Alf Evers to characterize the Colony as a romantic vision of "Camelot"—coincidentally the name given to one of the farms incorporated in the East Riding. He recounted how Jane Whitehead and Marie Little, clad in Pre-Raphaelite flowing gowns and floating veils, would swoop down on the haymakers bearing bowls of mead, which was, in reality, unfermented honey.[105] While no

fig. 12 View from the west of the upper portion of the barn and the road leading to White Pines, ca. 1907. Winterthur Library, Downs Collection, 92x39.1140, 12b.

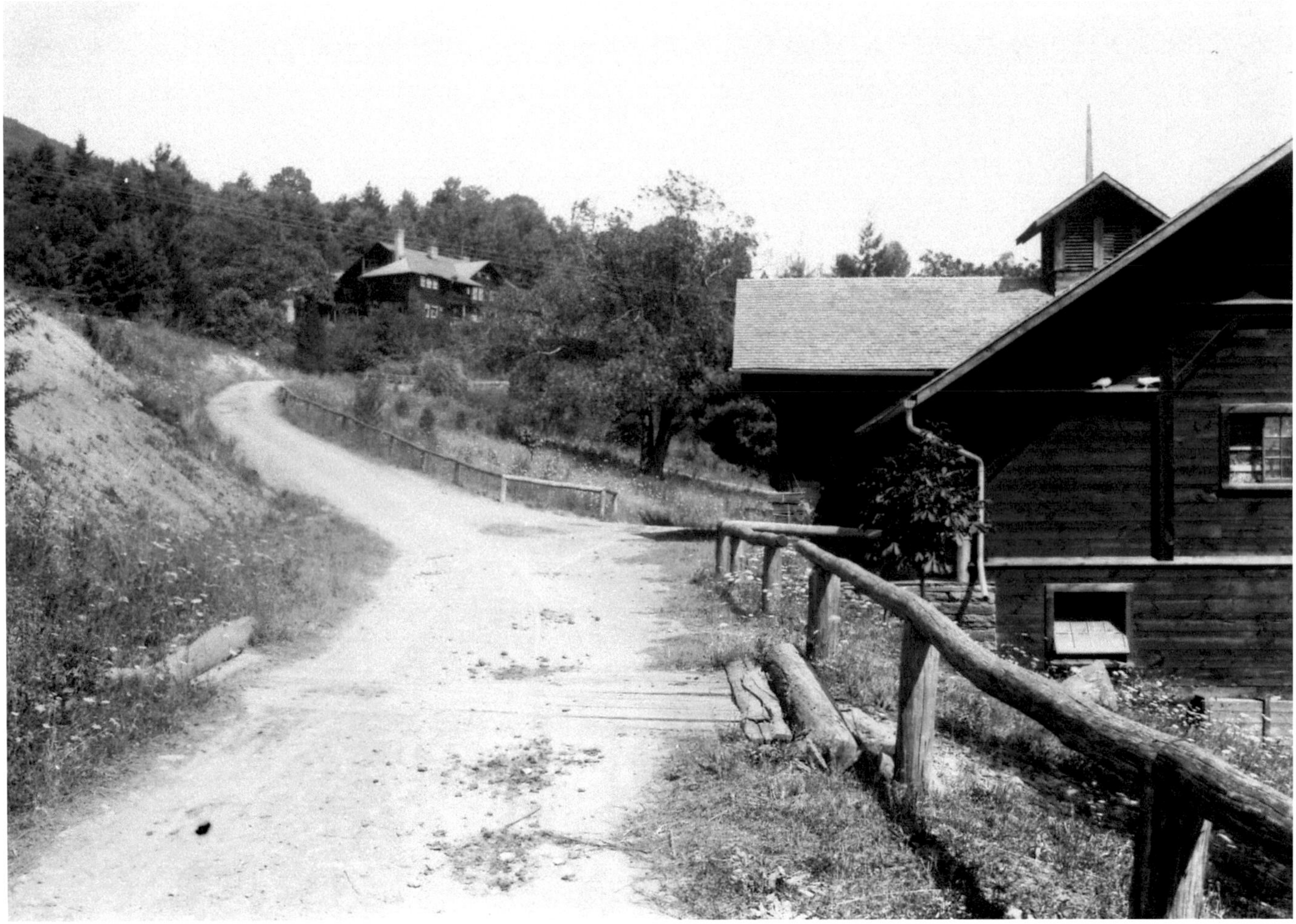

fig. 13 View from the southeast of the lower barn complex, ca. 1905. Winterthur Library, Downs Collection, 92x39.1140.13b. Part of the south façade of the upper barn is visible to the right.

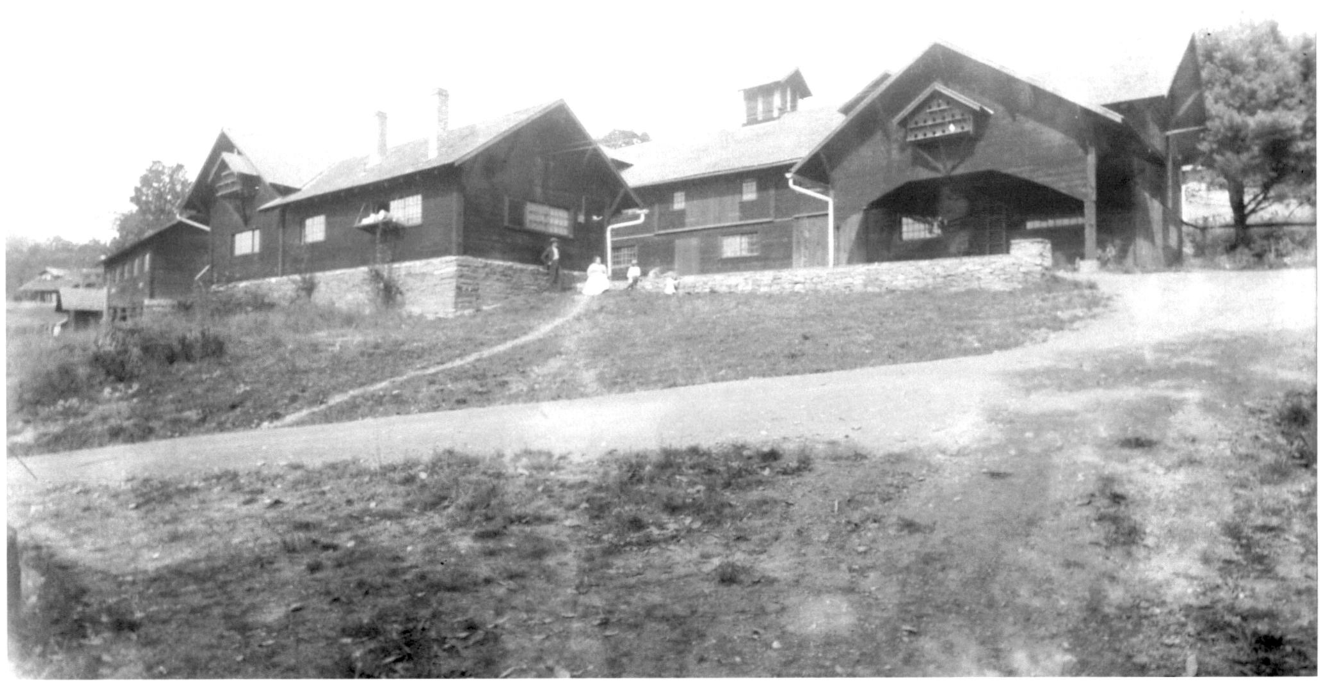

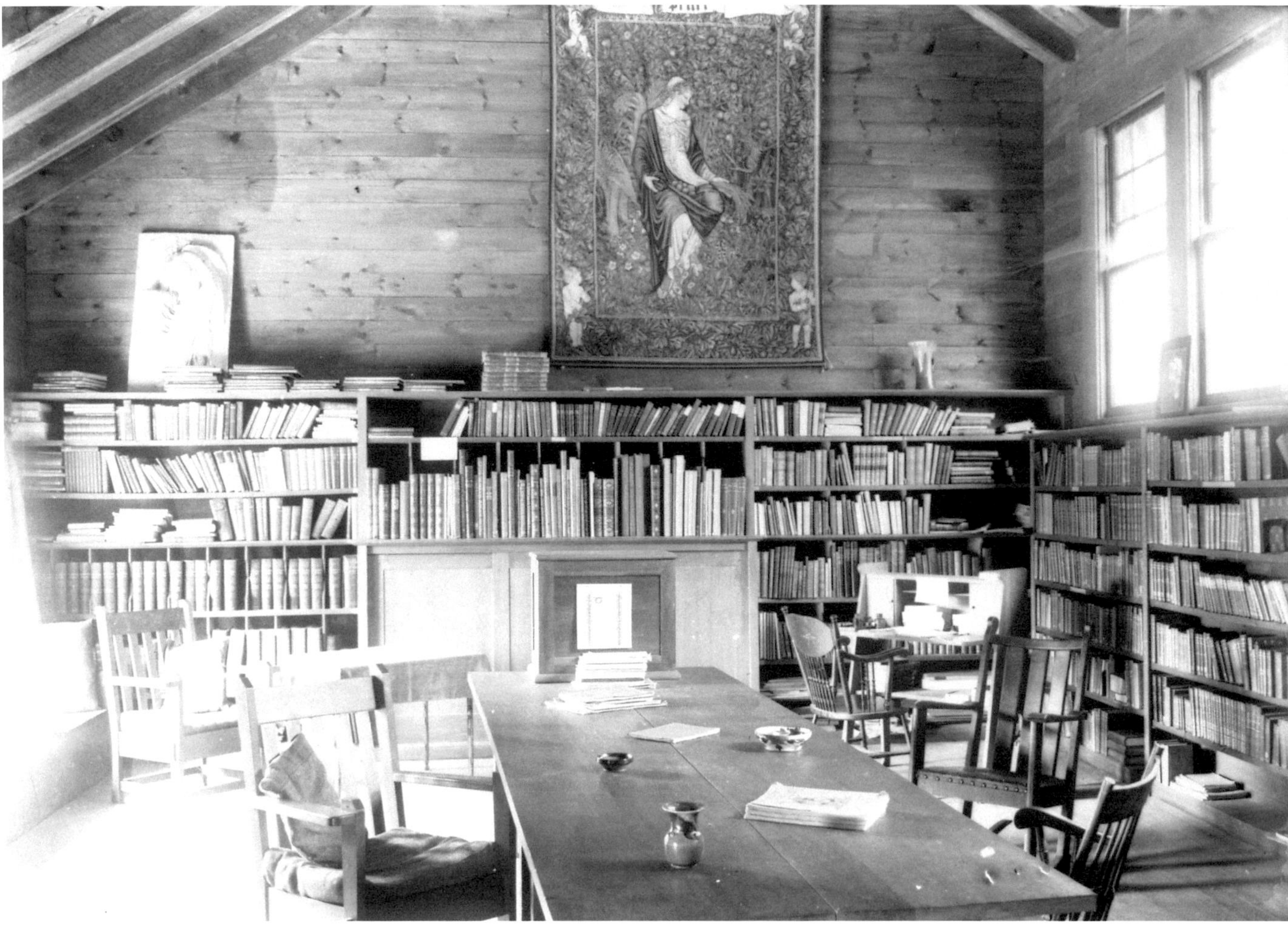

fig. 14 View of the west end of the library adjoining the Studio, ca. 1907. Winterthur Library, Downs Collection, 92x39.1140.11b

surviving accounts or photographs document beekeeping at Byrdcliffe, pigeon nesting-houses were prominently arrayed on cross gables of the barn. During the Middle Ages, dovecotes were equated with the lord of the manor, who retained the sole right to keep pigeons.[106] Crowning the broad roof of Byrdcliffe's composite barn, and visible from miles around, was a louvered wooden cupola capped by a gable roof with generous eaves and a lightning-rod spire. In late nineteenth-century America, the cupola was the prime status symbol of the sophisticated gentleman farmer.[107]

Poultney Bigelow proclaimed Ralph Whitehead to be "a mighty farmer in addition to his many other accomplishments," although not on a par with the celebrity gentleman farmers of the Vanderbilt clan.[108] Beginning in the late 1880s, the construction of Shelburne Farms by Lila Vanderbilt and husband William Seward Webb, in Vermont, and of Biltmore by her brother George at Asheville, North Carolina, received regular press coverage. The latter derived its name from *Bildt*, the region in Holland from whence the Vanderbilt family hailed, and *more*, an Old English word for rolling upland countryside. George Vanderbilt's sweeping plans involved the creation of model agricultural, forestry, and estate village programs, which lent credence to Ralph's prophetic words penned to Jane, from England, on August 26, 1891: "I have been much struck by the greater beauty of these parts of the country which are in the hands of large proprietors; where the trees have time to grow and the fields are not mere patches. In the future the large proprietors will be the communes."[109]

Whitehead was scouting for property in North Carolina in 1902; he also searched the Adirondacks as noted in the Byrdcliffe prospectuses of 1903 and 1907. Shelburne Farms's William Seward Webb was the largest "proprietor" in the Adirondacks, having opened up the region with his Adirondack Railroad in 1891–92. Shortly thereafter he constructed Nehasane, composed of a central lodge for his family, eleven guest cottages, several boathouses, barns and a working farm to provision the remote enclave with foodstuffs and ice. The estate was an outstanding representative of the Adirondack "great camp," a self-sufficient complex of functionally differentiated buildings deployed in an informal, picturesque manner.[110] Whitehead adopted just such a compound plan at Byrdcliffe for the same reasons wealthy Adirondack landowners embraced it; namely,

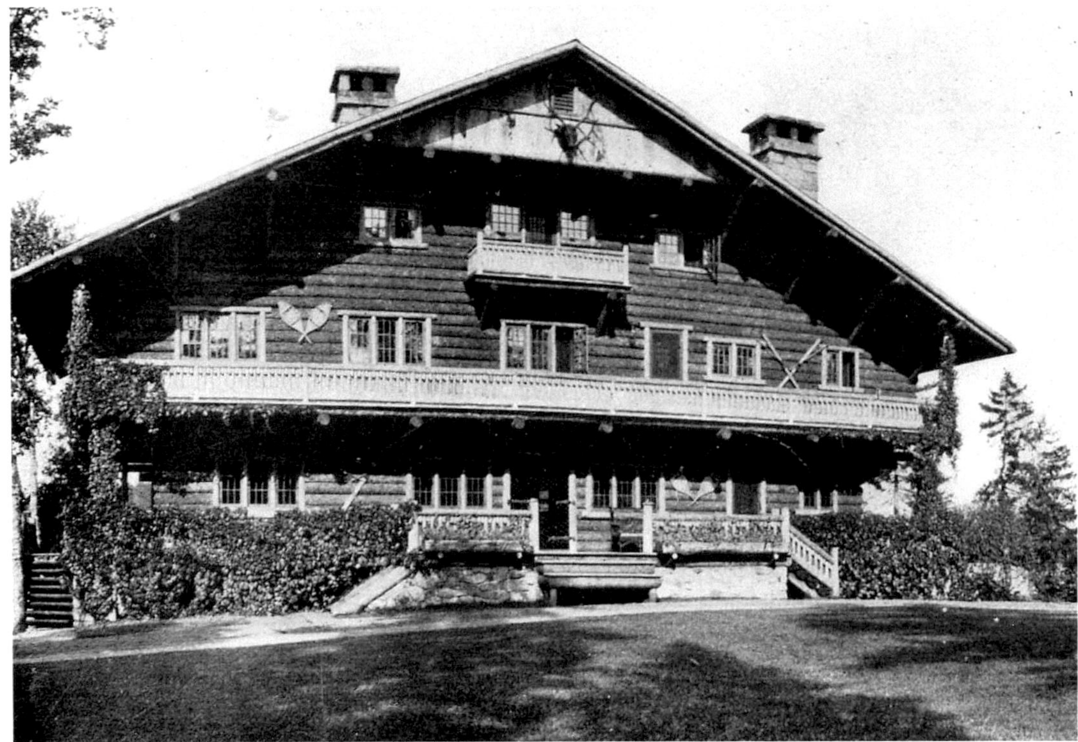

Left
fig. 15 Principal façade of Sagamore Lodge, designed by William West Durant, 1897. Courtesy of the Adirondack Museum.

Right
fig. 16 View from the southeast of White Pines. Webster family photograph, ca. 1918. Woodstock Guild.

the maximizing of mountain views and family privacy, combined with the pleasant prospect of a village community and structured sociability. Frequently the Adirondack camps featured roofed boardwalks or enclosed passageways converging on a social gathering place dubbed "the casino."[111] Byrdcliffe's Studio, where weekly concerts, dances, and art displays were held, was nicknamed "the casino," according to Lucy Brown.[112] Possibly the covered bridge between White Pines and the Loom Room (fig. 5) was inspired by the sheltered walkways of upstate New York's private mountainous preserves.

Adirondack log architecture may have been the source for the double-walled construction found at both White Pines and the Loom Room.[113] The 1895 inventory of Pine Knot, the first of four impressive estates William West Durant masterminded, included two different entries for "double frame cottage"; Durant's own Eagle Lake home boasted a double roof written up in a July 1902 *House Beautiful* article.[114] Double walls afforded insulation and an air space for various plumbing and heating utilities. Besides, a building made of logs would require a subsidiary framework to support inside walls finished with matched planks, sometimes in combination with a burlap covering for the upper section as at Sagamore.[115]

The last of Durant's elaborate great camps, Sagamore (fig. 15) was built in the years bracketing Whitehead's visits to the Adirondacks between June 1897 and September 1901, documented through his correspondence with Jane. The main lodge, on a site dotted with tall white pines, was habitable by the summer of 1897. White Pines—particularly the eastern façade (fig. 16)—with its broad gables, prominent overhanging eaves, and galleried balconies, bears more than a passing resemblance to Sagamore's central structure. Durant went on to build a stable, laundry, dining room, and boathouse before Alfred Vanderbilt purchased the property in 1901.[116] The precincts epitomized the six criteria Howard Lewis Applegate set forth for a great camp: 1) a single family estate; 2) on a lake shore; 3) with many buildings; 4) intended as a self-sufficient compound; 5) artistic in conception; and 6) notable for rustic materials and features.[117] Byrdcliffe lacked only the lake shore, and there was a swimming hole, at least, at the stream running between the farm and White Pines.

Whitehead generally eschewed the ostentatious hallmarks of Adirondack rusticity like peeled logs, birch-bark veneer, spruce-sapling appliqué, and twig- or boulderwork. The iconic rough stone fireplace was a rarity at Byrdcliffe, despite Bolton Brown's approximation of one in his Carniola abode.[118] Nevertheless, journalists reviewing Byrdcliffe connected it with Adirondack progenitors. Sanborn, for instance, writing about the interiors of the Colony's principal buildings in 1907, singled out the "spacious living rooms, monster fireplaces and raftered ceilings, which characterize the larger Adirondack camps."[119]

The Whiteheads might never have set foot inside one of Durant's great camps, but these were merely grander renditions of a local vernacular originating in the utilitarian structures associated with the area's logging heritage.[120] Ralph's letters to Jane indicate his familiarity with the environs of Saranac and Lake Placid, though he preferred Keene in the High Peaks region. He stayed at Glenmore, a rustic school of philosophy founded by a Scottish professor, Thomas Davidson. On June 5, 1897,

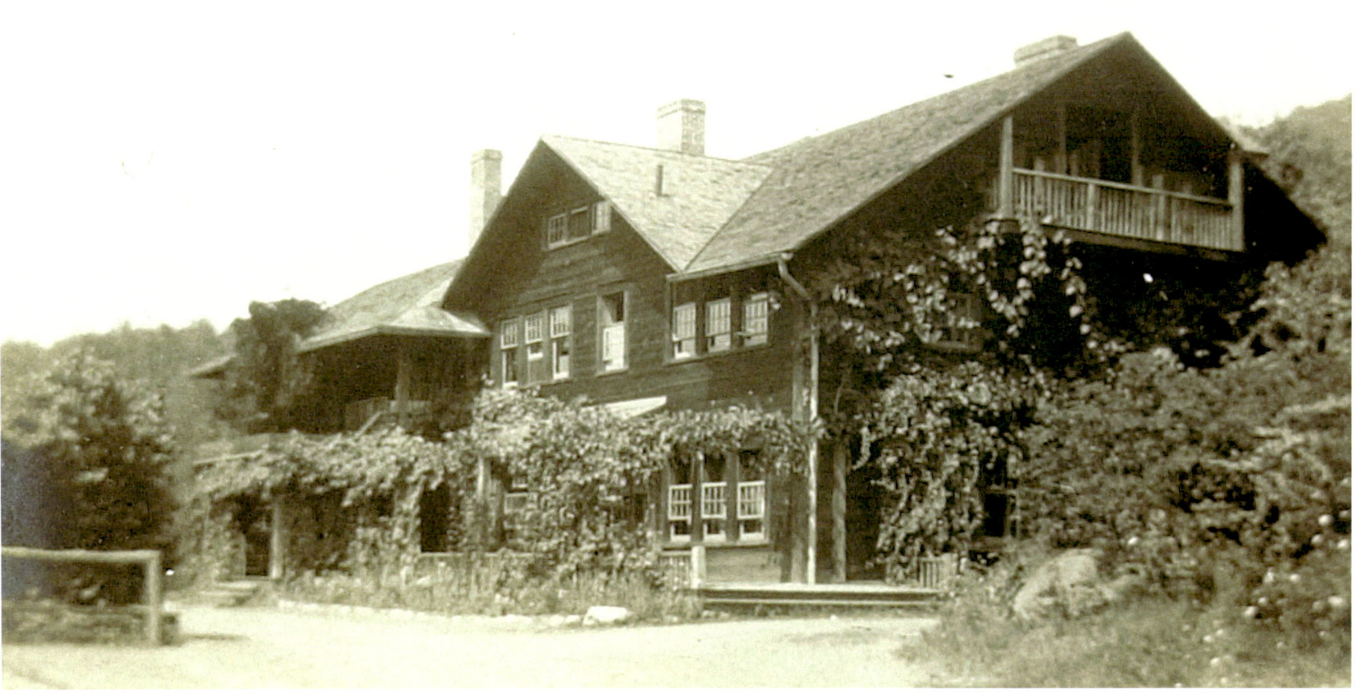

a month before Jane joined him there, Ralph described for her both Davidson—"rather too like a second-rate Ruskin"—and the accommodations, which consisted of a communal dining room and kitchen serving a half-dozen simple cottages.

A half-mile away was Summerbrook, the community presided over by Prestonia Mann and her husband, John Martin, an English Fabian. Here the Whiteheads met Marie Little, who would become a Byrdcliffe stalwart.[121] Ralph was contemplating a more permanent residency in the Adirondacks in 1897, for his June 5 letter informed Jane that Keene Valley "is 7 miles from here. It's said to be the best part of the Adirondacks but of course living there we could not have anything to do with either of these colonies."[122] He found a way to bring Keene to Woodstock by enticing Little to resettle at Byrdcliffe. The Looms studio-cottage he provided her (not extant) had an Adirondack flavor, for it was constructed along the lines of the "Lodge Designed to be Built at Jocks Lake, Adirondack Region" (figs. 17 and 18) in William Wicks's *Log Cabins and Cottages*.[123] The book, present in Byrdcliffe's library, was a fundamental primer for designers and owners of Adirondack camps.

Many of Wicks's sketches bore a resemblance to chalets because "the archetypal image of the mountain house," wrote Ramon Puig, is "an isolated dwelling, [with] steeply sloping eaves, wood, stone [. . .] the Swiss chalet."[124] It was the primary source, apart from log cabins, for Durant's Adirondack rustic style.[125] At Pine Knot, his first foray into artistic camp architecture in 1876, he named the main building "The Swiss Cottage." The imposing gable façade was overshadowed by an expansive low-pitched roof sporting very deep eaves, which protected the doors, windows, and porches, as in Swiss exemplars Durant may have seen on his European travels. There were, however, chalet pattern books already being printed in the United States at this date. The carefully drawn studies of rural Helvetic wooden houses by the Varin brothers were published by J. R. Osgood in 1875 (fig. 19). The introduction to the portfolio commended the exterior galleries, protected by the projecting roof, as particularly attractive features American architects might want to incorporate in their plans for modern country houses.[126]

Whitehead, whose devotion to Ruskin led him to the heights of the Alps, needed no introduction to chalets from American interpreters or publications. Although Ruskin disapproved of Englishmen's contemporary villas in a supposed Swiss taste, he had marveled at the genuine, site-specific vernacular shelters:

> Well do I remember the thrilling and exquisite moment when first, first in my life (which had not been over long), I encountered, in a calm and shadowy dingle, darkened with the thick spreading of tall pines, and voiceful with the singing of a rock-encumbered stream, and passing up towards the flank of a smooth green mountain, whose swarded summit shone in the summer snow like an emerald set in silver; when, I say, I first encountered in this calm defile of the Jura, the unobtrusive, yet beautiful, front of the Swiss cottage. I thought it the loveliest piece of architecture I had ever had the felicity of contemplating; yet it was nothing in itself, nothing but a few mossy fir trunks, loosely nailed together, with one or two grey stones on the roof; but its power was the power of association; its beauty, that of fitness and humility.[127]

Ruskin was describing the *mazot*, the temporary summer abode built by cowherds in the high alpine meadows. The more substantial and decoratively carved chalets of the valleys had a different "power of association," with medieval carpentry traditions and cottage industries. Gothic precepts still held sway in "wooden homes that need no paint to hide the deficiencies of workmanship" and familial wood-carving shops "in village homes.... Factories do not flourish in Switzerland."[128]

Whitehead had considered Switzerland a likely venue for realizing his and Jane's dream of a "convent" in the service of art and craft: "We want for the convent a decent population, a good climate, a country where work is the watch word, where there is not a superabundance of luxury, where public opinion is not blighted. For these reasons I thought of Switzerland."[129] Ralph wished to live there to await a divorce from his first wife, but he grudgingly relocated to Berlin in order to expedite the legalities. He was back in Switzerland in February 1892, writing to Jane of Ruskin and bemoaning the tourist company surrounding him at St. Moritz.

Whitehead brought along his own pleasant company, in the person of Hervey White, when he journeyed again to Switzerland in 1901.[130] From England he had written Jane, July 14, 1901, "someday you must share my mountains, the

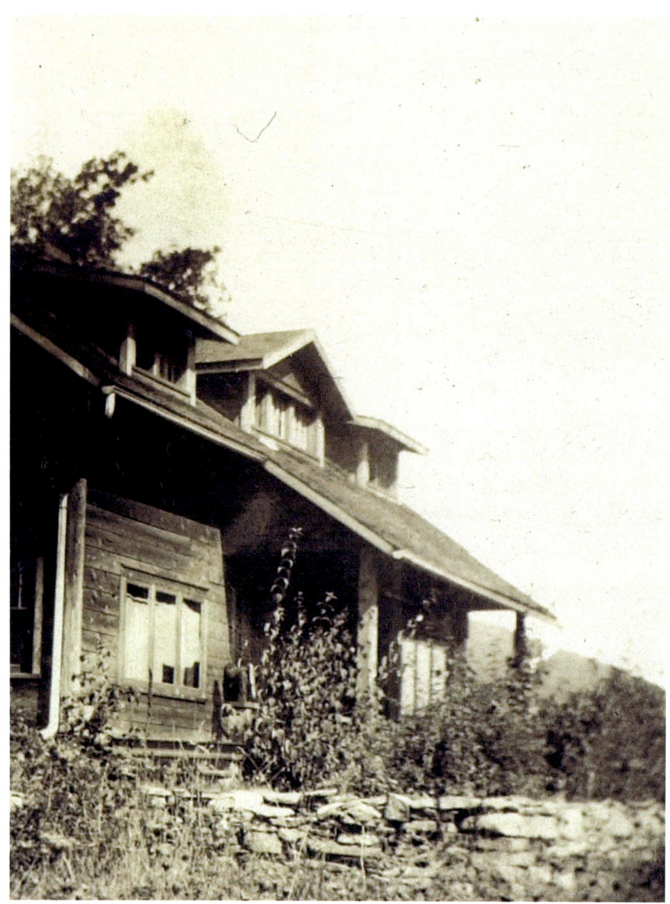

fig. 17 The Looms (burned, ca. 1950). Webster family photograph, ca. 1907. Woodstock Guild.

fig. 18 Design for lodge at Jocks Lake in the Adirondacks. Published in *Log Cabins and Cottages* by William S. Wicks (4th ed., 1900).

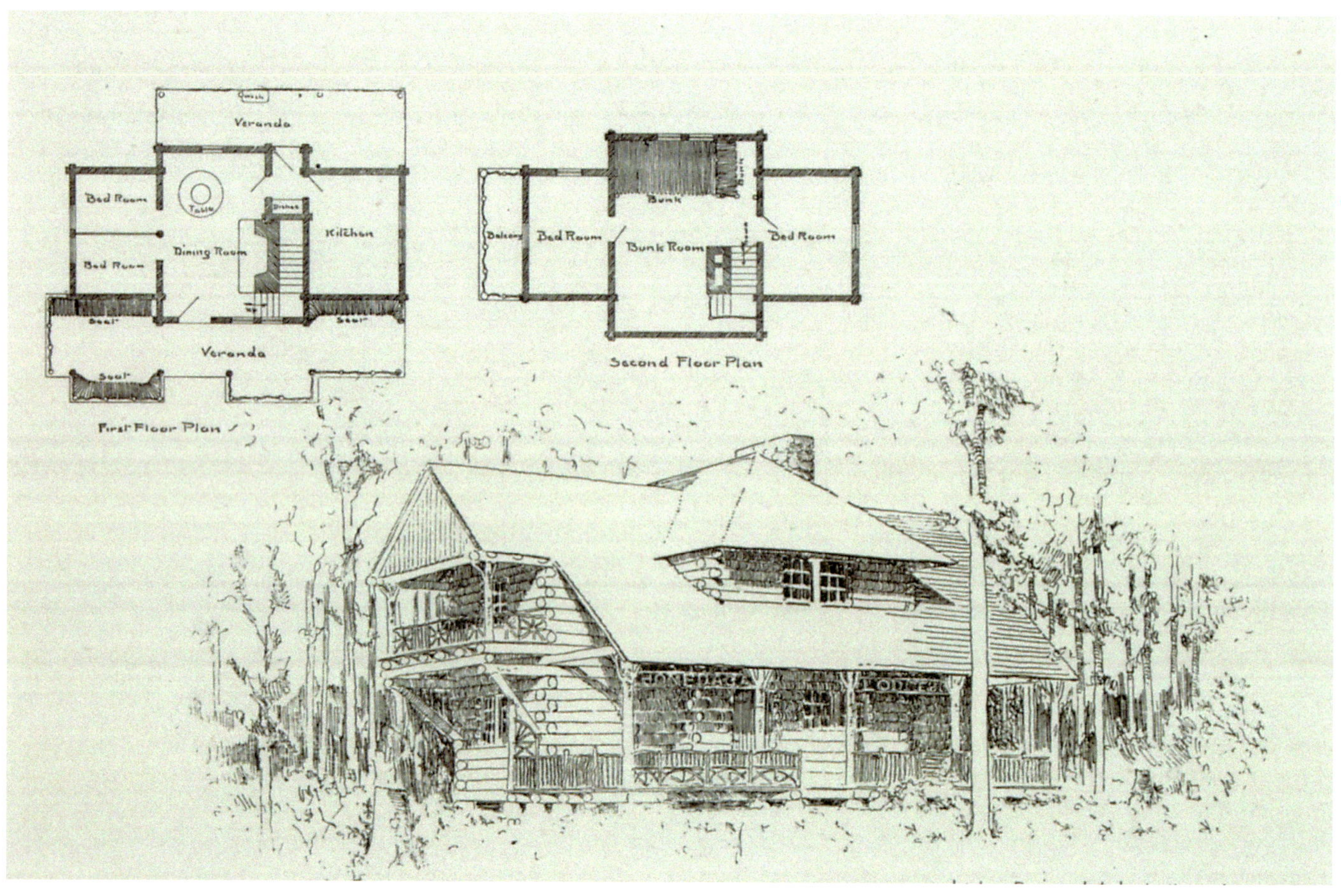

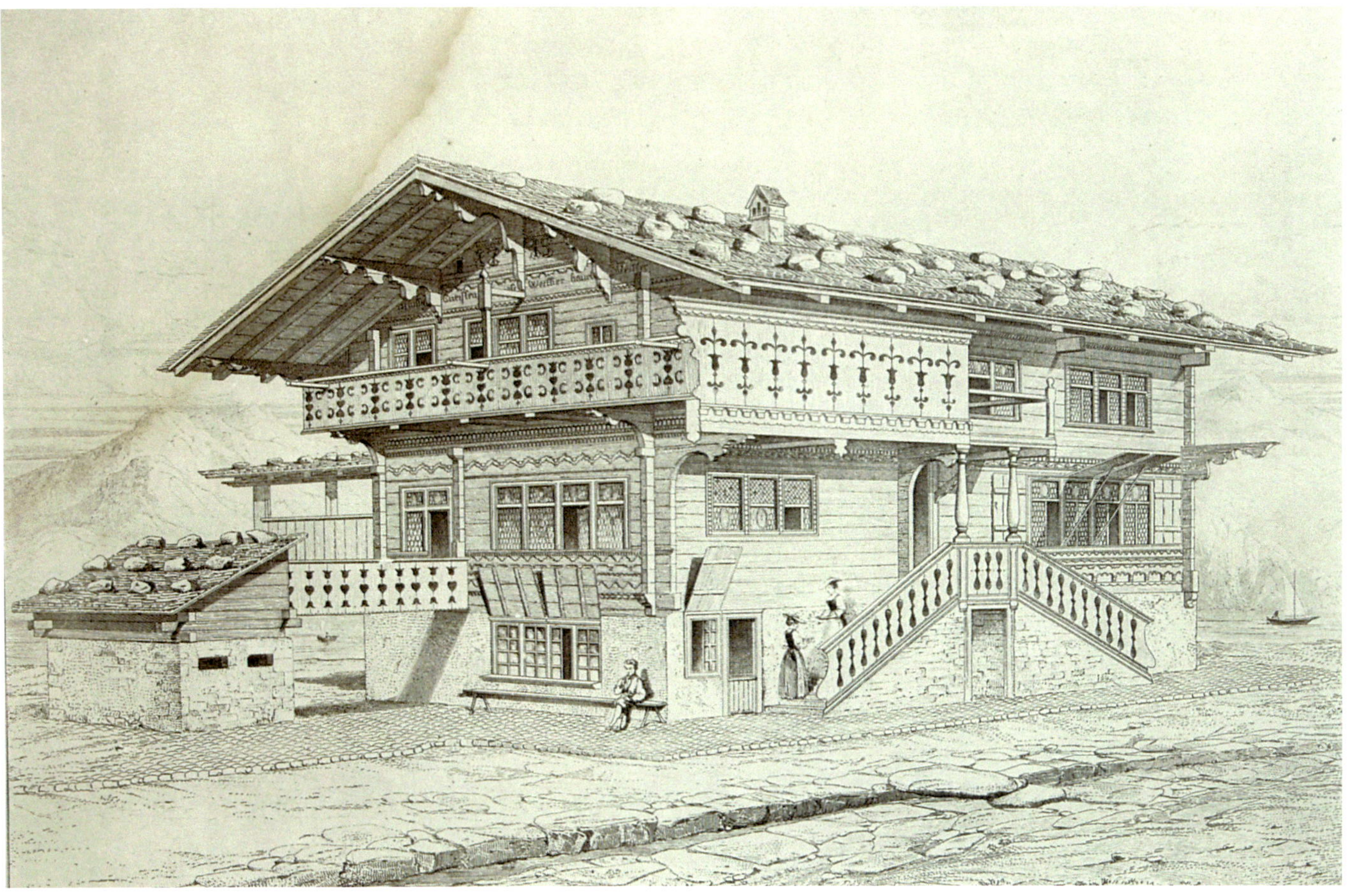

fig. 19 Valley chalet at Brienz, Bernese Oberland. Published in *The Picturesque Architecture of Switzerland* by A. and E. Varin (1875).

Alps." He was still thinking about Switzerland in 1902, while surveying Colony prospects with White in North Carolina. Ralph described for Jane a comfortable little boarding house "empty but for ourselves and the good people of the house who are quite as delightful as Swiss peasants."[131]

The other Byrdcliffe principal, Bolton Brown, had gone to Switzerland under his own auspices, mountaineering and sketching during the summers of 1887–88.[132] His residence at Byrdcliffe was christened "Carniola" after the Austrian Slavic province in the Jurian Alps. Whitehead's objections to Brown's original intention to make it an all-stone house may have stemmed from more than practical concerns about cost and timeliness in late fall of 1902. Alpine abodes typically utilized stone only for foundations and basements, and Whitehead wanted his art-village buildings to convey the unified appearance set forth in a Byrdcliffe brochure from the mid-1920s: "Their rustic lines and harmonious coloring, mostly in cool browns and greens, give the effect of Alpine chalets."[133]

The "cool greens," predominating in the Colony's interior architecture and furniture finishes as well, evoked the Austrian Alps in particular. Unlike the Swiss highlands, the Styria region of Austria, where Whitehead purportedly lived for seven years during his first marriage, was heavily wooded.[134] An 1867 English travelers' handbook quoted William Beckford in a section on Styria's forests:

> There seemed no end to these forests, except where little irregular spots of herbage, fed by cattle, intervened. Whenever we gained an eminence, it was only to discover more ranges of dark wood, variegated with meadows and glittering streams. White clover, and a profusion of sweet-scented flowers, clothe their banks; above waves the mountain ash, glowing with scarlet berries; and beyond rise hills and rocks and mountains, piled upon one another, and fringed with fir to their topmost acclivities. Perhaps the Norwegian forests alone equal these in grandeur and extent.[135]

Historically, Styria had functioned as a highway between Italy and Germany, absorbing influences from both cultures.[136] It comes as little surprise, then, that Whitehead put forth "Boscoverde" ("green woods" in Italian) as a potential name for the artisanal company he hoped to establish at Byrdcliffe.[137] Ralph also proposed a traditional German icon—the ceramic stove—as the centerpiece of Jane's bedroom at White Pines: "I am going to have a pretty stove in it built up of coloured tiles if I can get some made with a flange."[138]

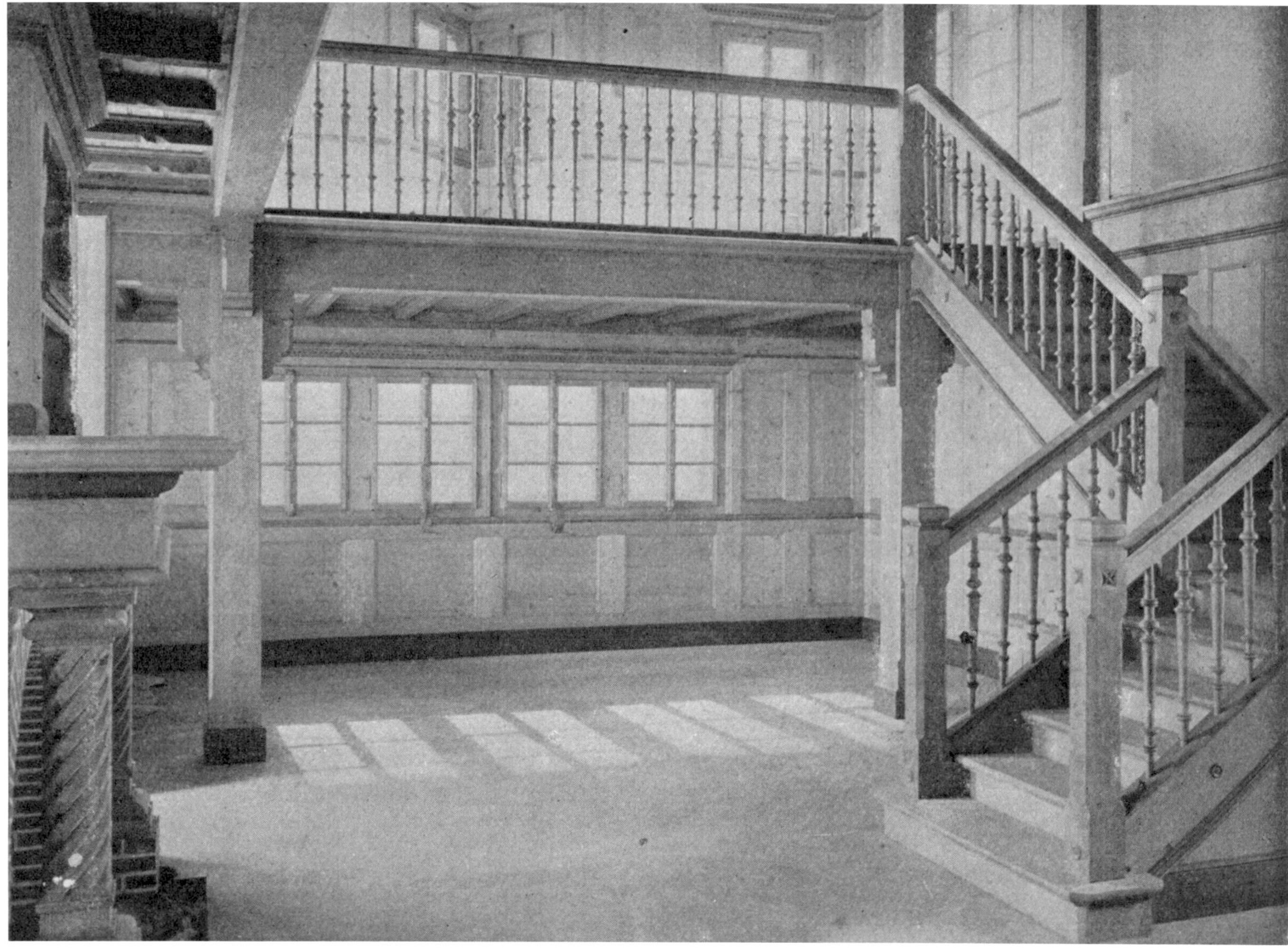

fig. 20 Hall of G. Fatio chalet, designed by Edmond Fatio, Lake Geneva, 1893. Published in *Architectural Record* (July–September 1897): 54, fig. 17. Courtesy of the Division of Rare and Manuscript Collections, Cornell University Library.

Although ethnically diverse, Europe's alpine regions shared a common vernacular timber-building tradition, which was taken up internationally and generically labeled "Swiss style" by 1900.[139] *Fachwerk*, or exposed heavy timber framing, is readily apparent on the western gable end of Byrdcliffe's barn (see fig. 12). The structure was Swiss in several other respects, beginning with its sitting on the side of a hill. The lower barn block incorporated a "forebay," a downhill arcaded aisle open to the elements on the southern exposure. The forebay, roofed but only partially enclosed, had evolved in Switzerland to provide refuge for livestock from the rain, high summer sun, and extremes of weather.[140] The upper barn component sprouted a porchlike forebay at the eastern end of the south façade (see fig. 13). Similarly, a breezeway yielded additional cover between the upper and lower barn masses (see the footprint in fig. 2, no. 4). The whole complex manifested the Swiss attribute of generous eaves, buttressed by brackets, to mitigate the weathering of the wooden walls and to shield the openings in inclement seasons.[141]

In accord with most of the buildings at Byrdcliffe, the barn was clad in Swiss-style horizontal flush-board siding, which Jean Schopfer found far superior to the Anglo-American preference for clapboards:

> Another cause of the inferiority of wood architecture in America is the manner of placing the boards on the walls, the upper ones usually overlapping the lower. The certain result of this is to prevent any decoration of the fronts, and to produce, by the numerous lines of the revetments, a fatiguing effect, which mars the appearance of the edifice. Besides, the joists are not visible and give no idea of the internal structure of the house.[142]

Schopfer had studied inside and out the meticulously reproduced chalets from various cantons of Switzerland brought together in a model village at the Geneva National Exposition in 1896. His comments about the interiors (see fig. 20), especially the dictum that "seeing the room, we can picture to ourselves the house and vice-versa," illuminate the wall treatments amd built-ins Ralph and Jane

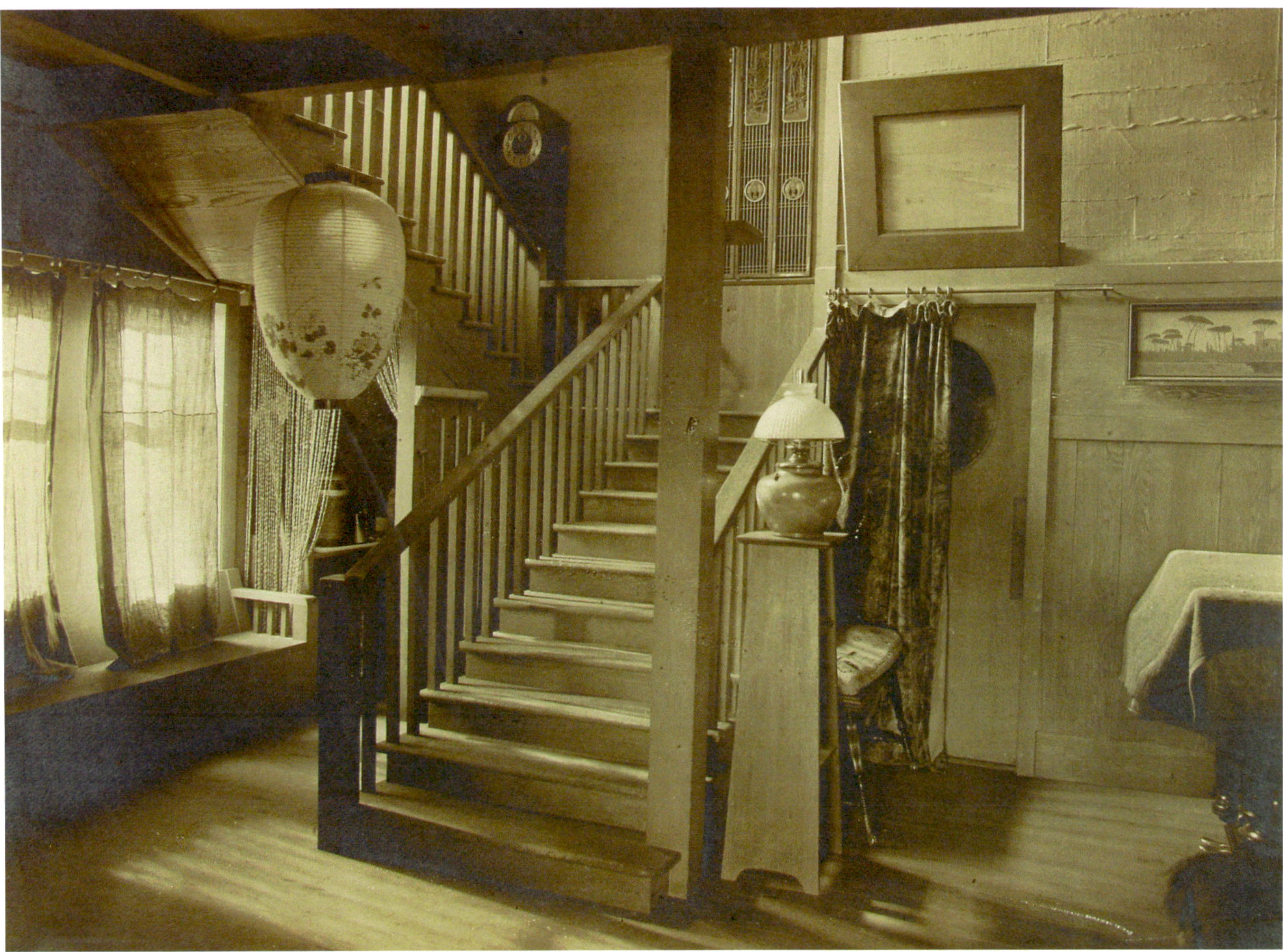

fig. 21 Stair hall at White Pines, photographed by Jessie Tarbox Beals. Winterthur Library, Downs Collection, 92x39.546. Published in *American Homes and Gardens* (October 1909).

agreed upon for White Pines.[143] Wainscoting was characteristic of chalets, and Schopfer emphasized its unity with the ubiquitous dressers—"one with the wainscoting of which they seem to be an extension." Dressers usually had display shelves, drawers, and both open and closed cupboard compartments. They became a leitmotif for the interior architecture at White Pines, commencing in the dining room with the case piece housing Jane's heirloom blue china and repeated in the living room and principal bedrooms, either as projecting or recessed architectonic units wedded to the wall (see fig. 32). On January 25, 1903, Ralph wrote regarding the southwest room on the second floor, which was to be Jane's chamber:

> In your bedroom it would be best I think to make a cupboard in the recess which I had intended for the bath[;] this cupboard can be 2 ft. 2 inches deep & 7 ft. 3 inches long. Then you could have a shallow cupboard on each side of the S. window & a window seat in this window . . . you see two sides of the room will be taken up with cupboards which is equivalent to paneling. . . .

The south window, with seat, was really a group of three windows treated en suite. Schopfer devoted considerable attention to the Swiss tendency to situate windows in combinations of two, three, or even four, united in a single frame; often a bench "extends from the wainscoting and is comprised in the frame of the group of windows."[144] The west wall of the living room at White Pines featured such an arrangement, as did the west wall of the first-floor stair hall (fig. 21). The seats' boxed bases echoed the wainscot of the living-room overmantel and the hall sheathing, while the ample window sills doubled as crest rails for the benches. The side moldings of the wide, flat frames encasing each three-window unit seemed to continue below the sills, effectively merging with boards of the same width at the ends of the angular backrests. The effect was akin to what Schopfer called the "prolongation of the frame" in exterior chalet windows.[145]

Voysey has been suggested as a source for White Pines's spacious stair hall with simple, spare woodwork, but the contemporary Swiss chalet was equally plausible.[146]

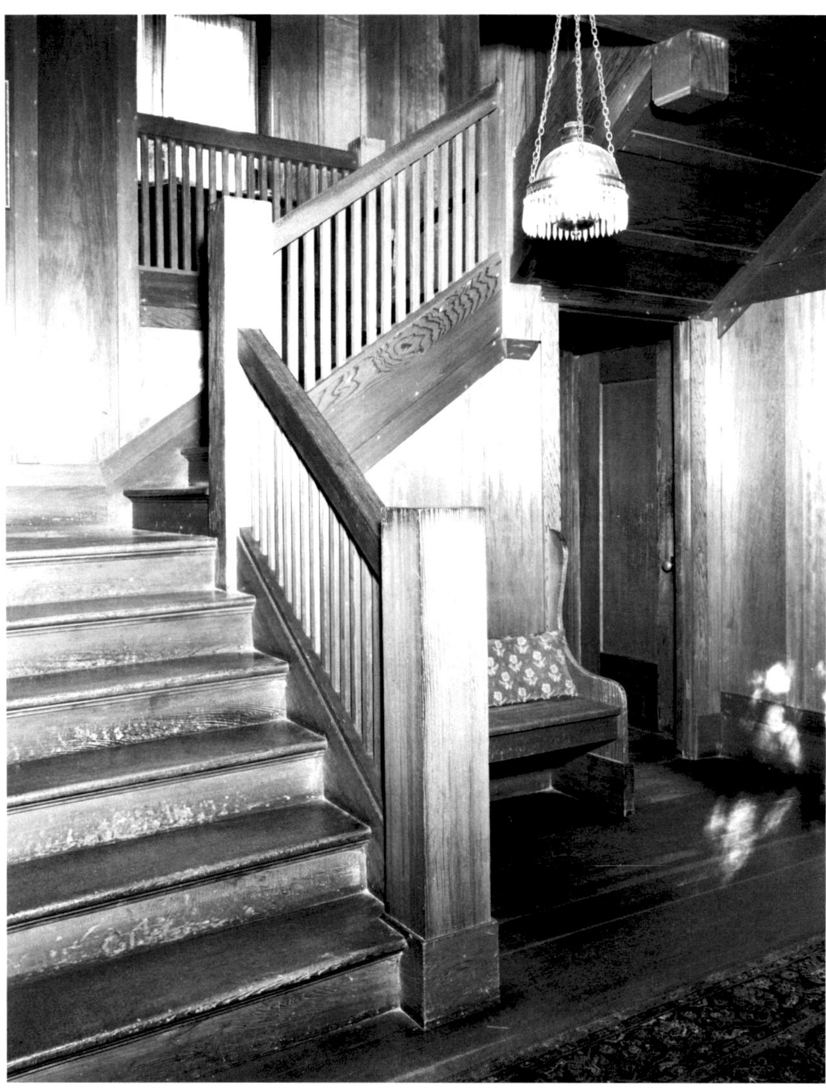

fig. 22 Stairway of Gifford H. McGrew House, designed by Bernard Maybeck with assistance from the owner and Charles Keeler, 1900. Courtesy of William S. Ricco and Kenneth Cardwell and the Berkeley Historical Society.

fig. 23 George H. Boke house, designed by Maybeck, 1901–2. Bernard Maybeck Collection, Environmental Design Archives, University of California, Berkeley.

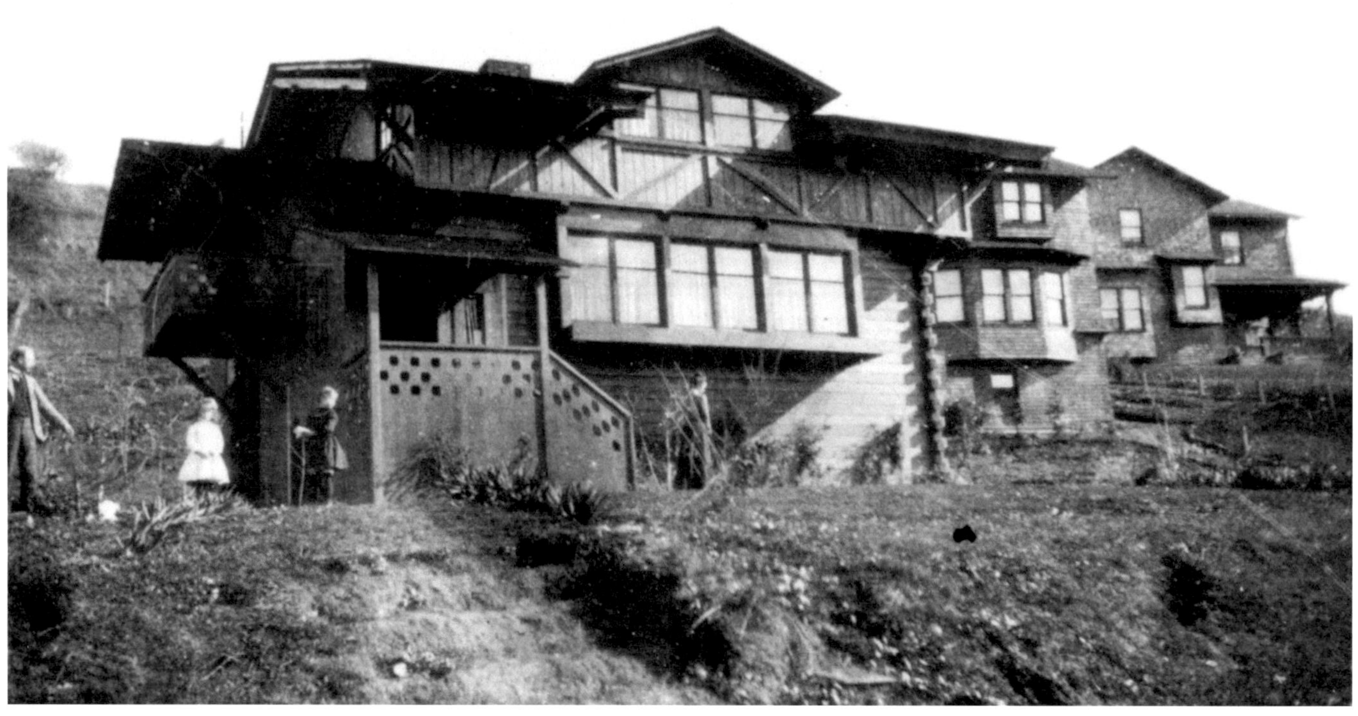

Schopfer pictured the modern-day interior, shown in figure 20. Though lacking a window bench, the chalet's fenestration and wainscot treatment, its frank expression of post-and-beam construction, and the open stairway, punctuated by emphatically horizontal landings, resonated with the Whiteheads' airy, woodsy space. Even more closely related was Bernard Maybeck's unpainted redwood entry and staircase (fig. 22), outfitted with squared hand rails, spindles, and newel posts, at the McGrew house in Berkeley, California. The ornamentation was natural and integral, derived from the play of light and the rhythmic grain pattern of the wall sheathing, allied with a built-in bench.[147]

Maybeck was the premier chalet architect in the United States at the turn of the century; he was lauded in Louis J. Stellmann's essay "The Swiss Chalet Type for America." Stellmann postulated that nowhere outside its native land was the Swiss chalet used to more advantageous effect than along the Pacific coast hills, especially around San Francisco Bay. Maybeck's Berkeley residences for Isaac Flagg (1901) and George Boke (fig. 23) boasted chalet rooflines and blocky massing in concert with redwood-sided walls, partially shingled in the former instance. Stellmann illustrated the latter, along with several subsequent chalet-style commissions by Maybeck, as examples of "simplicity, strength, economy, and the picturesque harmony with natural surroundings [which] mark the chalet in American architecture even more perhaps than they do, nowadays, in Switzerland, where the bizarre influence of foreign builders has added much intricate and fussy elaboration in the trimming of the houses."[148]

Maybeck reinterpreted the balconies overhung by the wide eaves of Swiss mountain houses as sleeping porches. These, in conjunction with spreading roofs and redwood construction, became distinctive attributes of the bungalows that mushroomed on California's hillsides in the years 1905–15.[149] A sleeping porch was still a novelty in 1902, when White Pines was equipped with one situated between Ralph's and Jane's bedrooms, right over the entrance porch[150] (see fig. 7). The first sleeping porch in Berkeley was at the residence of Charles Keeler (1895), Maybeck's earliest client. He commissioned the community's initial unpainted redwood house, shingled on the exterior and horizontally boarded inside. Skeletal redwood posts, girders, and rafters were purposefully exposed in the interior as ornament. The house was missionary since it led to the founding of the Hillside Club (1898) to promote Maybeck's architecture as a community-wide aesthetic.

Whitehead could have seen Keeler's dwelling and others like it in 1900, for the Santa Barbara *Morning Press* reported on August 8, "R. Radcliffe Whitehead has returned from a six weeks tour of the Northern part of the state."[151] Berkeley's unconventional hillside homes might have reminded him—as they did a physics professor from

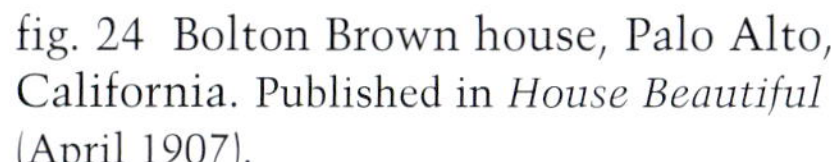

fig. 24 Bolton Brown house, Palo Alto, California. Published in *House Beautiful* (April 1907).

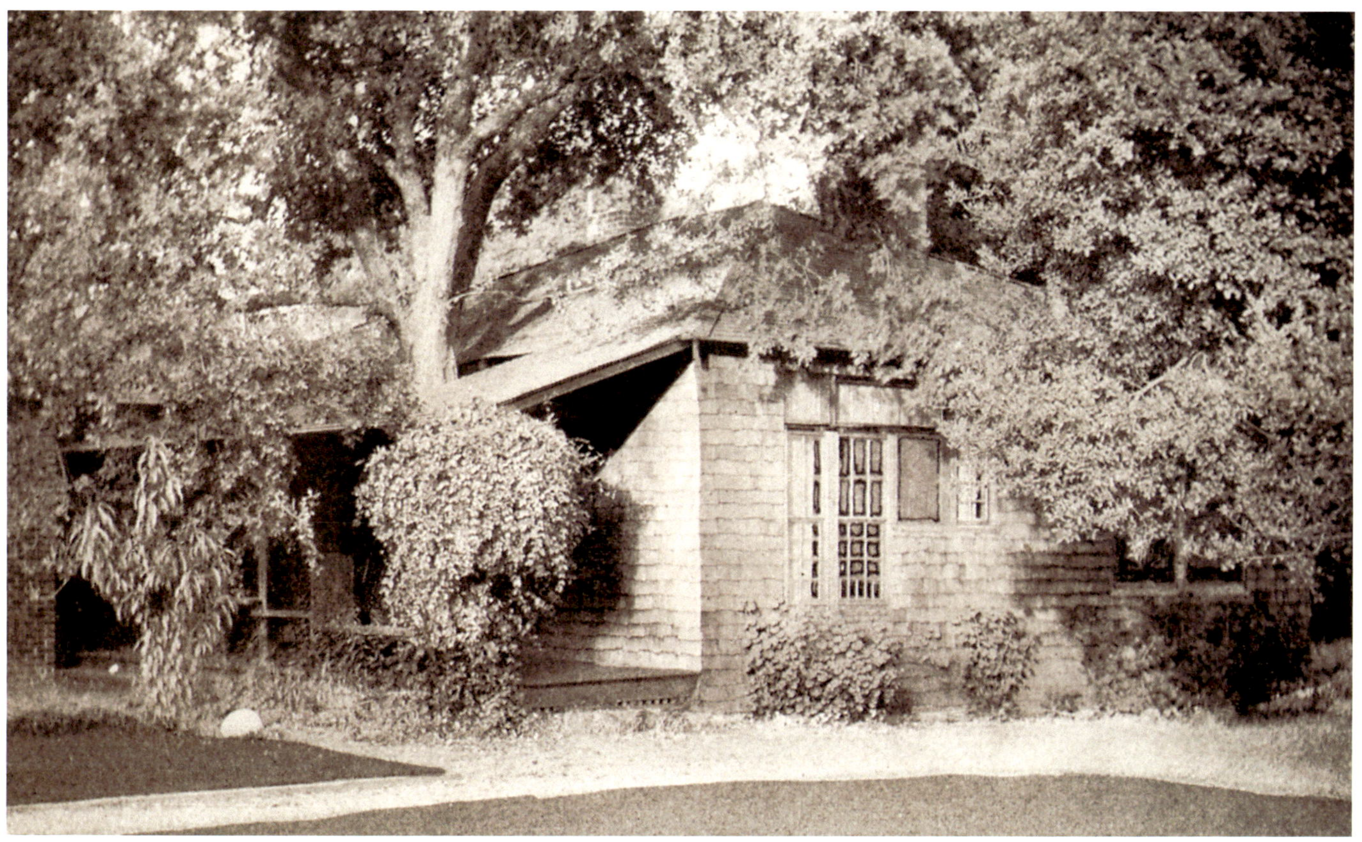

Germany—of the weather-boarded structures erected by Styrian peasants in the vicinity of Graz.[152] In any case, White Pines became a textbook example of what Keeler preached in *The Simple Home* (1904), dedicated to Maybeck and heralded in the preface as "the gospel of the simple life." Keeler urged his readers to commit to a natural house of rough-sawn boards, perhaps colored in a soft mossy green stain, and melded with the landscape via pergolas covered in climbing vines.[153]

Bolton Brown, who headed the art department at Stanford University in the 1890s, was living in Palo Alto when Maybeck designed two houses there for Emma Kellogg. *The Palo Alto Live Oak* (November 6, 1896) described the first as

> . . . the quaintest residence that has yet been built. . . . It is not large, covering but 20 x 36 feet of ground space, being a story and a half and having five rooms; yet the odd design of the exterior, with its covering of cedar shingles, its casement windows and broken outlines, makes it noticeable. The architect R.B. [*sic*] Maybeck, instructor in the State University, designates it Californian in style.[154]

By 1898 Brown occupied an equally quaint one-story "house of redwood within and without"; in other words, horizontally boarded on the interior and shingled outside[155] (fig. 24). The relatively large living room focused on a boulder-faced fireplace, nearly identical to the one Brown later built in his Carniola residence at Byrdcliffe. The low-pitched roof doubled as a sleeping porch of sorts, reached by means of an opening made in the porch overhang to accommodate a white oak growing through it.[156] Brown's "New Homie" was actually an early rendition of the fully developed California bungalow, highlighted by architectural historian Karen Weitze for its "retreat-to-nature

fig. 25 The Giglio (Italian for "lily") at Arcady. From a family album labeled "Photographs taken by Ralph Radcliffe Whitehead in 1892 on wedding trip in Paris, California, Arcady, New York, Byrdcliffe." Winterthur Library, Downs Collection, 92x39.1140.668.

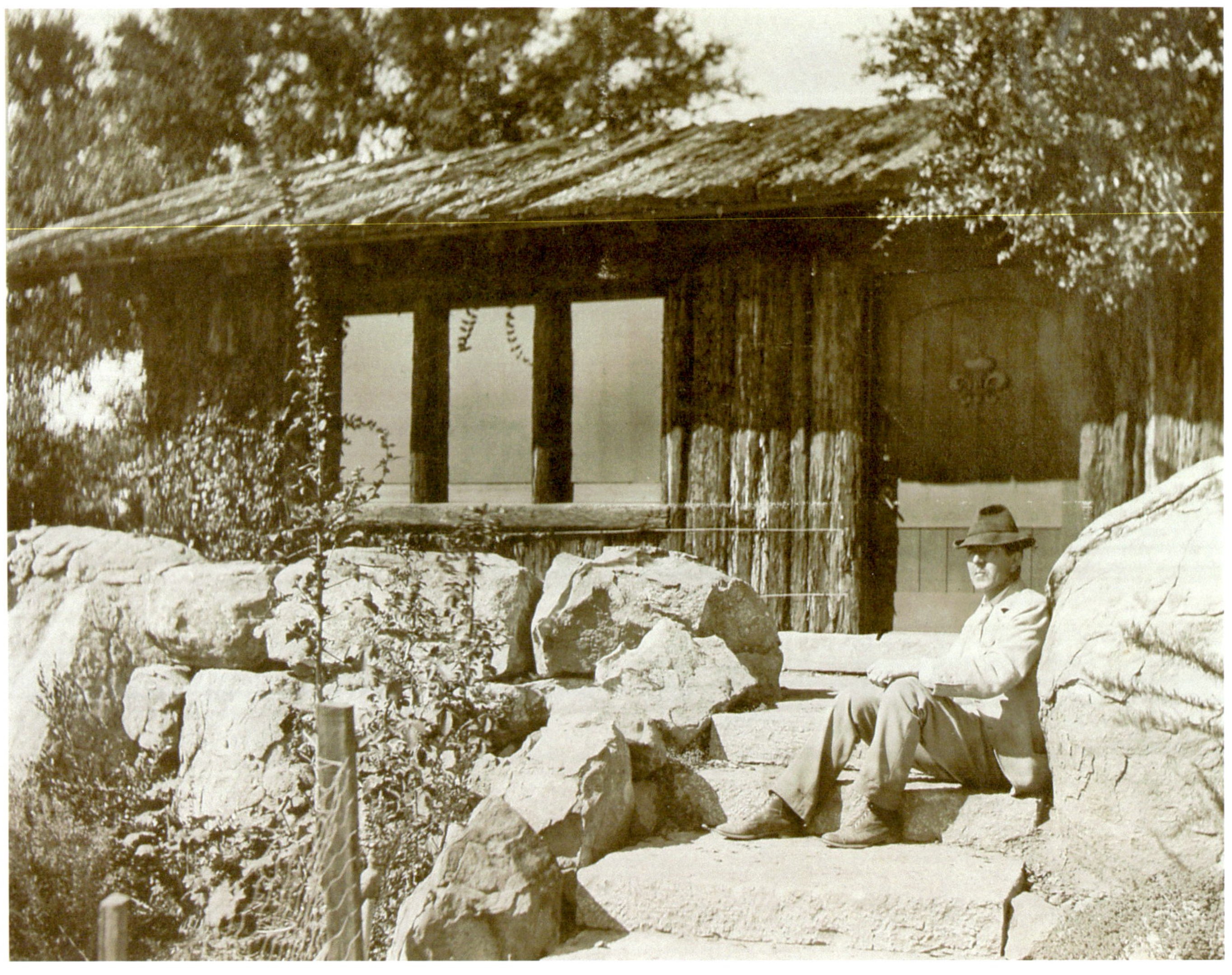

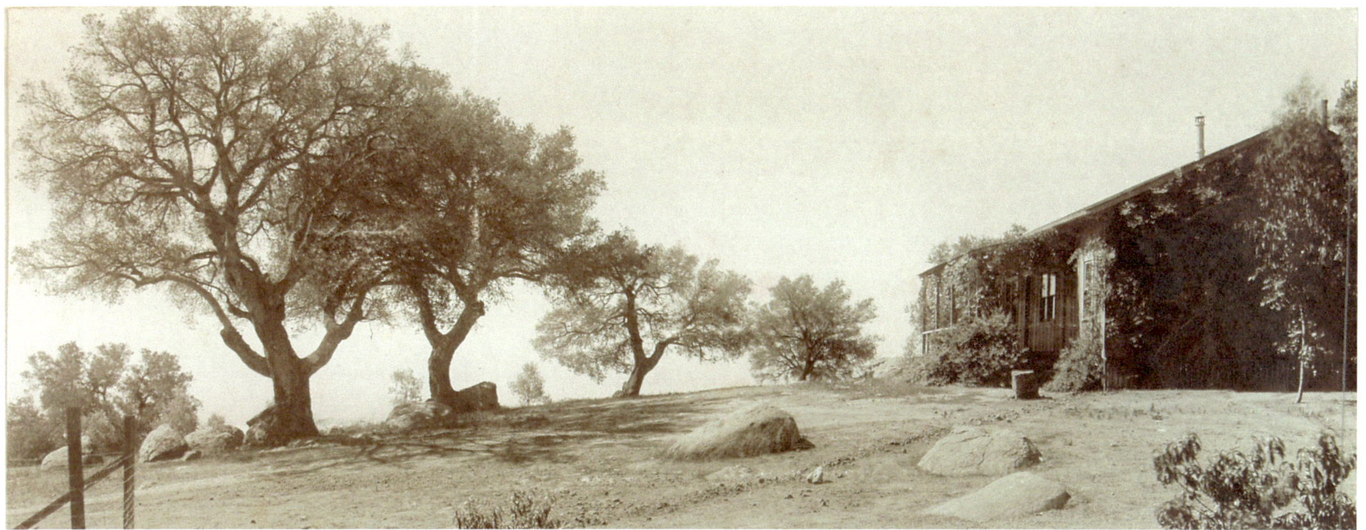

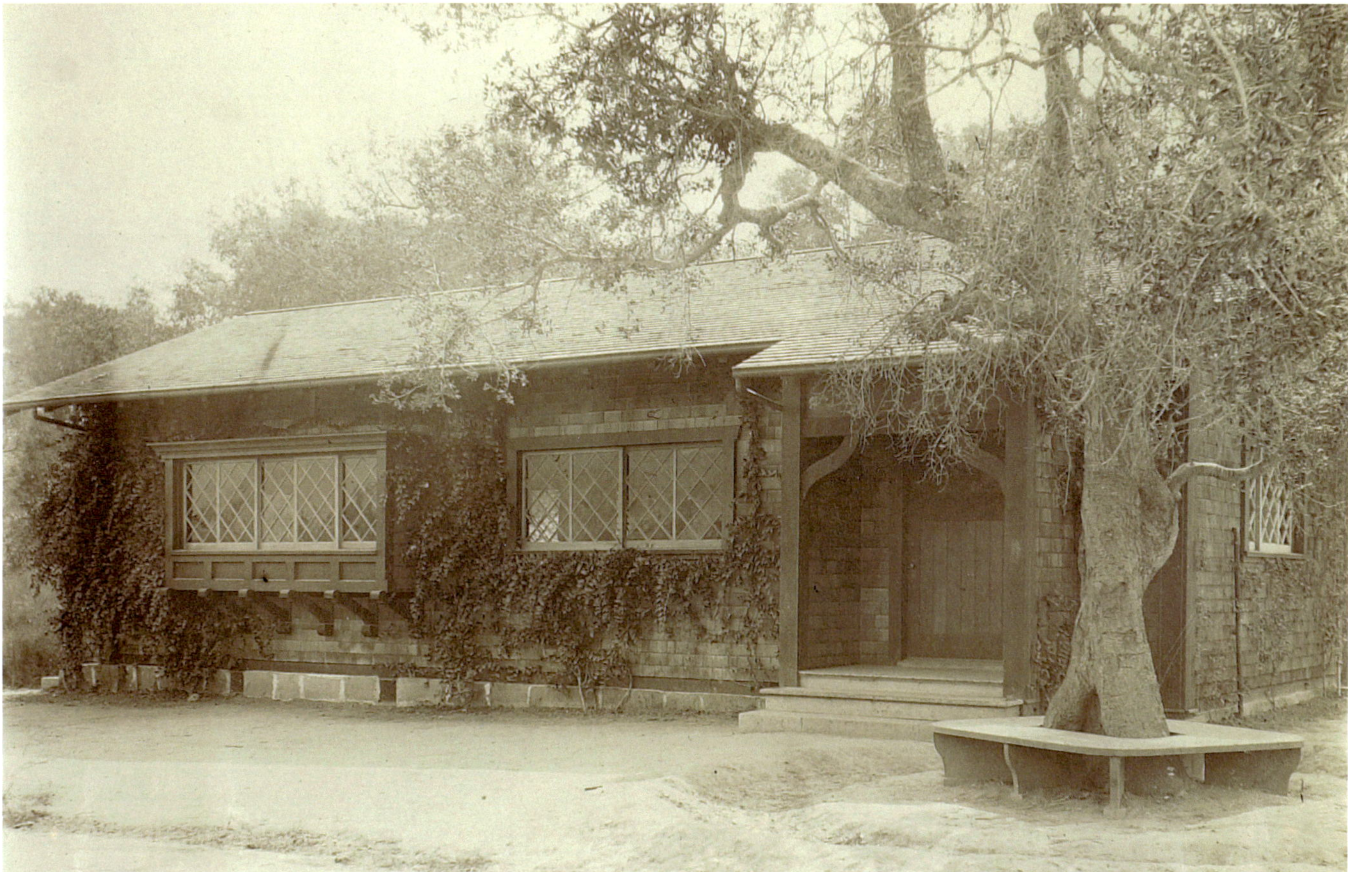

fig. 26 The Moon at Arcady, probably photographed by Ralph Whitehead, ca. 1900. From the family album begun in 1892. Winterthur Library, Downs Collection, 92x39.1140.668.

fig. 27 The Sloyd school at Arcady, built in 1898. Woodstock Guild. The school was moved and remodeled as a gardener's lodge by Arcady's subsequent owner.

quality. . . paralleling and possibly even contributing to the maturing of rustic design for the Victorian camps in the Adirondack and Catskill mountains in New York State. The bungalow in Palo Alto is among the earliest designs to establish a clear connection between Arts and Crafts centers on the East and West coasts. . . ."[157]

Bolton Brown was key, no doubt, in the implementation of Byrdcliffe's distinctive rustic architecture, dubbed "Edwardian redwood" by Woodstock locals and "bungalows" by Poultney Bigelow.[158] But Ralph and Jane Whitehead merit credit as California bungalow innovators, too. The redwood outbuildings they conceived for their Arcady estate (1895–98) were clearly forerunners of Byrdcliffe's straightforward wooden studio-residences.

The Giglio at Arcady (fig. 25) typified the fifth of Henry Saylor's ten bungalow categories: "the small, unusually

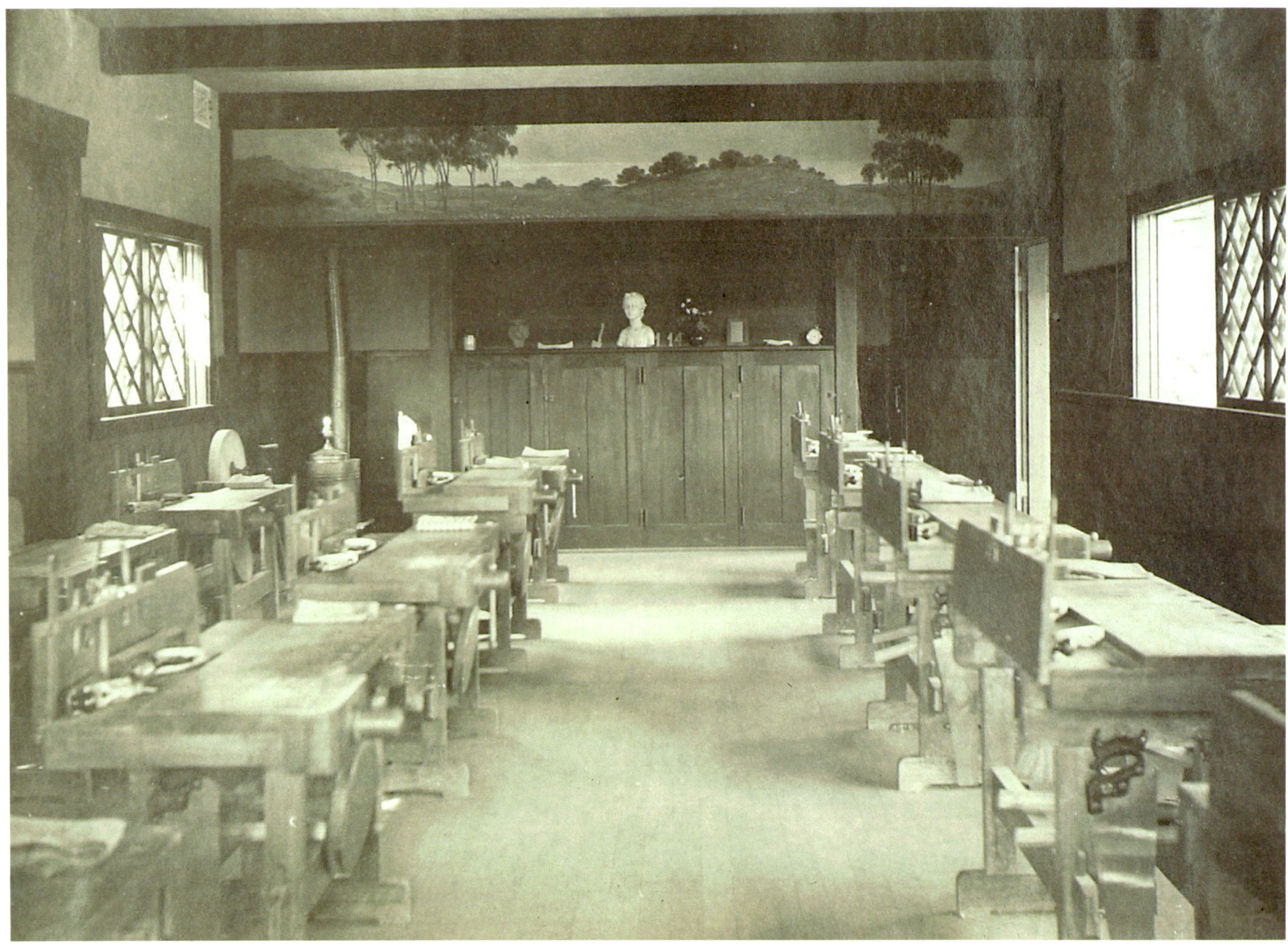

fig. 28 Woodworking studio of the Sloyd school at Arcady, ca. 1900. Winterthur Library, Downs Collection, 92x39.1140.603.

picturesque structure that is used as a retreat or perhaps merely as a summer house in connection with a larger house."[159] Built into a hill across the road from the main residence, and partly hidden among the trees, the Giglio was literally a tree house since the sides and roof were fabricated from redwood logs and slabs with the bark still adhered. The door was a board-and-batten affair, embellished with the Whiteheads' Florentine lily crest, set adjacent to windows organized as a tripartite unit.

The nearby "Moon" cottage (fig. 26) was conceived as a small, informal lodge-retreat for the family and/or select dependents. It functioned often as accommodations for guests, craftsmen, and students. In a letter to her mother in July 1895, Jane described the cottage as the gray-green "color of the rocks" surrounding it. The front porch did double duty as the dining room, decorated in a "natural" palette of orange and purple plantings:

> Under the front porch [is] a thick hedge of heliotrope[,] at intervals nasturtiums that climb. On the side 'Fortune's Yellow' rose & 'Tacinani' clematis. In the corner by the steps a certain orange creeper that is very prolific and beautiful.

The kitchen was sandwiched between the front porch and an even larger back porch equipped with a water closet. The rear part of the dwelling incorporated a large loft. Among the principal rooms was one "left in redwood & finished in green & white enamel." A light yellow enamel was used for Jane and Ralph's room, furnished in a yellow-and-blue cretonne. She concluded, "The Moon is almost done. It has taken a long time...I am never allowed to work, & directing others never goes fast. People are so curious about it—there is never an afternoon that more than half a dozen visitors don't come out of curiosity & putter about."

Jane recorded in her September 1898 calendar that the family of Christoph Tornoe, the Danish-born and German-trained contractor who had built the Whiteheads' Tuscan-style home, were in the Moon.[160] Presumably he was then constructing the Arcady Sloyd school (fig. 27), devoted to the teaching of a manual training system originated in Sweden. The shingle-clad school, really a woodworking studio, sported a low gable roof and diamond-mullioned sliding windows in three- or four-unit sets, with at least one companionate built-in seat on the inside (fig. 28).

A projecting bay, evidently built around a large picture window, sprouted from one of the gable ends and lent support for an arborlike framework on either side.[161] The rustic bench circumscribing a tree added interest to the entryway, which gave immediate access to the unpartitioned workroom. A broadly proportioned front door communicating directly with the primary interior space, as opposed to a vestibule or intermediate hall, was characteristic of California bungalows.[162] The same type of wide door with prominent horizontal rails and recessed vertical-plank panels was reused at the Villetta, where it opened into the communal living room from an expansive porch-pergola.

Jane's conventionalized grape-leaf-and-vine painting on the upper panel of the Sloyd school door effected a graceful transition from out-of-doors to indoors, as did Leonard Lester's tree-dotted frieze.[163] These decorations illuminated a point Ralph had made in his essay "From Tuscany to Venice": "Now let us premise that art shows us the beauties of nature which we had passed by unheeded. . . ."[164] He may have had Arcady's woodworking studio on his mind—its artful simplicity, open interior, and youthful students—when he wrote Jane on August 17, 1902, about the organization of White Pines. "How would it do not to have a drawing room at all but only a studio and a small dining room, and then a big play room for the children? The entrance to the house would perhaps be straight through to the studio. . . ."[165]

The Studio Archetype

Ralph Whitehead's conception of the house-as-studio bespoke his awareness of an international phenomenon whereby artists' material environments were viewed as art works in their own right, and as models for a more soulful, less consumption-oriented domesticity. Prior to his arrival in Woodstock, there were already a number of Catskill artist enclaves infused with this sensibility. Like photographs snapped at a family reunion, the illustrations printed in "Artists in Catskills" revealed a strong kinship among White Pines, the painter Charles Curran's Little Brown House at Cragsmoor, near Ellenville, and two cottages from Onteora Park, a summer colony at Tannersville initiated by the interior decorator Candace Wheeler.[166] The structures shared spreading gabled rooflines, prominent porches, grouped multipane windows, weathered-board-and-shingle building materials, and natural ornamentation achieved with climbing vines.

Wheeler was one of the leading lights of the American Aesthetic movement, which sought to elevate decorative art to the plane of fine art. While maintaining a formal, richly embellished studio in New York City, at Onteora she "put away all the tedious formalities and connections of urban . . . existence, and live[d] in happy simplicity without sacrificing any of the comforts and refinements."[167] Candace originally intended her Pennyroyal cottage (1883) to be built of logs, but the cost convinced her to substitute sawed lumber—the Whiteheads' choice for White Pines as well. Next door her daughter Dora erected a more rugged studio (1888), akin to Arcady's Giglio in its siding of bark-covered slabs.[168]

Jane Whitehead's affinity for Onteora was both personal, through her cousin May Clymer Bayard, and ideological.[169] Her 1906 calendar had July and August entries for "went to Onteora" and "preparing for Onteora [fair,] ticketing weavings." Certainly, the Wheelers and the Whiteheads were fellow believers in William Morris's dictum that a beautiful place was required in order to make beautiful things.[170] The motto Dora painted at Pennyroyal read, "Who creates a home creates a potent spirit which in turn doth fashion him that fashioned." Jane followed the recommendation given in Wheeler's *Household Art* to conceive decorations in relation to the situation and surroundings of the house. She reported "doing designs of balsam on bedroom," in keeping with *Household Art*'s contention that a mountain home "may become a far more real expression of its occupants than any city-house can be. . . . She [the mistress] may mount on ladders to stencil, or grovel on floors to stain."[171] "Balsam" was the name of the Onteora cottage frequented by Mark Twain, whose portrait Dora frescoed on Pennyroyal's walls, along with other Onteora-associated luminaries such as John Burroughs.[172]

Burroughs had links to yet another art colony located on Pakatakan Mountain, some thirty-five miles west of Onteora at Arkville.[173] The Arcady Sloyd school would have complemented Pakatakan's picturesque assemblage of shingled studios, distinguished by low horizontal massing and gable roofs, overhanging unboxed eaves, big northern

fig. 29 Parker Mann house/studio, Pakatakan Colony, Arkville, New York. Courtesy of Len Jenshel. The initial studio (1890) was converted to a residence when a new studio and breezeway were built (1902).

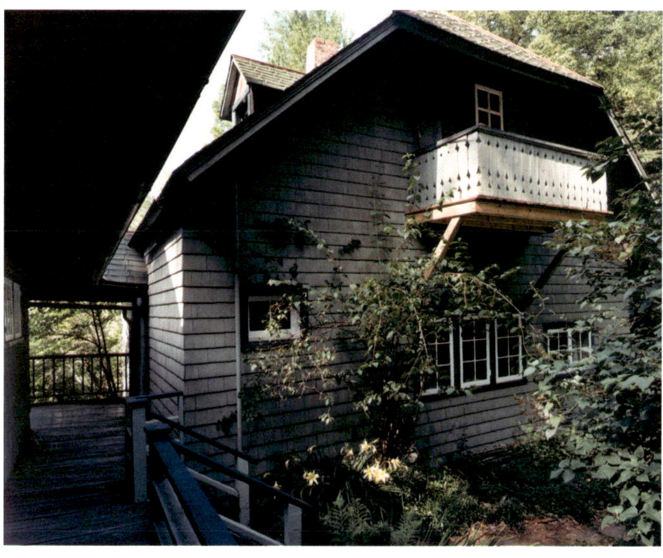

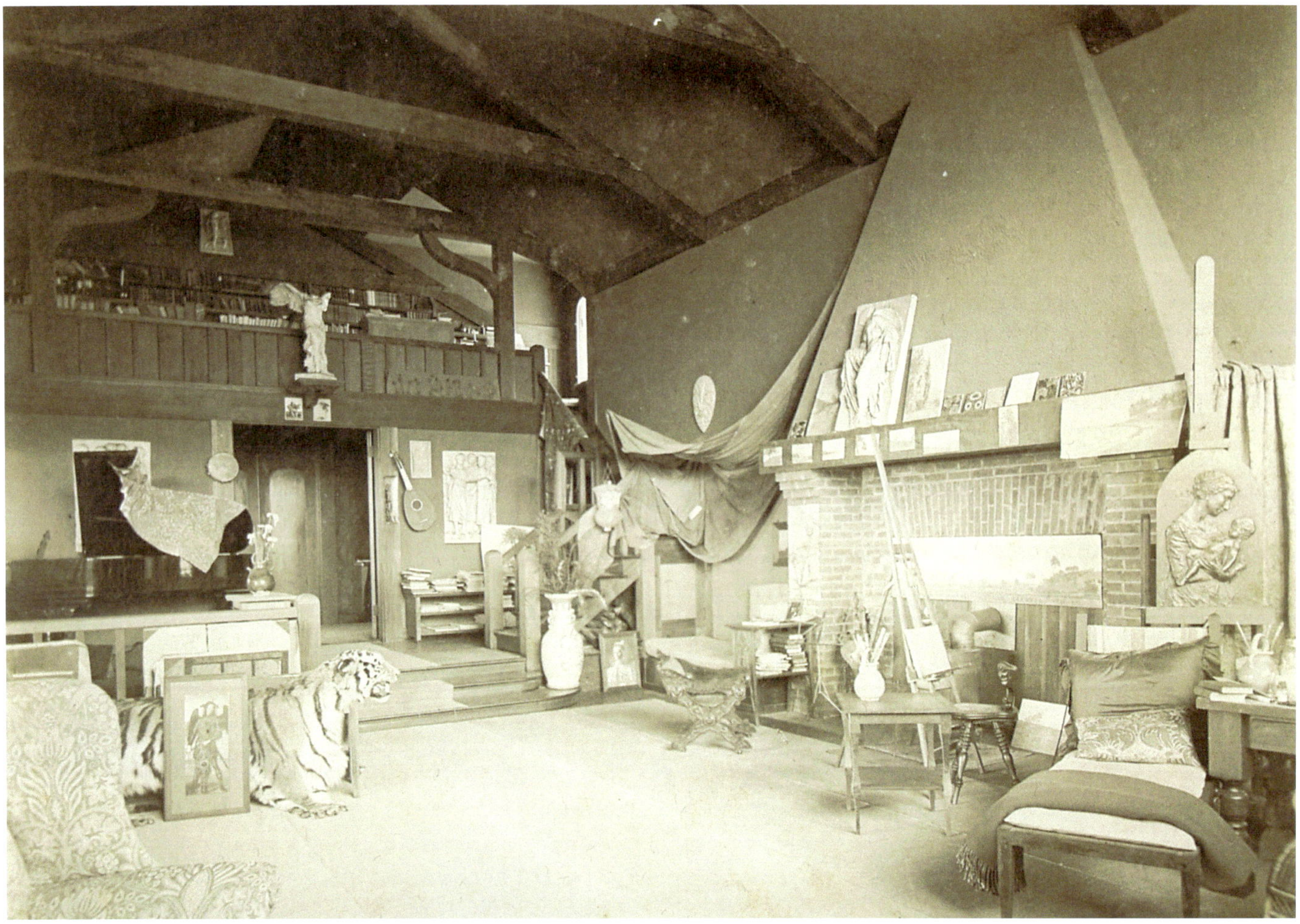

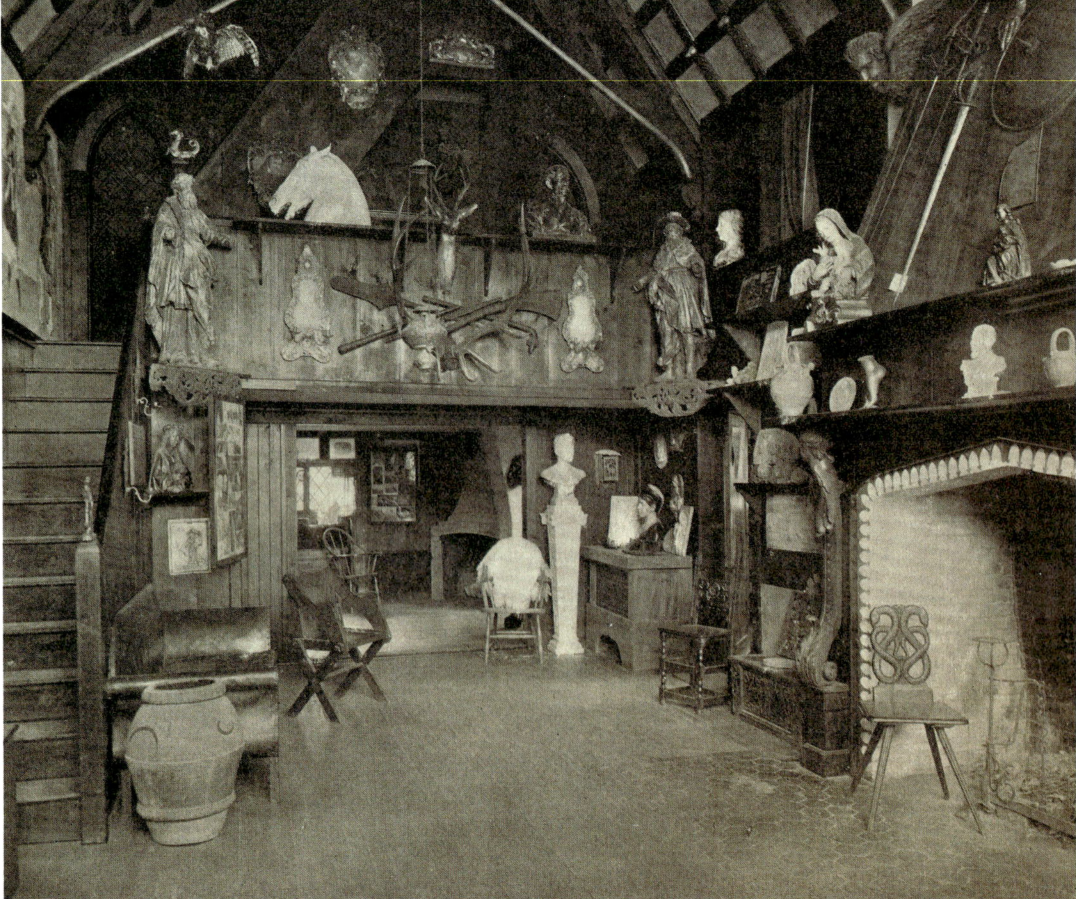

fig. 30 The studio in the main house at Arcady, ca. 1895. Winterthur Library, Downs Collection.

fig. 31 The Aldie studio of William Mercer, Doylestown, Pennsylvania. Published in *House and Garden* (October 1903).

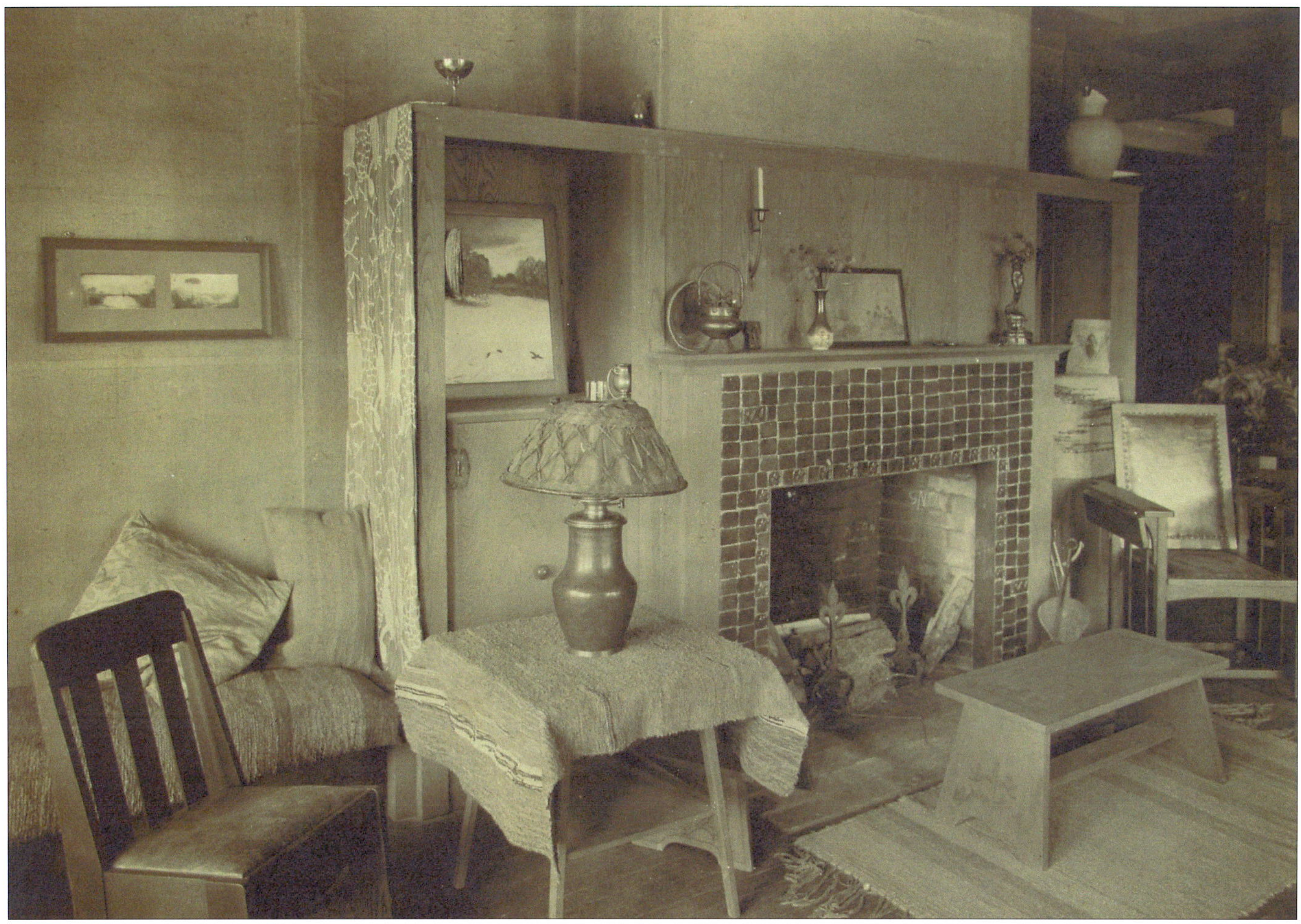

fig. 32 Living room, called the "Pine Tree Room," at White Pines. Winterthur Library, Downs Collection. Published in *Bungalows* by Henry H. Saylor (1911). The rug and low table were made at Byrdcliffe; the fleur-de-lys andirons complemented the border design of the fireplace tiles.

windows, and multipaned sash. The second-story balconies and covered passageway connecting Parker Mann's home and studio foreshadowed kindred features at White Pines and the Loom Room. By 1891, the Arkville colony of landscape painters was already a tourist landmark, for the Ulster and Delaware Railroad's guide to the Catskills alerted passengers that "several very attractive summer cottages . . . many of them by artists of note . . . may be seen . . . peering through the trees on the mountain slope."[174]

Pakatakan's best-known denizen was Alexander Wyant, who moved there in 1889 from Keene Valley, one of Whitehead's haunts in the Adirondacks. His initial "shanty" studio was supplanted by 1890 with a more substantial shingled house incorporating a Gothicized fireplace the Whiteheads would have approved. Enshrined on the wood-paneled overmantel, under a penthouse mounted on diagonal brackets, was a Madonna and Child in relief.[175] The chimneypiece treatment and such accessories as a tiger-skin hearth rug, an oriental carpet tacked up as a wall hanging, and a bust on a swathed pedestal signaled Wyant's participation in the phenomenon of the "aestheticizing studio."[176]

During the late nineteenth century, the artist's studio became not just an inspirational setting for its occupant but also an advertisement for his connoisseurship, depth of sentiment, and unconventionality. Ironically, certain conventions came to signify the "aestheticized studio," but the repetition enhanced rather than diminished their symbolic content. Jane outfitted her Arcady studio (fig. 30) with a tiger skin, *Winged Victory*, and a Voysey-designed "Tulip" textile draped casually over the stair railing. A mother-and-child bas-relief rested on an easel next to the imposing fireplace "in Gothic shape, coming into the room like the chimneys [of the Loire Valley chateau] at Blois." "Do you like that?" she quizzed her mother in late February 1895, then continued, "I want everything in the way of decoration to have a meaning, or what has not a meaning, to be beautiful in the way of colour or form. . . ."

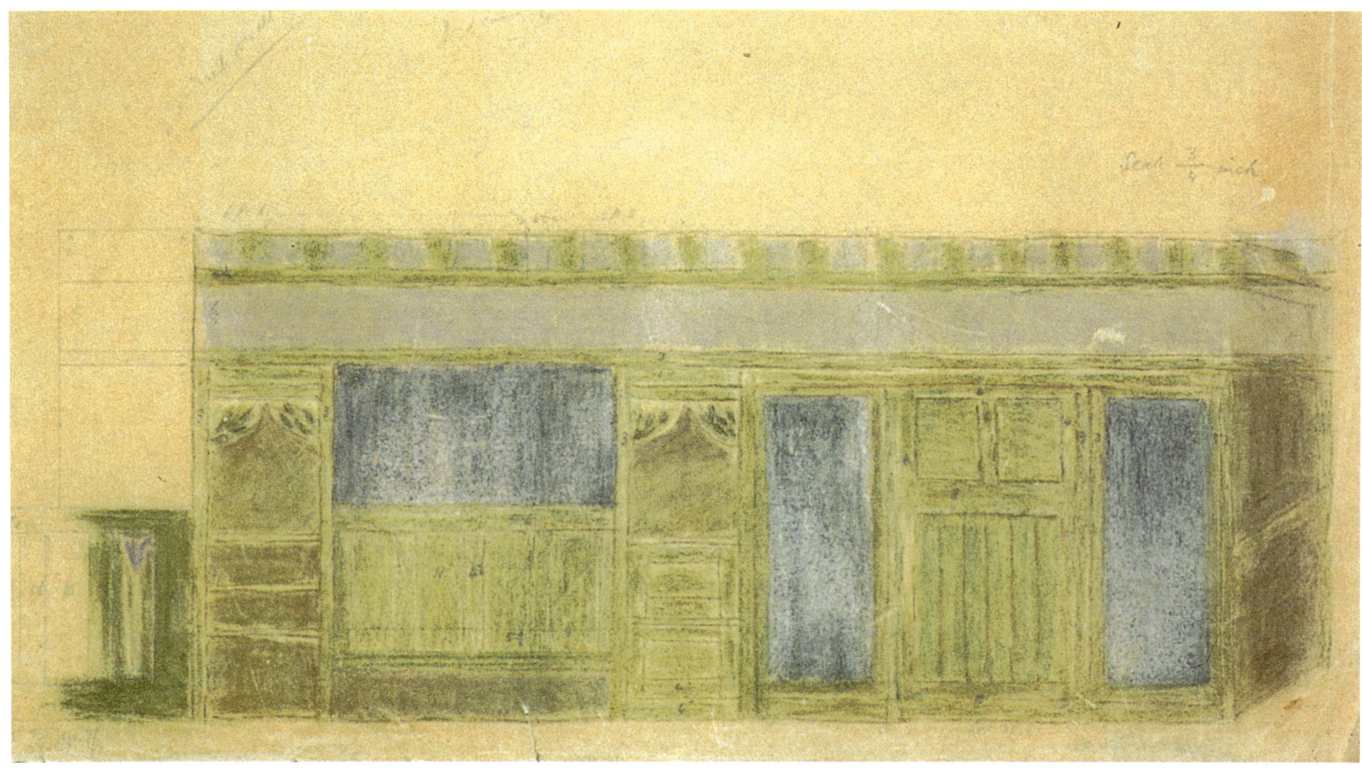

fig. 33 *White Pines Hall Elevation*. Winterthur Library, Downs Collection, 02x170.124

In a series of letters penned in February 1910, Ralph waxed sentimental about the adornments Jane had devised for Arcady. He pondered, "The Madonna in your room and the lily you painted beside it and the tower of the Palazzo and the Morris chintz, there lingers in them all the spirit of those days when we were in love with life and with each other . . . it is your taste, dear, that has made all the beauty here, and, without you, I don't seem to have the faculty of doing these things." At Byrdcliffe, Ralph depended on Jane, then, to supply "atmosphere," as defined in the opening paragraph of an article about the "Aldie" studio (fig. 31) of her cousin, the sculptor William Mercer:

> Wherever one goes one may see the effort on the part of workers in art to surround themselves with objects which by their lines and color will contribute to the atmosphere that is the breath of life to creative art. One feels this at once on visiting the studios, or work-rooms, of artists. One feels a different standard of life and success, and coming perhaps directly from the active strivings of commercial pursuits, one seems to enter another world, with different ideals and better ambitions.[177]

Usually an artist's country retreat was not so sumptuous or compartmentalized as an urban habitation. Hence the "atmosphere" of the workroom pervaded the dwelling, which contained fewer fashion-conscious items and more mementos representative of personality, individual experiences, and affiliations.[178] The tiled living-room fireplace at White Pines, illustrated but not identified in Saylor's *Bungalows* (fig. 32), was personalized in its iconography and commemorative of the Whiteheads' Aldie sojourns in southeastern Pennsylvania. During one Aldie visit without her husband, Jane toured the Moravian Tile Works operated by Henry Mercer, William's brother. She recounted to Ralph:

> Harry was nicer than ever . . . I sat up in his room after the rest had dispersed from the drawing room and we had an old time talk. He had taken me all through his works in the afternoon & I had chosen a tile fireplace of greeny blue oblong small bricks with occasional square tiles with a design on them. Two birds and a fleur de lys.[179]

The conspicuous irregularities of Mercer's tiles simultaneously accorded with the preindustrial aura of the "aestheticizing studio" and the reform agenda of the English Arts and Crafts movement.[180] Handmade tiles were recommended in *Modern British Domestic Architecture and Decoration*, a special 1901 number of *The Studio*.[181] This was the only publication specifically cited by Jane or Ralph as a source used in the planning of White Pines.[182] The Whiteheads copied the atmosphere as opposed to the particulars of the interiors illustrated; however, the green paneling and long-stemmed purple blossom shown in their hall elevation (fig. 33) clearly owed a debt to a dining-room scheme for Winscombe house by M. H. Baillie Scott (fig. 34). He associated colors with emotional states; for example, green was a "normal," satisfying hue that balanced out accents of red, orange, or yellow, appealing to the animal instincts.[183] Blue and purple, on the other hand, conveyed spiritual superiority, and a room done in those tones radiated refinement.

The last essay in *Modern British Domestic Architecture and Decoration* argued for stylized interpretations of nature, which communicated the feeling of a scene or the essence of a botanical specimen.[184] Jane heeded the advice in developing a frieze destined for the family's living room. She reported to Ralph on January 21, 1903:

> ... worked in pastel on a conventionalized frieze of pine trees ... I found I c[oul]d get the result I was thinking of with 5 colours[,] 2 blues 2 greens & a red brown. There is an upper sky and a lower sky[,] hills[,] near trees & far trees. Each mass of things having a flat tint, & in some cases two tints, one over another, for instance the lighter green of the further trees coming down over the hills, under a tint of "upper blue." The furthest trees having under their own tint a green one of the sky above. The beauty of it will depend a good deal on the drawing.

She followed up on February 25, "Drew the pines again—you will help me with the real frieze."

Although an extant pencil elevation of the living room's north wall depicts trees above the chimneypiece, no physical evidence of a painted mural has yet been uncovered.[185] Jane could have been too exhausted to carry out the ambitious project when she finally transplanted herself to upstate New York in April 1903. According to her calendar, she was "ill in bed," "melancholy," and the boys were sick, or "bad," after the move. Over the previous nine months she had packed and shipped furnishings from California, refurbished and remodeled Arcady in preparation for tenants, and endured numerous temper tantrums from children and servants.[186] Nevertheless, the Whiteheads' correspondence over many years consistently labeled the first-floor room with the customized Mercer tiles as the "pine tree room."[187]

Possibly Jane and Ralph came to view the conceptualization of the frieze, and of some of the other decorations suggested in the "five pastel interiors" she had worked on in early January, as sufficiently rewarding in itself.[188]

fig. 34 M. H. Baillie Scott, from *The Studio*, 1901.

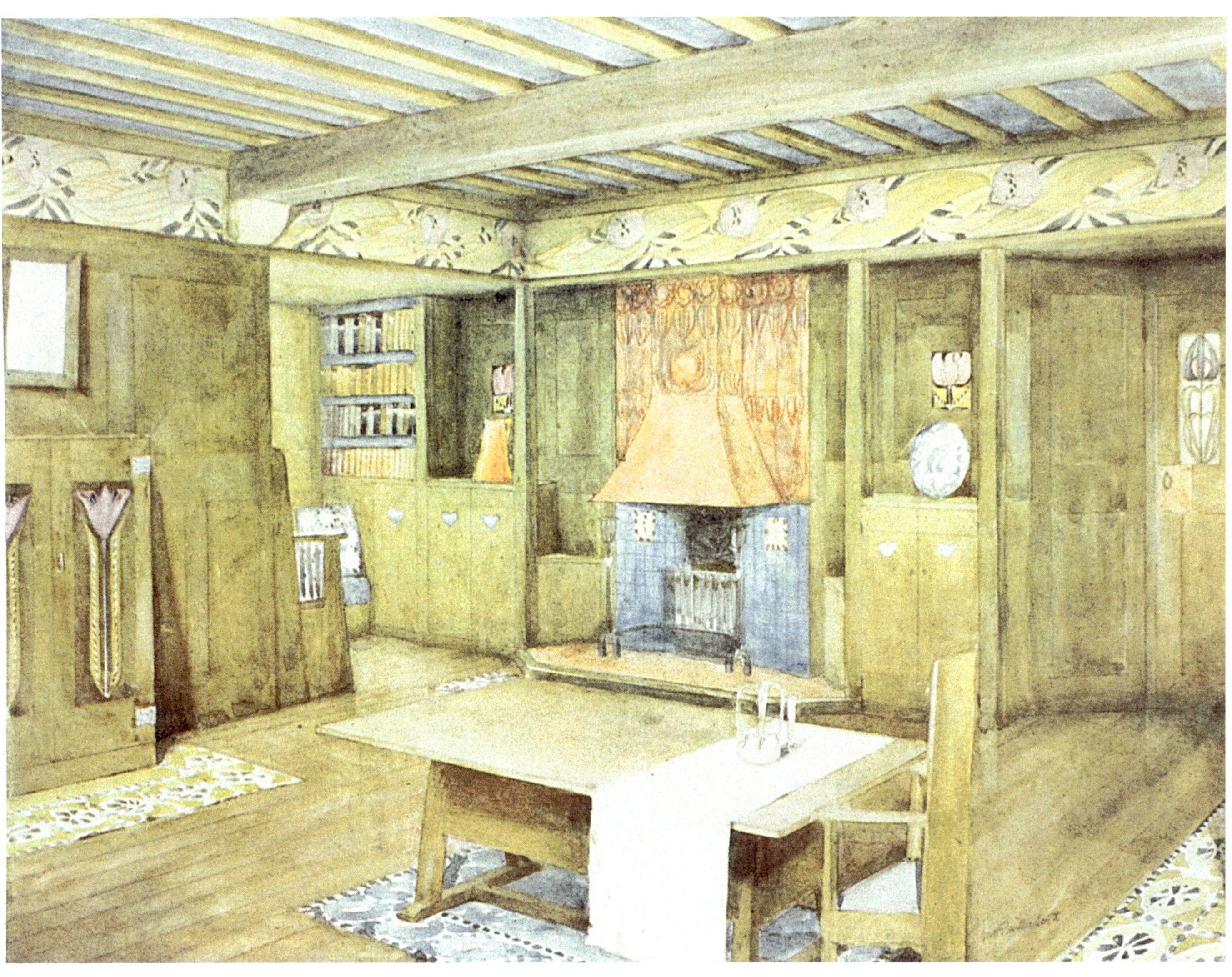

The Arts and Crafts movement, after all, did instruct its devotees to esteem process over product. Likewise, an aestheticized studio was really a work-in-progress, the design of which was supposed to foster reveries. From Arcady Jane mused to Ralph, in an undated letter seemingly written soon before she relocated to Byrdcliffe:

> The Studio is delightful now. I have made it over so to speak. Certainly the beauty of the place [Arcady] is great. The question of the possession of it comes to me often. One cannot possess anything material, & it passes from us—the sentiment of it & the experience it brought remains. We must not forget that. It was a great conception—this [Arcady] of yours.

Having existed in an aestheticized Tuscan idyll at Arcady, perhaps the Whiteheads actually began to "live" nature's beauty more fully at Byrdcliffe. The immediate experience of an ever-changing landscape—immersion in the moment—might yield greater fulfillment than the artifice of painted scenery. That message permeated Neroli, the Whiteheads' subsequent Montecito home (1912–26) (see pages 27 and 28)—simply built and appointed to foster communion with nature.[189] The following poem still graces the upper panel of a redwood door in the principal chamber:

> Listen to the Exhortation of the Dawn
> Look to This Day!
> For it is Life—the very Life of Life
> In its brief course lie all the
> Varieties and Realities of your Existence.
> The Bliss of Growth
> The Glory of Action
> The Splendour of Beauty
> For Yesterday is but a Dream
> & every Tomorrow is only a Vision
> But Today, Well-lived, makes
> Yesterday a dream of Happiness
> And every Tomorrow a vision of Hope
> Look well, therefore, to This Day,
> Such—is the Salutation of the Dawn[190]

Notes

1. This essay was a cooperative endeavor in that numerous colleagues, Winterthur librarians, and Byrdcliffe-affiliated staff, consultants, and collectors generously shared with me their expertise, insights, and comments, along with research notes, citations, and hard-to-come-by primary and secondary materials. I am particularly indebted to Robert Edwards, Nancy Green, Doug James, Evie Joselow, Arlette Klaric, Laura Parrish, Neil Larson, Rich McKinstry, David Schloerb, Bruce Smith, Carla Smith, Jeanne Solensky, Neville Thompson, Dot Wiggins, Mark Willcox, Tom Wolf, and Karen Zukowski. I am also grateful to the current occupants of Byrdcliffe cottages and of the Whiteheads' "Arcady" and "Neroli" properties in Montecito, California, who generously opened their houses for study. Jay Dooreck, Maria Herold, James Pattillo, Duffy and Maida Smith, and Harwood A. White Jr. merit special mention for facilitating my California investigations.

2. Bolton Brown, "Early Days at Woodstock," *Publications of the Woodstock Historical Society* 13 (August–September 1937): 4; Hervey White, "Woodstock in 1902—Enter the First Art Immigrants," typescript of paper read to the Woodstock Historical Society (1938), 1.

3. Depending on the context, subsequent references to "Arcady" may allude to either the main villa or the larger estate including subsidiary structures and gardens.

4. RRW to Jane, June 10, 1902: ". . . but the neighbors we know mean au fond as little to us as we do to them." When he was at Montecito seeking to sell Arcady (February 19, 1910), Ralph reiterated, "I would not want to bring up our boys here; the rich people who set the fashion have spoiled the life here. They drink and gamble at the club and the women play bridge in broad daylight. I stumbled into a tea party at the Eatons', which was just like the ones they used to have only more so. I could not live among these people who go round to teas and dinners all the time." Winterthur Library, Downs Collection. Arcady was sold in June 1911 to Union Carbide president George Knapp, who added a twelve-bedroom tower and formal water-gardens; it was published in Porter Garnett, *Stately Homes of California* (Boston: Little, Brown, & Co., 1915), 73–78.

5. Quotation in Neil Larson, "Historic Structures Report, White Pines, The Byrdcliffe Colony, Woodstock, NY," prepared by Argus Architecture & Preservation, P.C. (Troy, NY: October 2000), 5.

6. "A Plea for Manual Work," *Handicraft* 2/3 (June 1903): 59, 65.

7. "Woodstock of the Catskills and the Byrdcliffe Artists," *Christian Science Monitor*, January 8, 1924: 12. One of the seven farms purchased for the Byrdcliffe tract had belonged to the Snyders; it was renamed Camelot.

8. Alf Evers, *Woodstock: History of an American Town* (Woodstock: Overlook Press, 1987), 422, describes Whitehead's devotion to "the use of the tub." Whitehead believed, Evers continues, that "frequent bathing and brisk outdoor exercise helped account for the superiority of upper-class Britons. So every habitable structure at Byrdcliffe, however humble, had its bathroom, complete with an amply proportioned tub. The tubs were supplied by what [Hervey] White described as miles of water pipes running interminably under the soil of Byrdcliffe and in trenches cut through rocky ledges."

9. *Modern Painters by John Ruskin*, David Barrie, ed., vol. IV, *Of Mountain Beauty* (1856; reprint, London: Deutsch, 1987), 469.

10. *Modern Painters*, cited in *Ruskin Today*, Chosen and Annotated by Kenneth Clark (London: John Murray, 1964), 104–5.

11. The card catalogue from Byrdcliffe, in Winterthur Manuscripts 209, series 11, lists this discourse along with some seventy Ruskin titles—twice as many entries as for the second most popular author, William Morris.

12. Brown, "Early Days at Woodstock," 5–6.

13. The 1903 Byrdcliffe Summer Art School prospectus indicated, "It will be unique in being, not a temporary summer class, but an integral part of a permanent art village.... This is not a 'community,' but a welcome will be given to all true craftsmen, be they painters, musicians, writers, or what they may."

14. Whitehead owned a copy of this pamphlet, which is in the Winterthur Library, Downs Collection. Altogether there are six boxes of Ruskin lectures, poems, and articles.

15. *Modern Painters*, cited in *Ruskin Today*, 93.

16. RRW to Jane, June 5, 1902. Winterthur Library, Downs Collection.

17. A photograph is in W. G. Collingwood, *Ruskin Relics* (New York: T. Y. Crowell & Co., 1904), 5. On page 187, the author notes,

"Over the fire are no books, but as many pictures of the Brantwood study have shown, a della Robbia relief." White declared in "Woodstock in 1902," 7, that Ralph Whitehead's "first act" was to unpack the "image of the Virgin and Child and set it up in a shrine where his house was to be, and which still stands mysteriously by his grave."

18. Ruskin's first drawing of his house in the landscape (1871) and another of the domicile after additions are in James. S. Dearden, *Facets of Ruskin: Some Sesquicentennial Studies* (London: Chas. Skilton, 1970). See page 25 for Ruskin's correspondence with Thomas Carlyle about the environs: "It is a bit of steep hillside. . . . The slope is half copse, half moor and rock—a pretty field beneath, less steep—a white two-storied cottage, and a bank of turf in front of it—then a narrow mountain road and on the other side of that—Naboth's vineyard—my neighbor's field, to the water's edge."

19. Like White Pines, Müllersruhe, which will be identified hereafter as Eastover, once had a terraced garden. Grapevines still bear fruit on the western portion of the south façade of Serenata, one of the more commodious artists' cottages built along the edge of the forest (fig. 2, no. 25; and fig. 10). At Byrdcliffe's lower Riseley farm, the Lark's Nest (fig. 2, no. 5), frequented by Hervey White and his coterie, had vine-covered paths connecting the cabins and outbuildings; see Evers, *Woodstock*, 423.

20. *Modern Painters by John Ruskin*, 470–71.

21. Collingwood, *Ruskin Relics*, 4. "Ruskin's Chair" was the title for chapter 1; the book was in Byrdcliffe's library.

22. RRW to Jane, June 5, 1902. Winterthur, Library Downs Collection.

23. Woodstock Guild, Byrdcliffe walking tour brochure. Jane Whitehead moved into Yggdrasil after she was widowed, but it was originally the homestead of Hervey White and Fritz Van der Loo, the farm overseers, according to longtime Byrdcliffe craftswoman Bertha Thompson. An interior photograph is included with her unpublished typescript "Byrdcliffe—1904," Thompson family papers, Schlesinger Library. An exterior photograph is in Robert Edwards, "Byrdcliffe: Life by Design," in *The Byrdcliffe Arts and Crafts Colony* (Wilmington: Delaware Art Museum, 1984), 8.

24. Quoted in a description of the Ruskin Reading Guild's London-based journal, entitled "Igdrasil"; see Jeannine J. Falino, "Periodicals in Review 1880–1930," unpublished manuscript (Boston: Museum of Fine Arts, June 1984), 5.

25. Anita Smith, *Woodstock: History & Hearsay* (Woodstock: Stonecrop, 1959), 45.

26. RRW to Jane, September 12, 1912; citation and translation courtesy of Carla Smith. The motto was inscribed on the west-wall stuccoed fireplace, pictured in Larson, "Historic Structures Report," Appendix D, no. 75, and Winterthur Library, Down Collection.

Jane wrote to RRW on the same date, demanding as a prerequisite for returning to him "that you reduce your friendship with Miss Steele and Miss Walker to any ordinary acquaintance." She continued on November 4, "I found the situation at home all summer disagreeable, and at last I came away and left it. I know that you were vexed with me in NY for having talked with Miss Little of you." Winterthur Library, Downs Collection.

27. The nicknaming of intimates, often whimsically, was a persistent habit of Ruskin, according to Collingwood, *Ruskin Relics*, 224. Although a writer by the time he met Whitehead, White had grown up on a farm in Kansas. RRW to Jane, August 25, 1902: ". . . now I am going to Nicolo's farm. He and Fritz [Van der Loo] talk of a farm near us, and then I shant farm at all but rent them our fields [which] they will run and dairy and grow hay and corn for us."

28. "Morning Glories" was an alternate name for "Villetta." RRW asked Jane for advice, February 1, 1903: "The students boarding house could be 'Morning Glories' though I would rather find a shorter name. It should however have the sense of 'the morning' as it looks to the sunrise. How would 'Sunrise' do?" Winterthur Library, Downs Collection. "Sunrise" became the name of a smaller residence with three bedrooms (fig. 2, no. 37). Note that "Fleur de Lys" is sometimes spelled "Fleur-de-Lis."

29. S. F. A. Caulfield's *House Mottoes and Inscriptions: Old and New* (London: Elliott Stock, 1902) was in the Byrdcliffe library. The drawings are part of a group of hand-colored room suggestions on which Ralph and Jane evidently collaborated in the winter of 1902–3 (Winterthur Manuscripts 209, series 1). Jane confided to sister Gerty, December 26, 1902: "R and I are making decorations for the new house and are very busy."

A painting on canvas of three stalks of white "Madonna" lilies, symbolic of both virtue and motherhood, still adorns the lower portion of a master-bedroom door at the Whiteheads' "Neroli" home; it complements the Madonna-and-Child plaque framed into the nearby fireplace. Ralph contended in his essay "Tuscany to Venice," published in *Grass of the Desert* (London: Chiswick Press, 1892), 5: "It is the function of art to give expression to that which mere words cannot convey. . . . To take a simple instance in nature: the lily of the *Madonna* is to us something more than that which its classification by a botanist or the description of its growth by a gardener can ever tell us. They, as such, know nothing of the beauty of the lily."

Neroli was constructed shortly after the sale of Arcady. On July 2, 1911, the Santa Barbara *Morning Press* reported that Ralph Whitehead had "become re-enchanted with Montecito and will proceed with the improvement of his other properties here instead of selling them as planned." See also note 190.

30. RRW to Jane, August 12, 1901. Winterthur Library, Downs Collection.

31. Collingwood, *Ruskin Relics*, 9.

32. These were the captions for the two exterior photographs of White Pines included in Bigelow, "The Byrdcliffe Colony of Arts and Crafts," *American Homes and Gardens* 6/10 (October 1909): 389–90.

33. Annie Thompson, "Bertha and Byrdcliffe" (handwritten manuscript, Thompson family papers, Schlesinger Library), 20. Annie and her sister Bertha, a metalsmith and weaver, occupied Angelus for several summers after having lived in Serenata in 1908, Annie's first year at the Colony.

34. "Notes on Wood Stains from Encyclopedie—Roret—'Ebeniste' Paris," Winterthur Manuscripts 209, series 6. Encyclopédie Roret published manuals in the late nineteenth and early twentieth centuries on everything from the coloring and varnishing of metals and wood to iron founding, chair caning, sugar refining, and dry cleaning. Green and blue, as well as brown and gray, were prominent in the Byrdcliffe palette. Whitehead's notebook contained formulations for green from verdigris and copper sulfate, brown from walnut hulls, and gray from sumac. An indigo wood stain was obtained using sulfuric acid: "Warm acid in the sun, then add 8 parts acid to one indigo (powdered fine). Put in a glue pot for three hours boiling...add potash in quantity equal to indigo, leave for 24 hours—*this stain works very slowly.*"

35. Whitehead, "Modern Painters," in *Grass of the Desert*, 95. See also pages 14–15, where Whitehead quoted from *Stones of Venice* in his essay "Tuscany to Venice."

36. See Nikolaus Pevsner's summation of "Lamps" and other Ruskin writings in *Some Architectural Writers of the Nineteenth Century* (Oxford: Clarendon Press, 1972), especially pages 145, 151–52.

37. For illustrations, drawings, and a lengthy description of White Pines's floor plan, building materials, and the roof and façade treatments, consult Larson, "Historic Structures Report," 44–47, 64, 88, Appendices D–E.

38. "Notes to Review Plan A," Winterthur Library, Downs Collection.

39. An illustration of thatched cottages, at Baldon, is in Clifton Johnson, "The Charm of the English Country Cottage," *House & Garden* 4/1 (July 1903): 17. The Whiteheads owned this and other issues of *House & Garden* dating 1902–5.

40. "Notes to Review Plan A"; also "Bedroom No. 1," in Larson, Historic Structures Report, 81.

41. Naturalism is treated in *John Ruskin Selected Writings*, Philip Davis, ed. (London: J. M. Dent, 1995), 216–26. Bigelow's statement in "Byrdcliffe Colony," 392, resonated with the words of Ruskin's beloved William Wordsworth, whose *Guide through the District of Lakes* (1823) commended picturesque cottages and villas reminding "the contemplative spectator of a production of Nature and may . . . rather be said to have grown than to have been erected." Quotation found in Michael W. Brooks, *John Ruskin and Victorian Architecture* (New Brunswick: Rutgers University Press, 1987), 2–3.

42. *John Ruskin Selected Writings*, 217, 222.

43. Evers, *Woodstock*, 356.

44. Fleur de Lys today boasts vertical sheathing in the original bedroom interiors and horizontal boarding for the walls of the bathroom, closets, and the hallway between them. Shiplapping, meaning clapboarding that is beveled and overlapped to keep out water, was used on the outside of Yggdrasil, the large Studio, where art classes and exhibitions were held, and probably Carniola (destroyed by fire), but not on the exterior of Fleur de Lys, which was flush-board–sided

instead. The differences in construction might be indicative of the Colony's social hierarchy, as well as differing building crews or supervisors and year-round versus seasonal usage. Yggdrasil and Carniola, after all, were conceived as primary residences for White and Brown, respectively.

45. Quoted in Leland M. Roth, ed., *America Builds: Source Documents in American Architecture and Planning* (New York: Harper & Row, 1983), 108.

46. Evers, *Woodstock*, 160: "...until the 1960s there were still a few local men who had made hemlock shingles in the old way when they were young, and could show how it was done." Old wood shingles remain on one of the barn dovecotes.

47. On Whitehead's drawing, one of the building's outer doors exhibits diagonally boarded panels akin to Pattern B, door d, seen on another drawing labeled "Whitehead's Doors." This was the typical two-panel exterior door found at White Pines, according to Larson, "Historic Structures Report," 70. However, the actual Fleur de Lys doors represent the no. 2 sketch on a different drawing linked with the Loom Room, where Whitehead penciled in "flat panels running vertically." See fig. 11 for a door with two vertically boarded panels congruent with this drawing and notation. Both sheets of Whitehead's door designs are in the Winterthur Library, Downs Collection.

48. The bridge and its fenestration conjured up the weather-boarded sheds studded with multipaned windows at William Morris's Merton Abbey, where Whitehead had sought an apprenticeship before his marriage to Jane. Merton Abbey is illustrated in Philip Henderson, *William Morris: His Life, Work & Friends* (New York: McGraw Hill, 1967), pl. 50. Sliding windows with varying numbers of panes appeared in other Colony structures such as the barn, library, and Eastover. In a tripartite library grouping, the central 5/1 window slides over one of the stationary 4/1 side windows. Eastover's ample ground-floor studio features two east-facing pocket windows that slide into the wall on either side. The artistic desirability and possible origin of side-to-side sliding sash are discussed in Josephine Burleigh, "A Mountain Lodge," *American Home and Gardens* 8/11 (November 1911): 395. The article treats Ida Burgess's studio, located in Woodstock but not affiliated with Byrdcliffe: "...window openings were made wide rather than high with the old-time sliding sash of our Dutch forebears. Instead of the regulation upright window having pulleys and weights to raise the sash, these were built to slide back into the wall. . . . When open, these windows frame in bits of landscape that are veritable pictures in themselves."

49. See the Ruskin section in Roth, *America Builds*, 119.

50. Guild adherents were to work "with their hands and with such help of force as they can find in wind and wave." Electricity was installed at White Pines in 1914; see RRW to Ralph Jr., April 24. Winterthur Library, Downs Collection. He writes that Edwards, the chauffeur and mechanic, "has put in the electric light exceedingly well, but the lights are hardly strong enough & there are not enough of them to really light the rooms downstairs. . . ." Bigelow had mentioned the prohibition of automobiles in effect at Byrdcliffe in 1909. The first references to cars in the Whiteheads' correspondence occurred in 1912.

51. *Ruskin Relics*, 8–9.

52. Pevsner, *Some Architectural Writers*, 151.

53. Burroughs to "My Dear Friend" [RRW], August 30, 1905. Winterthur Library, Downs Collection. Contained in the same box are other letters from Burroughs (dated October 3, 1905, and January 2, 1906), a handwritten copy of Burroughs's poem "Waiting" (dated September 19, 1905), and a one-page endorsement of the simple life as manifested at Byrdcliffe. A one-room Byrdcliffe cabin across the road from Fleur de Lys was named "Wake Robin" (fig. 2, no. 23; and fig. 9), the title of Burroughs's first book (1871). Consult Elizabeth Burroughs Kelley, *John Burroughs's Slabsides* (Rhinebeck, NY: Moran Printing Co., 1974) for discussion and illustrations of the writer's retreat.

54. Whitehead returned to California in mid-June, leaving Brown, a native of upstate New York, to procure the farmland. Brown remembered Whitehead's directive: "If one of these farmers sees an Englishman in white flannels walking over his back fields, his price will double in the morning. I will put ten thousand dollars in the Kingston Bank to your credit, Mr. Brown, and leave you to do the buying." See Brown, "Early Days at Woodstock," 7.

55. "Ralph Radcliffe Whitehead," *Publications of the Woodstock Historical Society* 10 (August 1933): 21–22.

56. *Ruskin Relics*, 9; see also page 39: "Then suddenly forth of the wood you came upon the tennis-lawn—another concession to youthful visitors, for he played no athletic games. But in the creation of this glade he took the keenest delight, believing, as he said, in diggings of all sorts."

57. White, "Autobiography," 152–53; "Woodstock in 1902," 6–7. For plans, locations, and the siting of these buildings relative to each other, see fig. 2, nos. 1, 2, 7, 29; and fig. 9.

58. Brown, "Early Days at Woodstock," 11, chronicled how he handpicked the fireplace stones and kept the cement mortar from freezing by tending a fire all night for a week in zero-degree weather. White, "Autobiography," 153, recounted Whitehead's displeasure at Brown's choice of stone for his domicile, noting, "As it turned out, by the time the cellar was completed, Bolton found it had cost as much as he had planned for the whole house."

59. Brown, "Early Days at Woodstock," 10.

60. Smith, *Woodstock*, 1.

61. "The Woodstock Landscape," *Publications of the Woodstock Historical Society* 7 (July 1932): 20. Herrick was kept on as head of the woodworking shop, according to Edwards, "Byrdcliffe: Life by Design," 10.

62. "Bertha and Byrdcliffe," 31–32. Hillside is not within the confines of the Byrdcliffe property presently owned by the Woodstock Guild. In "Bought land and built my house" (unpublished manuscript, Thompson family papers, Schlesinger Library), 1, Bertha recalled, "Mr. Whitehead had made a fine road up to the flat below the site, and piped water from a spring at the top of my land."

63. "Bought land and built my house," 1.

64. RRW to Jane, August 25, 1902. Winterthur Library, Downs Collection.

65. RRW to Jane, January 25, 1903. Winterthur Library, Downs Collection.

66. RRW to Jane, October 23, 1902. Winterthur Library, Downs Collection.

67. White, "Autobiography," 152.

68. *Ibid.*, 154. Said White, "Bolton's enthusiasm was to receive its first check when Mr. Whitehead asked me to superintend the work of two houses; his own and the studio, Bolton's pet. I was reluctant. It was a job I was not fitted for, especially as I had not engaged the head carpenters and was not given authority to discharge them. Still, I was being paid a hundred dollars a month for other supervision and my time was not wholly taken up."

RRW to Jane, December 12, 1902: "I have taken the management of affairs entirely into my hands. The boss which I had is sick, Brown is incapable of being boss, and Nicolo with all the good will in the world can't manage as much as is going on here today. It stops next week, or rather is reduced to a small compass & then Nicolo who really helps me very much can manage the outside & Brown the inside work." Winterthur Library, Downs Collection.

69. Whitehead's "plans of fireplaces" differed from the rough boulder models Brown favored. Ralph preferred clean-lined stucco examples, combining the facing, mantelpiece, hood, and chimney flue into an integrated unit brought squarely into the room. The Villetta, Yggdrasil, Lark's Nest, and Loom Room chimneypiece designs were closely related. The Villetta surround was discretely decorated with tiles in the repeating cross pattern sketched, and numbered by color, on the back of an unlabeled chimneybreast drawing by Whitehead (catalogued as "Loom Room," Winterthur Library, Downs Collection). The Whitehead drawing for the west-wall Loom Room fireplace as built included an alternate elevation with a curved profile at the chimney base—like at Yggdrasil; for an illustration of the drawing, see Larson, "Historic Structures Report," Appendix C. Among the snapshots appended to Bertha Thompson's recollections are two marked "Lark's Nest," which highlighted the floor-to-ceiling stucco fireplace. The curved, beak-like profile of the mantel shelf approximated the one at Yggdrasil.

Whitehead may have derived certain of his ideas for fireplaces from adobe prototypes in California or the stucco work of modern British architects. A more direct influence was William Mercer, Jane's cousin, whose "Francis I Fireplace in the studio" was illustrated and so captioned in Oliver Coleman, "A Studio in Pennsylvania: The Workshop of Mr. Wm. S. Mercer, Jr.," *House Beautiful* 15/6 (May 1904): 365.

70. Collingwood, *Ruskin Relics*, 37, shows "Ruskin's Reservoir, Brantwood," complete with an artistically shaped handle for controlling a sluice gate. He elaborates on page 43, "One would have thought, sometimes, to see his eagerness over these inventions that he had missed his vocation; and he had indeed a keen admiration for

the civil engineer, wherever the road and bridge, mine and harbour, did not come into open conflict with natural beauties which he thought just as essential to human life as the material advantages of business."

71. David F. Myrick, *Montecito and Santa Barbara*, vol. 2: *The Days of the Great Estates* (Glendale, CA: Trans-Anglo Books, 1991), 510–11.

72. A letter from Vulcanite Paving in Philadelphia, July 14, 1904, referred to Whitehead's wanting to build a 100 x 50 ft. reservoir. Winterthur Library, Downs Collection. The White Pines standpipe is treated in Larson, "Historic Structures Report," 72. Collingwood, *Ruskin Relics*, 43, describes Ruskin's series of reservoirs at Brantwood as "useful in case of drought or fire."

73. White, "Autobiography," 162.

74. RRW to Jane, February 21, 1903. In a letter to her mother from Arcady, February 22, 1895, Jane described the process she and Ralph had adopted for designing furniture together. Her job was to sketch out the contours of table legs from books of decoration they had collected: "He gets a drawing board & pins up on it architectural paper & indicates the proportions. I then fill in, as a child does in a drawing book the table leg, which he takes to a mill or has turned." Winterthur Library, Downs Collection.

75. White portrayed Brown as a "disagreeable teacher of drawing" in "Autobiography," 145.

76. Brown, "Early Days at Woodstock," 10. Brown was not a self-effacing personality; the "we" in his statement bolsters Peter Whitehead's contention that the siting and basic design of the buildings were largely his father's, even if drafted by Brown. See Evers, *Woodstock*, 416; Clinton Adams, *Crayonstone: The Life and Work of Bolton Brown* (Albuquerque: University of New Mexico Press, 1993), 58. Apparently, Whitehead and Samuel Ilsley, his Arcady architect, had an analogous relationship, for Jane wrote to her mother in January 1895, "Ilsley is downstairs making architectural plans with Ralph." Winterthur Library, Downs Collection.

77. The boarding house might be Eastover; in any case, Byrdcliffe's 1903 prospectus promised, "There will be two boarding-houses on the property of Byrdcliffe in which board and lodging can be obtained. In one of them the charge will be $6.00 per week. Accommodation at a lower rate can be had at farm houses in the district." Which "farmhouse" Whitehead had in mind to alter is difficult to ascertain because seven former farms comprised the Byrdcliffe estate.

The "barn" could mean the combined livestock, granary, and vehicular storage facilities listed as "The Farm" on the Byrdcliffe map (see fig. 2, no. 4). A rudimentary barn elevation is in the Winterthur Library, Downs Collection. The "barn" might have been connected with Lark's Nest, where Hervey White and his chums gathered. White, "Autobiography," 157, reported their procuring the "best farmhouse on the property . . . [and] joined it to one of the barn buildings." Among the architectural drawings at Winterthur is a plan for the first and second floors of a home similar in size and configuration to Lark's Nest. The plan focuses on the kitchen and a combination living-dining area—they are the only spaces sketched with furniture. The latter is outfitted with a central table seating eight and a semicircular grouping of chairs around a substantial fireplace, flanked on the right by a long wall bench. A kindred furnishings scheme is documented at Lark's Nest by a photograph in the Winterthur Library, Downs Collection.

Ralph and Jane carried on a dialogue about the arrangements for the family's rooms on the second floor of White Pines. Room assignments were still undecided in mid January 1903. Ralph wrote Jane on January 18, referring to "her plan," which has not survived. Evidently she had expressed a preference for the middle bedroom. Ralph responded, "I took Nicolo up there yesterday to talk it over. He agrees that though the middle room is a good room you will like the S.W. room with the western window better for your room." Jane wrote back on January 21, "Do the rooms as you think best on the spot. If you don't follow my suggestions I shant mind . . . ." The elevation drawing of "Mrs. R. W.'s room—E. wall," with built-in cupboard dimensions noted, is for the southwest room; illustrated in Larson, "Historic Structures Report," Appendix C. Although Brown probably did the drafting, the marginalia appear to be Ralph's.

78. *Woodstock*, 45–46.

79. Loom Room elevations, sections, floor plan, fireplace and door sketches in Whitehead's hand are in the Winterthur Library, Downs Collection. In 1912, Whitehead enlarged the back dining room at White Pines without enlisting an architect's services (RRW to Jane, September 12). In the same year, Neroli—the Whiteheads' Montecito bungalow erected on land originally bought to supply water for Arcady—surfaced for the first time in the couple's correspondence. | A pen-and-ink drawing at Winterthur, labeled "Suggestion of Front Elevation of our house," shows projecting, cross-gabled end pavilions paralleling those at Neroli. The connecting middle section of the home as executed, however, is more rambling, more ranchlike than the depiction in the sketch.

80. *Art and Handicraft* (London: Kegan Paul, Trench, Trübner & Co., Ltd., 1893; reprint, New York: Garland, 1977), 166–67. Sedding trained in the office of George Edmund Street, whose pupils included William Morris and Philip Webb.

81. Quoted in Alf Evers, Foreword to Michael Perkins, *Woodstock Guild and its Byrdcliffe Arts Colony: A Brief Guide* (Woodstock: Woodstock Guild, 1991), 13. Ashbee came to Byrdcliffe in 1915. Whitehead had visited him in June 1901, and bought two silver cups for his sons (see fig. 32 for an Ashbee-designed cup above the fireplace on the left). The boys' births prompted Ralph to comment to Jane on June 21, 1901, "To be a country gentleman is no longer sufficing."

82. According to his daughter May, William Morris viewed Kelmscott Manor, his country house, as his one true home: "No house in London could ever be invested with the passionate delight he had in our dear riverside home, the home of his dreams, with its poet's garden." Cited in Wendy Hitchmough, *The Arts & Crafts Home* (London: Pavilion Books, 2000), 37.

Ashbee moved his Guild of Handicraft from London to the pastoral Cotswolds in 1902. "All the work we do can, I am convinced, be better done in the country," Ashbee wrote. He went on to endorse the healthfulness of transplanting London workmen to the countryside to engage in some agricultural activity. He credited Ruskin's neo-feudal Guild of St. George for attempting such reform; he suggested its failure was due to timing, insufficient resources, and being too small in scale. Ashbee was ready to try again in the new century: "Perhaps some day, some English landlord who has watched...his farms dying away, & his small tenantry and labourers gradually dispersed, may hold out the hand to us [the Guild], & make it possible for us to carry out our works in combination with some form of agriculture by small holdings, market gardening, or co-operative farming." See C. R. Ashbee, *A Few Chapters in Workshop Reconstruction and Citizenship* and *An Endeavor Towards the Teaching of Ruskin & Morris* (London: Essex House Press, 1894/1901; reprint, New York: Garland, 1978), 39.

83. Quotation found in Hitchmough, *The Arts & Crafts Home*, 37.

84. "Ralph Radcliffe Whitehead," 20. White told the same story but with different wording in his "Autobiography," 147. There Whitehead asked only for a "distant glimpse" of the sea.

85. White, "Autobiography," 119–20; Evers, *Woodstock*, 409.

86. The 1907 Byrdcliffe prospectus spelled out two provisos. First, no hotel, saloon, or factory was allowed. Second, when the purchaser wished to sell, the owner of Byrdcliffe had the right to buy back the lot at a price determined by arbiters. Bertha Thompson's handwritten deed is in the Winterthur Library, Downs Collection. She actually built in the West Riding, having acquiesced to Whitehead's request to exchange her initial plot.

Albert and Mary Webster were renters at Byrdcliffe as early as 1904. She was interested in progressive causes and communal experiments. By 1910, the couple had decided to commit to a parcel in the East Riding. On May 10, Whitehead answered their questions about the real estate covenant and negotiation of a repurchase agreement. "Yes, I shall make identical or *more stringent* regulations for other purchasers of land in the East Riding," he wrote; "I can think of no better way as to the appointment of a third arbiter than the one I have suggested, which is an usual one in Europe." He continued, "I am open to suggestions as to restrictions being limited to a long term of years instead of perpetuity." They finally settled on a deed specifying a fifty-year time frame. The Webster data is courtesy of Carla Smith.

87. "Leaders in American Arts and Crafts," *Good Housekeeping* 44/2 (February 1907): 148.

88. Hitchmough, *The Arts & Crafts Home*, 15. Gertrude Jekyll, *Old West Surrey: Some Notes and Memories* (London: Longman's Green & Co., 1904), 6, underscored the "pictorial value" of "the older cottages." Her *Wood and Garden* (1899) was in the Byrdcliffe library. An illustration and discussion of historic terraces from Gloucestershire, Cambridgeshire, and Lincolnshire, can be found in Olive Cook, *English Cottages and Farmhouses* (London: Thames and Hudson, 1982), 83.

89. Lawrence Weaver, *The "Country Life" Book of Cottages Costing from £150 to £600* (London: Country Life, Ltd., 1913), chapter XI. On page 203, he illustrates an Ashbee-designed block of four dwellings at Catbrook, Campden. The photograph shows two picturesque cross gables, a feature Whitehead also utilized at Byrdcliffe and Neroli, his home in Montecito during the first and second decades of the twentieth century. Ashbee produced his own *Book of Cottages and Little Houses* in 1906.

90. Bigelow, "Byrdcliffe Colony," 393. "Serenata," sometimes spelled "Serenada," derives from "serenade," a musical composition for a small ensemble. The extant cottage is an "ensemble" of three separate bedrooms, each with independent outside access. Yggdrasil likewise provides direct egress outdoors from the two ground-floor bedrooms. Its east façade sports dual gables, one of several traits the building shared with "A Bungalow of Irregular Form and Unusually Interesting Features," published in Gustav Stickley's *Craftsman* magazine, April 1907: "The house is somewhat irregular in design, but is so admirably proportioned and planned that the broken lines impress one as they do when seen in some old English house that has grown into its present shape through centuries of alteration in response to changing needs."

91. Ricardo to RRW, March 10, 1915. Winterthur Library, Downs Collection. Some of the earliest correspondence from Ralph to Jane mentioned his friend Ricardo; for example, RRW to Jane, April 27, 1891. Among the Whiteheads' possessions was a Ricardo-designed stylized landscape executed in ceramic tile by William De Morgan.

Like Ricardo, Whitehead worried about the financial feasibility of Arts and Crafts reform projects. RRW to Jane, February 22, 1903: "It is an important question in the development of our [Byrdcliffe] scheme to make the industries pay their expenses. I don't put a profit except a small interest on the capital invested in the industry itself—not in the land or the studio building. But the men who work for us have to be paid out of the proceeds of the industry and the men include the designers."

92. Brown, "Early Days at Woodstock," 13.

93. William Claiborne dubbed White Pines a "manor house" in "Byrdcliffe at Crossroads: Utopian Art Colony in the Face of Reality," *The Washington Post*, March 16, 1976: B13 (partial copy, courtesy of Tom Wolf). Karal Ann Marling used the "sprawling manor house" phrase in her introduction to *Woodstock: An American Art Colony*, 1902–77 (Poughkeepsie, NY: Vassar College Art Gallery, 1977), unpaged copy. Nick Evers, "Byrdcliffe's heritage is difficult to grasp," *Tempo* (March 11 1970): 6, maintained that Jane "made life tedious for some on Sunday afternoon when she summoned the artists and crafts people in residence for Morris dancing on the lawn of White Pines...some ruminated that Jane played the role of lady of the manor with too heavy a hand."

94. Frank Miles Day, preface to *American Country Houses of Today* (New York: Architectural Book Publishing Co., 1912), p. iv. He claimed that an American looking at the plan of a modern English house would be struck by its allocation of half or more of the first floor to kitchen, scullery, larders, store rooms, and other servant spaces. The Englishman, he continued, would be just as surprised to find these departments compressed in American homes of similar size, due to the higher wages and relatively fewer numbers of servants available in the United States.

95. Quoted in Jill Franklin, *The Gentleman's Country House and Its Plan, 1835–1914* (London: Routledge & Kegan Paul, 1981), 103.

96. Winterthur Library, Downs Collection; also Larson, "Historic Structures Report," 55, 57, and Appendix C. Whitehead and LeBoutillier both had ties to the Society of Arts and Crafts, Boston, but little else is known about their relationship. Ralph on his own enlarged the subsidiary dining area during Jane's absence in 1912, reporting to her on September 12, "the improvement in the back dining-room is a very great improvement. It is so much brighter and larger. The 2½ feet have made a great difference...."

97. Larson, "Historic Structures Report," 70, 79. Various first- and second-floor rooms in the rear half of the house are now painted. A scientific analysis of the finishes and paint history has not yet been undertaken. See also Winterthur Library, Downs Collection.

98. Hitchmough, *The Arts & Crafts Home*, 140. Franklin, *Gentleman's Country House*, 19, contends Voysey had more success in garnering Arts and Crafts country-house commissions than contemporaries like W. R. Lethaby, C. R. Macintosh, and M. H. Baillie Scott.

99. Elric Endersby, Alexander Greenwood, and David Larkin, *Barn: The Art of a Working Building* (Boston: Houghton Mifflin, 1992), 10. William N. Van Kleeck, whose family came to Byrdcliffe in 1951 to manage the agricultural operations, explained the layout and specialized aspects of the farm on a tour with the author (October 20, 2002).

100. Myrick, *Montecito and Santa Barbara*, vol. 2, 305. Whitehead purchased another twenty-eight acres by October 1894, and then an additional 250 acres in 1896, to ensure an adequate water supply for his home and gardens.

101. This enumeration of essential characteristics of a country estate appeared on a print entitled *Oxen Hoath, Seat of Leonard Bartholomew, Esq.*, engraved by Johannes Kipp, London, ca. 1715. It was shown in the 2001–2 Winterthur Museum exhibition "Life at Winterthur, 1902–51."

102. Sanborn, "Leaders in American Arts and Crafts," 148. Perkins, *Woodstock Guild and its Byrdcliffe Art Colony*, 25, puts the number of volumes at seven thousand. Bolton Brown's wife fondly recalled, "I read William Morris then, out of that library in the beautiful Kelmscott edition." See Lucy Brown, "The First Summer in Byrdcliffe, 1902–3," *Publications of the Woodstock Historical Society* 2 (August 1930): 20.

In his foreword to the Folger Shakespeare Library exhibition catalogue *The Compleat Gentleman: Books from English Country Houses* (1985), 7, director Werner Gundersheimer stated: "London, Florence, and Rome are remarkably comparable during their periods of high literary attainment, in that a strong symbiotic relationship connects the metropolis to the countryside. The intensity, the competitiveness, the risk of the cities come to be offset—in imagination as well, perhaps, as in reality—by the bucolic serenity and pastoral tranquility which writers and their patrons located in the Roman *compagna*, the Tuscan villa, and the English country house. In all of these settings, the book held an honored place, for it helped to fashion 'The Compleat Gentleman.'"

103. Burroughs to RRW, August 30, 1905.

104. The Morris citation and the attributes of barns in the Middle Ages are taken from Endersby, Greenwood, and Larkin, *Barn*, 12–13, 26, 29. Only the interior framing at Great Coxwell was timber; the outer walls were stone. A late sixteenth- or early seventeenth-century wood-sided barn, complete with protruding porch entrance, survives at the Weald and Downland Museum in southern England. English barns traditionally had the principal entryway on a long wall; whereas Continental barns tended toward gable-end entries.

105. Evers, *The Catskills*, 622; Smith, *Woodstock*, 46.

106. Cook, *English Cottages and Farmhouses*, 33.

107. Endersby, Greenwood, and Larkin, *Barn*, 112–13.

108. Bigelow, "Byrdcliffe Colony," 392.

109. Since the Webbs had started their model farm in Vermont several years before Biltmore was begun, Vanderbilt was probably influenced by their undertaking. The Webbs' five-story farm barn, topped by a miniature clock-tower cupola, contained stalls for eighty teams of horses and mules, estate-management offices, and various shops for blacksmiths, carpenters, and painters. See the illustration in Joe Sherman, T*he House at Shelburne Farms: The Story of one of America's Great Country Estates* (Middlebury: Paul S. Eriksson, 1986), 23. For an overview of Biltmore, consult Susan M. Ward and Michael K. Smith, eds., *Biltmore Estate* (Asheville: The Biltmore, Co., 1989). On craft endeavors, starting with woodcarving at Biltmore Village's Boys Club in 1901, see Kelly H. L'Ecuyer, "Uplifting the Southern Highlander: Handcrafts at Biltmore Estate Industries," *Winterthur Portfolio* 37/2-3 (Summer–Autumn 2002): 131–41. Closer to Byrdcliffe, Frederick Vanderbilt established a gentleman's farm at Hyde Park.

110. Harvey H. Kaiser, *Great Camps of the Adirondacks* (Boston: David R. Godine, 1982), 65, 183–87.

111. *Ibid.*, 65.

112. "The First Summer in Byrdcliffe," 19. RRW to Jane, February 1, 1903, referred to "Kelly's farm[,] which is what we called the casino for fun." Winterthur Library, Downs Collection.

113. Larson, "Historic Structures Report," 46, gives a brief account of the double walling but does not suggest any prototype in an American or European context. Ice houses do provide a precedent; they are discussed in William S. Wicks, *Log Cabins and Cottages: How to Build and Furnish Them*, 4th ed. (New York: Forest & Stream, 1900), 41.

114. Craig Gilborn, formerly affiliated with the Adirondack Museum, suggested a "double frame cottage" was most likely a log structure with a secondary frame to support the interior sheathing;

telephone conversation with the author, December 23, 2002. Waldon Fawcett, "Houses in the Woods," *House Beautiful* 12 (July 1902): 75, explained that Durant's inner roof, sheeted and tinned, was separated by an air space from the shingled outer roof. Perhaps Whitehead was familiar with double roofs in California to ward off heat. They were installed on early cottages at Santa Barbara's San Ysidro Ranch, where Arcady architect Samuel Ilsley had been engaged to draw plans for a small hotel in 1892. See Myrick, *Montecito and Santa Barbara*, vol. 1: *From Farms to Estates* (Glendale, CA: Trans-Anglo Books, 1987), 98–99.

115. Kaiser, *Great Camps*, 90; Craig Gilborn, *Adirondack Furniture and the Rustic Tradition* (New York: Harry N. Abrams, 1987), 65. White Pines, too, was finished with wainscot and burlap in some areas.

116. Kaiser, *Great Camps*, 91.

117. Cited by Michael Wilson, "Bewildered: The Origin and Future of the Adirondack Great Camps," lecture for Victorian Society Metropolitan Chapter, New York (January 18, 2000). Wilson credited Applegate with coining the term "great camps." See Applegate's three studies (*The Story of Minnowbrook*, *The Story of Pinebrook*, and *The Story of Sagamore*) published by Syracuse University in 1962.

Stick furniture of the Indiana "Old Hickory" sort, often encountered on Adirondack verandas, bedecked the porch of White Pines (fig. 7). There was a rustic bridge by the della Robbia shrine (fig. 3), reminiscent of an example at Brantwood described in Collingwood, *Ruskin Relics*, 32.

118. Illustrated in Bigelow, "Byrdcliffe Colony," 390. Only the ruined fireplace remains after a fire at Carniola in 1964. Whitehead's initial handwritten specifications for White Pines had called for "fireplaces plain rock." Those actually installed were more refined—done in brick, tile, or plaster. The specifications, titled "Notes to Review Plan A," are in the Winterthur Library, Downs Collection.

119. "Leaders in American Arts and Crafts," 148. Claiborne reported, "Byrdcliffe looks like a fading Adirondack hunting camp," in "Byrdcliffe at Crossroads," B1.

120. Gilborn, *Adirondack Furniture*, 53. Fawcett, "Houses in the Woods," 69, maintained that "restful simplicity . . . constitutes the chief charm of the perfect woodland haven, and thus it comes about that the wealthy man's lodge, if constructed in accordance with refined artistic taste and with a proper regard for the eternal fitness of things, does not differ greatly, save in detail, from that of his neighbor who is possessed of less of this world's goods."

121. Jane's calendar for July 1897, when she was with Ralph in Keene, has an entry for "Miss Little" on the 20th. Jane's calendars dating between 1885 and 1935 are in the Winterthur Library, Downs Collection. White, "Autobiography," 165, mentioned Little as a neighbor of the Martins and a Davidson aficionado. RRW to Jane, September 24, 1901, assessed the Martins ("Too much is of 'reform' about them.") as well as Little. "It's a pleasure," Ralph declared, "to escape to Miss Little's hut to see the colors of her warps. They refresh me after a desert of intellectualism." Winterthur Library, Downs Collection.

122. Later, while visiting her family in Pennsylvania, May 25, 1901, RRW wrote Jane, "They and others seem to think that our best plan would be to have a place in the Adirondacks and then to go for three months to the sea or to the pines down south." Winterthur Library, Downs Collection.

123. Kaiser, *Great Camps*, 66, illustrates the same lodge drawing but captions it "Honnedaga Lodge, a Wicks design for the Adirondack League Club." Another Wicks perspective, labeled "Cottage in Herkimer County N.Y." in *Log Cabins and Cottages*, relates to the dormer treatment of the Looms. Sanborn, who linked Byrdcliffe's architecture to Adirondack prototypes, selected the Looms as the sole architectural illustration for the Colony in "Leaders in American Arts and Crafts," 147. An elevation resembling the front façade of the Looms is among the Whitehead papers at Winterthur (series 1).

124. Ramon M.ª Puig, *Mountain Houses*, trans. Graham Thomson (Barcelona: Editorial Gustavo Gili, S.A., 1991), 8.

125. Paul Malo, "Adirondack Architecture and the Culture of Exurbia," in *Forever Wild: The Adirondack Experience* (Katonah, NY: Katonah Museum of Art, 1991), 25–26. Adirondack camp builders had an affinity for the chalets of the Bernese Oberland, according to Kaiser, *Great Camps*, 77, 109.

126. A. and E. Varin, *The Picturesque Architecture of Switzerland* (Boston: J. R. Osgood, 1875), 9.

127. Kata Phusin [John Ruskin], *The Poetry of Architecture: Cottage, Villa, Etc.* (New York: John W. Lovell Co., ca. 1873), 25–26. The book is a series of articles Ruskin wrote for Louden's *Architectural Magazine*, 1837–38, using the penname Kata Phusin (Greek for "according to nature").

128. Wendell G. Corthell, "The Use of Wood in Switzerland," *Craftsman* 5/1 (October 1903): 35.

129. RRW to Jane, August 11, 1891. Winterthur Library, Downs Collection.

130. White, "Autobiography," 136–37.

131. RRW to Jane, May 11, 1902. Winterthur Library, Downs Collection.

132. Adams, *Crayonstone*, 20–23.

133. "Byrdcliffe, Woodstock, Ulster County, New York, 'Gateway to the Catskills,'" Winterthur Manuscripts 209, series 6. On the use of stone, see Jean Schopfer, "Swiss Chalets II," *Architectural Record* 7/1 (July–September 1897): 40.

134. White, "Ralph Radcliffe Whitehead," 19–20.

135. *Handbook for Travelers in Southern Germany: Being a Guide to Wurtemberg, Bavaria, Austria, Tyrol, Salzburg, Styria, & c., the Austrian and Bavarian Alps, and the Danube from Ulm to the Black Sea* (London: John Murray, 1867), 405.

136. A. S. Levetus, "Austria, Introduction," in *Peasant Art in Austria and Hungary*, Charles Holme, ed. (London: The Studio, Ltd., 1911), 8.

137. RRW to Jane, June 5, 1902: "Our house then 'White Pines' and the 'company's' house 'Boscoverde' shall it be, or just 'Silva'?" Winterthur Library, Downs Collection.

138. RRW to Jane, December 2, 1902. Winterthur Library, Downs Collection.

139. Werner Blaser, *Fantasy in Wood: Elements of Architectural Style, c. 1900* (Basel: Birkhäuser Verlag, 1987), 7.

140. Endersby, Greenwood, and Larkin, *Barn*, 58, 74.

141. Jean Schopfer, "Wooden Houses in Switzerland," *Architectural Record* 6/4 (April–June 1897): 423.

142. *Ibid.*, 416.

143. Schopfer, "Swiss Chalets II," 46, 48–50. The 1896 Geneva Exposition created a sensation and was reprised at the Exposition Universelle held in Paris in 1900. See Albert Lévy, "Le chalet, lieu de mémoire helvétique," in *Le chalet dans tous ses états: La construction de l'imaginaire helvétique* (Geneva: Éditions Chênoises, 1999), 95. Whitehead was in Europe in 1896, but tracking his itinerary through correspondence with Jane is difficult because the couple's relationship was troubled at the time.

144. Schopfer, "Swiss Chalets II," 50.

145. "Wooden Houses in Switzerland," 426. Schopfer elaborated, "It [the frame] does not merely surround the window, but extends below it as far as the floor, thus giving it a larger place in the *ensemble* of the façade." The west-wall seat of the White Pines living room is illustrated in Larson, "Historic Structures Report," Appendix D, no. 31. The bench in the library at the Studio also neatly aligns with the wood frame surrounding a group of three south-facing windows at the western end of the room.

146. Larson, "Historic Structures Report," 48, referenced Voysey's "Remarks on Domestic Entrance Halls," published in *The International Studio* in 1901. See the illustration of the staircase at The Orchard, Chorley Wood, in Charles Holme, ed., *Modern British Domestic Architecture and Decoration* (London: The Studio, 1901), which Whitehead owned.

147. The McGrew stairwell configuration appeared consistently in Maybeck's ensuing work, according to Kenneth H. Cardwell, *Bernard Maybeck: Artisan, Architect, Artist* (Santa Barbara and Salt Lake City: Peregrine Smith, 1977), 69.

148. "The Swiss Chalet Type for America," *House & Garden* 20/5 (November 1911): 292. Maybeck's Rees house (Berkeley, 1906) was captioned ". . . built from a model executed in Switzerland. The [protruding] timber ends and balconies show a similar construction to those in the [Swiss] picture above." Cardwell, *Maybeck*, 105, stressed that those details were the only aspects of the Rees dwelling borrowed directly from the owner-supplied Swiss prototype.

149. Sleeping porches were not a Maybeck invention per se although he introduced them to Berkeley. Consult Dimitri Shipounoff, Introduction to Charles Keeler, *The Simple Home* (San Francisco: Paul Elder, 1904; reprint, Santa Barbara and Salt Lake City: Peregrine Smith, 1979), xxiv. Maybeck's homes were closely allied with the "California bungalow" house type; however, Henry H. Saylor defined true bungalows as one-story structures in *Bungalows*

(New York McBride Winston & Co., 1911), 9, 45. Yet Saylor (29, 31) made the Swiss chalet the third of his ten bungalow classifications: "The chalet in Switzerland is by no means confined to one floor, so that it is not surprising to find the American development of this building making more of the attic than in the true bungalow type." While architects Charles and Henry Greene are frequently credited with developing the California redwood boarded-and-shingled chalet, Maybeck was working in this mode earlier. See Cheryl Robertson, "The Resort to the Rustic: Simple Living and the California Bungalow," in Kenneth R. Trapp, *The Arts and Crafts Movement in California: Living the Good Life* (New York: Abbeville Press, 1993), 101–4, for an analysis of bungalows in general, their Swiss characteristics, and their great popularity in southern California during 1905–15.

150. The Villetta and Eastover had sleeping balconies as well. Figure 7 was published without identification in T. E. Whittlesey, "Building a Sleeping-porch," *House & Garden* 17/1 (January 1910): 44; and Frederick N. Reed, "The Problem of the Sleeping Porch," *House & Garden* 25/6 (June 1914): 462. The respective captions were, "Be sure the sleeping porch connects with a warm dressing-room," and "The designer of this house has succeeded in making a sleeping porch which is an integral part of the house and does not spoil its architectural scheme."

151. Whitehead, in fact, spent most of July in Oregon; on July 24, from Alsea, Oregon, Ralph informed Jane he was preparing to come home. Her calendar noted a trip to San Francisco on New Year's Eve, 1900. She also logged previous visits there on October 18, 1895, and July 23, 1896. "Oakland" was mentioned on July 24.

152. Ludwig Boltzmann, "Summer in Berkeley—1904," trans. Irene Jerison, *Westways* 68/9 (September 1976): 78.

153. *The Simple Home*, 13, 15, 32. Whitehead and Keeler had much in common. The latter founded a Ruskin Club and a Morrisian press christened "Sign of the Live Oak." Both men were friends of John Burroughs. With his wife, Louise, Keeler created a home-based Arts and Crafts guild to produce their own furniture designs for sale. Consult Shipounoff, Introduction to *The Simple Home*, xxv, xxxi-ii, xxxvi. The Keelers may have visited or corresponded with the Whiteheads because a sketch of Arcady headed the "Santa Barbara" chapter of the guidebook they compiled for the Santa Fe Railway. See Charles A. Keeler, *Southern California, Illustrated with Drawings from Nature and from Photographs by Louise M. Keeler* (Chicago: H. O. Shepard Co. for the Santa Fe Passenger Department, 1902), 121.

Paul Elder served as publisher for Keeler's *The Simple Home* and Whitehead's essay "Pictures for Schools" (1901). The latter was printed by Stanley-Taylor Co., a firm Elder often used (David Mostardi to author, July 22, 2003). RRW to Jane, July 26, 1901: ". . . write to Elder and Shepherd [*sic*] to have that bookplate made from the block used for my pamphlet." Elder was in partnership with Morgan Shepard from 1898–1903.

154. Quoted in Cardwell, *Maybeck*, 66. This house burned and was replaced by a second Maybeck design in 1899.

155. The quotation, though uttered by Keeler in regard to his own abode, aptly summarized Brown's dwelling. Cited in Shipounoff, Introduction to *The Simple Home*, xxi. On Whitehead's visiting the Browns in Palo Alto, probably in the winter of 1901–2, consult Adams, *Crayonstone*, 53.

156. E. A. Needles, "A Little House with Five Fireplaces," *House Beautiful* 21/5 (April 1907): 23–24.

157. Karen Weitze, "Utopian Place Making: The Built Environment in Arts and Crafts California," in Trapp, *The Arts and Crafts Movement in California*, 62. Brown's drawing titled *The New Homie*, along with an excerpt about the domicile from a letter he sent to his aunt, June 7, 1898, is in Adams, *Crayonstone*, 48.

158. Bigelow, "Byrdcliffe Colony," 389; "Edwardian redwood," appeared in Claiborne, "Byrdcliffe at Crossroads," B1, and Marling, *Woodstock*, n.p.

159. *Bungalows*, 37. Arcady's next owner retained the Giglio but renamed it the Hut; see Garnett, *Stately Homes of California*, 75. The present rustic dwelling across the street from the remodeled stucco villa preserves the spirit, if not the actual fabric, of the Giglio. The Arcady estate was subdivided in 1951, according to correspondence from R. A. Miller, Librarian, Santa Barbara Historical Society, to Mark Willcox, May 1, 1981.

160. Tornoe, who subsequently became known as an Arts and Crafts metalsmith, had been in Germany during 1897. Upon his return he built a chalet-studio along the lines of the school. Both structures are pictured in Cleek, "Tale of Two Studios," 62, 64. Later, Frederick Hürten Rhead, with whom Jane studied ceramics, set up shop on Tornoe's property. Rhead Pottery was incorporated in 1914; Tornoe and Ralph Whitehead were shareholders.

161. These architectural elements are illustrated in a deteriorated photograph, mounted in an album, in Winterthur Manuscripts 209, series 7.

162. On "our California custom of entering the living room directly from the front door," see Bungalowcraft Co., *California Bungalow Homes* (Los Angeles, 1910): 93. The self-styled "Bungalow Man" Henry L. Wilson pinpointed ten California bungalow determinants, including broad door and window openings, fenestration in groupings of three or more units, the "artistic subdivision of windows" into multiple panes of glass, and pergolas of rough-sawn pine. See "The California Bungalow: What It Is, What It is Not, and What It May Be," *Bungalow Magazine* 1/4 (June 1909): 117–18.

163. "Design for school door" is written in Jane's calendar for November 18, 1898. The ornamentation relates to the grape carving on an historic door shown in the Whitehead-owned *Die Zimmergotik in Deutsch-Tirol* (Leipzig: E. A. Seeman, 1889–1900), pl. 2. The two-volume publication is in Winterthur Manuscripts 209, series 3. A mural study by Lester is illustrated in color in Robert Edwards, "Arcady to Byrdcliffe: The Whiteheads' Circle of Artists" (Boston: James R. Bakker Gallery, 1999), n.p.

164. Whitehead, *Grass of the Desert*, 6.

165. He continued in a postscript, "We might make a dining room like that at Arcady but smaller . . . just big enough to have a sitting place for strangers so that they don't have to go to the studio and for us on cold nights, and then a studio and have the piano in the studio as at Arcady." White Pines as executed had a living/sitting room next to the entrance, and the piano was in the adjoining large stair hall. An ample studio was finally realized with the addition of the Loom Room in 1906. Among its accoutrements was a Chickering & Sons spinet, documented by a photograph in Winterthur Manuscripts 209, series 7.

166. "Artists in Catskills: Palette and Brush Busy in Quaint Mountainside Homes," *New-York Daily Tribune*, August 30, 1908: 4–5. The clipping is in Winterthur Manuscripts 209, series 11. Edward Lamson Henry initiated Cragsmoor, ca. 1879. It was a mountaintop venue where many artists lived, but Onteora was started with a conscious intent to form an art-minded community. See Karen Zukowski, "Creating Art & Artists: Late 19th-Century American Artists' Studios," (PhD dissertation, City University of New York, 1999), 69–70. For a biography of Wheeler, consult Doreen Bolger Burke, et al., *In Pursuit of Beauty: Americans and the Aesthetic Movement* (New York: Rizzoli and the Metropolitan Museum of Art, 1986), 481–83.

167. Elizabeth Bisland, "A Nineteenth-Century Arcadia," *Cosmopolitan* 7 (September 1889): 516, quoted in Amelia Peck and Carol Irish, *Candace Wheeler: The Art and Enterprise of American Design, 1875-1900* (New York: Metropolitan Museum, 2001), 57. Wheeler's New York studio is depicted in Eileen Boris, *Art & Labor: Ruskin, Morris & the Craftsman Ideal in America* (Philadelphia: Temple University Press, 1986), 110.

168. Candace Wheeler, *Yesterdays in a Busy Life* (New York: Harper & Bros., 1918), 293; William Rhoads, "The Artist's House and Studio in the Nineteenth-Century Hudson Valley," in *Charmed Places: Hudson River Artists and Their Houses, Studios, and Vistas* (New York: Harry N. Abrams, in association with Bard College and Vassar College, 1988), 92. Photographs of the studio and Wheeler's house are on page 137.

169. Jane explained to son Peter (May 22, 1915), "her [May's] husband was [a] statesman, the State of Delaware sent him to the Senate and finally he was our ambassador to England after he married Cousin May." An undated Jane to RRW letter at Winterthur, filed immediately after one written January 18, 1903, mentions her receipt of a letter "from May Clymer Bayard at Onteora." However, Onteora historian and current resident Jane Bayard Curley believes that May, her step-great-grandmother, first came to Onteora in July 1907. Winterthur Library, Downs Collection.

170. Marling, *Woodstock*, n.p., characterized Onteora as indebted to "the anachronistic, fairy-tale medievalism of William Morris' *News from Nowhere*." Regarding the Whiteheads at Arcady, Gail Harrison remembered, "They established a William Morris cult school." The oral history transcript is at Santa Barbara Historical Society.

171. Florence Morse, "About Furnishings," in Wheeler, ed.,

Household Art (New York: Harper & Bros., 1893): 190; Jane's calendar, November 16, 1905. A list at the back of Jane's calendar indicates plans for various furnishing updates. Although a frieze of balsamlike trees is sketched in a nursery elevation (Winterthur Manuscripts 209, series 1), no balsam-themed ornamentation is now in evidence at White Pines. The family bedrooms were altered substantially in 1914, after Ralph Jr. and Peter had gone off to school in California.

172. Wheeler, *Yesterdays*, 279–80. Onteora and Byrdcliffe each had a "Wake Robin" cottage, in honor of Burroughs's book so titled.

173. Pakatakan means "the meeting of the waters"; whereas Onteora signifies "hills of the sky." The best resource on the colony at Arkville is Robert D. Kuhn, "National Register of Historic Places Registration Form for Pakatakan Artists Colony Historic District" (filed with the National Register of Historic Places, New York State Office of Parks, Recreation and Historic Preservation, Albany, 1989).

174. Cited in Rhoads, "The Artist's House and Studio," 96.

175. Documented by a photograph in a private collection; see Rhoads, "The Artist's House and Studio," fig. 95. For his part, Ralph attached a Madonna-and-Child cast to the chimney on the east wall in the Loom Room. Other Whitehead fireplaces with comparable images centered on the overmantel were in Arcady's dining room and, later, Neroli's master bedroom.

176. Zukowski, "Creating Art & Artists," 83.

177. Coleman, "A Studio in Pennsylvania," 364. Mercer experimented with the unusual medium of pigmented cement for the execution of statuary, pottery, and architectural elements adapted from antique models. See "Cement Casting at 'Aldie,' " *House & Garden* 4/4 (October 1903): 175–80. The sole interior photograph (178) depicted the studio, focusing on the balcony-loft that was a prime feature of "aestheticizing studios." Similar balconies were in the Arcady studio and Byrdcliffe's Yggdrasil, where Jane dwelt in later life.

178. In an 1885 article on "The Summer Haunts of American Artists," Lizzie Champney explained that the artist often yielded to the temptation of a studio for show in the city, "a museum of rare bric a brac and artful effect of interior decoration; in the country he surrounds himself rather with necessary conditions of work." Quoted in Zukowski, "Creating Art & Artists," 59; see pages 125, 130, on the subject of personal memorabilia.

179. Jane to RRW, February 23, 1903. The extant fireplace displays several asymmetrically placed tiles bearing "RW" initials, which Jane did not mention (see page 69). Winterthur Library, Downs Collection.

180. Zukowski, "Creating Art & Artists," 375–78, discusses antimodernism and Arts and Crafts, especially the artist's conception of his work as craft and of his studio as an intentionally anachronistic workshop bedecked with antiques and handmade objects.

181. Edward S. Prior, "Upon House-building in the Twentieth Century," in *Modern British Domestic Architecture and Decoration*, 13.

182. RRW to Jane, January 20, 1903: "Send me too The Studio, that thick number, an extra number, called 'British Domestic Architecture and Decoration.' I will let you have it back again." Winterthur Library, Downs Collection.

183. Hitchmough, *The Arts & Crafts Home*, 83.

184. "A Few Words on Decoration and Embroidery," 29, complained, "But perhaps the hardest task of the missionary in decoration is to commend and justify convention in design. Suburbia . . . will still cry obstinately for a 'natural' leaf or flower. . . . And no argument will persuade the ignorant mind that it is not the object of the designer to copy actual roses, but to formulate a type, to sum up in a few eloquent lines the habit and character of roses, as the musician sums up in his *leit-motif* the essential utterance of his work."

185. Winterthur Manuscripts 209, series 1. More than one burlap layer is present on the living room walls. Some resurfacing would have been required when the door leading to the western pergola was deleted.

186. A week before Jane and the boys were due to arrive at Byrdcliffe, she wrote RRW that Mackie, the nanny, was quitting (March 30, 1903). In a previous letter (1902), Jane had chronicled some of her efforts at Arcady: "The things we made at home are fine—they just go, but we have to make more—curtains in the studio for instance. I have taken up the matting in the Daffodil room and stained the floor and waxed it. Had the seats of the stoa painted and the den porch. . . ." On November 25, 1902, Jane admitted her fatigue and urged Ralph to stay at Byrdcliffe until Christmas: " I like very much being alone. I can't do half as much for the babies if I weren't. What time I don't spend on them I rest myself, for when you went away I was sadly in need of rest & so for a little while yet I had best do what I am doing now. . . ." Winterthur Library, Downs Collection.

187. See Jane's calendar entry for April 11, 1904, "sitting in Pine Tree room"; on September 21, 1923, she told Ralph Jr., "I am sitting in the 'pine tree room.'" Winterthur Library, Downs Collection.

188. Jane's calendar notes, January 8, 1902: "At work. 5 pastel interiors." These are no doubt among the colored room views given to Winterthur in 2002 by Jane's nephew, Mark Willcox (series 1).

189. The house is relatively intact, having remained in the White family (not related to Hervey), who purchased it in 1926. The boarded walls of the interior, the patterns and proportions of doors and windows, as well as the porches laced with vines, are redolent of White Pines. The exterior walls are novel, being fabricated from a white asbestos material nailed in sheets to the exposed timber frame (Maria Herold, Montecito History Committee, to author [December 9, 2003]). The effect is not unlike a tent house made of canvas stretched on frames, which Saylor classified as a bungalow subtype. He called it "an ideal outdoor sleeping room" in *Bungalows*, 33. Tent camps were a hallmark of the California mountain resorts the Whiteheads frequented.

190. From the Sanskrit, the verse is attributed to Kalidasa, a fifth-century poet. Nail holes and stains on the door imply the poem may have replaced a damaged canvas complementing the lily study affixed to the lower panel (see endnote 29). Yet Harwood A. White Jr. claims the door's present decoration dates to the Whiteheads' occupancy (telephone conversation with the author [December 30, 2003]). The decorated door was an exception to the norm of leaving the redwood at Neroli in a natural state.

Jane wrote to Peter from Neroli on January 24, 1915: "This morning before daybreak I was waked up by two linnets on the rafter of the open roof in my bedroom, they chirped & twittered & sang so loudly chasing each other around, & then flew out again, having settled that they would not nest there. The sun came up all deep orange & made the sea look so blue. Some of the mandarins on the terrace are deliciously sweet now. . . ." The word "Neroli" means the essential oil from the flowers of the bitter orange, according to Myrick, *Montecito and Santa Barbara*, vol. 2, 307. Sketched in a notebook in Winterthur Manuscripts 209, series 1, is a Neroli logo depicting an orange tree framed by the motto "I Know a Place Where the Sun Is Like Gold." At the bottom, two rows of orange disks are arrayed on either side of a wavy line. Coincidentally, the wood cornice of the studio-living room at Yggdrasil, where Jane resettled at Byrdcliffe after Ralph's death, is painted with a simple meandering border of stylized oranges. Maybe this was a mnemonic for Neroli, which had been Jane's refuge during a temporary separation from Ralph in 1912–13. Later she wrote Ralph Jr. (March 22, 1924): "Father created a beautiful thing when he made this place." Winterthur Library, Downs Collection.

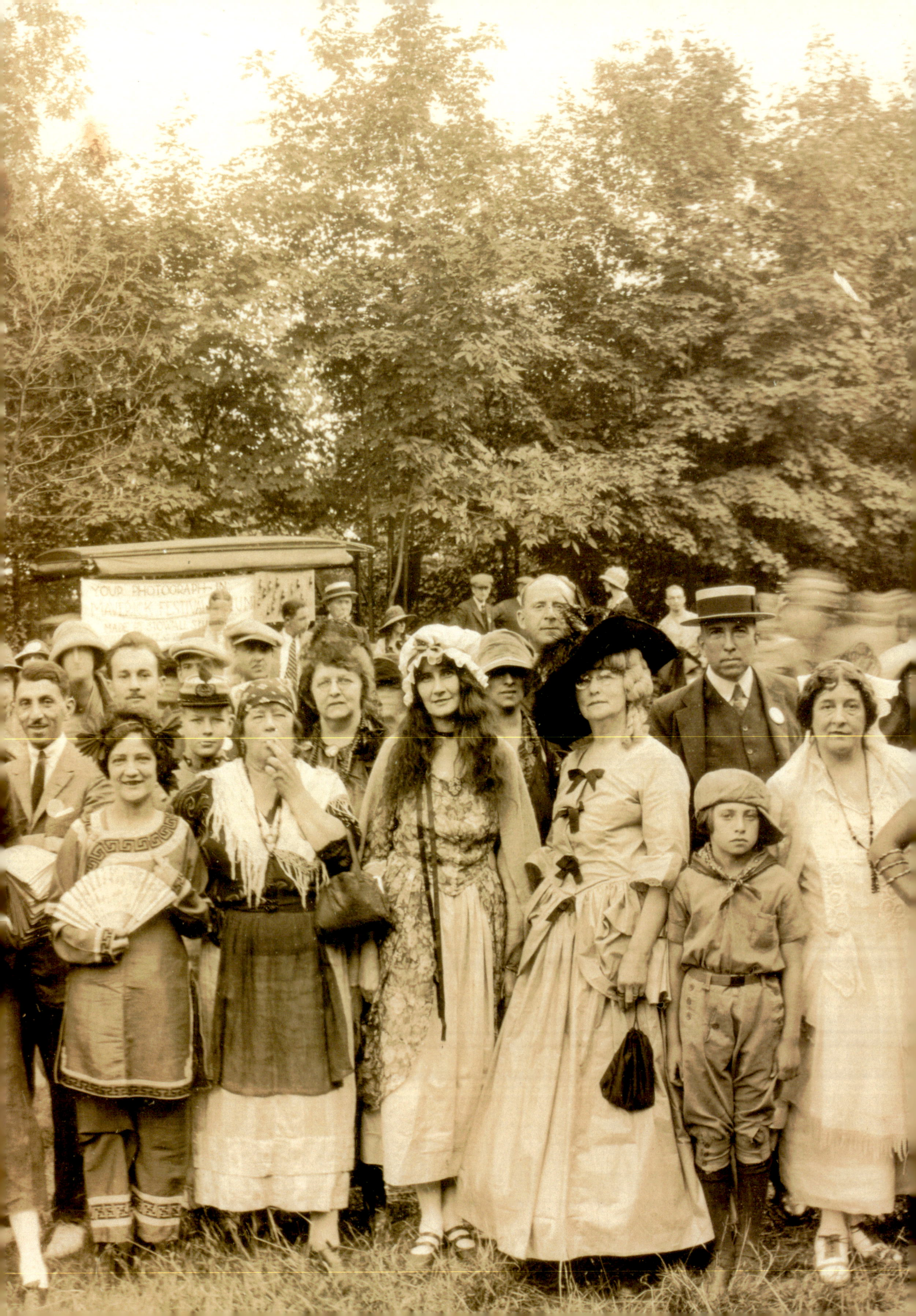
YOUR PHOTOGRAPH IN

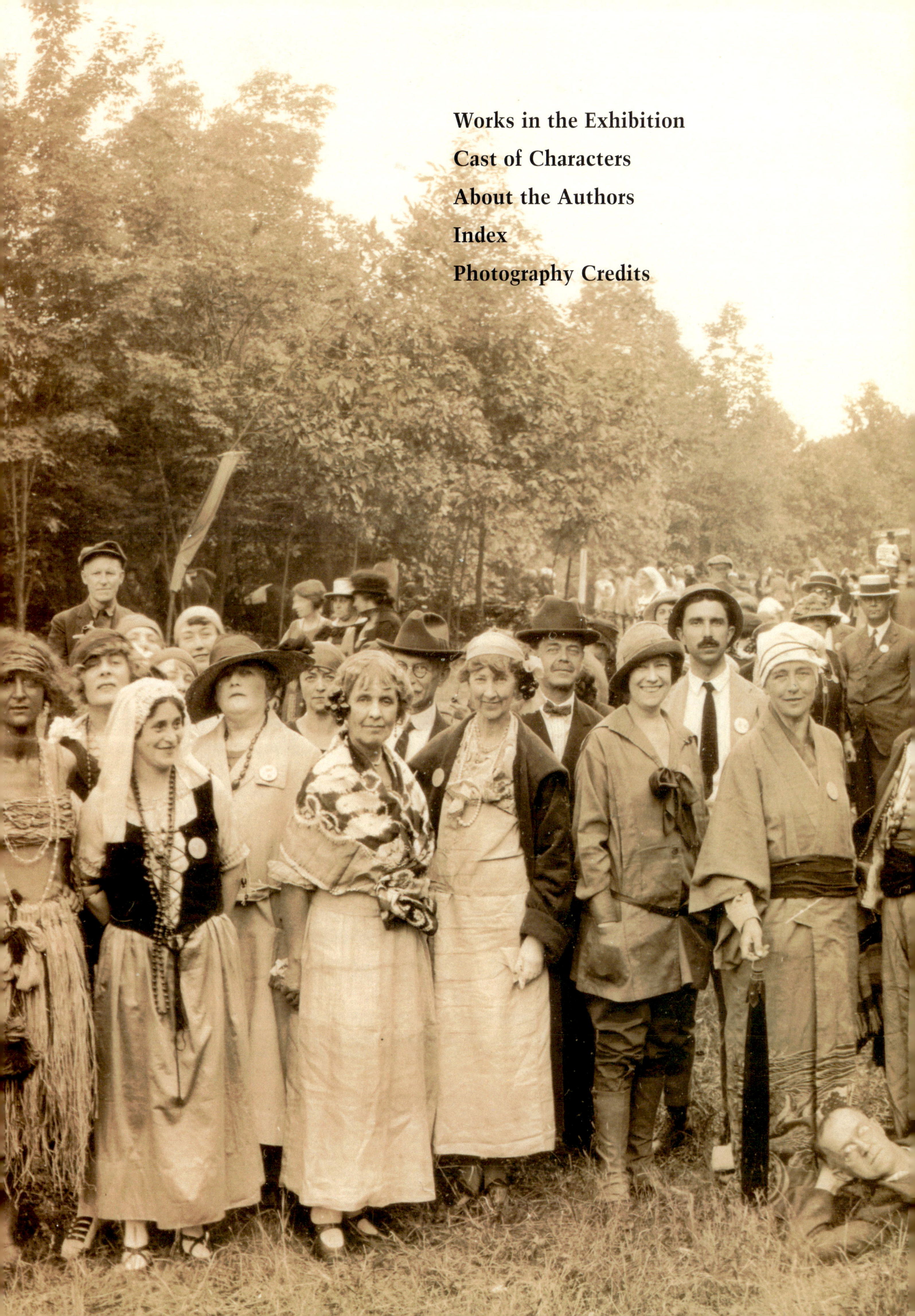

Works in the Exhibition

Books/Sketchbooks/Magazines

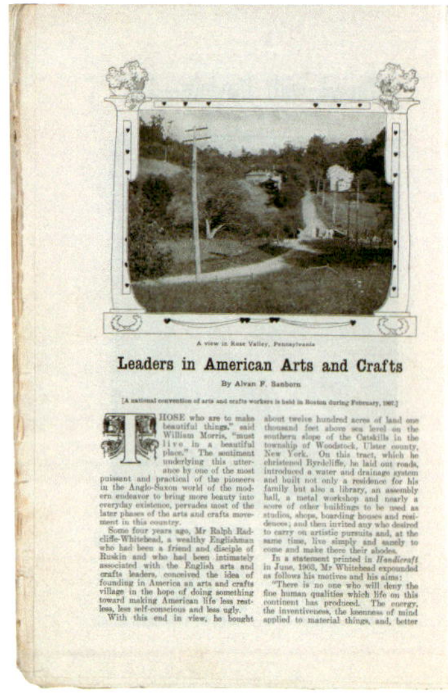

A view in Rose Valley, Pennsylvania

Leaders in American Arts and Crafts

By Alvan F. Sanborn

[A national convention of arts and crafts workers is held in Boston during February, 1907.]

THOSE who are to make beautiful things," said William Morris, "must live in a beautiful place." The sentiment underlying this utterance by one of the most puissant and practical of the pioneers in the Anglo-Saxon world of the modern endeavor to bring more beauty into everyday existence, pervades most of the later phases of the arts and crafts movement in this country.

Some four years ago, Mr Ralph Radcliffe-Whitehead, a wealthy Englishman who had been a friend and disciple of Ruskin and who had been intimately associated with the English arts and crafts leaders, conceived the idea of founding in America an arts and crafts village in the hope of doing something toward making American life less restless, less self-conscious and less ugly.

With this end in view, he bought about twelve hundred acres of land one thousand feet above sea level on the southern slope of the Catskills in the township of Woodstock, Ulster county, New York. On this tract, which he christened Byrdcliffe, he laid out roads, introduced a water and drainage system and built not only a residence for his family but also a library, an assembly hall, a metal workshop and nearly a score of other buildings to be used as studios, shops, boarding houses and residences; and then invited any who desired to carry on artistic pursuits and, at the same time, live simply and sanely to come and make there their abodes.

In a statement printed in *Handicraft* in June, 1903, Mr Whitehead expounded as follows his motives and his aims:

"There is no one who will deny the fine human qualities which life on this continent has produced. The energy, the inventiveness, the keenness of mind applied to material things, and, better

1. *Good Housekeeping,* February 1907
Alvan F. Sanborn, "Leaders in American Arts and Crafts," pages 146–52
$9\frac{7}{8}$ x $6\frac{7}{8}$ inches
Collection of the Byrdcliffe Art Colony of the Woodstock Guild

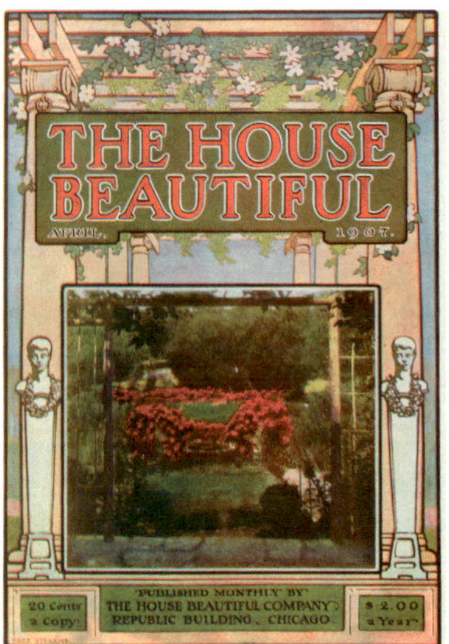

2. E. A. Needles, "A Little House with Five Fireplaces," *The House Beautiful,* April 1907 (with images of Bolton Brown's Palo Alto House)
$12\frac{3}{4}$ x $9\frac{5}{8}$ inches
Collection of Tom Wolf

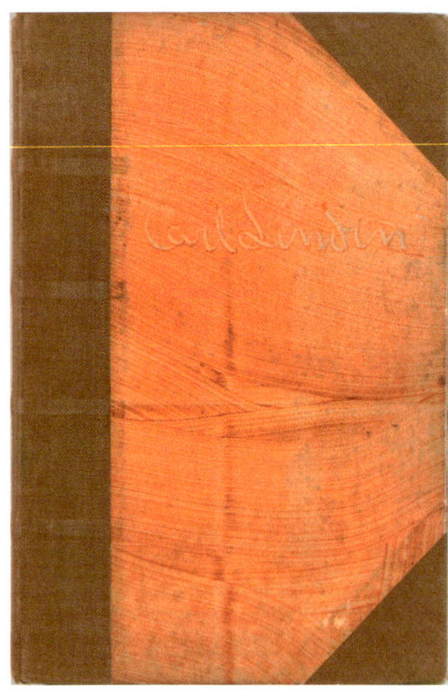

3. Louise Lindin, binder
Carl Lindin Sketchbook
Paper and linen binding
Height: $11\frac{1}{2}$ inches; width: $7\frac{5}{8}$ inches; depth: $\frac{3}{4}$ inch
Courtesy of David Cook Fine Art, Denver

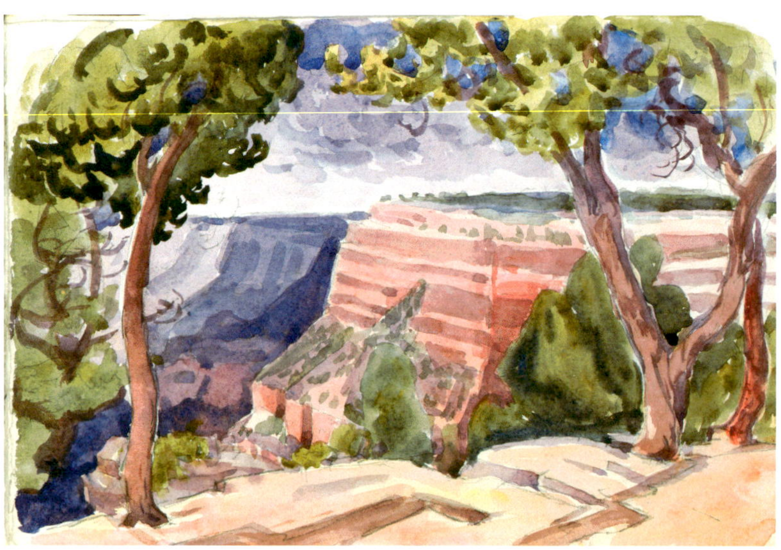

Carl Lindin
Grand Canyon, watercolor from Sketchbook

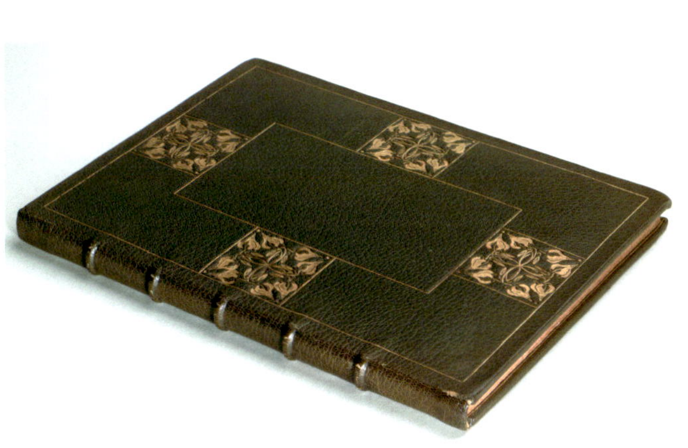

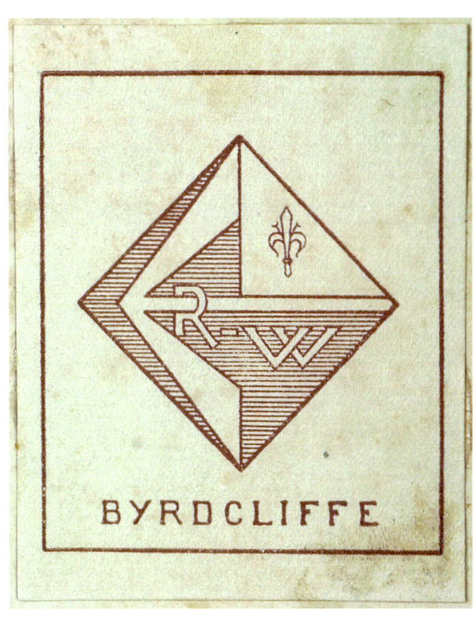

4. Louise Lindin, binder
Carl Lindin Sketchbook
Leather binding, gold-embossed
Height: $11^{3}/_{8}$ inches; width: $8^{7}/_{8}$ inches; depth: $^{1}/_{2}$ inch
Courtesy of David Cook Fine Art, Denver

5. John Ruskin
Modern Painters, Volume I with Byrdcliffe bookplate (illustrated)
Leather bound
Height: $7\,^{1}/_{8}$ inches; width: $4^{7}/_{8}$ inches; depth: 1 inch
Bookplate: 2 x $1\,^{1}/_{2}$ inches
On loan from Morgan Anderson Consulting

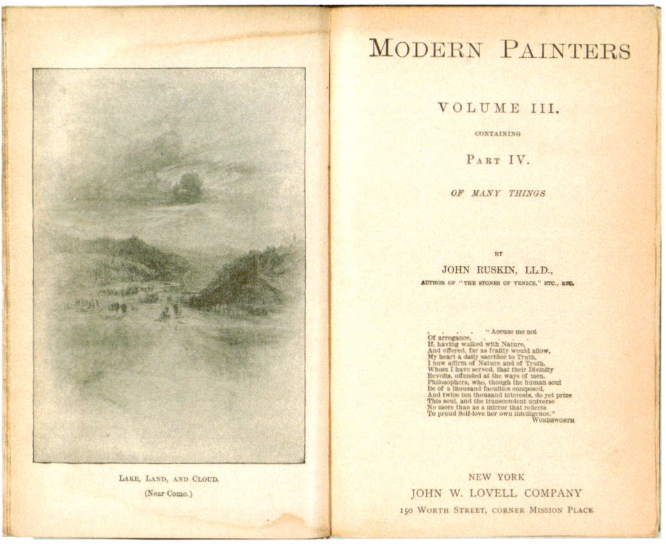

LAKE, LAND, AND CLOUD.
(Near Como.)

MODERN PAINTERS

VOLUME III.

CONTAINING

PART IV.

OF MANY THINGS

BY

JOHN RUSKIN, LL.D.,
AUTHOR OF "THE STONES OF VENICE," ETC., ETC.

. . . . . "Accuse me not
Of arrogance, ...
If, having walked with Nature,
And offered, far as frailty would allow,
My heart a daily sacrifice to Truth,
I now affirm of Nature and of Truth,
Whom I have served, that their Divinity
Revolts, offended at the ways of men.
Philosophers, who, though the human soul
Be of a thousand faculties composed,
And twice ten thousand interests, do yet prize
This soul, and the transcendent universe
No more than as a mirror that reflects
To proud Self-love her own intelligence."
WORDSWORTH

NEW YORK
JOHN W. LOVELL COMPANY
150 WORTH STREET, CORNER MISSION PLACE

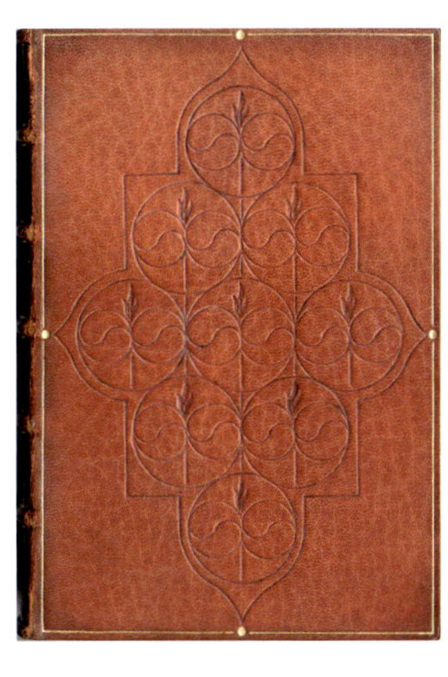

6. John Ruskin
Modern Painters, Volume III with Byrdcliffe bookplate
Leather bound
Height: $7\,^{1}/_{8}$ inches; width: $4^{7}/_{8}$ inches; depth: 1 inch
On loan from Morgan Anderson Consulting

7. Ellen Gates Starr, binder
Crux aetatis, and other poems, by Martin Schütze, 1904
Leather bound
Height: $7\,^{9}/_{16}$ inches; width: $5\,^{5}/_{16}$ inches; depth: $^{1}/_{2}$ inch
University of Chicago Library, Special Collections Research Center

8. Ellen Gates Starr, binder
Hero and Leander, a tragedy, by Martin Schütze, 1908
Leather bound
Height: $7\,^{5}/_{8}$ inches; width: $5\,^{5}/_{16}$ inches; depth: $^{3}/_{4}$ inch
University of Chicago Library, Special Collections Research Center

Ralph Radcliffe Whitehead

A friend had written me from a Socialist colony in the Adirondacks, (I was then a librarian with a salary,) ~~Chicago~~, I am sending you a Yankeeized Englishman who is ~~to spend~~ a few days in Chicago His name is Whitehead "Be nice to him, you may find him interesting." "He will probably be hungry" I thought dropping the letter in the waste basket.

He came up the long room toward my desk with that half apologetic, hesitating step peculiar to him. The day was hot, he did look hungry. I invited him at once to have lunch with me.

What he needs is a good feed I thought. I took him to a basement Cafeteria and blew him to a thirty five cent lunch

9. Hervey White
Ralph Radcliffe Whitehead
Unbound manuscript
12 x 9 inches
Collection of the Historical Society of Woodstock

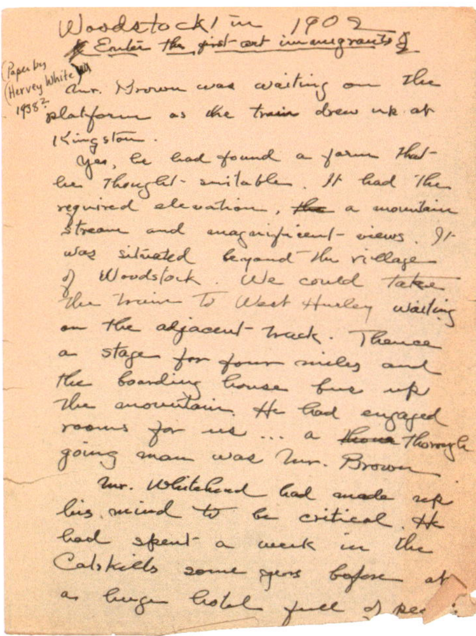

Woodstock in 1902
Enter the first art immigrants

(Paper by Hervey White 1938?)

Mr. Brown was waiting on the platform as the train drew up at Kingston.

Yes, he had found a farm that he thought suitable. It had the required elevation, a mountain stream and magnificent views. It was situated beyond the village of Woodstock. We could take the train to West Hurley waiting on the adjacent track. Thence a stage for four miles and the boarding house five up the mountain. He had engaged rooms for us ... a thorough going man was Mr. Brown.

Mr. Whitehead had made up his mind to be critical. He had spent a week in the Catskills some years before at a huge hotel full of

10. Hervey White
Woodstock in 1902
Unbound manuscript
11 1/2 x 8 1/2 inches
Collection of the Historical Society of Woodstock

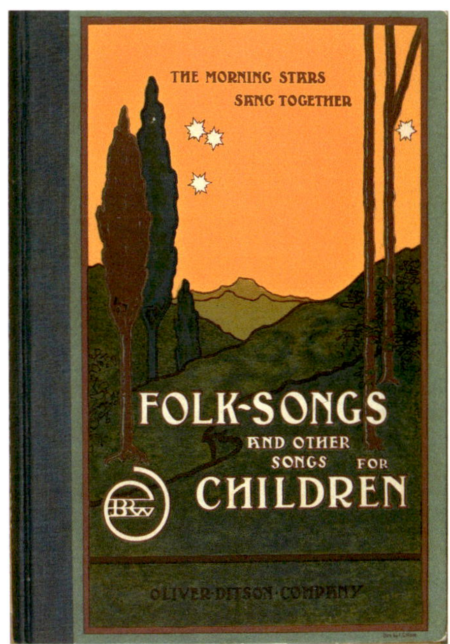

11. Compiled by Jane Whitehead and Ralph Whitehead
The Morning Stars Sang Together: Folk-Songs and Other Songs for Children, 1903
Cloth-bound book with paper cover design attributed to Jane Whitehead
Height: 11 15/16 inches; width: 8 9/16 inches; depth: 13/16 inch
Collection of the Byrdcliffe Art Colony of the Woodstock Guild

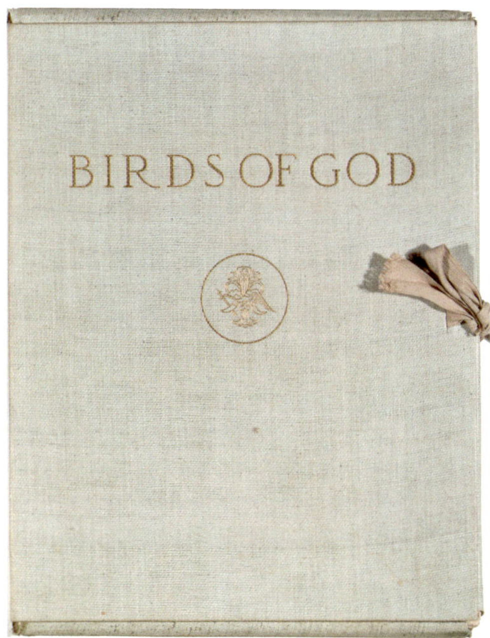

12. Jane and Ralph Radcliffe Whitehead
Birds of God, 1902
Linen-bound book
Height: 15 1/4 inches; width: 11 5/8 inches; depth: 1/2 inch
Private collection

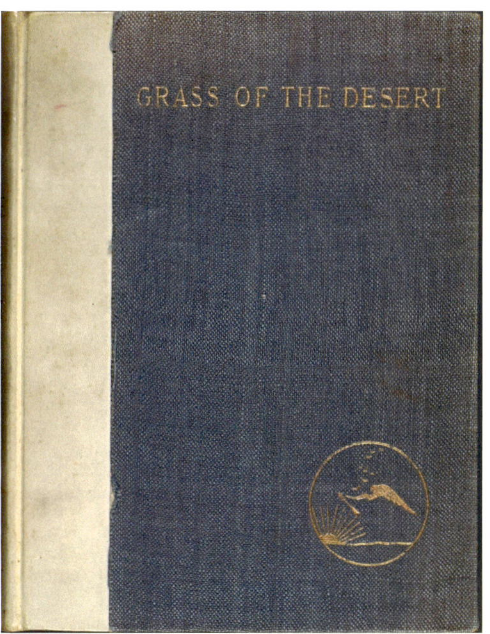

13. Ralph Radcliffe Whitehead
Grass of the Desert, 1892
Leather- and burlap-bound book
Height: 8 5/8 inches; width: 6 3/4 inches; depth: 7/8 inch
Collection of the Byrdcliffe Art Colony of the Woodstock Guild, Alf Evers Collection
Gift of the Douglas C. James Charitable Trust

Furniture and Related Drawings

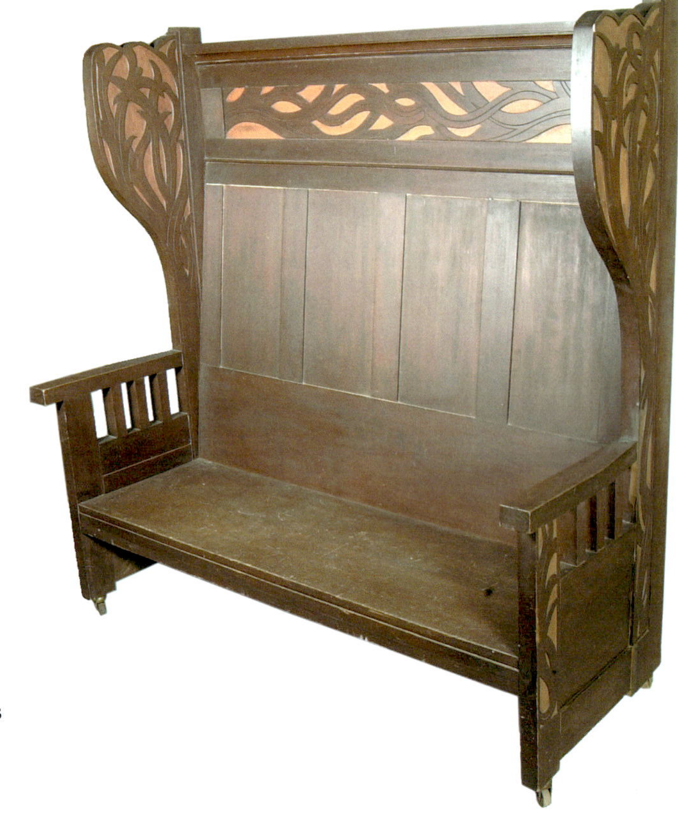

14. Dawson Dawson-Watson, designer
Settle, ca. 1904
Poplar
Height: 70 1/4 inches; width: 69 1/2 inches; depth 28 3/8 inches
Private collection

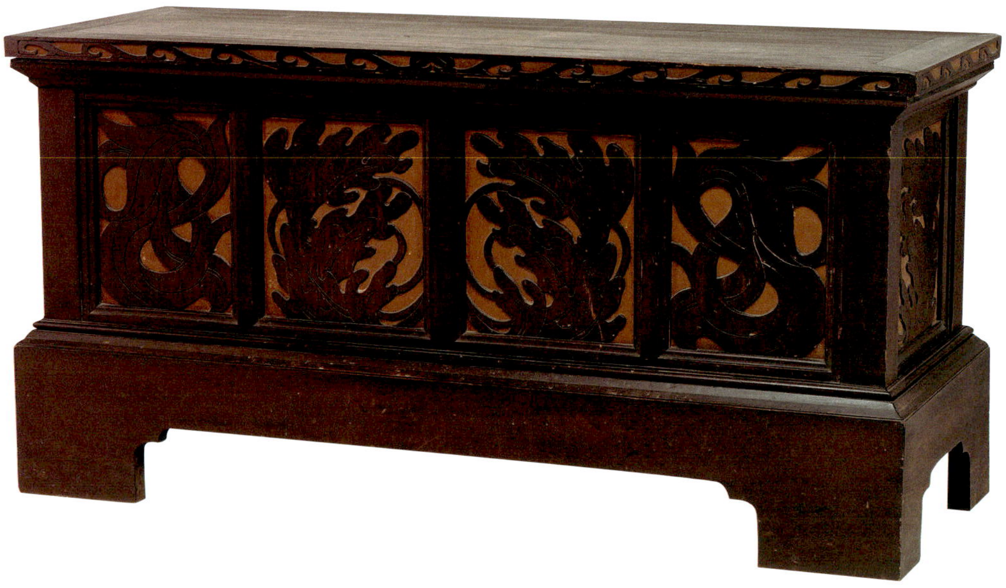

15. Dawson Dawson-Watson, designer
Blanket Chest, ca. 1904
Oak
Height: 26 1/4 inches; width: 59 1/4 inches; depth: 21 1/4 inches
Private collection
Courtesy of the Detroit Institute of Art
*Shown only at Milwaukee, Ithaca, and Albany

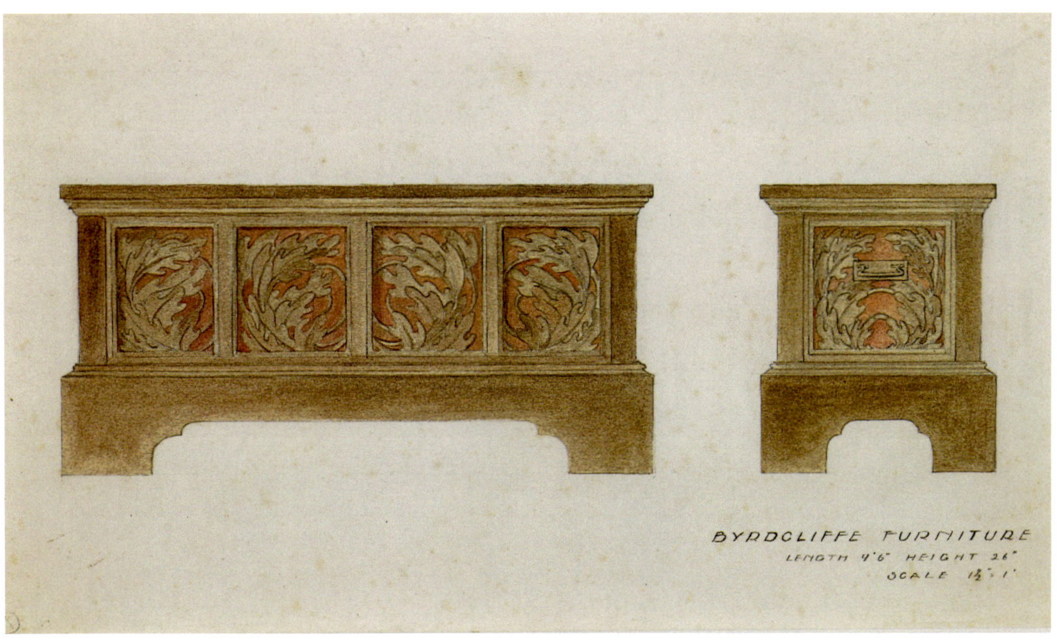

16. Dawson Dawson-Watson, designer
Blanket Chest, ca. 1904
Colored pencil
14 x 19 1/2 inches
Private collection
*Shown only at Milwaukee, Ithaca, and Albany

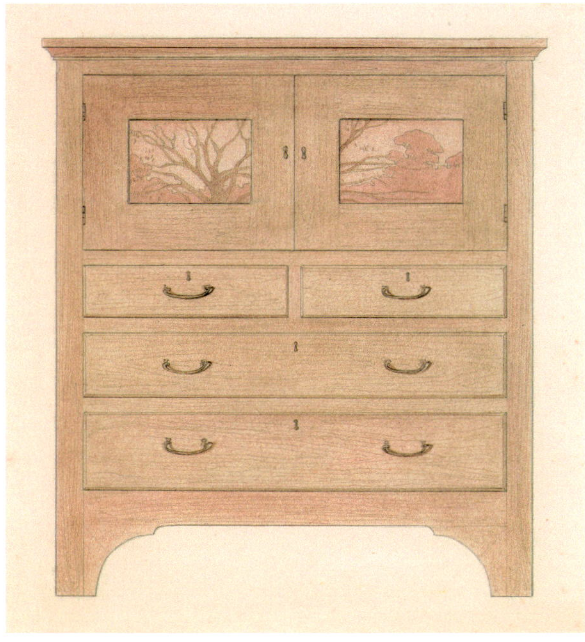

17. Attributed to George Eggers
Design for Chest with Winter Landscape
Pencil and colored pencil
12 x 10 inches
Collection of the Byrdcliffe Art Colony of the Woodstock Guild
Gift of Jill and Mark Willcox Jr.

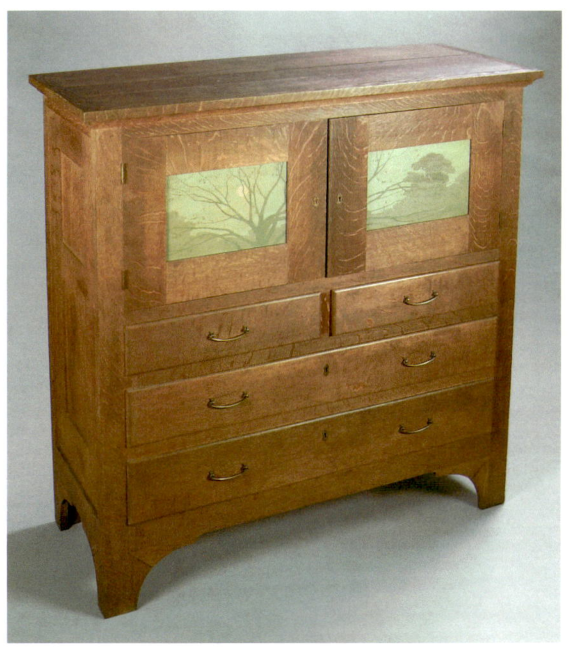

18. Attributed to George Eggers
Chest with Winter Landscape, ca. 1904
Oak with painted panels
Height: 64 3/8 inches; width: 60 inches; depth: 23 3/4 inches
Collection of the Byrdcliffe Art Colony of the Woodstock Guild

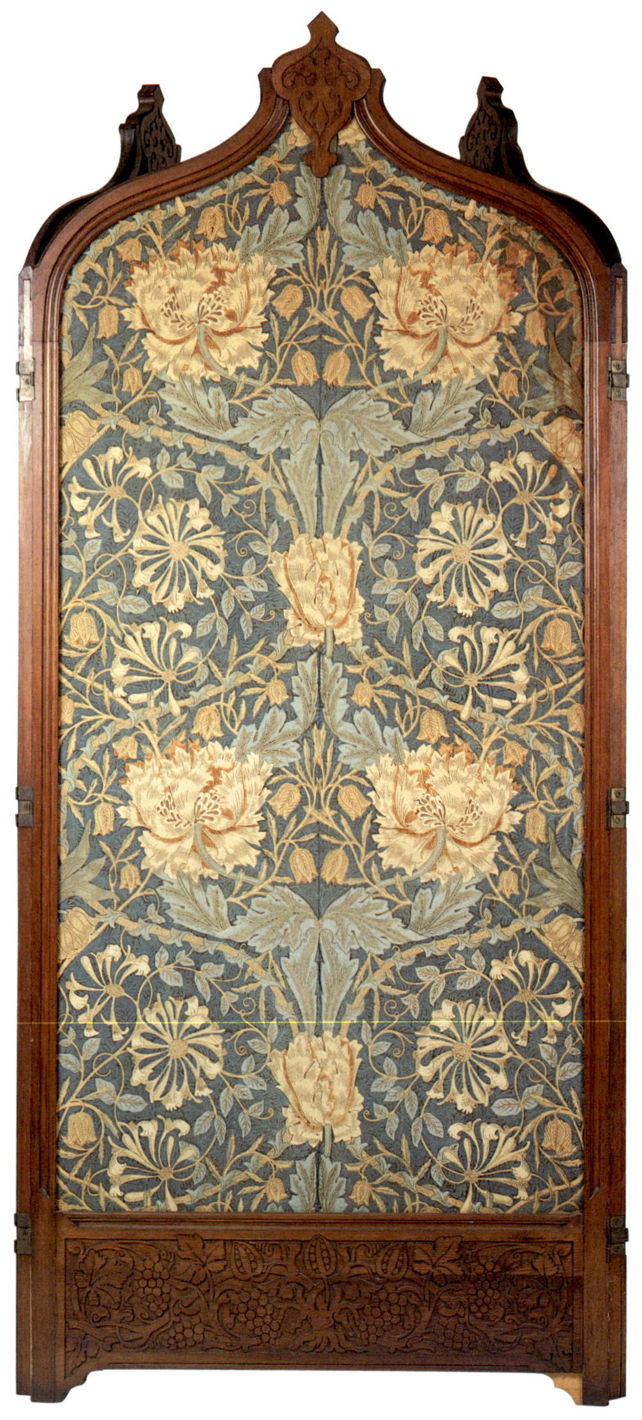

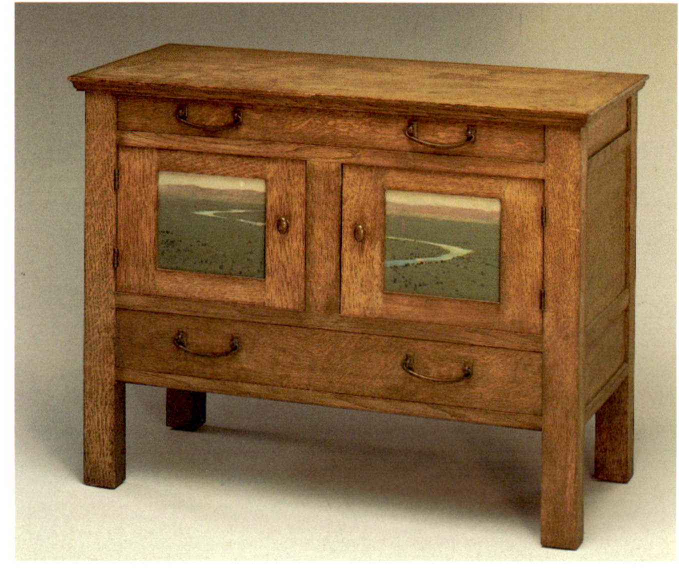

20. Hermann Dudley Murphy, panel designer
Chiffonier, ca. 1904
Oak with painted panels
Height: 27 3/8 inches, width: 36 7/8 inches, depth: 14 5/8 inches
Private collection

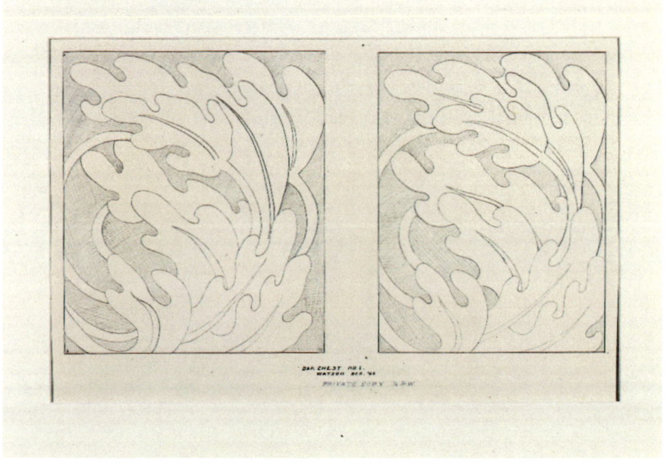

19. Morris & Company
William Morris "Honeysuckle" cretonne fabric, mounted in a Gothic-style screen, ca. 1890
Pine frame with cotton printed fabric
Height: 86 1/2 inches; width: 37 3/8 inches
Private collection

21. Zulma Steele, designer
Drawing for Dawson-Watson Chest, ca. 1904
(see cats. 15 and 16)
Pencil
22 x 28 inches
Private collection
*Shown only at Milwaukee, Ithaca, and Albany

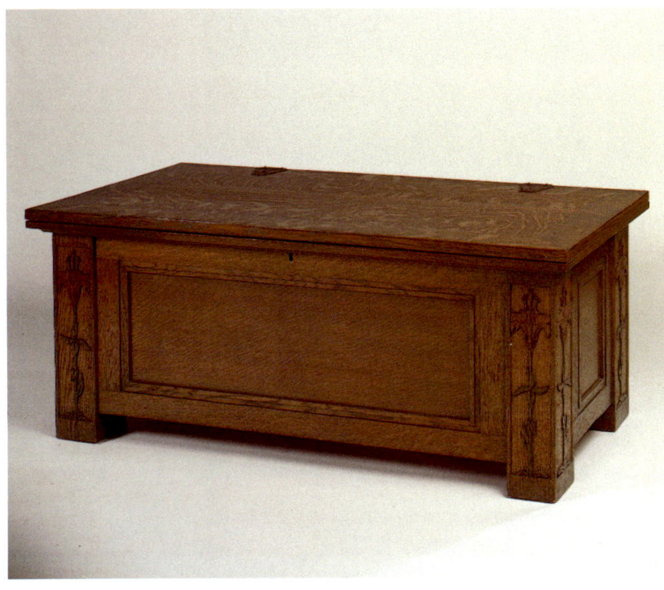

22. Zulma Steele, designer
Lily Blanket Chest, ca. 1904
Oak with carved panel design
Height: 20 1/4 inches; width: 50 1/4 inches; depth: 22 1/4 inches
Private collection

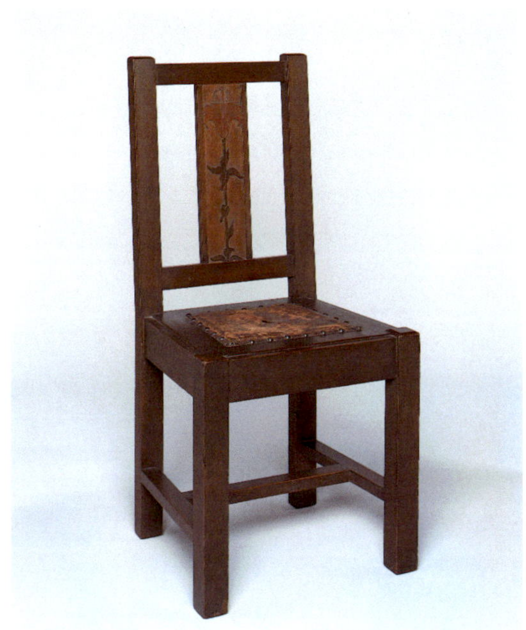

24. Zulma Steele, designer
Side Chair, ca. 1904
Cherry with leather upholstery
Height: 37 7/8 inches; width: 18 inches; depth: 16 inches
Milwaukee Art Museum, Layton Art Collection

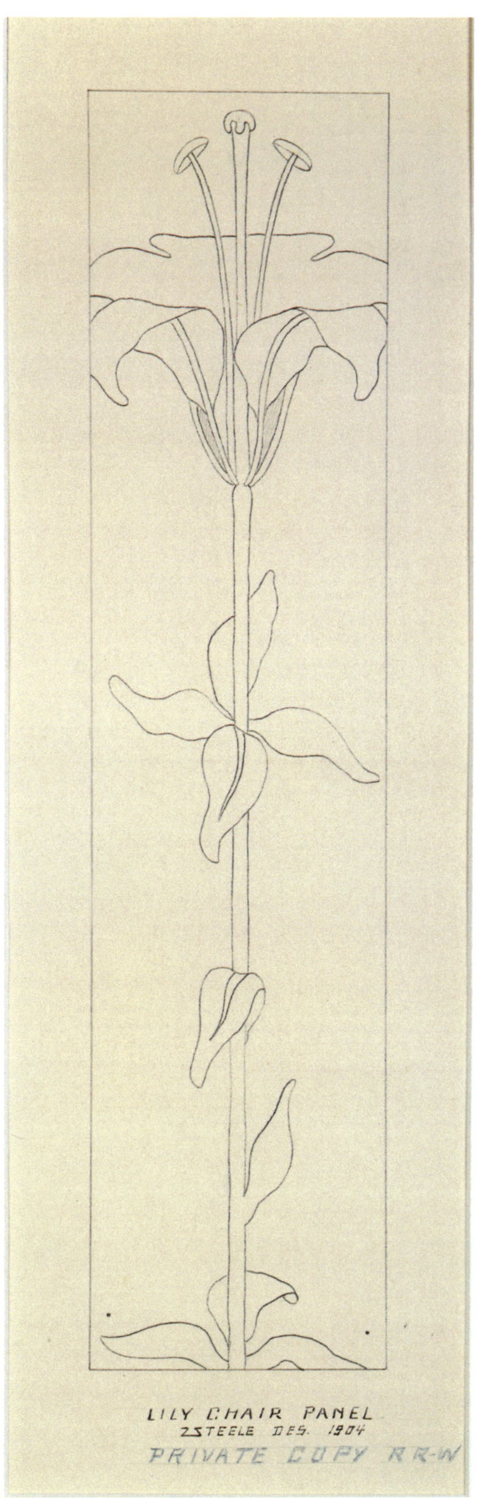

23. Zulma Steele, designer
Drawing for a Side Chair, ca. 1904
Pencil
12 3/8 x 6 3/8 inches
Milwaukee Art Museum, Layton Art Collection

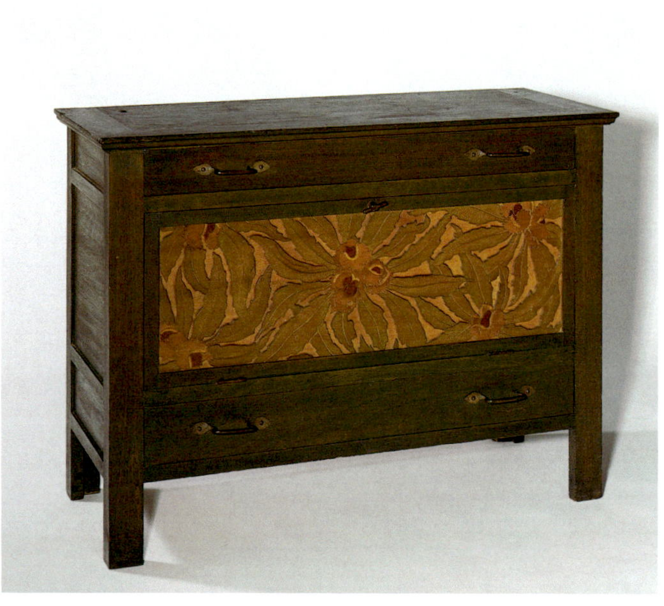

25. Zulma Steele, panel designer
Chiffonier with Chestnut Relief, ca. 1904
Poplar with copper hardware
Height: $27\,^{1}/_{4}$ inches; width: $38\,^{3}/_{4}$ inches; depth: $14\,^{5}/_{8}$ inches
Milwaukee Art Museum, Layton Art Collection

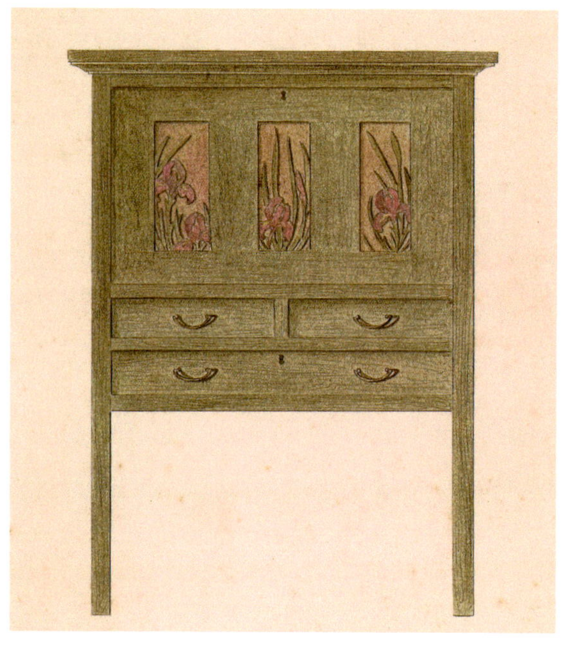

26. Zulma Steele, designer
Iris Desk Drawing, ca. 1904
Graphite and colored pencil
$9\,^{1}/_{8}$ x 7 inches
Collection of the Byrdcliffe Art Colony of the Woodstock Guild
Gift of Jill and Mark Willcox Jr.

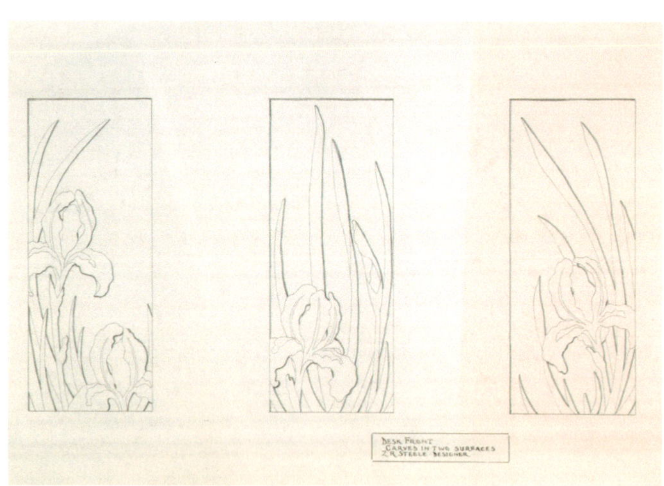

27. Zulma Steele, designer
Iris Desk Panel Drawing, ca. 1904
Graphite
$18\,^{1}/_{2}$ x $28\,^{1}/_{2}$ inches
Collection of the Byrdcliffe Art Colony of the Woodstock Guild

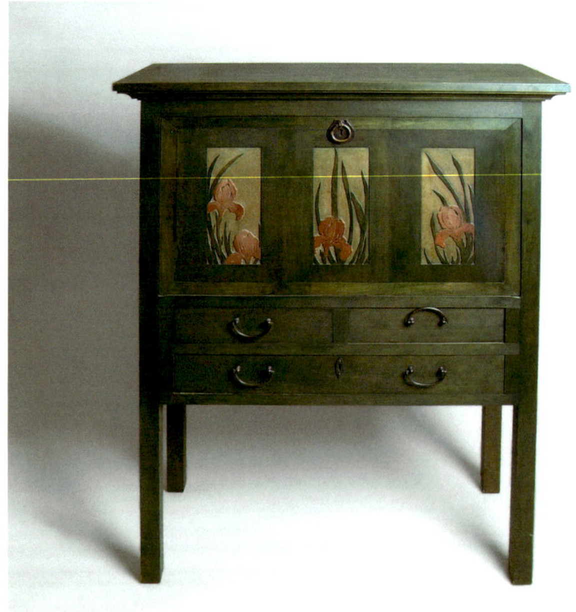

28. Zulma Steele, designer
Desk with Three Panel Iris Design, ca. 1904
Green-stained cherry with three painted panels
Height: $50\,^{3}/_{8}$ inches; width: $38\,^{3}/_{4}$ inches; depth: 16 inches
Collection of the Byrdcliffe Art Colony of the Woodstock Guild
Gift of Elise Genne and the Douglas C. James Charitable Trust

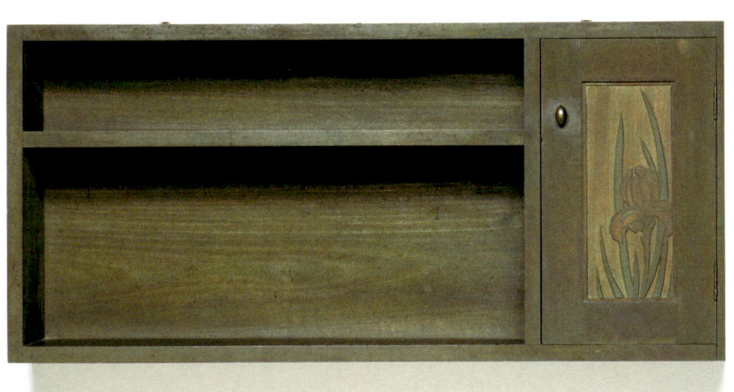

29. Zulma Steele, designer
Iris Hanging Wall Cabinet
Stained poplar
Height: 18 inches; width: 39 1/2 inches; depth: 8 inches
The Nelson-Atkins Museum of Art, Purchase, Nelson Trust (by exchange)
*Shown only at New York and Winterthur

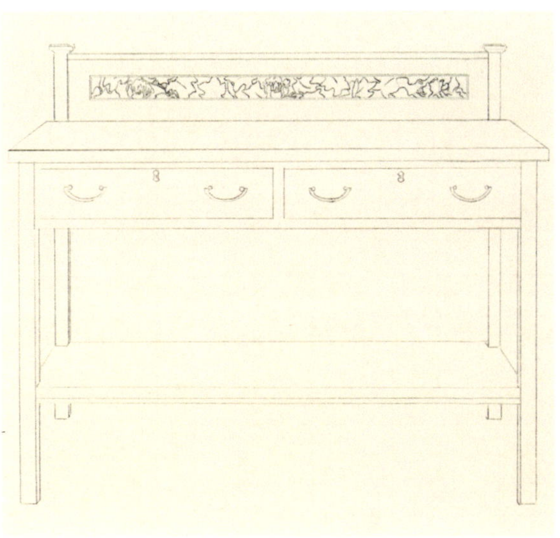

30. Zulma Steele
Design for Maple Leaf Sideboard
Pen and ink
7 1/2 and 8 1/2 inches
Collection of the Byrdcliffe Art Colony of the Woodstock Guild, Alf Evers Collection
Gift of the Douglas C. James Charitable Trust

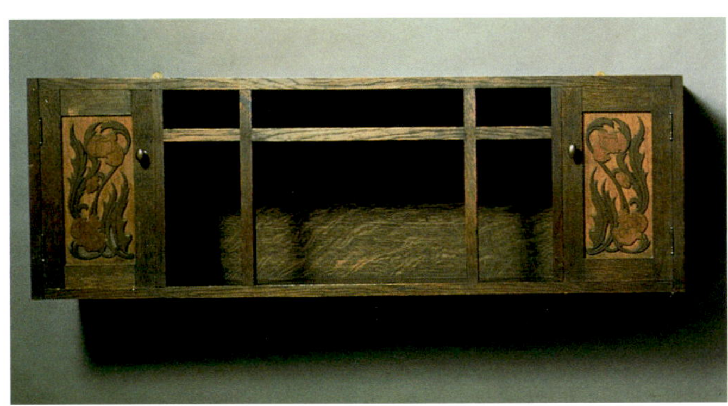

31. Zulma Steele, designer
Hanging Cabinet with Carved Poppy Design, ca. 1904
Oak
Height: 14 inches, width: 42 1/2 inches; depth: 8 inches
The Henry Francis Du Pont Winterthur Museum Inc.

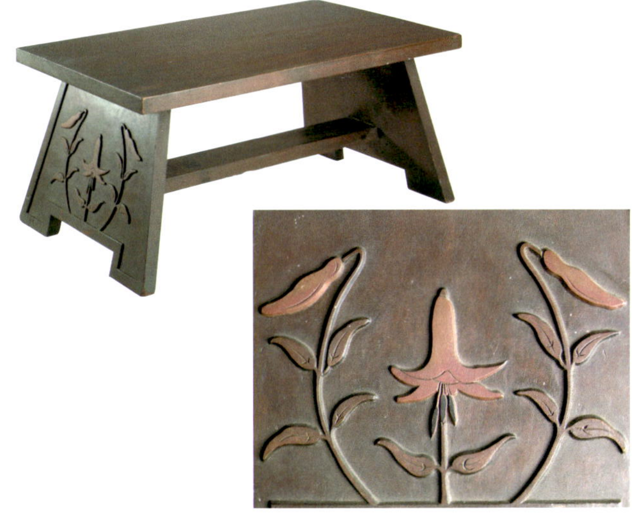

32. Zulma Steele, designer
Footstool with Lily Motif, ca. 1904
Poplar
Height: 9 3/4 inches; width: 20 7/8 inches; depth: 13 1/2 inches
Collection of the Woodstock Artists Association

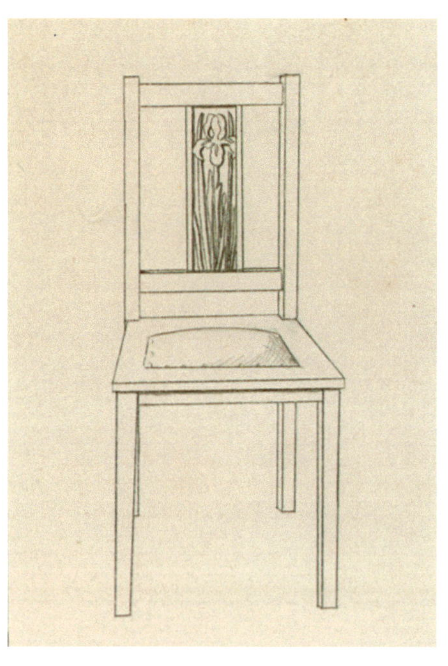

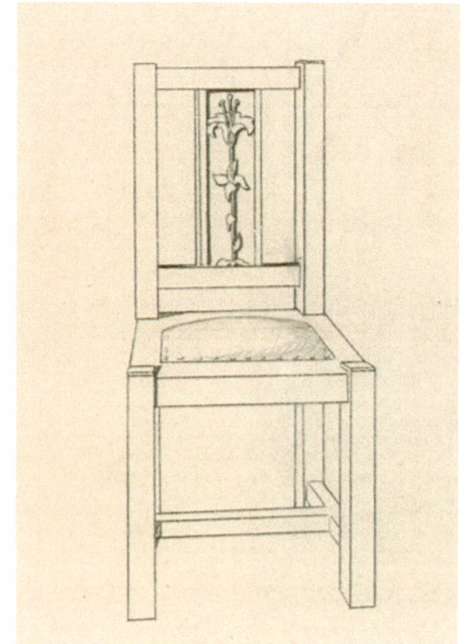

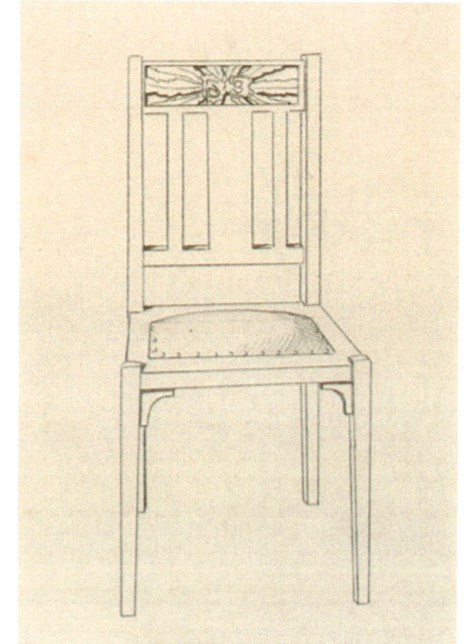

33. Zulma Steele
Designs for Three Chairs
Pen and ink
Each sheet approx. 6 3/4 x 5 inches
Collection of the Byrdcliffe Art Colony of the Woodstock Guild, Alf Evers Collection
Gift of the Douglas C. James Charitable Trust

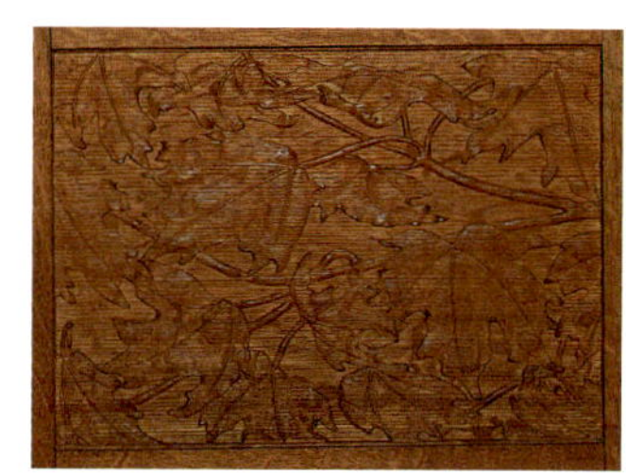

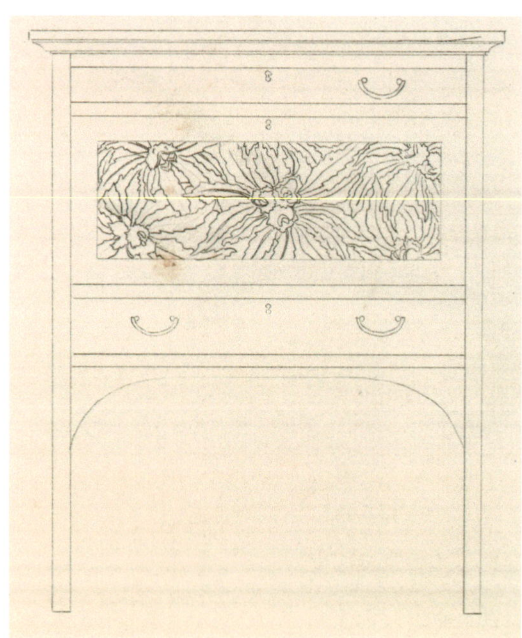

34. Zulma Steele
Chestnut Chest Design
Graphite
8 x 7 inches
Collection of the Byrdcliffe Art Colony of the Woodstock Guild, Alf Evers Collection
Gift of the Douglas C. James Charitable Trust

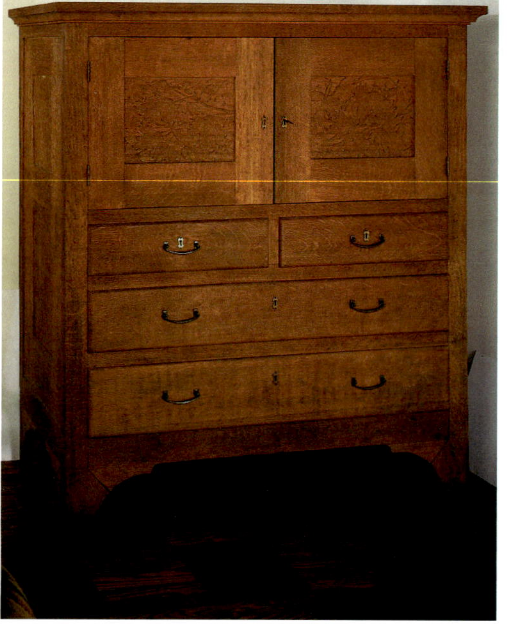

35. Attributed to Giovanni Battista Troccoli
Linen Press with Carved Maple-Leaf Design, 1904
Oak
Height: 60 inches; width: 40 inches; depth: 23 3/4 inches
Private collection

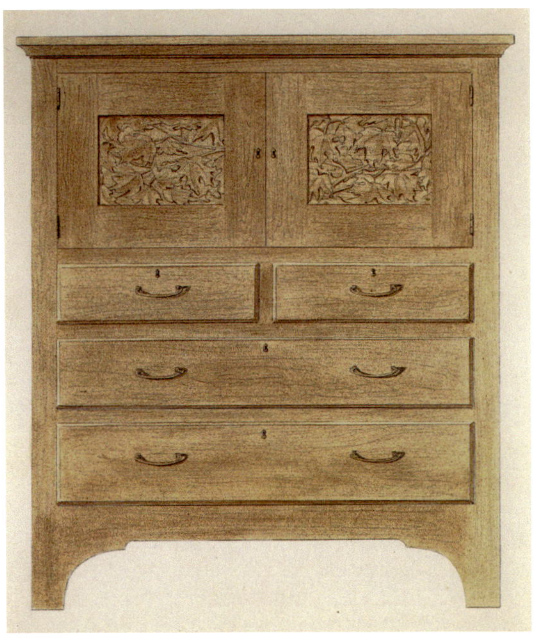

36. Unidentified designer
Drawing for Linen Press with Carved Maple-Leaf Design
Colored pencil
11 x 9 1/2 inches
Private collection

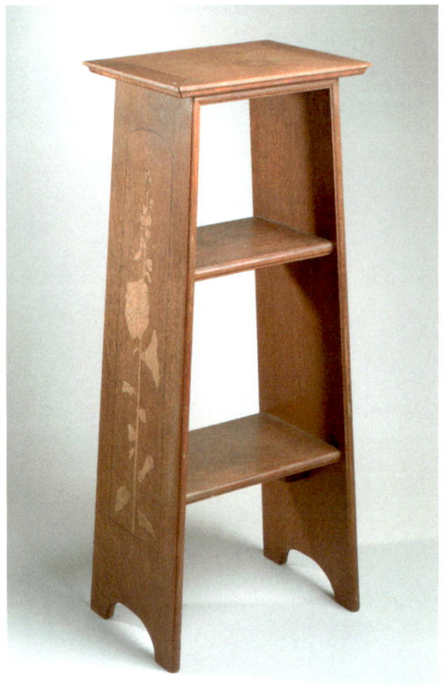

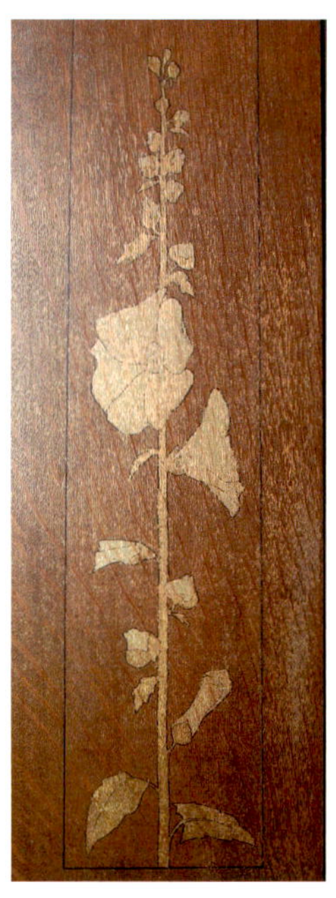

37. Unidentified artist
Lamp Stand with Hollyhock Design
Oak with polychromed sides
Height: 35 7/8 inches; width: 15 1/4 inches; depth: 10 1/16 inches
Collection of the Byrdcliffe Art Colony of the Woodstock Guild
Gift of Gioia Timpanellie

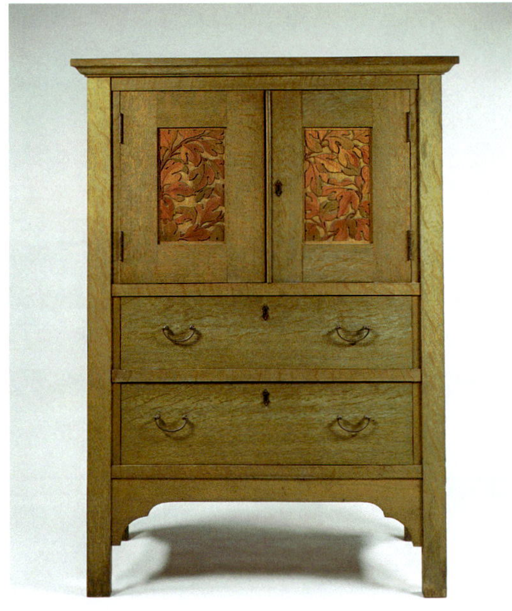

38. Edna Walker, designer
Linen Press with Sassafras Panels, ca. 1904
Carved oak, tulip poplar, and brass
Height: 55 inches; width: 41 inches; depth: 18 3/4 inches
The Metropolitan Museum of Art, Purchase,
Friends of the American Wing Fund, and
Mr. and Mrs. Mark Willcox Jr. Gift, 1991. (1991.311.1)
Photograph ©1992 The Metropolitan Museum of Art

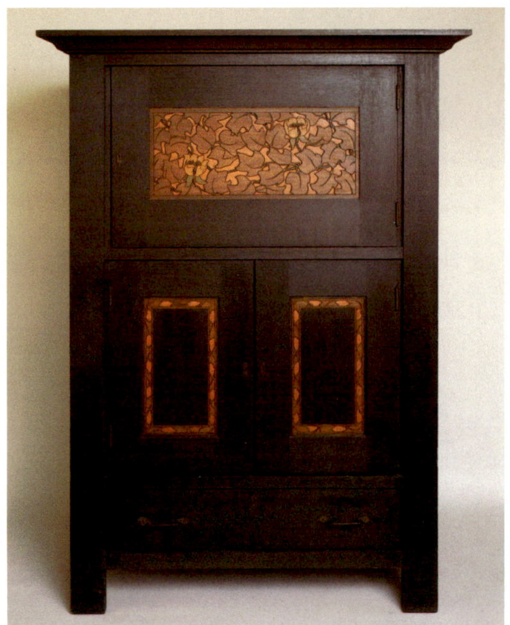

39. Edna Walker, designer
Tulip Chest, ca. 1904
Poplar
Height: 72 1/2 inches; width: 48 inches; depth: 21 inches
The Museum of Fine Arts, Boston
Museum purchase with funds donated anonymously and
Frank B. Bemis Fund

Metal

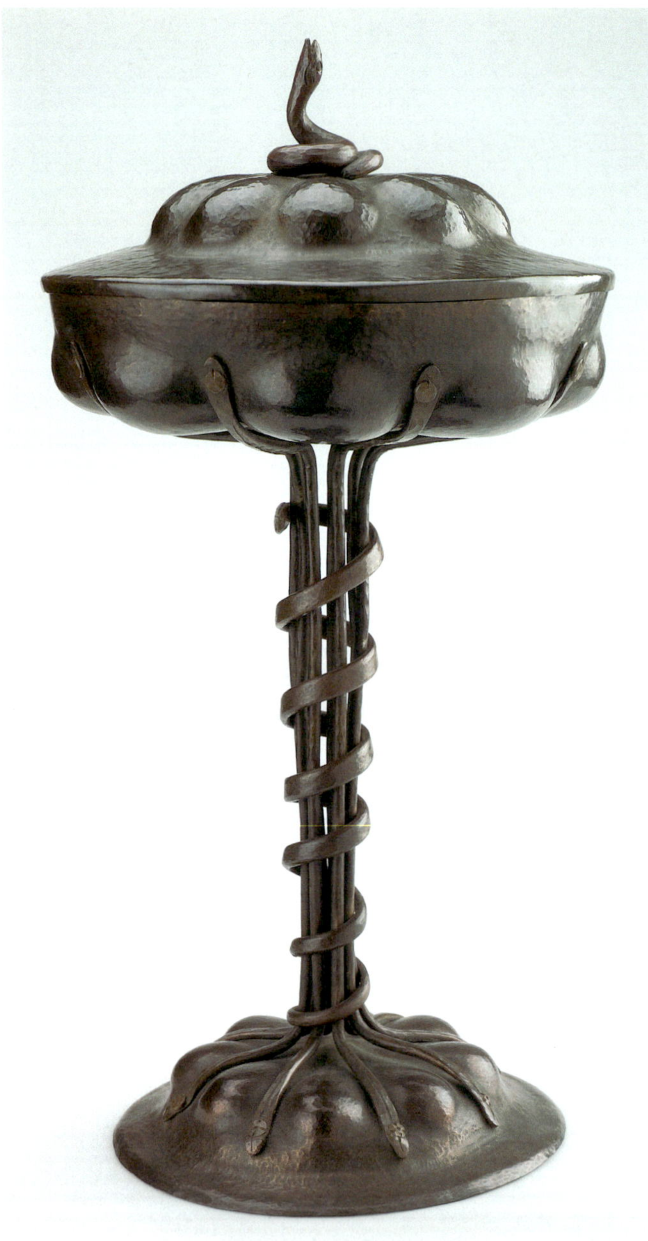

40. Laurin Hovey Martin
Covered Tazza, 1897–1902
Copper
Height: 13 1/4 inches; diameter: 7 1/4 inches
The Museum of Fine Arts, Boston
Gift of the artist's family, 1997

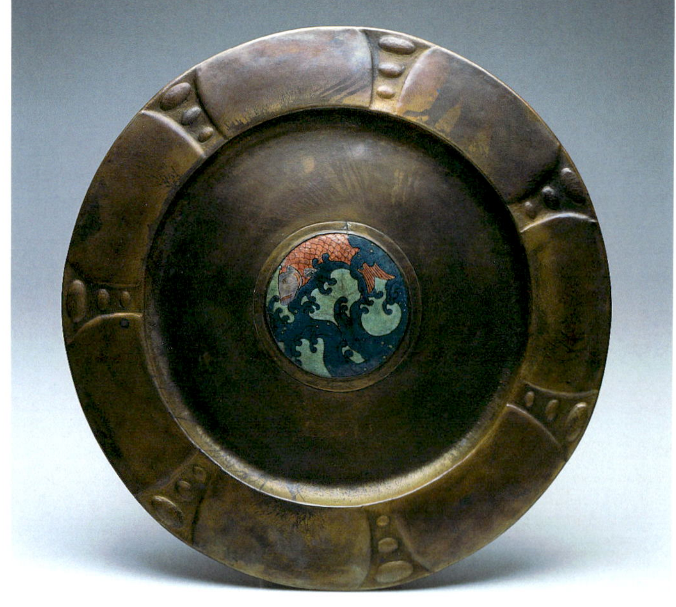

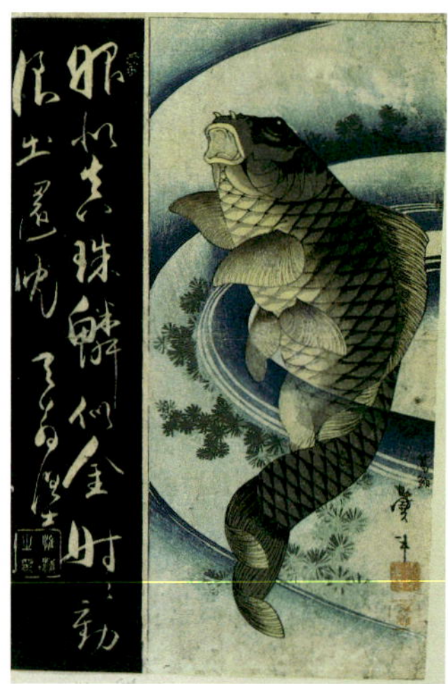

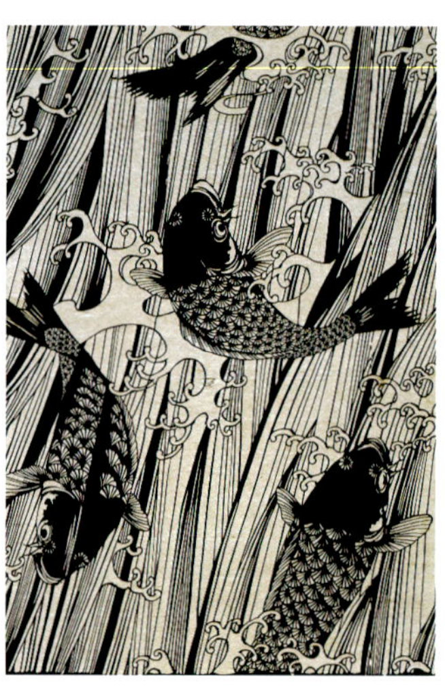

41. H. Stuart Michie
Charger, ca. 1905
Copper and enamel
Diameter: 15 1/2 inches
Collection of Henry T. Michie
(The two illustrations and Michie's own drawing [cat. 166] were used as inspiration for the charger design.)

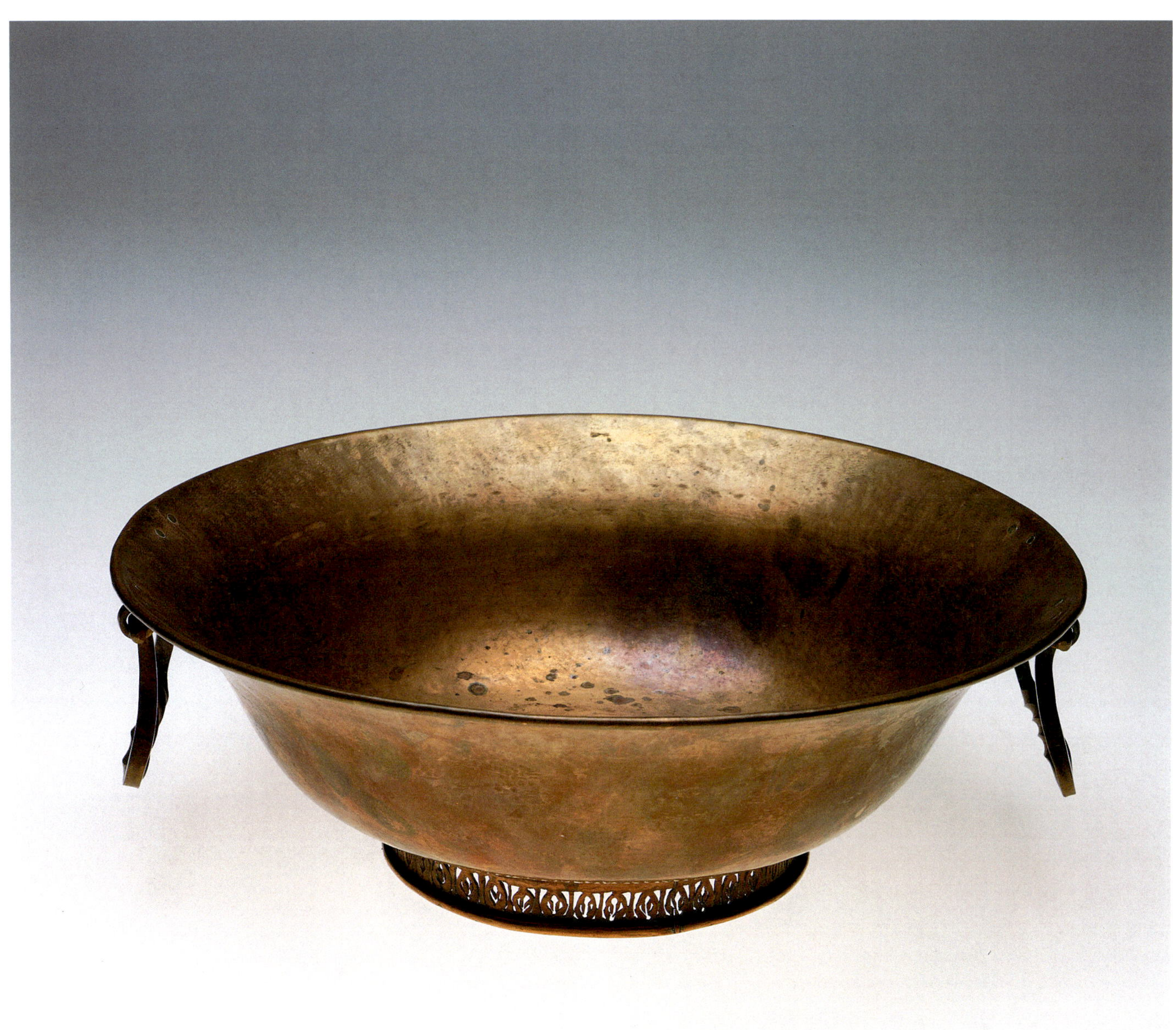

42. H. Stuart Michie
Two-Handled Bowl, ca. 1905
Copper
Diameter: 15 1/2 inches
Collection of Henry T. Michie

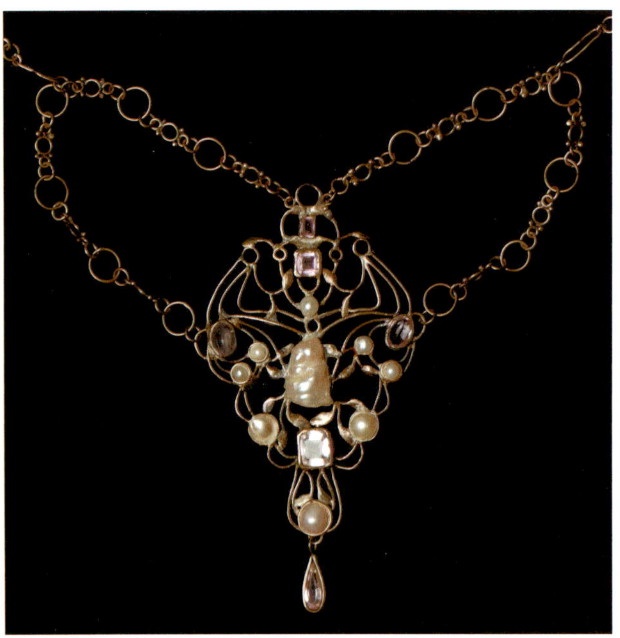

43. Edmund Rolfe
Necklace
10k gold and freshwater pearls
Pendant: $3\,^{3}/_{8}$ x 2 inches; chain: $7\,^{1}/_{2}$ inches
Collection of Maribeth Harmes

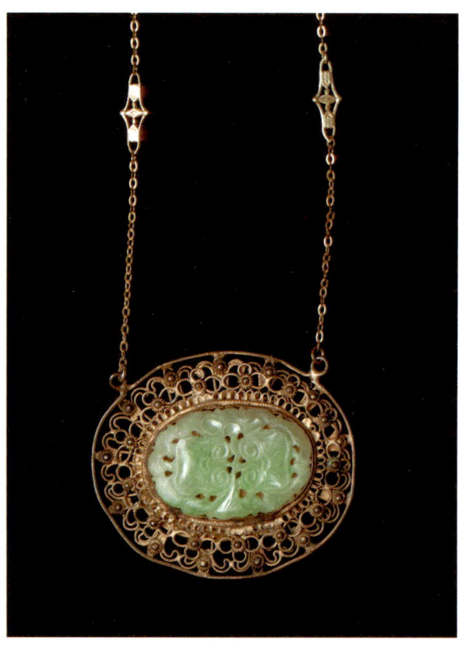

44. Edmund Rolfe
Pendant
10k gold with green opals
Pendant: $1\,^{7}/_{8}$ x $1\,^{5}/_{8}$ inches; chain: 15 inches
Collection of Maribeth Harmes

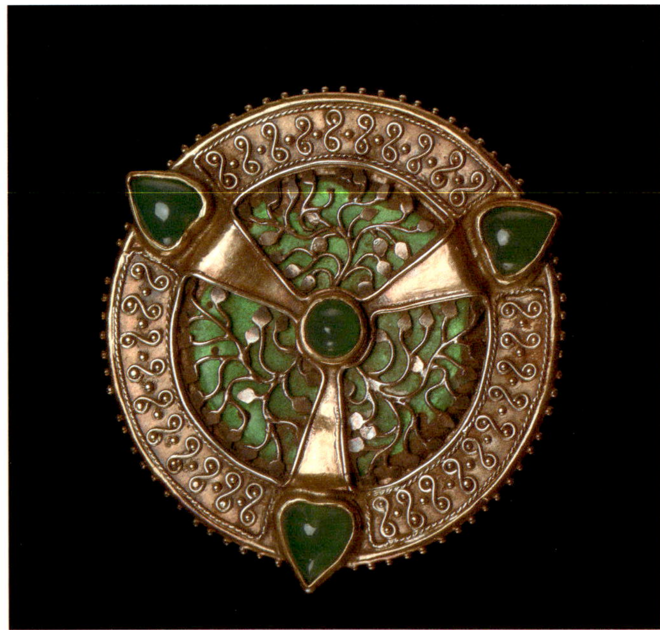

45. Edmund Rolfe
Brooch
Silver with jadeite
Diameter: $1\,^{5}/_{8}$ inches
Collection of Maribeth Harmes

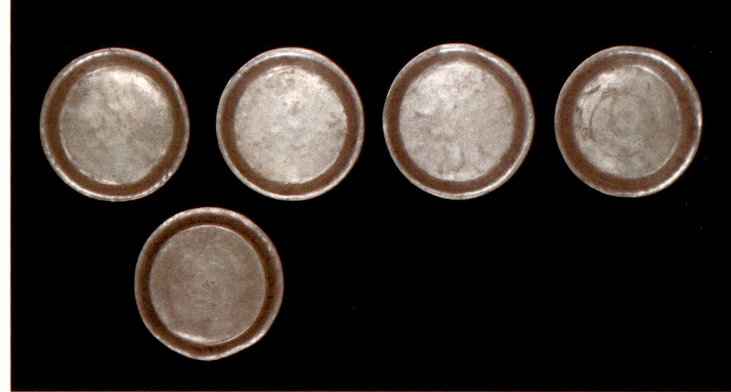

46. Edward Thatcher
Five Coasters
Pewter
Diameter: $3\,^{7}/_{8}$ inches (each)
Collection of Lawrence Webster

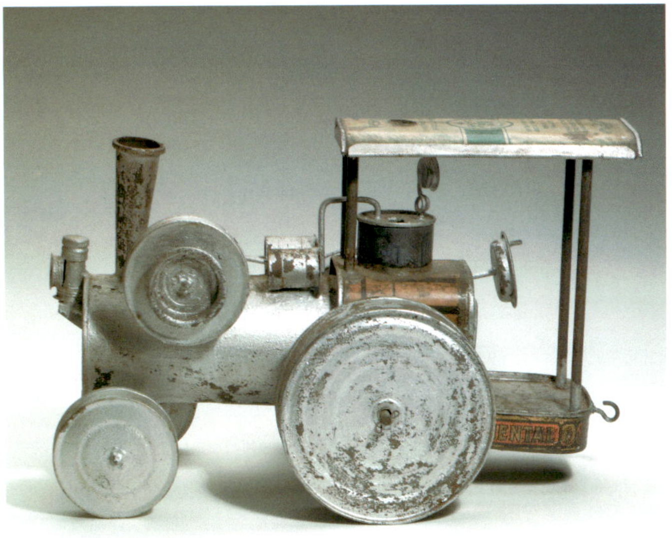

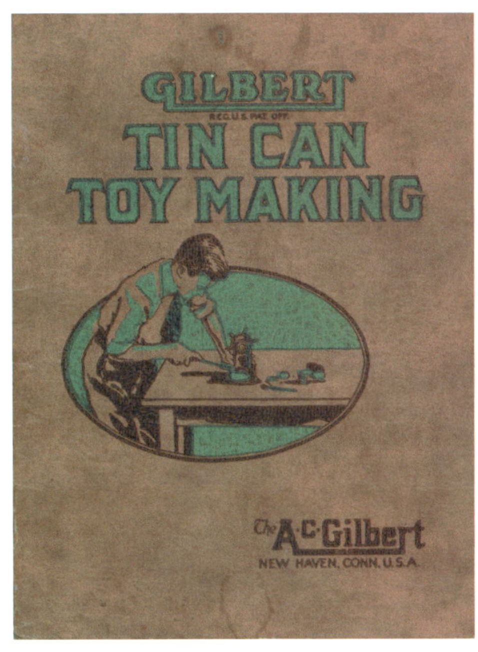

47. Edward Thatcher
Tin Train Engine Toy and Booklet
Toy height: 11 inches; width: 7 1/4 inches; depth: 5 3/4 inches
Collection of the Historical Society of Woodstock

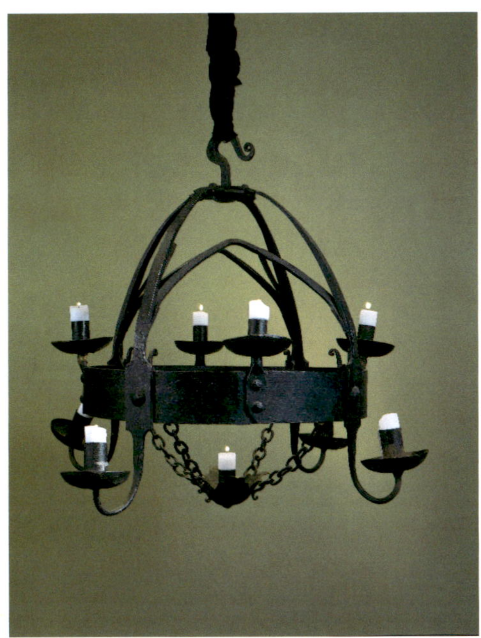

48. Edward Thatcher
Chandelier, ca. 1905
Wrought iron
Height: 35 inches; diameter: 39 inches
Collection of Jean and Jim Young

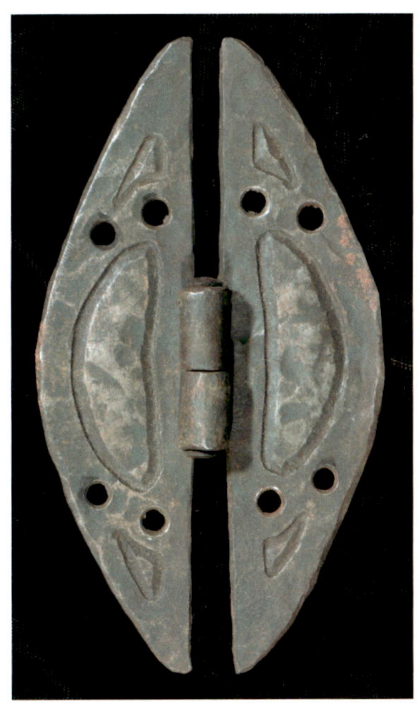

49. Attributed to Edward Thatcher
Metal Hinge
Iron
Height: 5 3/8 inches; width: 3 inches
Collection of the Byrdcliffe Art Colony of the Woodstock Guild

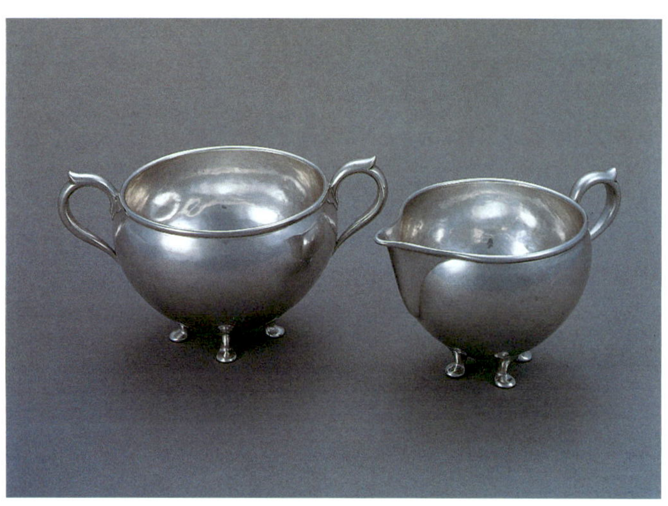

50. Bertha Thompson
Sugar Bowl and Creamer
Silver
Sugar Bowl: Height: 2 3/4 inches; width: 5 1/4 inches; diameter: 3 1/2 inches
Creamer: height: 2 5/8 inches; width: 4 1/2 inches; diameter: 3 1/4 inches
Collection of Janet Keep

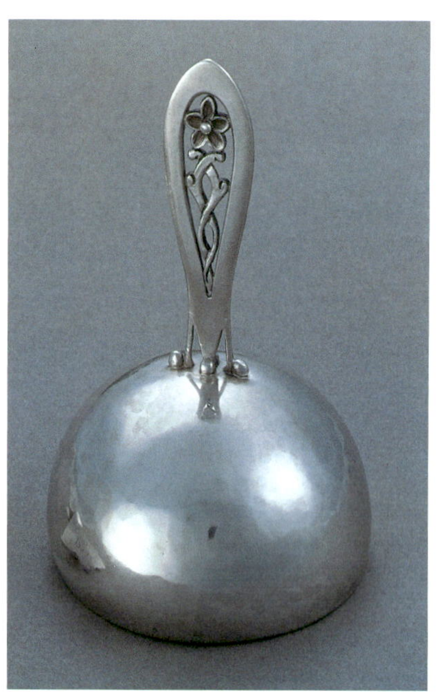

51. Bertha Thompson
Bell
Silver
Height: 3 1/2 inches; width: 2 1/2 inches; diameter: 2 1/2 inches
Collection of Janet Keep

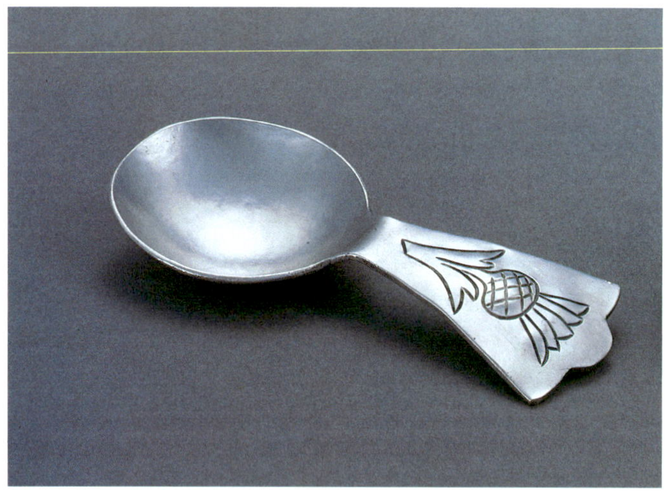

52. Bertha Thompson
Spoon
Silver
Height: 3 1/2 inches; width: 1 1/2 inches
Collection of Janet Keep

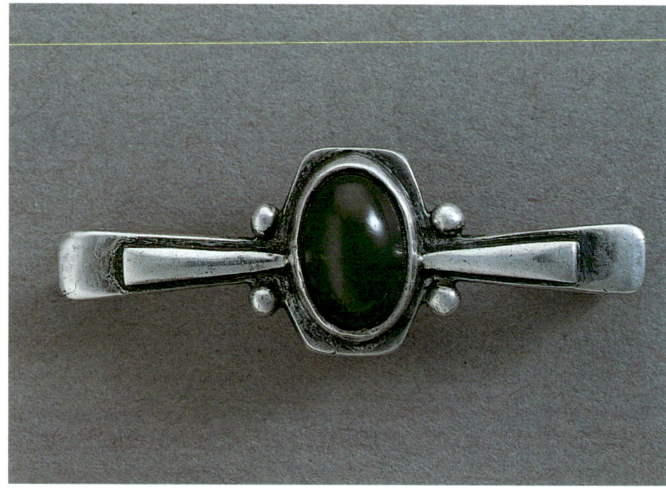

53. Bertha Thompson
Nacre Cape Fastener/Buckle
Silver with nacre cabochon
Height: 1 1/2 inches; width: 1 5/16 inches; diameter: 3/8 inch
Collection of Janet Keep

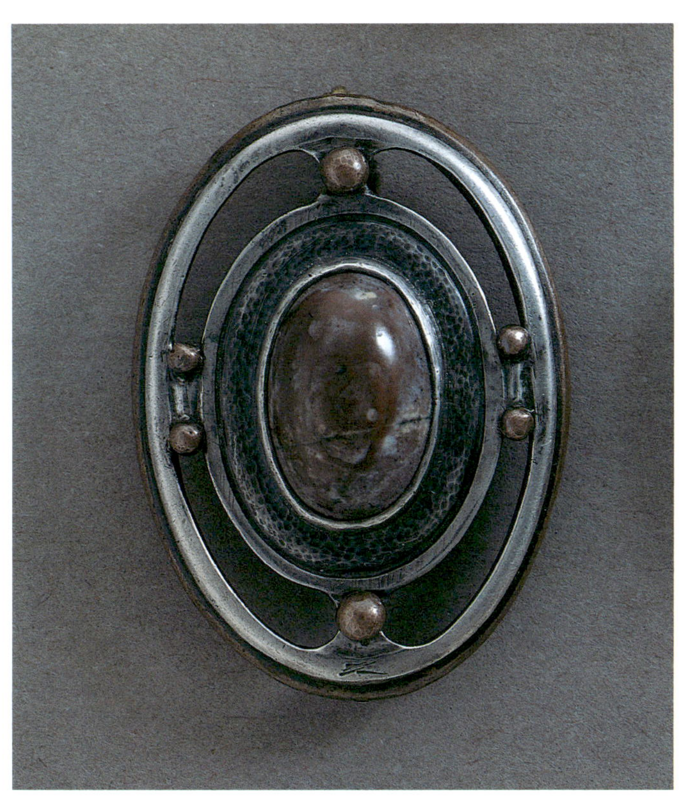

54. Bertha Thompson
Brooch
Silver and agate cabochon
Height: 1 $^5/_8$ inches; width: 1 $^1/_4$ inches; diameter: $^1/_2$ inch
Collection of Janet Keep

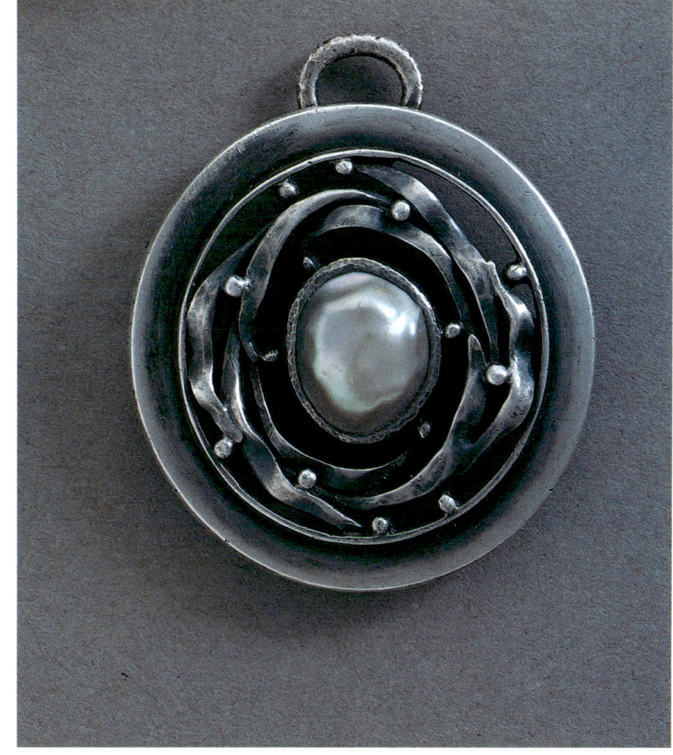

55. Bertha Thompson
Brooch
Silver and greenstone cabochon
Diameter: 2 inches
Collection of Janet Keep

Painting

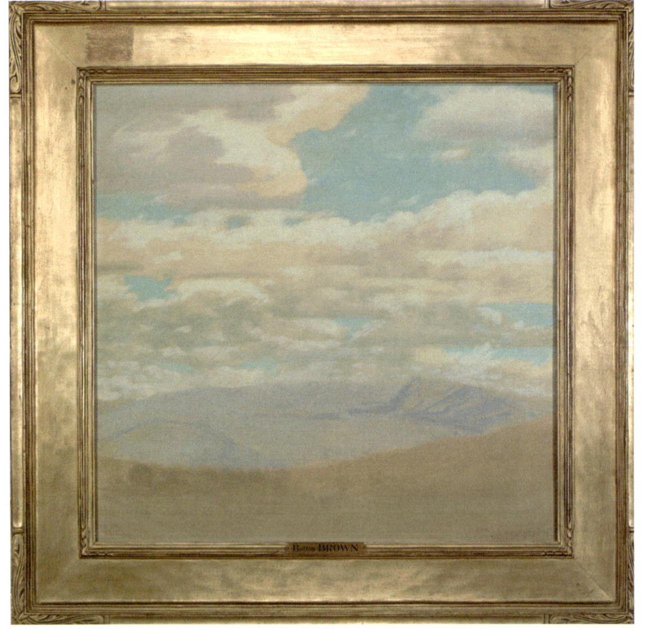

56. Bolton Brown
Landscape, in Carrig-Rohane frame
Oil on canvas
21 1/4 x 22 1/2 inches
On loan from Morgan Anderson Consulting

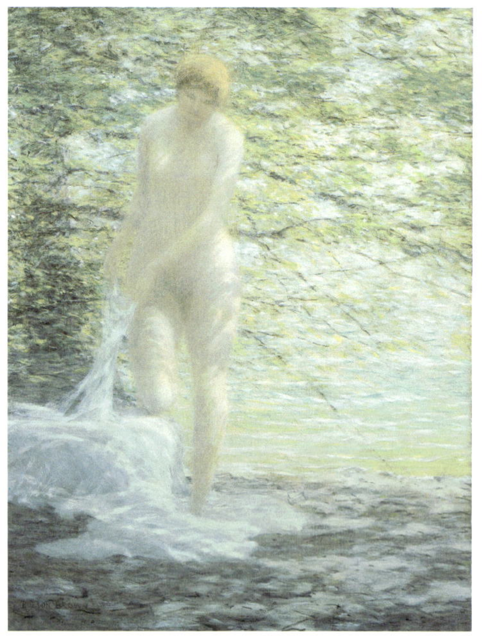

57. Bolton Brown
Sifting Shadows, ca. 1903
Oil on canvas
35 x 27 inches
Brooklyn Museum of Art
Gift of Quill Jones

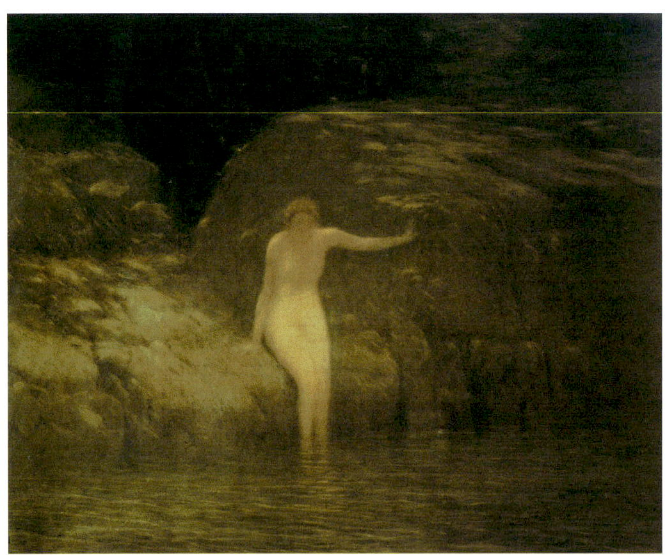

58. Bolton Brown
Nude by Pond, ca. 1910
Oil on canvas
25 x 35 inches
National Arts Club Permanent Collection, New York

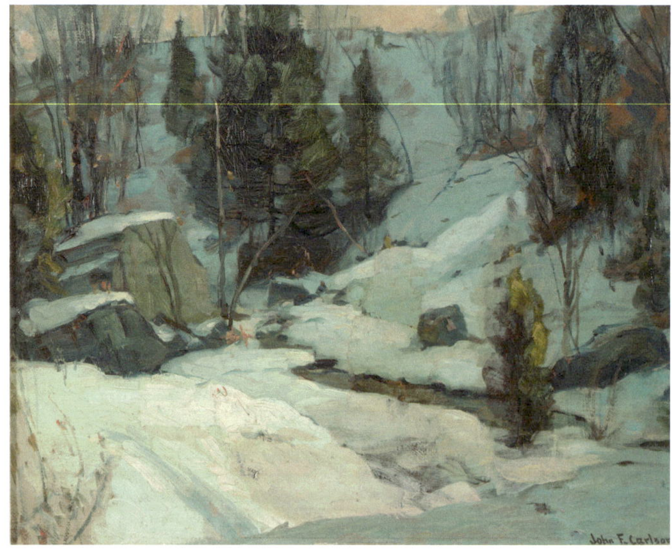

59. John Carlson
Wintry Glen, ca. 1922
Oil on canvas
12 x 16 inches
Collection of the Woodstock Artists Association
Gift of David and Robert Eric Carlson

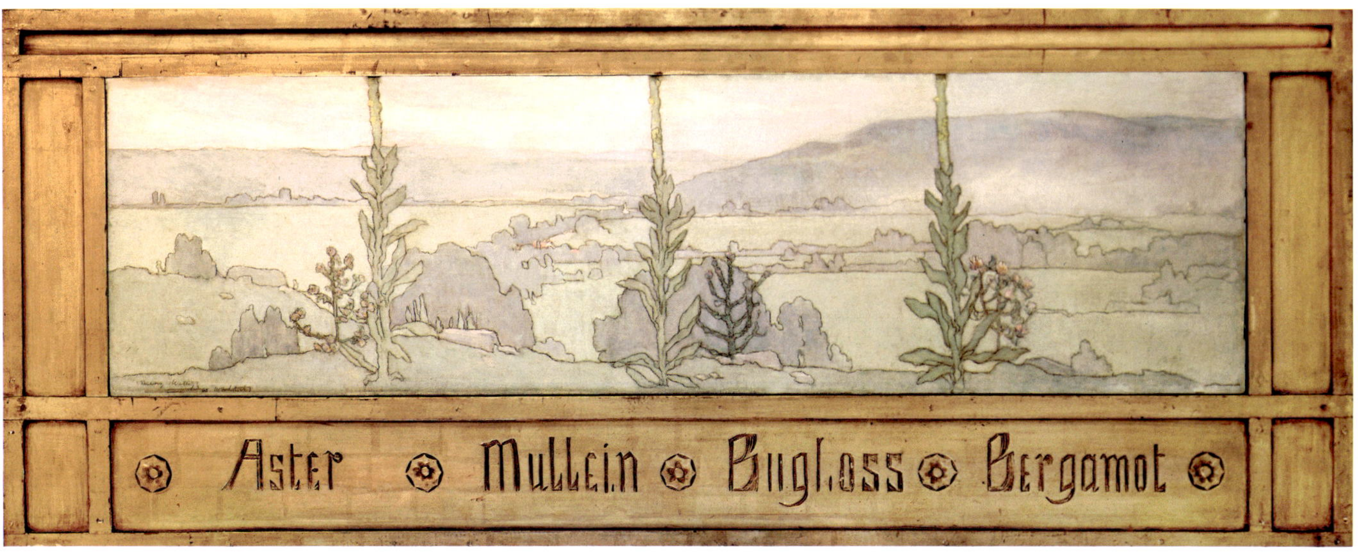

60. Dawson Dawson-Watson
Aster, Mullein, Burgloss, Bergamot, 1903
Oil on canvas
24 1/2 x 63 1/4 inches
Private collection
Courtesy of Berry-Hill Galleries, New York

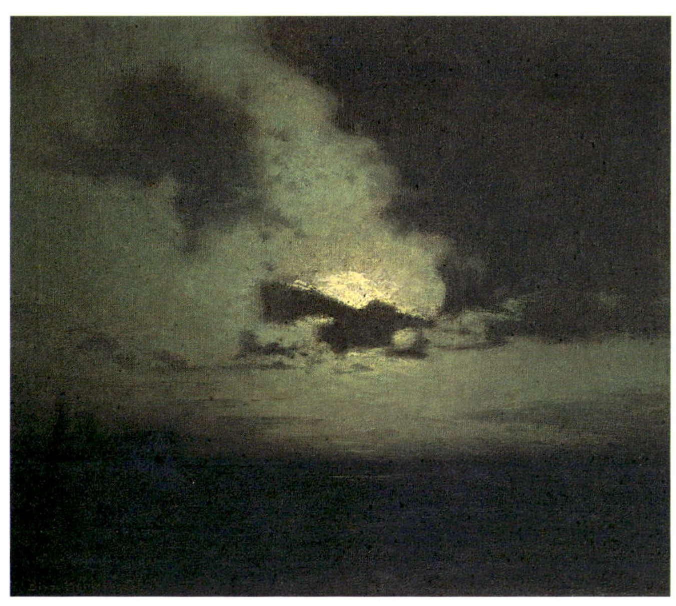

61. Lovell Birge Harrison
The Hidden Moon
Oil on canvas
25 1/4 x 30 1/8 inches
Collection of the National Academy of Design, New York

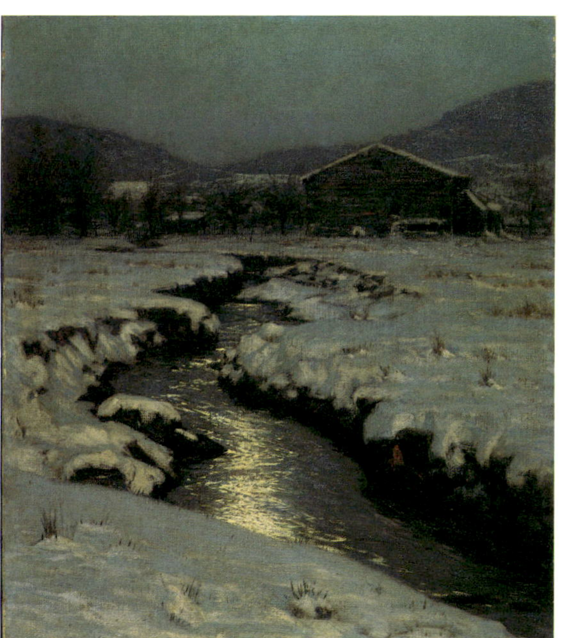

62. Lovell Birge Harrison
Woodstock Meadows in Winter, 1909
Oil on canvas
46 x 40 1/4 inches
Collection of the Toledo Museum of Art
Gift of Cora Baird Lacey, in memory of Mary A. Dustin

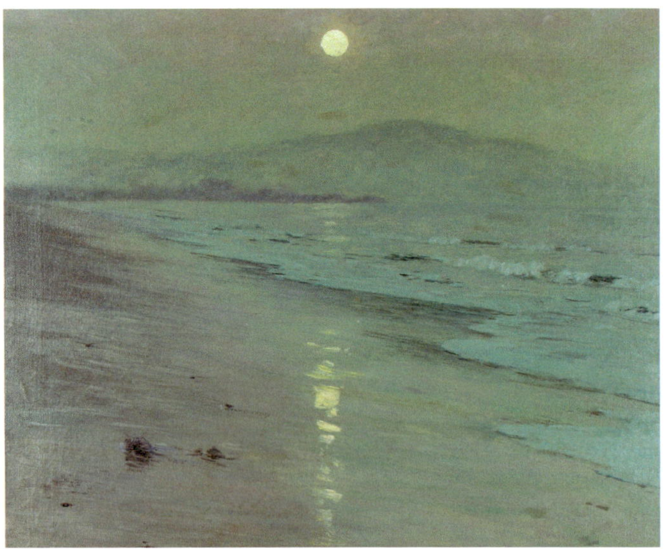

63. Lovell Birge Harrison
Moonrise on the Sea, 1896
Oil on canvas
19 x 24 inches
Private collection

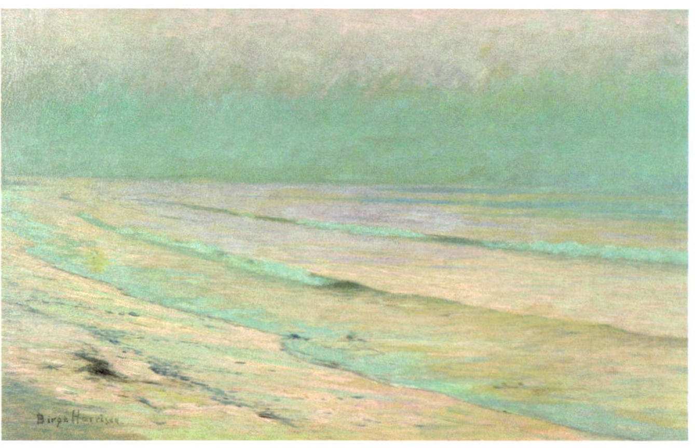

64. Lovell Birge Harrison
Serenity on the Pacific, ca. 1896
Oil on canvas
29 x 41 inches
Collection of the Woodstock Artists Association
Gift of Peter Whitehead

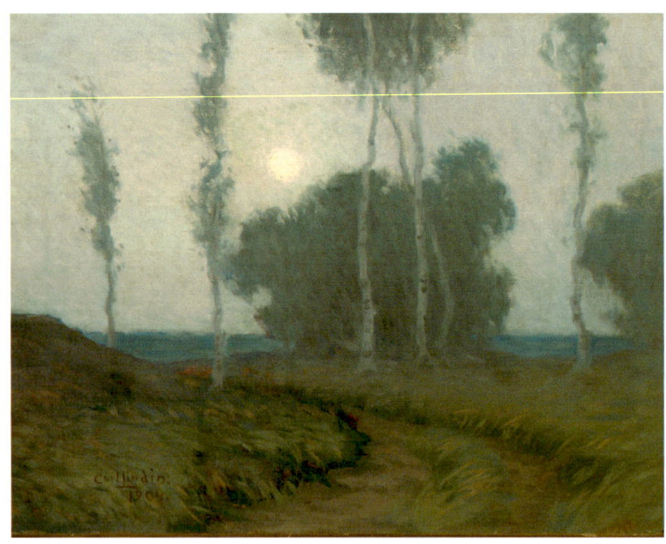

65. Carl Eric Lindin
Landscape
Oil on canvas
23 5/8 x 29 3/4 inches
On loan from Morgan Anderson Consulting

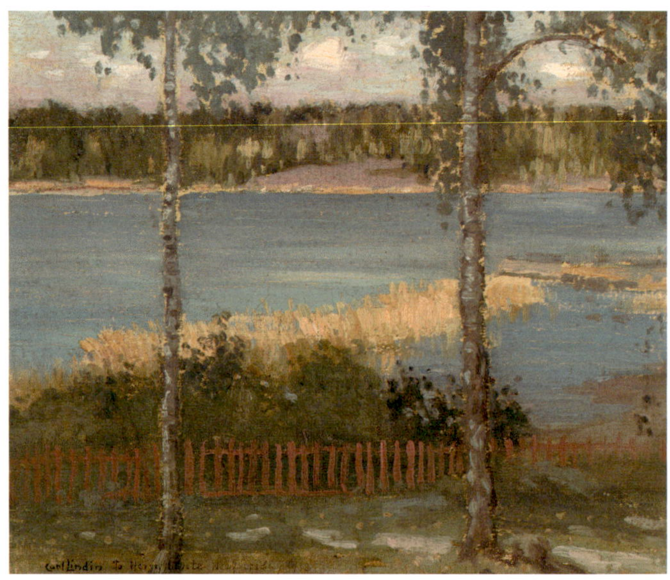

66. Carl Eric Lindin
Landscape, ca. 1913
Oil on canvas
19 x 22 inches
Woodstock Artists Association
Gift of Ruth Drake in memory of Pansy Drake Copeland and Franklin Ross Drake

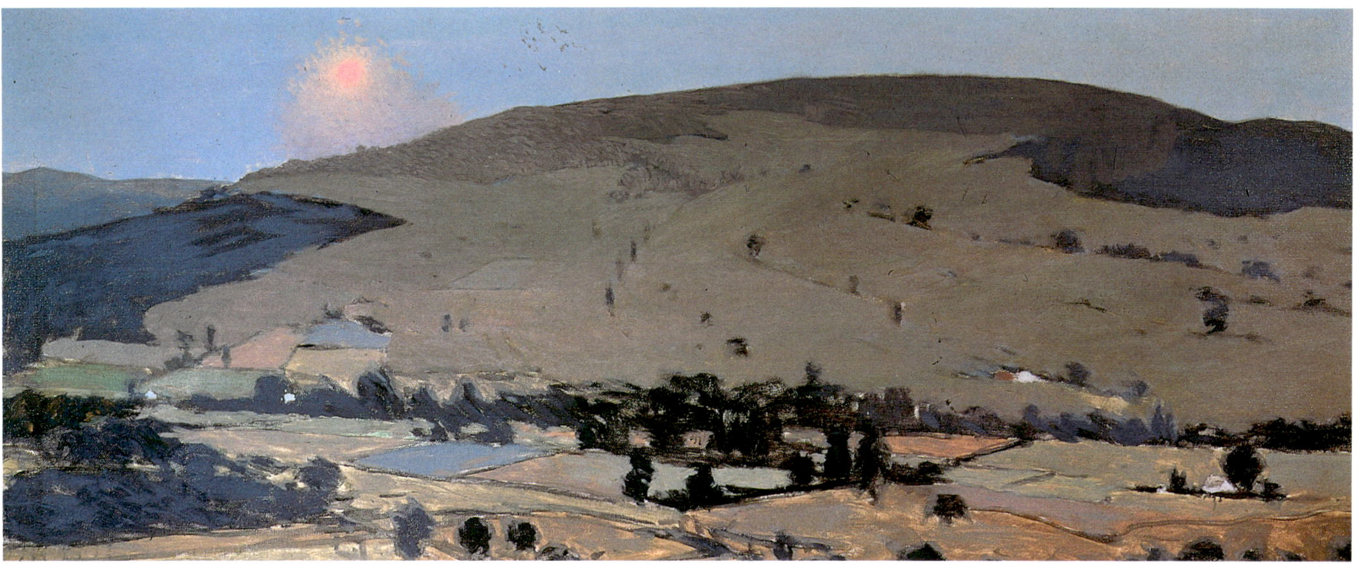

67. Hermann Dudley Murphy
Landscape, ca. 1903
Oil on canvas
28 x 69 inches
Private collection
Courtesy of Debra Force Fine Art, Inc., New York

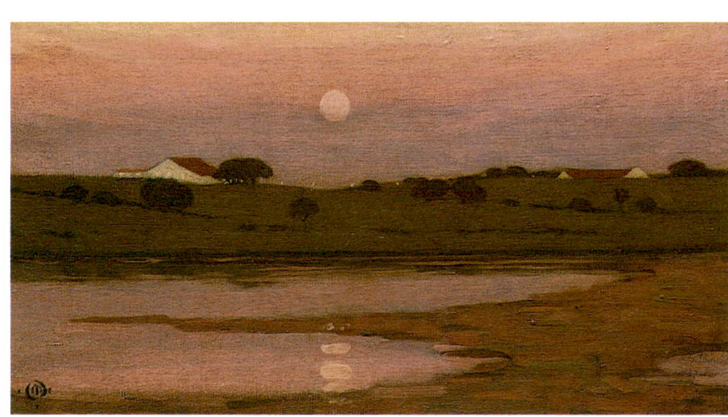

68. Hermann Dudley Murphy
Evening Glow, ca. 1905
Oil on canvas
10 x 18 inches
Private collection
Courtesy of Hirschl & Adler Galleries

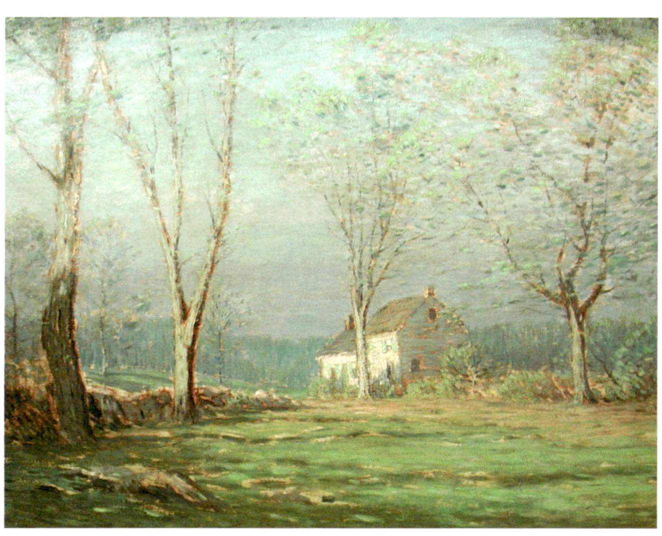

69. Leonard Ochtman
In May, 1907
Oil on canvas
40 1/2 x 50 1/2 inches
On loan from the Previti Gallery, New York

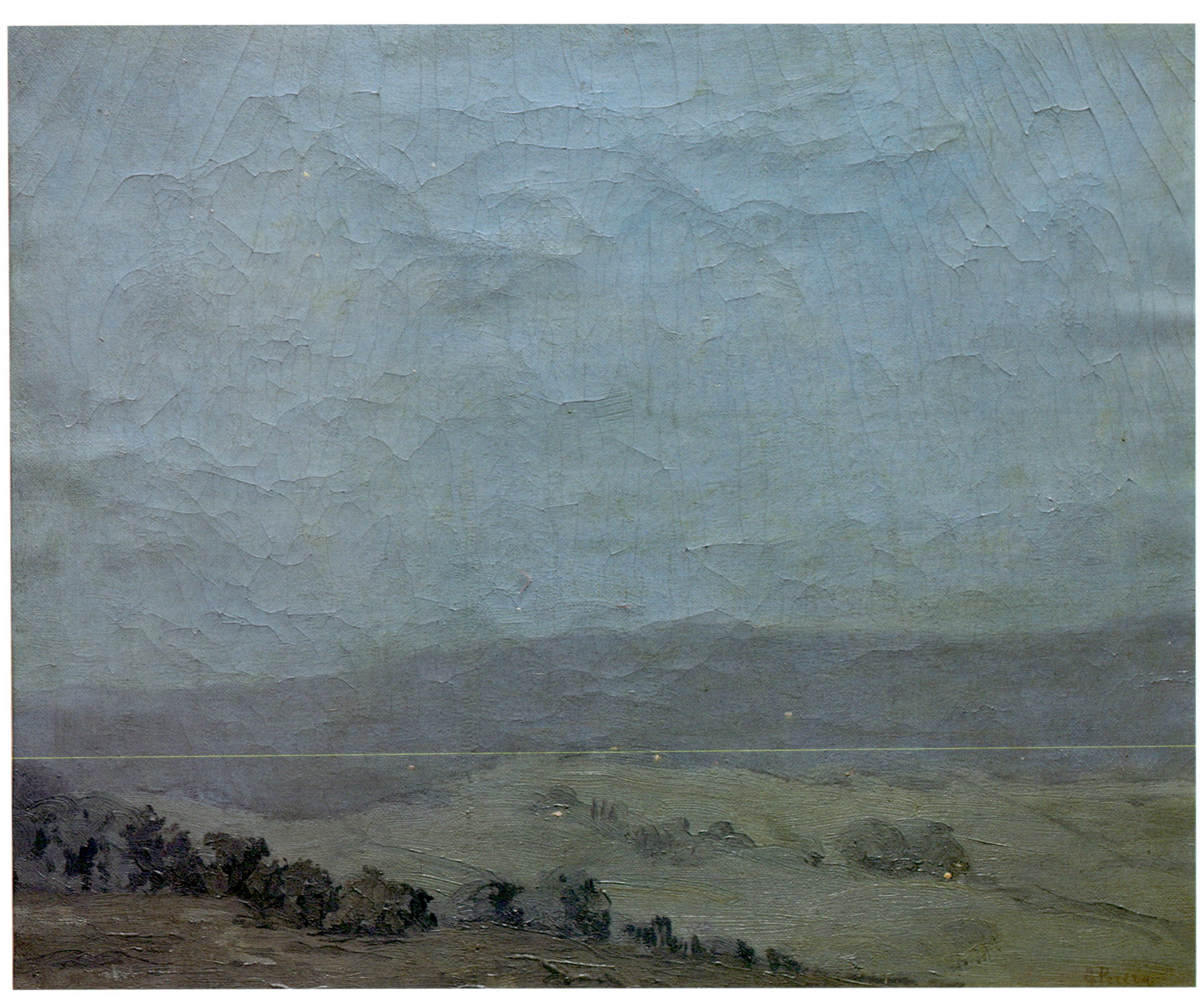

70. Gino Perera
Moonlight
Oil on canvas
$20\,^{7}/_{8}$ x $23\,^{7}/_{8}$ inches
Collection of Guido R. Perera Jr.

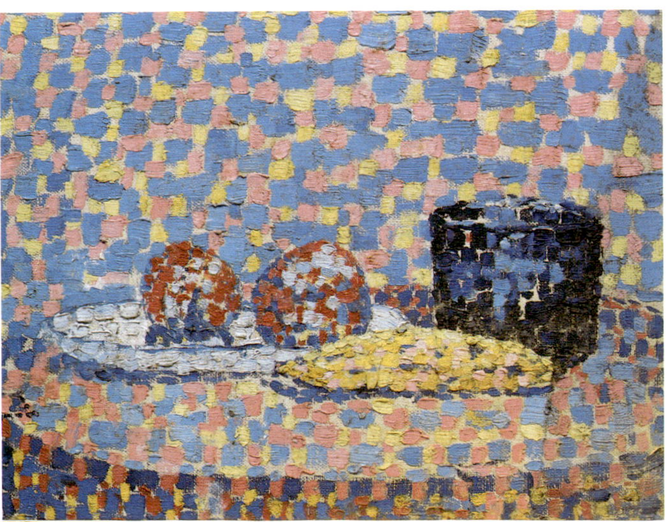

71. Gino Perera
Study, 1911
Oil on canvas
19 5/8 x 22 5/8 inches
Collection of Dr. Frederica P. D. Perera

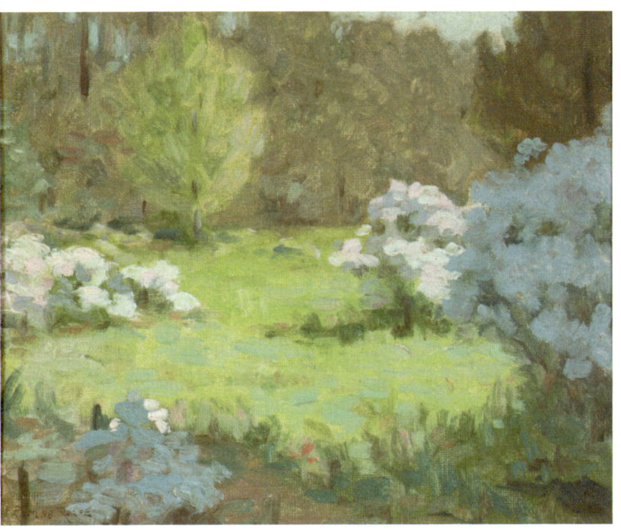

72. Edmund Rolfe
Landscape, ca. 1916
Oil on board
9 1/16 x 11 inches
Collection of Maribeth Harmes

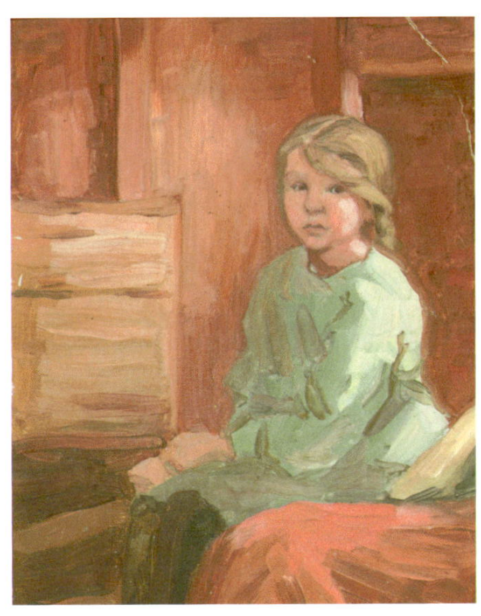

73. Edmund Rolfe
Girl in Interior, ca. 1914
Oil on board
8 x 6 15/16 inches
Collection of Maribeth Harmes

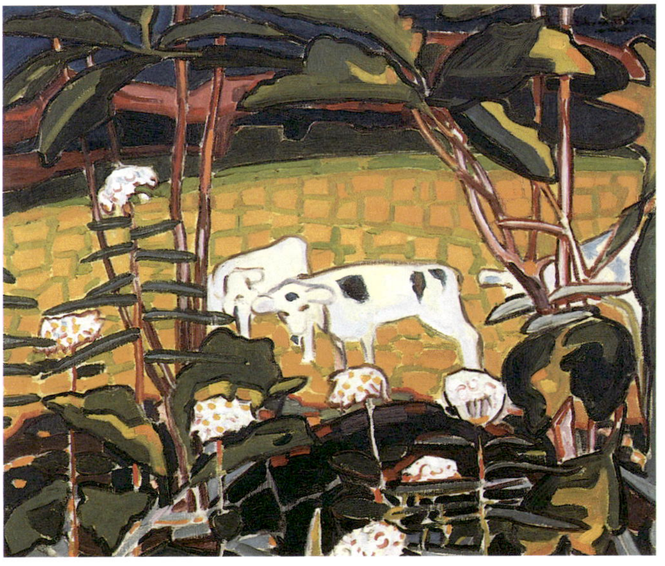

74. William Schumacher
Landscape with Cows, ca. 1917
Oil on canvas
24 x 32 inches
Collection of Suzanne Schutz

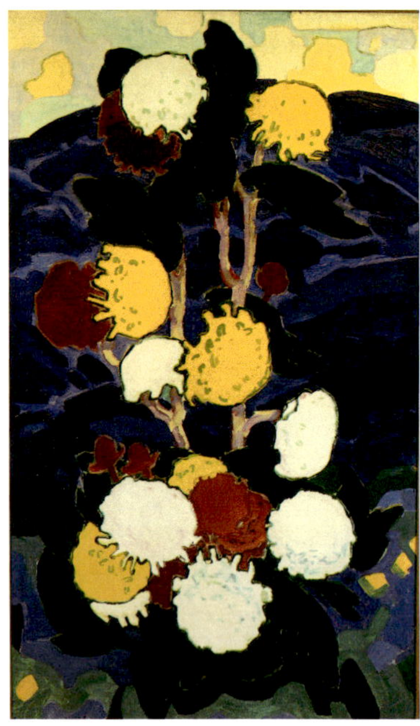

75. William Schumacher
Floral Landscape, 1916
Oil on canvas
42 x 25 inches
Courtesy of Hollis Taggart Gallery, New York

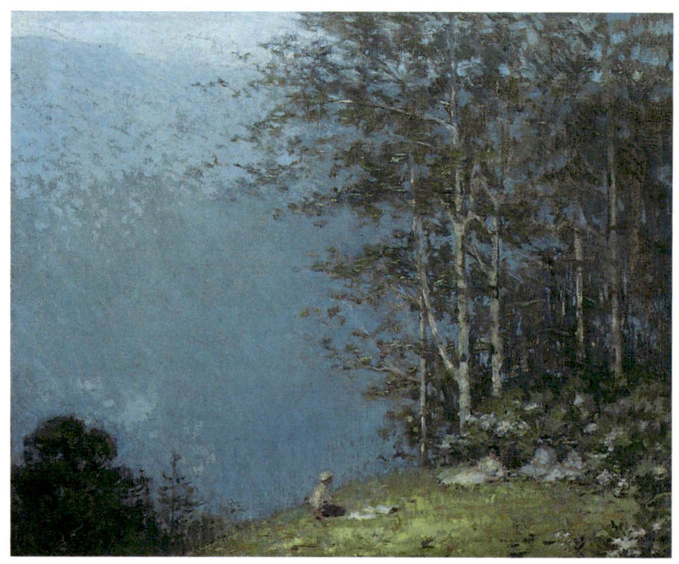

76. Zulma Steele
Summer, 1904
Oil on canvas
24 x 30 inches
Collection of Abby and Mark Lerner, New York

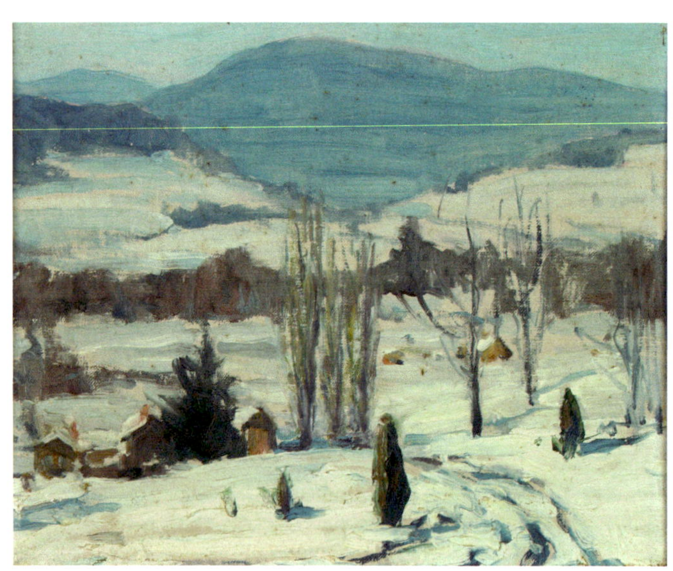

77. Zulma Steele
Byrdcliffe in Snow, ca. 1910
Oil on canvas
12 x 14 inches
Private collection

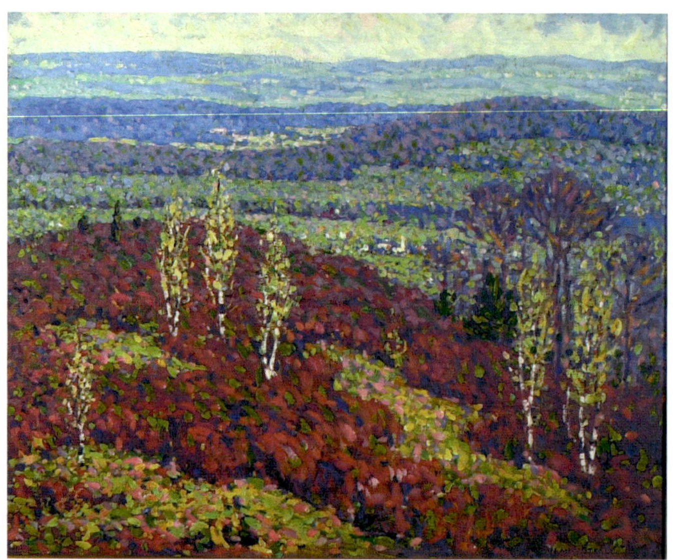

78. Zulma Steele
Autumn Landscape
Oil on canvas
$33\frac{15}{16}$ x $39\frac{7}{8}$ inches
Collection of Jean and Jim Young

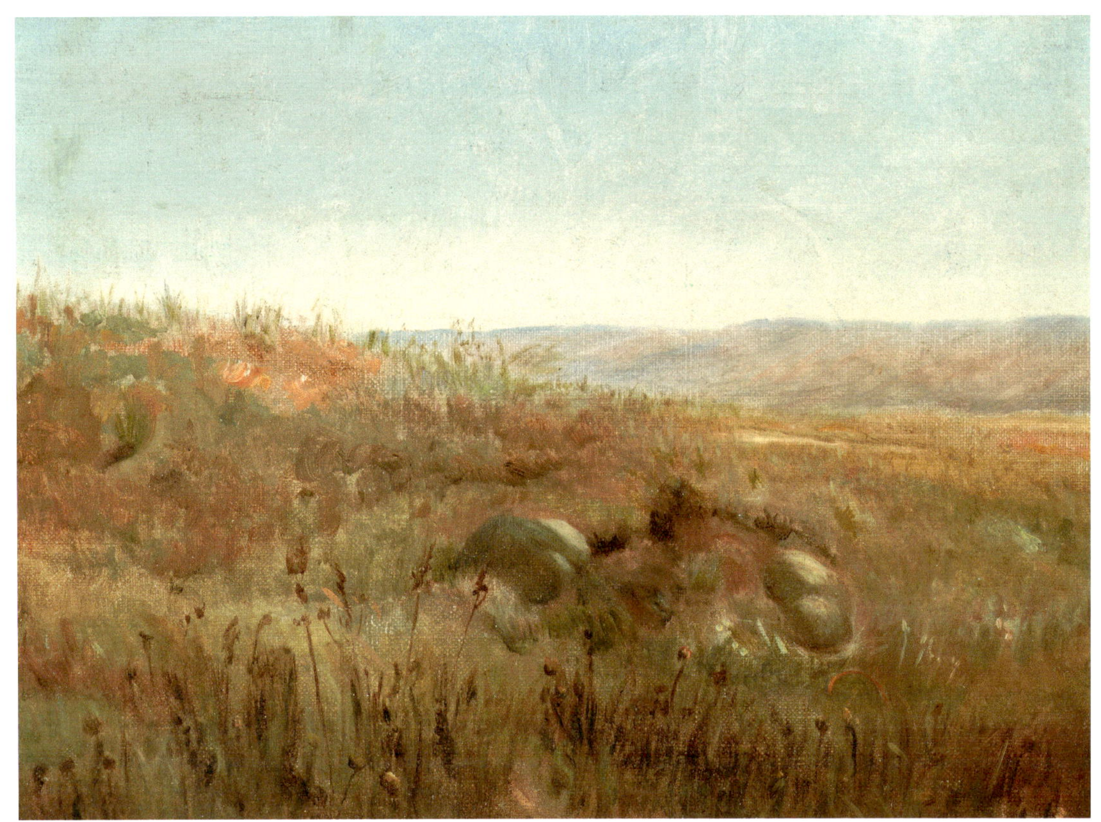

79. Jane Whitehead
Landscape, 1890s
Oil on canvas
14 1/4 x 18 1/4 inches
Private collection

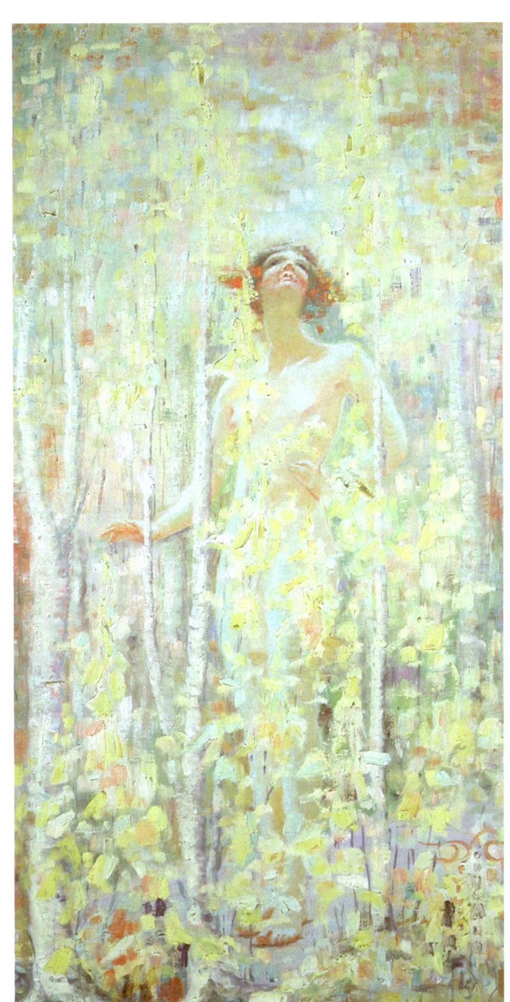

80. Dewing Woodward
Listening to the Footsteps of Autumn
Oil on canvas
48 x 25 3/8 inches
Collection of the Bigelow Homestead

Photography

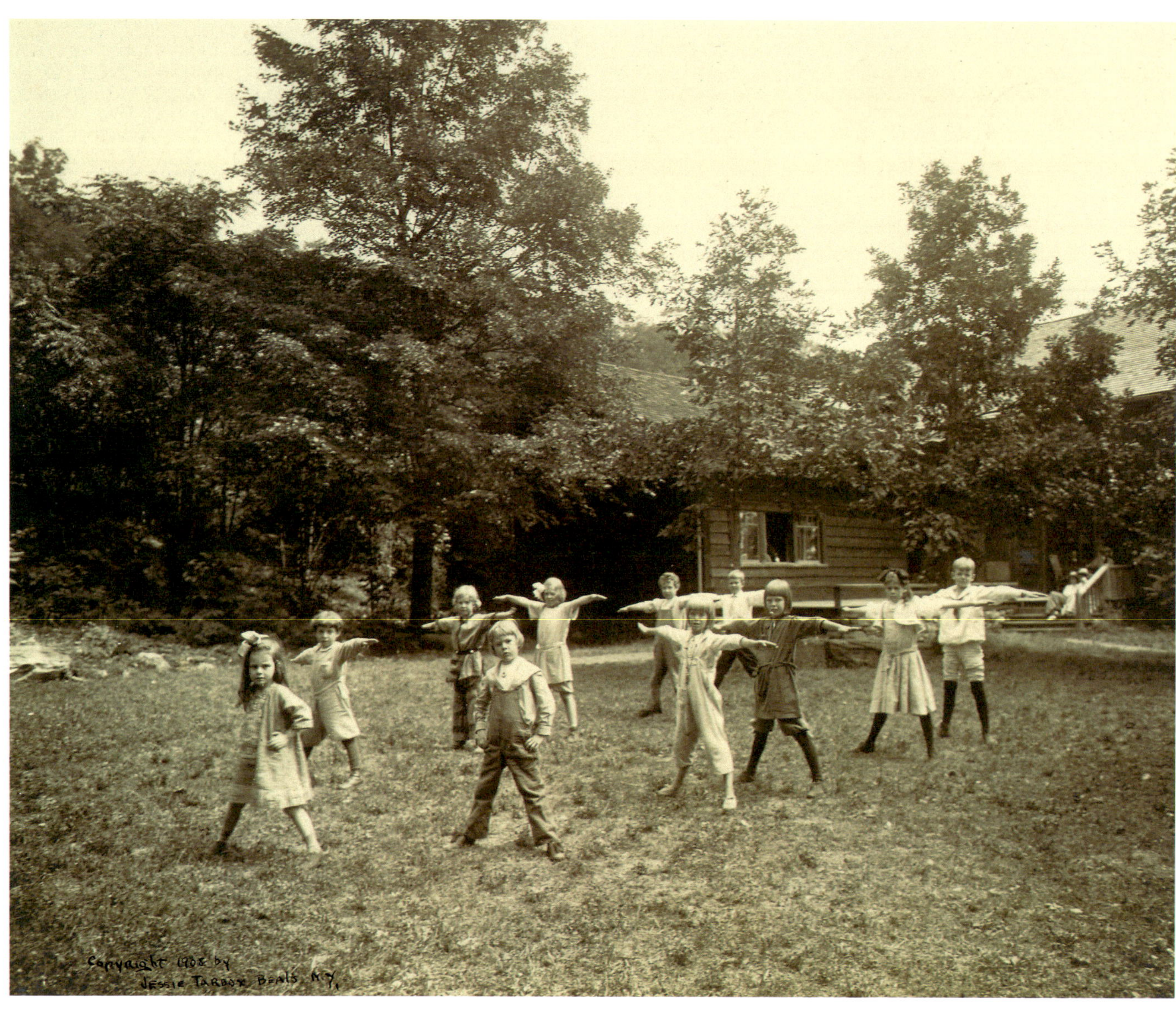

81. Jessie Tarbox Beals
Exercise Class, 1908 (Peter and Ralph Whitehead Jr. are in the front row, third and fourth from the left)
Silver print
7 1/2 x 8 3/4 inches
Collection of the Byrdcliffe Art Colony of the Woodstock Guild
Gift of Jill and Mark Willcox Jr.

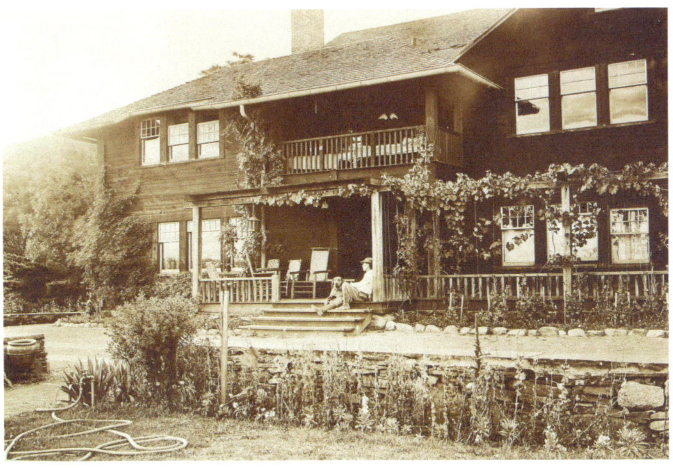

82. Jessie Tarbox Beals
White Pines, 1908
Silver print
5 1/4 x 7 1/4 inches
Collection of the Byrdcliffe Art Colony of the Woodstock Guild
Gift of Jill and Mark Willcox Jr.

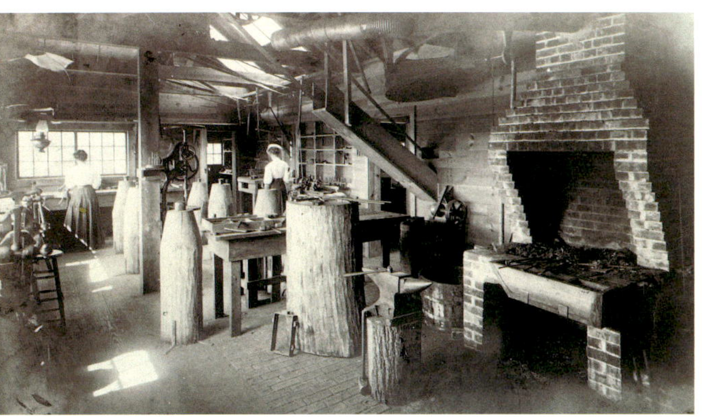

83. Jessie Tarbox Beals
Metal Shop, 1908
Silver print
7 1/2 x 9 1/2 inches
Collection of the Byrdcliffe Art Colony of the Woodstock Guild
Gift of Jill and Mark Willcox Jr.

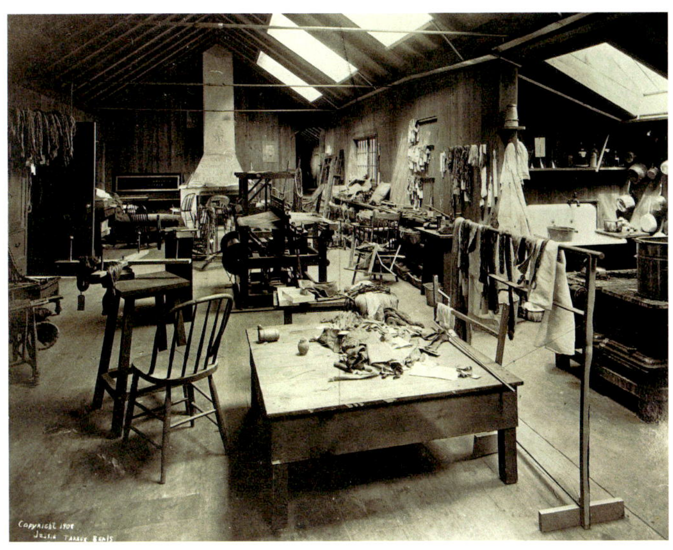

84. Jessie Tarbox Beals
Loom Room, 1908
Silver print
7 1/2 x 9 1/2 inches
Collection of the Byrdcliffe Art Colony of the Woodstock Guild
Gift of Howard Greenberg

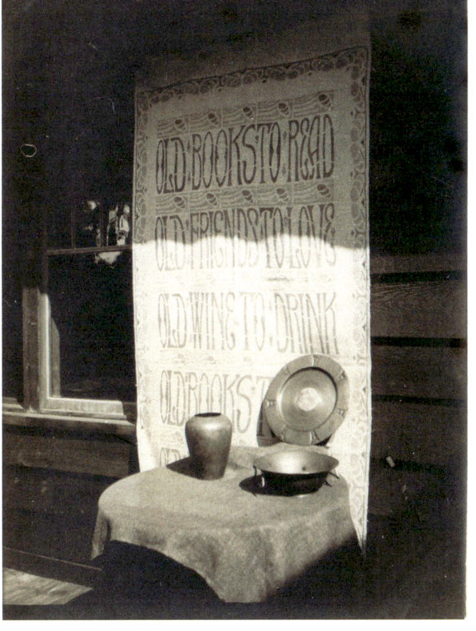

85. H. Stuart Michie
Byrdcliffe photograph, 1905
Silver print
4 1/4 x 3 1/4 inches
Collection of Thomas Michie
(see cat. 41 for charger; cat. 42 for bowl; cat. 157 for hanging)

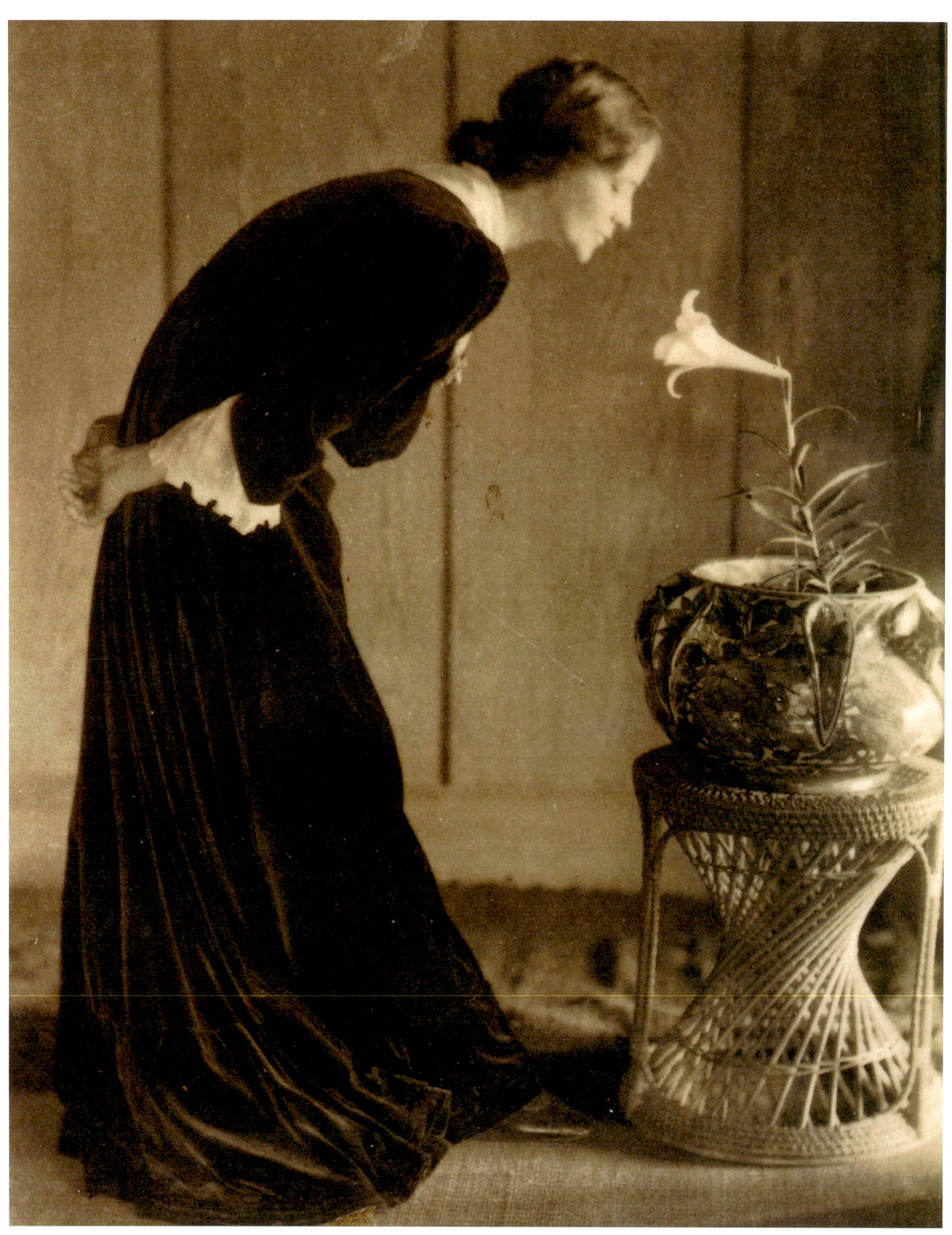

86. Eva Watson-Schütze
Jane Whitehead and Lily, 1905
Platinum print
8 x 6 1/4 inches
Collection of the George Eastman House
Gift of Frieda Schütze

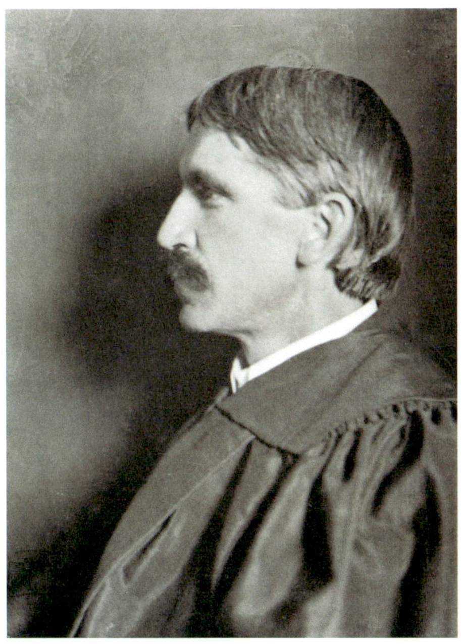

87. Eva Watson-Schütze
John Dewey, 1905
Platinum print
8 x 6 inches
Collection of the George Eastman House
Gift of Frieda Schütze

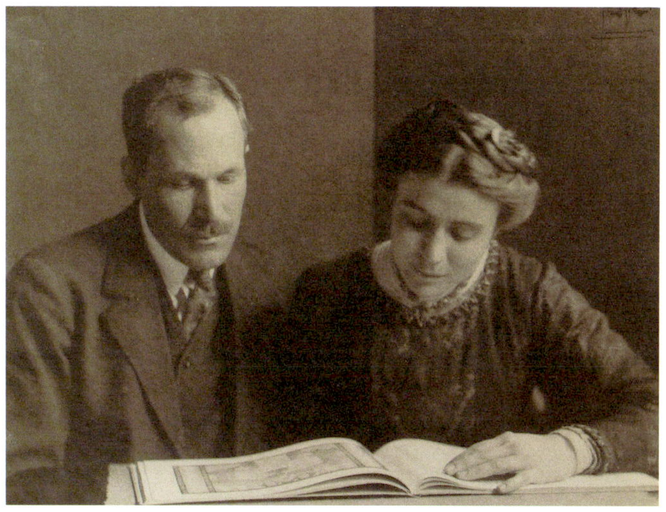

88. Eva Watson-Schütze
Carl and Louise Lindin, ca. 1905
Platinum print
6 1/8 x 8 inches
Collection of Howard Greenberg Gallery, New York

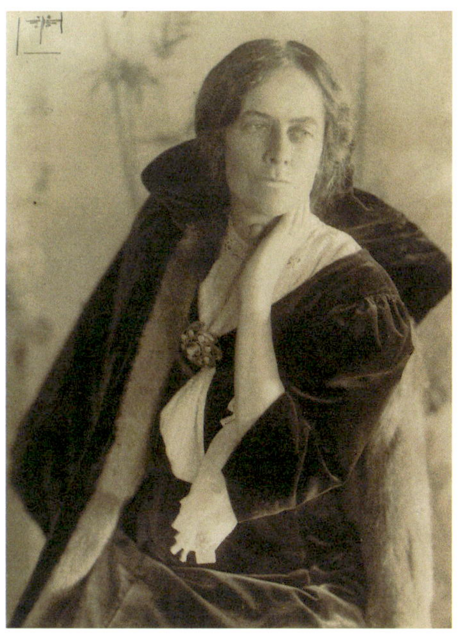

89. Eva Watson-Schütze
Jane Whitehead Seated, ca. 1905
Platinum print
8 x 6 inches
Collection of Howard Greenberg Gallery, New York

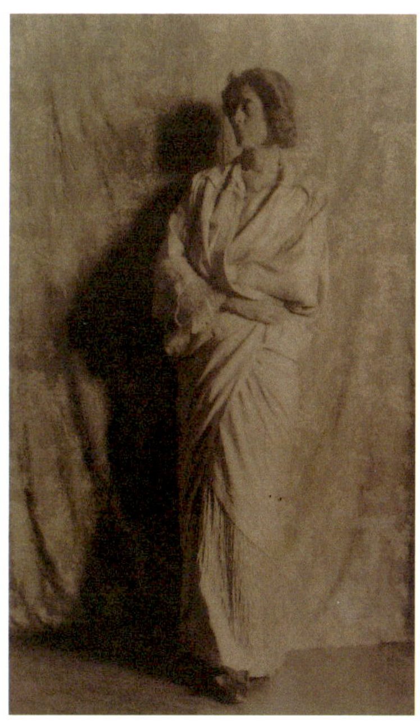

90. Eva Watson-Schütze
Jane Whitehead Standing, ca. 1905
Platinum print
8 x 5 inches
Collection of Howard Greenberg Gallery, New York

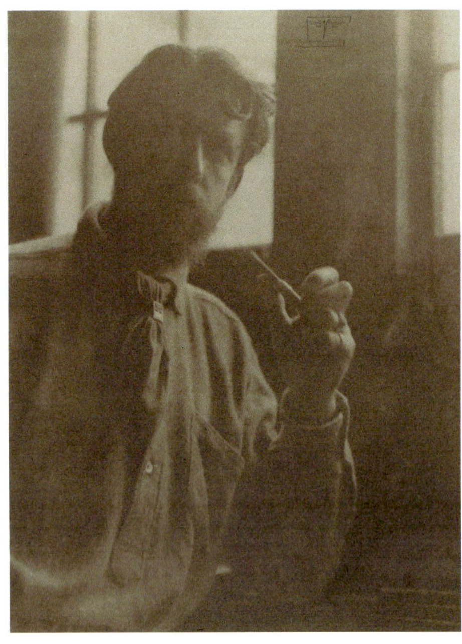

91. Eva Watson-Schütze
Bolton Brown, ca. 1905
Platinum print
8 x 6 1/4 inches
Collection of Howard Greenberg Gallery, New York

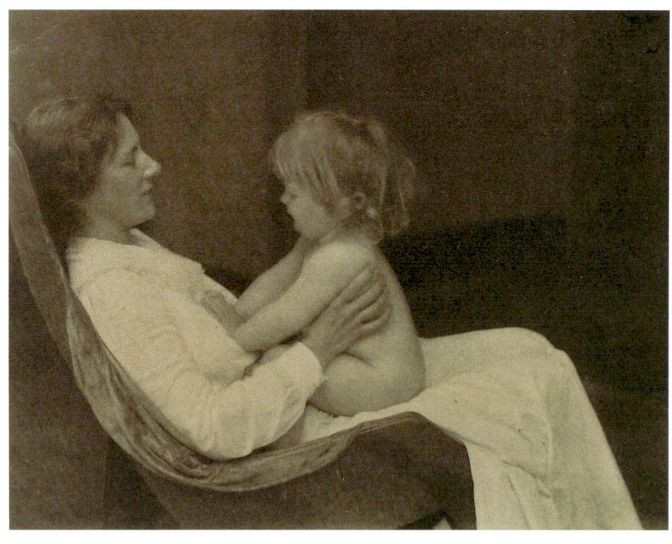

92. Eva Watson-Schütze
Lucy Fletcher Brown and Daughter in Rocking Chair, ca. 1905
Platinum print
6 1/4 x 7 7/8 inches
Collection of Howard Greenberg Gallery, New York

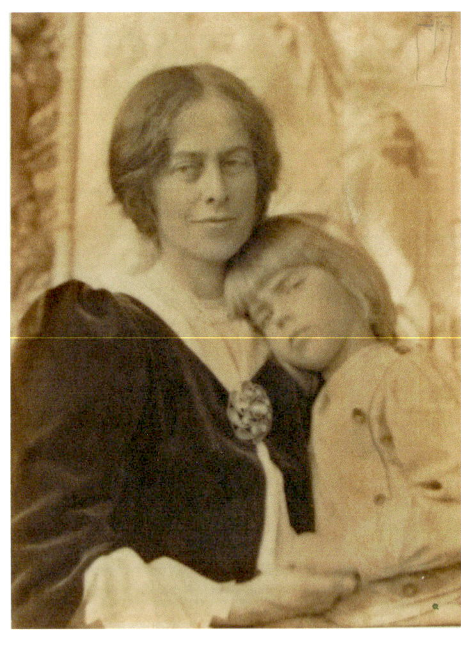

93. Eva Watson-Schütze
Jane Whitehead Holding Peter, ca. 1905
Platinum print
7 3/4 x 6 inches
Collection of Howard Greenberg Gallery, New York

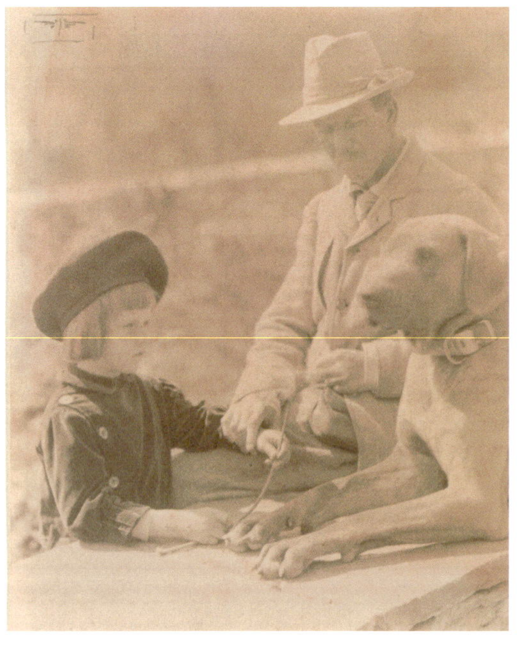

94. Eva Watson-Schütze
Ralph and Ralph Jr. with Dog, ca. 1905
Platinum print
7 1/2 x 7 1/2 inches
Collection of Douglas C. James

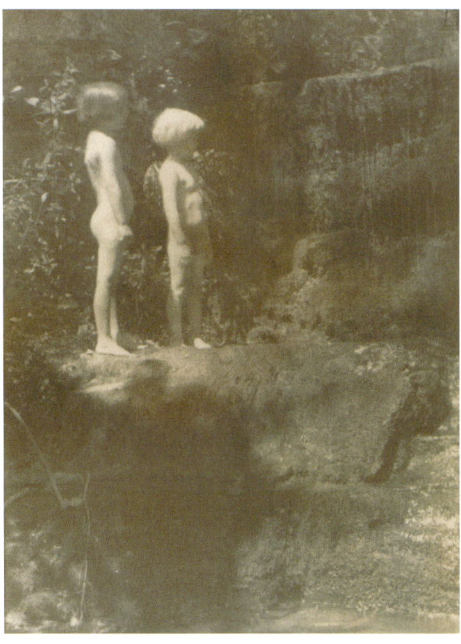

95. Eva Watson-Schütze
Untitled (probably Ralph Jr. and Peter at the watering hole), ca. 1905
Silver print
8 1/8 x 6 1/8 inches
Collection of Douglas C. James

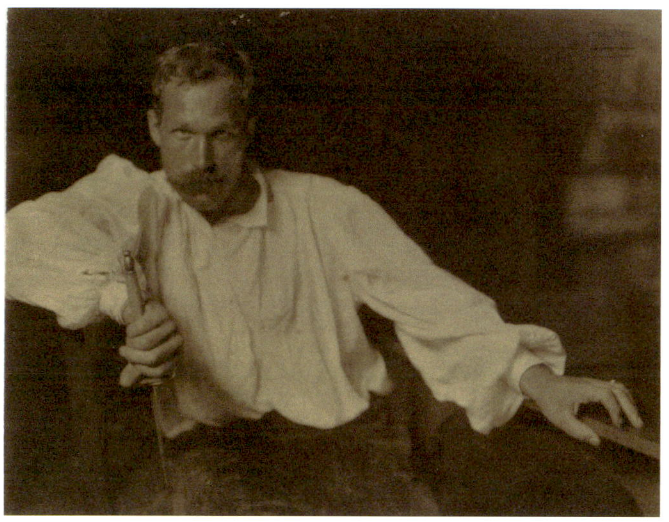

96. Eva Watson-Schütze
Carl Lindin
Platinum print
6 1/8 x 8 1/8 inches
Collection of Gregory E. and Eleanor Lindin

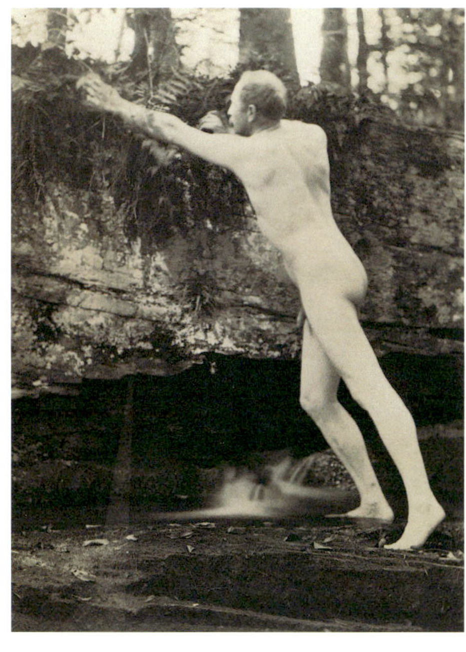

97. Eva Watson-Schütze
Martin Schütze in Quarry
Platinum print
8 x 6 inches
On loan from Morgan Anderson Consulting

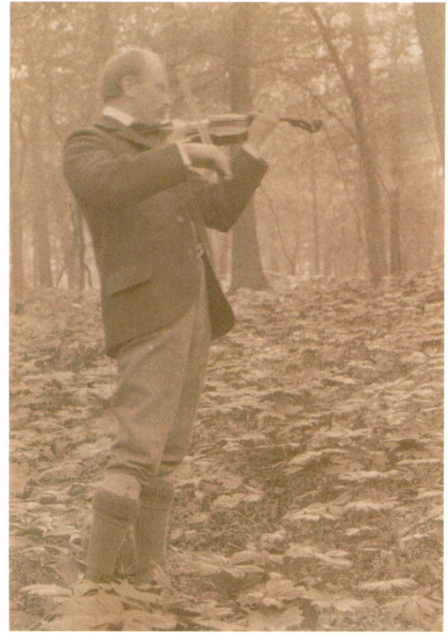

98. Eva Watson-Schütze
Martin Schütze with Violin
Platinum print
6 1/2 x 4 1/2 inches
On loan from Morgan Anderson Consulting

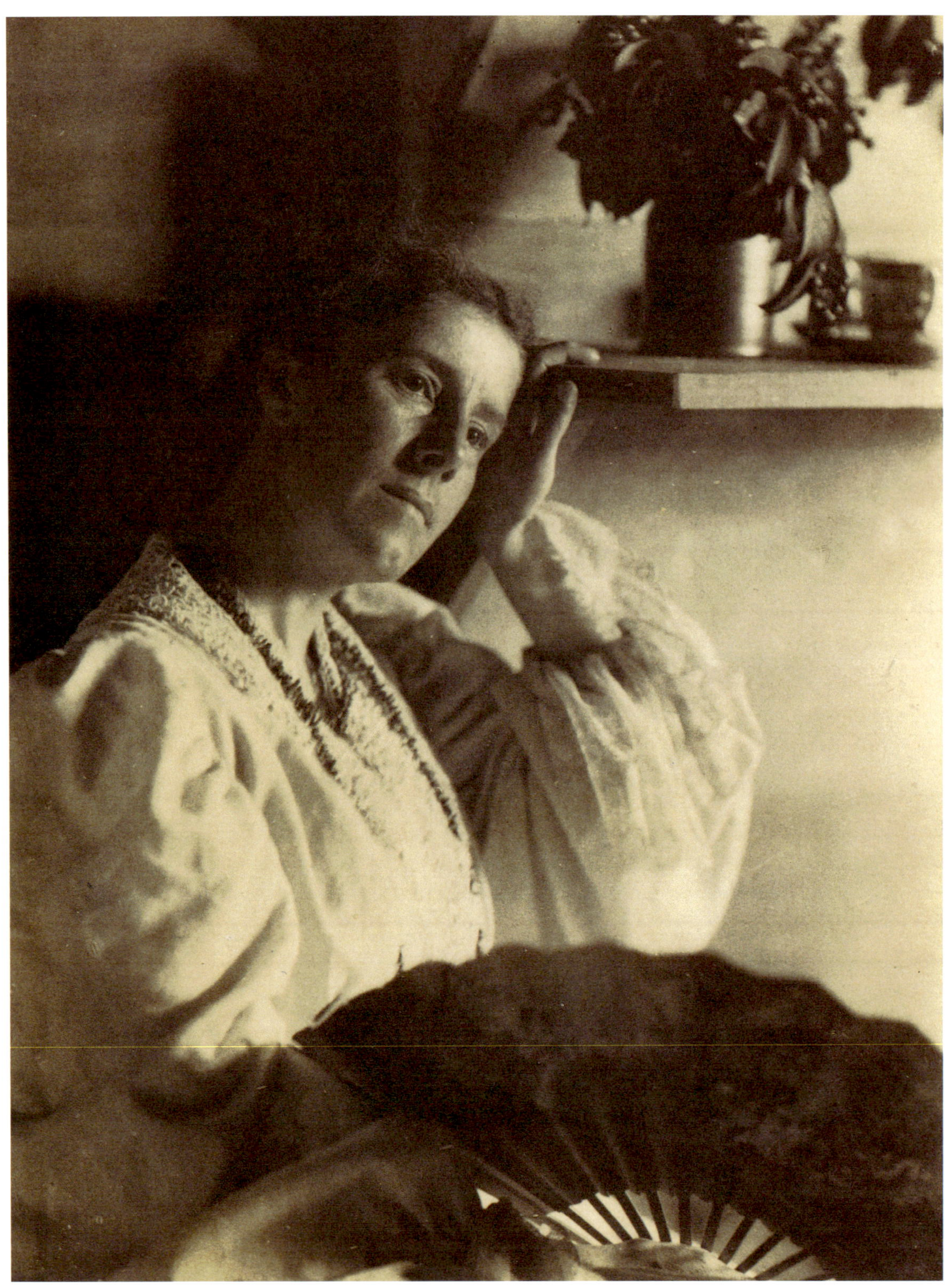

99. Eva Watson-Schütze
Charlotte Perkins Gilman, ca. 1915
Silver print
6 1/2 x 8 inches
Collection of the Schlesinger Library, Radcliffe Institute,
Harvard University

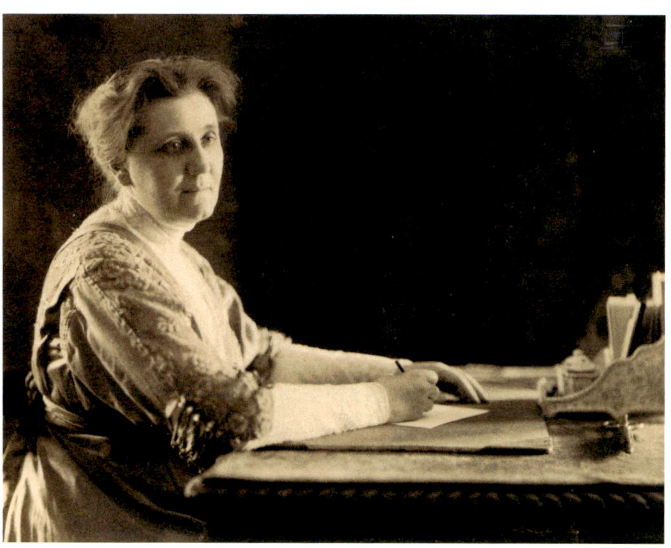

100. Eva Watson-Schütze
Jane Addams, ca. 1910
Platinum print
8 x 6 $^{5}/_{16}$ inches
University of Chicago Library, Special Collections
Research Center

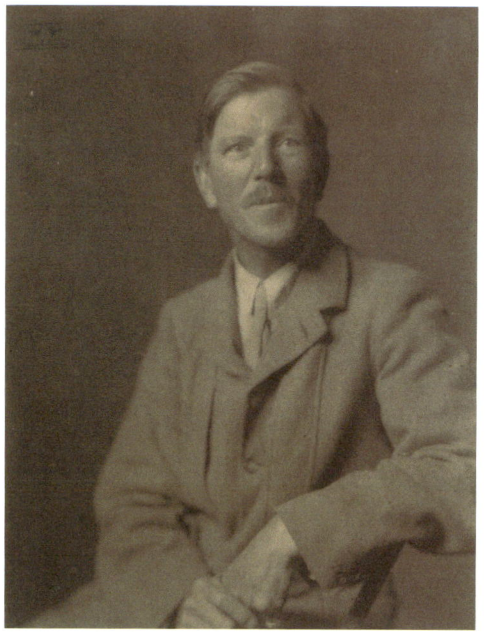

101. Eva Watson-Schütze
Ralph Whitehead, ca. 1905
Platinum print
8 x 6 inches
Private collection

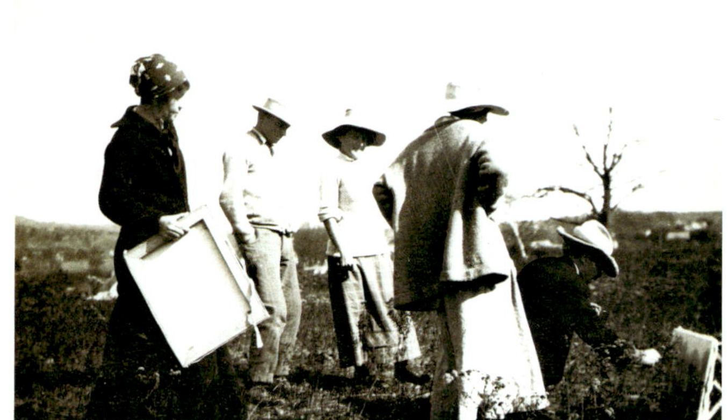

102. Unidentified photographer
Painting Class, en plein air, ca. 1910
Silver print
6 $^{3}/_{4}$ x 10 inches
Collection of the Byrdcliffe Art Colony of the Woodstock Guild,
Alf Evers Collection
Gift of the Douglas C. James Charitable Trust

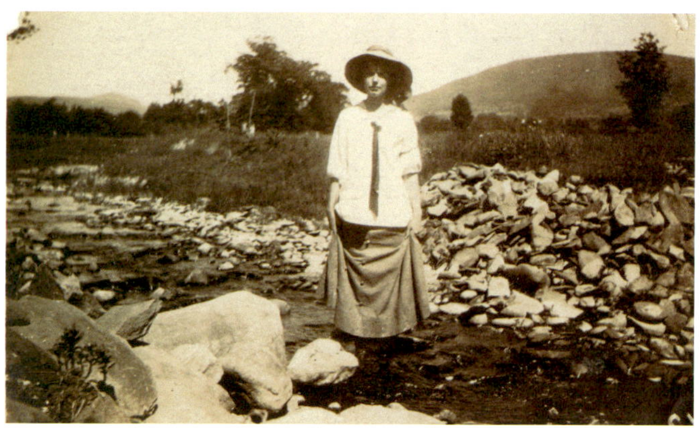

103. Unidentified photographer
Girl in Stream, ca. 1910
Silver print
3 $^{1}/_{8}$ x 4 inches
Collection of the Byrdcliffe Art Colony of the Woodstock Guild,
Alf Evers Collection
Gift of the Douglas C. James Charitable Trust

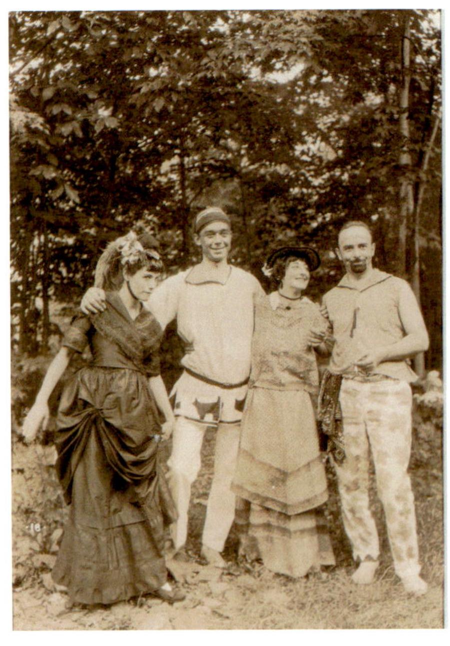

104. Unidentified photographer
Lucile Blanch, Rudolph Wetterau, Eugenie Gershoy, John Striebel at Maverick Festival, ca. 1920
Silver print
6 7/8 x 5 inches
The Jean Gaede Archives, Center for Photography at Woodstock, Permanent Print Collection
On extended loan to the Samuel Dosky Museum of Art, State University of New York at New Paltz

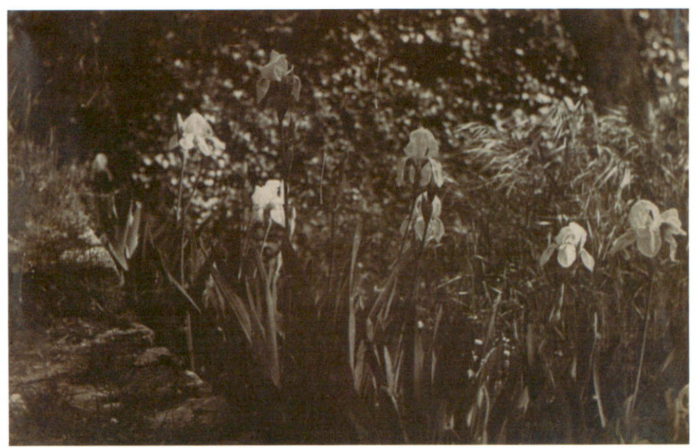

106. Ralph Radcliffe Whitehead
Irises
Albumen print
12 1/4 x 15 inches
Collection of Douglas C. James

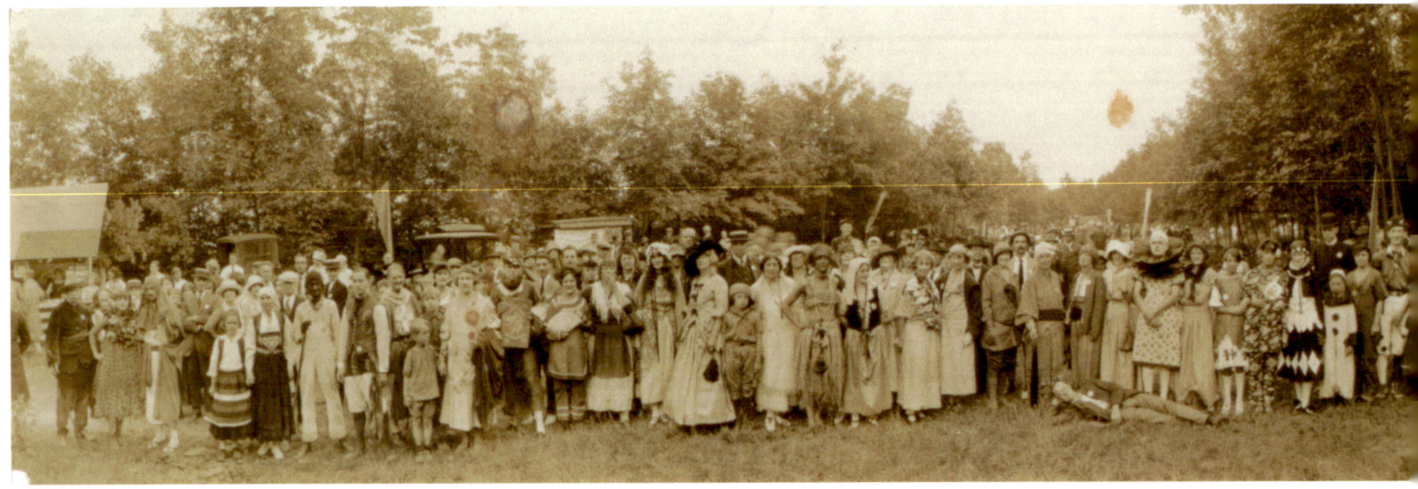

105. Unidentified photographer
Maverick Festival, ca. 1920
Silver print
6 x 36 inches
The Jean Gaede Archives, Center for Photography at Woodstock, Permanent Print Collection
On extended loan to the Samuel Dosky Museum of Art, State University of New York at New Paltz

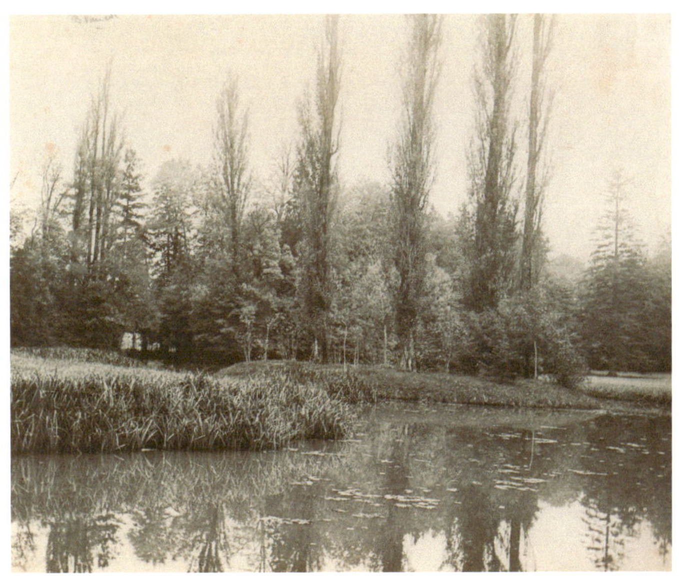

107. Ralph Radcliffe Whitehead
Winter Landscape
Albumen print
12 1/4 x 15 inches
Collection of Douglas C. James

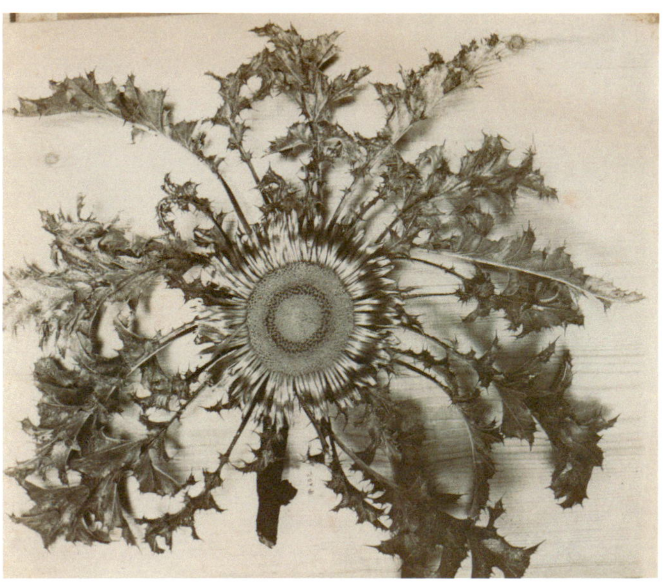

108. Ralph Radcliffe Whitehead
Botanical: Dried Flowers
Albumen print
12 1/4 x 15 inches
Collection of Douglas C. James

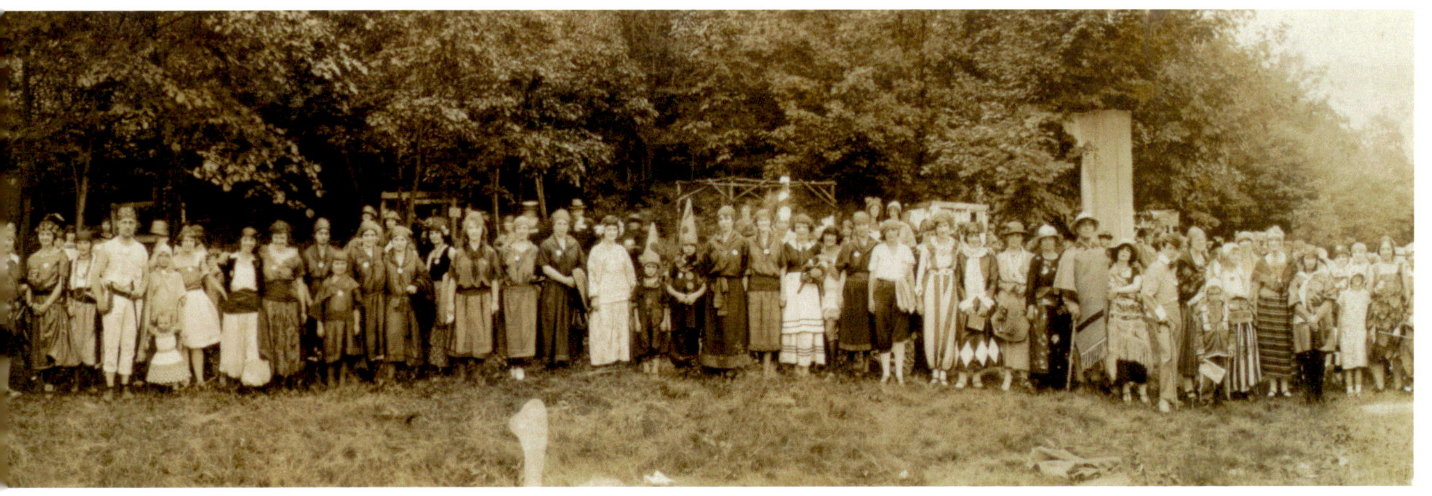

Pottery and Stoneware

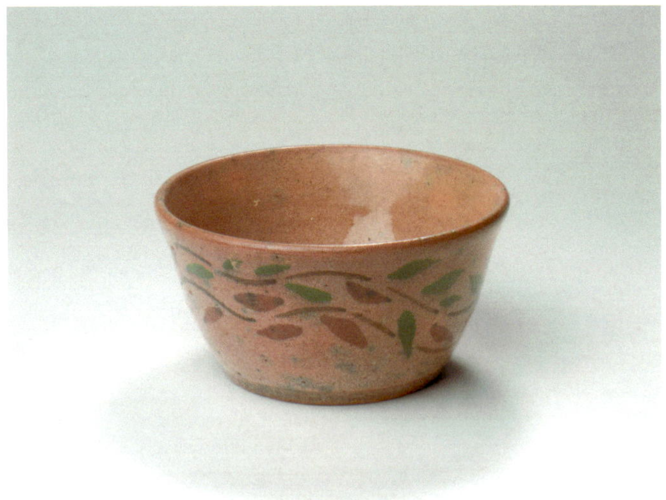

109. Bolton Brown
Bowl with stenciled decoration
Ceramic
Height: 2 1/2 inches; diameter: 5 inches
Courtesy of Linda and Donald Gregorius

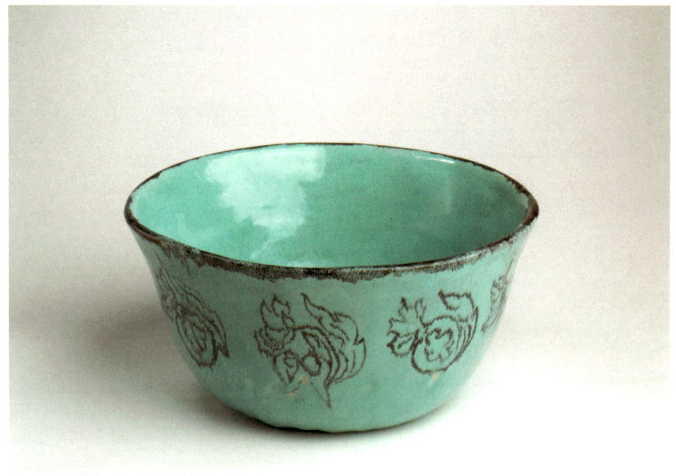

110. Byrdcliffe Pottery, 1903–22
Edith Penman and Elizabeth Hardenbergh
Small Bowl
Ceramic
Height: 5 inches; diameter: 10 1/4 inches
Courtesy of the Arts and Clay Company

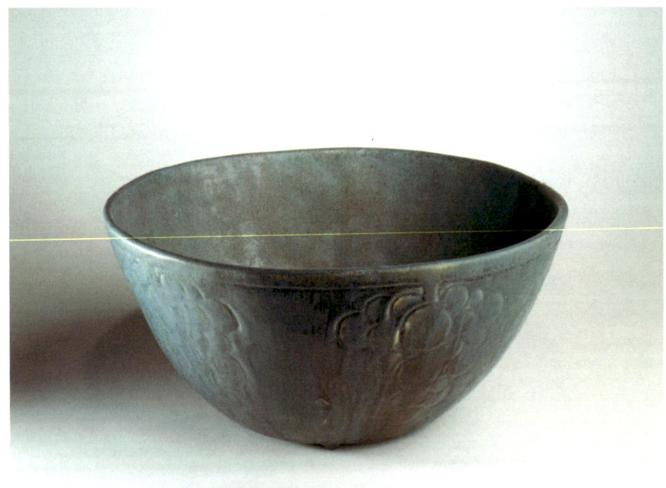

111. Byrdcliffe Pottery, 1903–22
Edith Penman and Elizabeth Hardenbergh
Large Bowl
Ceramic
Height: 5 3/4 inches; diameter: 12 3/4 inches
Courtesy of the Arts and Clay Company

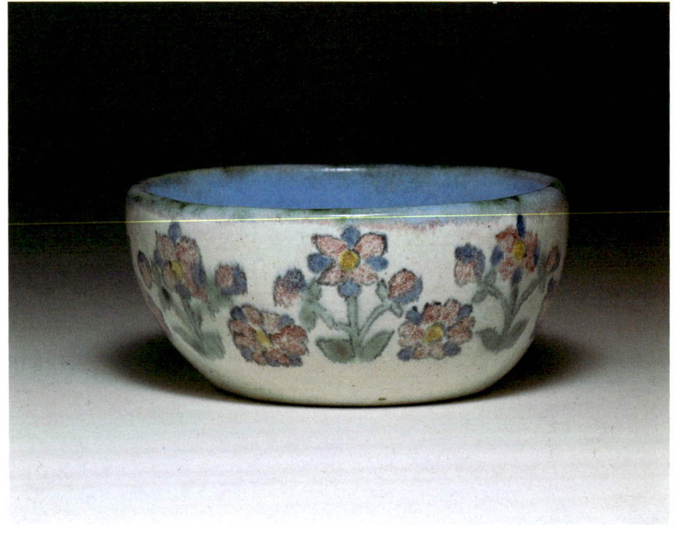

112. Byrdcliffe Pottery, 1903–22
Edith Penman and Elizabeth Hardenbergh
Bowl with Painted Flowers, ca. 1913
Ceramic
Height: 3 inches; diameter: 5 1/2 inches
Collection of Amy and David Dufour

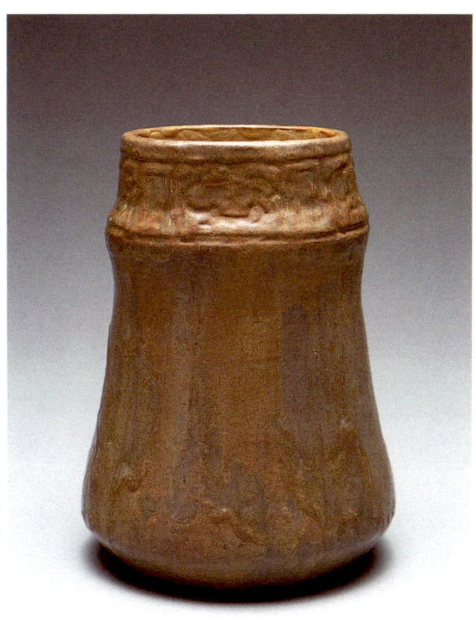

113. Byrdcliffe Pottery, 1903–22
Edith Penman and Elizabeth Hardenbergh
Vase
Ceramic
Height: 11 inches; diameter: $8\,{}^{1}/_{4}$ inches
Collection of Robert Ellison

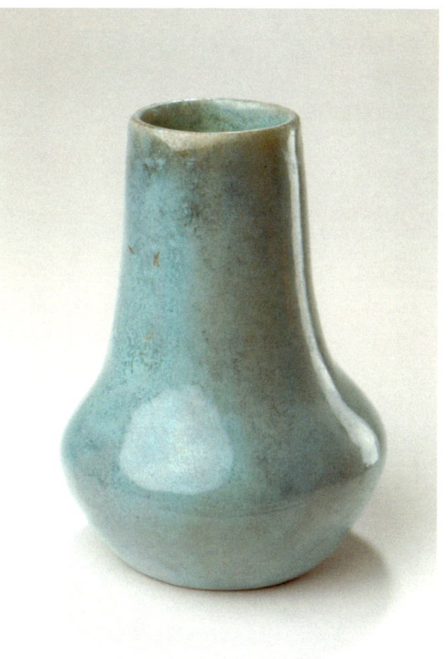

114. Byrdcliffe Pottery, 1903–22
Edith Penman and Elizabeth Hardenbergh
Vase
Ceramic
Height: 8 inches; diameter: 6 inches
Courtesy of Linda and Donald Gregorius

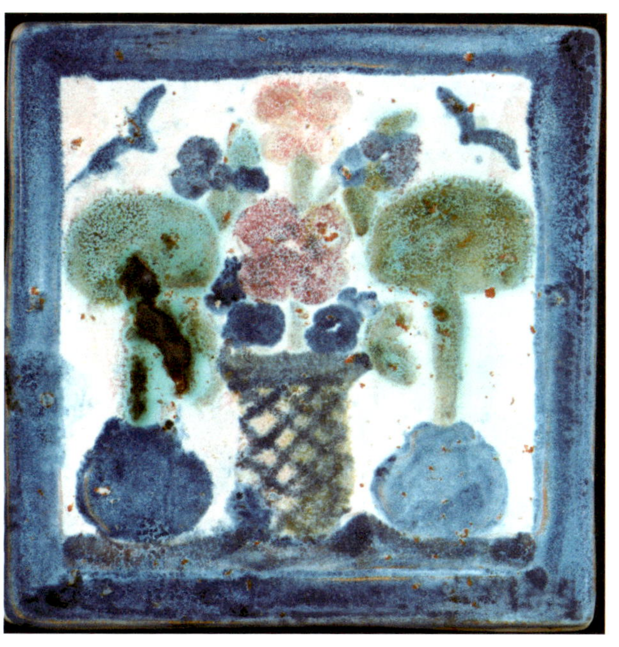

115. Byrdcliffe Pottery, 1903–22
Edith Penman and Elizabeth Hardenbergh
Tile: Flowers in a Vase
Glazed ceramic with painted design
Height: $5\,{}^{7}/_{8}$ inches; diameter: 6 inches; width: ${}^{5}/_{8}$ inches
Collection of Robert Inglish and Craig Wood

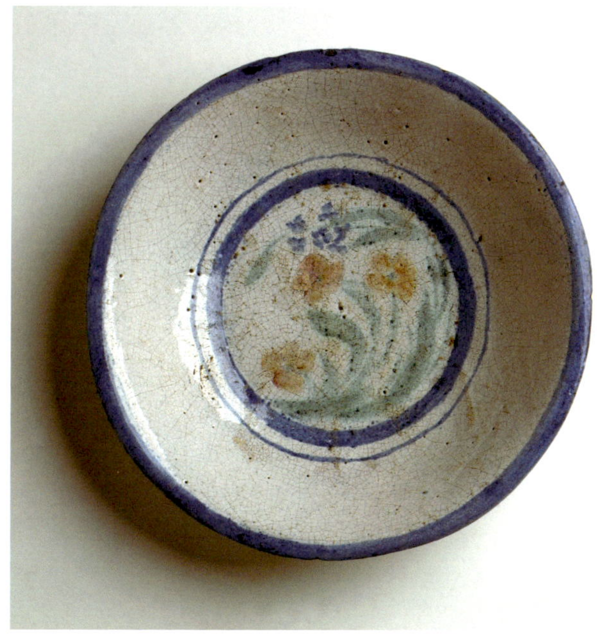

116. Byrdcliffe Pottery, 1903–22
Edith Penman and Elizabeth Hardenbergh
Bowl with Floral Painted Design
Ceramic
Height: $1\,{}^{5}/_{8}$ inches; diameter: $7\,{}^{5}/_{8}$ inches
Collection of Douglas C. James

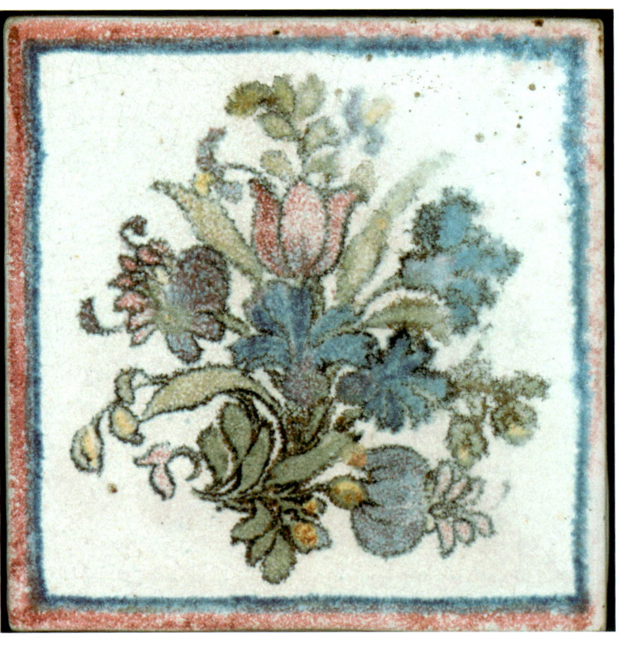

117. Byrdcliffe Pottery, 1903–22
Edith Penman and Elizabeth Hardenbergh
Tile, ca. 1920
Ceramic
Height: 5 3/8 inches; width: 5 3/8 inches; depth: 5/8 inches
Collection of Greg and Kathleen Eagen Johnson

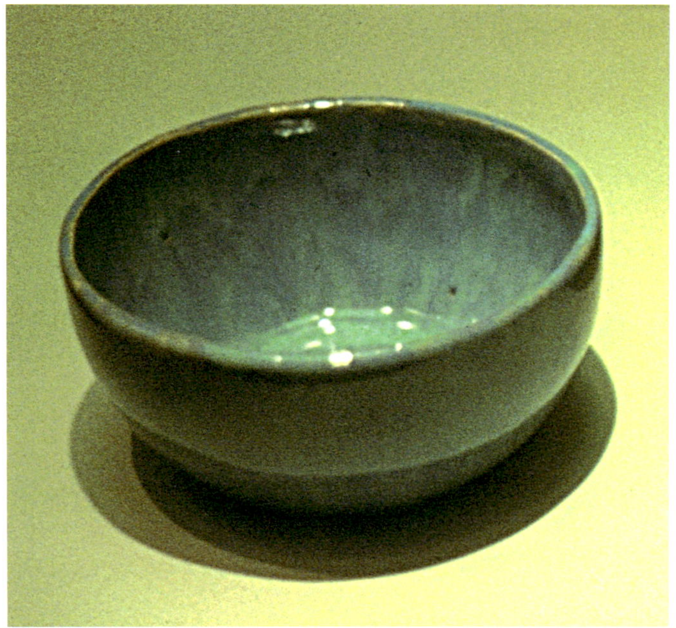

118. Byrdcliffe Pottery, 1903–22
Edith Penman and Elizabeth Hardenbergh
Glazed Earthenware Bowl, ca. 1917–18
Height: 2 3/4 inches; diameter: 6 inches
Collection of the Newark Museum, Purchase 1918

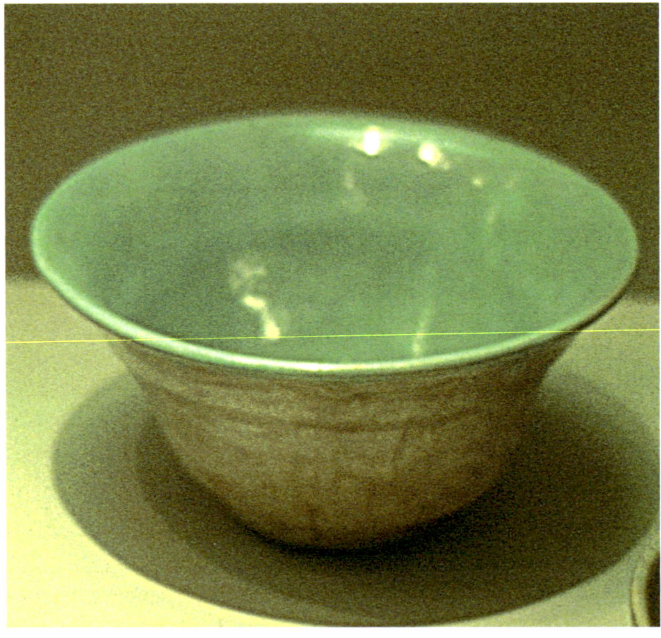

119. Byrdcliffe Pottery, 1903–22
Edith Penman and Elizabeth Hardenbergh
Flared Bowl with Gray-tan Crackle Glaze, ca. 1917–18
Height: 3 1/2 inches; diameter: 7 5/8 inches
Collection of the Newark Museum, Purchase 1918

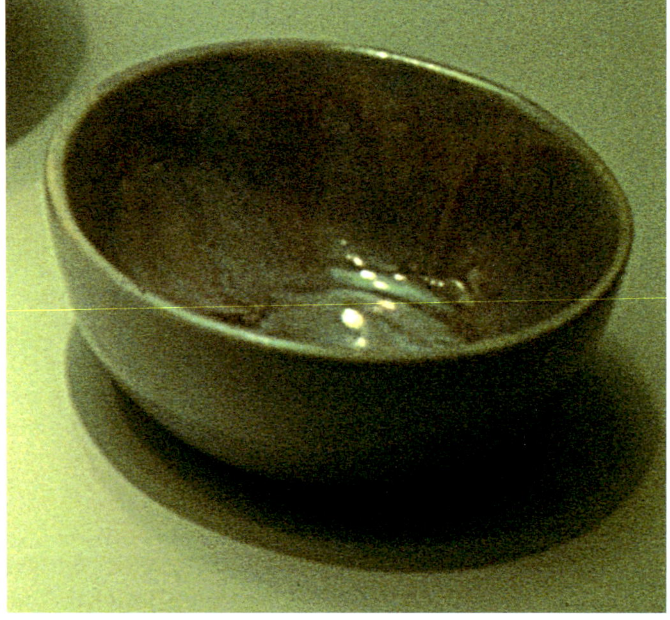

120. Byrdcliffe Pottery, 1903–22
Edith Penman and Elizabeth Hardenbergh
Bowl with Lavender-blue Glaze with Tan, ca. 1917–18
Height: 2 1/4 inches; diameter: 5 1/2 inches
Collection of the Newark Museum, Purchase 1918

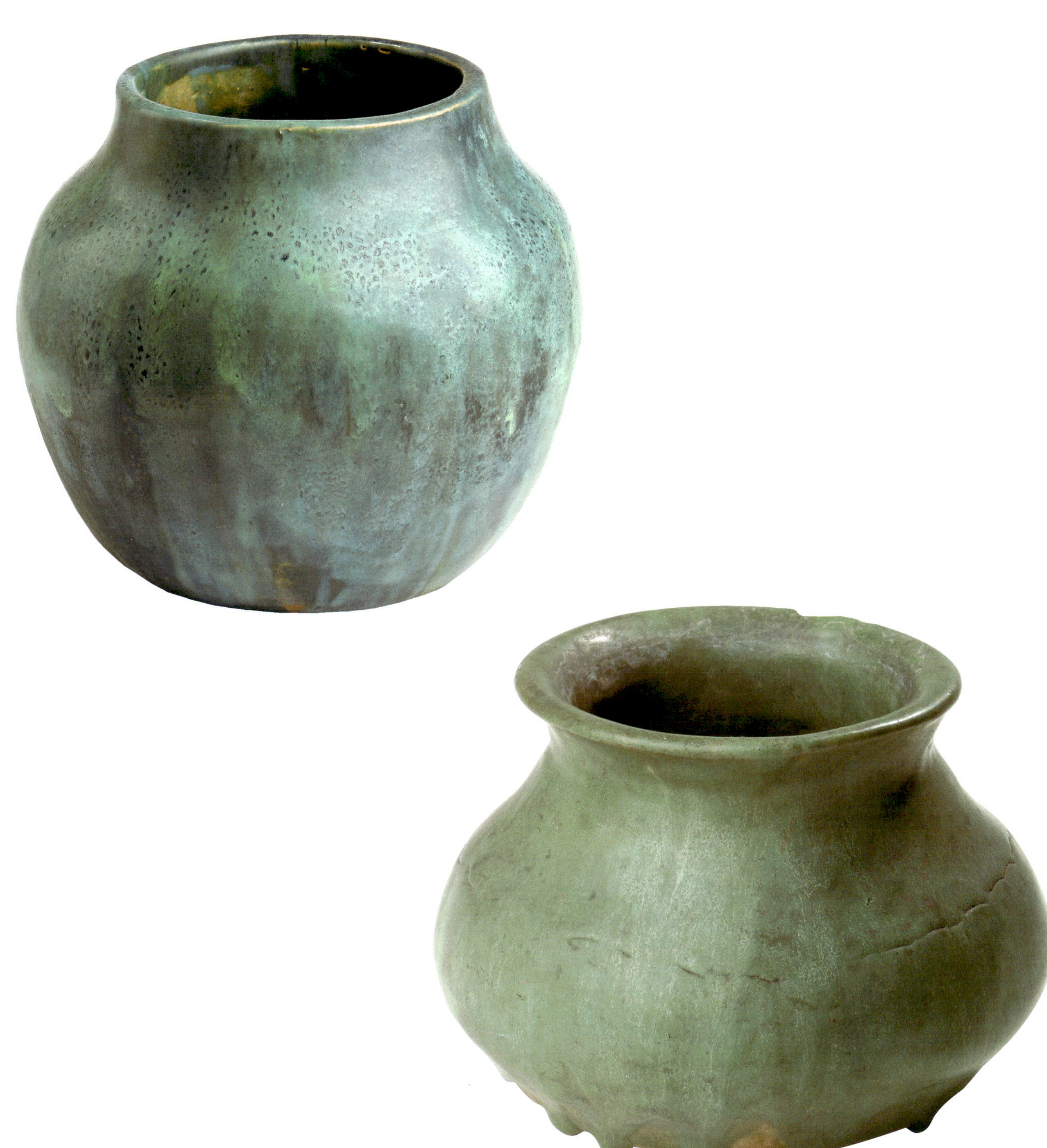

121. Byrdcliffe Pottery, 1903–22
Edith Penman and Elizabeth Hardenbergh
Bowl
Ceramic
Height: 7 3/4 inches; diameter: 8 1/2 inches
Collection of Edward Shlasko
Courtesy of the Arts and Clay Company

122. Byrdcliffe Pottery, 1903–22
Edith Penman and Elizabeth Hardenbergh
Byrdcliffe Vase
Ceramic
Height: 4 1/4 inches; diameter: 7 inches
Private collection

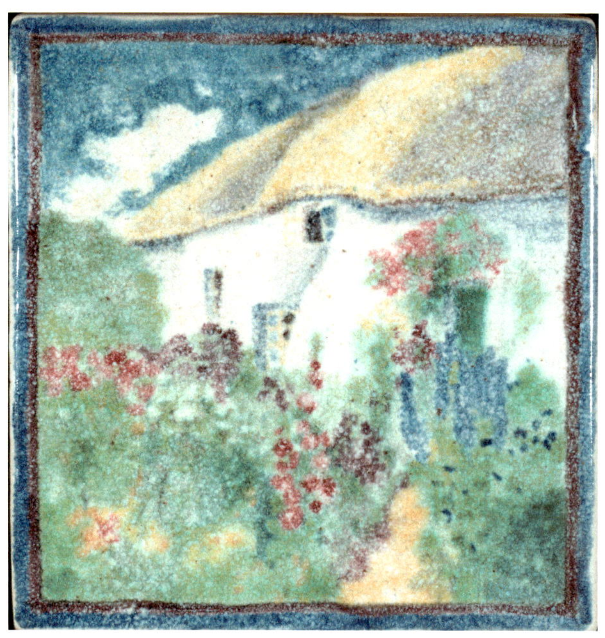

123. Byrdcliffe Pottery, 1903–22
Edith Penman and Elizabeth Hardenbergh
Tile: English Country Scene
Ceramic
Height: 11¾ inches; width: 11¾ inches; depth: ½ inch
Collection of Robert Inglish and Craig Wood

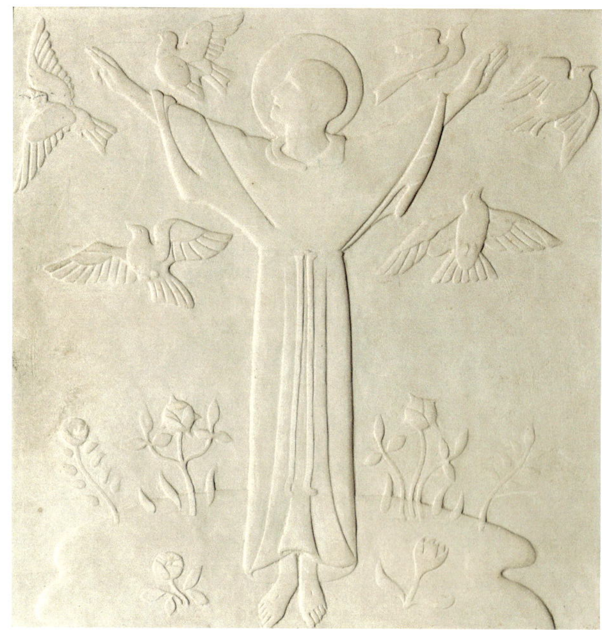

124. John Duncan, designer,
and **Vivian Bevans,** modeler
St. Francis, ca. 1904
Plaster relief
Height: 6½ inches; width: 6½ inches; depth: ⅜ inch
Collection of the Byrdcliffe Art Colony of the Woodstock Guild,
Alf Evers Collection
Gift of the Douglas C. James Charitable Trust

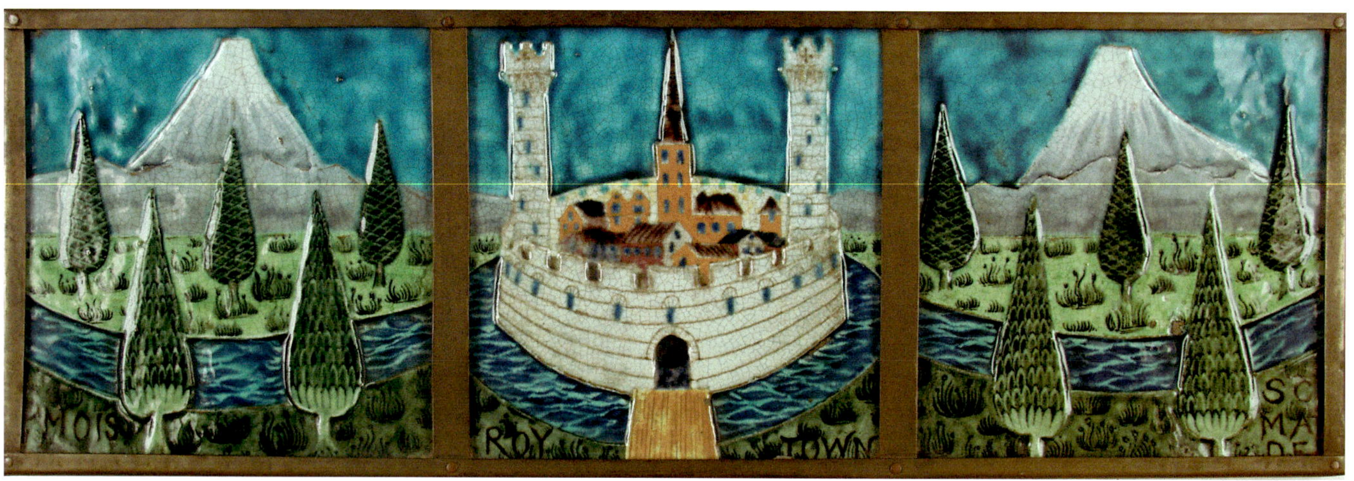

125. Halsey Ricardo, designer
British, 1854–1926
Troytown
Ceramic tiles
Height: 9⅜ inches; width: 28 inches; depth: 1 inch
Private collection

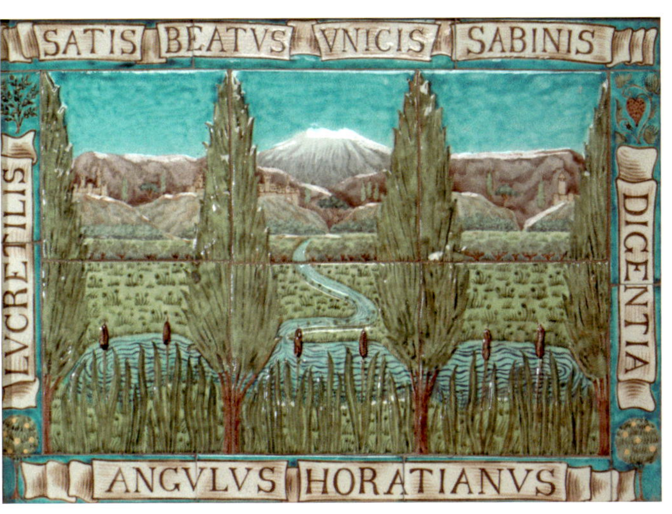

126. Halsey Ricardo, designer
British, 1854–1926
Landscape
Ceramic tiles
Height: 18 inches; width: $23\,^{3}/_{4}$ inches; depth: 1 inch
Private collection

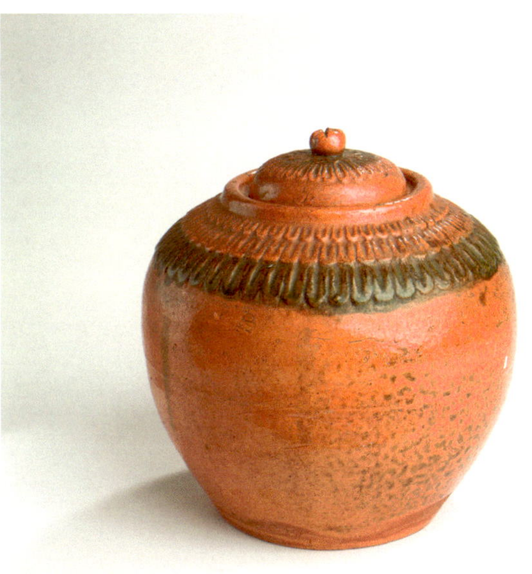

127. Zulma Steele
Ginger Jar
Ceramic
Height: 8 inches; diameter: $7\,^{3}/_{4}$ inches
Courtesy of Linda and Donald Gregorius

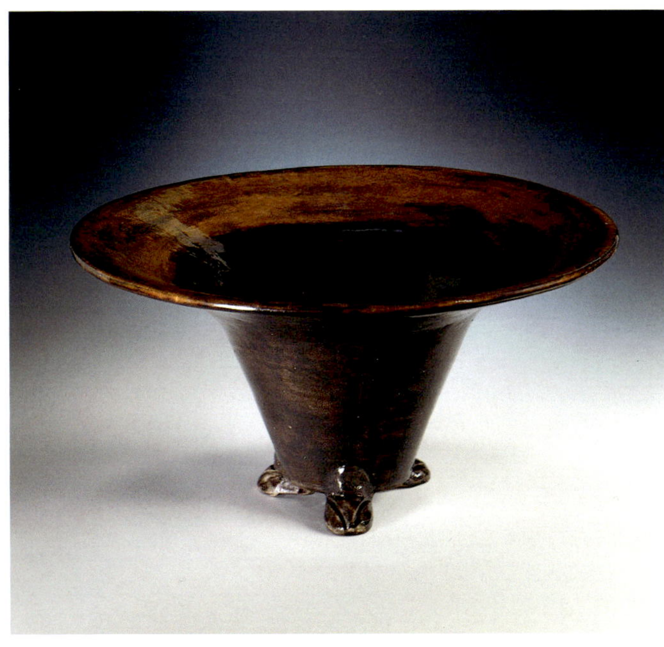

128. Zulma Steele
Zedware Bowl
Glazed ceramic
Height: $6\,^{1}/_{4}$ inches; diameter: $12\,^{5}/_{8}$ inches
On loan from Morgan Anderson Consulting

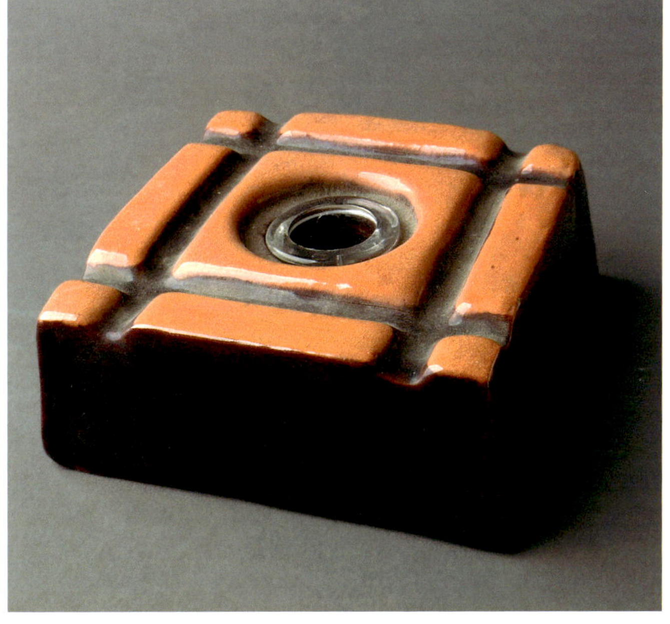

129. Zulma Steele
Ink Stand
Ceramic
Height: $1\,^{3}/_{4}$ inches; width: $4\,^{7}/_{8}$ inches; depth: $4\,^{15}/_{16}$ inches
Collection of Jean and Jim Young

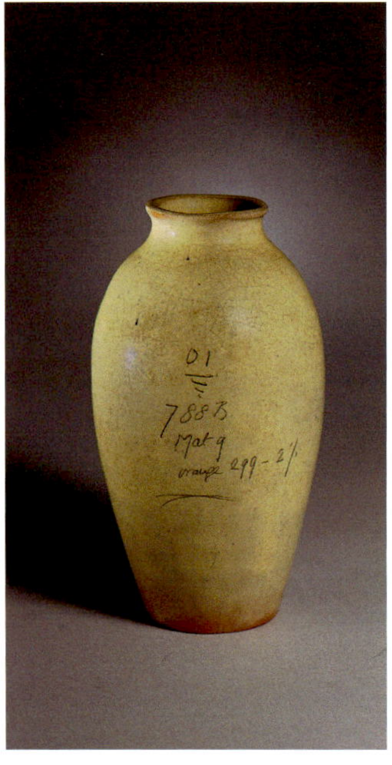

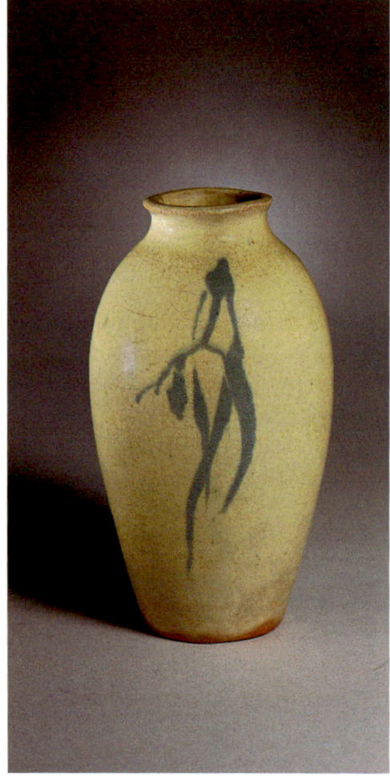

130. White Pines Pottery, 1915–26
Jane and Ralph Whitehead
Eucalyptus Pot
Ceramic
Height: 5¾ inches; diameter: 3¾ inches
Private collection

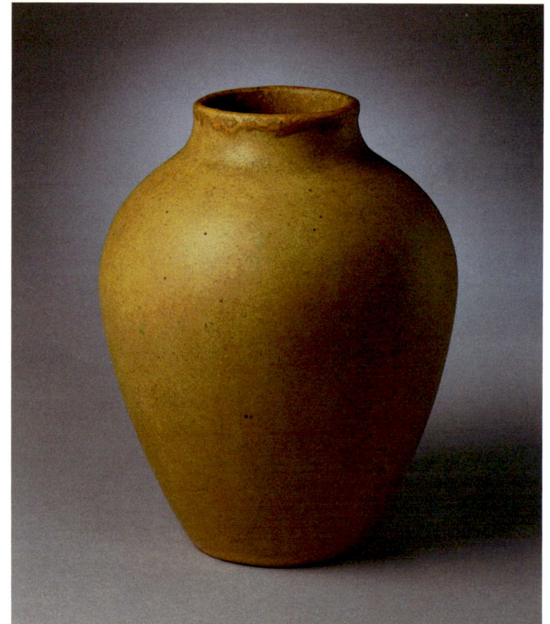

131. White Pines Pottery, 1915–26
Jane and Ralph Whitehead
Yellow vase
Ceramic
Height: 7 inches; diameter: 5¾ inches
Private collection

(not illustrated)

132. White Pines Pottery, 1915–26
Jane and Ralph Whitehead
Model for Vase
Wood
Height: 18 inches; diameter: 11 inches
Milwaukee Art Museum, Layton Art Collection

133. White Pines Pottery, 1915–26
Jane and Ralph Whitehead
Bisque (unglazed) Vase
Ceramic
Height: 16½ inches; diameter: 11 inches
Milwaukee Art Museum, Layton Art Collection

134. White Pines Pottery, 1915–26
Jane and Ralph Whitehead
Three-part Plaster Mold
Ceramic
Height: 21 inches; diameter: 16¼ inches
Milwaukee Art Museum, Layton Art Collection

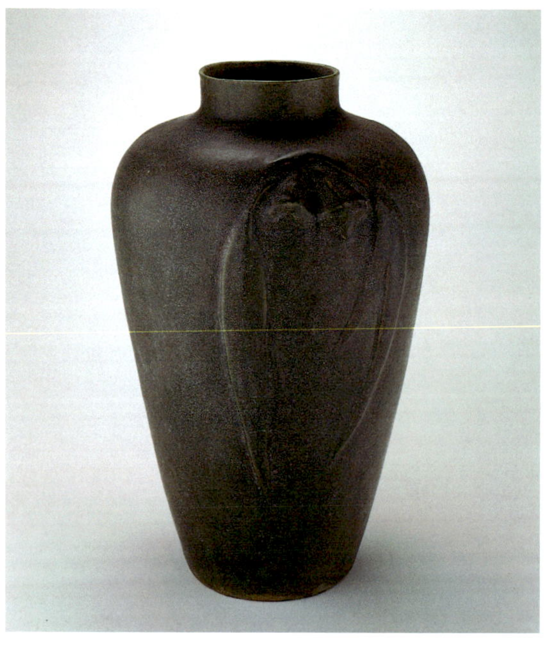

135. White Pines Pottery, 1915–26
Jane and Ralph Whitehead
Vase, ca. 1915–26
Ceramic
Height: 15¾ inches; diameter: 10½ inches
Milwaukee Art Museum, Layton Art Collection

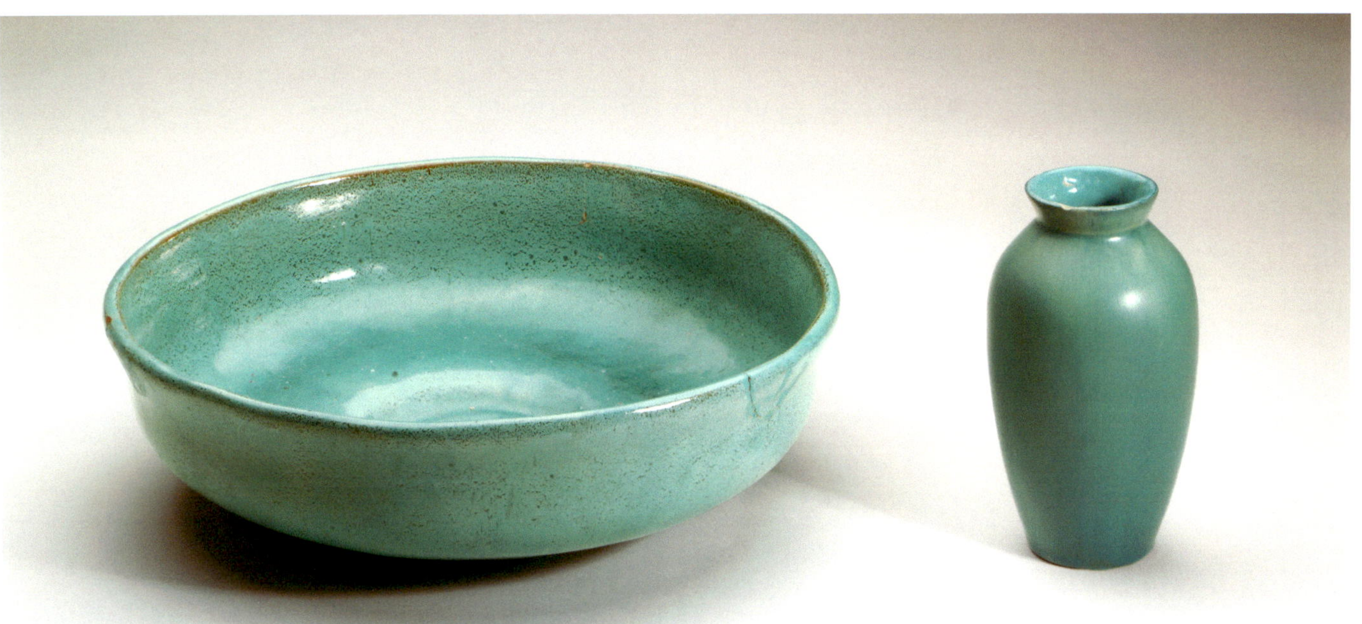

136. White Pines Pottery, 1915–26
Jane and Ralph Whitehead
Low Bowl
Ceramic
Height: 3 inches; diameter: 10 inches
Collection of Lawrence Webster

137. White Pines Pottery, 1915–26
Jane and Ralph Whitehead
Vase with Outflaring Rim
Ceramic
Height: 4 3/4 inches: width: 2 3/4 inches
Collection of Lawrence Webster

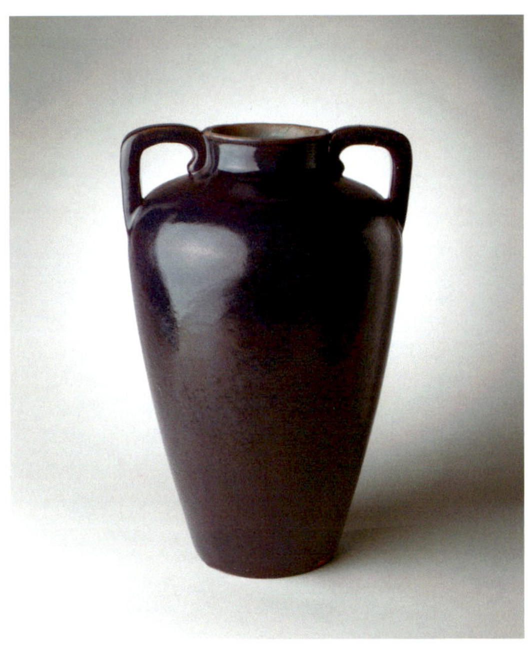

138. White Pines Pottery, 1915–26
Jane and Ralph Whitehead
Tall Vase with Handles
Ceramic
Height: 15 inches; diameter: 9 1/2 inches
Private collection

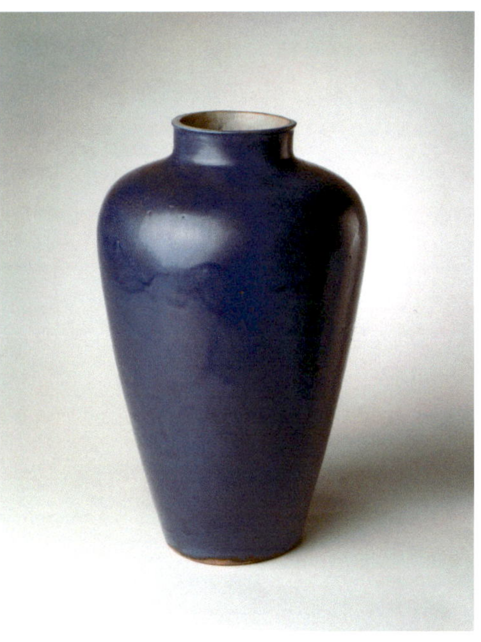

139. White Pines Pottery, 1915–26
Jane and Ralph Whitehead
Tall Vase without Handles
Ceramic
Height: 15 inches; diameter: 9 1/2 inches
Private collection

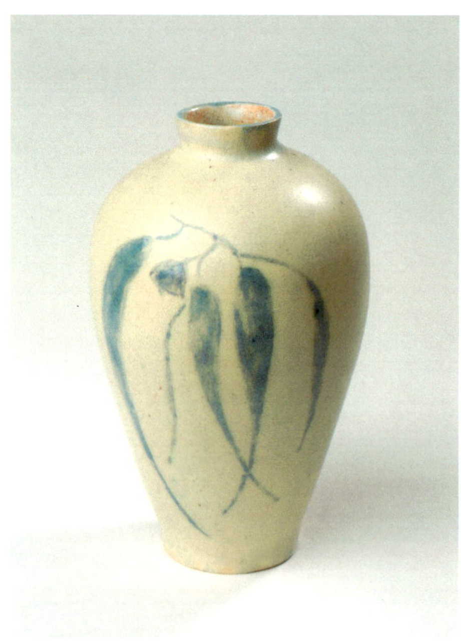

140. White Pines Pottery, 1915–26
Jane and Ralph Whitehead
Eucalyptus Vase
Ceramic
Height: 6 3/4 inches; diameter: 3 inches
Private collection

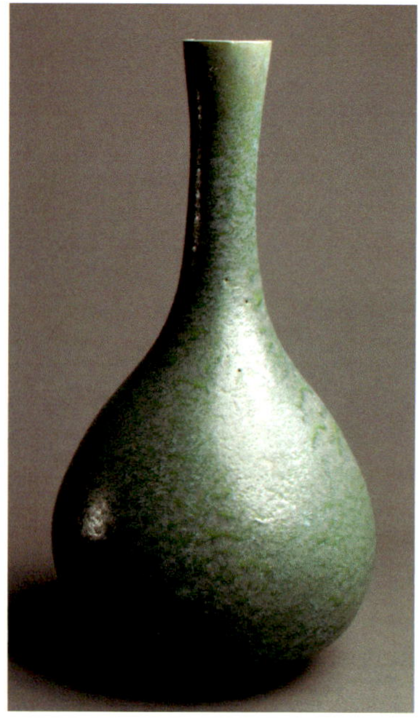

141. White Pines Pottery, 1915–26
Jane and Ralph Whitehead
Vase, Persian Shape
Ceramic
Height: 13 inches; diameter: 8 inches
Private collection

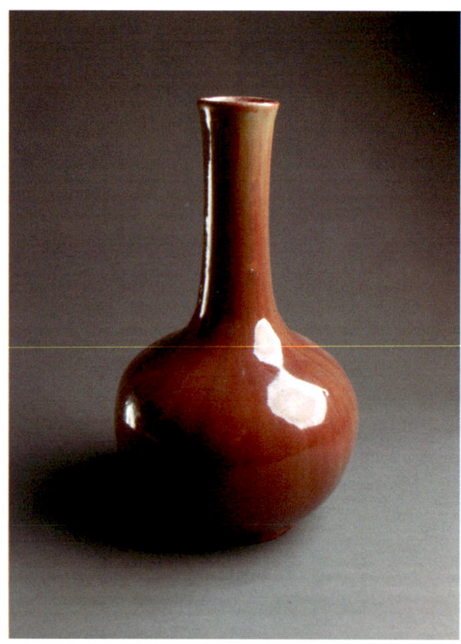

142. White Pines Pottery, 1915–26
Jane and Ralph Whitehead
Red vase, Chinese Shape
Ceramic
Height: 12 1/2 inches; diameter: 7 1/2 inches
Private collection

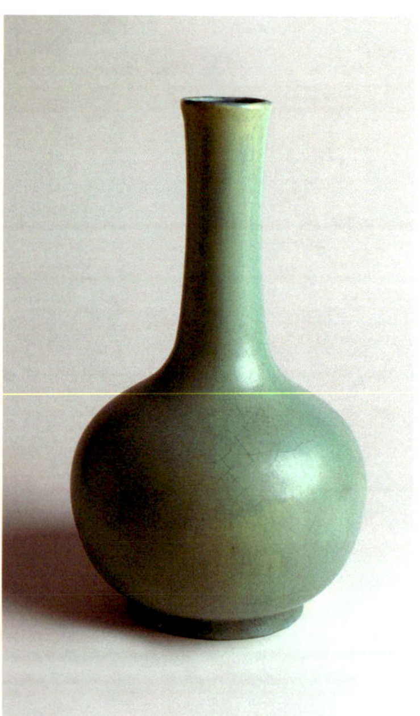

143. White Pines Pottery, 1915–26
Jane and Ralph Whitehead
Vase with turquoise glaze
Ceramic
Height: 13 inches; diameter: 7 1/2 inches
Collection of the Byrdcliffe Art Colony of the Woodstock Guild
Gift of the Douglas C. James Charitable Trust in honor of Carla Smith

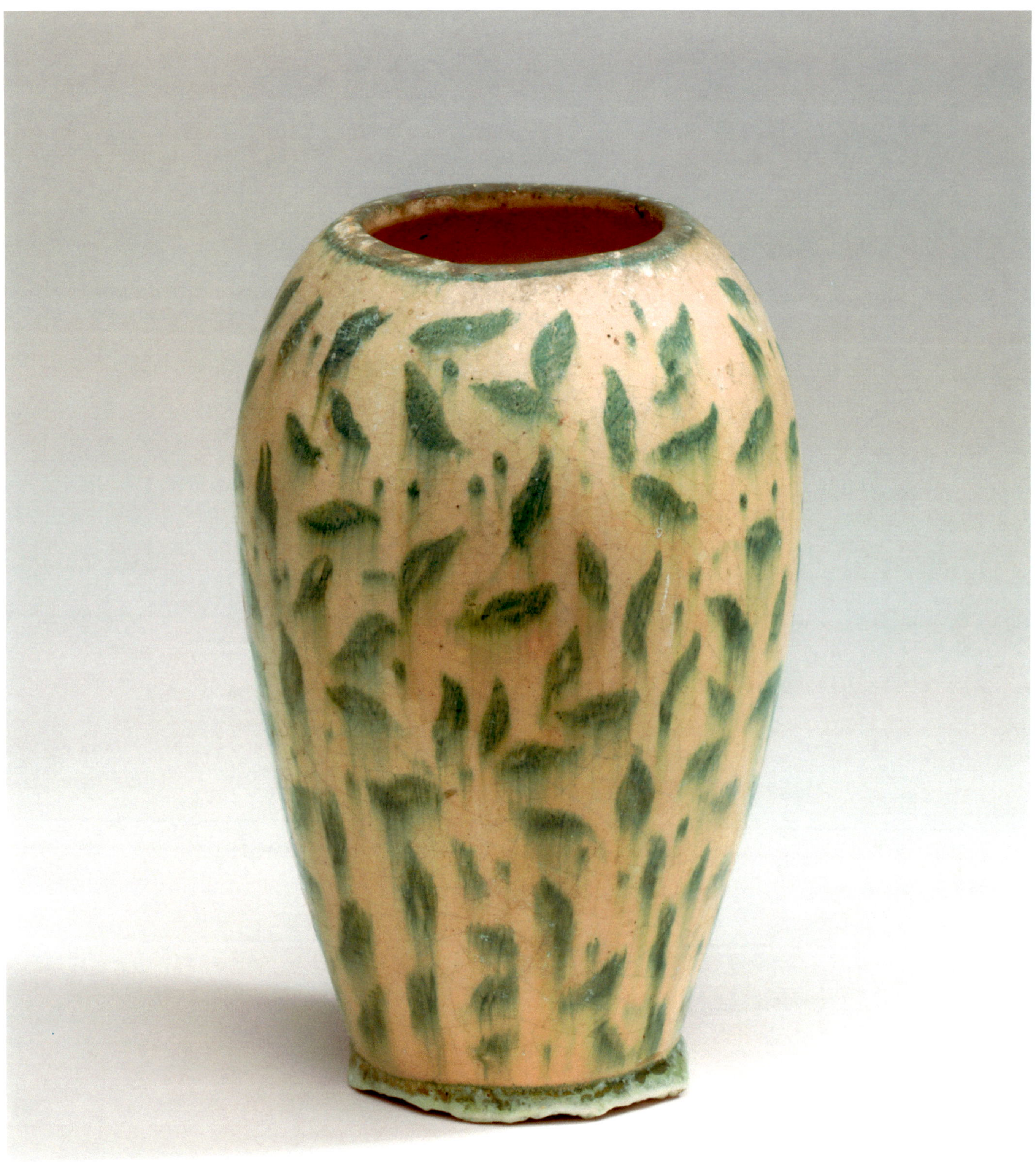

144. White Pines Pottery, 1915–26
Jane and Ralph Whitehead
Vase with Leaf Pattern Overall
Stoneware, cream-glazed with painted pattern
Height: 5 1/2 inches; diameter: 3 1/2 inches
Collection of the Byrdcliffe Art Colony of the Woodstock Guild

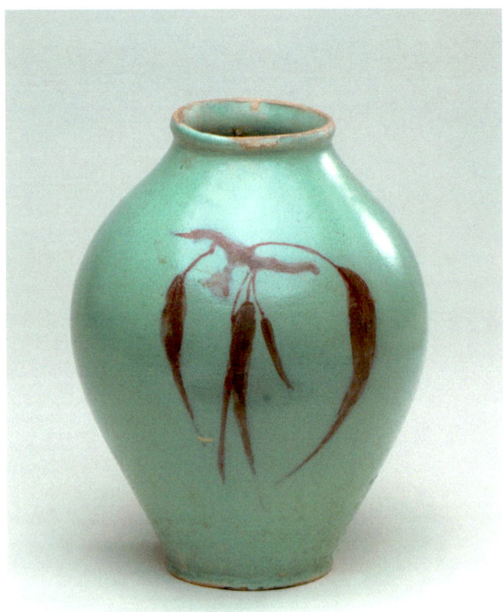

145. White Pines Pottery, 1915–26
Jane and Ralph Whitehead
Vase with Eucalyptus Painted on Turquoise Ground
Height: 8 1/8 inches; diameter: 6 1/2 inches
Collection of the Byrdcliffe Art Colony of the Woodstock Guild
Gift of Carol Cohen

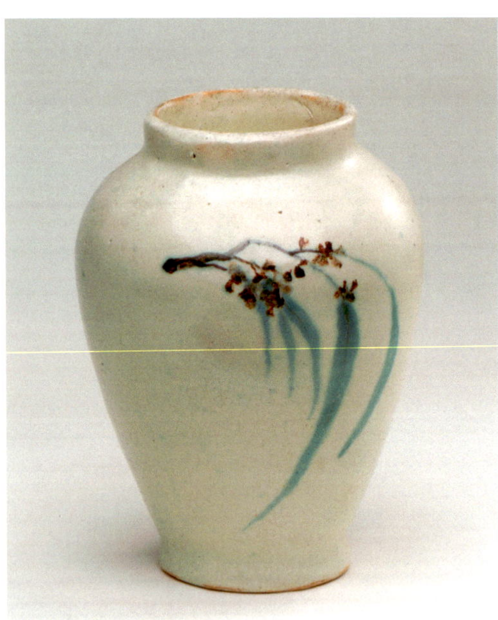

146. White Pines Pottery, 1915–26
Jane and Ralph Whitehead
Vase with Eucalyptus Branch Painted on White Ground
Painted stoneware
Height: 7 inches; diameter: 5 3/8 inches
Collection of the Byrdcliffe Art Colony of the Woodstock Guild

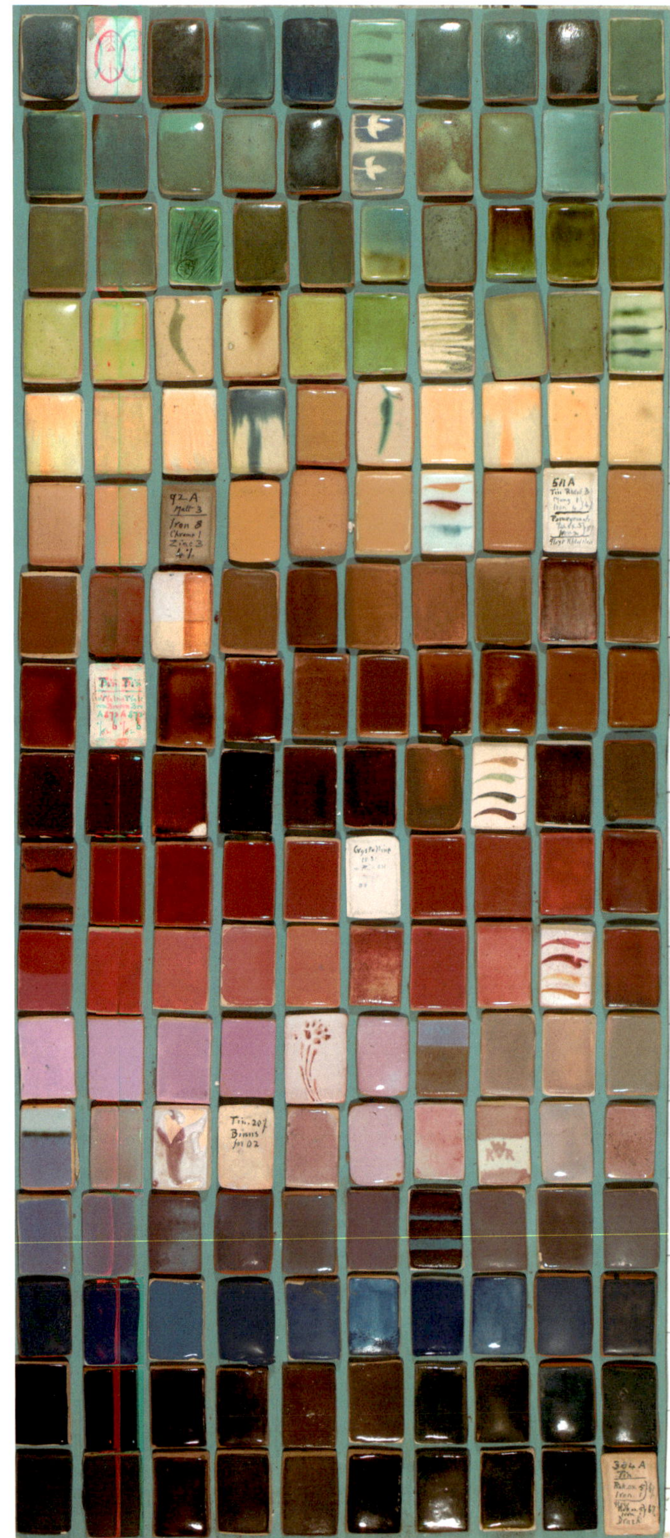

147. White Pines Pottery, 1915–26
Jane and Ralph Whitehead
Sample tiles
Glazed ceramic
Height: 41 inches; width: 18 inches; depth: 1 inch
Collection of the Byrdcliffe Art Colony of the Woodstock Guild

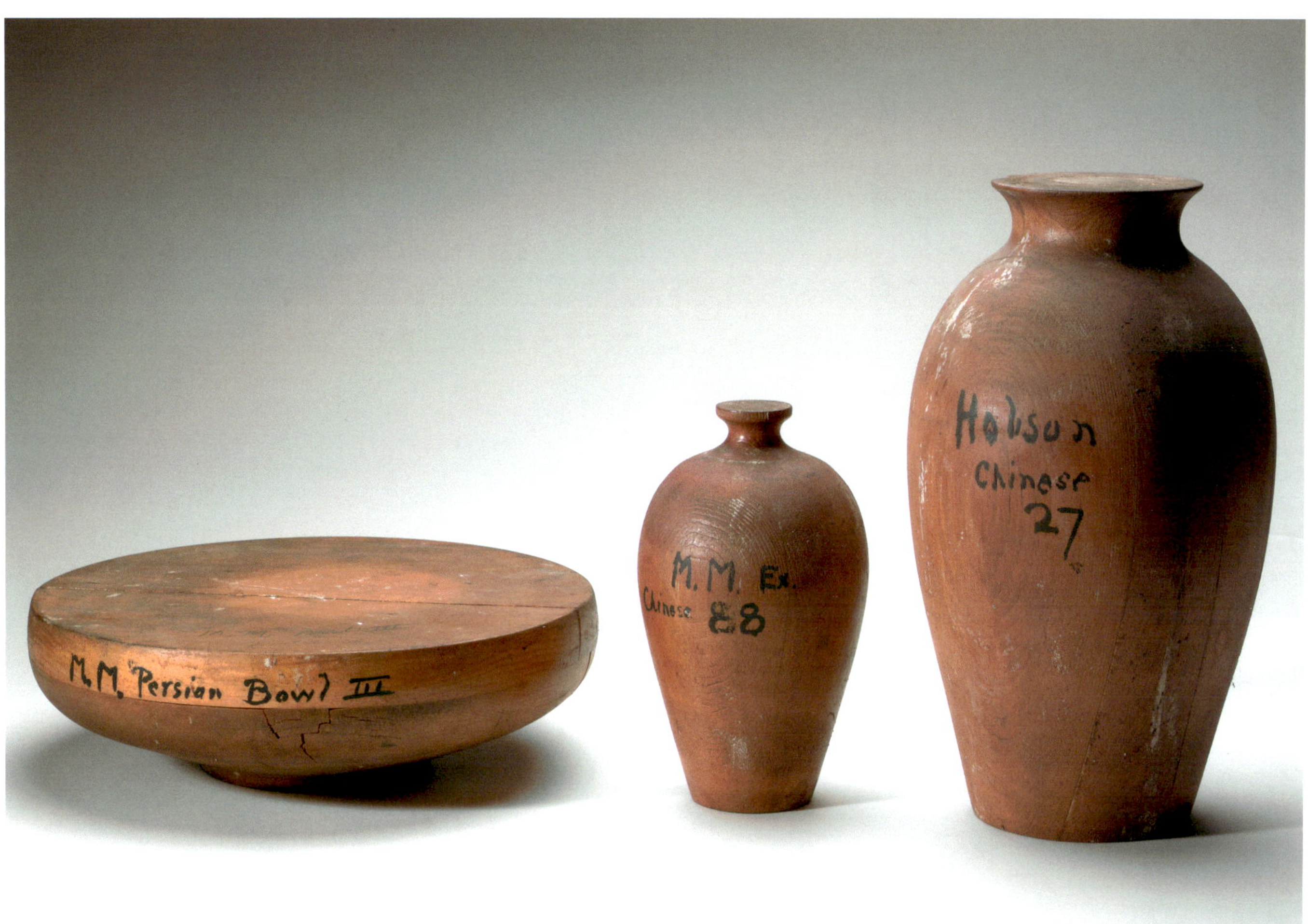

148. White Pines Pottery, 1915–26
Jane and Ralph Whitehead
Persian-Shape Wooden Model
Poplar
Height: 3 1/2 inches; diameter: 11 3/8 inches
Collcction of the Byrdcliffe Art Colony of the Woodstock Guild

149. White Pines Pottery, 1915–26
Jane and Ralph Whitehead
Chinese-Shape Wooden Model
Poplar
Height: 8 inches; diameter: 4 1/2 inches
Collection of the Byrdcliffe Art Colony of the Woodstock Guild

150. White Pines Pottery, 1915–26
Jane and Ralph Whitehead
Chinese-Shape Wooden Model
Poplar
Height: 12 inches; diameter: 7 1/2 inches
Collection of the Byrdcliffe Art Colony of the Woodstock Guild

Textiles

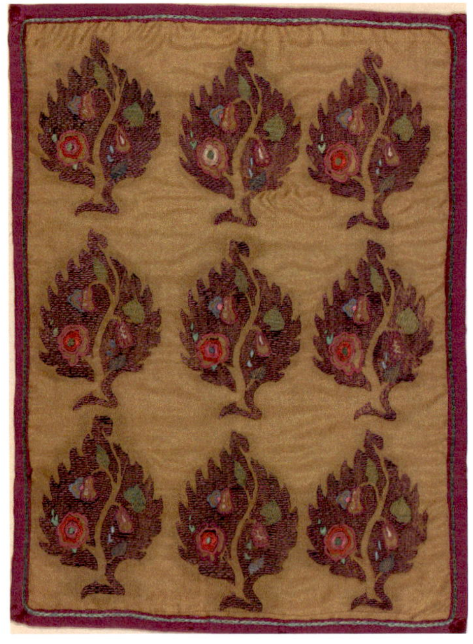

151. Helen Buttrick
The Pear Tree Garden
Woodblock and embroidery on silk
11 x 8 inches
Collection of the Historical Society of Woodstock

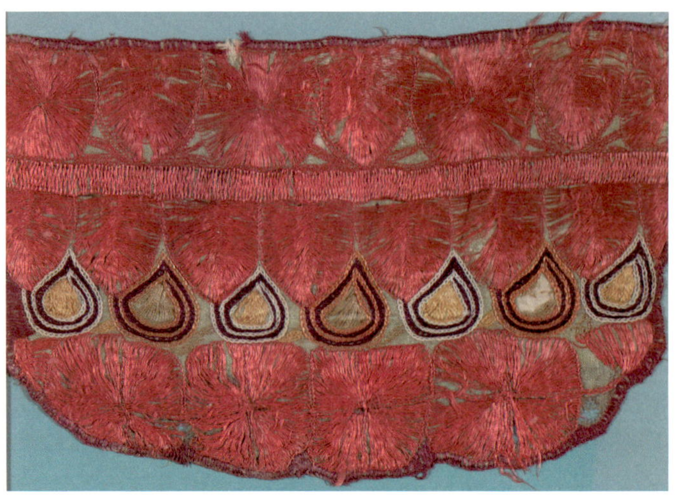

152. Helen Buttrick
Practice Piece
Embroidery on silk
7 x 10 3/4 inches
Collection of the Historical Society of Woodstock

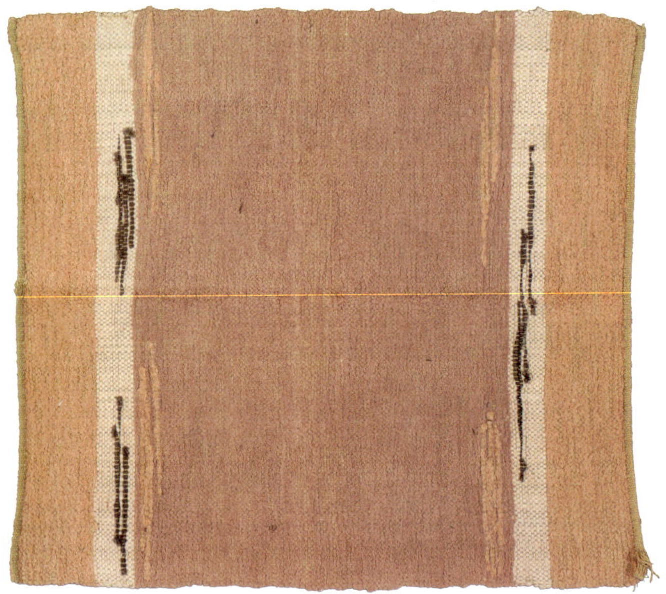

153. Marie Little
Weaving (striped)
Cotton
25 3/4 x 29 inches
Collection of Lawrence Webster

154. Marie Little
Weaving
Cotton
34 x 39 inches
Collection of Lawrence Webster

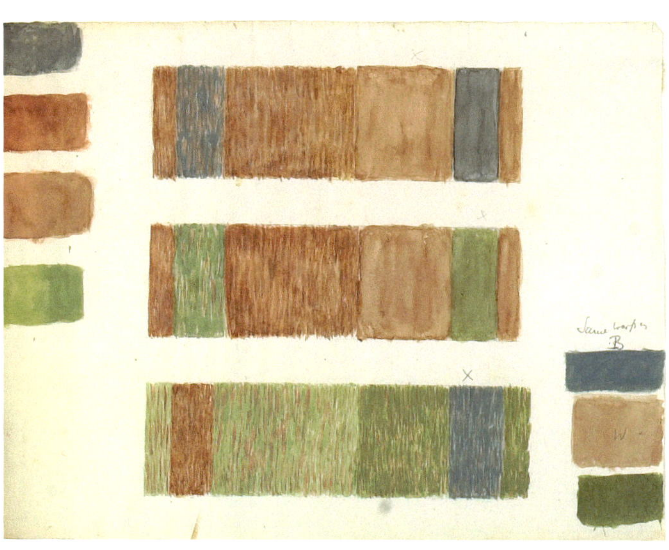

155. Marie Little
Designs for Rag Rugs, ca. 1910
Watercolor and colored pencil
11 x 14 inches
Collection of The Woodstock Artists Association
Gift of Mark Willcox Jr.

156. Marie Little
Wall Hanging
Blue silk
20¾ x 41 inches
Collection of the Historical Society of Woodstock
Gift of Judy Lund and Ted Wassmer

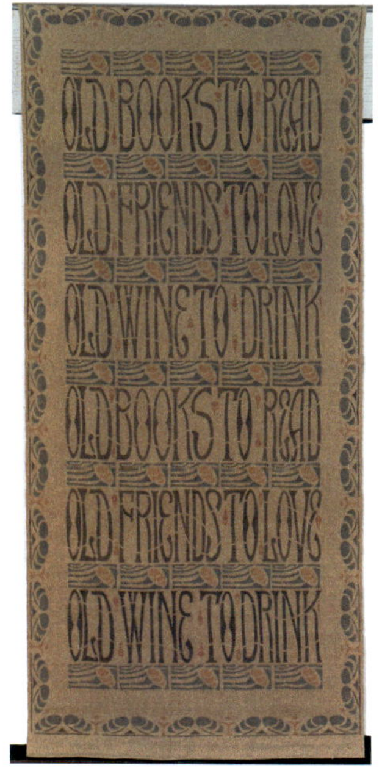

157. H. Stuart Michie
Wall Hanging, ca. 1905
Linen with stencil decoration
101 x 48½ inches
Collection of Thomas Michie

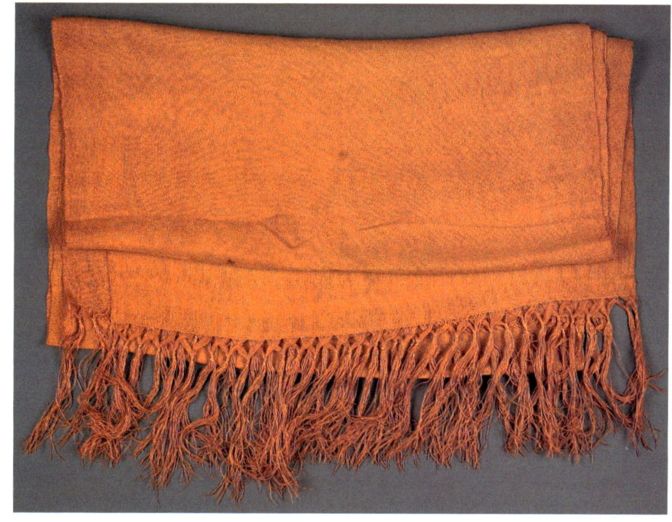

158. Ralph Radcliffe Whitehead
Woven Runner, ca. 1915
Silk
80 x 19 inches
Collection of the Woodstock Artists Association
Gift of Mark Willcox Jr.

Works on Paper

159. Vivian Bevans
City at Night, ca. 1902
Color wood-block print
4 x 5 inches
Collection of the Byrdcliffe Art Colony of the Woodstock Guild,
Alf Evers Collection
Gift of Douglas C. James Charitable Trust

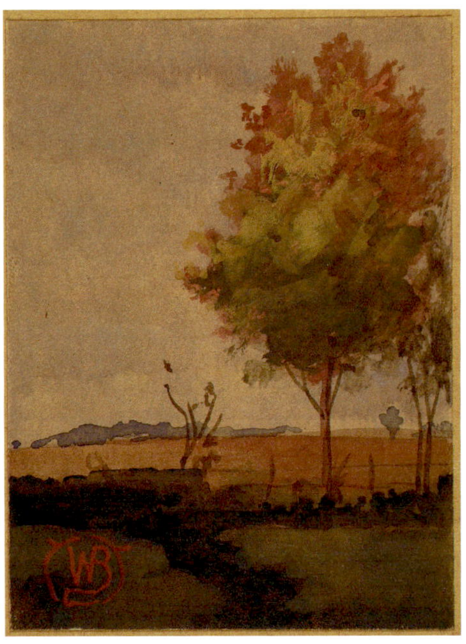

160. Vivian Bevans
Landscape
Watercolor
4 x 3 inches
Collection of the Byrdcliffe Art Colony of the Woodstock Guild,
Alf Evers Collection
Gift of Douglas C. James Charitable Trust

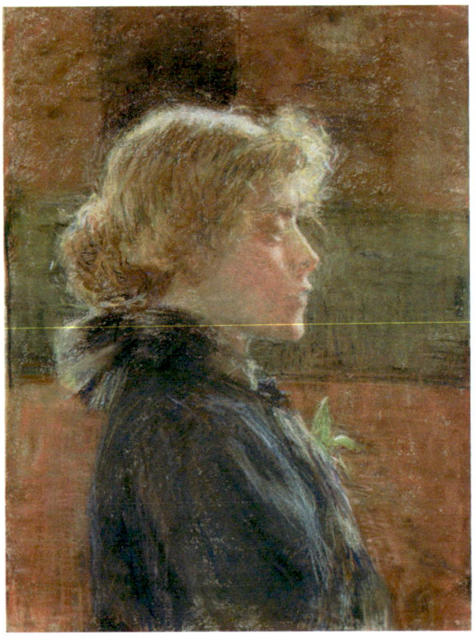

161. Attributed to Madeleine Fleury
Jane Byrd Whitehead, ca. 1891
Pastel on board
12 x 9 inches
Private collection

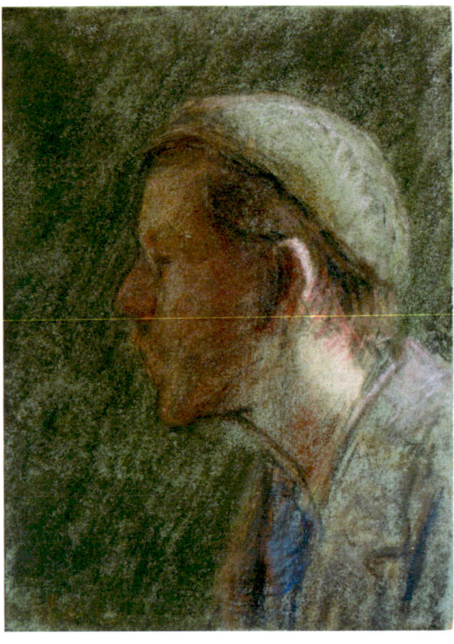

162. Attributed to Madeleine Fleury
Ralph Radcliffe Whitehead, ca. 1891
Pastel on board
8 x 6 inches
Private collection

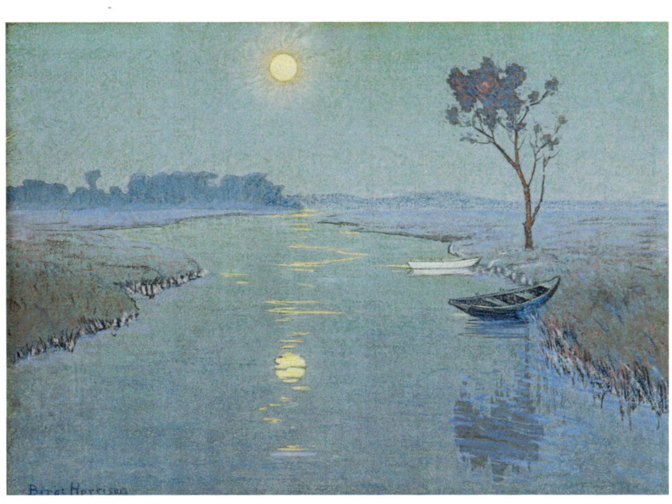

163. Lovell Birge Harrison
Untitled (view of a stream), ca. 1904
Pastel with touches of graphite over wood-block print
$10\frac{13}{16}$ x $15\frac{3}{8}$ inches
Collection of Douglas C. James

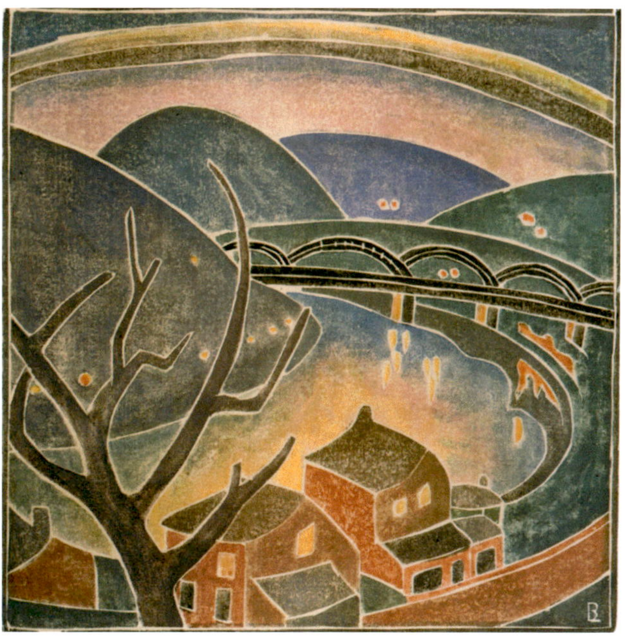

164. Blanche Lazzell
The Monongahela, 1919, printed 1930
Color wood-block print
12 x $11\frac{1}{2}$ inches
Collection of Johanna and Leslie Garfield
*Shown only at Milwaukee, Ithaca, and New York

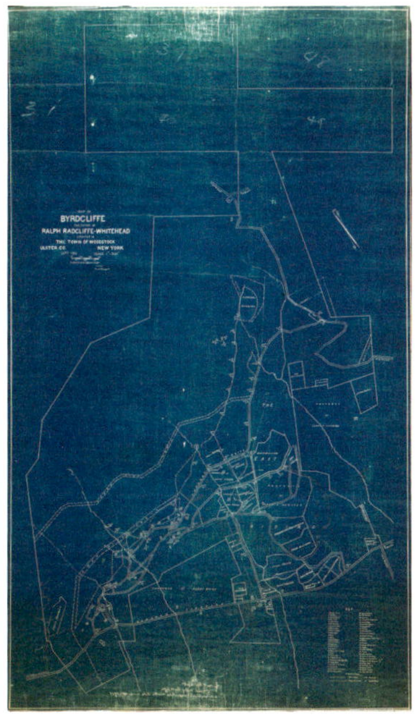

165. A. S. Low and David Reichgatt,
survey and drawing
Map of Byrdcliffe
Blueprint
$47\frac{1}{4}$ x $27\frac{3}{4}$ inches
Collection of the Historical Society of Woodstock

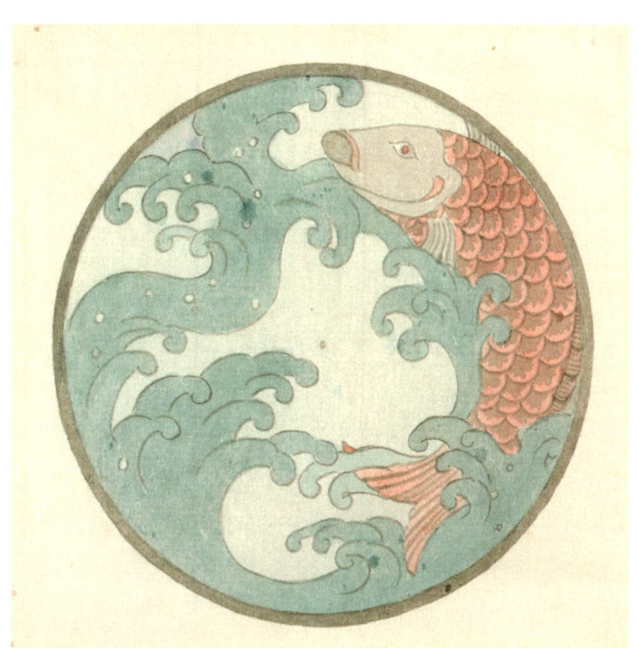

166. H. Stuart Michie
Enamel Design, ca. 1905
Watercolor
$6\frac{3}{8}$ x $5\frac{3}{4}$ inches
Collection of Thomas Michie
(see cat. 41)

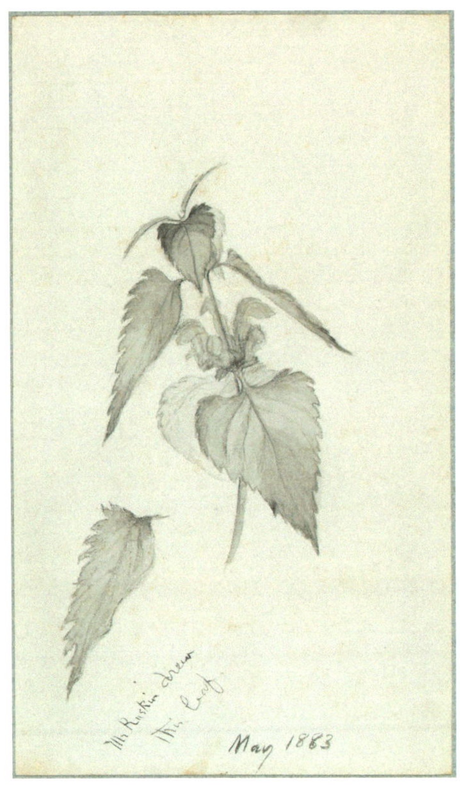

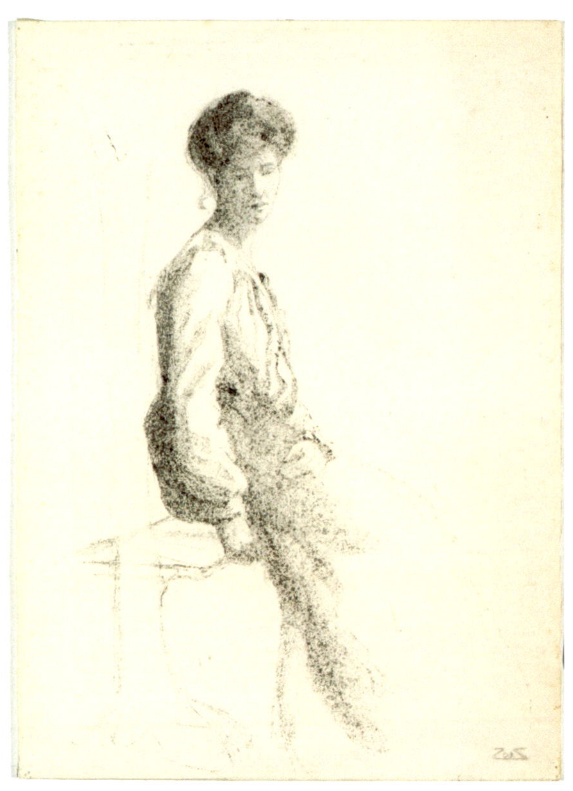

167. John Ruskin
Leaf Study, 1883
Pencil
8 7/8 x 5 1/4 inches
Private collection

168. Zulma Steele
Portrait, 1903
Charcoal
15 1/8 x 11 1/8 inches
On loan from Morgan Anderson Consulting

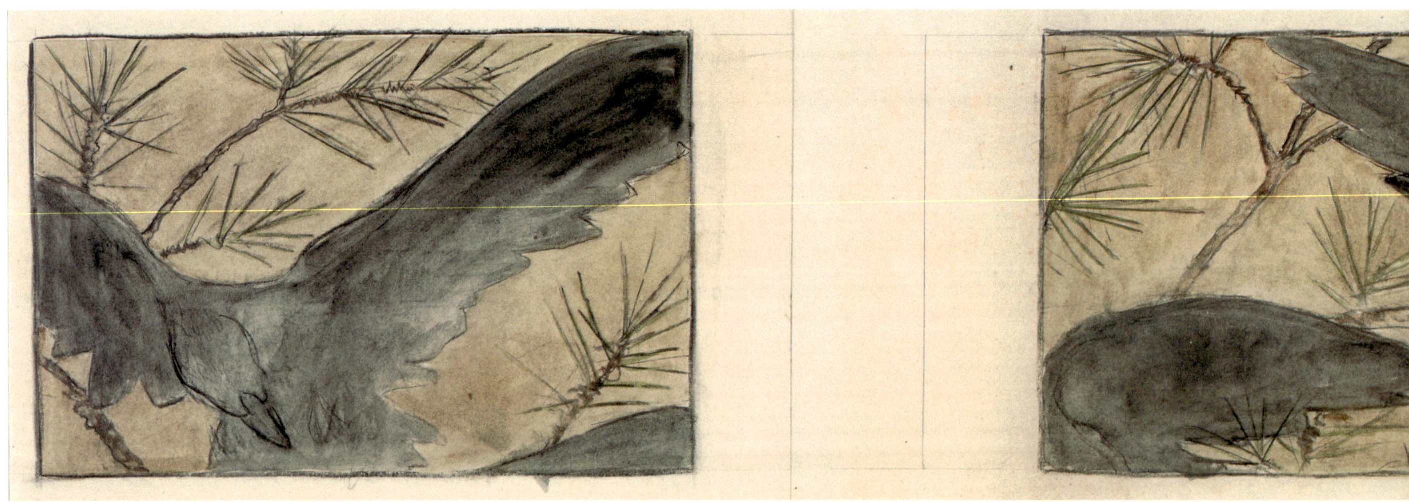

171. Zulma Steele
Crows Panel
Charcoal and watercolor
15 x 68 inches
Private collection

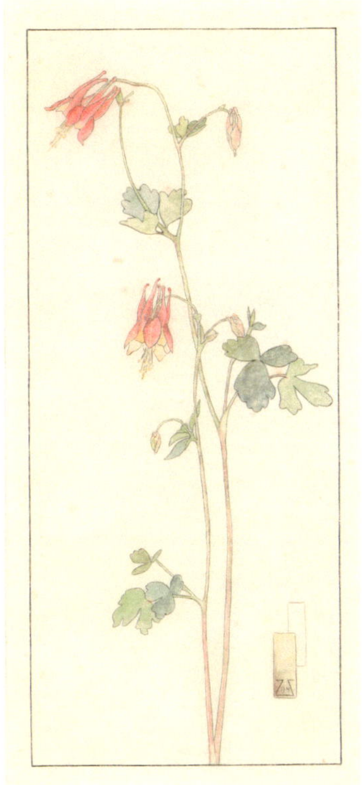

169. Zulma Steele
Columbine
Pen, ink, and watercolor
14 1/2 x 7 1/2 inches
Private collection

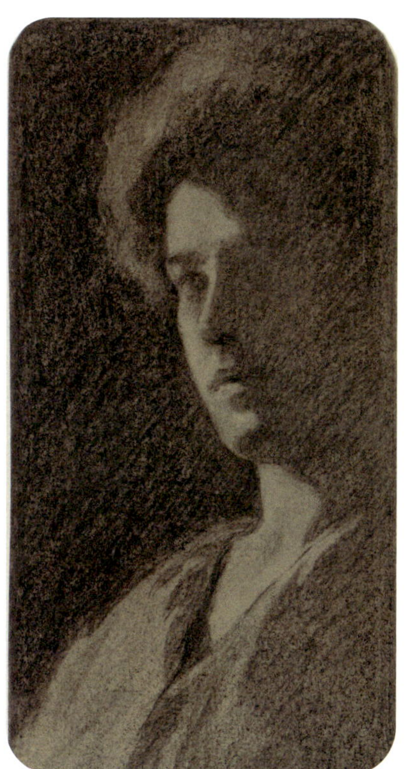

170. Zulma Steele
Self-Portrait, 1901
Charcoal
7 3/4 x 3 5/8 inches
Collection of Tom Wolf

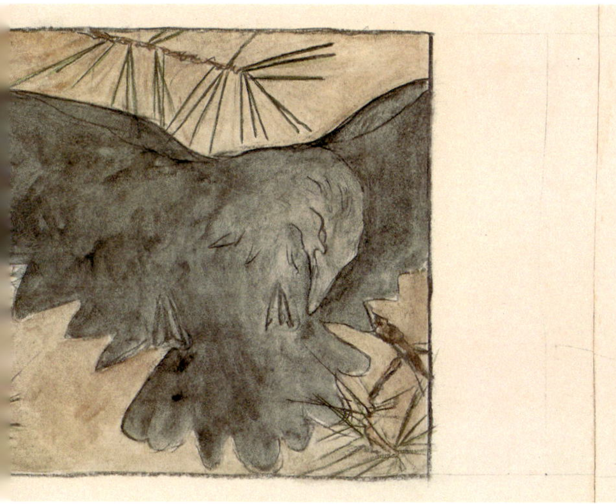

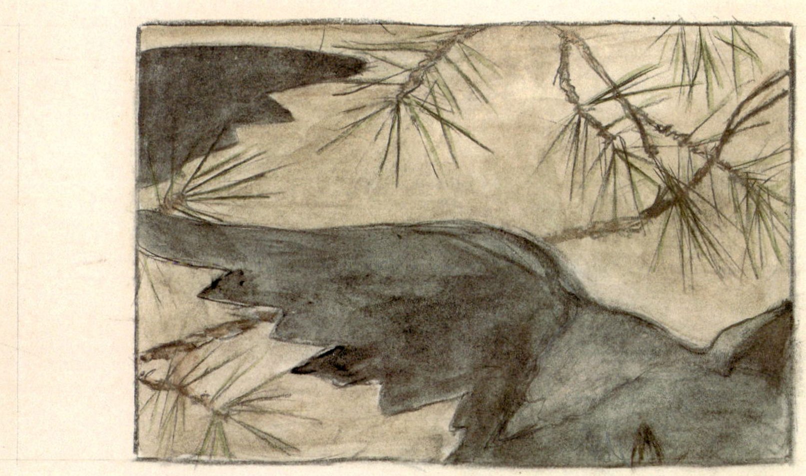

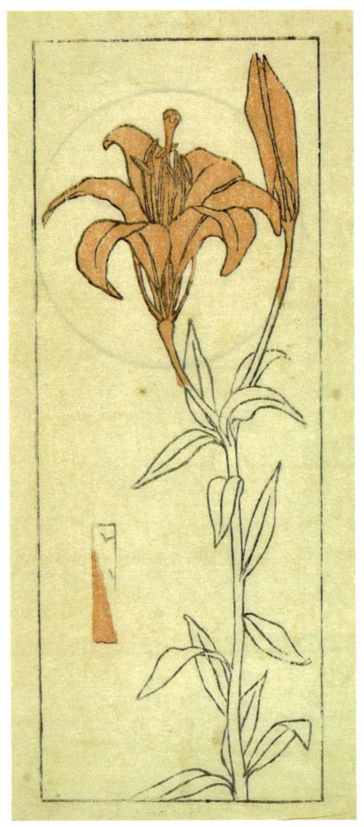

172. Zulma Steele
Lily, ca. 1904
Hand-colored wood-block print
12 1/2 x 4 3/4 inches
Collection of the Byrdcliffe Art Colony of the Woodstock Guild,
Alf Evers Collection
Gift of the Douglas C. James Charitable Trust

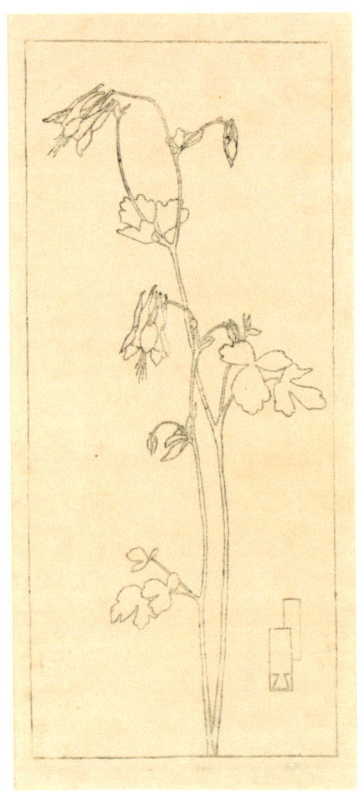

174. Zulma Steele
Columbine
Wood-block print
14 1/2 x 7 1/2 inches
Collection of the Byrdcliffe Art Colony of the Woodstock Guild

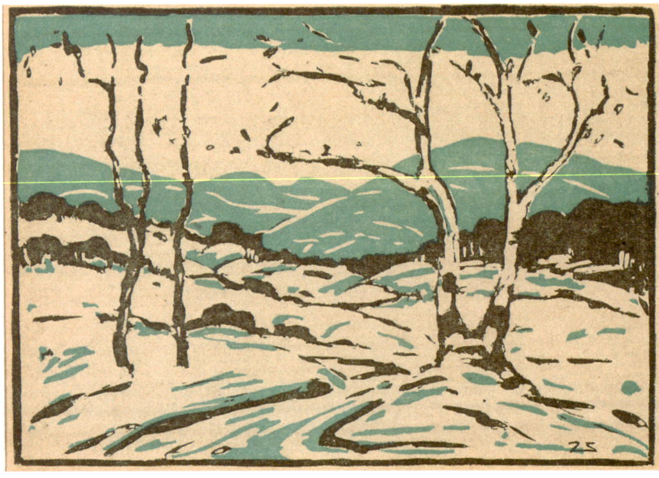

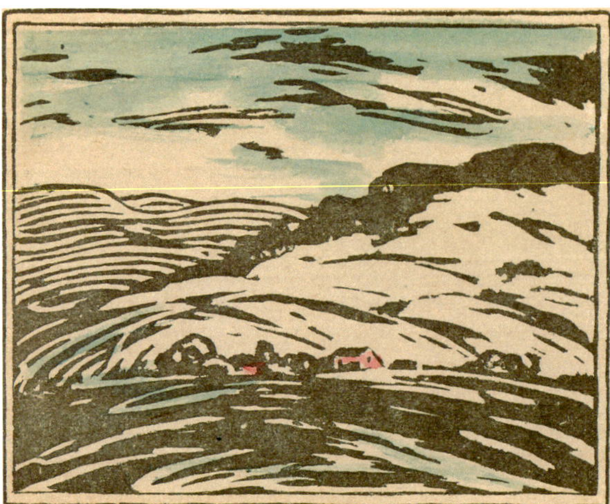

173. Zulma Steele
Landscapes
Woodcuts
Left to right: 3 x 4 5/8 inches; 3 1/8 x 4 inches; 2 3/4 x 4 1/8 inches;
3 x 3 5/8 inches
Collection of the Byrdcliffe Art Colony of the Woodstock Guild,
Alf Evers Collection
Gift of the Douglas C. James Charitable Trust

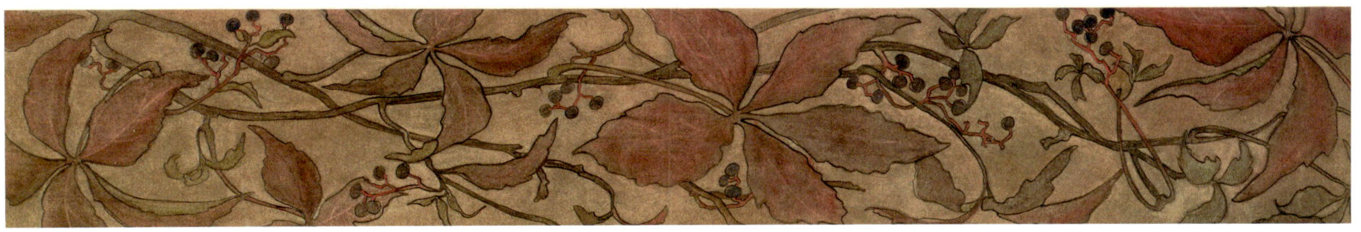

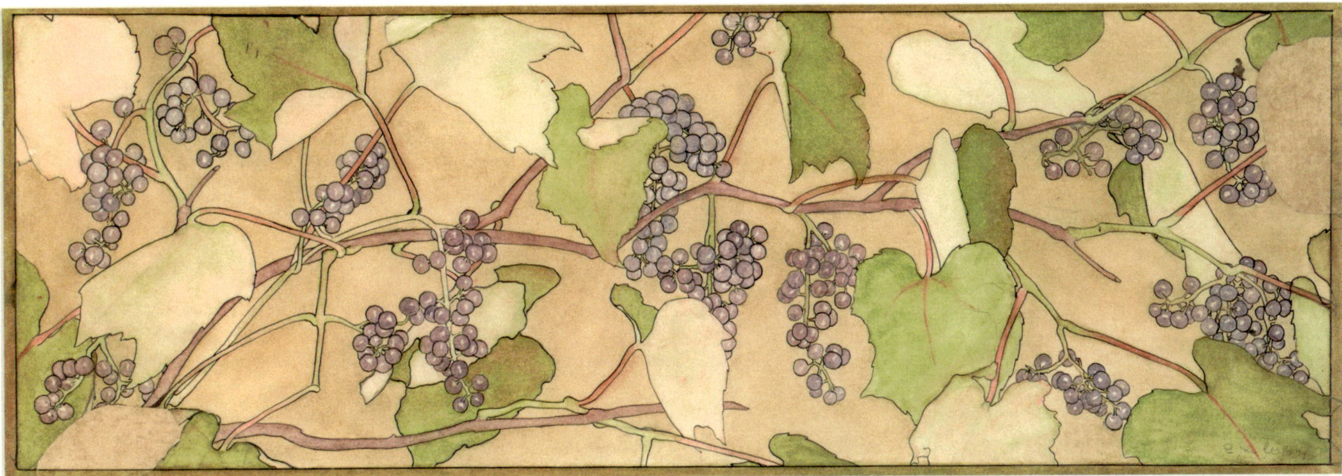

175. Zulma Steele and Edna Walker
Woodbine
Pen, ink, and watercolor
5 1/2 x 34 3/8 inches
Collection of the Byrdcliffe Art Colony of the Woodstock Guild, Alf Evers Collection
Gift of the Douglas C. James Charitable Trust

176. Zulma Steele and Edna Walker
Wild Grape Leaves
Watercolor on tracing paper
10 3/4 x 28 inches
Collection of the Byrdcliffe Art Colony of the Woodstock Guild

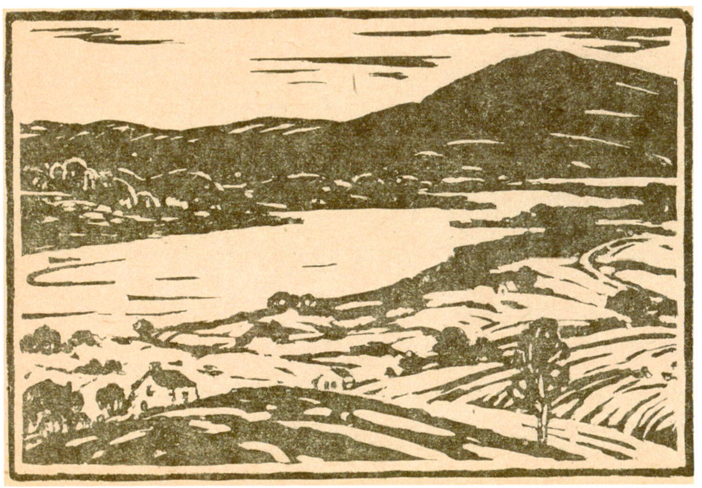

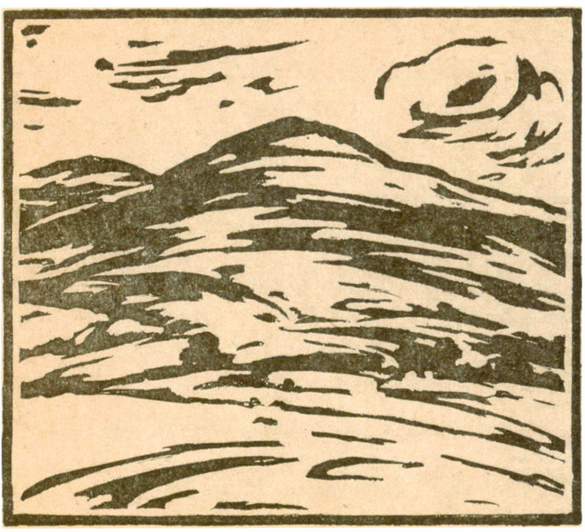

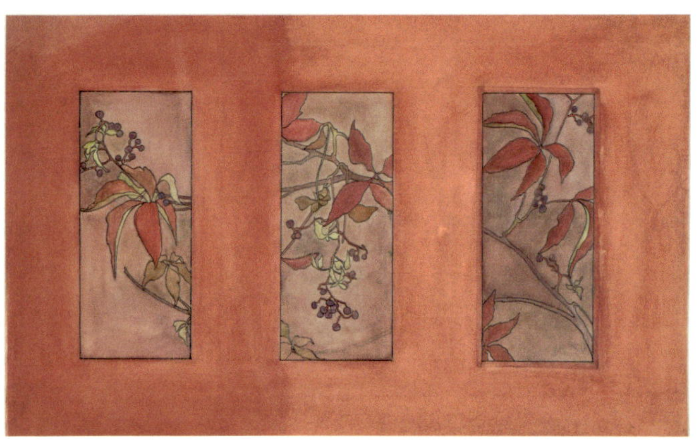

177. Zulma Steele and Edna Walker
Woodbine (three panels)
Watercolor
31 x 18 1/2 inches
Collection of the Byrdcliffe Art Colony of the Woodstock Guild, Alf Evers Collection
Gift of the Douglas C. James Charitable Trust

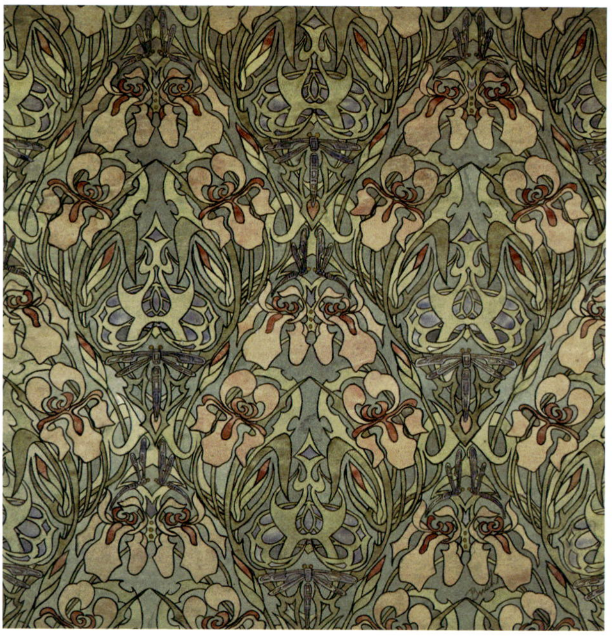

178. Zulma Steele
Dragonfly Wallpaper, ca. 1905
Watercolor, pen and ink, and gold paint
17 1/2 x 17 1/2 inches
Collection of Jean and Jim Young

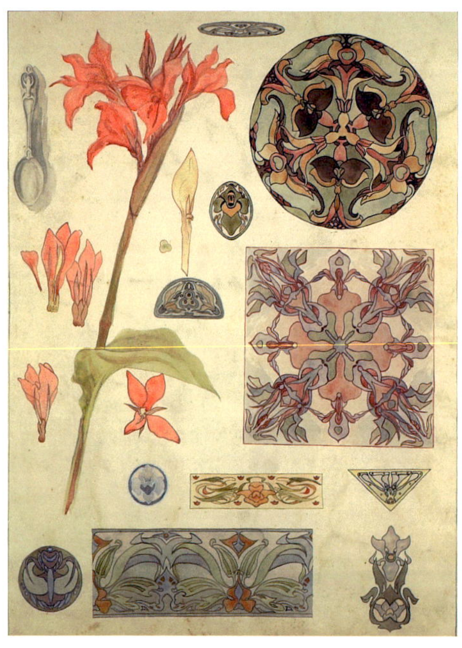

179. Zulma Steele
Sheet of Plant Studies and Border Designs
Pencil and watercolor
23 x 17 inches
Collection of Jean and Jim Young

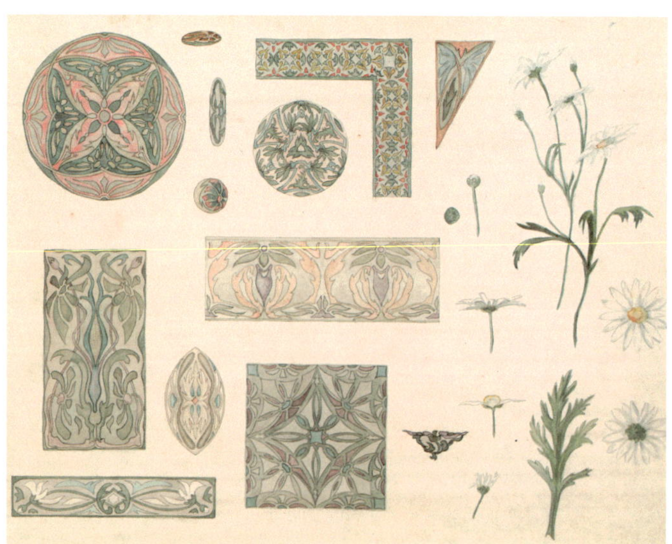

180. Zulma Steele
Sheet of Plant Studies and Border Designs
Pencil, pen, and watercolor
19 x 24 inches
Collection of Jean and Jim Young

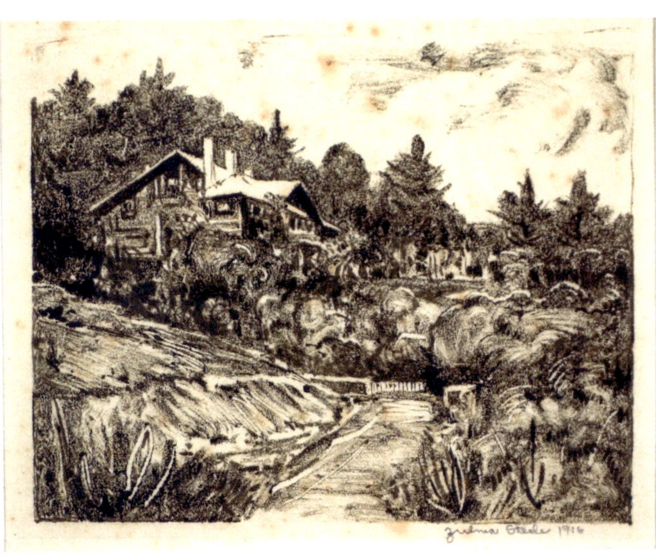

181. Zulma Steele
White Pines, 1918
Monotype
3 x 3 1/2 inches
Collection of Jean and Jim Young

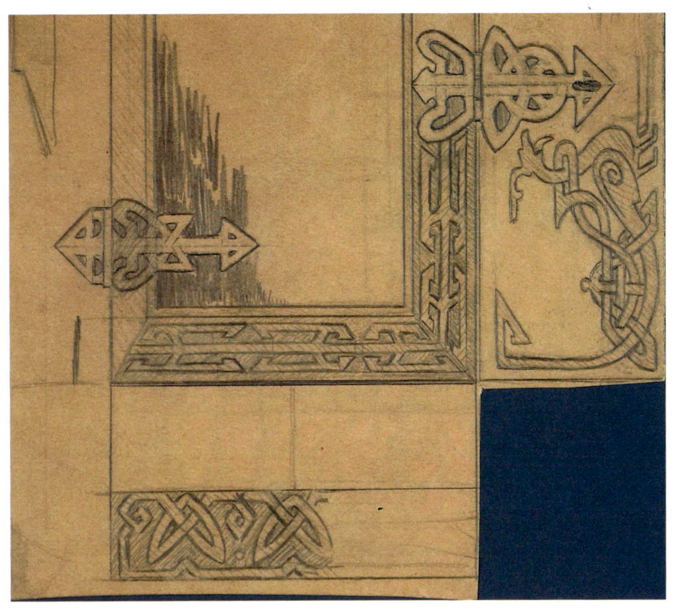

182. Edward Thatcher
Drawings for hinges
Pencil
8 1/2 x 7 1/2 inches (irregular)
Collection of the Byrdcliffe Art Colony of the Woodstock Guild,
Alf Evers Collection
Gift of the Douglas C. James Charitable Trust

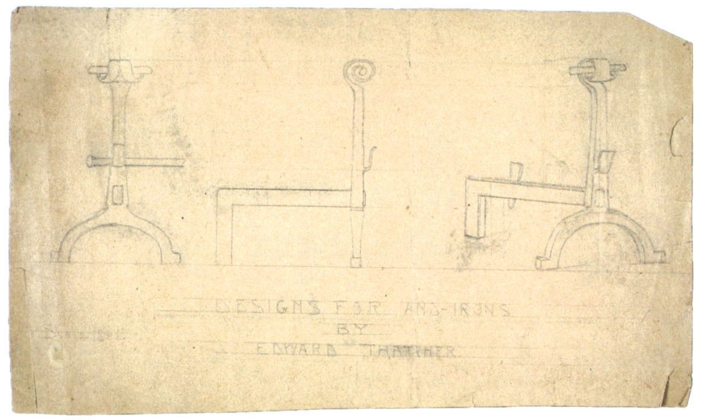

183. Edward Thatcher
Design for Andirons
Graphite
6 5/8 x 11 5/8 inches
Collection of the Byrdcliffe Art Colony of the Woodstock Guild
Gift of Jill and Mark Willcox Jr.

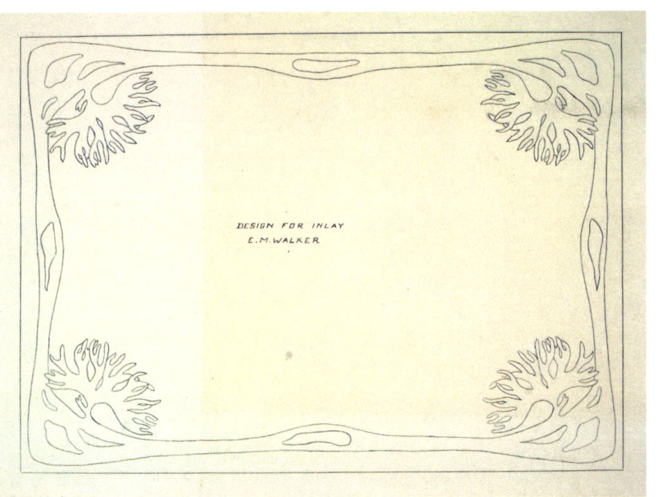

184. Edna Walker
Design for Inlay
Graphite
11 1/4 x 15 inches
Collection of the Byrdcliffe Art Colony of the Woodstock Guild
Gift of Jill and Mark Willcox Jr.

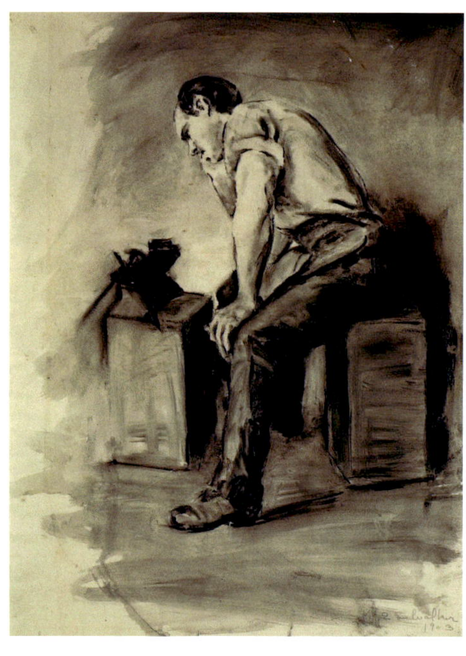

185. Edna Walker
Ned Thatcher at Forge
Charcoal
21 x 16 inches
Collection of Jean and Jim Young

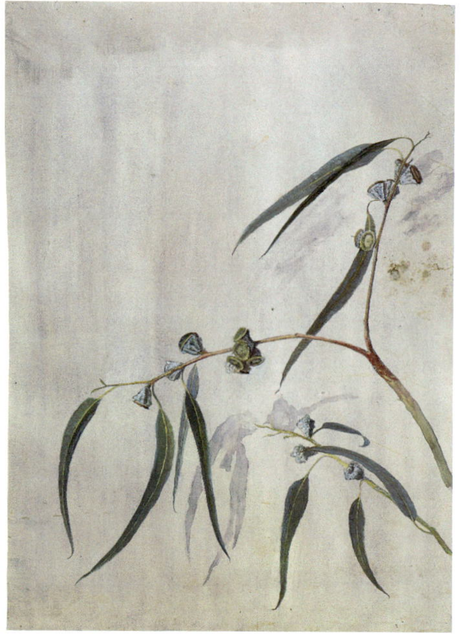

186. Jane Whitehead
Eucalyptus drawing
Pastel
$21^{7}/_{8}$ x $16^{1}/_{4}$ inches (irregular)
Collection of the Milwaukee Art Museum

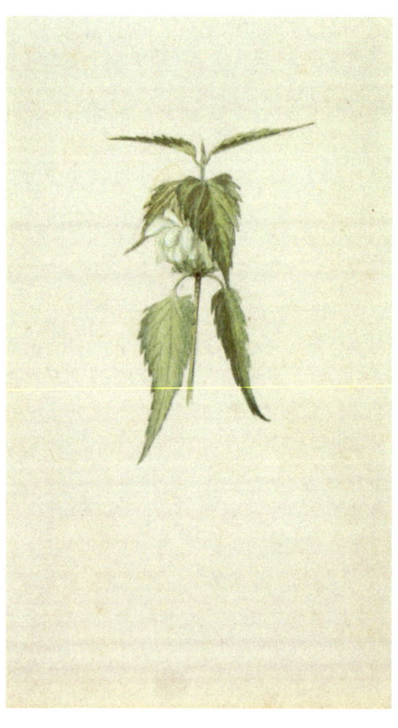

187. Jane Whitehead
Leaf Study, after John Ruskin, 1883
Watercolor and pencil
$8^{7}/_{8}$ x $5^{1}/_{4}$ inches
Private collection

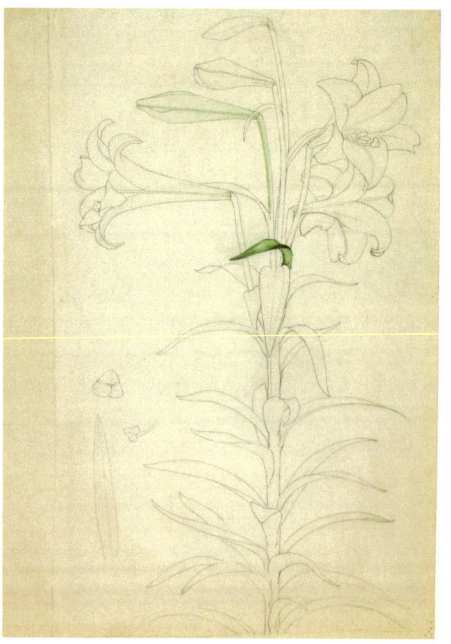

188. Jane Whitehead
Lilies
Pencil and watercolor
25 x 15 inches
Private collection

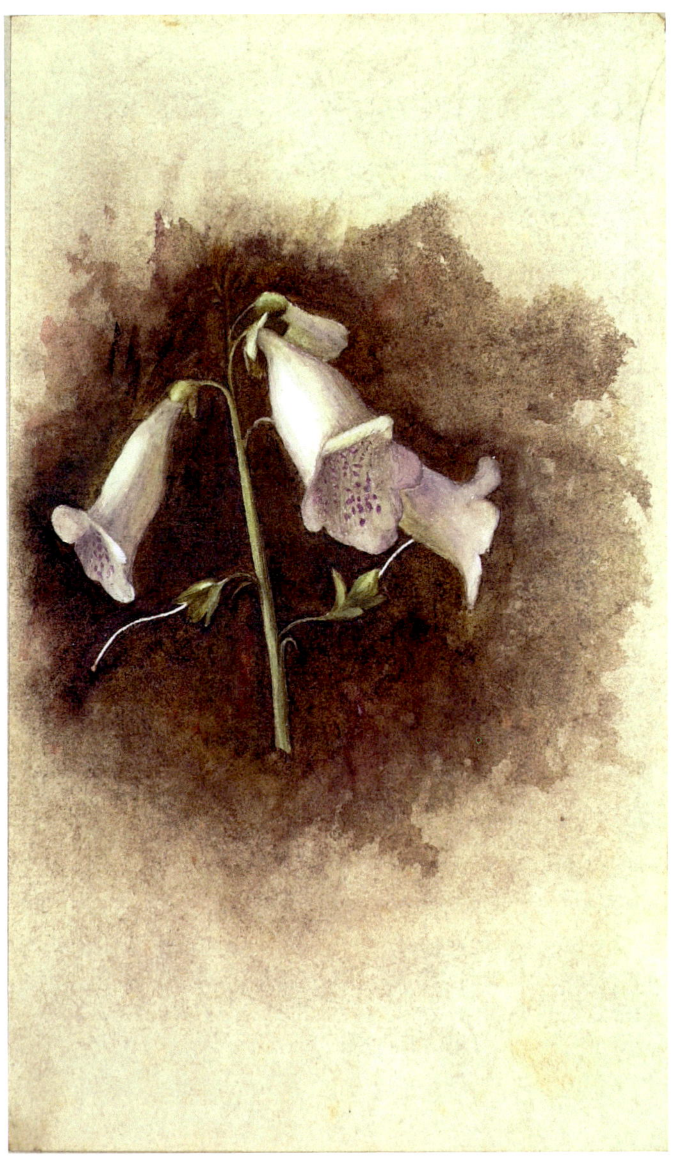

189. Jane Whitehead
Foxgloves
Watercolor
$8\,^{7}/_{8}$ x $5\,^{1}/_{4}$ inches
Collection of the Byrdcliffe Art Colony of the Woodstock Guild
Gift of Jill and Mark Willcox Jr.

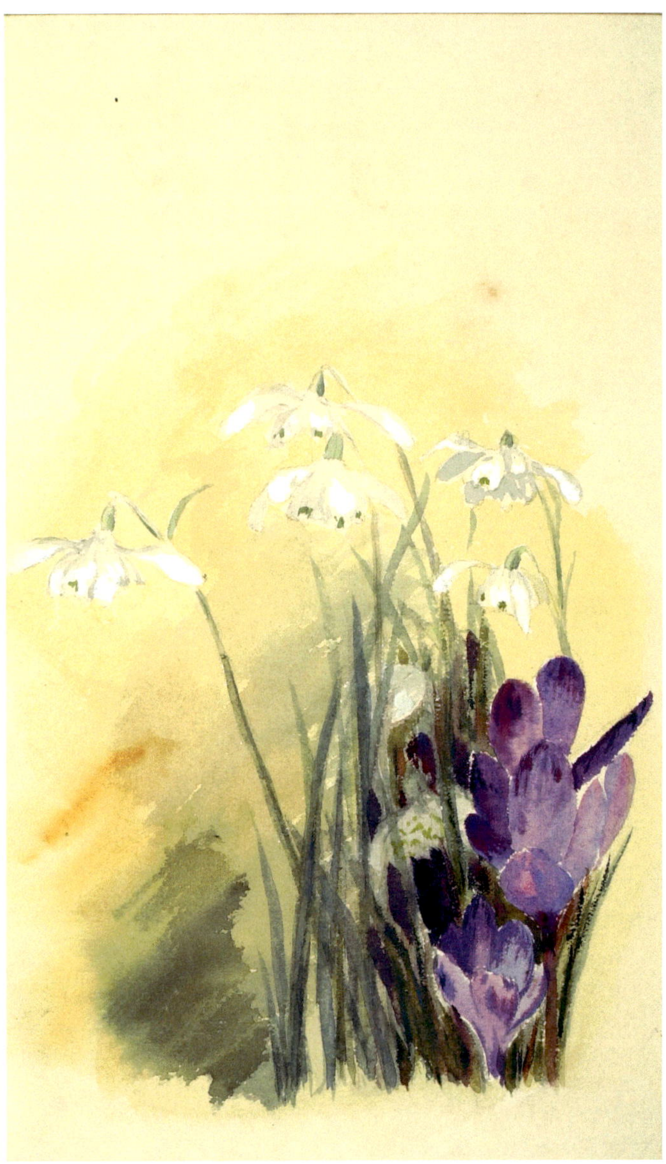

190. Jane Whitehead
Crocuses
Watercolor
$8\,^{7}/_{8}$ x $5\,^{1}/_{4}$ inches
Collection of the Byrdcliffe Art Colony of the Woodstock Guild
Gift of Jill and Mark Willcox Jr.

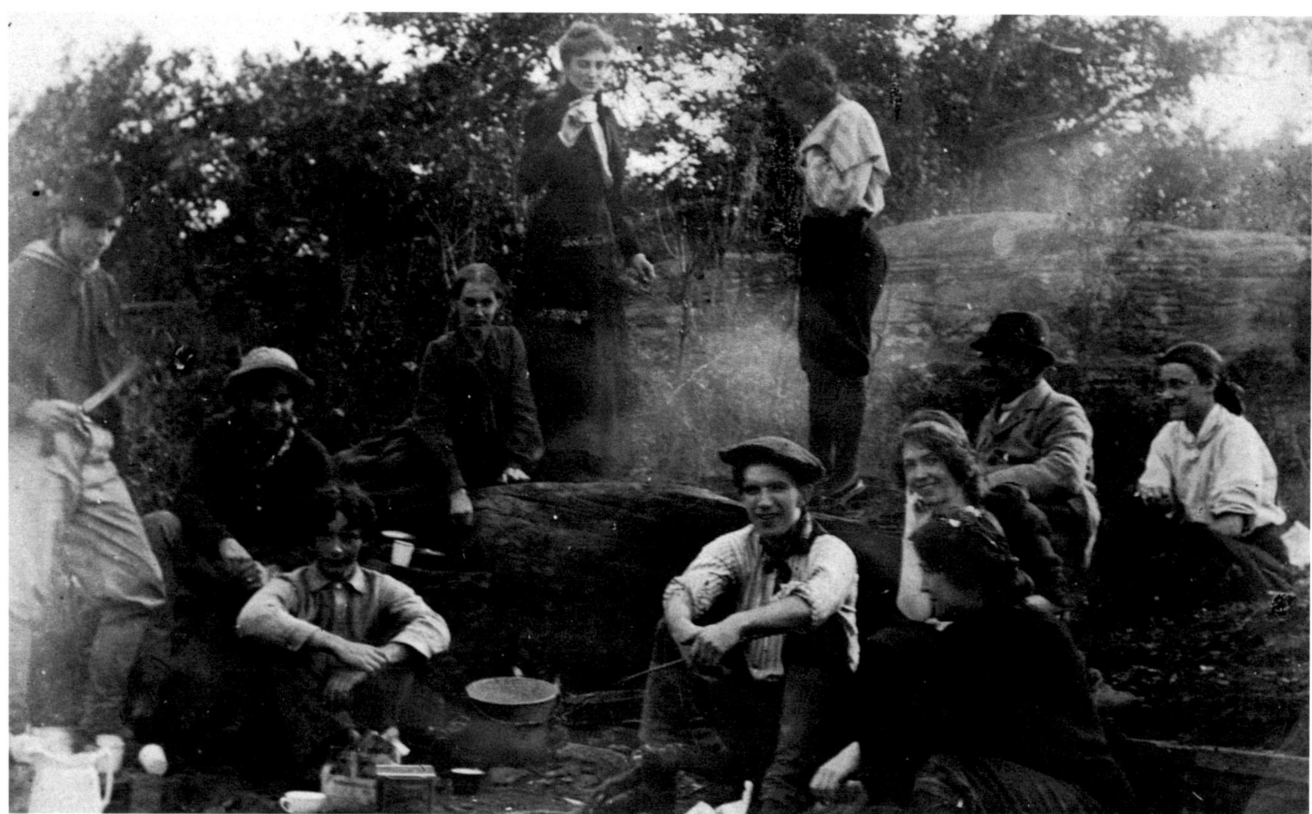

fig. 1 Attributed to Bertha Thompson, *Picnic on Overlook Mountain*, 1904. Silver print. Schlesinger Library, Radcliffe Institute, Harvard University.

Cast of Characters

NANCY E. GREEN

> Art Colonies, those disreputable bastions of Bohemia that began in the 1890s to infiltrate our rural landscape, are a fascinating chapter in the history of American culture. Hotbeds of talk, theory, and aesthetic politics, they have attracted some of the best names, gone through some of the most interesting "isms", and—not peripherally—spawned some of the most cheerful events in the annals of merrymaking[1] (fig. 1).

So many people affected the ideas and growth of the Byrdcliffe colony; Whitehead traveled widely, seeking out advice and searching for qualified artists of like-minded temperament to work and colonize Byrdcliffe. Many came and visited, spending time at the Villetta Inn or as guests of the Whiteheads at White Pines; some stayed, buying land from Whitehead and building their own homes or moving nearby, staying outside the periphery of Whitehead's restrictions for his colony yet remaining involved. And from afar, advice was offered from some of the leading intellectuals, educators, art teachers, social thinkers, and historians of the day.

Although ultimately the colony did not end up as Whitehead had wished, his legacy has endured. Byrdcliffe remains today a functioning art colony, dedicated to promoting fine art, music, theater, and literature—the longest lasting colony of its type.

There may never be a complete list of who came to Byrdcliffe and when, and many of the objects made there are no longer extant. This roster provides information about some of the known participants as well as many of the influential advisors, recognizing their involvement with Whitehead's dream.

John Quincy Adams

American

Adams was a friend of Charlotte Perkins Gilman's who was invited to come to the Lark's Nest the first summer Byrdcliffe was open. A member of the New York Civic Art Committee and secretary to New York's Fine Art Commission, he hired White one winter to work as an assistant with him. White recollected in his autobiography that Adams was considered "worthy" because he had written a book on art.

Jane Addams

American, 1860–1935

Addams, with her friend Ellen Gates Starr, established Hull House in Chicago in 1883, based on Toynbee Hall in London, which she visited in the 1880s. It was the first settlement house in Chicago and offered many "firsts" for Chicagoans: the first public baths, the first public playground, the first citizenship preparation classes, first free art exhibitions, first public swimming school, and first college extension courses, among much else. Hull House also instigated investigations that led to the first factory laws and the first model tenement code. It was a model of its type and gave people from the poorest walks of life exposure to culture and education and fair representation in society. Addams was awarded the Nobel Peace prize in 1931. Many of the residents and workers at Hull House went to Byrdcliffe during its formative years, and Addams herself visited as well.

C. R. Ashbee

British, 1863–1942

Ashbee began his career at Toynbee Hall in the 1880s; in the early 1900s he moved his crafts business to Chipping Camden, but the market for handmade crafts wasn't favorable and he was forced to close the shops in 1908. Whitehead knew his work in metal and visited him in Chipping Camden on his 1901 trip to Europe and purchased cups for each of his sons and a belt buckle for Jane. Ashbee participated in several lecture tours to the United States, and he visited Byrdcliffe in 1915.

Katharine Babbitt

American, died 1925

Whitehead first met Babbitt at Summerbrook; Jane soon became good friends with her and they occasionally traveled together. She apparently worked in the furniture shop at Byrdcliffe but came more as a friend of the Whiteheads than as a practicing artist. Babbitt and Marie little shared a resiidence for a while which became a focal meeting place for residents to talk about art and literature. She was hit by a car and died in 1925.

Jessie Tarbox Beals

American, born Canada, 1870–1942

At the age of eighteen, Beals moved to Williamsburg, Massachusetts, to begin a career as a schoolteacher. After nearly ten years, she quit and became one of the first notable women photojournalists, documenting American life for nearly four decades. In 1909 her pictures of Byrdcliffe were published in *American Homes and Gardens*, accompanying Poultney Bigelow's article on the colony. They remain some of the best archival images of the colony in its early days of operation.

Vivian Bevans

American, 1881–1947

Vivian Bevans and Bertha Thompson knew each other at the Art Institute of Chicago where they studied under Bror Nordfeldt, the woodcut artist, as well as taking classes with John Duncan. The girls became acquainted with Carl Lindin at this time as well and Bertha remembered the murals he was painting for Hull House. Bevans's sister Laura married Thorstein Veblen. Thompson recalls that Whitehead, "on the strength of her work with Nordfeldt (and her unusual beauty and charm) . . . invited Vivian to 'Byrdcliffe' to teach woodblock printing." She married Hervey White in 1904 and had two sons. She worked at the Herter Looms in New York, and later left White and remarried. White described Vivian as having "a wild sort of beauty that drew attention wherever she went. I was breathless the first time I saw her and my mind made up on the instant"[2] (fig. 2; see fig. 13).

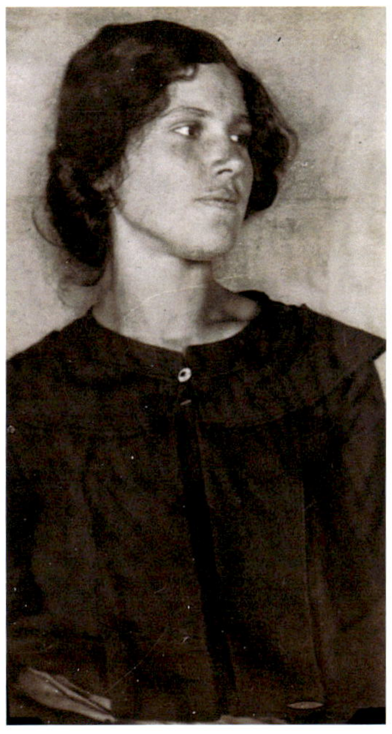

fig. 2 Attributed to Bertha Thompson, *Vivian Bevans*, 1904. Silver print. Thompson Family Papers, Schlesinger Library, Radcliffe Institute, Harvard University.

Poultney Bigelow

American, 1855–1954

Poultney Bigelow came from Malden, New York; his father had been ambassador to France and Poultney was educated in Paris with the future Kaiser Wilhelm II, with whom he remained friends. At his home in Woodstock, he occasionally entertained royalty, friends, and acquaintances from his youth. Despite being trained as a lawyer, he sailed around the world and was shipwrecked off the coast of Japan. He later published numerous books and was known for his puckish sense of humor. His annual birthday celebrations were memorable events, celebrated in a splendid manner, with lots of visitors. He wrote an article on Byrdcliffe for *American Homes and Gardens* published in October 1909; it was accompanied with haunting photographs by photojournalist Jessie Tarbox Beals. Jane's diary mentions many social activities with the Bigelows and her friendship with the family seems to go back to her early years, before she married Ralph.

Thérèse Kruger Bourgeois

(also known as Marie-Therese Duncan)
American, born Germany, 1895–1987

Kruger was one of the six "Isadorables," students of dancer Isadora Duncan. All orphans, Duncan legally adopted the six girls and they became teachers of the Duncan style of dancing, traveling around Europe and Russia propagating her methods and winning new students for Duncan's school. Theresa was known as impulsive and spirited; Isadora herself claimed, "My girls are like the Knights of the Grail! And come to earth when there are wrongs to be redressed."[3] In June 1921 she danced for the last time with Duncan in London and then returned to New York, where she married art dealer Stephen Bourgeois. Jane Whitehead's calendar note for July 26, 1923, reads: "Duncan dancing—Miss Bourgeois."[4] She may have come to Woodstock with Mary Desti, a friend of both Duncan's and Bourgeois's, who bought land at the Maverick.

Bolton Brown

American, 1864–1936

Brown was born in Dresden, New York, and went to Syracuse University. After graduation he taught at Cornell University briefly before going to Stanford, where he established the department of drawing and painting in 1894. It was here that he met Ralph and Jane. Though very different in personality from Whitehead and White, he shared many of the same ideals, and he quickly became one of the founding quartet, in search of a site for the colony. In the spring of 1902, White and Whitehead traveled south while Brown, due to his familiarity with the northeast, spent much of his time hiking through the Berkshires into the Catskills. It was Brown who discovered Woodstock and recognized its suitability for their venture. On June 8, 1902, Ralph wrote to Jane: "You say that I have told you nothing much of Brown lately. Well, I like him better & so does Niccolo, the more we are with him. Of course he is what he is, that he is not a Southerner! But he is a good man to deal with, unassuming & fair-minded; he is very active, almost too quick for me!"[5] Eventually this assessment would change and by the end of the first year, the two men decided to part ways. He remained friends with White who remembered him as an affectionate husband and indulgent father. Brown, however, remained in the area and became a well-known lithographer in the second decade of the twentieth century after learning the art in England. He wrote several books, including *The Painter's Palette* and *Lithography for Artists*. Brown was a charter member of the Sierra Club as well as a skilled mountain climber, and a peak in the Sierra Nevada Mountains was named for him after his death.

Lucy Brown

American, 1870–1949

Lucy Fletcher met Bolton Brown in California, and they were married in 1896. They spent their honeymoon on a two-month camping trip in the Sierra foothills. In the

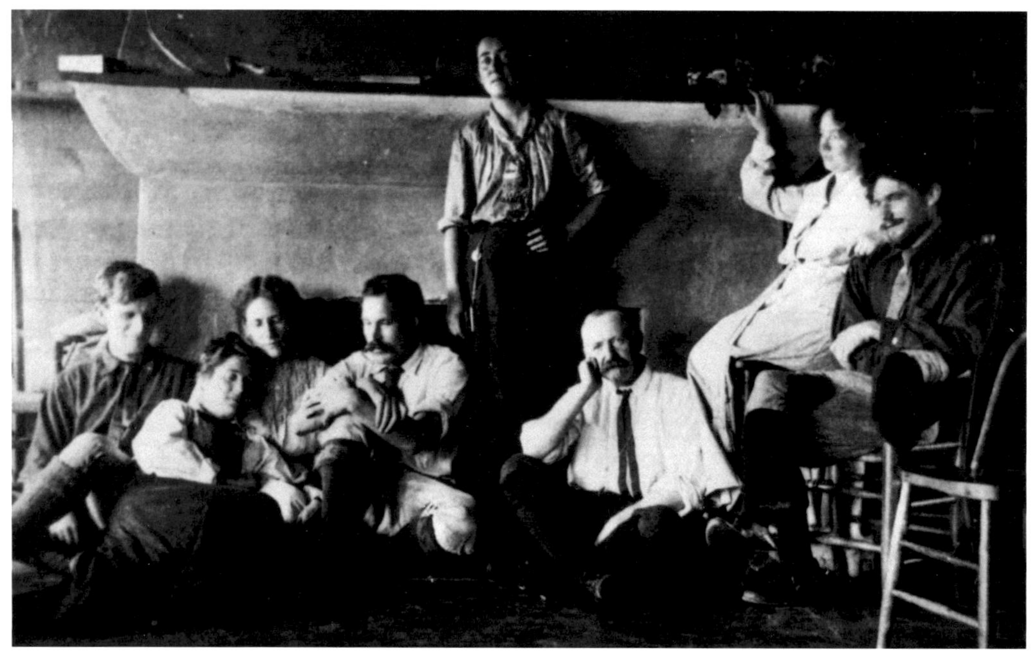

fig. 3 Unidentified photographer, *At the Lark's Nest*, ca. 1904. Left to right: Ned Thatcher, Isabel Moore, Lucy Brown, Carl Lindin, Ethel Canby, Riulf Erlenson, unidentified woman, and Olaf Westerling. Silver print. Collection of the Woodstock Historical Society.

winter of 1902 they moved to Woodstock to be part of Ralph Whitehead's founding group of colonists at Byrdcliffe (fig. 3). As Anita Smith remembers, "No one who knew Lucy Brown could ever forget her beautiful face which revealed a keen mind as well as compassion, which are not always mates. She had traveled far and experienced much and could talk about it in picture making sentences with the well-chosen word."[6] Lucy attempted weaving but found that her talents were not in this line. She and Bolton ran a Japanese print business in New York for several years before they were divorced in 1912. Despite the divorce, they remained close until his death in 1936.

John Burroughs

American, 1837–1921

John Burroughs, who lived close by, visited Byrdcliffe many times. In a letter to an unknown recipient, he described the pace of the colony and its benefits:

> You ask me to tell you about my visit to "Byrdcliffe." Well, I spent a thoroughly enjoyable ten days there. You know, when I went I thought I might stand it three days, but I found the ten days all too short. In the first place, the situation is very beautiful, high on the flank of Overlook Mountain above the small & picturesque Woodstock valley & commanding a superb mountain panorama. . . . Then the place, unlike some of the Catskill Camps I have visited, is not too much in the woods, but shows a delightful mingling of the sylvan & the pastoral. The various cottages & buildings are as picturesque as [. . . *unreadable*. . .], both outside & in; low & rambling, of undressed boards & timbers, & stained a rich tan color. The landscape has been no where marred or defaced; the modesty & privacy of nature has in all things been guarded. And the people, upwards of fifty of them, go well with this kind of background: very democratic, free & informal in their intercourse & thoroughly serious & earnest, each one with some work or pursuit that occupies the greater part of each day—young men & women painting landscapes or portraits or modeling in clay, or working in leather, or in metals, or weaving, or designing or taking music lessons, or working at cabinet work in carpentry—public school teachers spending their vacation learning some craft, some well known artists with their families, two or three women authors reading up on some subject in the large up-to-date library—all happy & all too busy to loan one idle hand to the devil. I liked the whole spirit & atmosphere of the place immensely. In the large hall which serves as a dance room & picture gallery, the paintings of the week are hung on Saturday morning & criticized by some artist of established reputation . . . . The dances Tuesday & Saturday nights give just the right feeling & social touch to the life there. . . . The large solid library was a surprise to me. Few colleges have as good, I should like nothing better than to spend a season here seated on the secluded upper veranda, reading up on certain subjects . . . . Mr. and Mrs. Whitehead are the perfection of host & hostess, & their hearts are thoroughly in this work . . . . If you now have an invitation to "Byrdcliffe" accept it. I assume you will not regret having done so.[7]

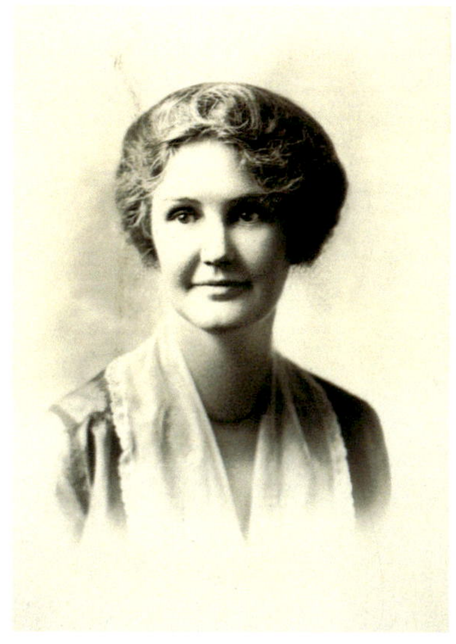

fig. 4 Unidentified photographer, *Helen Goodrich Buttrick*, ca. 1905. Silver print. Thompson Family Papers, Schlesinger Library, Radcliffe Institute, Harvard University.

Annette Butler

American

Butler was one of the teachers at the Sloyd school on the Whiteheads' property in California. The Sloyd system trained students in weaving, woodworking, modeling and other crafts. She visited Byrdcliffe the first summer and is listed in the Villetta ledger as a 1903 visitor.

Helen Goodrich Buttrick

American

Helen Buttrick was a childhood friend of Bertha Thompson's from Chicago and the two had classes in design together at the Chicago Art Institute. She came to Byrdcliffe in the early years and Thompson remembers her at Dow's summer school one summer while she was there. She also took classes with her at Pratt in 1912 (fig. 4). She received her degree from the University of Chicago and wrote a book, *Principles of Clothing Selection*, published in 1924.

Ethel Canby

American

Hervey White remembered Ethel Canby among the Byrdcliffe guests that first year; she came with her mother and her sister. Canby married etcher Orville Peets and stayed on in Woodstock, becoming actively involved in the community. During World War I she

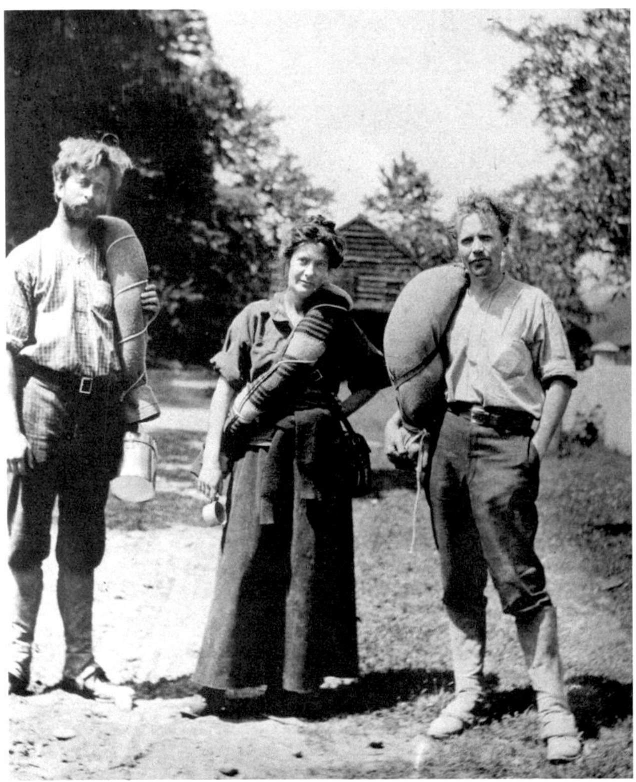

fig. 5 Unidentified photographer, *Unidentified man, Lou Wall Moore, John Carlson*, ca. 1905. Silver print. Collection of the Historical Society of Woodstock.

was organized local fairs in the town and with the aid of many of the resident artists raised funds for the Red Cross.

Arthur Beecher Carles

American, 1882–1952

Carles, best known today for his modernist style related to German Expressionism and Fauvism, came to Byrdcliffe in the summer of 1906. He was a friend of Alfred Stieglitz, John Marin, and Max Weber and was a popular teacher at the Pennsylvania Academy of Fine Arts from 1917 to 1925. He had studied there himself, with William Merritt Charles, Anshutz, and Cecelia Beaux. A member of the extensive Beecher clan, he may have come to Byrdcliffe with his Gilman relatives as they are listed next to each other in the Villetta register.

John Carlson

American, born Sweden, 1874–1945

Carlson (fig. 5, see also fig. 9) moved with his family to Buffalo, New York, from Sweden in 1884. He was the first scholarship student at Byrdcliffe, arriving in 1904, and studied painting under Birge Harrison and Carl Lindin. He also joined in the musical life of the colony as a player of the harmonium. In 1905 he rented a barn/studio in Rock City, near Woodstock, and lived "precariously for months on beer and cheese."[8] He is also listed as staying at the Villetta that summer. Harrison opened the Art Students League Summer School in Woodstock in 1906 and Carlson joined him the following year as his assistant, succeeding him as head of the school in 1911. Eventually Carlson operated his own summer school of landscape painting in Woodstock from 1922 to 1945, and during the winter months he traveled extensively around the United States. Carlson said he liked painting trees best because they were "excellent friends and, for me, the most fascinating sitters! Trees are a lot like human beings; rooted men, possessing character, ambitions, and idiosyncrasies. Those who know trees, see their struggles too; struggles with the wind and the weather; struggles to adjust themselves to their society. For nature will not allow them to run amuck, heedless to their neighbors; their individual propensities must conform to the cosmic rhythm in a wood."[9]

Rinaldo Carnielo

Italian, 1853–1910

Carnielo met Whitehead in 1889 and thereafter the two became close friends, particularly after Whitehead moved to Florence in 1890. On a visit in 1901 Whitehead purchased the sculpture *Christ on the Cross with Angels* that still resides outside White Pines today. The sculpture of his youngest son, "Bimbo," was done when the Whiteheads visited Carnielo for the last time, in 1906 (see page 94). Though born in Venice, Florence, and knowledge of the art of that city, proved a greater influence on Carnielo. He was known for his numerous bas-reliefs as well as his commemorative monuments, done in a realistic style. His former home in a nineteenth-century Art Nouveau building is now the Carnielo Museum, Florence.

Ernest Chapman

New Zealander, born 1864

Chapman was an experienced artist when he came to Byrdcliffe; he had exhibited at the Art Institute of Chicago in 1901, and again in 1904; and at the Boston Society of Arts and Crafts in 1906. At the colony he worked in brass and iron in the forge, alongside Thatcher, and was known as the "Brassbeater."

Elizabeth Colwell

American, 1881–ca. 1956

Born in Michigan, Colwell, a noted woodcut artist, was a student of B. J. O. Nordfeldt at the Chicago Art

Institute (as were Vivian Bevans and Bertha Thompson). She showed her woodcuts in group exhibitions in the second and third decades of the twentieth century in Chicago, Boston, and New York, though she is best known for her bookplates and fancy lettering, having designed the typeface cut by the American Type Founding Co. called "Colwell Hand Letter." She is listed in the Villetta ledger as a visitor in 1921 and again in 1924. She most likely knew about Byrdcliffe through the Chicago connection provided by Bevans and Thompson.

Paul Cornoyer
American, 1864–1923

Born in St. Louis, Cornoyer studied in Paris at the Académie Julian and received a gold medal from the American Art Association. One of the founders of the North Shore Arts Association in Gloucester and an early president of that organization, he was also a member of the National Academy of Design and the Woodstock Artists Association. He came to Byrdcliffe the first year it was open and is listed in the Villetta ledger as a boarder that fall.

Clarence Darrow
American, 1857–1938

Best remembered today for his role as defense lawyer in the 1925 Scopes trial, Darrow was also a distinguished orator and writer. Born in rural Ohio, he moved to Chicago in 1887 and in 1891 he took a job in the law department of the Chicago and Northwestern Railway. He also served as an advocate for the United Mine Workers in the early 1900s. A friend of Hervey White's, he was associated with Hull House and it was probably through this connection that he was drawn to spend time at Byrdcliffe.

Mabel Davidson
American

Davidson is listed in the Villetta ledger for 1912 and 1919 though she visited more frequently than is recorded. She is known to have worked with Hardenbergh and Penman on the Byrdcliffe Pottery.

Dawson Dawson-Watson
American, born England, 1864–1939

Dawson-Watson first studied art with the American Mark Fisher, an expatriate working in London, then went to Paris where he studied with Carolus-Duran, Chartran, and others. In 1893 he moved to the United States where he was the director of the Hartford Art Society. He was skilled in a variety of media, and besides painting he worked as a designer in textiles as well as being a woodworker. He was in St. Louis from 1904 to 1915, teaching at the School of Fine Arts, then moved to Springfield, Illinois, and finally San Antonio, Texas. He was recommended to Whitehead by Birge Harrison, who had met Dawson-Watson in Canada, and he taught at Byrdcliffe in the first season. In a letter to Jane, Whitehead explained, "Harrison . . . writes me about a painter who is in Quebec whom he most strongly recommends as a decorator & designer in woodwork."[10]

Matilde de Cordoba
American, 1871–1942

De Cordoba was the child of a French mother and Cuban father. Her siblings included a sister, Mercedes, who was an artist, and a brother, Pedro, who became a stage and screen actor. Both visited her at Byrdcliffe in 1905. She studied at the Art Students League under Cox and Whittemore, with William Merritt Chase at Shinnecock, and with Aman-Jean in Paris. Known as a portrait painter and printmaker, she came to Byrdcliffe for a commissioned etching portrait of John Burroughs. She returned, many years later, in 1917.

John Dewey
American, 1859–1952

A philosopher and education reformer, Dewey came to Byrdcliffe in 1906 and built a playhouse with his children on the property of Bolton Brown's former residence, Carniola. White and Whitehead both knew him when he taught at the University of Chicago; he came to Columbia University in 1904 where he worked with Arthur Wesley Dow, the newly appointed head of Teachers College. He brought the Shotwells and the Weyls to Byrdcliffe.

William Hunt Diederich
American, born Hungary, 1884–1953

Diederich, a noted sculptor in both stone and metal, was in Woodstock in the late teens through the early 1930s. He made pottery at Byrdcliffe, dated 1930, and the Whitehead family owned some of his silhouette works.

Arnold Dolmetsch
British, 1858–1940
Dolmetsch revived old music and the craft of making almost forgotten instruments like the viol, the recorder,

and the harpsichord. Not surprisingly, he was sought out by the Whiteheads, who themselves had an active interest in old music. Dolmetsch and his wife came to Byrdcliffe in 1908, staying at the Villetta and giving concerts for the residents on the clavichord and harpsichord. His credo, "A beautiful instrument that is to produce beautiful sounds will inevitably be beautiful in appearance,"[11] aptly fulfills the agenda of the Arts and Crafts aesthetic and made him popular among artists of this period.

Paul Dougherty
American, 1877–1947

Bertha Thompson clearly remembers Dougherty as one of the artists at Byrdcliffe during one of her first summers there. Trained as a lawyer, Dougherty changed to an art career in the late 1890s, studying first with Robert Henri and then in Europe for five years. He moved to California in the 1930s and is best remembered today for his marine paintings.

Arthur Wesley Dow

Dow was a painter and printmaker who is best remembered today for his work in art education. He taught at Pratt Institute for many years and he sent several of his students to Byrdcliffe, among them Zulma Steele, Ned Thatcher, Edna Walker, George Eggers, and Warren Wheelock. Bertha Thompson attended his summer school in Ipswich (fig. 6) during its last year of operation, 1907, and was visited there by Thatcher, Steele, Westerling, and Vivian Bevans White. Dow's influence was multiplied by his books, of which *Composition*, initially published in 1899, is the best known. In Whitehead's correspondence with Jane he mentions planning a trip to Ipswich, but it does not appear that he actually went—though he did go to Pratt, in search of qualified teachers to work at the colony.

Olivia Dunbar
American, 1873–1953

Dunbar graduated from Smith College in 1894 and went to work for the *New York World* two years later. In 1902 she quit newspaper work to concentrate on writing articles, short fiction, ghost stories, and biography. She came to Byrdcliffe the first summer, invited to the Lark's Nest by Carl Lindin and Hervey White. In 1914 she married the poet/playwright Ridgeley Torrence; both were avid supporters of black rights, and Dunbar also spoke out in support of women's suffrage, a topic which she frequently addressed in her fiction.

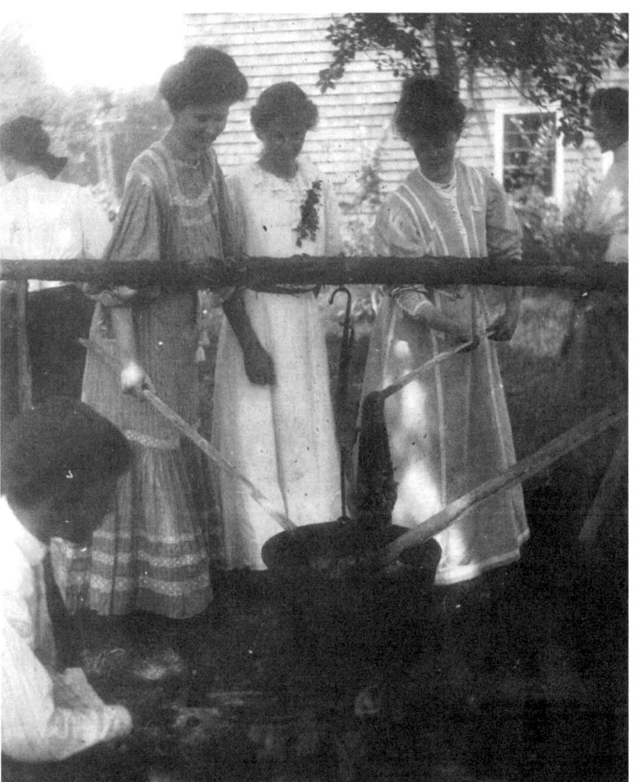

fig. 6 Unidentified photographer, *Helen Buttrick and Bertha Thompson Stirring Dye Pots at Arthur Wesley Dow's Ipswich Summer School*, 1907. Silver print. Thompson Family Papers, Schlesinger Library, Radcliffe Institute, Harvard University.

John Duncan
Scottish, 1866–1945

Scottish artist John Duncan came to the United States in 1900 to be associate professor of art at the University of Chicago; in 1903 he went to Byrdcliffe to organize printmaking efforts there. He had set up a lithographic press at Hull House in 1895 and had planned on doing something similar in Woodstock. Whitehead, however, refused to get a press, associating lithography with commercial enterprises. His hope had been to set up something more artistic, using the example of Arthur Dow's Ipswich prints as a prototype. This never came to pass. White noted that he was "a good artist and draughtsman as well as craftsman also, a teacher and splendid fellow." Duncan then returned to Edinburgh where he continued painting in the Celtic Revival/Pre-Raphaelite tradition for which he was known. His commissions included stained glass, altarpieces, and church murals.

Charles Frederick Eaton
American, 1842–1930

A painter, craftsman, and landscape architect, Eaton was a neighbor of the Whiteheads in Montecito, on his estate called Riso Rivo. Handmade books were one of the specialties produced in his studio there, complete with wrought-metal mounts. The metalwork harks back to a medieval concept, heavy in its realization. Like most Arts and Crafts practitioners, he emphasized the use of local floral and fauna in his crafts. He is also known for his lamps that incorporate translucent shells as the shade. He exhibited in many of the major Arts and Crafts exhibitions in the early part of the twentieth century.

Abastenia St. Leger Eberle
American, 1878–1942

Born in Iowa, Eberle grew up in Canton, Ohio. An accomplished violinist, she became interested in clay modeling at a young age. During the Spanish-American War, her family moved to Puerto Rico, where her father was a physician. In 1899 she moved to New York and studied for three years at the Art Students League with Kenyon Cox and George Grey Barnard. She made some collaborative sculpture with Anna Vaughn Hyatt and then, turning from the more traditional style she had been working in, Eberle began working more abstractly. At the same time she became interested in settlement work in Manhattan's Lower East Side and she used many of the children she met there as models for her work. She exhibited widely and was elected an associate of the National Academy of Design in 1929. She came to Byrdcliffe during the teens.

George William Eggers
American, 1883–1958

Eggers was a student of Arthur Wesley Dow's at the Pratt Institute where he received a certificate in drawing, painting, and composition. He was one of the many Dow students to go to Byrdcliffe during the early years of its existence and is listed in the Villetta ledger for 1903 and 1904. While there he worked as a woodworker, doing carpentry projects to earn his keep. In 1906 he went to Chicago to serve on the faculty of the Chicago Normal College, where he remained until 1921. At that time he moved to Colorado as director of the Denver Art Museum; he later became director of the Worcester Art Museum and chairman of the City Colleges of New York. He most likely first met Bolton Brown at Byrdcliffe in 1903, and the two collaborated on several prints, probably in the second and third decades of the twentieth century when Brown became a celebrated lithographer.

Joseph Enneking
American, 1881–1942

The son of the famous nineteenth-century painter John Enneking, Joseph studied at the Cowles Art School and the Boston Museum of Fine Arts School with Frank Benson, Edward Tarbell, and Joseph DeCamp. Though his father discouraged him from becoming an artist, he persisted in his goal. His was a vivid personality and a friend remembered, "He loved people and could make the most unhappy person laugh."[12] He is listed in the Villetta ledger as a 1903 visitor to the Byrdcliffe campus.

Riulf Erlenson
Norwegian

Riulf Erlenson (alternately spelled "Erlandsen") exhibited at the Society of Independent Artists as a painter in the 1930s. He was known as one of the woodcarvers for the furniture at Byrdcliffe and is listed in the 1904 Villetta ledger. It is possible that he supervised the furniture making at Byrdcliffe, along with Fordyce Herrick. Like many of the early craftsmen at Byrdcliffe, he was from the Boston Society of Arts and Crafts (see fig. 3).

Madeleine Fleury
French

Little is known about Madeleine Fleury. She was born in Constantinople to French parents and exhibited at the 1889 Salon des Artistes Français where she received an honorable mention. She appears to have met Jane Whitehead while studying at the Académie Julian in Paris in the 1880s. The two remained friends and Jane usually visited her on trips abroad. There are pastel portraits of both Jane and Ralph by Madeleine Fleury from their early years together that show Fleury to be a talented artist, though she never received the recognition of her more famous father and brother, the artists Joseph Fleury and Tony Robert-Fleury, who taught for many years at the Académie Julian.

Richard le Gallienne
British, 1866–1947

An Englishman born in Liverpool, le Gallienne fancied himself an aesthete. He grew his hair long and cultivated an appearance of delicacy and grace after attending an Oscar Wilde lecture in 1893. He also added the more aristocratic sounding French article "le" to his surname. A poet and critic, he was also ethereally good-looking and photographed well, and he made sure his image was well circulated in the literary world. He is best remembered today for his prose, particularly for his book *Quest of the Golden Girl* (1896). He married Julie Norregard in 1897 and subsequently moved to the United States. For many years he was a Woodstock resident and his essay on the town (published in 1923 by the Woodstock Art Association) is a droll look at the community there and offers an amusing insider's view of both the town and Byrdcliffe itself.

Charlotte Perkins (Stetson) Gilman

American, 1860–1947

Feminist critic and author Gilman was the great-niece of Henry Ward Beecher and Harriet Beecher Stowe. She studied art at the Rhode Island School of Design and there met and eventually married artist Charles Stetson. Divorced in 1894, Stetson then married her best friend and the three remained on good terms. In 1898 she wrote *Women and Economics: A Study of the Economic Relation Between Men and Women as a Factor in Social Relations*; two years later she married her first cousin, George Houghton Gilman. A frequent visitor to Byrdcliffe, she first met Whitehead in the Adirondacks at Prestonia Mann's retreat, Summerbrook. She was invited to the Lark's Nest in 1903 by Hervey White and subsequently came and stayed often. She is listed in the Villetta ledger for 1904, 1905, 1906, and 1919. Her cousin, Lyman Beecher Stowe, visited in 1913.

Herbert J. Hall

American

Dr. Hall started the Marblehead Pottery in 1904 where crafts were taught as therapy for convalescing patients. The summer of 1907 when Bertha Thompson attended Dow's Ipswich school, she remembered several of the Dow students boarding at the Halls' home and that a "Miss Nash," one of the students, was responsible for breaking up the Halls' marriage. In 1915 Hall sold the Marblehead business to Arthur Baggs, the potter whose name has become synonymous with the style of Marblehead Pottery. Along with Mertice M. C. Buck, Hall wrote *Handicrafts for the Handicapped*, published in 1916. In 1920 Hall visited Byrdcliffe and signed the Villetta register.

H. Elizabeth Rutgers Hardenbergh

American, active 1890–1940

Hardenbergh was born in New Brunswick, New Jersey, and studied in New York with Henry B. Snell. Though known as a painter of floral still lifes, she was also a proficient potter and, with Edith Penman, set up the Byrdcliffe Pottery on the Byrdcliffe campus in 1903. In the winter months she shared a space in the Van Dyck studios with Penman until the 1920s. The 1910 Villetta ledger lists a Miss H. A. Hardenbergh and a Mrs. Warren Hardenbergh, visiting the campus from New Brunswick, New Jersey, most likely relatives of Elizabeth's.

Lovell Birge Harrison

American, 1854–1929

"Harrison more than anyone else led the transformation from Ruskin-Morris goals of Byrdcliffe to the lusty, uninhibited art colony of Woodstock."[13] An old friend of the Whiteheads from Santa Barbara, Harrison became head of the art school at Byrdcliffe in 1904. "Harrison's relations with art students were marked by kindness and thoughtfulness; his manners were polished without being stiff; and he radiated warmth and goodwill."[14]

Franz Hazenplug

American, 1873–1931

Hazenplug was a staff artist at Stone & Kimball along with Will Bradley. He designed Chap-Book posters and several book and exhibition placards. A book

fig. 7 Unidentified photographer, *Fordyce Herrick in Front of White Pines*, ca. 1910. Silver print. Collection of the Historical Society of Woodstock.

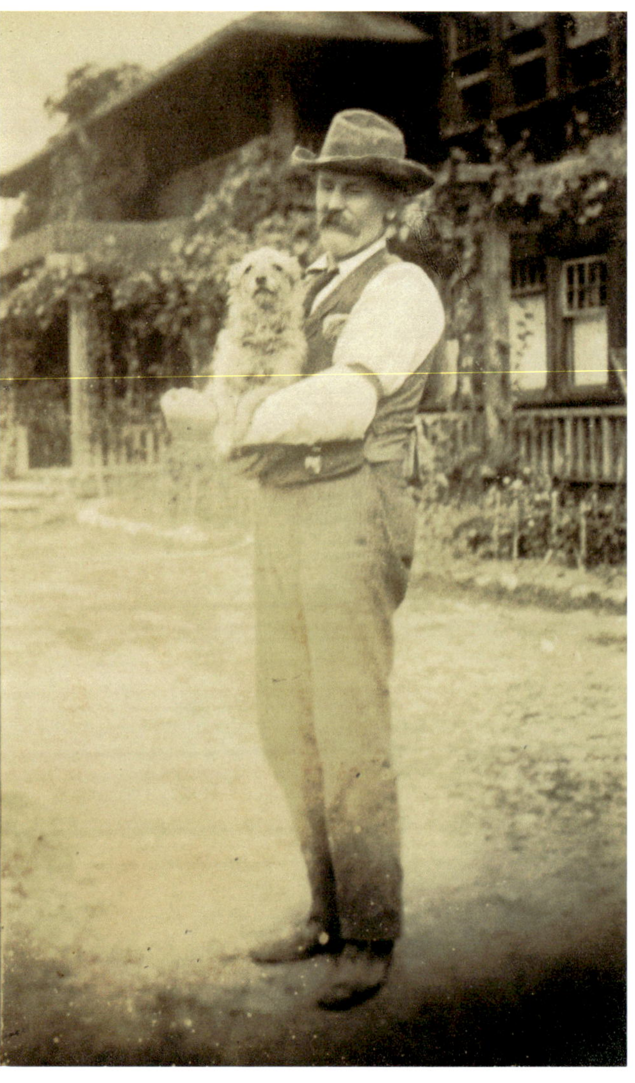

illustrator and poster designer for other companies, he was also associated with Jane Addams's Hull House and the University of Chicago, which is probably how he came to Whitehead's attention. After the turn of the century he concentrated his talents on designing and illustrating books. He headed the metalwork at Byrdcliffe in 1909 and is listed in the Villetta as staying there that year. Around 1920 he changed his name to Hazen.

Fordyce Herrick

American

Herrick was head architect and boss carpenter for White Pines and many of the other Byrdcliffe buildings. He was one of the few Woodstock locals to work on the campus for many years, including time as the furniture shop foreman and, afterwards, as all-around handyman (fig. 7).

Adele McGinnis Herter and Albert Herter

American, 1869–1946; American, 1871–1950

The Herters met in Paris where he was working on a mural and she was studying with Courtois, Bouguereau, and Tony Robert-Fleury (Madeleine's brother). They were married in 1893 and in 1896, upon their return to the United States, Albert taught at the Art Institute of Chicago. Later they founded Herter Looms in New York, which specialized in elegant tapestries and textiles. Byrdcliffe artists Edna Walker and Vivian Bevans White would eventually work there. Adele worked with her husband on many of his important commissions. When Albert's mother died in 1913 in Santa Barbara, they began to convert her estate, El Mirasol, into an exclusive hostelry for wealthy travelers. The Herters established a second residence there in 1914, where they became extremely involved with the arts community. At El Mirasol, the young Jesse Arms (later Botke), who was a Herter Looms designer and a friend of Bertha Thompson's, helped with the murals for the Desert Room.

Albert studied with Carroll Beckwith at the Art Students League and with Cormon and J. P. Laurens in Paris. (Jane Whitehead also studied with Laurens in Paris and this may be how they originally met.) Jane's diaries from the second decade of the twentieth century onward frequently mention visits to El Mirasol.

Ted Hinton

American

Hinton was a mathematician, and nephew of Ada Nettleship. Hinton taught mathematics in Tokyo and wrote a book about the fourth dimension, "involving the construction by the reader of hundreds of cubes with differently coloured surfaces and edges."[15] At Byrdcliffe, he worked on the farm but took time out of his duties to demonstrate a machine that explained his theories of the fourth dimension. Many of the participants who knew him doubted his sanity. It is most likely that he came to know the Whiteheads through the Nettleship connection and through his father, whom Whitehead had known in England. He was a frequent visitor in the early years to Byrdcliffe and married Carmelita Chase; Whitehead gave them the house Camelot as a wedding present. White recalled in his autobiography, "When Mr. Hinton died, he died in an elevator. I think he was suddenly whisked into the fourth dimension."

Harriet Howe

American

Howe and Charlotte Perkins Stetson meet in Los Angeles in 1891 and shared a home for a short period in 1892. The two remained lifelong friends and Howe came to visit Byrdcliffe in the early years of its operation. She wrote a book called *Pastels* and published poems in the 1913 *Plowshares* journal, edited and published by Hervey White.

Paul Kefer

Belgian

Hervey White remembered in his autobiography, "One evening shortly before the season opened, Mr. Whitehead and I went to an orchestra concert by Sam Franco to hear a program of early Italian music. A cello solo interested us both very much and I suggested we find out the name of the artist and ask him to give a recital in the Byrdcliffe studio. It was arranged; the cellist's name was Paul Kefer, a young French Belgian, and an offer of fifty dollars was accepted." Kefer came to Byrdcliffe with his wife and baby for several weeks; he was also an early investor in the Maverick enterprise and later became first resident there. In 1913 he formed the Trio de Lutece along with Carlos Salzedo and Georges Barrere.

Arthur Harold Knott

American, born Canada, 1883–1977

Though born in Canada, Knott's family moved to Vermont when he was three years old; from 1903 to 1905 he studied at the Pratt Institute, coming under the influence of Dow's training in decorative design. It was probably also through Dow and the various Pratt students that were infiltrating Byrdcliffe, that Knott heard about the colony (fig. 8). He studied painting there under Murphy and Harrison and went on to become an

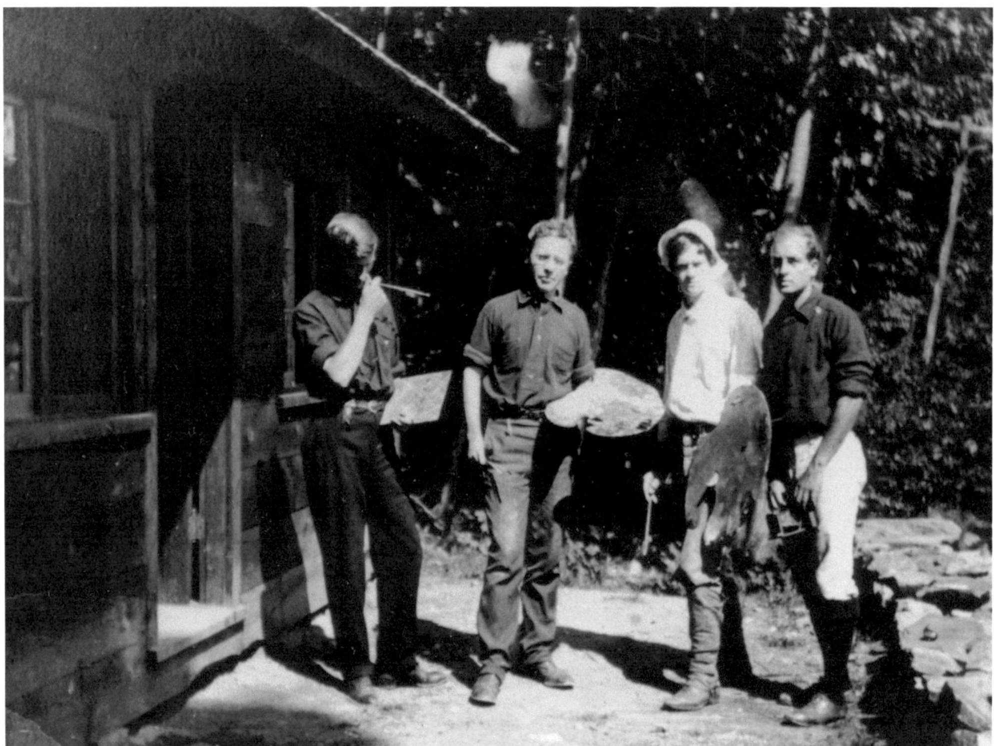

fig. 8 Unidentified photographer, *Harold Knott, John Carlson, two unidentified artists, at Byrdcliffe*, 1907. Silver print. Collection of Harleigh Knott.

interior designer in New York. In 1921 he moved to California where he continued to work and paint for the rest of his life.

Blanche Lazzell

American, 1878–1956

Lazzell was born in West Virginia and earned a degree in drawing, painting, and art history from West Virginia University in 1905. She went to New York and studied with William Merritt Chase at the Art Students League in 1908; this was followed by two years in Paris at the Académie Moderne. With the outbreak of the war, she came back to the States, settling in Provincetown and learning the white line color woodcut technique, which has since become synonymous with her name. But it was at Byrdcliffe in 1917, under the guidance of painter William Schumacher, that she cut her first color print. She is listed in the 1917 Villetta ledger. In 1923 she returned to Paris to study with Fernand Léger, Albert Gleizes, and André Lhote; thereafter her style was more definitively abstract. In the 1930s she was a W.P.A. artist and in the 1940s she studied with Hans Hofmann.

Leonard Lester

American, born England, 1870–1952

Lester began his art training in England, emigrating to Canada in 1889. In the early 1890s he moved to Pasadena and he was one of the artists to take advantage of the studio space offered by Whitehead on his Santa Barbara property. For many years he taught art in Cuba, returning to California in 1916 where he would remain the rest of his life. Whitehead owned a massive mural by Lester that was hung in the Sloyd school.

Augusta Leyendecker

American, born Germany, 1872–1957

Augusta and two of her brothers, the illustrators Frank and Joseph Leyendecker, came to Woodstock in 1904, the second summer it was open. Augusta studied dance with the artist and dancer Lou Wall Moore and was one of the witnesses at the wedding of Vivian Bevans and Hervey White that fall in New York. In her later years she kept house for her brothers at their home in New Rochelle, New York. The Leyendeckers probably heard about Byrdcliffe through their Chicago connections.

Frank Leyendecker

American, born Germany, 1877–1924

The Leyendeckers immigrated to Chicago from Germany in 1882. Both Frank and his older brother Joseph showed artistic talent at a young age, and Frank was apprenticed to the stained-glass artist Carl Brandt. In 1896 the brothers traveled to Paris and studied at the Académie Julian under Benjamin Constant and Jean Paul Laurens. When they returned to Chicago two years later, they achieved quick success as magazine illustrators. They visited their sister at Byrdcliffe in the summer of 1904.

Joseph Leyendecker
American, born Germany, 1874–1951

Joe Leyendecker, like his brother, was an illustrator and advertising artist. He studied at the Art Institute of Chicago and learned engraving in a commercial firm. In 1896 he went to Paris with Frank and, that same year, won the Century Poster competition. His best-known ads were for Chap-Book; after 1900 he worked extensively for *Collier's*, *The Saturday Evening Post*, Arrow collars, and Chesterfield cigarettes. He visited Byrdcliffe with his siblings in 1904. His popular success allowed him to maintain a studio in the Beaux Arts Building on Bryant Park and 41st Street as well as an opulent home in New Rochelle where he lived with his brother and sister.

Carl Eric Lindin
American, born Sweden, 1860–1942

Like many of the Byrdcliffe artists, Lindin studied in Paris with Laurens, Constant, and Aman-Jean. In 1887 he arrived in the United States and was associated with Hull House in Chicago for many years, where he painted some of the decorations. In 1902 he set up house in the unused Lutheran Church there with Hervey White and Fritz Van der Loo, where the three unorthodox founders slept on pews and Lindin used the pulpit for an easel. His polished manners and charm made him an engaging asset to the colony during its early days. He married Louise Hastings, a bookbinder, also from Hull House, and they remained in Woodstock, remodeling the Lutheran Church into a home. He remembered the first days of Byrdcliffe romantically, recalling, "the birds sang as if the earth had just then been newly created. And the Byrdcliffers sang too, and danced and made love to each other, just like the birds."[16] He was known for his portrait paintings and landscapes (fig. 9). White wrote a novel about Lindin's experiences at Byrdcliffe, placing it in California and changing all the names.

Louise Hastings Lindin
American, 1882–1968

Hastings was associated with Hull House and this is where she met Carl Lindin, considered the most eligible bachelor among the young Byrdcliffe participants. They married in 1905 and she moved into the renovated Lutheran Church in Woodstock. She had studied bookbinding with Ellen Gates Starr at Hull House and it was this skill that she contributed to the Byrdcliffe venture.

Marie Little
American, 1866–1949

Marie Little was a student at the Pratt Institute where she studied from 1895 to 1898, coming under the influence of Arthur Wesley Dow in her latter years. Whitehead met her in 1898 at Prestonia Mann's Fabian

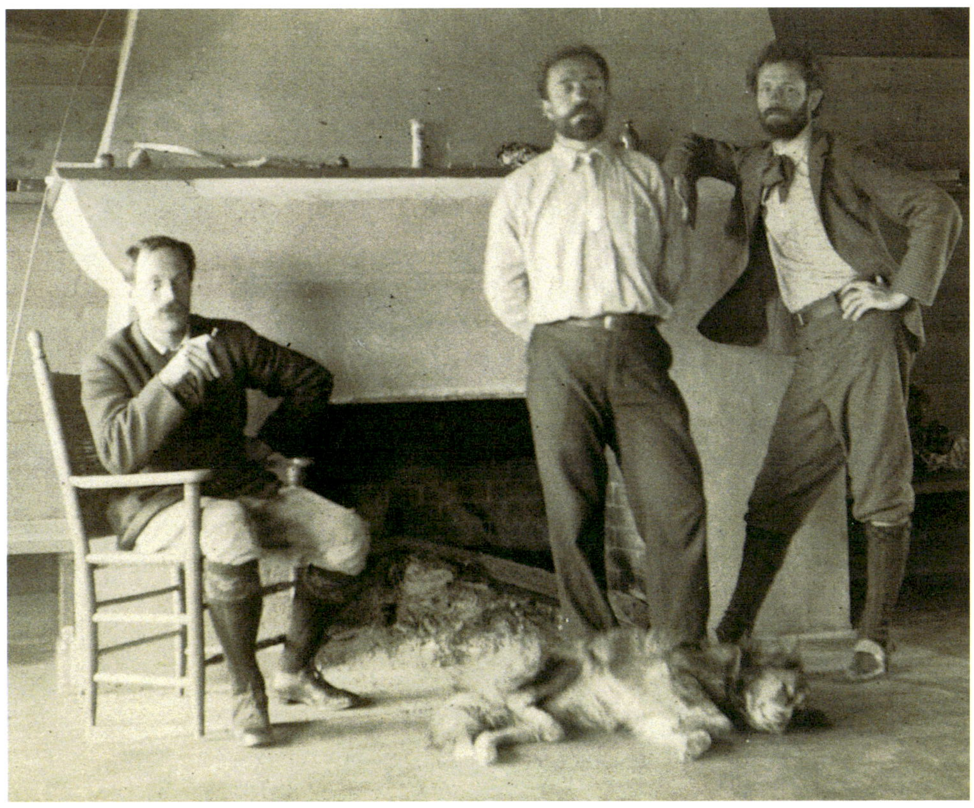

fig. 9 Unidentified photographer, *At the Lark's Nest*, ca. 1905. Left to right: Carl Lindin, Fritz Van der Loo, Hervey White. Silver print. Thompson Family Papers, Schlesinger Library, Radcliffe Institute, Harvard University.

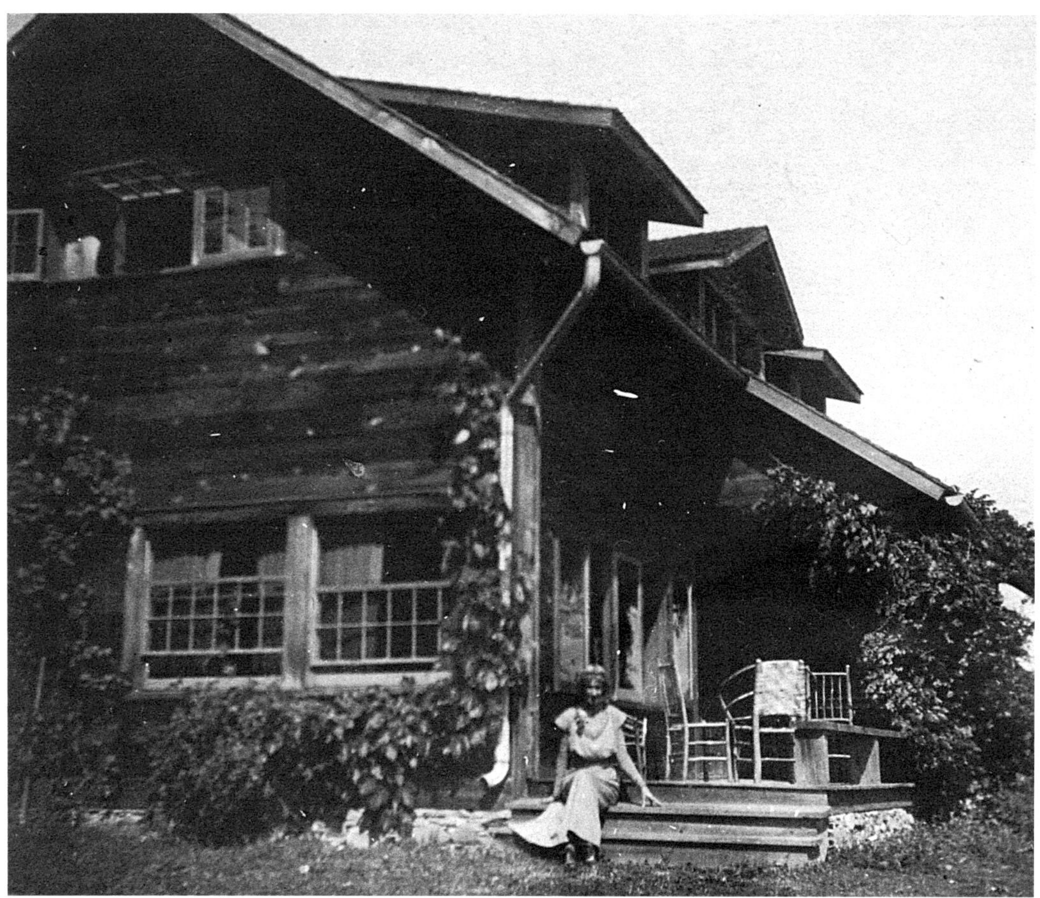

fig. 10 Unidentified photographer, *The Looms, home of Marie Little*, ca. 1908. Silver print. Thompson Family Papers, Schlesinger Library, Radcliffe Institute, Harvard University.

retreat, Summerbrook, in Keene Valley. She was a talented weaver and Whitehead actively sought to include her in his plans for his colony. He wrote to Jane in 1902, "I have collected quite a number of chair patterns & some information as to materials. I think there is a good market for painted burlap & handwoven carpets such as Miss Little makes."[17] In a postscript to the same letter he adds, "I am so glad we are to have Miss Little. She must come & teach Mrs. Brown fine weaving next summer." Little's weaving studio was called "The Cricket," or "The Looms" (fig. 10), a simple one-room studio, which burned in the 1920s. Anita Smith remembers how she worked, "Most of her dyes she made herself from barks and berries which gave her materials the tones of the woods and fields."[18] Annie Thompson also remembers Little's weavings, remarking on the lovely autumn colors. "As we passed her house we'd see quantities of material hanging in chunks on the line. After a while this material became finished products and we'd wander in to see what she had made."[19] Little had studied music in Italy in her youth where her "poplar-like figure and quivering voice had been admired."[20] Whitehead would have been attracted to this musical talent and her familiarity with his favorite haunts in Italy. Little was one of the stalwart Byrdcliffe residents, staying there until the middle of the second decade of the twentieth century, when she moved into the town of Woodstock.

Marie Manning
American, 1873–1945

Manning was a newspaper writer and friend of Hervey White's who came to Byrdcliffe the first summer of 1903. Born of English parents, she was educated in private schools in London and New York. In 1893 she became a cub reporter for the *New York World*; four years later she joined the staff of the *New York Evening Journal* and began a famous advice column called "Beatrix Fairfax." Her literary career began in 1902 with the publication of a novel, *Lord Alingham*; this was followed in 1903 with the popular *Judith of the Plains*. She married a real estate dealer, Herman Gasch, in 1905 and gave up her career to raise her two sons, but she continued to be involved with women's rights issues. In 1929 she revived her advice column and later worked for the International News Service. She signed the Villetta guest book in 1909 but probably visited earlier as well.

Prestonia Mann Martin
American, 1862–1945

A cousin of the educator Horace Mann, Prestonia Mann attended Glenmore School for the Culture Sciences with her parents. She was so impressed that around 1895 she purchased land from Davis Dewey (John Dewey's brother) next to Glenmore and started a "camp" that became an informal summer colony for a group of prominent social reformers. Her experiment was called Summer Brook Farm (later changed to Summerbrook) and visitors included Upton Sinclair, Clarence Darrow, Maxim Gorky, Jane Addams, and Charlotte Perkins Gilman. Mann, like Ruskin, believed that true socialists must do physical labor, and this was incorporated into the daily life of Summerbrook. She met her future husband, Dr. John Martin, in 1899 and they were married the following year. Newly arrived from England, he was teaching at Columbia and soon became a leader of the Fabian Society in the United States. Mann was against women's suffrage and, with her husband, wrote *Feminism: Its Fallacies and Follies* (1916) in which she attacked both Gilman and Addams.

Laurin Hovey Martin

American, 1875–1939

Martin's art education began in Lowell, Massachusetts, where he took evening classes. This was followed by a program at the Cowles Art School in Boston and three semesters at the Birmingham School of Art in England. He took private enameling lessons with Alexander Fisher before returning to the United States around 1900. From then on he taught at the Massachusetts Normal School, which is probably where Whitehead met him when he was in Boston scouting for teachers and participants for his colony. Martin is listed in the Villetta ledger for 1904, 1905, 1907, and 1908, and in the 1907 prospectus as teaching metalwork there. In the summers of 1909 and 1913 he taught metalwork at the Chautauqua Institute. He was a member of the Handicraft Society and the Boston Society of Arts and Crafts.

Maud Mason

American, 1867–1956

Born in Russellville, Kentucky, Maud Mary Mason studied with William Merritt Chase, Henry Snell (who also taught Penman and Hardenbergh), and Arthur Wesley Dow in New York and with Frank Brangwyn in Paris. She was a painter of floral still lifes and landscapes as well as an experienced ceramist. She exhibited at the Panama Pacific International Exposition in 1915 and won a gold medal there. At her home in New Canaan, Connecticut, she maintained beautiful flower beds, often used as subjects for her art. She is listed in the 1920 Villetta ledger as a visitor but Jane Whitehead notes earlier visits in several diary notations from February 1916. Apparently Jane was taking informal pottery lessons from Mason at Byrdcliffe. Mason was also very active as an exhibiting artist and in artist organizations. In 1933 she opened her own ceramics school and was named honorary president of the New York School of Ceramic Art; the following year she was elected an associate member of the National Academy of Design.

Henry Chapman Mercer

American, 1856–1930

Mercer was Jane McCall Whitehead's cousin and was known for his careers in archeology as well as tile making. After graduating from Harvard in 1879 he received a law degree from the University of Pennsylvania, but he never practiced. He preferred to travel extensively and collect prodigiously, and he periodically met with the McCalls on European travels. From 1893 to 1897 he was associate editor for the *American Naturalist* and he wrote his first archaeological monograph, *The Lenape Stone, or the Indian and the Mammoth*, in 1885. He moved to Doylestown in 1896 and opened his Moravian Pottery and Tile Works there in 1898. In 1907 he became an architect and designed three reinforced concrete buildings that formed the Tileworks campus, including his home, Fonthill. He was a master craftsman of the Boston Society of Arts and Crafts and played a key role in reviving decorative ceramic tile interest at the turn of the century. The fireplace at White Pines was made of Moravian tiles.

H. Stuart Michie

American, born Canada, 1871–1943

Michie came to the United States in 1898 and studied at the Pratt Institute under Arthur Wesley Dow. From 1905 to 1906 he studied at the Central and Camberwell Schools of Arts and Crafts in London, and the following summer, upon his return to the States, he went to Byrdcliffe with his friend the metalsmith Laurin Martin (both are listed in the Villetta ledger for that summer). He also taught at Columbia with Dow and at Dow's Ipswich Summer School before becoming head of the Arts and Crafts Department at George Washington University (1907–9). Thereafter he settled in Worcester, Massachusetts, where he became principal of the School of the Worcester Art Museum; he was a multitalented artist, producing work in metal, textile, printing and lettering, and woodwork.

Anne Carroll Moore

American, 1871–1961

Moore was a librarian, editor, and author of children's books who frequently visited Byrdcliffe. An 1896 graduate of the Library School of Pratt, she was the children's librarian there from 1897 to 1906. She also wrote critiques of children's books for *The Bookman* (1918–27); the *New York Herald Tribune* (1924–30); and the *Atlantic Monthly* (beginning in 1930). It is most likely that she met Whitehead in the early days of the colony when he was looking for congenial participants and visited Pratt looking for both students and teachers to join the effort. Moore was an advocate of the benefits of oral storytelling for children, and she staged programs in drawing rooms and libraries in New York.

Isabel Moore
American

Chicagoan Moore (see fig. 3) was a freelance magazine editor for Putnam's and an active suffragist. A friend of Marie Manning and Olivia Dunbar, she came to Byrdcliffe for several summers and eventually bought land and built various homes. She had a doctorate and several other degrees of higher learning "... but it only made her laugh when, in later years, as she was working for women's Suffrage, the digger of ditches whom she was trying to enlist in the support of the nineteenth amendment looked up from his pick to say 'What's the use of that? Women ain't edicated enough to vote!'" (A. Smith, *It Happened in Woodstock*, 99)

Lou Wall Moore
American

Moore was both a sculptor and a dancer from Chicago, and she came to Byrdcliffe the first summer at the invitation of Hervey White. She appears to have been there for at least two summers and is remembered as visiting the colony with her daughter, Bessie, also a dancer, and as being a popular hostess among the artists. She was a member of the Chicago Society of Artists and exhibited at the Art Students League from 1899 to 1913. At the St. Louis Exhibition of 1904 she won a bronze medal (see fig. 5).

William Morris
British, 1834–1896

A student of Ruskin's at Oxford in the 1850s, Morris went on to establish the firm of Morris, Marshall, Faulkner & Co. in 1861 and work in a variety of media, including mural decoration, carving as applied to architecture, stained glass, metalwork, furniture, embroidery, and stamped leather. In 1875 the firm became Morris & Co. and produced everything from tapestries to glassware, with Morris designing most of the surface decorations, like the textiles and wallpapers, himself. In 1884 he founded the Socialist League, a political commitment that showed him to be in a completely different camp than Whitehead. Morris felt strongly that the furnishing of one's own house was never a morally neutral choice: "It is not possible to dissociate art from morality, politics and religion."

Rockwood Moulton
American, born 1881

Moulton was another of the visitors who arrived after graduating from the Pratt Institute, where he was one of Dow's students. He is listed in the Villetta ledger as a 1905 visitor.

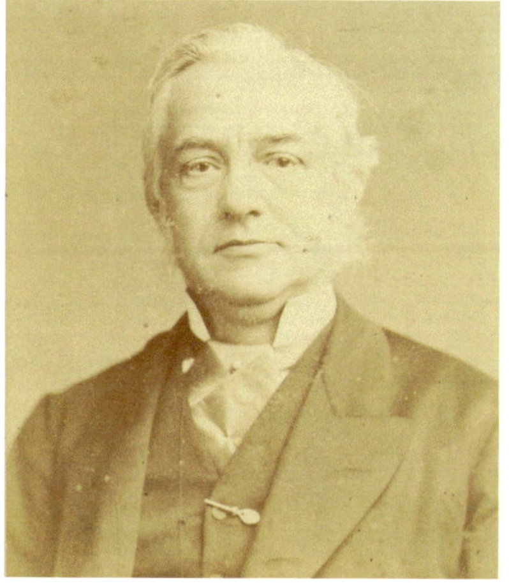

fig. 11 Elliott & Fry, British, active 1860s–1900s, *Max Müller*, ca. 1886. Albumen print. Winterthur Library, Downs Collection, 92x39.1140.512.

Max Müller
German, 1823–1900

Jane Whitehead met and became good friends with Max Müller and his wife while staying near Oxford in the 1880s. The famed philologist and Orientalist came to Britain as a student at Oxford where he remained for the rest of his life. His series of lectures, *Science of Language*, popularized the idea of myths as metaphors for describing natural phenomena. His wrote on many subjects and the last twenty-five years of his life were devoted to the editing of the fifty-one volume *Sacred Books of the East* (fig. 11).

Hermann Dudley Murphy
American, 1867–1945

Murphy was born in Marlboro, Massachusetts, and studied at the Museum of Fine Arts School under Otto Grundman and Joseph DeCamp. He worked as an illustrator for two years, but in 1891 he went to Paris where he studied at the Académie Julian with Laurens and Benjamin Constant. From 1901 to 1937 he taught drawing at the Harvard School of Architecture; he was friends with Charles and Maurice Prendergast, Denman Ross, and Charles Woodbury. In 1903 he formed a framing business with Charles Prendergast and W. Alfred Thulin called Carrig-Rohane. Murphy was striking in appearance and was described as "very tall, very straight. He has a Viking's beard, a deep voice, and the strong, supple hands of his profession. He is as industrious as any hard-working business man. His is always engaged in a piece of work, smoking long black cigars, throwing the ashes about luxuriously, and growling because the light doesn't last longer."[21] Murphy taught at Byrdcliffe the first two summers, and there are several mentions of him in later years in the Whiteheads' correspondence and in Jane's calendar, indicating that they kept in touch. While at Byrdcliffe, Murphy supposedly also ran a frame-making shop with the help of Edwin Slater but attributable samples are no longer extant. Murphy was also a renowned athlete, winning the American Canoe Association championships in 1902, 1909, 1910, and 1931 and was a member of canoe clubs both in America and England.

Leonard Ochtman

American, born the Netherlands, 1854–1934

When Birge Harrison left Byrdcliffe to take over the running of the summer school of the Art Students League in Woodstock, Ochtman, who painted in a similar Tonalist style, was hired to replace him. He is listed in the 1907 Byrdcliffe prospectus as teaching painting there. Brought to America in 1866, his parents settled in Albany; though apprenticed to an engraver, as a painter he was self-taught. In the 1870s he traveled to Europe where he was influenced by the work of Corot; he returned to France again in 1887 and upon his return to New York he opened a studio with Charles Warren Eaton. He probably met the Whiteheads through Harrison, who brought him to Woodstock to teach. He also painted at Cos Cob, Connecticut, along with other American Impressionists such as Theodore Robinson, Childe Hassam, and J. Alden Weir.

Edward Penfield

American, 1866–1925

Penfield, like the Leyendecker brothers, was a highly successful illustrator. He worked ten years (1891–1901) for *Harper's* and his style was characterized by pared-down images presented in a clean, graphic style. He did freelance projects in Holland and Spain, and when he returned to the United States he became a regular contributor to the leading magazines of the day, including the *Saturday Evening Post*, *Collier's*, and *Literary Digest*. Penfield was among those who had a studio in New Rochelle, and after his death in 1925 Augusta Leyendecker mounted a memorial exhibition of two hundred works at the New Rochelle Public Library. He visited the Byrdcliffe campus in 1919 and 1920, staying at the Villetta. It is possible he had heard about the colony through his friends (and New Rochelle neighbors) the Leyendeckers.

Edith Penman

American, born England, 1860–1929

A painter, etcher, and potter, Penman came to the United States as a child and studied at the Cooper Union School of Design for Women in New York from 1879 to 1880. She also studied with Swain Gifford in England and Henry B. Snell, and this may have been where she first met Elizabeth Hardenbergh. She learned to etch around 1887 and exhibited in the Woman's Building at the 1893 Columbian Exposition in Chicago. She had a winter studio in the Van Dyke Studio Building in New York that she shared with Hardenbergh. She exhibited with the Women's Art Club of New York, and with the National Association of Women Painters and Sculptors until 1926.

Gino Perera

American, born Italy, 1872–1961

Perera was a sculptor and a painter who had studied art at the Boston Museum of Fine Arts School. He came to Byrdcliffe for many summers, building a house on the property. A noted musician, his skill in this area added to the cultural evenings held at Byrdcliffe. He was also a collector and owned the painting *The Golden Hour*, by John Enneking, that was exhibited in the Boston Arts Club memorial exhibition in 1917.

Evelyn Perry

British

Bertha Thompson recalled in her notes that Ralph Whitehead brought the dancer Evelyn Perry to Byrdcliffe from England "to teach folk dancing to the children." As it turned out, he encouraged all of the residents, young and old, to participate. Annie Thompson remembered Perry as a delightful leader and a friend with whom her sister kept in touch afterward. Perry is listed as a resident at the Villetta in 1909 and 1910.

J. Aldo Randegger

Italian

Bertha Thompson remembers Randegger being at the colony the second year of operation, 1904. He was a pianist who resided in one of the smaller cottages, Serenata, and was Byrdcliffe's resident pianist.
He visited again in 1907 with his wife.

Frederick Hürten Rhead

American, born Britain, 1880–1942

Rhead studied at the Wedgwood Institute and became head of the Wardle Art Pottery in 1899. In the early 1900s he moved with his wife to the United States, working at both the Weller Pottery and Roseville Pottery in Zanesville, Ohio. He also worked at the Jervis Pottery and at University City pottery in Missouri before setting up the Arequipa Pottery at the sanatorium in Fairfax, California. In 1914 the Rhead Pottery was incorporated by its directors, Ralph Whitehead and Christoph Tornoe, the two shareholders. Formally known as Rhead Pottery, it was referred to as the Pottery of Carmarata. In 1915 Rhead received a gold medal at the Panama Pacific International Exposition and in 1934 he was awarded the Charles Fergus Binn Medal for his contributions to the advancement of ceramic art. Jane studied ceramics with him during his years in Santa Barbara. Today his best known work is Fiestaware, which he developed late in his career.

Halsey Ricardo

British, 1854–1928

Ricardo was trained as an architect, and though he was the same age as Whitehead it is not known exactly when the two met. They remained lifelong friends, corresponding intermittently until Ricardo's death in 1928. Ricardo was part of the tile-making revival in England, in partnership with William De Morgan for ten years. He was also a teacher at the Central School and designed Debenham House, probably his finest architectural achievement. "If a man really likes what he has got to do, he will make great shifts to express and realise his pleasure; he will choose carefully his materials and . . . will put the stamp of individuality on his work."[22] He was remembered as "a man of wide culture and of very quick intelligence, an ardent musician, a keen and appreciative student of art in all forms, and withal a most kindly, generous-minded, humorous, genial man."[23]

Edmund Rolfe

American, 1877–1917

Rolfe came to Byrdcliffe in the summer of 1905 to replace Laurin Martin as the metalwork teacher. He boarded at the Villetta that year and stayed at Byrdcliffe until he built his own studio workshop on the mountain to the west. One of the first auto fatalities in Woodstock, Rolfe was later remembered by Thompson: "His untimely death meant the loss to Woodstock of a craftsman of unusual promise. His work had already found recognition in Boston and elsewhere." Both a jeweler and a painter, Rolfe was listed in the prospectus as "Lives at Byrdcliffe year round."[24]

Denman Ross

American, 1853–1935

Denman Waldo Ross was a collector of art, particularly Asian art, and an art educator. The son of a prosperous Cincinnati family, he trained under Harvard's first art historian, Charles Eliot Norton. He went on to earn a PhD in economics a few years later, before turning to the study of art. He became a painter himself, and taught in the architecture and fine arts departments at Harvard starting in 1899 and eventually joining the fine arts faculty formally in 1909.

In 1907 Ross wrote *On Drawing and Painting*, a book which described a nine-step value system for painters. In Whitehead's papers at Winterthur is a copy of Ross's *The Neutral Scale*, which charts this value system from white (1) to mid-value (5) to black (9), an easy and useful system for teaching beginning artists. Whitehead met with Ross in Boston before hiring his teachers for the newly founded Byrdcliffe campus; it was through Ross that he met H. D. Murphy and engaged him for the first year to head the painting department.

John Ruskin

British, 1819–1900

Ruskin was the only child of well-to-do parents who traveled abroad extensively during his formative years. He wrote *Modern Painters* in several volumes, published over seventeen years (1843–60), and *Stones of Venice*, published in three volumes with the first volume appearing in 1851 and the last in 1853. In the second volume of *Stones* he wrote a chapter on the "Nature of Gothic" in which he described Gothic ornament as the natural expression of the joy of the laborer content in his work, prescient of what would become the Arts and Crafts aesthetic. In 1869 Ruskin was named Slade Professor of Fine Art at Oxford where Whitehead would study with him in the early 1870s. In January 1871 Ruskin developed the idea for a series entitled *Fors Clavigera: Letters to the Workmen and Labourers of Great Britain* (these would continue on and off until 1884) inspiring philanthropists, artists, and political radicals in the late nineteenth century. His proposition for the Guild of St. George as an alternative, collaborative society employing manual labor was the basis of Whitehead's initial vision of Byrdcliffe.

William Emile Schumacher

American, 1870–1931

Like many of the Byrdcliffe participants, Schumacher hailed from Boston and studied in Paris, but his influences were the more modern ones of Matisse, the Fauves, and Paul Gauguin. His work reflects these influences, with bold, broad patterns and abstracted forms, and he exhibited in the 1913 Armory Show. Schumacher spent many summers from the middle of the second decade of the twentieth century to the early 1920s at Byrdcliffe and was Blanche Lazzell's teacher there, helping her to make her first color woodcut in 1917, a process for which she would become internationally known.

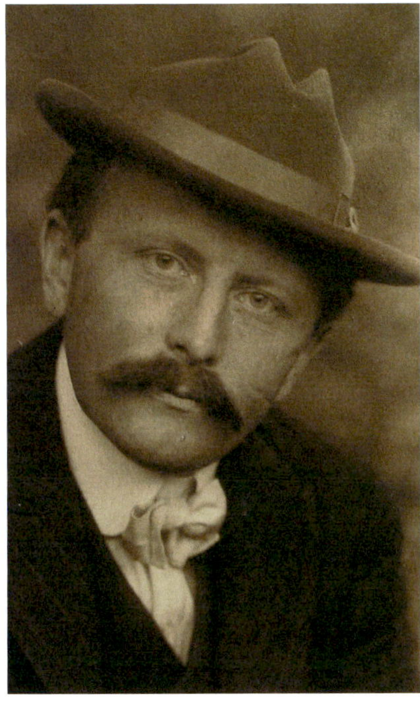

fig. 12 Eva Watson-Schütze, *Martin Schütze*, ca. 1905. Platinum print. Courtesy of the Howard Greenberg Gallery, New York.

Martin Schütze

German, 1867–1950

Born in Mecklenburg, Schütze studied law in Rostock and Freiburg. He came to the United States as a Fellow in German at the University of Pennsylvania where he met Walter Weyl as well as his future wife, Eva Watson. He was the chair of German literature for many years at the University of Chicago and spent his summers at Byrdcliffe, beginning in the inaugural year, 1903. He became the first president of the Woodstock Historical Society and organized many of its early programs. He also initiated the series of talks called the "Byrdcliffe Afternoons" in the late 1930s (fig. 12).

Mary Sheerer

American, 1865–1954

Mary G. Sheerer, who had come to the Newcomb Pottery in New Orleans in the 1890s to supervise the women and teach pottery design, had studied at the Cincinnati Art Academy and had been involved with developing the Rookwood Pottery there. She was also a summer visitor to Dow's school in Ipswich. She remained at Newcomb for her entire career, retiring in 1931, the same year she was named a fellow of the American Ceramics Society. She came to Byrdcliffe the summer of 1917, probably at the urging of the Whiteheads whom she had met the previous February when they made a detour to New Orleans on their annual trip westward, in order to visit the Pottery.

James Shotwell

American, born Canada, 1874–1965

A teacher of history at Columbia from 1900 and professor from 1908 to 1942, Shotwell came to Byrdcliffe in 1907 on the recommendation of John Dewey and thereafter built a house nearby where he spent summers with his family. He was a tireless promoter of international understanding and an active member of several national and international labor, peace, and historical conferences, including the Paris Peace Conference (1918–19) and the conference at San Francisco (1945). Among his many works are *An Introduction to the History of History* (1922), *Plans and Protocols to End War* (1925), *The Origins of the International Labor Organization* (1934), *On the Rim of the Abyss* (1936), and *The Long Way to Freedom* (1960). A prolific writer, Shotwell also coauthored studies on international relations and was editor of the 150-volume *Economic and Social History of the World War* (1919–29).

Edwin Slater

American, 1884–after 1929

Slater was at Byrdcliffe in 1904, 1905, 1906, 1909, and 1913 and was remembered by Bertha Thompson as good-looking and a particular pet of Jane Whitehead's. He seemed to have worked largely under the direction of Hermann Dudley Murphy in the frame-making shop and in August 1916 he published an article in *Arts and Decoration* called "The Future of Picture Framing in America." He studied painting with Chase, Thomas Anschutz, Cecilia Beaux, Henry Poore, and Harrison and was known for his landscapes (fig. 13).

Anita M. Smith

American, 1893–1968

Like Jane Whitehead, Smith came from a wealthy Philadelphia family but rebelled in 1912 when she came to Woodstock with money that had been intended for a ball gown. She was a painter and craftsperson, a writer, and an herbalist, and she chronicled the bohemian life of Woodstock in her book *Woodstock: History and Hearsay* (1959). She studied at the Art Students League and with John Carlson, and exhibited her work at the Maverick in the 1920s. She also showed her work at the

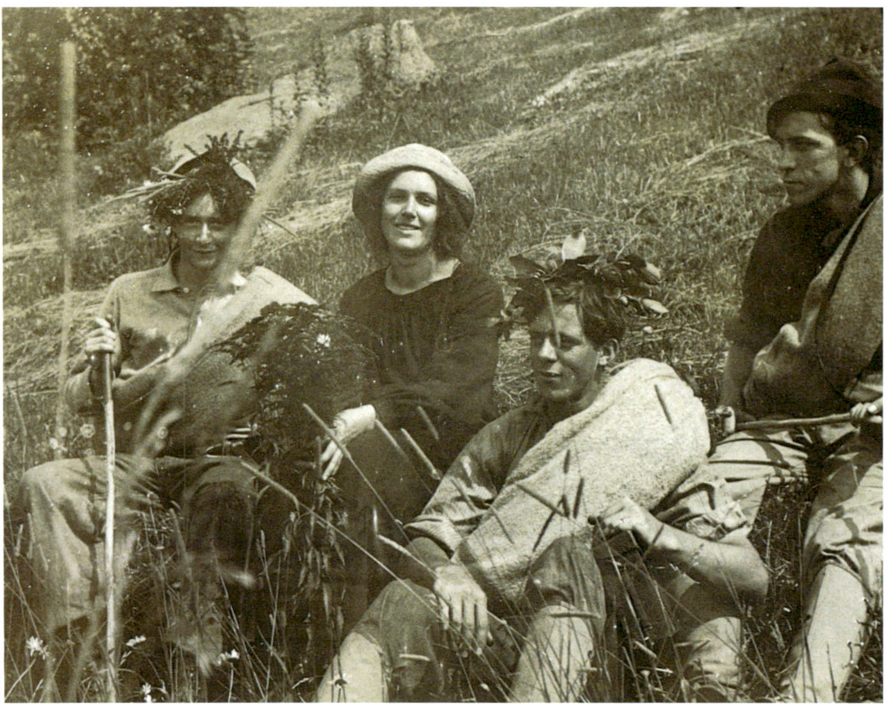

fig. 13 Attributed to Bertha Thompson, *Byrdcliffe Picnic*, 1904. Left to right: Edwin Slater, Vivian Bevans, two unidentified artists. Silver print. Thompson Family Papers, Schlesinger Library, Radcliffe Institute, Harvard University.

National Academy of Design and at the Pennsylvania Academy of Fine Arts. An active member of the Woodstock community, she was appointed the Chief Observer for the Woodstock Observation Post for the Aircraft Warning Service when it became active in December 1941. She was also secretary of the France Forever organization, begun by Philip Buttrick in the same year.

Ellen Gates Starr

American, 1859–1940

Starr, with her close friend Jane Addams, founded Hull House in 1883; she first put art to a social reformist purpose with a class in the history of art. A student of the famed British bookbinder T. J. Cobden-Sanderson, she was largely responsible for the craft program at Hull House which included the Hull-House Shops and the Hull-House Kilns. She was invited to the Lark's Nest the first summer by White and Lindin; she moved up to the Villetta (she is listed in the ledger for that summer) and worked and taught in the building called Skylights.

Zulma Steele

American, 1881–1979

Zulma Steele (fig. 14) was one of the most talented of the students to come to Byrdcliffe in the summer of 1903, and she became a lifelong Woodstock resident. She worked as a painter, potter, and designer and was the sister of the well-known illustrator Frederick Dorr Steele. Described by Bolton Brown as "an outstanding lady both visually and in quality we call style,"[25] she had ancestral ties to the Catskills. In 1904 she and Edna Walker moved into the home they had designed for themselves called the Angelus, where they lived together for many years. Jane Whitehead actively disliked both women and considered them a wayward influence on her husband. Steele studied painting with Harrison and continued her work in crafts. During World War I she was in France with the Red Cross; she studied in Paris with André Lhote and took classes at the Grande Chaumière and Colorossi art ateliers. In 1923 she took over the Byrdcliffe Pottery and later made her own line of ceramics called Zedware. In 1926 she married the twice-widowed businessman Nelson Parker, who died in 1928.

Charles Walter Stetson

American, 1858–1911

Stetson was one of the artists who worked in the Arcady studios in the 1890s. Married to feminist writer Charlotte Perkins Stetson, they divorced in 1894 and both remarried. Their daughter, Katharine Beecher Stetson, divided her time between both households and became an artist and frequent visitor to Byrdcliffe with her mother and stepfather. Largely self-taught, Stetson's style was influenced by European symbolist art.

Katharine Beecher Stetson

American, 1885–1979

Stetson was a sculptor and landscape painter and daughter of Charlotte Perkins Gilman and painter Charles Walter Stetson. She came to Byrdcliffe many times in

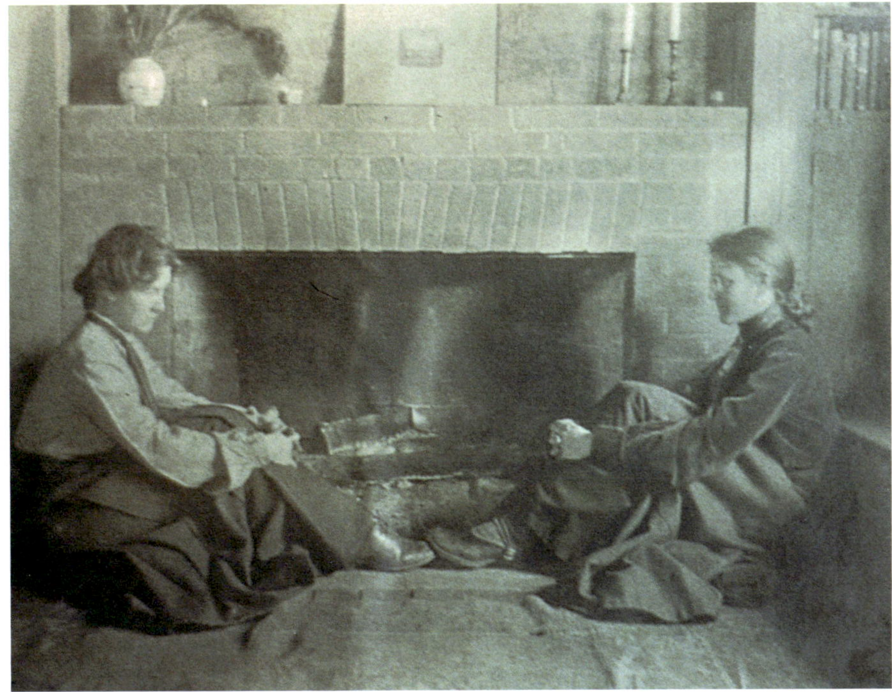

fig. 14 Unidentified photographer, *Zulma Steele and Edna Walker in their Byrdcliffe home, Angelus,* ca. 1910, from the Steele Family Photograph Album. Silver print. Courtesy of Robert G. Steele.

the early years with her mother and stepfather and is listed in the Villetta ledger as a guest in 1904 and 1907. She studied with William Merritt Chase and Cecilia Beaux as well as with Harrison, Murphy, and Ochtman and her husband, F. Tolles Chamberlin. She settled in Pasadena in 1925 where she taught from 1919 to 1962.

Wallace Stevens

American, 1879–1955

Wallace Stevens visited Byrdcliffe for the first time in the summer of 1915 when his wife, Elsie, was studying art there. They returned two summers later. A lawyer and businessman, Stevens became publishing his poetry in 1914, in a special wartime issue of *Poetry*. His first book of poetry, *Harmonium*, was published in 1923. He continued as a bonding lawyer his entire life, moving to Connecticut in 1916 to join the home office of the Hartford Accident and Indemnity, eventually being promoted to vice president of the company in 1934. He continued to write poetry, often composing verses on his way to and from work, and is today considered one of the great American poets of the twentieth century.

Edward (Ned) Thatcher

American, 1883–1933

A 1902 graduate of the Pratt Institute with a Certificate in Design, Thatcher (fig. 15) came to Byrdcliffe the first summer it was open and spent summers in Woodstock for most of the remainder of his life. He was an

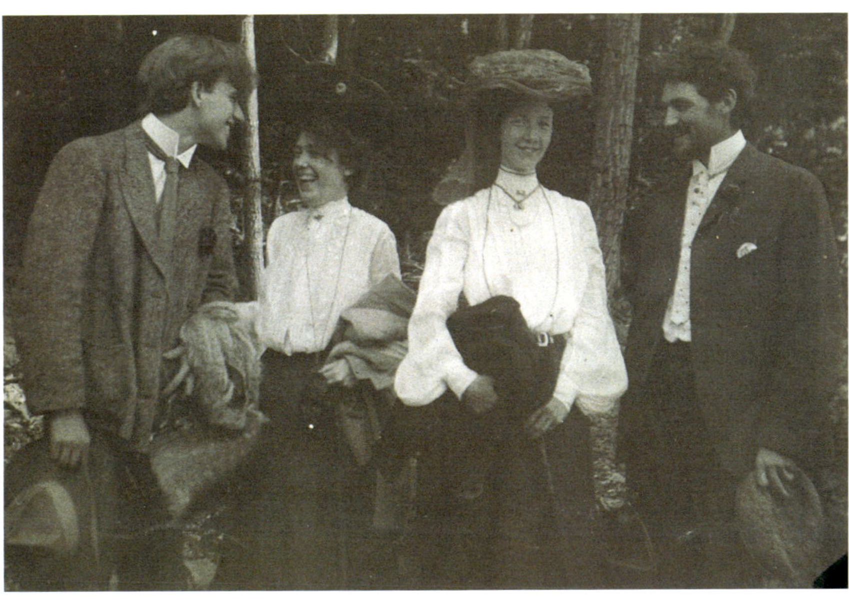

fig. 15 Attributed to Bertha Thompson, *Ned Thatcher, two unidentified women, Olaf Westerling,* 1904. Silver print. Thompson Family Papers, Schlesinger Library, Radcliffe Institute, Harvard University.

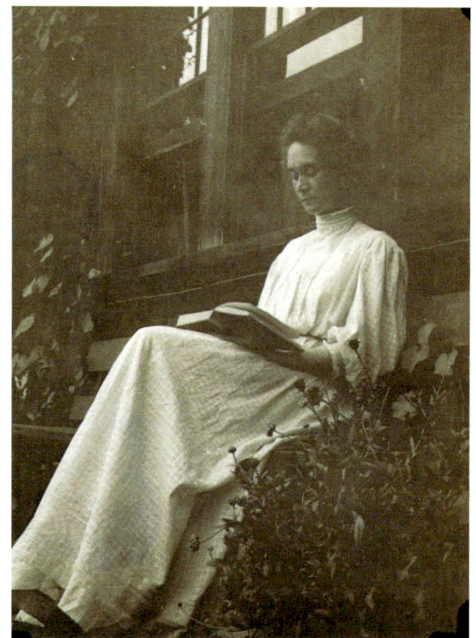

fig. 16 Attributed to Bertha Thompson, *Annie Thompson on Terrace*, ca. 1910. Thompson Family Papers, Schlesinger Library, Radcliffe Institute, Harvard University.

accomplished metalworker, painter, and writer and was known for his sense of humor. He contributed humorous prose and poetry to the local paper under the byline of Iddie Flitcher. During the winter months he taught at Columbia University's Teacher College with Arthur Wesley Dow, and also made tin-can toys, publishing brochures on how to make them and turning it into an occupational therapy program after World War I. Around 1911 he opened the Thatcher Summer School of Metalwork in Woodstock which taught jewelry making, enameling, and handwrought metalwork. He is listed in the Villetta ledger for 1903, 1904, and 1906, though he was in residence other years as well, eventually becoming a prominent Woodstock character.

Annie Thompson

American, born Britain, 1875–1955

Both Annie Thompson and her sister Bertha spent many years in Byrdcliffe. Bertha arrived in 1904 and returned again in 1908, building a house there in 1913. Annie, who was a teacher, visited during the summer months, and both of the sisters kept diaries that tell us much about life at the Colony during the early years. Annie did some weaving and basket making, at Bertha's instigation, and even mentioned selling some of her wares in the Byrdcliffe sales (fig. 16).

Bertha Thompson

American, born Britain, 1882–1974

Thompson came from Chicago to study metalwork under Laurin Martin in 1904. After that summer she went to Boston for three years, spending the intervening summers at Dow's Ipswich Summer School where she remembered visits from Olaf Westerling, Ned Thatcher, Edna Walker, Zulma Steele, and Vivian Bevans White, as well as Helen Buttrick, who joined the classes one summer. She took classes in Boston for two years with the master silversmith George Gebelein (fig. 17). Annie remembered her sister's "spirit of adventure" and "her self-forgetfulness and helpfulness to others was a constant way of life . . . . She was impulsive but rarely faulty in her relation to people."[26] Bertha had polio as a child and her accomplishments seem all the more remarkable because of her determination to succeed. In 1908 she was back staying at the Villetta; the next five summers she rented a cottage and in 1914 she designed and built her own cottage on property that Whitehead sold to her, above White Pines. In the winter of 1912, Thompson, Steele and Walker were in New York, staying in an apartment owned by Mrs. Whitehead on East 19th Street and taking classes at Pratt. During the early war years she was back in Chicago, taking bookbinding classes with Ellen Gates Starr and learning weaving at Hull House; in 1917 she became an occupational therapist, serving at Kenilworth in Biltmore, North Carolina. She became friends with printmaker Jesse Arms Botke, one of the most important designers for the Herter Looms, and ultimately she went to California for a few years and taught in the Ojai school system. While in California, she visited the Whiteheads at their home in Carmel.

fig. 17 Unidentified photographer, *Bertha Thompson in her Boston Studio*, ca. 1906. Silver print. Thompson Family Papers, Schlesinger Library, Radcliffe Institute, Harvard University.

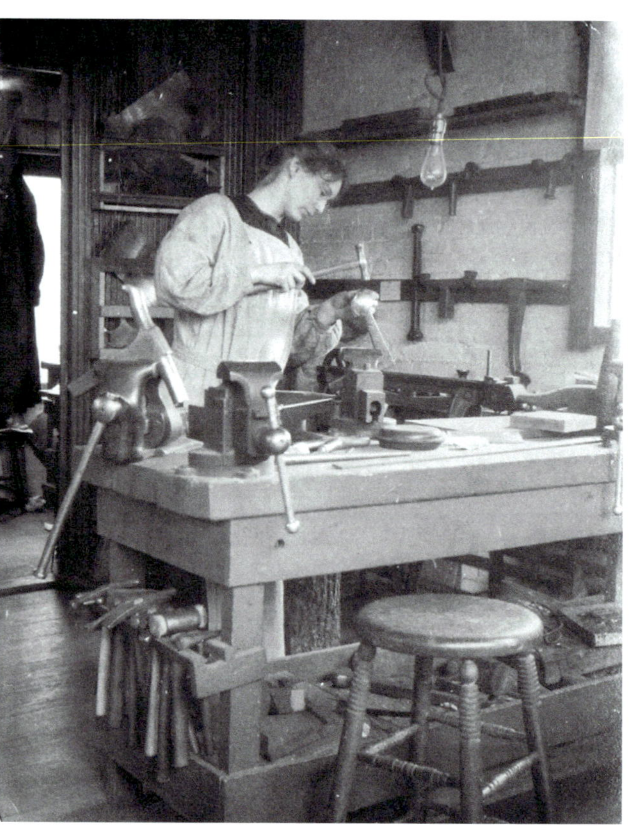

Mary Bradish Titcomb
American, 1856–1927

Titcomb first studied art in Boston with Edmund Tarbell and Frank Benson before going to Paris in 1895 where she studied under Lefébvre. Known as a painter and illustrator, she came to Byrdcliffe in 1905 as a scholarship student and stayed at the Villetta. Born in Windham, New Hampshire, she was for many years a teacher in the Massachusetts public school system at a time when there was a law that prohibited public school teachers from marrying. In 1901 she left teaching to become a full-time artist. There are many connections between the Whiteheads and Boston; Ralph made several trips there in the early 1900s to search out teachers for his school at Byrdcliffe. He mentions visiting the Boston Normal School in his letters to Jane and it is possible that this is where he met Titcomb. She was a member of "The Group," seven women artists from the Boston area, which included Lilian Wescott Hale, Margaret Patterson, Jane Peterson, and Laura Coombs Hills.

Christoph Tornoe
Danish, ca. 1860–1915

Tornoe and Ralph Whitehead were the shareholders in Frederick Hürten Rhead's pottery established near Santa Barbara in 1914. The pottery itself was located on Tornoe's property in Mission Canyon. Tornoe was a craftsman himself, working both as a cabinetmaker and metalworker and was involved with the creation of Arcady.

Oscar Lovell Triggs
American, 1865–1930

Triggs, an Arts and Crafts advocate and authority as well as a teacher, was an instructor at the University of Chicago, a post he lost after gaining notoriety as a promoter of free love, free verse, and socialism. He was founder of the Saugatuck Press and editor of the "Bulletin of the Morris Society of Chicago" but, like many other American Arts and Crafts practitioners, he later broke with Morrisian ideals over the role of the machine in artistic production. He was invited to the Lark's Nest during Byrdcliffe's first summer and stayed there with his friends Lindin and White.

Giovanni Troccoli
Italian, 1882–1940

Troccoli was both a woodworker and a painter who came from the Boston Society of Arts and Crafts to work at Byrdcliffe in the early years and taught crafts there as well as supervising the carving. He had studied at the Académie Julian in Paris and then with

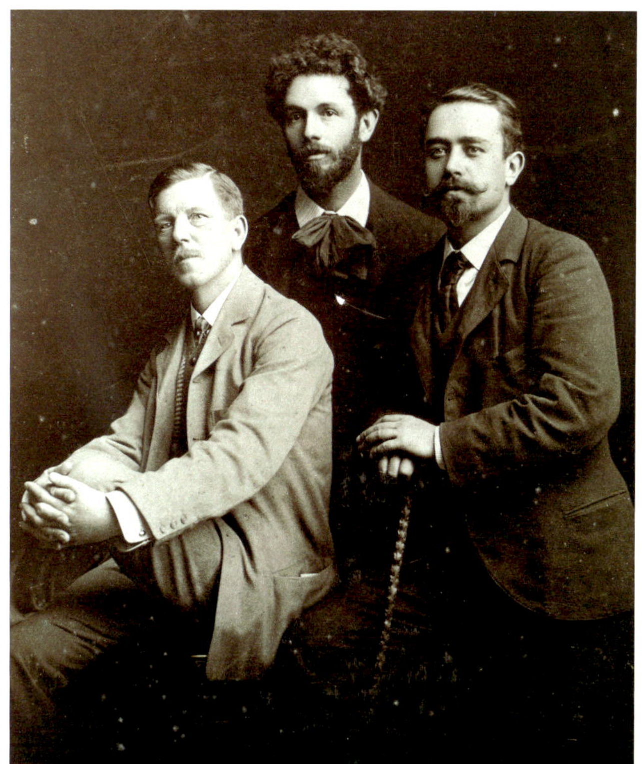

fig. 18 Unidentified photographer, *Ralph Whitehead, Hervey White, Fritz Van der Loo*, ca. 1903. Silver print. Collection of the Woodstock Historical Society.

Denman Ross in Boston. A 1915 article in *House Beautiful* featured a candlestick by him: "Mr. Giovanni B. Troccoli, a painter as well as a wood carver . . . has produced an unusual design among modern candlesticks, suggested by an old Spanish example. Metal or glass is nowadays so generally used for this purpose that Mr. Troccoli's wooden candlestick would seem unusual even without the oddity of his design."[27] He won a gold medal at the Panama Pacific International Exposition in 1915; as did Maud Mason. From 1926 until his death in 1940 he maintained a residence in Santa Barbara. After his death, H. D. Murphy, who was in Santa Barbara at the time of Troccoli's death, tried to help his impoverished widow by contacting the Vose Gallery to see if they would be interested in selling some of the paintings left in the artist's possession.[28]

Fritz Van der Loo
Dutch

Van der Loo (fig. 18) fought in the Boer War with De Wits's raiders and henceforth was easily recognizable by the bits of his Boer War uniform that he sported with his everyday clothing. He met White and Whitehead on a transatlantic trip in 1901 and came to Byrdcliffe to help out White in 1902. He helped in the building and road-building of that first year. Soon after he married a woman who was rumored to be heiress to a vast Central American coffee fortune, bringing her back to Woodstock. Whitehead put Van der Loo in charge of transportation, moving people and goods back and forth by carriage and wagon, but when White decided to leave and form the Maverick, Van der Loo sold out and sailed for China, where he worked successfully as agent for a British line of patent medicines.

Thorstein Veblen

American, 1857–1929

Noted political economist Thorstein Veblen taught at the University of Chicago (1892–1906), Stanford (1906–9), the University of Missouri (1911–18), and the New School for Social Research (1918–26). He wrote many scathing indictments against capitalism, among them his best-known book, *The Theory of the Leisure Class* (1899), an attack on the corrosiveness of upper class society. He coined the phrase "conspicuous consumption," a chapter title in his first book. A strange but brilliant man, he spoke twenty-five languages and pursued studies in history, literature, art, science, technology, pedagogy, agriculture, labor relations, and industrial development and was proficient to the point of expertise in all these areas. He was invited to Byrdcliffe by fellow Chicagoan Hervey White.

Peter Verburg

American

A noted Arts and Crafts bookbinder, Verburg came to Byrdcliffe with Ellen Gates Starr, staying at the Villetta in 1903.

Charles Volkmar

American, 1841–1914

Best known for his ceramics work, Volkmar was also a landscape painter and teacher. He was responsible for setting up the pottery shop and kiln at Byrdcliffe, probably around 1904. At the age of twenty, Volkmar had gone to Europe where he stayed for nearly fifteen years, studying painting, sculpture, and pottery, returning permanently to the States in 1879. His son, Leon, formed a flourishing ceramics partnership with him that lasted until 1911 when ill health forced Volkmar to close the business.

Elizabeth von Arnim

British, 1866–1941

Von Arnim was born Mary Beauchamp in Sydney, Australia. She was brought up in England and met her first husband, Count Henning August von Arnim-Schlagenthin, in Italy in 1889. After several years of living in Pomerania where she wrote her first book, *Elizabeth and Her German Garden*, the family moved to London in 1908. In 1910 the Count died and Elizabeth moved to Switzerland where she entertained friends such as H. G. Wells and her cousin the writer Katherine Mansfield. In 1916 she married Francis, the second Earl Russell (known as the "wicked earl" and brother to mathematician Bertrand Russell) who had been tried for bigamy in 1901. When this marriage quickly unraveled, she ran away to America and frequently visited the Whiteheads during the summers of 1916 and 1917 at Byrdcliffe. There are many notes in Jane's diaries from the 1880s referring to social occasions with the Russells and it was probably through this connection that Jane came to meet Elizabeth. Von Arnim's other books include *The Enchanted April* and her autobiography, *All the Dogs of My Life*.

Edna Walker

American, born 1880

Walker (fig. 19) received a certificate in painting and design from the Pratt Institute in 1903. During her summers she had taught art in the public schools and after graduation she was one of several of Arthur Wesley Dow's students to go to Byrdcliffe. She is listed as staying at the Villetta in the summer of 1903 but thereafter she and her friend Zulma Steele shared a house called the Angelus. They worked together on many of the furniture designs, based on the flora and fauna found in the area. It is not known how many years she remained at the colony although she is listed in the 1909 Villetta ledger and Bertha Thompson men-

fig. 19 Attributed to Bertha Thompson, *Edna Walker*, 1904. Silver print. Thompson Family Papers, Schlesinger Library, Radcliffe Institute, Harvard University.

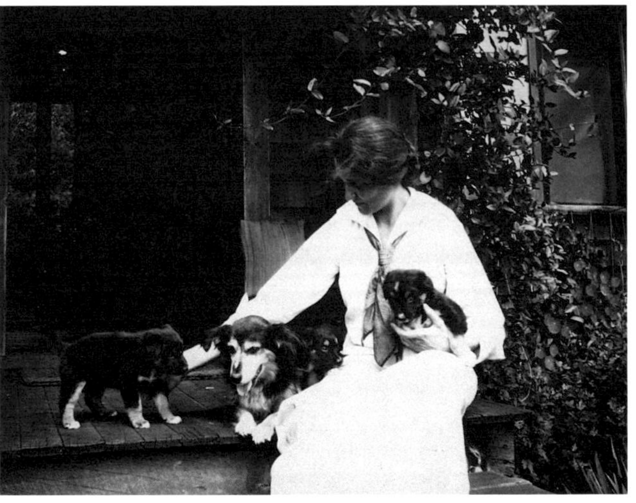

tions Steele and Walker in her recollections as being still in residence in the second decade of the twentieth century. Walker worked as director of weaving at the Herter Looms in New York during the winter months; it is thought that she eventually moved to Scotland.

Eva Watson-Schütze

American, 1867–1935

Born in New Jersey, Watson-Schütze entered the Pennsylvania Academy of Fine Arts at the age of fifteen, taking classes in modeling and painting with Thomas Eakins and Thomas Anschutz. Fellow pictorialist Joseph Keiley remembered her at this time: "quick and nervous of motion, reserved and self-reliant in bearing, and in speech quiet, thoughtful, and to the point."[29] Watson married her husband, University of Chicago professor Martin Schütze, in 1901 and accompanied him to Byrdcliffe the first summer it was open. The two became permanent summer residents of the colony, spending winters ensconced in the intellectual milieu of Chicago. A pictorialist photographer, Watson-Schütze was part of the Stieglitz group of Photo-Secessionists and was featured in his journals *Camera Notes* and *Camera Work*. Her portraits of the people she knew both in Chicago and in Woodstock form a poignant paean to these people who were her friends. Her darkroom at Byrdcliffe was in the building called Skylights.

Mary Say Lawrence Webster and Albert Lowry Webster

American, 1872–1944; American, 1859–1930

The Websters first came to Byrdcliffe in 1904. Mary Webster was the daughter of Cyrus J. Lawrence, a New York banker and collector of Barye bronzes and French Impressionist paintings. There are Mary Cassatt portraits of Mary and of two of her nieces, Cyrus's grandchildren, at the Clark Art Institute in Williamstown, Massachusetts. Mary was a musician, and she and her husband were remembered for their sense of fun and whimsy, creating a warm meeting place for other members of the Byrdcliffe colony.

After graduating from Yale in 1880, Albert was a topographer with the U.S. Geological Survey working out west. He did graduate studies in sanitary engineering at Johns Hopkins and in Frankfurt, Germany. Upon his return, he started practice as a civil engineer in New York City and helped design such important projects as the Manhattan sewers and the water system in the Chrysler building. During World War I he was a member of the Council of National Defense and a member of the Building Code Committee, appointed by President Hoover. He also wrote and illustrated a children's book, *Caleb and the Friendly Animals*, which is clearly set in a Byrdcliffe-like magic land.[28]

William Wendt

American, born Germany, 1865–1946

Wendt came to the United States when he was fifteen, joining an uncle in Chicago. He took night classes at the Art Institute and during the day worked in a commercial art shop. He made his first trip to California in 1894 and continued to visit over the next twelve years when he finally moved there permanently, settling in Los Angeles with his new wife, the sculptress Julia Bracken. He was one of the artists who used the offered studio space at the Whiteheads' home Arcady in the later part of the 1890s. White remembered him in his autobiography as "tawny, but slender, an artist type in looks and ways. He was never quite sure about his stories—which were proper for ladies' ears and which were not."

A. Olaf Westerling

Swedish, 1877–1938

Westerling was a woodcarver at Byrdcliffe and is listed as a visitor in the 1904 Villetta ledger. He kept up with some of the other 1904 visitors, visiting Bertha Thompson at Ipswich, 1907, along with Thatcher, Steele, and Vivian Bevans White (see fig. 15).

Walter Weyl

American, 1874–1919

Weyl earned his PhD in economics in 1897 and is remembered today as both an economist and a writer. He was extremely interested in labor issues and called for a redistribution of wealth. He wrote *The New Democracy* (1912) and also started *The New Republic* in 1914 with Herbert Croly and Walter Lippmann. He believed the middle classes were the best chance of creating the "new democracy," and Richard le Gallienne said of Weyl that "he could make political economy almost as attractive as a love affair."[31] He met his future wife, magazine journalist and social activist Bertha Poole, at Hull House and it was most likely through this connection that he eventually decided to relocate to Woodstock. He died of cancer in 1919 and was remembered as saintly; his colleagues at the *New Republic* said, "His method was to comprehend, no matter where it led him. He asked questions and always when he honestly could, he gave the benefit of the doubt."[32]

Candace Wheeler

American, 1827–1923

Bereaved after a daughter's death, Wheeler was inspired by the work she saw at the 1876 Philadelphia World's Fair and the following year she helped to organize the Society of Decorative Art of New York, a charity group

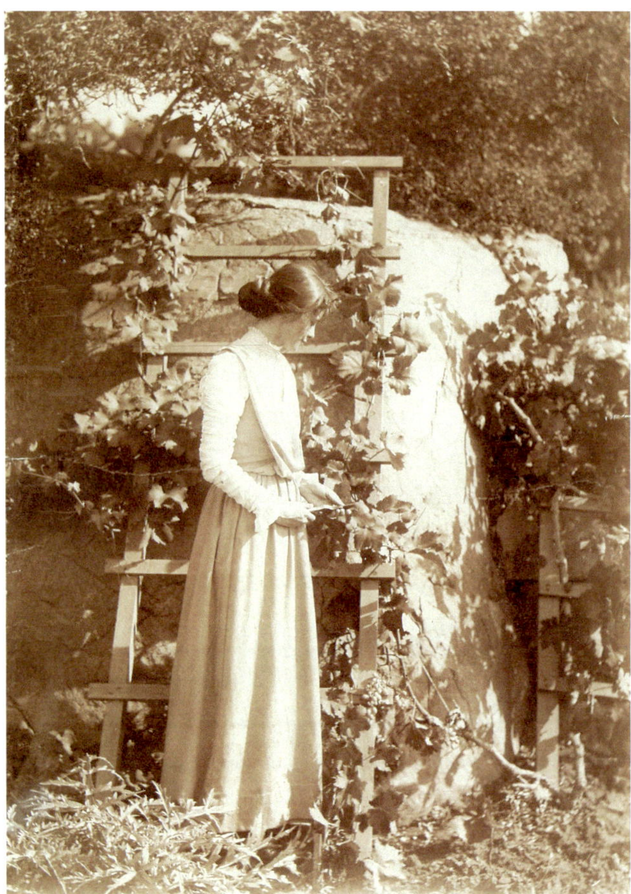

fig. 20 Ralph Whitehead, *Jane at Arcady*, ca. 1895. Albumen print. Winterthur Library, Downs Collection, 92x39.327

that exhibited and sold women's handicrafts. Two years later, Wheeler, with Louis Comfort Tiffany, established the design firm of Associated Artists. She was in charge of the textile division and in 1883 she opened her own business, of the same name. She was director of the planning committee's Bureau of Applied Arts for the Woman's Building at the Chicago World's Fair in 1893. Her daughter Dora also was an artist and the two worked together at their estate, Onteora Park, near Byrdcliffe. There are several mentions in Jane's diaries of visiting Onteora.

Warren (Frank) Wheelock

American, 1880–1960

Born in Sutton, Massachusetts, Wheelock was a 1905 graduate of Pratt with a certificate in drawing, painting, and composition; he probably learned about Byrdcliffe through Arthur Wesley Dow. Like George Eggers, he worked as carpenter around Byrdcliffe to earn room and board and later became known for his direct carving of geometric shapes and his work in sculpture, as well as his paintings and illustrations. He was a drawing instructor at Pratt from 1905 to 1910 and divided the remainder of his time between Linville Falls, North Carolina; Albuquerque; New York; and Woodstock, where he had a solo show of his work in 1925. He was one of the founders (with John Sloan) of the Society of Independent Artists. During the 1930s he was an artist for the W.P.A.

Edith Wherry

American, born 1876

Edith Wherry is best remembered for her books *The Red Lantern* (1911), *The Wanderer on a Thousand Hills* (1917), and *The Lamp Still Burns* (1955). The daughter of missionaries, she was born in China and lost family members in the Boxer Rebellion in 1900. She visited Byrdcliffe the first summer and boarded with the Browns. She was remembered as eccentric (nicknamed "the flamboyant bat") and, according to Bolton Brown, "she could entertain Byrdcliffers by reciting the Lord's Prayer in Chinese."[33] Lucy Brown remembers her coming to stay for two weeks and spending the summer and "when the dew fell and the stars began to twinkle over the hilltops she would wrap herself in a somber cape and flitter up and down the hill roads, joining parties of night riders or walkers, doing Overlook, or haunting moonlit meadows and streams on the lookout for a pixie or two."[34] Three years later she returned to Byrdcliffe from France and married a Canadian under an oak tree, "which she considered to be the loveliest spot in the world." Later, in 1911, she moved to Hollywood and married Harold Struan Muckleston.

Hervey White

American, 1866–1944

Hervey White (see fig. 18) was a man of many talents who was born to a farm family in New London, Iowa. He received a degree from Harvard in 1894, traveled abroad for a period, then returned to the Midwest, settling in Chicago where he was associated with Jane Addams's Hull House. It was here that Whitehead met him, introduced through Charlotte Perkins Stetson (later Gilman). Though from a much different social background than Whitehead the two quickly became friends, and Whitehead fondly nicknamed White "Nicolo." Over the years, White wrote many books and articles; he was also a poet and musical enthusiast. His book *Quicksand* (1900) was hailed by Theodore Dreiser "as one of the six great American novels."[35] He married Vivian Bevans in 1904 and the same year he left Byrdcliffe to establish his own colony nearby, called the Maverick, which became renowned for its summer music festivals and its outdoor theater. White also funded the Maverick Press and was editor of *Wild Hawk* and *Plowshare*, periodicals published between 1911 and 1929. Richard le Gallienne's description of White rings true: "No figure is better known in Woodstock than that of Hervey White, combining as he does in a sort of shaggy preciosity of appearance all the elements of a varied life. Hirsute as his own 'Maverick' hillside, thatched with rough curls, and 'bearded like the pard,' he suggests the God Pan in a pink blouse and workmen's trousers. Eager, young-eyed, keen and yet dreaming, shy and yet forceful, he comes along the open road, like one of Whitman's 'Cameradoes,' always loafing and gay, and always at work on his thousand and one schemes."[36] In his first book, *Differences*, published soon after his initial meeting with Whitehead, White named his heroine Genevieve Radcliffe. At Hull House he formed a cooperative to make furniture but disbanded the group after the completion of only one piece. He and Gilman collaborated on an unpublished play at Hull House. White's sons Caleb and Dan, and Van der Loo's son, Kees, ran the Maverick after White's death.

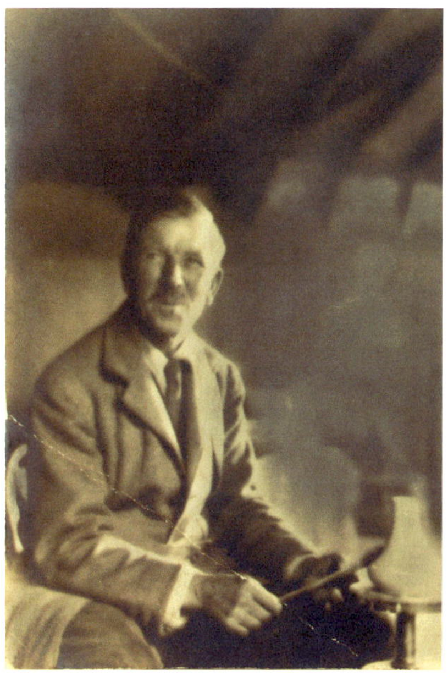

fig. 22
Unidentified photographer, *Ralph Whitehead in Pottery*, ca. 1920. Silver print. Winterthur Library, Downs Collection, 92x39.1140.235.

Jane Whitehead

American, 1861–1955

Jane Byrd McCall (fig. 20) came from a prominent Philadelphia family and spent much of her early years traveling around Europe with her sister, Gerty, and their mother. She was presented to Queen Victoria in 1886 and was part of a social set that included many of the distinguished writers, artists, and educators of the day. In 1885 she met Whitehead; he was married to Marie at the time and it seems that his relationship with Jane didn't take any real form until 1890 when they met again in Italy. Thereafter they began to make long-term plans and in the spring of 1892, after Whitehead received his divorce, he came to America where they were married. Jane was an accomplished artist in her own right and had studied at the Académie Julian in Paris in the 1880s and under J. P. Laurens and Edmond Aman-Jean in the 1890s. She continued to draw and paint after her marriage and at Byrdcliffe she became actively involved in both the weaving and pottery ventures. She was remembered by many of the residents as being very much the "lady of the manor," wearing flowing gowns and veils and ordering the artists to participate in Morris dances, held on the lawn of White Pines. She was very particular in those she chose to associate with and was known to avoid unwanted visitors by calling out from an upstairs window "Mrs. Whitehead is not at home."[37] White, who first met her in the 1890s, recalled that she "was a lady of rare charm." She and her younger son, Peter, remained at Byrdcliffe after Ralph's death. She moved into Yggdrasil and died there in 1955.

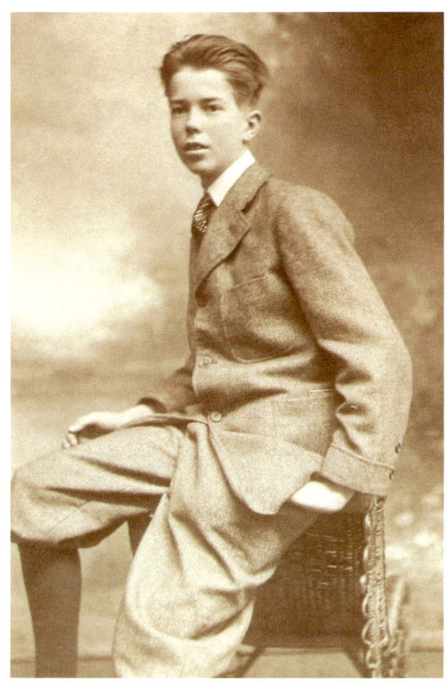

fig. 21
Unidentified photographer, *Peter Whitehead*, ca. 1915. Silver print. Winterthur Library, Downs Collection, 92x39.1140.649.

Peter Whitehead

American, 1901–1976

The younger son of Jane and Ralph Whitehead, Peter (fig. 21) features prominently in several of Eva Watson-Schütze's photographs. Named Geoffrey at birth, he seems to have changed his name to Peter in his early teens. Always close to his mother, the two remained at Byrdcliffe after the deaths of Ralph Jr. and Ralph Sr. Although trained in several fields, Peter seems never to have actively worked. White Pines remained his primary residence until his death in 1976.

Ralph Whitehead

American, born Britain, 1854–1929

Whitehead was born in Saddleworth, Yorkshire, and went to Balliol College, Oxford, where he came under the influence of John Ruskin, then Slade Professor. This influence and that of Arts and Crafts practitioner William Morris would remain the largest influences on his desire to construct his own Arts and Crafts community. He wrote *Grass of the Desert* (1892), which was published by Chiswick Press; Walter Crane was director of the Press at the time. After his 1892 divorce from his Austrian wife, Marie, he moved to America and married Jane Byrd McCall. They built a home in Montecito, California, called Arcady and established a Sloyd school on the property. Although considered by some of his colleagues as dictatorial in manner, Whitehead was also noted for his kindness, generosity and intelligence. Greatly interested in music as well as fine art, Whitehead published two books of folk songs with his wife, *The Morning Stars Sang Together: Folk-Songs and Other Songs for Children* (1903) and *Folks Songs of Eastern Europe* (1912). Emotionally bereft after his older son, Ralph, Jr., died in the sinking of the SS *Vestris* in 1928, Whitehead died of pneumonia only a few months later, in February 1929 (fig. 22).

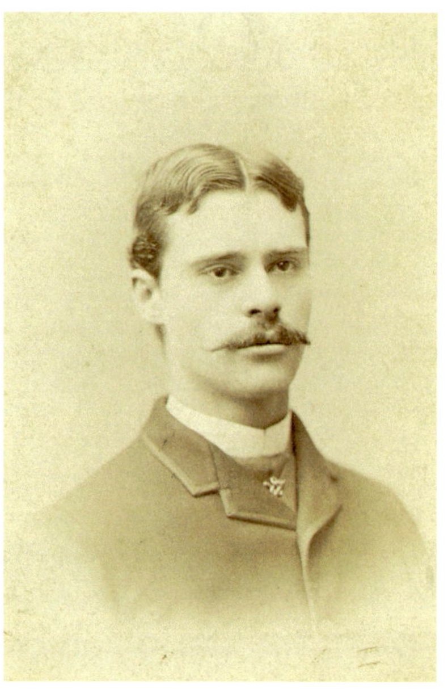

fig. 24 Unidentified photographer, *Owen Wister*. Albumen print. Winterthur Library, Downs Collection, 92x39.1140.515.

Ralph Whitehead Jr.

American, 1899–1928

Ralph Jr. (fig. 23), like his brother, seems to have had trouble focusing on a career and was often in trouble. His father's letters to him (in the Winterthur Library, Downs Collection) provide a glimpse into the difficult relationship between the two. Returning from Europe in 1919, after serving in World War I, Ralph Jr. seems to have tried to turn over a new leaf. Though still somewhat uncontrollable in temperament, by the time of his death in 1928 he had settled down to serious work in South America. It was after a visit home, on a return voyage to his work aboard the SS *Vestris* that he drowned when the boat sank near the Bahamas. His father never really recovered from this loss and died three months later.

fig. 23 Unidentified photographer, *Ralph Jr.*, 1919. Silver print. Winterthur Library, Downs Collection, 92x39.1140.209.

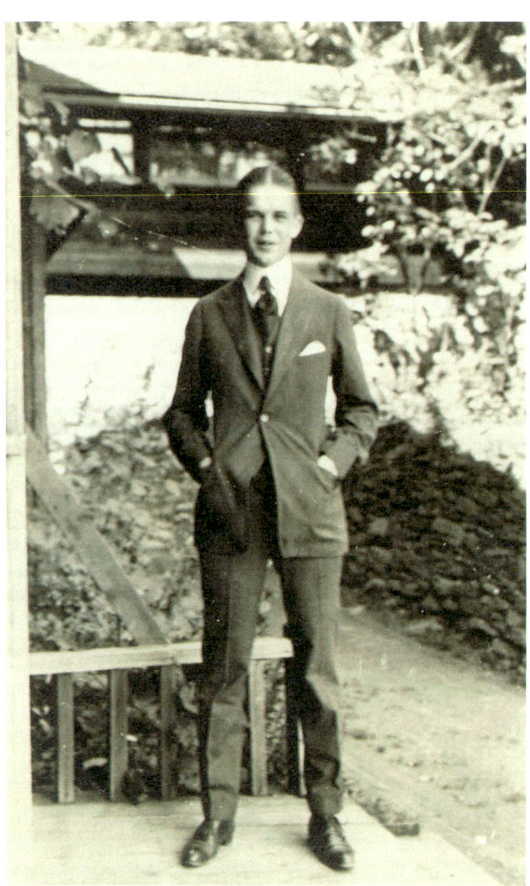

Owen Wister

American, 1860–1938

A family friend of the McCalls, Wister (fig. 24) grew up in Philadelphia and graduated from Harvard in 1882, where he met his future lifelong friend, Theodore Roosevelt. His main interest was music and after graduation he went to Europe, planning to continue in this career. After writing two operas, his father steered him toward a business career, but he rejected this and took to writing. His first book, *The New Swiss Family Robinson*, was written in 1882 and thus followed a long career. His most famous book was *The Virginian* (1902). Jane's sister, Gerty, who never married, supposedly cared deeply for Wister.

Dewing Woodward

American, 1856–1950

Born in Pennsylvania, Woodward studied at the Pennsylvania Academy of Fine Arts and then went to Europe for fifteen years where she studied with Tony Robert-Fleury, Jules Lefébvre, and Bouguereau at the

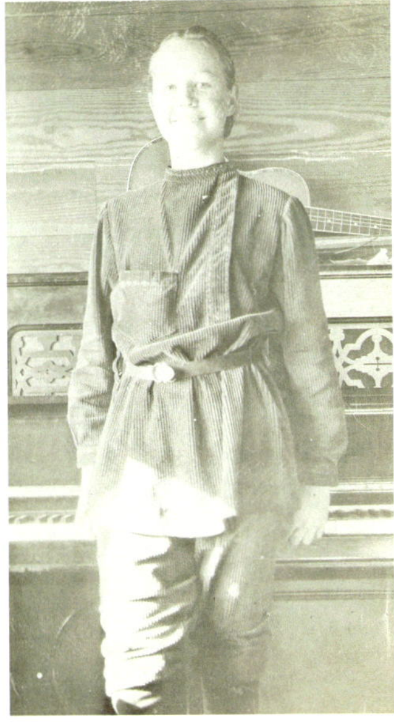

fig. 25 Unidentified photographer, *Byrdcliffe Participant*. Silver print. Lucy Brown remembered evenings of dancing in the studio: "Denim and corduroy were the vogue in dress, and I think of the lamp-lit studio, the pre-jazz music and our quaint gyrations with vast pleasure." Winterthur Library, Downs Collection, 92x39.1140.371.

Académie Julian. In 1894 she was awarded the Grand Prix for her work in the Salon. In 1907 she returned to the United States and moved to Shady, near Byrdcliffe, where she established the Blue Dome Fraternity in 1913 for the purpose of painting the nude out of doors. She was for many years Dean of Fine Arts at Bucknell College and later held the same position at the University of Miami. She was known for her paintings of birds, nudes, portraits, genre scenes, and townscapes.

fig. 26 Unidentified photographer, *Women artists at Byrdcliffe*, ca. 1910. Silver print. Winterthur Collection, Downs Collection, 92x39.1140.272.

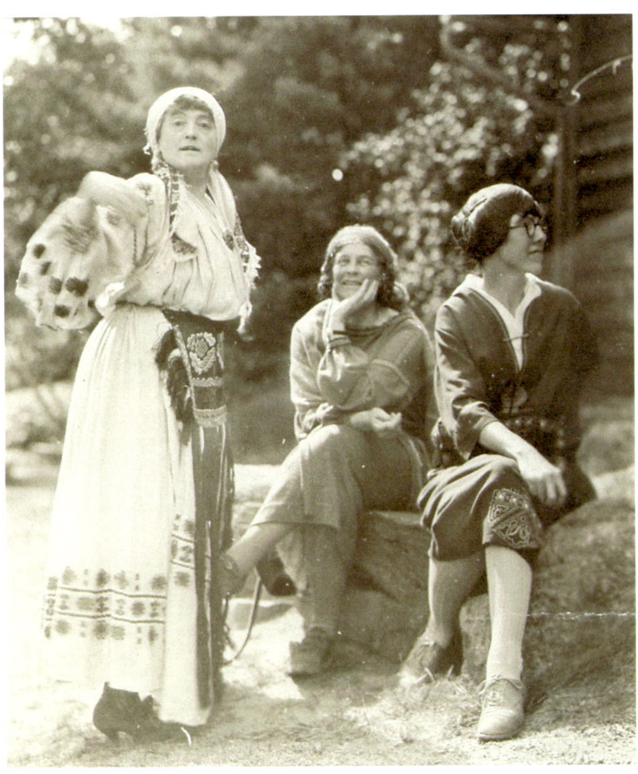

Notes

1. "Woodstock Colony: 75 Years in Art," *The New York Times*, February 4, 1877.
2. White, *Autobiography*, 169.
3. Quoted in Peter Kurth, *Isadora: A Sensational Life* (Boston: Little, Brown and Company, 2001), 329.
4. Winterthur Library, Downs Collection.
5. RRW to Jane, June 2, 1902. Winterthur Library, Downs Collection.
6. Anita Smith, *Woodstock: History and Hearsay*, 44.
7. John Burroughs, August 30, to "My Dear Friend" (unknown) from West Point. Winterthur Library, Downs Collection.
8. Anita M. Smith, *Woodstock: History and Hearsay* (Woodstock, NY: Catskill Publishing Company, 1959), 48.
9. John Carlson, *Guide to Landscape Painting* (New York: Dover Publishing), 123.
10. RRW to Jane, February 22, 1903. Winterthur Library, Downs Collection.
11. Quoted in Lionel Lambourne, *Utopian Craftsmen: The Arts and Crafts Movement from the Cotswolds to Chicago* (Salt Lake City: Peregrine Smith, Inc., 1980), 197.
12. Quoted in Patricia Jobe Pierce and Rolf H. Kristenson, *John Joseph Enneking: American Impressionist Painter* (Hingham, MA: Pierce Galleries, Inc., 1972), 119.
13. Alf Evers, *Woodstock*, 426.
14. Alf Evers, *The Catskills*, 628.
15. See Michael Holroyd, *Augustus John* (New York: Penguin Books, 1976), 101–2 footnote.
16. Quoted in Alf Evers, *The Catskills*, 622.
17. RRW to Jane, December 7, 1902, New York, Kensington Hotel. Winterthur Library, Downs Collection.
18. Smith, *Woodstock: History and Hearsay*, 45.
19. Bertha M. Thompson, unpublished diary, 19. Schlesinger Library, Radcliffe Institute, Harvard University.
20. Smith, *Woodstock: History and Hearsay*, 45.
21. R. K. Davis, *Boston Sunday Post*, February 19, 1928.
22. Halsey Ricardo, "Of the Room and Furniture," *Arts and Crafts Essays* (New York & London: Garland Publishing, Inc., 1977), 278.
23. Edward Warren, "Obituary: Halsey Ricardo," *Journal of the Royal Institute of British Architects* (March 10, 1928): 312.
24. Bertha Thompson, "The Craftsmen of Byrdcliffe," *Publications of the Woodstock Historical Society* 10 (July 1933): 11.
25. Smith, *Woodstock: History and Hearsay*, 43.
26. Annie Thompson, unpublished diary, 40. Schlesinger Library.
27. *House Beautiful* vol. 38, no. 1 (June 1915): 18.
28. Vose Gallery files, letter from Murphy to Robert Vose, March 3, 1940.
29. Quoted in Jean F. Block, *Eva Watson-Schütze: Chicago Photo-Secessionist* (Chicago: The University of Chicago Library, 1985), 3.
30. I am grateful to Lawrence Webster for providing valuable information about her family.
31. Smith, *Woodstock: History and Hearsay*, 169.
32. John A. Garraty and Mark C. Carnes, eds., *American National Biography*, vol. 23 (Oxford: Oxford University Press, 1999), 104.
33. Alf Evers, *Woodstock: History of an American Town* (Woodstock, NY: The Overlook Press, 1987), 432.
34. Smith, *Woodstock: History and Hearsay*, 44.
35. "Hervey White, 78, Author and Editor," *The New York Times*, October 21, 1944.
36. Richard le Gallienne, *Woodstock* (Woodstock, NY: Woodstock Art Association, 1923), 17.
37. Anita Smith, *It Happened in Woodstock*, 65.

About the Authors

Ellen Paul Denker is an independent scholar, writer, and exhibition curator of American decorative arts, specializing in ceramics history. Among her recent projects, she organized the exhibition *On the Streets: New York's Trolleys and Buses* for the New York Transit Museum. She is the 2003 recipient of the Robert C. Smith Award from the Decorative Arts Society.

Robert Edwards has managed the Willcox collection of Byrdcliffe-related objects from the Whitehead Estate since 1976. He was consultant and essayist for *A Poor Sort of Heaven, A Good Sort of Earth: The Rose Valley Arts and Crafts Experiment* (1983) and *"The Art That is Life": The Arts and Crafts Movement in America, 1870–1920* (1987). He was curator for and produced *Life by Design: The Byrdcliffe Arts and Crafts Colony* (1984) at the Delaware Art Museum. He wrote about the Byrdcliffe colony and the furniture made there for *The Magazine Antiques* (January 1985 and May 2002) and has edited and published widely on various aspects of the Arts and Crafts movement. He was a 2000 Winterthur Research Fellow.

Heidi Nasstrom Evans is a PhD candidate at the University of Maryland, Department of American Studies. Her forthcoming dissertation, for which she received research support from the Winterthur Museum, is on Jane Byrd McCall Whitehead. She is curating an exhibition on the stylization of Jane's life, scheduled to open at the Georgia Museum of Art in Athens in October 2004. Ms. Nasstrom Evans is on the faculty at the Cooper-Hewitt/Parsons sister program in the decorative arts at the Smithsonian Associates in Washington, DC. She also teaches classes on nineteenth- and twentieth-century decorative arts; material culture; and women, art, and culture at the University of Maryland.

Nancy E.Green is senior curator of prints, drawings, and photographs at the Herbert F. Johnson Museum of Art. She joined the staff in 1985 and has organized dozens of exhibitions at the Johnson Museum and elsewhere. She has published numerous articles, exhibition guides, and catalogues, including *Arthur Wesley Dow and American Arts and Crafts*, which was circulated nationally by the American Federation of Arts. In 2000 she received a Winterthur Fellowship to pursue her research on the Byrdcliffe colony, as well as a three-month Getty Curatorial Research Fellowship in 2002 to continue work on the Byrdcliffe project.

Cheryl Robertson, an independent scholar, consultant, and museum professional, is a recognized authority on the Arts and Crafts movement as well as domestic interiors and family living patterns in the United States between 1870 and 1940. She has contributed essays to two landmark Arts and Crafts books: *The Arts and Crafts Movement in California: In Pursuit of the Good Life* and *"The Art That is Life": The Arts and Crafts Movement in America, 1870–1920.* She was awarded a Winterthur Fellowship for this project.

Tom Wolf is a professor of art history at Bard College and has published widely in the area of twentieth-century American art, particularly on artists who have worked in Woodstock, such as Konrad Cramer, Yasuo Kuniyoshi, and Arnold Blanch. He has been awarded several fellowships, including a Research Fellowship at the J. Paul Getty Museum in 1989 and an Andrew W. Mellon Fellowship at the Metropolitan Museum of Art in 1992–93. In 1999 and 2000 he received fellowships from Winterthur to pursue research on the Byrdcliffe colony. He has been associated with this project since its earliest inception at the Woodstock Guild and is co-curator of the exhibition.

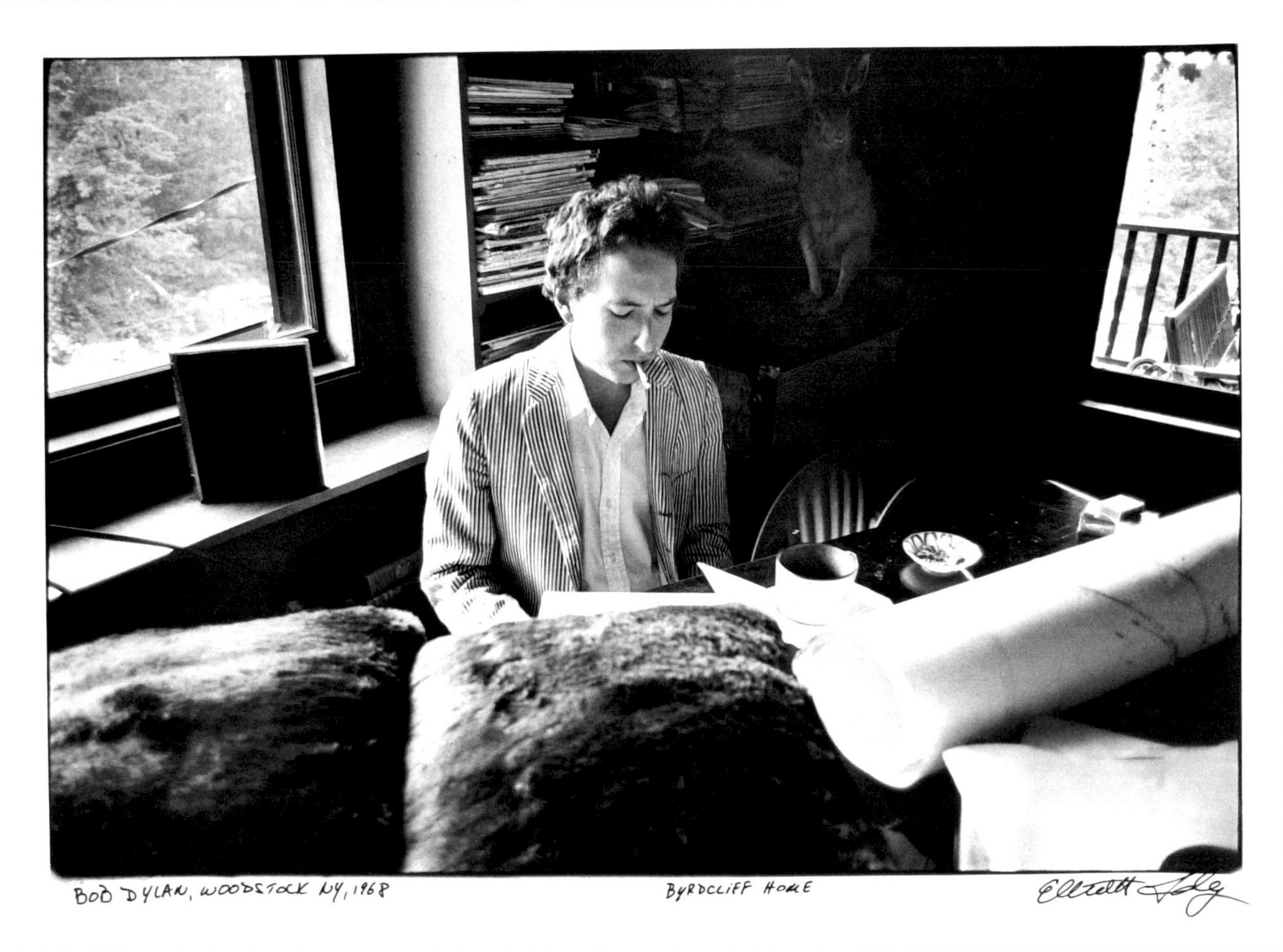

191. Elliott Landy
American, born 1942
Bob Dylan at Hiloha, Byrdcliffe, 1968
Silver print
16 x 20 inches
Collection of Douglas C. James

Index

Photography Credits

Unless otherwise indicated in the catalogue and below, all photographs were taken by Matthew Ferrari, Johnson Museum of Art, Cornell University.

Byrdcliffe's History

fig. 7 Photograph by Sebouh Kizirian, PRO Photo & Imaging
fig. 9 Les Walker
fig. 17 Tony DeCamillo, Art/Science Photographics

Byrdcliffe Furniture: Imagination Versus Reality

figs. 2, 3, 4, 6, 8, 9a, 9b, 12, 15, 20b, 24, 26 Rick Echelmeyer, courtesy of Robert Edwards
fig. 24 Dion Ogust, Woodstock
fig. 26 Los Angeles County Museum of Art © 1993 All rights reserved

Art at Byrdcliffe

fig. 2 Rick Echelmeyer, courtesy of Robert Edwards

Purely for Pleasure: Ceramics at Byrdcliffe

fig. 18 Tony De Camillo, Art/Science Photographics

Nature and Artifice in the Architecture of Byrdcliffe

fig. 22 Courtesy of William Ricco, Kenneth Caldwell, and the Berkeley Historical Society
fig. 23 Environmental Design Archives, University of California, Berkeley © UC Regents
fig. 31 Courtesy of Robert Edwards

Works in the Exhibition

15 ©2003 Detroit Institute of Art
16, 21, 22, 30, 35, 36, 74, 76, 97, 98, 128, 130, 131 Tony DeCamillo, Art/Science Photographics
19, 20, 126 Rick Echelmeyer, courtesy of Robert Edwards
23, 24 John R. Glembin
38 ©1992 Metropolitan Museum of Art, New York
39 Christie's Images Ltd.
40 ©2003 The Museum of Fine Arts, Boston
41, 42, 85, 157, 166 Erik Gould
48, 112, 117 Courtesy of Spanierman Gallery LLC, New York
50, 51, 52, 53, 54, 55 Michael Agee
56 Bob Wagner
57 Courtesy of the Brooklyn Museum/Central Photo Archive
60 Ali Elai
70, 71 Clive Russ
80 Courtesy of the Bigelow Homestead
113 Robert Ellison
163 R. Lorenzson
164 Lisa Martin
191 © Elliott Landy/Landyvision.com